**LIFETIME LEARNING CENTRE
LINCOLN COUNTY BOARD OF EDUCATION
ADULT BUSINESS**

92-11

LIFETIME LEARNING CENTRE
LINCOLN COUNTY BOARD OF EDUCATION
AGRI-BUSINESS

Accounting Principles

A SKILL-BUILDING APPROACH

Dwight L. Gibson
Administrative Head
West Carlton Secondary School
Dunrobin, Ontario

Contributing author: **Norman J. Shoemaker**
Head, Business Education
Sir Winston Churchill Secondary School
Vancouver, British Columbia

John Wiley & Sons

Toronto   New York   Chichester   Brisbane   Singapore

To our parents, and our children, Corrie, Michael.   D.G.

To those who are the true constants in my life:
       My Mom and Dad
    My Sons, Scott and Rob   N.S.

Copyright © 1992 by John Wiley & Sons Canada Limited.

All rights reserved. No part of this work covered by the copyrights hereon may be reproduced or used in any form or by any means — graphic, electronic or mechanical — without the prior written permission of the publisher.

Any request for photocopying, recording, taping or information storage and retrieval systems of any part of this book shall be directed in writing to the Canadian Reprography Collective, 379 Adelaide Street West, Suite M1, Toronto, Ontario M5V 1S5.

Care has been taken to trace ownership of copyright material contained in this text. The publishers will gladly receive any information that will enable them to rectify any reference or credit line in subsequent editions.

Canadian Cataloguing in Publication Data

Gibson, Dwight L., 1944-
    Accounting principles: a skill-building approach

Includes index.
ISBN 0-471-79658-1

1. Accounting. I. Shoemaker, Norman J., 1942- II. Title.

HF5635.G52 1991   657   C91-094700-7

Production Credits

DEVELOPMENTAL EDITOR: Marg Bukta
COPY EDITOR: Debbie Davies
COVER DESIGN: Brant Cowie/ArtPlus Limited
TYPESETTING: Q Composition

Printed and bound by John Deyell Company

10 9 8 7 6 5 4 3 2 1

Contents

TO THE TEACHER *vii*

TO THE STUDENT *xi*

CHAPTER ONE
The Balance Sheet
1.1 The Role of an Accountant *1*
1.2 A Personal Balance Sheet *7*
1.3 Balance sheet for a Business *10*
1.4 Generally Accepted Accounting Principles *17*
   Chapter Review and Skill Development *22*
   Accounting at Work – Controller *27*
   Computer Accounting – Spreadsheets ... A Powerful Accounting Tool *30*

CHAPTER TWO
Analyzing Transactions for Balance Sheet Accounts
2.1 Transactions *34*
2.2 Analyzing Transactions *46*
2.3 The General Ledger *57*
2.4 Balancing Accounts and the Trial Balance *70*
   Chapter Review and Skill Development *76*
   Accounting at Work – Assistant Auditor General *86*
   Computer Accounting – Creating a Spreadsheet Template (Model) *88*

CHAPTER THREE
Analyzing Transactions Related to the Income Statement
3.1 The Income Statement *93*
3.2 Transactions Involving Income Statement Accounts *103*
3.3 The Owner's Drawings Account *110*
3.4 Month-End Procedures *115*
   Chapter Review and Skill Development *128*
   Accounting at Work – Chartered Accountant *128*
   Computer Accounting – Using a Spreadsheet to Analyze Accounting Data *133*

CHAPTER FOUR
The General Journal
4.1 The General Journal *135*
4.2 Posting to Running-Balance Ledger Accounts *143*
4.3 The Trial Balance Revisited *152*
   Chapter Review and Skill Development *163*
   Accounting at Work – Certified Management Accountant *169*
   Computer Accounting – No Business That Can Afford a Personal Computer Should Be Preparing Accounts Manually *172*

Chapter Five
The Worksheet
5.1 The Worksheet *184*
5.2 Preparing Financial Statements from the Worksheet *193*
5.3 Working Capital and Current Ratio *198*
5.4 Comparative Financial Statements *199*
    Chapter Review and Skill Development *205*
    Accounting at Work – Certified General Accountant *210*
    Computer Accounting – Spreadsheets Revisited *213*

PROJECT 1 — THE ACCOUNTING CYCLE *216*

Chapter Six
Special Transactions
6.1 Debit and Credit Memos *220*
6.2 Sales Tax *238*
6.3 Credit Cards, Debit Cards, and Prepaid Cards *248*
    Chapter Review and Skill Development *259*
    Accounting at Work – Collection Officer *264*
    Computer Accounting – And Now . . . The Computerized Restaurant *266*

Chapter Seven
End-of-Period Procedures — 1
7.1 Adjusting Entries for Prepaid Expenses *270*
7.2 Depreciation of Fixed Assets *280*
7.3 The Eight-Column Worksheet *293*
    Chapter Review and Skill Development *303*
    Accounting at Work – Entrepreneur *309*
    Computer Accounting – Adjustments and the Computer *311*

Chapter Eight
End-of-Period Procedures — 2
8.1 Adjustments for Unrecorded Expenses *314*
8.2 Adjustments for Unearned Revenue and Unrecorded Revenue *321*
8.3 Closing Entries and the Post-Closing Trial Balance *329*
    Chapter Review and Skill Development *339*
    Accounting at Work – Public Accountant *345*
    Computer Accounting – The Power of Accounting Software *347*

CHAPTER NINE
The Merchandising Business
9.1 Purchase Transactions for a Merchandising Business Using a Periodic Inventory System   352
9.2 Sales Transactions for a Merchandising Business Using a Periodic Inventory System   364
9.3 Completing the Accounting Cycle for a Merchandising Business Using a Periodic Inventory System   383
9.4 Accounting System for a Merchandising Business Using a Perpetual Inventory System   401
   Chapter Review and Skill Development   415
   Accounting at Work – Computer Analyst/Programmer   422
   Computer Accounting – Inventory Control   424

PROJECT 2 — THE ACCOUNTING CYCLE   434

CHAPTER TEN
Subsidiary Ledger Systems
10.1 The Subsidiary Ledger System   438
10.2 The Purchasing Department and Accounts Payable   443
10.3 The Credit Department and Accounts Receivable   457
10.4 Other Design Aspects of Subsidiary Ledger Systems   471
   Chapter Review and Skill Development   479
   Accounting at Work – Accounts Receivable Clerk   486
   Computer Accounting – Subsidiary Ledgers And Computer Accounting Software   490

CHAPTER ELEVEN
Columnar Journals
11.1 Designing an Accounting System: The Columnar Journal   494
11.2 Posting Procedures Using a Columnar Journal   509
11.3 Designing an Accounting System: Special Journals   518
   Chapter Review and Skill Development   534
   Accounting at Work – Systems Analyst   542
   Computer Accounting – Computerizing the Columnar Journal   545

PROJECT 3 — THE ACCOUNTING CYCLE   549

Chapter Twelve
Internal Control Over Cash
12.1 Internal Control   555
12.2 Petty Cash Fund   556
12.3 Internal Control Over Cash Receipts   565
12.4 Bank Reconciliation   568
    Chapter Review and Skill Development   581
    Accounting at Work – Bank Manager   589
    Computer Accounting – Internal Control — A Concern Of All Companies   591

Chapter Thirteen
Payroll Accounting
13.1 Calculating Gross Pay   595
13.2 Calculating Net Pay   610
13.3 Recording Payroll in the Payroll Register   623
13.4 Updating the Books for Payroll   630
    Chapter Review and Skill Development   645
    Accounting at Work — Payroll Supervisor   649
    Computer Accounting — Payroll Accounting   653

Chapter Fourteen
Analyzing Financial Statements
14.1 Ratios   667
14.2 Trends   680
    Chapter Review and Skill Development   689
    Accounting at Work — Financial Analyst   696
    Computer Accounting — Getting Down To Business   699

Index   702

To the Teacher

Two main goals of *Accounting Principles: A Skill-Building Approach* are:
1. to provide a learning environment that is relevant to an accounting-related career, and
2. to allow students to take an active role in that learning environment. The activities in the text allow the teacher to move away from the didactic approach to teaching accounting and towards experiential learning. Emphasis is placed on building skills needed by an accountant. Curricula place emphasis on students' analytical, problem-solving, writing, and value judgement skills. These and the many other skills required for success in an accounting-related job are emphasized throughout the text and reinforced in an experiential, practical, hands-on approach. These skills are not only useful in the students' careers, but also in the development of positive life skills.

Accounting Principles: A Skill-Building Approach presents the above skills in the context of many current issues: entrepreneurship, harassment, discrimination, the environment, the global economy, and pay equity. The following skills have been emphasized:

1. COMMUNICATION SKILLS

The ability to communicate effectively is a prime skill in all careers. *Accounting Principles: A Skill-Building Approach* uses brainstorming, business letter writing, report and memo preparation and presentation, interviewing, class discussion and debate, and collaborative learning opportunities to help students develop and improve their business communication skills. Some strategies are best learned by the use of a model. Below are two models that could be used by students.

Memo Writing
The following model is suggested for memo writing:
Memo to:
Memo from:
Date:
Subject:

Report Writing
The following model is suggested for writing:
To: The name and position of the person to whom you are sending the report.
Date: The date of the report.
Subject: The subject matter to be discussed.
Originators: The name of the report writers.
Purpose: Indicate the reason for the report.
Rationale: Outline the reason for your proposal or recommendation, and related comments.
Background: Give any data that is necessary, or procedures that have been followed, that would support your proposal.
Recommendation: Summarize your report and state your recommendations.

2. TECHNICAL SKILLS

An accountant in today's business milieu must have not only the traditional accounting skills but must also be able to use a computer to execute accounting practices. This course presents accounting and computer skills as well as a number of other technical skills. Analytical skills are developed through cognitive skill development problems in the "evaluate and assess" and "synthesize and conclude" activities which appear at the end of every chapter.

The principles of accounting are clearly presented, first in the context of a service business, and then in the context of a merchandising business. Then such systems as multi-column journals and subsidiary ledgers designed to meet specific criteria are studied. In all cases, the logic within the process is emphasized. To enhance students' understanding, flowcharts are provided and business policy manuals developed.

Accounting principles for such typical accounting problems as the federal goods and services tax, debit cards, and prepaid or cash cards are included.

Computer Accounting

The Computer Accounting sections provide the ideal introduction to applied microcomputer accounting applications for the high school students. Students gain practical, hands-on experience with two application areas — the spreadsheet and the accounting software package.

The sections are designed and organized to provide performance-based instruction. In each section, students read a narrative description of the purpose and function of a specific operation and then perform the operations in the exercises that follow.

3. MANAGEMENT SKILLS

Throughout the text, students see the accountant in supervisory and managerial roles. Management skill, such as leadership, time management, organization, and team building, are introduced in the text through a number of different strategies. Extra attention has been paid to decision making and goal setting, problem solving, and value analysis and clarification. Outlined below are models for decision-making and problems-solving techniques. Both of these models lead to value analysis and clarification.

Problem Solving

One of the key skills required of an accountant is problem solving. *Accountant Principles: A Skill-Building Approach* provides many opportunities for students to develop a logical approach to problem solving. The strategy for problem solving includes individual analysis and conclusion, or group brainstorming and consensus seeking. The following model is one form the problem-solving strategy could use.

Identify and state problem	What evidence exists that there is a problem?
Define why it is a problem	Is it really a problem? What is happening, as opposed to what should be happening?
Accumulate information.	Collect relevant data.
Establish criteria.	What objectives must the solution facilitate?
Create alternative solutions.	Prepare a list of alternative solutions (use brainstorming and creative thinking techniques).
Adopt best solution.	Evaluate solutions. Select the one considered best.
Make a plan of implementation.	How will the solution be put into effect? Prepare and implement an action plan.
Monitor and evaluate the results.	Action plan must include a detailed monitoring system.

Decision Making

Parallel to problem solving is decision making. Decision-making situations present a predefined objective that must be met. For example, a business objective may be to add a dental plan to the benefits package of management and employees or to purchase a major piece of equipment. The analysis is similar to that of problem solving. The model below illustrates the decision-making process a business might follow to obtain a new automobile.

Objective.	State the objective that will be the result of the decision. In this case, the objective is to study the positive and

	negative effects for the business if it decides to obtain a new automobile.
Establish criteria.	The limits that are placed on the decision should be stated. For example, the business may only want to spend a specified amount on the automobile.
List alternatives.	The various alternatives available to the business should be listed. For example, the business could buy, lease, or not obtain the automobile.
Compare alternatives.	Detailed analysis should be made to compare the alternatives. For example, the financial implications of each alternative should be compared, as should each alternative's impact on the company's business.
Identify risks.	The risks involved under each of the alternatives should be identified. For example, what are the financial risks should the company enter into a leasing agreement and discover, after two months, that the automobile is unnecessary?
Assess risks.	Each risk's impact on the business should be assessed for each alternative. For example, what will be the cost to the business of operating without the automobile?
Make a decision.	A decision must be made based on the assessment of the risks and the potential benefits.
Evaluate decision.	After the decision is implemented, its effect on the business should be monitored. Businesses learn by experience, and therefore monitoring decisions is a necessary element of decision making in business.

The text provides numerous opportunities to employ these decision-making and problem-solving models.

ACCOUNTING AT WORK

Each chapter includes an accounting-related career profile that illustrates accounting in action. The accompanying questions encourage students to examine the entry requirements for, the activities involved in, and the benefits of, specific careers. Questions also assist in the development of research skills.

SELF-DIRECTED LEARNING

Accounting Principles: A Skill-Building Approach provides a complete outline in the Teacher's Resource Package to allow a student to work through the text at his or her own pace. This package for individualized instruction includes:
a) text correlation
b) self-evaluation instruments
c) assignments
d) evaluation instruments

EVALUATION

The Teacher's Resource Package includes a variety of materials for evaluation. They include unit tests, sample examinations, a bank of multiple choice questions, and group and self-evaluation activities.

PRESENTATION

Accounting Principles: A Skill-Building Approach is written to allow students to gain access to the accounting information without the reading

level becoming a barrier. Visual materials in the text enhance understanding of concepts. A number of other strategies have been employed to ease access to the information.
1. Each chapter begins with list of objectives.
2. Accounting terms are presented at the beginning of each chapter.
3. Accounting procedures are presented in a narrative so that the student uses an inquiry approach.
4. Each chapter is broken down into lessons, with lesson review and applications following.
5. Each new accounting term is defined in the margin when it is introduced.
6. Each chapter ends with a summary of generally accepted accounting principles and concepts introduced in the chapter.
7. Progressive levels of cognitive skill development are included at the end of each chapter.

All transactions have been presented from the perspective of the business. This enables students to visualize what is taking place from the perspective of the accountant for the business. For example, instead of stating that "the owner invested in the business", the transaction will read "Received an investment from the owner". Articles and data from Canadian business have been presented where possible to give the students more knowledge of accounting in action.

THE PROGRAM

Accounting Principles: A Skill-Building Approach is a complete system. It contains this text, a set of students working Papers, a Teacher's Resource Package, and a data disk.

ACKNOWLEDGEMENTS

We are grateful to a number of people who assisted us in preparation of this text. Our students provided insights by class testing much of the material. Teachers across the country welcome us at seminars and provided suggestions and criticisms. These comments helped us to stay on track and prepare a textbook that would be user friendly in the classroom. We are especially thankful to the following reviewers who evaluated our manuscripts to ensure that the text meet the needs of their classrooms.

Muriel Berry
Co-operative Education Coordinator
General Vanier S. S.
Oshawa, ON

Heather Doyle
F. W. Johnson Collegiate
Regina, SK

Sharon Wilson, C. M. A.
Business Education Department Head
Maples Collegiate
Winnipeg, MB

Robert Cameron
St. Patrick's H. S.
Halifax, NS

Ray Carroll
School of Business
Dalhousie University, NS

Dolorosa Dollard
Western Community College
Stephenville, NF

Ron Hansen
Paul Kane Composite H. S.
St. Albert, AB

Ron Kaziuk
Salisbury Composite H. S.
Sherwood Park, AB

Richard Lander
Jarvis C. I.
Toronto, ON

Howard Lear
Business Department Head
Killarney Secondary School
Vancouver, BC

Dorothy Lukkien
Walter Murray Collegiate
Saskatoon, SK

Jim McCracken
Britannia S. S.
Vancouver, BC

Sharon McCrae
St. Boniface Diocesan H. S.
Winnipeg, MB

Diane Mavety
Magee S. S.
Vancouver, BC

Dennis Moffat
Evan Hardy Collegiate
Saskatoon, SK

Karen Wood
Woburn C.I.
Scarborough, ON

We would also like to recognize the contribution made in special ways by the following people: Kay Petch, a research assistant, fulfilled every request enthusiastically and expeditiously; Margo Murchison spent many hours proofreading and making suggestions that gave clarity to the text; John Priddle for his valuable comments and suggestions.

We would also like to recognize the staff at John Wiley & Sons Canada Limited, who provided us with the support and encouragement which are so necessary in completing a project of this magnitude. John Lynch originally supported the project. Others who made a significant contribution, and provided daily encouragement and direction, were Linda Scott, Oliver Salzmann, Jeffrey Aberle, and Madhu Ranadive. Special thanks are due to Joseph Gladstone, Acquisitions Editor, who took over the project and brought it to its conclusion. Our editors were instrumental at every stage of the project, providing encouragement, direction, suggestions, and criticism. Debbie Davies, our copy editor, perused the various stages to ensure that the detail, which is so important in an accounting project, was correct. Marg Bukta, our developmental editor, was very precise in her comments, and brought special insights and talents to the project. She worked with enthusiasm, dedication, patience, and interest, and her efforts are reflected in many aspects of the book.

Finally, we would like to thank our families, who gave up quality time with us while we were working on this text. Their love, understanding, and patience were a source of constant encouragement.

To the Student

Accounting Principles: A Skill-Building Approach is designed to help you understand accounting terms, principles, and procedures used in today's business environment. The text also demonstrates the usefulness of those skills in your everyday life.

By following the growth, problems, and development of the Algor Computer Company, you will learn how to present business information both orally and in writing, and to assess critically business information presented to you. The format of presentation of the ideas, skills, and knowledge in the text encourages initiative, problem solving, and critical analysis.

The Book Plan

The text is divided into 14 chapters. Each chapter's title states the overall accounting function to be studied. The specific learning objectives for that chapter are listed as skills to be acquired by the end of the chapter. Any new vocabulary, concept, or special accounting term introduced in the chapter is presented at the beginning of the chapter under the heading "Language of Accounting".

The chapters are divided into sections, which are numbered for easy reference. Each section is followed by two sets of activities: "Lesson Review" questions are factual, recall questions, and "Lesson Applications" are practical applications that give you the opportunity to use the information and skills you have just learned.

Throughout each section, new vocabulary, concepts, or accounting terms (those identified at the beginning of the chapter) first appear in boldface type. All such new vocabulary items are defined in the margin beside their first use. Thus, you are alerted to the term at the beginning of the chapter, see it used and defined in context, and defined formally in the margin.

Often, in the text, there are interesting facts under the heading "The Facts Speak". These are sets of data that provide a connection between the information being presented in the chapter and the real world of business.

At the end of each chapter, there is s a set of activities designed for skill development and application. They are presented under the following headings.

Accounting Principles and Concepts: a review of the major accounting ideas presented in the chapter in point form.

Food for Thought: a set of mini problems that require consideration of, and response to, a single issue. Each problem relates to a specific accounting concept developed in the chapter and gives you the opportunity to demonstrate your understanding of the underlying principle.

Organizing: These questions ask you to present information from the chapter in a different format.

Applications: In this section, you use the skills and information you have gained from the chapter to complete a series of accounting procedures.

Focussing: This section takes a major skill or concept from the chapter and investigates it further. For example, Chapter 4 focusses on the trial balance.

Evaluate and Assess: This section presents actual office situations. You are asked to analyze the information provided and prepare an evaluation of the system.

Synthesize and Conclude: In this section, general information, often of a statistical nature, is given. You are asked to draw conclusions based on your understanding of the data.

Accounting at Work is a feature that appears in every chapter. Here, a specific individual is highlighted and his or her career path is examined. Each person is in an accounting-related job or uses accounting to better accomplish his or her work objectives. One or two newspaper ads for this type of job appear along with the profile. The accompanying questions focus on the relationship between the skills you are learning in this course and your future career choices.

Business Career Skills is a set of activities designed to sharpen and increase business communication skills and to introduce you to real work management problems.

Each chapter ends with a **Computer Accounting** section.

We hope you enjoy using this text and wish you luck in this course and in your future endeavours.

CHAPTER ONE

The Balance Sheet

LEARNING OBJECTIVES

At the end of this chapter you should be able to
- distinguish between bookkeeping and accounting;
- describe the role of an accountant;
- describe skills required of an accountant;
- prepare a personal balance sheet;
- prepare a balance sheet for a business;
- discuss basic generally accepted accounting principles;
- load a spreadsheet program and use it to format a balance sheet model;
- use the spreadsheet model to enter assets and liabilities and automatically calculate the owner's equity.

LANGUAGE OF ACCOUNTING

You will see the following terms in this chapter:

assets	electronic spreadsheet program
audit	entrepreneur
balance sheet	equities
cells	financial worksheet
collateral	liabilities
creditor	marketable securities
debtor	

> "*Luca Pacioli first wrote about accounting in 1494.*"

Accounting: the gathering of information about a business and the subsequent recording, summarizing, and interpreting of it.

Bookkeeping: the gathering and recording of financial information about a business.

1.1 The Role of an Accountant

The practice of accounting goes back to ancient civilizations. The technique currently used, however, was first written about by Luca Pacioli, in 1494 in Italy. Since that time accounting has evolved to include many concepts not considered in those days. However, the basic concept of double-entry accounting that you will learn in this book is that which was documented by Pacioli.

Accounting has many purposes, and has been given many definitions. We shall broadly define **accounting** as gathering financial information about a business, and then recording, summarizing, and interpreting it. That information is then made available to interested persons. In actual fact, accounting is broken down into two types of functions: the bookkeeping function and the accounting function. The **bookkeeping** function is the gathering and recording of financial information. Bookkeepers record the day-to-day activities of a business, keeping track of all items related to the two main activities of any business: buying and selling. At the end of certain time periods, the bookkeeper, under the direction of an accountant, will prepare summaries in order to meet the requirements of those persons interested in the financial position of the business.

The accounting function includes more sophisticated tasks. The accountant is responsible for designing the system that the bookkeeper uses. Furthermore, the accountant uses the summaries provided by the bookkeeper to make more specialized reports, and to interpret the information included in these reports. The interpretation of information is necessary in order to determine the current financial situation of a business, and to make sound plans for its future.

> *"Accounting is the language of business."*

Accounting is frequently referred to as "the language of business". Your study of accounting will not only provide you with the basic skills of accounting, but it will also propel you into the world of decision making that influences the success or failure of a business.

The role of an accountant is described in our definition of accounting: a provider of information to interested users, and an interpreter of that information for the business itself.

Who are these users of financial information? The most important group of users of the financial information prepared by accountants is the management of the business. Financial reports are an accumulation of the past history of the business, and the wise interpretation of these reports by the accountant allows management to properly plan for the future of the business.

> *"Profit is the main goal of most businesses."*

The main goal of most businesses is to make a profit. To meet this goal, many decisions must be made. Should the business change its prices, perhaps, or reduce costs by laying off workers, or find other ways

"You seem to have the qualifications we're looking for in a bookkeeper."

HERMAN copyright (1976) Jim Unger. Reprinted with permission of Universal Press Syndicate. All rights reserved.

to cut costs? Should it expand? If so, how? By buying out existing businesses, by franchising additional outlets, or by opening branches? The decisions required in a business are many, and most of them are based on financial information. The following summary of a news digest highlights the results of not obtaining and using financial information properly.

THREE BUOYS

Three Buoys houseboats was created in 1982 by two commerce graduates. They built and sold hundreds of houseboats to Canadian investors, becoming one of the most successful companies in the early 1980s. The investors rented the houseboats to those looking for a place in the sun and on the water during the summer. However, by 1987 the success story had turned to a disaster, and the firm was in receivership. Two reasons were given for the collapse. Buyers of the boats were initially able to take advantage of a tax break that was subsequently eliminated by Revenue Canada. However, the main problem, according to a management consultant, was that the two owners were geniuses only in marketing and sales, and did not rely on others to make up for their weaknesses in accounting and cost analysis. The two apparently had no time for detail, accounting, and number-crunching.

Creditor: *a person or business to whom others are financially indebted.*

Many other users of financial information are found outside of the management team of the business. Certainly anyone who has loaned money to that business (a **creditor**) wants to know its financial position. For example, businesses frequently borrow money from financial institutions, such as banks or trust companies. Also, the government requires that data be provided, the most important of which is information regarding earnings for income tax purposes. Prospective investors looking for future returns on their investment will base their investment decision mainly on the past history of the business. Other users of the financial information are listed in the following table:

USERS OF ACCOUNTING INFORMATION	
Inside the Business	**Outside the Business**
Owners	Creditors
Managers	Prospective investors
Employees	Suppliers
	Labour unions
	Competitors
	Customers
	Government
	Political parties

Organization chart: *a chart showing the lines of authority and responsibility in a business.*

The accountant's prime task is to provide financial information for the use of the business itself. The accountant is a member of the management team whose expertise is relied on by the managers responsible for other areas of the business. Most businesses prepare an **organization chart** that illustrates the authority and responsibility belonging to each area of the business. A typical organization chart is shown here for Algor Computer Services, after it had become a very large business.

FIGURE 1-1 ORGANIZATION CHART FOR A COMPUTER SERVICES BUSINESS

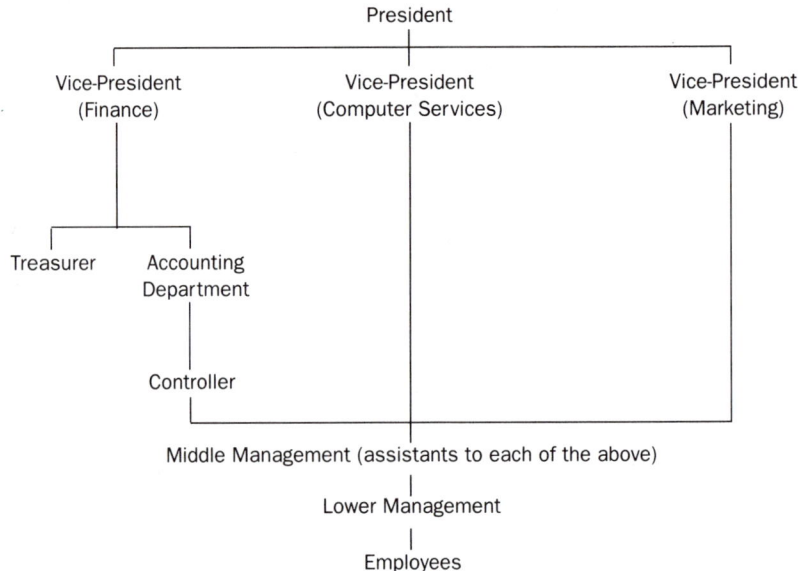

Controller: *the chief accountant of a business.*

Treasurer: *the person responsible for handling cash, making payments, and all dealings with financial institutions.*

The department heads meet regularly to decide upon the future course of the business. The **controller** is the chief accountant, and represents the accounting department at such times. Each department relies upon the accounting department to complete a variety of tasks related to the accounting function. The **treasurer** is responsible for handling cash, making payments, and all dealings with financial institutions.

The various tasks within the accounting department itself are illustrated in Figure 1-2. Each of the tasks will be examined in detail in later chapters in the text.

The tasks carried out by the accounting department vary from business to business, depending upon the needs and size of the business.

FIGURE 1-2 ORGANIZATION CHART FOR AN ACCOUNTING DEPARTMENT

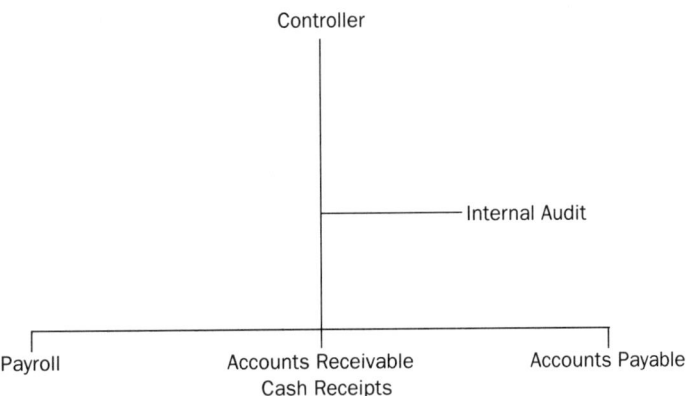

> **An audit:** a check of the financial records to ensure their accuracy, and to ensure that generally accepted accounting principles are being followed.
>
> **Accounts receivable:** claims the business has on customers to whom the business sold goods or services on credit.
>
> **Accounts payable:** amounts owing to other businesses for goods or services bought on credit.

For example, in some businesses the purchasing department, credit office or budgeting department may be part of the accounting department. At Algor Computer Services, the controller oversees the work of all members of the department, and decides what accounting procedures will be followed and what reports will be prepared. She provides the reports to other departments so that decision making can occur.

The Internal **Audit** division is responsible for checking the accuracy of the employees' accounting work, and for ensuring that the established policies are being followed. The Payroll division keeps a record of hours of work, pay levels, and deductions made, and prepares paycheques. As well, this division makes payments on behalf of employees for various deductions taken from their pay. These deductions include income tax, unemployment insurance, and Canada Pension among others.

The **Accounts Receivable** division keeps records of all customers who buy on credit, and sends them monthly statements. Related to this division is the Cash Receipts division, which records payments received from the credit customers and receipts from all cash sales. The **Accounts Payable** division maintains records of amounts owing to suppliers, and payments made.

As you can see from the above organization charts, the accounting department performs a service to all aspects of the business. Accountants must have many skills at hand in order to perform the many tasks required. The following is a list of skills that are emphasized throughout this text.

Skills of an Accountant		
Communication	**Technical**	**Management**
Interviewing	Accounting	Chairperson
Reading	Analyzing	Decision Making
Research	Budgeting	Leadership
Speaking	Computer	Organization
Writing	Forecasting	Problem Solving
	Mathematics	Supervision
		Time Management

The controller at Algor not only has to perform the accounting tasks listed above, but, among other things, must
- supervise the people in her department, and demonstrate leadership skills;
- keep up with changes in the accounting profession;
- have personal organization skills;
- communicate with other departments;
- solve problems and make decisions;
- co-ordinate the computerized accounting system as it applies to the total business.

In order to fulfill these various requirements, it is important that the controller develop and maintain the skills shown above.

Lesson Review

1. Distinguish between bookkeeping and accounting.
2. Why is accounting referred to as the language of business?
3. What are the two main roles of an accountant?
4. What is the main goal of most businesses? Can you name businesses that would not have it as their main goal?
5. What is a business organization chart? Why are these charts prepared?
6. Describe the function of each division of the accounting department at Algor Computer Services.
7. What information would the Vice-Presidents in charge of Computer Services and of Marketing want from the accounting department?
8. Why must an accountant have so many skills in order to be successful?

Lesson Applications

9. For each of the users of financial information listed on page 3, indicate what information they would need to know about the business.

10. For each skill listed on page 6, indicate a task that you think the controller at Algor Computer Services performs that requires the skill.

1.2 A Personal Balance Sheet

Entrepreneur: a person who perceives a business opportunity, organizes a plan to take advantage of it, and raises capital to finance it.

Service business: a business that sells a personal skill or the use of something.

Merchandising business: a business that buys goods for resale.

Proprietorship: a business owned by one person.

Balance sheet: a financial statement that shows what a business or person owns, owes and is worth at a specific date.

Vijay Marshall decided a number of years ago that he wanted to be an entrepreneur. (An **entrepreneur** is one who perceives a business opportunity, organizes a business plan to take advantage of the opportunity, and raises capital to finance the project. In effect, an entrepreneur is a risk taker.) Vijay had enjoyed the business courses he had taken in high school. He subsequently went to university and specialized in computer math and to college for computer technology courses. Vijay worked for a number of years, and had accumulated some savings. He also inherited some money, which finally made it possible for him to plan the opening of his own business, Algor Computer Services.

His business plan was to operate a service business, repairing certain brands of computers and installing computer networks. (A **service business** provides either a personal skill, such as that of a repairman, or the use of something, such as a bowling alley.) As finances would permit, he hoped to expand his business activities to include merchandising. (A **merchandising business** buys goods for the purpose of reselling them.) Vijay approached his bank manager for a loan because he did not think his own funds were sufficient to start the business. Moreover, he wanted to have a **proprietorship**, a business owned by one person. What financial information would the bank manager require from Vijay?

The bank manager asked Vijay to provide information concerning his financial position so that she could determine the risk to the bank in extending the loan. To show this information in a form consistent with that used by accountants, it was necessary for Vijay to prepare a balance sheet. A **balance sheet** is a financial statement that shows what a business or person owns, owes and is worth at a specific date. Vijay knew from his accounting courses that a balance sheet required a listing of his **assets** (things of value that he owned) and his **liabilities** (monies that he owed). He prepared the balance sheet shown in Figure 1-3.

FIGURE 1-3 PERSONAL BALANCE SHEET FOR VIJAY MARSHALL

Vijay Marshall
Balance Sheet
as at May 31, 1985

Assets		Liabilities	
Cash	$14 980	Charge Accounts	$ 850
Marketable Securities	45 000	Automobile loan	4 300
Loan to Brother	2 500	Total Liabilities	5 150
Personal Items	4 000		
Computer	9 500		
Stereo Equipment	3 400		
Furniture	7 200	**Net Worth**	
Automobile	12 500	V. Marshall, Capital	93 930
		Total Liabilities	
Total Assets	**$99 080**	**and Capital**	**$99 080**

An asset: *something of value that is owned.*

A liability: *an amount that is owed.*

Marketable Security: *an investment that can be readily converted to cash.*

Investment: *a financial asset that the owner intends to keep for more than a year.*

Debtor: *a business or a person that another business or person owns a claim on.*

In preparing his personal balance sheet, Vijay recorded the assets at the cost price, which is the price that he paid for them. He included the marketable securities that he had received as an inheritance, for he now had control over them. Let us examine all the items on Vijay's balance sheet in detail.

Assets

Assets are things of value that are owned. Cash, the first asset that Vijay listed, is common to all of us. Whether it is cash on hand in the business or on deposit at a financial institution, it is listed as cash. Cash includes coins, bills, cheques, and money orders. The **marketable securities** that Vijay listed are Canada Savings Bonds, which he received as an inheritance. Marketable securities include any investment that can be readily converted to cash. In Vijay's case, Canada Savings Bonds can be cashed at any financial institution. If the investments cannot be readily converted to cash, or if it is the intent of the owner to keep them for longer than a year, they are usually listed on the balance sheet as **Investments**. If Vijay had purchased shares in a company, they too would be listed as an investment.

The claim that Vijay has on his brother is collectable at some future date. His brother is a **debtor**: someone on whom Vijay owns a claim. The other assets that Vijay listed were either bought by Vijay or given to him. They are referred to as fixed assets: assets that he will keep for a long time. He also had other things in his possession, such as compact discs that he had borrowed from a friend. Since Vijay did not own them, he did not include them in his list of assets.

Liabilities

The debts owed by Vijay are his liabilities. The people or businesses to whom the money is owed are called creditors. People borrow money in order to buy assets. In this case, Vijay had borrowed money by using his VISA card to purchase a new amplifier. Although he had repaid part of the amount, at the time of making his balance sheet he still owed $850. He had also obtained a loan from the bank to buy his car.

Owner's Equity

The difference in value between Vijay's assets and his liabilities is his **net worth**, or **owner's equity**. As is evident from Vijay's balance sheet, the total of his assets is equal to the total of his liabilities plus owner's equity.

Net worth or *owner's equity:* the difference in value between assets and liabilities.

$$\text{ASSETS} = \text{LIABILITIES} + \text{OWNER'S EQUITY}$$

Fundamental accounting equation: Assets = Liabilities + Owner's Equity.

The equation Assets = Liabilities + Owner's Equity is referred to as the **fundamental accounting equation**. It is the basis for many of the concepts that we will learn in the following chapters. The relationship is always true, for what you own (assets) minus what you owe (liabilities) is equal to your worth. As is also evident, the left side of the balance sheet is equal to the right side, which is the reason for the name *balance sheet*.

LESSON REVIEW

11. What is the purpose of a balance sheet?

12. What is an asset?

13. What is a liability?

14. What is owner's equity? How is it calculated?

15. What is the fundamental accounting equation?

16. Why is the financial statement called a balance sheet?

LESSON APPLICATIONS

17. Prepare your personal balance sheet.

18. Indicate which of the following should be included on a personal balance sheet, and explain why or why not.
    (a) a bicycle
    (b) textbooks borrowed from the school for the year

(c) an old book that has been read, and is no longer wanted
(d) a portable radio that has been partly paid for
(e) money owed to a parent, who does not expect to be paid back
(f) an old tent received from a neighbour who was throwing it in the garbage

19. Prepare a fictitious balance sheet for the person you admire most.

20. Indicate whether the following are service and/or merchandising businesses, and, where applicable, indicate the service that each provides.
    (a) Petro-Canada Inc.
    (b) Sears Canada Inc.
    (c) Royal Bank of Canada
    (d) Canadian National
    (e) Morton's Chiropractic Clinic
    (f) Wilson, Easton, and Billings, Law Office
    (g) Double Decker Golf Range
    (h) Loblaws Supermarkets

1.3 Balance Sheet for a Business

The balance sheet for a business looks very much like the one prepared by Vijay to show his personal financial position. After a few years of being in business, Algor Computer Services has the balance sheet shown in Figure 1-4. Note that it only includes items related to the business, it does not include any of Vijay's personal items. Vijay's personal items and business items are looked upon as separate entities. An **entity** is referred to as a unit of accountability, and for accounting purposes they should not be mixed.

An entity: *a unit of accountability.*

Steps in Preparing a Balance Sheet

The format for the balance sheet, as for all accounting documents, is consistent from business to business. This enables users to make better comparisons of the financial information in the documents. For balance sheets, the following rules apply:

1. A three-line heading answers the questions
   Who? — the name of the business, Algor Computer Services
   What? — the name of the document, in this case a Balance Sheet
   When? — the date on which the balance sheet was made, June 30, 1988
   Note: A balance sheet provides a snapshot of the financial condition of the firm after the close of business on the date shown on the statement. As soon as the date changes, the balance sheet is no longer valid.

FIGURE 1-4 BALANCE SHEET FOR ALGOR COMPUTER SERVICES

Algor Computer Services
Balance Sheet
as at June 30, 1988

Assets		Liabilities	
Cash	$ 97 843	Accounts Payable	$ 24 503
Accounts Receivable	37 901	Short-Term Loans	17 302
Office Supplies	1 239	Mortgage Payable	248 000
Land	124 600	Total Liabilities	289 805
Building	228 000		
Office Equipment	14 500		
Computer Equipment	45 600	**Owner's Equity**	
Automobile	12 500	V. Marshall, Capital	272 378
		Total Liabilities and	
Total Assets	**$562 183**	**Owner's Equity**	**$562 183**

2. The heading Assets is centred on the left half of the page, with the assets and their values listed, followed by a single line and the total title, Total Assets.

3. The heading Liabilities is centred on the right half of the page, with the liabilities and their values listed, followed by a single line and the total title, Total Liabilities.

4. The heading Owner's Equity is centred after the Total Liabilities. The owner's name, followed by the word Capital is entered, with the amount of the owner's equity. This value should be calculated using the fundamental accounting equation. The amount is followed by a single line, and the liabilities and owner's equity are then added to get Total Liabilities and Owner's Equity. (Blank lines should be left after the Total Liabilities line so that the Total Assets will be on the same line as the Total Liabilities and Owner's Equity.)

5. The final totals are double ruled. Dollar signs should be placed at the top of each column, and beside the final totals. When using columnar paper, dollar signs and decimals are not necessary.

6. The balance sheet is one of the most important business statements, and is therefore usually typed. Because of its importance, there should be no errors or corrections on the statement, and no abbreviations. Your teacher will tell you whether to use pencil or ink for your course work.

Columnar paper: vertically-ruled paper used in accounting to record amounts.

Columnar paper, or accounting paper, is commonly used for accounting. The paper is designed with vertically ruled lines to accomplish the particular purpose of the accountant. Observe how the amounts are written in the money columns on the balance sheet in Figure 1-5. Dollar signs, commas, and decimals are usually not used. When there are no cents, a – or 00 may be written in the cents column. (When columnar paper is not used, dollar signs and decimals are added. Dollar signs are placed beside the first figure in a column and beside final column totals.)

FIGURE 1-5 BALANCE SHEET ON COLUMNAR PAPER

Algor Computer Services
Balance Sheet
as at June 30, 1988

Assets		Liabilities	
Cash	97 843 –	Accounts Payable	24 503 –
Accounts Receivable	37 901 –	Short-Term Loans	17 302 –
Office Supplies	1 239 –	Mortgage Payable	248 000 –
Land	124 600 –	Total Liabilities	289 805 –
Building	228 000 –		
Office Equipment	14 500 –		
Computer Equipment	45 600 –	Owner's Equity	
Automobile	12 500 –	V. Marshall, Capital	272 378 –
Total Assets	562 183 –	Total Liabilities and Owner's Equity	562 183 –

At all times, in order to show that a mathematical operation has taken place, a single line precedes the total. To show that a total is the final total, a double-ruled line is placed under it.

Abbreviations are not used on financial statements unless they are part of the official name of the business. The firm Sears Canada Inc. does have an abbreviation in its official name, so it is written using the short form. The firm Willson Automobile Parts Limited does not use the short form of Limited (Ltd.) in its name, so the word should be written out. No abbreviations of account names such as A.P. for Accounts Payable should be used.

Neatness is extremely important in accounting, for all users of the financial information must be able to read the names and numbers. A great deal of time can be wasted trying to find errors caused by illegible numbers. To correct errors, one of two procedures is followed. If the error is more than one digit, a straight line is drawn through the entire number, and the correct number is written above. If the error is only one digit, a diagonal is used. The diagonal is used so that there is no confusion with the number 7, which is sometimes written as a 7. The following illustrates the procedure for correcting:

$$579.41$$
$$\overline{-462.98\text{-}}$$

$$9\overset{2}{\cancel{8}}3.67$$

A great deal of time may be spent reading numbers, especially during an audit. One person reads numbers from a document to another person who checks the numbers: possibly for half a day. In order to do this quickly, a standard way of reading numbers is followed. The amount $1 567.83 will commonly be read one thousand five hundred and sixty-seven dollars and eighty-three cents: a total of ten words. However, the number of words that are read can be reduced by following one of two rules:

1. Break the number down into pairs of digits working from right to left: the above number will then be read fifteen sixty-seven eighty-three, a total of three words. The person visually checking the entry knows that the last word indicates the cents. If there are no cents, as in $934.00, the number is read nine thirty-four dollars.

2. Read the number in groupings according to where the space(s) and decimal fall: the above number will then be read one five sixty-seven eighty-three, a total of four words.

Balance Sheet Items

The *left side* of the balance sheet lists the assets, that is, items of value owned by the business. They include each of the following:

Cash for the business balance sheet includes the same items as for Vijay's personal balance sheet. In addition, businesses have VISA and MasterCard credit card drafts, which will be discussed in Chapter 6.

Accounts Receivable are claims that Algor Computer Services has on customers who did not pay at the time a service was rendered. As with Vijay's brother, these customers are referred to as debtors. These claims are usually collectable within thirty days of the date of the sale. The claims may be listed individually with surnames or business names in alphabetical order, such as B. Cameron, D. Martino, etc., or they may be lumped together under the heading Accounts Receivable, or they may be listed as Accounts Receivable/B. Cameron.

Office Supplies are items purchased for use within the office, such as paper, and computer ribbons.

Fixed Assets are items that are tangible and are going to remain in the business for some time. These include items such as land, buildings, equipment, and automobiles.

Cash: this asset includes cash on deposit, coins, bills, cheques, money orders, and credit card drafts.

Equities: the claims against the assets of the business.

The *right side* of the balance sheet lists the **equities**, or claims against the assets of the business. Equities are divided into two categories: liabilities, which are amounts owed to others, and owner's equity, which represents the owner's claim on the business.

$$\text{ASSETS} = \text{EQUITIES}$$
$$\text{ASSETS} = \underset{\text{(creditors)}}{\text{LIABILITIES}} + \underset{\text{(owner)}}{\text{OWNER'S EQUITY}}$$

Liabilities are the debts owed by the business. The businesses, governments, or employees to whom they are owed are called creditors. Each creditor has a claim on the business for the amount owing to them. Liabilities include the following:

Accounts Payable are amounts owing to creditors for goods or services that the business purchased. These amounts must be paid within a specified time, usually within thirty days. As with Accounts Receivable, they may be listed individually or lumped together under the heading Accounts Payable, or they may be listed as Accounts Payable/Willson Office Supplies Ltd.

Loans are amounts owing to a financial institution, such as loans obtained from a bank or a trust company. Such loans are usually repayable in one of two ways: over a number of years, or on demand by the financial institution.

Mortgage Payable is an amount borrowed to purchase an expensive item such as land or a building. The borrower signs a pledge to pay back the sum owed at a specified payment and frequency and within a specified length of time. If the borrower is unable to pay, the mortgage agreement entitles the creditor to seize the asset for which the loan was given. The asset is the **collateral**, or security, for the loan. Mortgages are repayable over many years.

Collateral: the security given as a pledge for repayment of a loan.

The other equity is the claim that the owner has on the business. In the event of bankruptcy or closing of the business, the creditors have first claim on the assets. The owner has a claim on whatever remains, which is referred to as a **residual claim**. If there are not enough assets to satisfy the claims of the creditors, the owner of a proprietorship is personally responsible for them. For example, if a firm owed $90 000

Residual claim: the last claim on the business.

THE FACTS SPEAK...

Assets as at December 31, 1989
Dominion Textile Inc. and subsidiary companies, $1 368 379 000
McDonald's Corporation, $8 158 674 000
Canadian National Railway System, $6 906 035 000

The Facts Speak...

Liabilities as at December 31, 1989
Dominion Textile Inc. and subsidiary companies, $822 821 000
McDonald's Corporation, $4 745 864 000
Canadian National Railway System, $3 531 180

---

and its assets could only be sold for $70 000 when closing, the owner would be personally responsible for the $20 000 difference.

V. Marshall, Capital represents the net worth of the business, or the claim that the owner has on the business. It is calculated by subtracting the value of the claims of the creditors — the liabilities — from the value of the assets.

Order of Liquidity

For the purpose of consistency, assets that are quickly converted into cash, or used within the year, are listed in what is referred to as the **order of liquidity**. The order of assets for Algor Computer Services and the reason for the position of each are as follows:

Cash — most liquid of all assets
Accounts Receivable — converted to cash, usually within 30 days
Office Supplies — used up during the year

In the case of physical assets that last a long time, the listing is usually done in the inverse order of liquidity. Therefore, on Algor Computer Services' balance sheet, Land is listed first, followed by Building, Office Equipment, Computer Equipment, and Automobile.

Liabilities are listed according to when they are due, or mature, with those due within a year listed first. This is referred to as the **maturity rule**. It is therefore possible to have two listings for a loan or a mortgage: one for the amount due in the current year, another for amounts due in later years. Frequently, all loans are lumped into two categories: short-term debt and long-term debt.

Order of liquidity: the order in which assets are used up or converted to cash.

Maturity rule: liabilities are listed in the order of maturity date.

Lesson Review

21. What questions do the three-line headings of a statement answer?
22. What is done to the final totals on all financial statements?
23. Distinguish between the use of dollar signs, commas, and decimals on typewritten statements and statements on columnar paper.

24. Write the following numbers as they would be read aloud by an accountant: $834.23; $4 392.88; $103.65; $429.00; $23.00; $83.93; $0.03

25. What items are included in the term "cash"?

26. What do you call a person or business for whom you set up an account receivable?

27. Distinguish between office supplies and other physical assets.

28. What are equities? What are the two categories of equities?

29. What do you call a person or business for whom you set up an account payable?

30. Distinguish between a loan and a mortgage.

31. What is collateral?

32. Who has first claim on the assets of a business?

33. How is the claim of the owner on the business calculated?

34. Describe how the order of liquidity applies to assets on a balance sheet.

35. In what order are physical assets listed on a balance sheet?

36. In what order are liabilities listed on a balance sheet?

LESSON APPLICATIONS

37. (a) Give the name of a business in your area, and list seven assets it has.
    (b) Using the same business mentioned in (a), list three liabilities that it might have.

38. Complete the following equations by calculating the unknown amount.

Assets	=	Liabilities	+	Owner's Equity
$40 000	=	$20 000	+	?
?	=	$30 000	+	$10 000
$49 000	=	?	+	$18 000
$68 000	=	$49 000	+	?
?	=	$68 000	+	$23 000

39. Christine Boyko was preparing the balance sheet for her business, Chris's Craft Shop. Indicate which of the following items should be included on the business's balance sheet.
    (a) Cash in her personal account.

(b) Cash in the business's bank account.
(c) The building she rents for her business.
(d) Display cases for the store bought using the business's funds.
(e) A friend's wood crafts, which Chris's Craft Shop is trying to sell for her.
(f) A car rented from a car leasing agency, but used in the business.
(g) A cash register that was purchased using a trust company loan. The loan has not been fully repaid.

40. Given the following items for Willett Building Cleaning, prepare a balance sheet in accepted accounting form as at August 31, 19–8. The firm is owned by A. Willett.

Cleaning Supplies	$ 780	Office Building	$29 000
Cleaning Equipment	12 000	Land	54 000
Accounts Payable	3 290	Trucks	29 080
Cash	4 325	Bank Loan	2 100
Accounts Receivable	2 489	Mortgage Payable	36 760
A. Willett, Capital	89 524		

41. The following balance sheet was prepared by Erin Vollrath, for the business which she owned, Erin's Dance Studio.

Balance Sheet of
Erin Vollrath
as at Sept. 30, 19–3

Accounts Payable	$ 2 000	Mortgage Payable	$110 000
Building	90 000	Accounts Receivable	5 000
Land	20 000	Bank Loan	2 000
Stereo Equipment	8 000		
Personal Automobile	12 500	Vollrath, Equity	24 500
Cash	9 000	Total Equities	$141 500
Total Assets	$141 500		

State ten errors that Erin has made in the preparation of the balance sheet, and indicate why each is an error.

1.4 Generally Accepted Accounting Principles

The reason for preparing financial documents of any type is to provide information to someone: the owner, management, creditors, prospective investors, the government, or others. Yet, for financial information to be meaningful, all accountants must follow the same rules. For example, if Vijay Marshall decides to expand Algor Computer Services and needs a loan to do so, it will be necessary for him to provide prospective creditors with statements that indicate the financial position of the business, and its prospects for the future. He will be competing with other borrowers, for any lending institution has only so much money available to lend. The preparation of these statements requires that the accountant know the rules, and apply them to the best of his or her ability.

The Rule Makers

In Canada, the accounting profession has developed a set of principles that are referred to as "generally accepted accounting principles" (**GAAPs**). These principles are referred to as generally accepted because they have been adopted by the accounting profession. The *Canadian Business Corporations Act* states that the principles established by the Canadian Institute of Chartered Accountants (CICA) are those that will apply in Canada. The establishment of these rules follows in-depth study by the CICA's Accounting Standards Committee. The principles established by the CICA are set out in the *CICA Handbook*. It should be noted, however, that there are increased pressures on this organization to adopt rules that apply on an international basis.

The trend toward globalization is going to affect Canada's accounting standards. The International Accounting Standards Committee has been formed to give recognition to the new global economy. Businesses are getting larger, opening offices in foreign countries, or merging with foreign companies. There is a need, therefore, to have accounting standards that apply on a worldwide basis. This process has resulted in the proposal of twenty-nine changes to international accounting standards, thirteen of which affect Canada directly.

There are a number of advantages to having international standards. It will be much easier to assess a balance sheet, for the same worldwide accounting standards will be applied in its preparation. It will be much easier for multinational corporations to obtain audits when there are globally uniform rules. As well, it will reduce the costs to firms of following the different national standards when companies sell stocks and bonds in a number of countries at the same time.

Other accounting organizations also recommend principles that are followed in their specialized areas. The Society of Management Accountants of Canada (SMAC) prepares *Management Accounting Guidelines*. The Canadian Certified General Accountants Association (CCGAA) publishes professional literature for its members, including a *GAAP Guide*. We will examine many of the principles followed in the profession throughout the text. Some of the principles are outlined here.

Business Entity Concept

The **business entity concept** assumes that the financial information provided about a business is exclusive, that is, it does not include any

GAAPs: generally accepted accounting principles.

Business entity concept: the financial information about one entity must be kept separate from that of other entities.

data about the owner or other businesses. The balance sheet for Algor Computer Services, for instance, should therefore not include any personal items belonging to Vijay Marshall.

Historical Cost Principle

When Vijay Marshall prepared his personal balance sheet for the bank, he had a number of options for the dollar amount to use for the various asset items. He could use the value of the item when he purchased it, the value that it represents to him, or the value he thought that he could get if he sold it. The **historical cost principle**, however, states that assets are to be recorded on the balance sheet at original cost. Since this is a GAAP, users of balance sheets know that all items are recorded at their cost price. Certainly this means, however, that the values on the statement are not realistic. We will learn later how to make adjustments to the statement and add explanatory notes, such that the statement provides more meaningful information.

> **Historical cost principle:** assets are recorded on the balance sheet at their original cost.

Monetary Unit Concept

The **monetary unit concept** assumes that money is the common denominator for measuring economic activity, and that amounts appearing in financial statements are in Canadian dollars. It is also assumed that the dollar remains relatively stable. All items on Algor Computer Services' balance sheet are expressed in Canadian dollars. Simple as that idea may seem, it causes difficulties at times, because inflation causes the purchasing power of the dollar to decline. As well, some assets, such as land, increase in value due to inflation. Combining this concept with the historical cost principle leads to financial statements that may be distorted. The same type of office equipment, for example, may be recorded on two different balance sheets at two different values merely because the items were purchased in different years. Much discussion has taken place in the accounting profession about whether changes in price levels should be reflected in the valuation of assets in the financial statements. Current policy is not to change the values to reflect changes in the value of money.

> **Monetary unit concept:** money is the common denominator for measuring economic activity. Canadian money is the unit of measure.

Going Concern Assumption

The **going concern assumption** states that it is assumed that a business has an unlimited life. The value of many assets shown on a balance sheet would not have meaning if this assumption were not followed. For example, a hotel that uses monogrammed linens would record them on the balance sheet at cost price. If the hotel were going out of business, however, the linens might have very little value, especially if the new owner planned to change the name or logo of the business. This

> **Going concern assumption:** it is assumed that the business entity has an unlimited life.

assumption also supports the historical cost principle. Since most assets are for use in the business, and are not for resale, it is rational to record them at cost price and not market value.

Full Disclosure Principle

You might ask whether a balance sheet is of any value if the items are recorded at cost and one does not know what the true value is. In order to provide the users of the financial information with more meaningful data, other relevant information is disclosed along with the statement. The **full disclosure principle** states that information that will influence the judgement and decisions of an informed user must be presented. The information can be presented either as a note to accompany the financial statement, or in other financial information. The significance of providing full disclosure has not been lost on some investors, for they have sued businesses for not fully disclosing relevant information.

> *Full disclosure principle:* information that will influence the judgement and decisions of an informed user must be presented.

LESSON REVIEW

42. Why is it necessary that generally accepted accounting principles be followed?

43. What Canadian organization is legally authorized to establish the generally accepted accounting principles?

44. What other accounting organizations are involved in the preparation of accounting principles?

45. What does the business entity concept state? Why is it important?

46. What is the historical cost principle? Why is it significant to users of the balance sheet?

47. What does the monetary unit concept state? Give examples of assets that become more expensive over time, and assets that decrease in value.

48. What is the going concern assumption? What relationship does it have to the historical cost principle?

49. What is the full disclosure principle?

LESSON APPLICATIONS

50. Mikio Kiuchi was preparing a balance sheet. On it, he listed all his personal assets, and the assets of his proprietorship. What generally accepted accounting principle has not been followed?

Why would the users of his balance sheet want to know that he has combined two entities on his balance sheet?

51. Suppose that the CICA required that businesses provide one balance sheet using cost, and one balance sheet using current value. What would businesses have to do in order to meet this requirement? What benefits, if any, would it provide to users of balance sheets?

52. Company A purchased a computer in 19–3 for $150 000. In a few years the cost of computers decreased significantly, while the functions they could perform increased significantly. The same model of computer could be purchased by Company B in 19–8 for $90 000. Can these balance sheets be realistically compared? What accounting principles must the user of the balance sheets be aware of in order to compare these two items?

53. Royal Insurance Canada, in its *1988 Annual Report*, added the following notes to its financial reports:
    "1. Operations and balance sheet . . . are presented in accordance with generally accepted accounting principles.
    2. Investments are carried at book value. Market values at December 31, 1988 exceeded book in the aggregate by $70.8 million."

    (a) What principle is being followed by the inclusion of the notes?
    (b) Why is Note 1 important to users of the report?
    (c) The book value of the investments was $1.2 billion. Of what value is the additional information given in Note 2 to users of the report?
    (d) The *1988 Annual Report* for CN indicates that, for the pension fund that it holds in trust for its employees, the investments are shown at market value. The market value used was that of December 31, 1988. What significant GAAP change has occurred? Why would a pension fund show investments at market value and not cost price?

54. Bart owns two small businesses, one for the repair of small engines and the other is an automobile service centre. He wishes to borrow $15 000 from a trust company to expand the small engine business. What principle should Bart be certain to follow when preparing the balance sheet for the small engine business? What other information would the trust company want from Bart? Why?

55. Indicate what you, as a prospective investor in a business, would want to have disclosed to you concerning
    (a) accounts receivable
    (b) land
    (c) building
    (d) accounts payable
    (e) mortgage payable
    (f) automobile

CHAPTER REVIEW AND SKILL DEVELOPMENT

Accounting Principles and Concepts
- According to the **order of liquidity**, assets are listed in the order in which they will be converted to cash or used up.

- According to the **maturity rule**, liabilities are listed in the order of maturity date.

- The **business entity concept** states that the financial information about one entity must be kept separate from that of other entities.

- The **historical cost principle** states that assets are shown on the balance sheet at their cost price.

- The **monetary unit concept** states that Canadian dollars are used as the monetary unit for financial information. The amounts are not adjusted to reflect inflation.

- The **going concern assumption** states that the business entity is assumed to have an unlimited life.

- The **full disclosure principle** states that all information that will influence the judgement and decisions of an informed user of the financial data must be disclosed.

Knowing the Terms
For each of the following statements, indicate the term being defined.
(a) Something of value owned by the business.
(b) The gathering, recording, summarizing, and provision of financial information to interested persons.
(c) Amount due from a debtor.
(d) Security given for a loan.
(e) A creditor's claim against the assets of the business.
(f) A financial statement that shows the assets, liabilities and owner's equity of a business at one point in time.
(g) The owner's claim against the assets of the business.
(h) The order in which assets will be converted to cash or used up.
(i) A business owned by one person.
(j) GAAP that indicates the order in which liabilities will be paid.

Food for Thought
1. Geneviève Rondeau used the current value of the assets in her business when preparing the balance sheet. What effect does this have on other items on the balance sheet? In what way might users of the balance sheet be misled due to her procedure?

2. A business is about to go bankrupt. As a user of its balance sheet, what values would you want the assets to be recorded at? Why? What GAAP would this violate?

3. The 1988 inflation rate for Argentina was over 1 400%. What effect did this have for users of the balance sheets of firms in that country?

4. The owner of a business has purchased supplies for his own use and has the accountant charge these purchases to the business. What GAAP does this violate? What can the accountant do about the owner's request?

5. An accountant is hired to be the controller for a business. She says

that she is going to be part of the management team. What does this mean?

6. For what businesses are the financial reports available to the public?

7. A student who wishes to become an accountant states that the only skills that will be important to him are the accounting skills that he learns. Indicate why the student should learn as many skills as possible while in school.

8. If businesses were to record assets at market value, what would have to be done each year in order to obtain that value? Why would it not be beneficial to use market value on the balance sheet?

9. It would be possible to increase each year all the assets on the balance sheet by an amount equal to the rate of inflation. What weaknesses would there be in this approach?

10. A Canadian company that has branches in other countries wishes to prepare one balance sheet for all of its branches. How will it convert the figures of the foreign branches, which are in foreign currencies, to Canadian dollars?

11. The word capital has many meanings. Give five of them.

Organizing — Steps in Preparing a Balance Sheet

Assume that you are producing a slide show in order to explain to your peers in your class (a) the preparation of a balance sheet, and (b) the purpose of a balance sheet.
In order to do this, you are to draw six slides. Beside the first five slides put the dialogue that you would use to explain the preparation of the balance sheet. The last slide is to be used to show the purpose of a balance sheet.

Applications

1. A. Payne, Investigator, maintains an office with a secretary. Using Figure 1-6, prepare a balance sheet in proper form as at August 31, 19–1.

FIGURE 1-6

Office Equipment	$ 5 000
Automobile	29 875
Surveillance Equipment	9 870
Accounts Receivable	2 459
Cash	12 765
Accounts Payable	3 985
Bank Loan	3 278
Office Supplies	546
Land	44 900
Building	64 870
Mortgage Payable	39 876
Marketable Securities	2 280
Investments	6 000

2. Parkway Bowling Lanes is owned by Kris Shwaykowski. The firm has the following assets and liabilities as at June 30, 19–2. Prepare a balance sheet for the firm.
Cash $53 900; Accounts Receivable $1 540; Marketable Securities $12 000; Office Supplies $320; Land $110 000; Building $76 000; Office Equipment $3 900; Bowling Equipment $31 200; Investments $25 000; Accounts Payable $12 900; Short-Term Loans $15 300; Mortgage Payable $123 900.

Applications — Comprehensive

Ahamad's Accounting Services is owned by Keith Ahamad. The firm rents its premises. The assets and liabilities are as follows, as at August 31, 19--. Prepare a balance sheet, and answer the questions that follow.
Accounts Payable $14 200; Cash $16 200; Bank Loan $14 800; Automobile $13 590;

Computer Supplies $8 750; Office Equipment $3 290; Computer Equipment $35 080; Trust Company Loan $22 400; Office Supplies $1 386; Accounts Receivable $22 410.
(a) Discuss what the $3 290 figure for Office Equipment represents.
(b) Discuss how the business entity concept applied to the preparation of the balance sheet.
(c) What principle should be followed in order to give more information about the items on the balance sheet?
(d) What items on Ahamad's Accounting Services' balance sheet would you as a creditor like to know more about?
(e) One of the computers in the business is no longer usable. Should it be listed as an asset at cost price? Justify your decision.
(f) Should Keith wish to close the business at this time, what figure indicates his equity in the business? Would he actually receive that amount? Explain your answer.

Focussing — Equities

Chris Yzerman is the accountant for Jung's Video Corner. He prepares a balance sheet at year end as shown in Figure 1-7.

Chris tells the owner that equities means "claims" on the business, and that they must always be equal to the assets. He also states that it is not necessary to have the equities listed individually, since all claims are the same.
(a) Comment on Chris's statements to the owner.
(b) Why do some creditors have claims ahead of other creditors?
(c) If you were going to make a $15 000 loan to the business, why would you want the creditors to be listed individually?
(d) If the liabilities on Jung's Video Corner balance sheet were $115 000, on what percentage of the business assets would creditors have a claim?
(e) If you were going to loan the firm the $15 000, would you prefer that the creditors or the owner have a higher claim on the assets? Explain your position.

Evaluate and Assess — Accounting Principles

Cindy McIntyre was preparing a balance sheet for her dry cleaning business, McIntyre's Cleaning. She noticed that the value on her balance sheet for the car the business owned

FIGURE 1-7

Jung's Video Corner Balance Sheet as at May 31, 19--			
Assets		**Equities**	
Cash	$ 9 000	Owner and creditor claims	$184 000
Accounts Receivable	800		
Supplies	300		
Equipment	12 000		
Videos	89 000		
Video Equipment	72 900		
		Total Liabilities and	
Total Assets	**$184 000**	**Owner's Equity**	**$184 000**

was $14 000, which was the amount that she paid for it. She knew that it was only worth about $4 000 now. She also noticed that the building and land were valued at $80 000 and $30 000 respectively, which were the amounts that she had originally paid for them. She believed them to be presently worth $65 000 and $48 000 respectively. Cindy thought the balance sheet should show the current value for all of these assets.

(a) What principle should be followed in presenting the value of the assets on the balance sheet? What does the principle state?

(b) Why are the values of assets not changed to reflect current values? Give at least two reasons.

(c) If Cindy were to approach a lending institution in order to obtain a loan, would the institution be interested in the current value of the assets? Why or why not?

Synthesize and Conclude
Statement Analysis

1. Diane Evason has approached you for a loan for her business. She wishes to borrow $10 000 in order to increase her inventory of videos. She presents you with the balance sheet shown in Figure 1-8.

   (a) Ms. Evason tells you that, in the short term, her cash position is good. Is there any information that you would like to know before commenting on her statement?

   (b) Ms. Evason tells you that, in the long term, prospects look good for her business. What item(s) might indicate that? What other information would help you evaluate this statement?

   (c) Write a brief report to Diane Evason, indicating whether or not you would approve the loan, and give reasons for the decision.

2. The balance sheets for two cleaning services are shown in Figures 1-9 and 1-10. Indicate which firm, in your opinion, has the better financial position and why. Cheung's monthly payments are $1 200 on the bank loan and $2 600 on the mortgage. MacDonald's monthly payments are $2 600 on the bank loan and $5 400 on the mortgage.

FIGURE 1-8

The Corner Video
Balance Sheet
as at March 31, 19–9

Assets			Liabilities		
Cash		$ 3 980	Accounts Payable		$ 1 209
Accounts Receivable		6 480	Bank Loan		8 410
Office Supplies		425	Mortgage Payable		18 000
Videos		42 090	Total Liabilities		27 619
Land		38 900			
Building		21 000	**Owner's Equity**		
			D. Evason, Capital		85 256
			Total Liabilities and		
Total Assets		**$112 875**	**Owner's Equity**		**$112 875**

FIGURE 1-9

Cheung's Cleaning Services
Balance Sheet
as at October 31, 19--

Assets		Liabilities	
Cash	$ 40 000	Accounts Payable	$ 13 000
Marketable Securities	10 900	Bank Loan	22 900
Accounts Receivable	4 500	Mortgage Payable	112 300
Office Supplies	300	Total Liabilities	148 200
Land	92 000		
Building	87 000		
Equipment	17 400	**Owner's Equity**	
Automobiles	32 000	B. Cheung, Capital	135 900
		Total Liabilities and	
Total Assets	**$284 100**	**Owner's Equity**	**$284 100**

FIGURE 1-10

MacDonald's Cleaning Services
Balance Sheet
as at October 31, 19--

Assets		Liabilities	
Cash	$ 60 000	Accounts Payable	$ 33 000
Marketable Securities	5 000	Bank Loan	69 400
Accounts Receivable	14 500	Mortgage Payable	187 500
Office Supplies	950	Total Liabilities	289 900
Land	129 700		
Building	147 000		
Equipment	21 150	**Owner's Equity**	
Automobiles	47 000	M. MacDonald, Capital	135 400
		Total Liabilities and	
Total Assets	**$425 300**	**Owner's Equity**	**$425 300**

Owner's Claim

3. John Yablonski, who owns Capital Management Consulting, has decided to retire. He has hired a liquidator to assist in the closing of the business. The liquidator has sold the assets on behalf of Capital Management Consulting. The business has $43 290 in cash. The liquidator has received the amounts shown in Figure 1-11.

The liabilities of the firm total $145 300. The firm had to pay a $500 fee for paying off its mortgage, and the liquidator charged $2 400 for the service.

(a) Calculate the owner's equity before the liquidation.
(b) Calculate the residual claim of John Yablonski on the business after it has been liquidated.
(c) What would Mr. Yablonski's claim have been had the land not been sold for a profit, but rather at the value shown on the balance sheet? Is the amount more or less than the owner's equity before the liquidation?
(d) Would it have been to Mr. Yablonski's advantage to sell the whole business to someone, rather than liquidating? Explain.

FIGURE 1-11

Accounts	Listed on Balance Sheet	Amount Received
Receivable	$ 45 600	$ 39 200
Supplies	1 340	720
Land	139 200	195 000
Building	223 980	198 000
Equipment	35 800	24 300

ACCOUNTING AT WORK

Kim Lanthier
Controller

Kim Lanthier has been employed as Controller by John Wiley & Sons Canada Limited, the Canadian division of an international publishing company. In this position she was responsible for supervising the accounting functions of the business. "Generally," she says, "I had been charged with providing up-to-date and accurate financial information to internal and external users of the data." Internal users include company managers who require the information in order to make product decisions and to analyze the success of past actions. External users are auditors, the American parent company, and bankers. Hiring and training of staff was also a significant part of her job.

After high school, Lanthier entered Queen's University and graduated with a Bachelor of Commerce degree. She took a position with a public accounting firm as a student in accounts. Here she took advantage of the in-house training program to move up to the role of senior auditor. At the same time, she completed the work and exams leading up to the Chartered Accountant exam. The CA credentials, along with the on-the-job experience, gave her the qualifications to apply for the Controller's job at the publishing company. "The company demanded an accounting designation — either a Chartered Accountant (CA), Certified General Accountant (CGA) or Certified Management Accountant (CMA) — as a minimum requirement for the position," Lanthier says. "As well, applicants needed to have three to five years of experience and a thorough knowledge of

Giltspur is North America's leading manufacturer and marketer of exhibit products and services for trade shows, expositions, and related events. Our Toronto division is seeking a confident, high energy individual for the key position of

CONTROLLER

Reporting to the President, the Controller will have broad financial and administrative responsibilities including reporting and financial systems, planning, financial analysis, and office management.

The successful candidate will possess a professional accounting designation, 5 to 10 years of senior financial experience, preferably gained in a custom manufacturing environment, and strong communication skills. Familiarity with *ACCPAC* and *dBase* is a definite asset.

You must be able to work in a dynamic, team-oriented environment and relate well with computerized systems.

If you possess these qualities and want to be part of an aggressive, successful organization within the North American trade show industry, please mail or fax your résumé immediately to:

Giltspur

GILTSPUR EXHIBITS
OF CANADA INC.
120 Carrier Drive
Rexdale, Ontario
M9W 5R1

Attn.: Lorraine Goodson
Tel.: (416) 674-0845
Fax: (416) 674-1228

Controller

We are a leading retailer in the home improvement business with a number of home improvement centres in the Ottawa area.

Reporting to the President, the Controller's responsibilities include:

- all accounting for retail store operations;
- budgeting and cash management;
- development of management information systems;
- certain compliance reporting and liaising with external auditors; and
- daily supervision of accounting staff

The successful candidate will have a CGA or a senior CGA student designation, excellent communication skills, and be proficient at operating in a computerized environment. Retail experience, particularly in the home improvement industry, would be a definite asset.

Salary will be commensurate with previous experience.

accounting systems." Her combination of training and experience earned her the Controller's job at John Wiley & Sons.

Lanthier has just taken another step up the corporate ladder, to become vice-president (finance) at Wiley. There is little accounting training that will prepare her for the position; instead, courses in management skills are more appropriate, along with more experience. Eventually, her skills and abilities could lead to a Chief Executive Officer (CEO) job.

"It took a lot of work and effort to become a Controller," warns Lanthier, "but it's worth it." She clearly finds accounting a rewarding career.

Using the career profile for Kim Lanthier, and the two advertisements for controllers, answer the following questions.

1. What tasks are identified as being part of the job of controller?

2. What educational requirements are required for each of the advertised positions?

3. What skills other than accounting are identified as being necessary for a controller?

4. What salary could a controller expect to receive?

Business Career Skills

1. Problem Solving — Entrepreneurship

Barbara Klooster had taken many business studies courses while in high school, and had gone on to university where she earned a degree in Business Administration. She subsequently became a Chartered Accountant, and then took a job as controller with a major Canadian company.

Barbara had, however, always wanted to be an entrepreneur. Her mother was well known for her baking recipes and especially for her cookies. Barbara thought that she might open a cookie shop, making use of her mother's recipes. Her plan was to focus on outlets in large office buildings; the outlets would also provide drinks. If successful, she hoped to franchise other establishments. Barbara's dilemma was whether to stay in her present position, where she was earning $70 000 annually, or open her business. If she decided to open her own business, she would have to cease working for her present employer. Barbara had saved $24 000 and estimated that she needed $42 000 to open her first location.

(a) Using the problem-solving method outlined in the Introduction to the Teacher, decide whether Barbara should become an entrepreneur and open Klooster's Kookies.

(b) Write a paragraph outlining your decision.

2. Consensus Seeking — Proprietorship

In the text, we learned that Vijay Marshall had wanted to go into business since he was in high school. He specifically wanted to be a proprietor, that is, the owner of his own computer-related business. When he accumulated enough assets he was able to do so.

(a) In groups, brainstorm to create a list of reasons why a person would want to be a proprietor.

(b) After creating your list of reasons, each student should rank them from most important to least important.

(c) In your group, try to reach a consensus on a ranking of the reasons.

(d) Your teacher will indicate what you are to do with your ranking.

COMPUTER ACCOUNTING
SPREADSHEETS... A POWERFUL ACCOUNTING TOOL

In most of your work you have encountered problems that you probably answered by using a calculator, a pencil, an eraser, and a sheet of paper. Attaining the answer was probably tedious and time-consuming, perhaps involving numerous rewrites of the data as well as the finished result. Sales projections, income tax calculations, budgets, cost estimates, financial statements, and so on can also be done with these tools, but there are the same concerns about time involved and repetition of data.

Electronic spreadsheet programs substitute a computer for the calculator, a keyboard for the pencil, and automatic recalculation for the eraser. They also replace paper by turning a video-screen window into a gigantic worksheet. This window can be moved in any direction.

The electronic spreadsheet is far too large for you to be able to see the entire worksheet at one time. For example, the *Microsoft Works* spreadsheet program is a grid, or matrix, consisting of in excess of one million **cells**, which are formed by the intersection of 256 columns and 4 096 rows. In each of these cells, you can enter a title, a number, or a formula to be calculated. In this way you can set up your own charts, tables, and records.

Once you have set up your electronic spreadsheet with titles, numbers, and formulas, you can utilize its real power. The computer uses your formulas to calculate and recalculate data on the worksheet. If you change a number on the worksheet, all other related numbers will change before your eyes as the program *automatically* recalculates all

FIGURE 1-12 ELECTRONIC SPREADSHEET WINDOW

File	Edit	Print	Select	Format	Options	Chart	Window
	A	B	C	D	E	F	G
1							
2							
3							
4							
5							
6							
7							
8							
9							

relevant formulas. With this valuable aid, you can easily correct mistakes and omissions and examine various alternatives.

What Is an Electronic Spreadsheet?

Prior to the development of the computer spreadsheet in 1979, all financial planning (comparative financial reports, budgets, and detailed analyses) was done manually on worksheet analysis paper (using a calculator, a pencil, and correcting material — namely the eraser). If an error was made, all calculations made after that error had to be erased and recalculated. Many times it was frustrating and time-consuming.

An electronic spreadsheet (basically a computer worksheet program) is modelled after the standard **financial worksheet**: a blank piece of paper marked with rows and columns. The space at the intersection of each row and column is called a cell. Cells are the main element of the spreadsheet, ready to take, store, and present several kinds of data.

On the standard paper worksheet, cells can contain only information entered by hand. Statistics must be calculated and, if necessary, recalculated on an electronic calculator.

An electronic spreadsheet, on the other hand, has the power to interpret different kinds of entries and perform useful operations automatically.

In the electronic spreadsheet, the contents of individual cells can consist of three kinds of information.

FIGURE 1-13 WORKSHEET FOR MANUAL ACCOUNTING

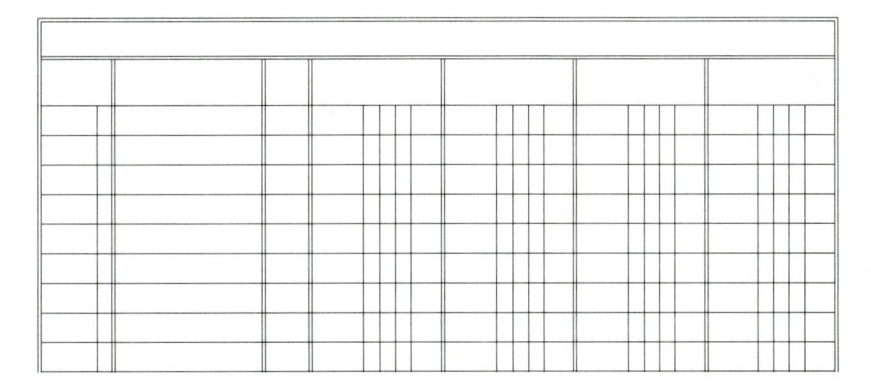

FIGURE 1-14 TYPES OF WORKSHEET INFORMATION

```
    File  Edit  Print  Select  Format  Options  Chart  Window
=SUM(C5:C8)
             A         B         C         D         E         F         G
 1
 2
 3     Assets  ←——— Label
 4
 5     Cash                     4500  ←——— Value
 6     AR/T. Smith               300
 7     Supplies                  600
 8     Equipment                2000
 9     Total Assets             7400  ←——— Formula
10
11
```

Labels (or headings) help you establish and describe the identity of rows, columns, or other portions of the spreadsheet. Labels are defined as text, borders, and other entries to the spreadsheet that are not used for the actual calculations that the spreadsheet performs. Label examples include:

Assets
=============== (border of equal signs)

Values (such as dollar amounts, weights and measures, and rates of pay) are the raw data on which the mechanics of the spreadsheet work. Numbers can be displayed on the worksheet in several forms:

45 (general)
10.98 (fixed number of decimal places)
$2 456.89 (currency)
78.5% (percentage)
2.675E6 (scientific)

Formulas give the spreadsheet its actual power: the reason that it is such a popular business accounting and analytical tool. Formulas may contain specific numbers, references to other cells, or a combination of both. Any of the standard mathematical operators (+, −, *, or /) can be used in formulas to manipulate the data on a spreadsheet in a useful way. Also, because the spreadsheet is intended to do a variety of calculations simply and easily, its designers have built into the program a series of mathematical operations that can be accessed with short key words.

The ability to store formulas with text and numbers is what makes the electronic spreadsheet such a powerful aid for answering **what-if questions**, which require numerous calculations to give a meaningful result. Using linked formulas, it's easy to set up large, interactive, numerical and financial models. Then you can enter various numbers through these models to see the effects of a variety of situations.

In addition, invoices, income statements, balance sheets, and other important accounting forms can be quickly set up on a computerized spreadsheet and then called-up when needed.

Let us see how this tool can be used in an accounting context.

FIGURE 1-15 SPREADSHEET MODEL OF A BALANCE SHEET

```
   File   Edit   Print   Select   Format   Options   Chart   Window

        A         B       C         D        E        F       G         H
  1                                Heading                            Formulas
  2                                Balance Sheet
  3                                Date
  4              Assets                      Liabilities
  5                                0                                0
  6                                0                                0
  7                                0                                0
  8                                0                                0
  9                                0                                _____
 10                                0  Total Liabilities             0        1
 11                                0
 12                                0         Owner's Equity
 13                                0                                0        2
 14                                0
 15                                0
 16                             _____
 17                                   Total Liabilities and Owner's
 18         Total Assets           0  Equity                        0     3 & 4
 19                             ======                           ======
 20
```

In this chapter you were introduced to the purpose and preparation of the balance sheet. Load your spreadsheet program into your computer and develop a spreadsheet model that will allow you to enter assets and liabilities and will then calculate the owner's equity. It is always a good practice to make a rough plan of what you want the spreadsheet to do and how it might be formatted. You could use Figure 1-15 to develop your balance sheet spreadsheet model.

Remember to include formulas to calculate the capital, total assets, total liabilities, and total liabilities and owner's equity.

Exercises

Complete each of the following activities by making any necessary changes on your computer program. Save each exercise on diskette and print out copies to submit to your teacher.

1. Prepare a balance sheet for Artona Studios using today's date. Assets include Cash $7 800; Photographic Equipment $24 670; Supplies $3 400; Land $50 000; Building $78 000. Liabilities include two separate suppliers: Skana Photo Lab Suppliers $3 560; and Kodak Canada Ltd. $6 500. Your spreadsheet should automatically calculate the capital investment of the owner, James Cheng.

2. Prepare a balance sheet for Mark's Plaza Pharmacy using today's date. Assets include Cash $10 600; Medical Supplies $15 600; Furniture $4 690; Store Equipment $12 400; Store Supplies $34 000. Liabilities include Bank Loan $25 000; and Accounts Payable to Pharmascience Co. $5 685, East Coast Drug Co. $2 400, and Ayerth & Wyeth $3 200. Your spreadsheet should automatically calculate the capital investment of the owner, Mark Dymentryko.

3. Prepare a balance sheet for Tony O's Restaurant, owned by Tony Pasquale, on September 30, 19--. Assets include Building $150 000; Land $56 000; Equipment $43 000; Furniture $18 790; Supplies $5 630; Cash $15 000. Liabilities include Mortgage $40 000; Bank Loan $14 000; Can Am Imports $3 750; Qwest Foods Ltd. $2 456; WestCoast FoodPak Systems $2 390. Your spreadsheet should automatically calculate Tony's investment in Tony O's. Note that in this exercise, both the assets and the liabilities must be rearranged according to generally accepted accounting principles.

CHAPTER TWO

Analyzing Transactions for Balance Sheet Accounts

LEARNING OBJECTIVES

At the end of this chapter you should be able to
- describe a transaction;
- outline the most common types of transactions;
- state the purpose of source documents;
- describe the concept of "on account";
- distinguish between a debit and a credit;
- state the rules of debit and credit for balance sheet accounts;
- describe the double-entry principle;
- state the purpose of a trial balance;
- load a spreadsheet program and use it to design and set up a source document form (template).

LANGUAGE OF ACCOUNTING

You will see the following terms in this chapter:

account	on account
audit	purchase/sales invoice
chart of accounts	remittance slip
credit	source document
debit	spreadsheet template
hard copy	transactions
invoice	trial balance

2.1 Transactions

One of the most important accounting skills to learn is to analyze and record transactions. Each day many events change the financial position of a business — these are called **transactions**. Every purchase is a transaction, and every sale is a transaction.

Transaction: an exchange of goods and/or services that results in a change in the financial position of an entity.

TRANSACTIONS

Purchaser
Money
⟷
Supplier
Goods and/or Services

> "To analyze a transaction means to decide what was gained by the business, and what was given."

Think about the largest store you have ever visited, and imagine the number of purchases and sales — transactions — that take place in that store in a single day. Each of these transactions must be "analyzed" and recorded. Even though the same type of transaction might be repeated thousands of times a day, or the analysis might be done by computer (as is done in larger stores), it is still necessary for the accountant to understand the theory related to the transaction.

Types of Transactions

Basically, every business engages in two activities: buying and selling. These two activities make up over ninety percent of the transactions that occur in most businesses. Businesses buy goods and services, either to sell or use, and, in turn, they sell either goods or services. These two basic activities result in five common business transactions.

> "Buying and selling are the two basic activities of most businesses."

THE FIVE BASIC TRANSACTION ACTIVITIES OF A BUSINESS

Buying:

(1) purchase of items, such as supplies, equipment, and merchandise for resale (usually done on account, which means that payment takes place at a later date);

(2) payment for items purchased, either at the time of purchase or later, which is a payment on account.

Selling:

(3) sale of a good or service for cash;

(4) sale of a good or service on account;

(5) receipt of cash from sales on account.

> **On account:** a buying or selling transaction has occurred, with payment to be made or received at a later date.

Let us examine the concept of **on account**. Frequently, a person or business buys goods but prefers not to pay for them at the time of purchase. They "open an account" with the seller and are sometimes given a credit card. When customers buy without paying they are buying "on account." At some future date, payment will be made "on account." Businesses also sell goods and/or services on account. When a business sells on account, it requires that the customer pay on account at a later date, usually within thirty days.

To summarize:
- businesses buy on account and later pay the supplier on account;
- businesses sell on account and later receive money from the customer on account.

It is important to recognize that a transaction only records what is occurring at that moment, and not something that occurred previously or will occur in the future. For example, Algor Computer Services may sign a contract to purchase $10 000 worth of network equipment from a supplier. At the time of signing, no transaction has occurred; there has only been an agreement. Later, Algor actually purchases the equipment, and agrees to pay in thirty days. A transaction has then occurred, for Algor's balance sheet will change: it has more equipment, and owes the creditor on account. In thirty days, another transaction will occur when Algor actually pays the creditor. The balance sheet will change again, for it will show less cash and reduced liabilities. Each of these transactions will be recorded on the date that it occurs. In reality, they are two related transactions which are recorded at different times.

No transaction	**Transaction**	**Transaction**
Contract signed	Goods/service received, amount owed	Payment made

Source Documents

Source document: *the original source of information indicating that a transaction has occurred.*

Invoice: *a bill that lists the goods or services sold by the supplier and indicates when payment is to be made.*

Purchase invoice: *the source document that indicates goods or services have been purchased, and will be paid for at a later date.*

A business must record a transaction the moment it takes place. Otherwise, the fact that it occurred may be forgotten. The paper it is first recorded on is called a **source document**: the document (piece of paper) that is the source of information to indicate that a transaction has occurred. This source document must be completed accurately, for it will be used as the source of information for recording the transaction in the books of the business. For each of the five basic types of transactions, a business either receives or completes one of the following source documents. In order to readily identify the various types of documents it completes, a business will use forms of different colours.

1. Purchase Invoice: For a purchase made on account, a **purchase invoice** is received from the supplier. The term **invoice** is another name for a bill: it means that the amount of the transaction has not yet been paid. Businesses buy most items on account: they will be paid for at a later time. Figure 2-1 is a purchase invoice, showing that Algor Computer Services purchased some brackets and screws from Westend Hardware Limited. The terms on the purchase invoice indicate when the invoice must be paid. When the invoice arrives at Algor Computer Services, it is stamped to show the date it was received. An entry is made in the books to record its receipt, and it is either paid immediately or filed according to the date by which it must be paid. When it has been paid, it will be filed in alphabetical order, according to the name of the supplier.

Chapter 2: Analyzing Transactions for Balance Sheet Accounts

```
                    Invoice Received
                          │
            ┌─────────────┴─────────────┐
            ▼                           ▼
     Paid Immediately          Filed According to Due Date
            │                           │
            │                           ▼
            │                    Paid on Due Date
            │                           │
            └─────────────┬─────────────┘
                          ▼
         Filed Alphabetically According to Supplier
```

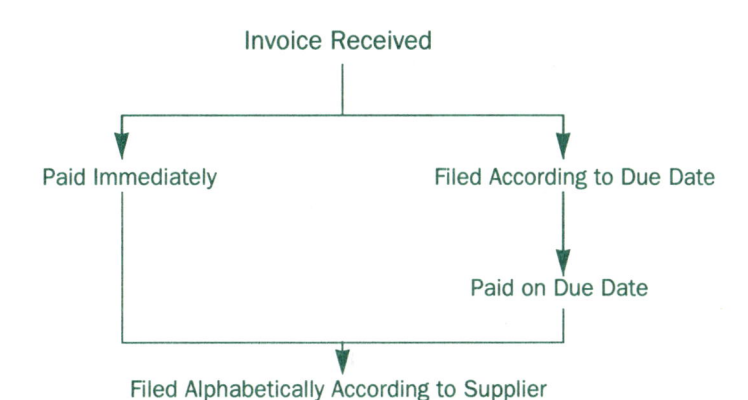

FIGURE 2-1 A PURCHASE INVOICE RECEIVED BY ALGOR COMPUTER SERVICES

INVOICE			No. 443
	Westend Hardware Limited		
	2593 Cedarview Road, Nepean, ON K1Z 3B9		
	Phone (613) 500-5222		
SOLD TO: Algor Computer Services 55 Eastern Parkway Kanata, ON K2L 2B1		DATE: Sept. 4, 1988 RECEIVED SEP 06 1988	
Our Order No.: 264B	Your Order No.: 11-212	Terms: 30 days	
Quantity	Item	Unit Price	Amount
14	L-shaped corner brackets	$2 50	$35 00
24	pkg. 1 1/2 #8 wood screws	80	19 20
		TOTAL	$54 20

Note that the federal goods and services tax and the provincial sales tax will be excluded from most source documents until the topics are studied in Chapter 6.

***Cheque copy** or **cheque stub:** the source document that indicates a payment has occurred.*

2. Cheque Copy: When a business pays for a purchase, the treasurer issues a cheque. The creditor receives the original, and the accountant receives a **cheque copy** from which to record the transaction. Some businesses complete a cheque stub showing the information concerning the cheque issued instead of keeping

a cheque copy. The cheque and stub are originally attached to one another in a book of cheques; the completed cheque is detached and sent to the creditor. A cheque stub is shown in Figure 2-2.

FIGURE 2-2 A CHEQUE STUB, OF A CHEQUE ISSUED BY ALGOR COMPUTER SERVICES

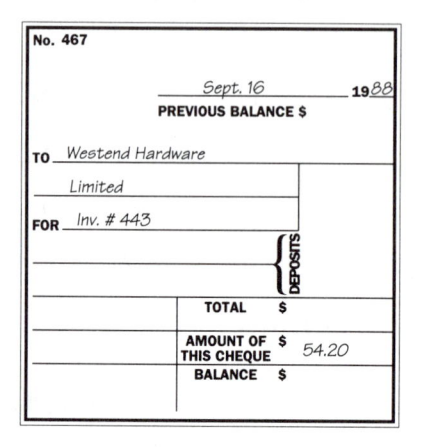

No. 467	
	Sept. 16, 19_88_
	PREVIOUS BALANCE $
TO _Westend Hardware_	
Limited	
FOR _Inv. # 443_	
	DEPOSITS
	TOTAL $
	AMOUNT OF THIS CHEQUE $ 54.20
	BALANCE $

Cash sales slip: the source document that indicates a cash sale has occurred.

3. Cash Sales Slip: When a business makes a cash sale, it is recorded on a piece of paper, either by hand or by a machine. The seller

FIGURE 2-3 A CASH SALES SLIP, ISSUED BY ALGOR COMPUTER SERVICES

CASH SALE 99 - 0123

ALGOR COMPUTER SERVICES
Your One Stop for Computer Installations and Training
55 Eastern Parkway, Kanata, ON K2L 2B1
Phone (613) 500-1212

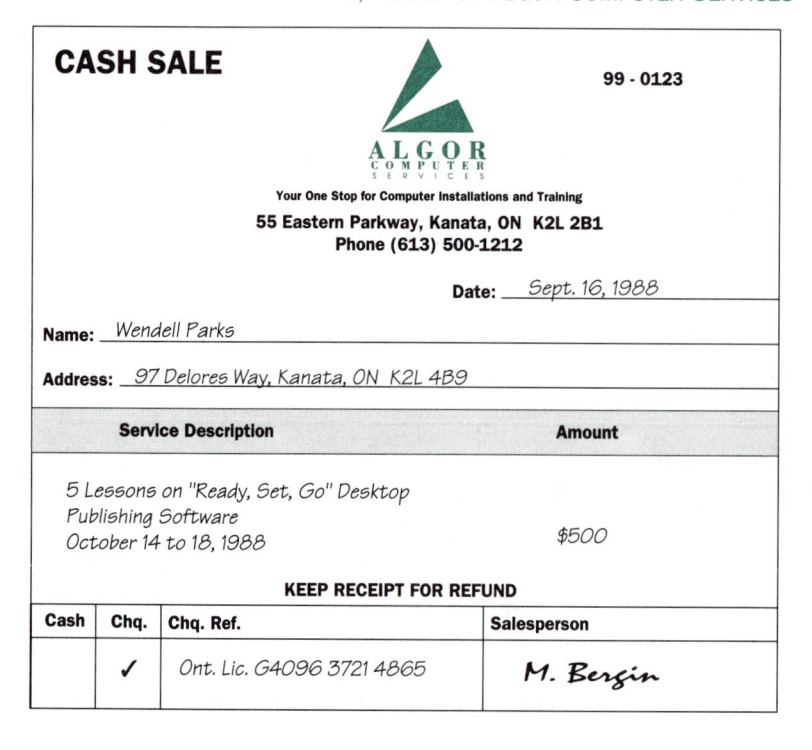

Date: _Sept. 16, 1988_

Name: _Wendell Parks_
Address: _97 Delores Way, Kanata, ON K2L 4B9_

Service Description	Amount
5 Lessons on "Ready, Set, Go" Desktop Publishing Software October 14 to 18, 1988	$500

KEEP RECEIPT FOR REFUND

Cash	Chq.	Chq. Ref.	Salesperson
	✓	Ont. Lic. G4096 3721 4865	_M. Bergin_

FIGURE 2-4 A CASH REGISTER RECEIPT, FROM SMITH HARDWARE

SMITH HARDWARE
241 Merivale Road
Kanata, ON

Retain this receipt as proof of purchase.

39922	2.45	
40392	38.84	
GST	2.89	FT
PST	3.30	PT
TOTAL	47.48	TO
CASH	48.00	CA
CHANGE	.52	CH
25/07/91	5:43 PM	

gives you a receipt or a **cash sales slip** as your proof of purchase. An example of a cash sales slip and a cash register receipt are provided in Figures 2-3 and 2-4.

Sales invoice: the source document that indicates a sale of goods and/or a service on account has occurred.

4. Sales Invoice: A **sales invoice** is completed when a sale has been made on account: the buyer is going to pay at a later date. The terms indicate when the customer must make payment. The sales invoice will be filed, for future reference, either in alphabetical order according to the customer name, or in order of the sales invoice number. A sales invoice is shown below.

FIGURE 2-5 A SALES INVOICE, ISSUED BY ALGOR COMPUTER SERVICES

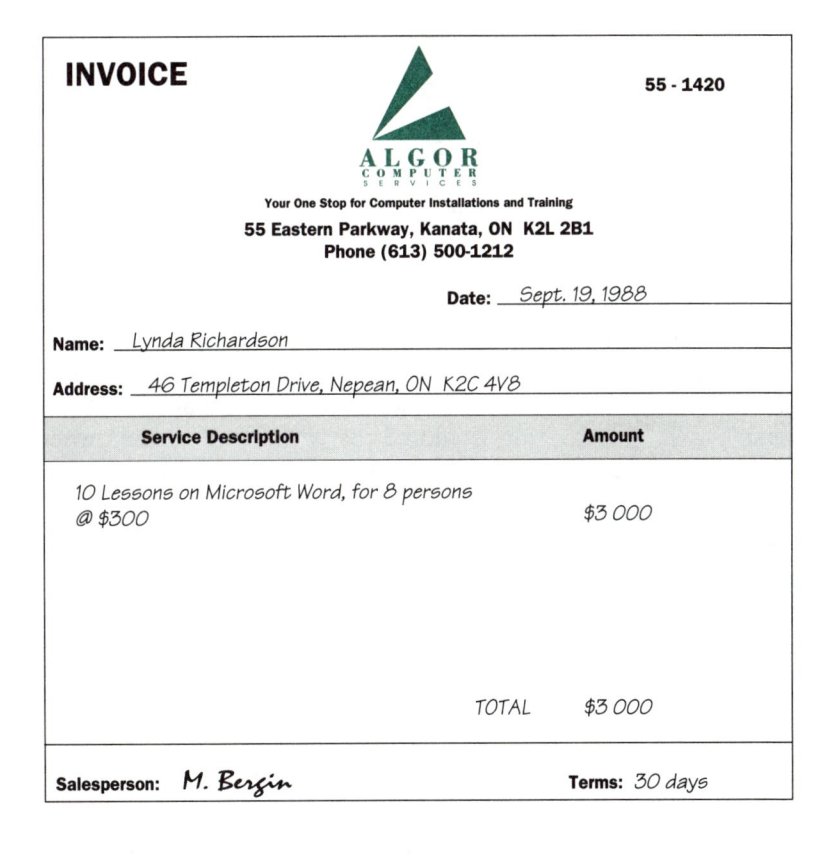

INVOICE

55 - 1420

ALGOR COMPUTER SERVICES

Your One Stop for Computer Installations and Training
55 Eastern Parkway, Kanata, ON K2L 2B1
Phone (613) 500-1212

Date: _Sept. 19, 1988_

Name: _Lynda Richardson_

Address: _46 Templeton Drive, Nepean, ON K2C 4V8_

Service Description	Amount
10 Lessons on Microsoft Word, for 8 persons @ $300	$3 000
TOTAL	$3 000

Salesperson: _M. Bergin_   **Terms:** _30 days_

Cash receipt slip: the source document that indicates that cash has come into the business from a source other than an immediate cash sale.

5. Cash Receipt Slip: A **cash receipt slip** records all cash that comes into the business other than from immediate cash sales. Most of these monies will be from debtors who pay their accounts. Cash receipt slips will be filed for future reference, either in alphabetical order according to the customer's name, or in numerical order according to the number of the cash receipt slip. A cash receipt slip is shown in Figure 2-6.

FIGURE 2-6 A CASH RECEIPT SLIP, ISSUED BY ALGOR COMPUTER SERVICES

```
CASH RECEIPT                                            33 - 1010

                         ALGOR
                         COMPUTER
                         SERVICES
               Your One Stop for Computer Installations and Training
               55 Eastern Parkway, Kanata, ON  K2L 2B1
                       Phone (613) 500-1212

                                        Date: Oct. 4, 1988

Received from: Lynda Richardson

On account: ✓           Other: _____

Cash: $1 500 xx   Chq.: _____  Chq. ref.: _____

Received by: M. Bergin
```

> **Memo** or **voucher**: the source document used to record "unusual" transactions.

6. Memo or voucher: There are certain transactions that do not fall within the five main types. These are transactions which do not occur frequently. A **memo** or **voucher** is a source document used to record one of these "unusual" transactions. One such transaction would be the withdrawal by the owner of equipment owned by the business. A memo is shown below.

FIGURE 2-7 A MEMO, USED BY ALGOR COMPUTER SERVICES

```
MEMO # 0005

DATE: Sept. 17, 1988

DESCRIPTION: Withdrawal of $5 000 in computer equipment by the owner,
             Vijay Marshall.


ACCOUNTS: Equipment                          V. Marshall, Capital

COMPLETED BY:  M. Bergin
```

All source documents are numbered. The numbers allow the originating business to ensure that all source documents are received by the accountant. For example, the cash receipt slips completed by a clerk will be forwarded to the accountant who will first ensure that they are all on hand. If some are missing, the accountant must find out why. When a source document has been spoiled due to an error made on it, the document should not be destroyed. The word "void" should be written on it, and it should be initialled and filed with all the other documents.

The following chart provides a summary of the six main source documents that are used in business:

THE SIX MAIN SOURCE DOCUMENTS USED IN A BUSINESS	
Document	**Use**
Purchase Invoice	To record purchases of goods or services on account.
Cheque Copy	To record all payments, whether on account or for cash purchases.
Cash Sales Slip	To record a sale of goods or services for cash.
Sales Invoice	To record a sale of goods or services on account.
Cash Receipt Slip	To record amounts received from customers on account, or investments of cash by the owner.
Memo or Voucher	To record unusual transactions that do not fall into the categories above.

Source documents provide the factual evidence an accountant needs to make an entry. Should such evidence not be available, the accountant must use some other objective evidence when recording a transaction. In some cases, it may be necessary to obtain the opinion of an appraiser. Source documents must be kept for at least six years. Then, application to destroy them must be made to Revenue Canada.

Objectivity Principle

Objectivity principle: accounting records must be kept on the basis of objective evidence.

The **objectivity principle** relates to source documents. The accountant must have objective evidence available in the form of a source document so that it is possible to record a dollar value for the transaction. If, for instance, a property is purchased for $5 000 and a cheque is issued, the accountant must record the transaction. But what if the accountant believes that the property is really worth $8 000? Should the entry be for $5 000 or for $8 000? The only objective figure is $5 000, and that is the amount that must be used.

LESSON REVIEW

1. What is a transaction? Name a store that you have visited, and list five different types of transactions that take place in it.

2. What are the two basic activities that every store is involved in?

3. What is a source document? Why is one completed for every transaction?

4. Name the source document completed or received by a business for each of the following transactions:
   (a) buying supplies but not paying for them immediately
   (b) payment of an amount on account
   (c) receipt of money on account
   (d) sale of an item on account
   (e) cash sale
   (f) withdrawal of supplies by the owner

5. Which of the six source documents that we have studied would be
   (a) issued by Algor Computer Services, and
   (b) received by Algor Computer Services?

6. Why are source documents numbered?

7. What is done with source documents that are filled out incorrectly?

8. What is the objectivity principle?

LESSON APPLICATIONS

9. Indicate whether each of the following is a transaction, and state why or why not.
   (a) Received $3 000 from the owner as an additional investment.
   (b) Paid $18 000 for an automobile.
   (c) Signed a $15 000 contract to perform services for Lothian Associates.
   (d) Paid the business's income tax, $15 400.
   (e) Purchased a business licence, $100.
   (f) Signed a contract to purchase $4 000 worth of computer supplies over the next year from Sisomphone Computer Supplies Ltd.
   (g) Hired a new employee, and agreed to pay her $3 000 per month.

10. Name the source document that will be completed or received by a business for each of the following transactions:
    (a) Provided a service to P. Lucht, $60 on account.
    (b) Purchased postage stamps and paid $60 by cheque.

(c) Received $496 on account from R. Switzer.
(d) The owner took home $57 worth of supplies.
(e) Provided a service to Aldo Urbisci for $120 cash.
(f) Received $5 000 as an additional investment by the owner.
(g) Paid $920 on account to Colonial Furniture Ltd.
(h) Provided $1 000 in services to Guy Vuonng in exchange for supplies.
(i) Sold land that was not being used by the business, $10 000 cash.
(j) Made a monthly mortgage payment on the shop by cheque, $1 000.

11. Assume that you are Algor Computer Services. Answer the questions below which apply to the following source document.

```
INVOICE 94-339
                    BARTON OFFICE FURNISHINGS
                        Phone (613) 500-5538
                        426 Parkdale Avenue
                        Nepean, ON  K2L 2B4

DATE: 10/07/88

SOLD TO:    Algor Computer Services
            55 Eastern Parkway
            Kanata, ON                      RECEIVED OCT 12 1988
            K2L 2B1
```

| Our Order No.: 28-746 | Your Order No.: 11-267 | Terms: 30 days |

Quantity	Item	Unit Price	Amount
1	#3998 Teak Desk	$1 290 —	$1 290 —
1	#987 Teak File Cabinet	430 —	430 —
1	#1882 Office Chair	680 —	680 —
		TOTAL	$2 400 —

THIS IS AN INVOICE

(a) What type of source document is it?
(b) Who is the seller?
(c) Who is the buyer? What is the buyer's order number?
(d) What is the seller's order number?
(e) On what date was the source document issued?
(f) How many days does the buyer have for paying the invoice?

12. Assume that you are Algor Computer Services. Answer the questions which apply to the following source document.
    (a) What type of source document is it? What number is it?
    (b) With whom does the transaction occur?
    (c) Who initiated the transaction?
    (d) Why did the transaction occur?

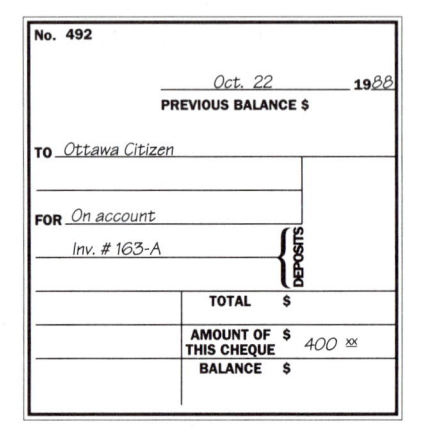

```
No. 492
                                  Oct. 22        1988
                        PREVIOUS BALANCE $
TO  Ottawa Citizen

FOR  On account
     Inv. # 163-A

                        TOTAL        $
                        AMOUNT OF $   400 xx
                        THIS CHEQUE
                        BALANCE    $
```

13. Assume that you are Algor Computer Services. Answer the questions which apply to the following source document.

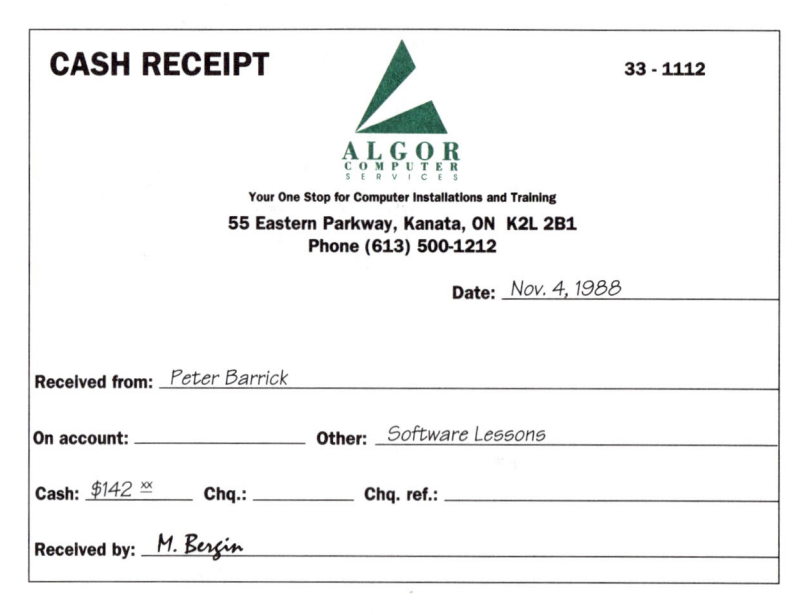

```
CASH RECEIPT                                    33 - 1112

                    ALGOR
                    COMPUTER
                    SERVICES
            Your One Stop for Computer Installations and Training
              55 Eastern Parkway, Kanata, ON K2L 2B1
                     Phone (613) 500-1212

                                  Date:  Nov. 4, 1988

Received from:  Peter Barrick

On account: _____   Other:  Software Lessons

Cash:  $142 xx    Chq.: _____   Chq. ref.: _____

Received by:  M. Bergin
```

(a) What type of source document is it? What number is it?
(b) With whom does the transaction occur?

(c) What was the reason for issuing the document?
(d) Who issued the document? Why is it important that this be included on the source document?
(e) What would be the effect on the balance sheet if the document had not been completed, and the cash receipts clerk had merely taken the money?

14. Assume that you are Algor Computer Services. Answer the questions below which apply to the following source document.

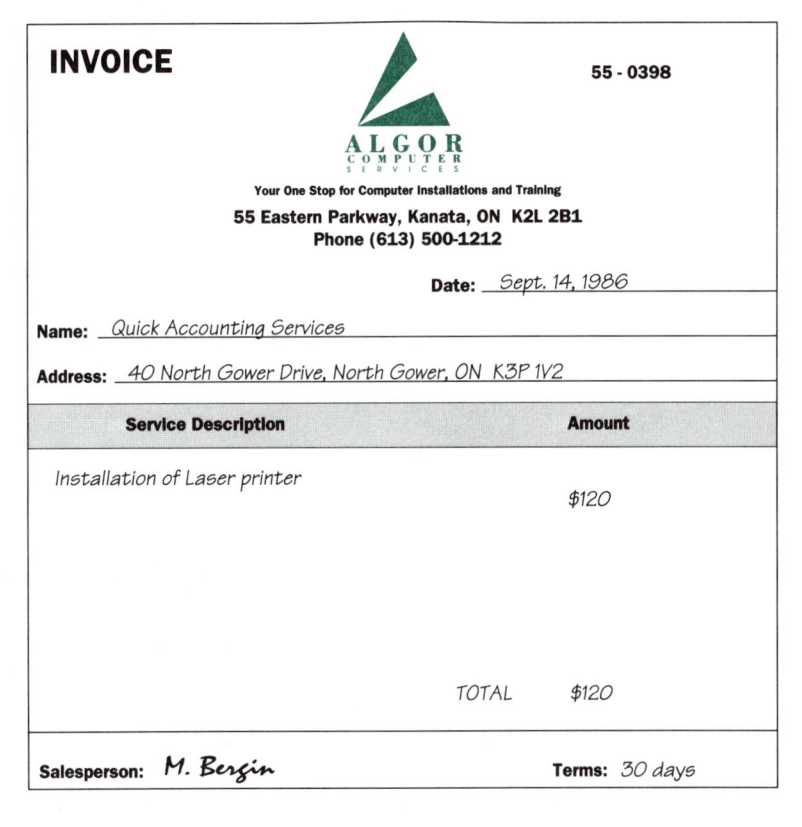

INVOICE 55 - 0398

ALGOR COMPUTER SERVICES

Your One Stop for Computer Installations and Training
55 Eastern Parkway, Kanata, ON K2L 2B1
Phone (613) 500-1212

Date: _Sept. 14, 1986_

Name: _Quick Accounting Services_

Address: _40 North Gower Drive, North Gower, ON K3P 1V2_

Service Description	Amount
Installation of Laser printer	$120
TOTAL	$120

Salesperson: M. Bergin   Terms: 30 days

(a) What type of source document is it? What number is it?
(b) Why was the document completed?
(c) When is payment due?
(d) What is the purpose of the document number?

15. Prepare a set of source documents, not including a cheque stub or cheque copy, for a business for which you would like to be the proprietor. Be certain that all relevant information is contained on each document.

2.2 Analyzing Transactions

"When analyzing transactions (1) consider how they affect the business, and (2) picture what took place in the transaction."

In order to facilitate the analysis of transactions, a document called a **transaction analysis sheet** will be used, as shown in Figure 2-8. This sheet is not used in business, but is introduced here for the purpose of teaching the concepts related to the analysis of transactions.

Here are a few hints to assist you in analyzing transactions. First, *always concern yourself only with how a transaction affects the business;* don't worry about its effect on the owner, customers, creditors or anyone else. Do you remember the balance sheets that we examined in Chapter 1? One was the personal balance sheet for Vijay Marshall, and the other was for his business, Algor Computer Services. Marshall and his business are separate entities. The owner will contribute certain assets to the business and withdraw other assets for personal use. It is best to focus on the business, and record the transactions according to how they affect the business, not the owner. Secondly, *try to picture what actually took place in the transaction.* When a purchase of supplies is made for cash by the business, picture supplies arriving at the business, and cash leaving.

Steps in Completing the Transaction Analysis Sheet

The following steps should be followed when entering a transaction on a transaction analysis sheet:

1. Enter the balance sheet on the transaction analysis sheet. The following is the balance sheet as it existed for Algor Computer Services on June 30, 1985, when it was a new business.

Algor Computer Services
Balance Sheet
as at June 30, 1985

Assets		Liabilities	
Cash	$ 2 340	Accounts Payable	$ 4 320
Accounts Receivable	9 493	Short-Term Loans	12 300
Office Supplies	401	Total Liabilities	16 620
Office Equipment	3 922		
Computer Equipment	18 320	**Owner's Equity**	
		V. Marshall, Capital	17 856
		Total Liabilities and	
Total Assets	**$34 476**	**Owner's Equity**	**$34 476**

The above items are entered into the various columns of the transaction analysis sheet in the order in which they appear on the balance sheet. The fundamental accounting equation, Assets = Liabilities + Owner's Equity, is shown on the sheet.

FIGURE 2-8 AMOUNTS TRANSFERRED FROM THE BALANCE SHEET

	TRANSACTION ANALYSIS SHEET							
	ASSETS					= LIABILITIES		+ OWNER'S EQUITY
	Cash	Accounts Receivable	Office Supplies	Office Equipment	Computer Equipment	Accounts Payable	Short-Term Loans	V. Marshall, Capital
Opening Balances	2340 –	9493 –	401 –	3922 –	18320 –	4320 –	12300 –	17856 –

2. Individual transactions are then entered on the sheet, and a new account total is calculated after each entry. The new total must be calculated because sometimes the amount will be increasing the balance of the account, and sometimes decreasing its balance. The transactions should be analyzed using the following format:

ITEM CHANGED	TYPE OF ITEM	INCREASE/DECREASE	AMOUNT

As we will see, at least two items must change for every transaction. The items can either be an asset, a liability, or the owner's equity. Some transactions are analyzed and entered on transaction analysis sheets that follow.

Transaction 1
July 2   Cheque Copy #16   Algor Computer Services purchased $400 worth of office supplies from Summerside Stationery Ltd.
- The business gained supplies, an asset. Did you picture the supplies arriving at the business? The amount, $400, is added to the Office Supplies column.
- The business lost cash, an asset. Remember that cheques are included as cash. Picture a cheque leaving the business. The Cash column must decrease by $400.

ITEM CHANGED	TYPE OF ITEM	INCREASE/DECREASE	AMOUNT
Office Supplies	Asset	Increase	$400
Cash	Asset	Decrease	$400

Note how these two items have been entered on the transaction analysis sheet. One asset has increased, and another decreased, so assets are still equal to liabilities plus owner's equity. Remember that after each transaction, a new total is calculated for each item.

FIGURE 2-9 TRANSACTION ANALYSIS SHEET ENTRY FOR TRANSACTION 1

	TRANSACTION ANALYSIS SHEET								
	ASSETS					=	LIABILITIES		+ OWNER'S EQUITY
	Cash	Accounts Receivable	Office Supplies	Office Equipment	Computer Equipment		Accounts Payable	Short-Term Loans	V. Marshall, Capital
Opening Balances	2340 -	9493 -	401 -	3922 -	18320 -		4320 -	12300 -	17856 -
July 2	-400 -		+400 -						
	1940 -	9493 -	801 -	3922 -	18320 -		4320 -	12300 -	17856 -

Transaction 2

July 3   Cash Receipt Slip #33-0076   Received $200 on account from Cheryl Smiley, a customer.
- The business gained cash, an asset: the Cash column increases by $200.
- The business no longer owns its claim on Smiley, for she has paid it. Thus, Accounts Receivable decreases by $200. Again notice that one asset has increased, and another decreased, such that assets are still equal to liabilities plus owner's equity.

ITEM CHANGED	TYPE OF ITEM	INCREASE/DECREASE	AMOUNT
Cash	Asset	Increase	$200
Accounts Receivable	Asset	Decrease	$200

FIGURE 2-10 TRANSACTION ANALYSIS SHEET ENTRY FOR TRANSACTION 2

	TRANSACTION ANALYSIS SHEET								
	ASSETS					=	LIABILITIES		+ OWNER'S EQUITY
	Cash	Accounts Receivable	Office Supplies	Office Equipment	Computer Equipment		Accounts Payable	Short-Term Loans	V. Marshall, Capital
Opening Balances	2340 -	9493 -	401 -	3922 -	18320 -		4320 -	12300 -	17856 -
July 2	-400 -		+400 -						
	1940 -	9493 -	801 -	3922 -	18320 -		4320 -	12300 -	17856 -
July 3	+200 -	-200 -							
	2140 -	9293 -	801 -	3922 -	18320 -		4320 -	12300 -	17856 -

Transaction 3

July 4   Cash Receipt Slip #33-0077   The business received an additional investment of $3 000 cash from the owner, V. Marshall.

Chapter 2: Analyzing Transactions for Balance Sheet Accounts   49

- The business received cash, an asset. The Cash column increases by $3 000.
- The claim that the owner has on the business has increased: V. Marshall, Capital increases by $3 000.

ITEM CHANGED	TYPE OF ITEM	INCREASE/DECREASE	AMOUNT
Cash	Asset	Increase	$3 000
V. Marshall, Capital	Owner's Equity	Increase	$3 000

Both the left and the right sides of the fundamental accounting equation have changed, but the equation is still in balance.

FIGURE 2-11 TRANSACTION ANALYSIS SHEET ENTRY FOR TRANSACTION 3

	Cash	Accounts Receivable	Office Supplies	Office Equipment	Computer Equipment	=	Accounts Payable	Short-Term Loans	+	V. Marshall, Capital
Opening Balances	2340 −	9493 −	401 −	3922 −	18320 −		4320 −	12300 −		17856 −
July 2	−400 −		+400 −							
	1940 −	9493 −	801 −	3922 −	18320 −		4320 −	12300 −		17856 −
July 3	+200 −	−200 −								
	2140 −	9293 −	801 −	3922 −	18320 −		4320 −	12300 −		17856 −
July 4	+3000 −									+3000 −
	5140 −	9293 −	801 −	3922 −	18320 −		4320 −	12300 −		20856 −

Transaction 4

July 5 Purchase Invoice #198 Bought computer equipment on account from Office Suppliers Ltd., $800.

- The business received computer equipment, an asset. The Computer Equipment column increases by $800.
- Since Algor wishes to pay at a later date, Office Suppliers Ltd. has a claim on Algor. Accounts Payable increases by $800.

ITEM CHANGED	TYPE OF ITEM	INCREASE/DECREASE	AMOUNT
Computer Equipment	Asset	Increase	$800
Accounts Payable	Liability	Increase	$800

Although both the left and the right sides of the fundamental accounting equation have changed, the equation is still in balance.

FIGURE 2-12 TRANSACTION ANALYSIS SHEET ENTRY FOR TRANSACTION 4

	TRANSACTION ANALYSIS SHEET							
	ASSETS					= LIABILITIES		+ OWNER'S EQUITY
	Cash	Accounts Receivable	Office Supplies	Office Equipment	Computer Equipment	Accounts Payable	Short-Term Loans	V. Marshall, Capital
Opening Balances	2340 -	9493 -	401 -	3922 -	18320 -	4320 -	12300 -	17856 -
July 2	-400 -		+400 -					
	1940 -	9493 -	801 -	3922 -	18320 -	4320 -	12300 -	17856 -
July 3	+200 -	-200 -						
	2140 -	9293 -	801 -	3922 -	18320 -	4320 -	12300 -	17856 -
July 4	+3000 -							+3000 -
	5140 -	9293 -	801 -	3922 -	18320 -	4320 -	12300 -	20856 -
July 5					+800 -	+800 -		
	5140 -	9293 -	801 -	3922 -	19120 -	5120 -	12300 -	20856 -

Transaction 5

July 6   Cheque Copy #17   The business paid $300 to Office Suppliers Ltd., on account.

- The business gained a reduction in the amount that it owes Office Suppliers Ltd., who are creditors. Thus, Accounts Payable decreases by $300.
- The business gave up cash, an asset. The Cash column decreases by $300.

ITEM CHANGED	TYPE OF ITEM	INCREASE/DECREASE	AMOUNT
Accounts Payable	Liability	Decrease	$300
Cash	Asset	Decrease	$300

There have been two changes to the transaction analysis sheet, but assets are still equal to liabilities plus owner's equity.

FIGURE 2-13 TRANSACTION ANALYSIS SHEET ENTRY FOR TRANSACTION 5

	TRANSACTION ANALYSIS SHEET							
	ASSETS					= LIABILITIES		+ OWNER'S EQUITY
	Cash	Accounts Receivable	Office Supplies	Office Equipment	Computer Equipment	Accounts Payable	Short-Term Loans	V. Marshall, Capital
Opening Balances	2340 -	9493 -	401 -	3922 -	18320 -	4320 -	12300 -	17856 -
July 2	-400 -		+400 -					
	1940 -	9493 -	801 -	3922 -	18320 -	4320 -	12300 -	17856 -
July 3	+200 -	-200 -						
	2140 -	9293 -	801 -	3922 -	18320 -	4320 -	12300 -	17856 -
July 4	+3000 -							+3000 -
	5140 -	9293 -	801 -	3922 -	18320 -	4320 -	12300 -	20856 -
July 5					+800 -	+800 -		
	5140 -	9293 -	801 -	3922 -	19120 -	5120 -	12300 -	20856 -
July 6	-300 -					-300 -		
	4840 -	9293 -	801 -	3922 -	19120 -	4820 -	12300 -	20856 -

Transaction 6

July 7   Cheque Copy #18/Purchase Invoice #933   Purchased office equipment from California Office Furnishings Ltd., $1 200. $500 was paid in cash, and $700 was to be paid in one month.
- The business received office equipment, an asset. The Office Equipment column increases by $1 200.
- Since Algor Computer Services wishes to pay some money now and the balance at a later date, two columns are affected. Algor wrote a cheque for $500, thus, the Cash column decreases by $500.
- Since Algor wishes to pay the balance, $700, at a later date, California Office Furnishings Ltd. now has a claim on Algor. Thus, Accounts Payable increases by $700.

ITEM CHANGED	TYPE OF ITEM	INCREASE/DECREASE	AMOUNT
Office Equipment	Asset	Increase	$1 200
Cash	Asset	Decrease	$500
Accounts Payable	Liability	Increase	$700

There are three items that change because of this transaction. The business gained office equipment, and gave up cash and a claim on itself. However, when the items are totalled, the fundamental accounting equation still applies. Remember that for every transaction *at least* two items must change, and that after analyzing the transaction, assets must equal liabilities plus owner's equity.

FIGURE 2-14 TRANSACTION ANALYSIS SHEET ENTRY FOR TRANSACTION 6

	ASSETS					=	LIABILITIES		+ OWNER'S EQUITY
	Cash	Accounts Receivable	Office Supplies	Office Equipment	Computer Equipment		Accounts Payable	Short-Term Loans	V. Marshall, Capital
Opening Balances	2340 -	9493 -	401 -		3922 -	18320 -	4320 -	12300 -	17856 -
July 2	-400 -		+400 -						
	1940 -	9493 -	801 -		3922 -	18320 -	4320 -	12300 -	17856 -
July 3	+200 -	-200 -							
	2140 -	9293 -	801 -		3922 -	18320 -	4320 -	12300 -	17856 -
July 4	+3000 -								+3000 -
	5140 -	9293 -	801 -		3922 -	18320 -	4320 -	12300 -	20856 -
July 5						+800 -	+800 -		
	5140 -	9293 -	801 -		3922 -	19120 -	5120 -	12300 -	20856 -
July 6	-300 -						-300 -		
	4840 -	9293 -	801 -		3922 -	19120 -	4820 -	12300 -	20856 -
July 7	-500 -			+1200 -			+700 -		
	4340 -	9293 -	801 -		5122 -	19120 -	5520 -	12300 -	20856 -

As can be seen on the transaction analysis sheet, the financial position of Algor Computer Services has changed. The result of any transaction is a change in the financial position of the business. The new data can be used to prepare a balance sheet, as shown below.

Algor Computer Services
Balance Sheet
as at July 7, 1985

Assets		Liabilities	
Cash	$ 4 340	Accounts Payable	$ 5 520
Accounts Receivable	9 293	Short-Term Loans	12 300
Office Supplies	801	Total Liabilities	17 820
Office Equipment	5 122		
Computer Equipment	19 120	**Owner's Equity**	
		V. Marshall, Capital	20 856
		Total Liabilities and	
Total Assets	**$38 676**	**Owner's Equity**	**$38 676**

LESSON REVIEW

16. What two hints were given to assist in the analyzing of transactions?

17. What is a transaction analysis sheet? What purpose does it serve in learning accounting?

18. Describe the process of entering transactions on a transaction analysis sheet.

19. What is done with the final totals on the transaction analysis sheet?

20. How many items must change for each transaction?

21. What relationship must exist after each transaction has been entered on a transaction analysis sheet?

LESSON APPLICATIONS

22. For each of the following transactions, complete a chart similar to the one shown below.

Transaction #	Item Changed	Type of Item	Increase/ Decrease	Amount

    (1) Purchase Invoice #745: Purchased $435 worth of supplies from McNabb Industries on account.
    (2) Cash Receipt Slip #329: Received $5 900 as an additional investment by the owner, R. Walters.
    (3) Cheque Copy #68: Paid $425 for a new office desk.
    (4) Purchase Invoice #942B: Purchased accounting documents, $253 on account.
    (5) Cash Receipt Slip #330: Received $212 on account from C. Mekki.
    (6) Cheque Copy #69: Paid $52 for office supplies.
    (7) Cheque Copy #70: Paid $435 to McNabb Industries on account.

23. For each of the following transactions, complete a chart similar to the one shown below.

Transaction #	Item Changed	Type of Item	Increase/ Decrease	Amount

    (1) Purchase Invoice #94-229: Purchased $435 worth of supplies on account from Edwards Business Suppliers Ltd.
    (2) Voucher #29: The owner, E. Susuki, took $55 worth of supplies for her personal use.
    (3) Cheque Copy #938: Paid $375 on account to Edwards Business Suppliers Ltd.
    (4) Cash Receipt Slip #835: Received $245 on account from B. Didak.
    (5) Cheque Copy #939: Paid $45 for supplies.
    (6) Cheque Copy #940: Paid $8 000 for purchase of government bonds.
    (7) Purchase Invoice #393: Purchased $558 worth of office equipment on account.
    (8) Cheque Copy #941: Paid $30 000 for purchase of property; land valued at $20 000 and building at $10 000.
    (9) Cheque Copy #942: Paid $954 to the bank to reduce the loan.

24. Warren Borinsky is the owner of his own dental practice. The balance sheet for the practice is as follows:

Warren Borinsky, Dental Practice
Balance Sheet
as at July 1, 19–7

Assets		Liabilities	
Cash	$12 000	Accounts Payable	$ 4 000
Accounts Receivable	6 000	Short-Term Loans	3 000
Supplies	3 700	Total Liabilities	7 000
Equipment	52 000		
Automobile	14 000	**Owner's Equity**	
		W. Borinsky, Capital	80 700
		Total Liabilities and	
Total Assets	**$87 700**	**Owner's Equity**	**$87 700**

(a) Enter the amounts from the balance sheet onto a transaction analysis sheet.
(b) Analyze the transactions given below, and record them on the transaction analysis sheet. (Total the transaction analysis sheet after each transaction.)

July 2 Purchase Invoice #943: Purchased $700 worth of equipment on account from Dental Suppliers Ltd.
  4 Cash Receipt Slip #93–338: Received $800 from the owner, W. Borinsky, as an additional investment.
  9 Cash Receipt Slip #93–339: Received $150 on account from L. Cavell.
  11 Cheque Copy #822: Paid $300 on the bank loan.
  15 Cheque Copy #823: Paid $220 on account to K. Murchison, a creditor.
  17 Cheque Copy #824: Paid $100 to W. Borinsky, the owner, for his personal use.
  17 Cheque Copy #825: Purchased a new automobile for $13 000. Paid $3 000 in cash, and obtained a bank loan for the balance.

(c) Check for the accuracy of the fundamental accounting equation, and double rule your totals if the transaction analysis sheet is in balance.
(d) Prepare a new balance sheet, as at July 17.

25. Tony Zaatar is the owner of Westway Golf Centre, a driving range where lessons are also provided. The balance sheet for the range is as follows:

Westway Golf Centre
Balance Sheet
as at August 1, 19–7

Assets		Liabilities	
Cash	$ 5 300	Accounts Payable	$ 1 302
Accounts Receivable	1 809	Short-Term Loans	4 200
Golf Balls	1 967	Total Liabilities	5 502
Golf Equipment	3 498		
Tractor	7 459	**Owner's Equity**	
		T. Zaatar, Capital	14 531
		Total Liabilities and	
Total Assets	**$20 033**	**Owner's Equity**	**$20 033**

(a) Enter the amounts from the balance sheet onto a transaction analysis sheet.
(b) Analyze the transactions given below, and properly complete the transaction analysis sheet.

Aug. 2 Cheque Copy #944: Paid $300 for 20 dozen practice balls.
   9 Cash Receipt Slip #840: Received $150 cash on account from T. Bishop.
   11 Cash Receipt Slip #841: Received $500 cash from the owner, Tony Zaatar, as an additional investment.
   15 Cash Receipt Slip #842: Sold the old ball washer for $300; received $200 cash, and the balance on account.
   18 Cheque Copy #945: Paid $240 on the bank loan.
   19 Cheque Copy #946: Purchased a new ball washer for $870; paid $270 cash, and the balance is owing on account to Future Shop.

(c) Prepare a new balance sheet, as at August 19.

26. The completed transaction analysis sheet for Norton's Sauna and Hot Tub Emporium is given in Figure 2-15. For each of the changes, you are to
(a) indicate the source document that would have been used, and
(b) describe the transaction that took place in the business.
Example: October 1 Memo — Borrowed $4 000 from Trust Company.

FIGURE 2-15

	TRANSACTION ANALYSIS SHEET								
	ASSETS					=	LIABILITIES		+ OWNER'S EQUITY
	Cash	Accounts Receivable	Supplies	Hot Tub Supplies	Equipment		Accounts Payable	Trust Co. Loan	C. Norton, Capital
Opening Balances	9320-	2921-	772-	4631-	24916-		3756-	14200-	24604-
October 1	+4000-							+4000-	
	13320-	2921-	772-	4631-	24916-		3756-	18200-	24604-
October 2	-9200-				+9200-				
	4120-	2921-	772-	4631-	34116-		3756-	18200-	24604-
October 3	+700-	-700-							
	4820-	2221-	772-	4631-	34116-		3756-	18200-	24604-
October 4	-400-		+1000-				+600-		
	4420-	2221-	1772-	4631-	34116-		4356-	18200-	24604-
October 5	+5200-								+5200-
	9620-	2221-	1772-	4631-	34116-		4356-	18200-	29804-
October 6	-500-						-500-		
	9120-	2221-	1772-	4631-	34116-		3856-	18200-	29804-
October 7				+1100-			+1100-		
	9120-	2221-	1772-	5731-	34116-		4956-	18200-	29804-

27. Debbie MacLean is the owner of Dunrobin Video Rentals. The balance sheet as at February 1 is as follows:

Dunrobin Video Rentals
Balance Sheet
as at February 1, 19–7

Assets		Liabilities	
Cash	$ 9 503	Accounts Payable	$ 3 402
Accounts Receivable	4 291	Bank Loan	23 982
Videos	34 938	Total Liabilities	27 384
Video Equipment	12 984		
Automobile	14 400	**Owner's Equity**	
		D. MacLean, Capital	48 732
		Total Liabilities and	
Total Assets	**$76 116**	**Owner's Equity**	**$76 116**

(a) Using the above balance sheet, and the following transactions, complete a transaction analysis sheet.

Feb. 4 Purchase Invoice #984: Purchased $4 000 worth of new videos on account from Video Warehouse Ltd.

   10 Cash Receipt Slip #492: Received $200 on account from Lise Terry, a customer.

   13 Memo #94: The owner, Debbie MacLean, took $115 worth of videos from the business to keep for her personal use.

   15 Cheque Copy #294: The owner, Debbie MacLean, used $30 worth of business funds for personal use.

18   Purchase Invoice #928: Purchased a new VCR for the business, $1 900. $900 was paid in cash, and the balance is owing on account to Future Shop.
24   Cheque Copy #295: Paid $700 on the bank loan.
28   Memo #95: Returned videos valued at $300 to Video Warehouse Ltd., because they were damaged by water.

(b) Prepare a new balance sheet, as at February 28, 19–7.

2.3 The General Ledger

General ledger: a book of accounts.

Algor Computer Services has hundreds of transactions a day. Picture each of these transactions being placed on a transaction analysis sheet. After each transaction new totals are calculated. From these totals, a balance sheet is prepared. The length of the transaction analysis sheet itself would be unmanageable. Algor Computer Services requires a better technique in order to record the changes resulting from transactions.

As indicated earlier, transaction analysis sheets are used only when learning the basics of analyzing transactions. In designing an accounting system, a special book called a **general ledger** is used. This book has one page for each item found on the balance sheet. The page is referred to as an **account** and on it the changes in the one item are recorded. Each page, or account, may take the form shown below, which has been set up as the Cash account.

Account: a page on which changes in any one item are recorded.

```
              Cash
       dr.    |    cr.
```

Debit side: the left side of the T-account.

The accounts are referred to as T-accounts, because of their resemblance to the letter T. The sides of the account are named, not left and right, but **debit** and **credit**. The left side of every T-account is the debit side, abbreviated to dr. The right side of every T-account is the credit side, abbreviated to cr.

Credit side: the right side of the T-account.

The general ledger pages are kept in the order in which the items are found on the balance sheet. The result is that first there are asset accounts, then liability accounts, and finally the owner's equity accounts. The ledger might take some other form, such as a set of cards, a computer disk, or a magnetic disk.

At the front of the ledger there is a **chart of accounts**, which is similar to a table of contents. The chart of accounts provides a numbering system for the accounts. As we noted in Chapter 1, it is necessary for a business to design an accounting system that provides it with the information it requires in order to make informed business decisions. One of these decisions is what account names the business will use in

Chart of accounts: a listing of all account names and numbers.

its ledger. For example, will putting all of the accounts receivable into one account called Accounts Receivable provide sufficient information, or should separate accounts be made for each customer? If so, should they be listed by name only, or preceded by "Accounts Receivable"? The more information that is available, the more valid the decisions that are made based on that information. However, generating data is a cost to the business, and to generate information that is not going to be used is a waste of the business's economic resources.

The following numbering system was used by Algor Computer Services after a number of years in business. You will learn to use each of these accounts in this course. Note that each account is given a number, and not a page number. Page numbers would not be appropriate, for it is not possible to know how many pages are going to be required to record changes in each account over the life of the business. Also, the account numbers are not consecutive, for the business may want to add new accounts. The accounts are grouped by number, with assets first followed by liabilities and capital. Notice that asset account numbers all start with the digit 1, liabilities with 2, and capital with 3. You may not understand the function of many of the accounts listed, but these will be explained in future chapters.

Algor Computer Services
Chart of Accounts

Assets
100 Cash
105 Petty Cash
108 Payroll Account
110 Marketable Securities
120 Accounts Receivable
125 Allowance for Doubtful Accounts
130 Merchandise Inventory
135 GST Recoverable
140 Prepaid Insurance
145 Prepaid Rent
150 Office Supplies
155 Computer Supplies
160 Land
170 Building
171 Accumulated Depreciation: Building
175 Office Equipment
176 Accumulated Depreciation: Office Equipment
180 Computer Equipment
181 Accumulated Depreciation: Computer Equipment
190 Automobile
191 Accumulated Depreciation: Automobile

Liabilities
200 Accounts Payable
205 Wages Payable
207 Vacation Pay Payable
210 Short-Term Loans
215 Interest Payable
220 Mortgage Payable
225 Long-Term Loans
230 GST Payable
240 PST Payable
250 CPP Payable
255 UI Payable
258 Health Tax Payable
260 Income Tax Payable
262 RPP Payable
265 Union Dues Payable

270 Health Insurance Payable
280 Group Life Insurance Payable

Owner's Equity

300 V. Marshall, Capital
310 V. Marshall, Drawings
320 Income Summary

Revenue

400 Computer Services
410 Software Lessons
415 Refunds
420 Sales
425 Sales Returns and Allowances
430 Sales Discounts
440 Bank Interest
450 Accounts Receivable: Interest on Overdue Accounts
460 Sales Tax Commission
470 Discounts Earned

Cost Accounts

500 Purchases
510 Freight-in
520 Purchases Returns and Allowances
525 Purchases Discounts

Expenses

600 Wages Expense
610 CPP Expense
615 Workers' Compensation Expense
620 UI Expense
622 Health Tax Expense
625 RPP Expense
630 Health Insurance Expense
640 Group Life Insurance Expense
650 Bank Expense
651 Interest Expense
655 VISA Discount Expense
660 Advertising Expense
670 Utilities Expense
675 Rent Expense
680 Automobile Expense
685 Delivery Expense
690 Depreciation Expense: Building
700 Depreciation Expense: Office Equipment
705 Depreciation Expense: Computer Equipment
710 Depreciation Expense: Automobile
715 Bad Debts Expense
720 Insurance Expense
730 Office Supplies Expense
740 Computer Supplies Expense
750 Cash Short and Over
760 Miscellaneous Expense

It is in the accounts that the transactions will now be recorded, instead of on a transaction analysis sheet.

Opening a Ledger

To open a ledger: to enter the opening balances.

To make an entry: to write the amounts for a transaction in a book.

In order to begin using the ledger to record transactions, the figures from the balance sheet for a business have to be transferred into the ledger accounts. This process is called **opening the ledger**. What would be a logical method? Amounts on the left side of the fundamental accounting equation will be put on the left side of the T-accounts, and amounts on the right side of the fundamental accounting equation will be put on the right side of the T-accounts. To put an amount in the ledger is **to make an entry**. There will therefore be debit entries and credit entries. The term entry sometimes refers to recording both the debit and credit parts of a transaction.

Opening balance: the first amount entered into an account.

Figure 2-16 shows that the balances have been transferred to the ledger accounts from the balance sheet as at June 30, 1988. The amount in each account when a set of accounting records is started is called the **opening balance**. As transactions occur, the balances of the accounts will change. Note that the date is recorded for each transaction.

Algor Computer Services
Balance Sheet
as at June 30, 1988

Assets		Liabilities	
Cash	$ 97 843	Accounts Payable	$ 24 503
Accounts Receivable	37 901	Short-Term Loans	17 302
Office Supplies	1 239	Mortgage Payable	248 000
Land	124 600	Total Liabilities	289 805
Building	228 000		
Office Equipment	14 500	**Owner's Equity**	
Computer Equipment	45 600		
Automobile	12 500	V. Marshall, Capital	272 378
		Total Liabilities and	
Total Assets	**$562 183**	**Owner's Equity**	**$562 183**

FIGURE 2-16 GENERAL LEDGER FOR ALGOR COMPUTER SERVICES WITH OPENING BALANCES

GENERAL LEDGER

Cash		100		**Accounts Receivable**		120		**Office Supplies**		150
dr.	cr.			dr.	cr.			dr.	cr.	
July 1 97 843				July 1 37 901				July 1 1 239		

Land		160		**Building**		170		**Office Equipment**		175
dr.	cr.			dr.	cr.			dr.	cr.	
July 1 124 600				July 1 228 000				July 1 14 500		

Computer Equipment		180		**Automobile**		190		**Accounts Payable**		200
dr.	cr.			dr.	cr.			dr.	cr.	
July 1 45 600				July 1 12 500					July 1 24 503	

Short-Term Loans		210		**Mortgage Payable**		220		**V. Marshall, Capital**		300
dr.	cr.			dr.	cr.			dr.	cr.	
	July 1 17 302				July 1 248 000				July 1 272 378	

This procedure leads to the following very important rule for each of the three types of accounts:
- Assets have debit balances because they are found on the left side of the fundamental accounting equation, and when the amounts are transferred to the T-accounts they are similarly put on the debit (left) side.
- Liabilities have credit balances because they are found on the right side of the fundamental accounting equation, and when the amounts are transferred to the T-accounts they are similarly put on the credit (right) side.
- Owner's Equity has a credit balance because it is found on the right side of the fundamental accounting equation, and when the amount is transferred to the T-account it is similarly put on the credit (right) side.

Assets		=	Liabilities		+	Owner's Equity	
dr.	cr.		dr.	cr.		dr.	cr.
balance				balance			balance

Entering Transactions into a General Ledger

Each day the transactions of a business are entered in the general ledger. The following transactions for Algor Computer Services will be entered in the general ledger accounts. In order to assist you in following the changes, the ledger accounts for each transaction will also be shown with the transaction analysis.

Transaction 1
July 2   Cash Receipt Slip #33-0829   The business received $500 cash from V. Marshall, the owner, as an additional investment. (The business gained $500 cash and gave the owner an increase of $500 in his equity claim.)

Now that ledger accounts have been introduced, it must be determined whether to enter the amounts on the debit side or the credit side of the account. Try to apply the following four questions when analyzing transactions:

> **QUESTIONS FOR ANALYZING TRANSACTIONS**
> What accounts change?
> What type of account are they?
> Does each account increase or decrease?
> Should the amount be entered on the debit or credit side of the account?

For Marshall's investment, the following analysis is made:

ACCOUNT CHANGED	TYPE OF ACCOUNT	INCREASE/ DECREASE	DEBIT/ CREDIT	AMOUNT
Cash	Asset	Increase	Debit	$500
V. Marshall, Capital	Owner's Equity	Increase	Credit	$500

GENERAL LEDGER

```
        Cash         100           V. Marshall, Capital    300
      dr.   |   cr.                     dr.   |   cr.
July 2  500 |                                  | July 2  500
```

In order to determine the debit/credit column, let us logically examine where the amounts should be entered.

- The Cash account already has a debit balance in it. The account should now be increased by $500. In order to add amounts, people normally put them under one another in a column. Therefore, the $500 should be put on the same side as the balance. A very important rule has thus been established: **in order to increase an asset, the amount is entered on the debit side of an account.**
- A rule can also be established for the owner's Capital account. The opening balance is found on the credit side. To add in this case, amounts are again recorded under one another. Thus, **to increase an owner's equity account, the amount is entered on the credit side of an account.**

```
      Assets      =     Liabilities    +    Owner's Equity
   dr.   |  cr.        dr.  |  cr.         dr.  |  cr.
 increase |                                      | increase
```

For this transaction, note that a debit and a credit were entered in the ledger accounts.

Transaction 2
July 3 Purchase Invoice #27C Office supplies in the amount of $200 are purchased on account from Westend Stationery Ltd.
(The business gained office supplies, and gave a claim on itself to a creditor, Westend Stationery Ltd.)
- We have already established the rule that in order to increase an asset, in this case Office Supplies, the amount is put on the debit side of the T-account.
- The Accounts Payable must also change. Since the liability has increased, we put the number under the previous amount. Therefore, the amount is put on the credit side. Note that again there has been a debit and a credit entry for the transaction.

ACCOUNT CHANGED	TYPE OF ACCOUNT	INCREASE/ DECREASE	DEBIT/ CREDIT	AMOUNT
Office Supplies	Asset	Increase	Debit	$200
Accounts Payable	Liability	Increase	Credit	$200

GENERAL LEDGER

Office Supplies		150	Accounts Payable		200
dr.	cr.		dr.	cr.	
July 3 200				July 3 200	

We have established the rule, therefore, that **to increase a liability, the amount is put on the credit side of an account.**

The following is a summary of the rules that we have learned:

Assets		=	Liabilities		+	Owner's Equity	
dr.	cr.		dr.	cr.		dr.	cr.
increase				increase			increase

Double-entry accounting: *for every transaction total debits must equal total credits.*

For the preceding transactions, there was a debit entry and a credit entry. This is **double-entry accounting**: for every transaction, total debits must *always* equal total credits. It is the accounting system documented by Luca Pacioli in Italy in 1494. Keep this important principle in mind as you work through the following examples in order to establish the remainder of the rules for recording debits and credits.

Transaction 3

July 4   Cheque Copy #441   The business paid $300 on account to Mortimore Professional Services. (The business gained a $300 reduction in what it owes one of its creditors, and gave $300 cash.)

ACCOUNT CHANGED	TYPE OF ACCOUNT	INCREASE/ DECREASE	DEBIT/ CREDIT	AMOUNT
Accounts Payable	Liability	Decrease	Debit	$300
Cash	Asset	Decrease	Credit	$300

GENERAL LEDGER

Accounts Payable		200	Cash		100
dr.	cr.		dr.	cr.	
July 4 300				July 4 300	

Note that again the principle of double-entry accounting has been followed: total debits are equal to total credits for the transaction.
- In order to increase the liability Accounts Payable, the amount is entered on the credit side. Thus, to decrease a liability as required in this transaction, the opposite is done. The rule is: **to decrease a liability, the amount is entered on the debit side of an account.**
- In order to increase an asset, the amount is entered on the debit side. Thus, to decrease an asset as required in this transaction, the opposite is done: **to decrease an asset, the amount is entered on the credit side of an account.**

Transaction 4
July 5   Memo #118   An error was discovered in the recording of the investment by V. Marshall. The amount of the investment was $400, not the $500 as recorded.

ACCOUNT CHANGED	TYPE OF ACCOUNT	INCREASE/ DECREASE	DEBIT/ CREDIT	AMOUNT
V. Marshall, Capital	Owner's Equity	Decrease	Debit	$100
Cash	Asset	Decrease	Credit	$100

GENERAL LEDGER

```
   V. Marshall, Capital    300         Cash                100
       dr.       |     cr.          dr.        |     cr.
   July 5  100  |              |  July 5  100
```

As for all transactions, the debits are equal to the credits for this transaction.
- The Capital account needs to be reduced. As we saw earlier, to increase the Capital account a credit is made. Therefore, the rule is: **to decrease owner's equity, the amount is entered on the debit side.**
- The asset Cash is reduced by making a credit entry.

We have now established the debit and credit rules for the three types of balance sheet accounts: assets, liabilities, and owner's equity.

DEBIT AND CREDIT RULES FOR BALANCE SHEET ACCOUNTS

Assets	=	Liabilities	+	Owner's Equity
dr. / cr.		dr. / cr.		dr. / cr.
increase / decrease		decrease / increase		decrease / increase

Now let us put these rules into effect by analyzing the following transactions. Remember to ask yourself the four questions for analyzing transactions!

Transaction 5
July 6   Cash Receipt Slip #33-0830   Received $300 on account from a customer, D. Lapkoft. (The business gained $300 in cash, and lost its $300 claim on the debtor, D. Lapkoft.)

ACCOUNT CHANGED	TYPE OF ACCOUNT	INCREASE/ DECREASE	DEBIT/ CREDIT	AMOUNT
Cash	Asset	Increase	Debit	$300
Accounts Receivable	Asset	Decrease	Credit	$300

GENERAL LEDGER

Cash	100		Accounts Receivable	120
dr.	cr.		dr.	cr.
July 6 300				July 6 300

Transaction 6
July 7   Cash Receipt Slip #33-0831   The owner, V. Marshall, invested $500 cash in the business, and gave to the business his personal computer worth $3 000. (The business gained $500 cash and a $3 000 computer, and gave to the owner an increased claim on the business.)

Instead of only two accounts changing, three change. However, the fundamental accounting equation will still hold true, for the total debits are equal to the total credits for the transaction.

ACCOUNT CHANGED	TYPE OF ACCOUNT	INCREASE/ DECREASE	DEBIT/ CREDIT	AMOUNT
Cash	Asset	Increase	Debit	$500
Computer Equipment	Asset	Increase	Debit	$3 000
V. Marshall, Capital	Owner's Equity	Increase	Credit	$3 500

GENERAL LEDGER

Cash	100		Computer Equipment	180		V. Marshall, Capital	300
dr.	cr.		dr.	cr.		dr.	cr.
July 7 500			July 7 3 000				July 7 3 500

Note the changes in the general ledger shown in Figure 2-17 for all of the previous transactions.

FIGURE 2-17 GENERAL LEDGER WITH TRANSACTIONS FOR JULY 1 TO JULY 7 ENTERED

GENERAL LEDGER

Cash			100
dr.		cr.	
July 1	97 843	July 4	300
2	500	5	100
6	300		
7	500		

Accounts Receivable			120
dr.		cr.	
July 1	37 901	July 6	300

Office Supplies			150
dr.		cr.	
July 1	1 239		
3	200		

Land			160
dr.		cr.	
July 1	124 600		

Building			170
dr.		cr.	
July 1	228 000		

Office Equipment			175
dr.		cr.	
July 1	14 500		

Computer Equipment			180
dr.		cr.	
July 1	45 600		
7	3 000		

Automobile			190
dr.		cr.	
July 1	12 500		

Accounts Payable			200
dr.		cr.	
July 4	300	July 1	24 503
		3	200

Short-Term Loans			210
dr.		cr.	
		July 1	17 302

Mortgage Payable			220
dr.		cr.	
		July 1	248 000

V. Marshall, Capital			300
dr.		cr.	
July 5	100	July 1	272 378
		2	500
		7	3 500

LESSON REVIEW

28. What is an account? What type of account was introduced in this section? Why is it called that?

29. What is meant by the term debit?

30. What is meant by the term credit?

31. In what book are all the accounts contained?

32. What is the chart of accounts? What purpose does it serve?

33. What is the process of transferring initial balances to the general ledger called?

34. What rule was followed for transferring the balances of the balance sheet items to the T-accounts?

35. Name the three types of accounts that we have studied to date.

36. Indicate the type of balance that each of the three types of accounts have, and describe why they have that type of balance.
37. State the four questions that one should answer when analyzing a transaction.
38. Describe the concept of double-entry accounting.
39. Draw a diagram to summarize the rules for increasing and decreasing the three types of accounts.

LESSON APPLICATIONS

40. For each of the following items, indicate the type of account, and whether the opening balance should be placed on the debit or credit side of the ledger account. The first one is done for you.
    (a) Cash   Asset   Assets have debit balances.
    (b) Supplies
    (c) Equipment
    (d) Bank Loan
    (e) Accounts Receivable
    (f) Building
    (g) Accounts Payable
    (h) Marketable Securities
    (i) Land
    (j) Elizabeth Imhof, Capital

41. Rob Veurtjes owns a business, Veurtjes Driving School, which provides driving lessons. For each of the transactions given below, fill in a chart similar to the following:

ACCOUNT CHANGED	TYPE OF ACCOUNT	INCREASE/ DECREASE	DEBIT/ CREDIT	AMOUNT

   (1) Purchased office supplies for $80 cash.
   (2) Received $90 cash on account.
   (3) Paid $50 on account.
   (4) Paid $200 to the owner, Robert Veurtjes, for personal use.
   (5) Purchased a computer hard disk on account, $6 000.
   (6) Received $5 000 from the owner, Robert Veurtjes, as an additional investment.
   (7) The owner withdrew a $3 000 monochrome monitor from the business.

42. Sandy Wyman is the owner of Wyman's Income Tax Service. For each of the transactions given below, complete a chart similar to the following:

ACCOUNT CHANGED	TYPE OF ACCOUNT	INCREASE/ DECREASE	DEBIT/ CREDIT	AMOUNT

   (1) Purchased office supplies, $480, from Watson Accounting Supplies on account.
   (2) Received $200 on account.
   (3) Purchased a new accounting software package, $2 500 on account, from Computer Suppliers Ltd.
   (4) Received $4 000 from the owner, Sandy Wyman, as an additional investment.
   (5) Paid $400 on the mortgage.
   (6) Purchased marketable securities for $5 000 cash.
   (7) Sold land for $17 000 cash.
   (8) Signed a $5 000 contract with Northern Management Consultants.
   (9) The owner invested $2 000 in cash and a $5 000 fax machine in the business.

43. K. Travis is the owner of a new business, Travis Real Estate Services.
   (a) Open a general ledger by entering each amount on the balance sheet into an account and supply an appropriate account number for each one.
   (b) Enter the following transactions in the business's general ledger. Put the transaction date before each entry.

Travis Real Estate Services
Balance Sheet
as at July 31, 19–7

Assets		Liabilities	
Cash	$43 800	Accounts Payable	$15 400
Accounts Receivable	11 300	Short-Term Loans	3 200
Office Supplies	987	Total Liabilities	18 600
Furniture & Equipment	3 402		
Automobile	18 490	**Owner's Equity**	
		K. Travis, Capital	59 379
Total Assets	**$77 979**	**Total Liabilities and Owner's Equity**	**$77 979**

Aug. 1 Cash Receipt Slip #1: Received $5 000 as an investment by the owner.
2 Purchase Invoice #248: Purchased $2 400 worth of office furniture on account from Willard's Office Furniture Ltd.
2 Purchase Invoice B693: Purchased $220 worth of office supplies on account from Slatery Stationery Ltd.
4 Voucher #1: Received a computer valued at $3 000 as an investment by the owner.
4 Cheque Copy #1: Paid $1 000 on account to Willard's Office Furniture Ltd.
4 Cash Receipt Slip #2: Borrowed $3 000 from Royal Trust Ltd.
5 Cheque Copy #2: Paid $100 on account to Slatery Stationery Ltd.

44. Barton Travel Agency books holidays for its clients. Selected transactions for the first part of January are given below.
(a) Open the general ledger assigning appropriate account numbers.
(b) Enter the transactions in the general ledger.

Barton Travel Agency
Balance Sheet
as at December 31, 19–7

Assets		Liabilities	
Cash	$17 300	Accounts Payable	$10 200
V. Wilson	4 300	Short-Term Loans	3 200
D. Yastremski	1 234	Total Liabilities	13 400
Office Supplies	755		
Furniture & Equipment	14 340	**Owner's Equity**	
		J. Barton, Capital	24 529
		Total Liabilities and	
Total Assets	**$37 929**	**Owner's Equity**	**$37 929**

Jan. 1 Cash Receipt Slip #483: Received $10 000 from Jackie Barton, the owner, as an additional investment.
2 Purchase Invoice #84: Purchased a new computer terminal on account from Compuware, $10 000.
3 Cash Receipt Slip #484: Received $220 on account from D. Yastremski.
4 Cheque Copy #83: Paid $1 000 on account to Compuware.
5 Purchase Invoice #B443: Purchased office supplies on account from Normand Office Supplies Ltd., $220.
7 Cash Receipt Slip #485: Borrowed $2 000, payable over six months, from the Royal Bank of Canada.

8   Purchase Invoice #42: Purchased a fax machine on account from Normand Office Supplies Ltd., $6 000.
9   Cheque Copy #84: Paid $400 on account to Normand Office Supplies Ltd.
9   Cheque Copy #85: Purchased $5 000 worth of Government of Canada Bonds as an investment. (A new account needs to be created.)

2.4 Balancing Accounts and the Trial Balance

Once the transactions for a period of time have been entered in the ledger accounts, it is necessary to calculate new account **balances**. This is the main advantage of having a ledger: it provides the new balances for the preparation of an up-to-date balance sheet.

To balance accounts, the following steps are carried out:

(1) Add each column of numbers. If you have been making the entries in ink, it will be handy to enter the totals in pencil so that they are not confused with an entry. These totals are usually written one half a line high, and are called **pencil footings** or **pin totals**. When they are called the former it is because they are written in pencil, and because to "foot" in accounting means to put a total at the bottom, where the foot is on a person. The term "pin total" comes from their being half a line high, smaller than the other numbers.

> **Pencil footings** or **pin totals:** the total of a column written in pencil, one half of a line high.

(2) Calculate the difference between the debit side total and the credit side total for each account. This is the balance of the account.

(3) Enter the balance on the larger side beside the last entry and circle the amount.

The accounts will have either a debit balance, a credit balance, or a nil balance. A debit balance results if the debit total is greater than the credit total. A credit balance results if the credit total is greater than the debit total. A nil balance, written ∅, results if the debit and credit totals are equal. The balanced general ledger for Algor Computer Services is shown in Figure 2-18.

Notice that all the asset accounts have debit balances, and that the liability and capital accounts have credit balances. Is it possible to have it any other way? Yes, but such a situation is not usual. If the business had a claim on Amy Fecteau, a debtor, for $400 and by error she remitted $500 to the business, the account would have a credit balance of $100. The account would then be treated as a liability because of its credit balance. It is also possible that the Cash account balance could

FIGURE 2-18 GENERAL LEDGER WITH ACCOUNTS PENCIL FOOTED AND BALANCED

GENERAL LEDGER

Cash			100
dr.		cr.	
July 1	97 843	July 4	300
2	500	5	100
6	300		400
7	500		
(98 743)		99 143	

Accounts Receivable			120
dr.		cr.	
July 1	37 901	July 6	300
(37 601)	37 901		300

Office Supplies			150
dr.		cr.	
July 1	1 239		
3	200		
(1 439)	1 439		

Land			160
dr.		cr.	
July 1	124 600		
(124 600)	124 600		

Building			170
dr.		cr.	
July 1	228 000		
(228 000)	228 000		

Office Equipment			175
dr.		cr.	
July 1	14 500		
(14 500)	14 500		

Computer Equipment			180
dr.		cr.	
July 1	45 600		
7	3 000		
(48 600)	48 600		

Automobile			190
dr.		cr.	
July 1	12 500		
(12 500)	12 500		

Accounts Payable			200
dr.		cr.	
July 4	300	July 1	24 503
	300	3	200
	(24 403)		24 703

Short-Term Loans			210
dr.		cr.	
		July 1	17 302
	(17 302)		17 302

Mortgage Payable			220
dr.		cr.	
		July 1	248 000
	(248 000)		248 000

V. Marshall, Capital			300
dr.		cr.	
July 5	100	July 1	272 378
	100	2	500
		7	3 500
	(276 278)		276 378

Exceptional balance: *an account balance opposite to that which the type of account normally has.*

be a credit caused by overdrawing the bank account. (It should be noted that it is a criminal offence to write a cheque knowing that there is not enough money in the account to cover it.) Such a balance is referred to as an **exceptional balance**: a balance opposite to that which the account would normally have.

GENERAL LEDGER

Amy Fecteau			
dr.		cr.	
Aug. 10	400	Aug. 19	500

Similar situations would arise if the business overpaid a liability, or if an item was returned on account after the account had already been paid.

The Trial Balance

Algor Computer Services prepared a formal balance sheet, and after calculating the total of liabilities and owner's equity, found that it was not equal to the total assets. As the balance sheet had been done in ink, many changes were needed after the error was found. Algor wanted to find a method of checking to provide that total debits equal total credits before preparing its balance sheet.

Many transactions will occur in a business during a single month. The accountant must be certain that the double-entry principle of accounting has been followed for each transaction: that total debits equal total credits. To determine whether the total debits in the ledger do equal the total credits, a **trial balance** is prepared, or "taken off." The trial balance can take several forms, as shown in Figure 2-19. These balances were prepared for Algor Computer Services using their ledger shown in Figure 2-18.

The first trial balance is an informal trial balance, with merely the account balances written in. The balances of accounts with debit balances on July 7 are entered in the debit column; credit balances are entered in the credit column. The columns are then totalled.

The second trial balance is a tape trial balance. To calculate the trial balance on the printing calculator, the debits are entered using the plus key, and the credits are entered using the minus key. When the total key is pressed, a 0 should be shown as a total if the ledger is in balance. For this reason the method is sometimes referred to as the zero proof method. However, if there is an amount shown when the total is taken, that amount represents the amount of the error. If the ledger is not in balance, it is necessary to find any errors and correct them. More on how to do that, later.

The third trial balance is a **formal trial balance** with account names and balances shown.

The trial balance has a second purpose: it provides the information for the preparation of a new balance sheet. The accountant could prepare a balance sheet directly from the accounts in the ledger, but it is much easier to use the summary of this information on the trial balance.

If the trial balance is in balance, does it mean that the accountant has done all the work correctly? Not necessarily. The following transaction takes place: Algor Computer Services sells a typewriter, listed under Office Equipment, for $400 cash. The accountant records the transaction as a $400 debit to Cash, and a $400 credit to Office Supplies. The credit should have been to Office Equipment. The ledger will still balance. However, the balance of the Office Supplies account is $400 too small and the balance of the Office Equipment account is $400 too large.

Formal trial balance: a list of account names and balances, with total debits and credits.

FIGURE 2-19 THREE TYPES OF TRIAL BALANCES: INFORMAL, TAPE, AND FORMAL

Algor Computer Services
Trial Balance
July 7, 1988

Debit	Credit
$ 98 743	$ 24 403
37 601	17 302
1 439	248 000
124 600	276 278
228 000	
14 500	
48 600	
12 500	
$565 983	$565 983

Algor Computer Services
Trial Balance
July 7, 1988

```
        *
98 743  +
37 601  +
 1 439  +
124 600 +
228 000 +
14 500  +
48 600  +
12 500  +
24 403  −
17 302  −
248 000 −
276 278 −
      0 *
```

Algor Computer Services
Trial Balance
July 7, 1988

	Debit	Credit
Cash	$ 98 743	
Accounts Receivable	37 601	
Office Supplies	1 439	
Land	124 600	
Building	228 000	
Office Equipment	14 500	
Computer Equipment	48 600	
Automobile	12 500	
Accounts Payable		$ 24 403
Short-Term Loans		17 302
Mortgage Payable		248 000
V. Marshall, Capital		276 278
	$565 983	$565 983

The trial balance will also balance if the only error is failing to enter a transaction in the ledger. The accounts related to the missing transaction will not be correct, but the trial balance will have total debits equal to total credits. We will study how to find errors in Chapter 4.

In many cases, the error will become evident in the future: the error in the recording of the transaction for the sale of the typewriter will be noticed when the business does a count (inventory) of its typewriters and notices that it has one less than recorded. Similarly, if an error is made in a customer's account, the customer will probably notify the business. That does not justify the original error; however, the error will be corrected.

Audits

Audit: an examination of the books by an accountant to see that GAAPs are being followed, and to see that the books have been done accurately.

A business should conduct an audit of its books regularly. An **audit** is the examination of the books by an accountant in order to see that generally accepted accounting principles are being followed, and to see that the books have been done accurately. One of the checks would be to see that all the source documents have been accounted for. As noted earlier, they are numbered. The accountant may also make recommendations to management concerning procedures that could be taken to operate the business more efficiently.

Internal and external audits can take place. In a larger business, an accountant may be on staff solely for the purpose of conducting audits in the various branches or divisions of the firm. In smaller businesses, an audit will be conducted by an accounting firm hired by the business. Limited companies must be audited by an outside auditor.

The need for audit procedures is evidenced by the life of Harold Jaggard. He became boss of Grays Building Society, a mortgage-and-loan institution in Britain. He instructed the bookkeeping staff to make entries in pencil, or an easily erased ink. Jaggard knew when the auditors would appear each year. He took the ledgers home just before they appeared and adjusted them to his liking. One year, the auditors showed up early, and Jaggard's forty-year ruse came to an end. He had taken over $6 million, which he had spent on a fast life. When caught at age seventy-nine, he ended his own life. He had $3 600 in the bank.

Auditors are also liable for any errors that they make, or for mistakes in judgement in performing the audit. For example, the Hong Kong Bank of Canada lent Vancouver's Synflex Industries Ltd. $1 million. Audited reports didn't indicate that there was unpaid federal sales tax. The federal government subsequently put Synflex in receivership for its inability to pay the taxes. The auditing firm was ordered to pay $602 000 to the Hong Kong Bank of Canada in the form of damages, for the bank had relied on the audited reports.

LESSON REVIEW

45. Describe the steps in balancing a ledger.
46. State the two names given to the total of a column, and describe why the names are used.
47. What are the three types of balances?
48. What is an exceptional balance? Give an example of two accounts that could have an exceptional balance. Give an example of two accounts that will never have an exceptional balance.
49. What is the purpose of a trial balance? What does it not prove?
50. Name the three possible types of trial balances, and describe each.
51. What is an audit?
52. Distinguish between an internal audit and an external audit.

LESSON APPLICATIONS

53. The ledger accounts for Noma Cleaning Service are given below.
    (a) Calculate the balance in each of the accounts.
    (b) Take off a formal trial balance.

GENERAL LEDGER

Cash			100
dr.		cr.	
Nov. 1	12 200	Nov. 6	700
3	6 000	12	800
4	200	13	500
8	4 000		
9	200		

J. Barton			110
dr.		cr.	
Nov. 1	750	Nov. 9	200

C. Malloy			120
dr.		cr.	
Nov. 1	600	Nov. 4	200

Supplies			130
dr.		cr.	
Nov. 1	4 320		
5	800		

Equipment			140
dr.		cr.	
Nov. 1	9 650		
10	3 200		

Automobiles			150
dr.		cr.	
Nov. 1	26 300		

Accounts Payable			200
dr.		cr.	
Nov. 6	700	Nov. 1	3 450
13	500	5	800
		10	3 200

Bank Loan			210
dr.		cr.	
Nov. 12	800	Nov. 1	16 200
		8	4 000

T. Bartholomew, Capital			300
dr.		cr.	
		Nov. 1	34 170
		3	6 000

54. The ledger accounts for Mascarenhas Towing Services are given below.
   (a) Calculate the balance in each of the accounts.
   (b) Take off a formal trial balance.

GENERAL LEDGER

Cash			10
dr.		cr.	
May 1	29 200	May 4	600
3	1 100	5	2 000
8	4 000	6	100
11	16 000	12	16 000
		13	1 400
		14	400

Accounts Receivable			12
dr.		cr.	
May 1	2 820	May 3	1 100

Supplies			14
dr.		cr.	
May 1	900		
6	100		

Furniture & Fixtures			16
dr.		cr.	
May 1	6 320		
10	900		

Communication Equipment			18
dr.		cr.	
May 1	16 300		
13	1 400		

Trucks			20
dr.		cr.	
May 1	42 300		
12	16 000		

Accounts Payable			30
dr.		cr.	
May 4	600	May 1	7 830
14	400	10	900

Short-Term Loans			32
dr.		cr.	
May 5	2 000	May 1	29 600
		11	16 000

T. Mascarenhas, Capital			50
dr.		cr.	
		May 1	60 410
		8	4 000

CHAPTER REVIEW AND SKILL DEVELOPMENT

Accounting Principles and Concepts

- According to the **double-entry principle**, for every transaction, total debits must equal total credits.

- Asset accounts have **debit balances**, and liability and capital accounts have **credit balances**. The rules for the types of balance were derived from their relationship to the fundamental accounting equation.

- According to the **objectivity principle**, accounting records must be kept on the basis of objective evidence.

- A **trial balance** is prepared to prove the accuracy of the general ledger.

Knowing the Terms

For each of the following statements, indicate the term being defined.

(a) A listing of all account names and numbers used by the business.
(b) To enter the opening balances in the general ledger.
(c) An account with a balance opposite to that which it would normally have.
(d) An exchange of goods and/or services that results in a change in the financial position of the business.
(e) The document that indicates that a transaction has occurred.
(f) Totals written one half of a line high, and in pencil.

(g) The left side of a T-account.
(h) A check of the books to ensure that generally accepted accounting principles are being followed.
(i) A form used to record changes in any one item.
(j) Source document used to record unusual transactions.

Food for Thought

1. A bookkeeper decided to put all similar source documents in a pile, and enter the transactions in the ledger once a week rather than daily. What is the disadvantage of this procedure?

2. A firm signs a contract with a supplier on November 1. The supplies are to be received on December 1, and payment is to be made on January 2. The bookkeeper makes an entry on November 1 to record all three events. She claims that it doesn't matter that the events are entered as one transaction on November 1, for eventually all the events will occur. Criticize her viewpoint.

3. Give three reasons why a transaction analysis sheet would not be used by a business.

4. Explain why the double-entry system of accounting should always result in a trial balance which is in balance.

5. A chart of accounts could be put in an order other than that found on the financial statement. In what other order could they be put? What would be the disadvantage of doing so?

6. When setting up a chart of accounts, an accountant decided to make a separate account for each debtor instead of putting them all into one account called Accounts Receivable. What are the advantages and disadvantages of designing the chart in this way?

7. A firm receives a piece of land as a donation from a municipality. In return, the firm must build its plant on the land. The land is valued at $220 000 on the books of the municipality. An appraiser indicates that the land would sell for $250 000 on the open market. What value should be used in the firm's books to record receipt of the land as a donation?

8. Comment on the following statement: "Since the trial balance is in balance, the accounts must be correct."

9. Rather than prepare a trial balance on a monthly basis, a firm decides to do it every three months. What are the advantages and disadvantages of this procedure? Do the disadvantages outweigh the advantages? Explain.

10. Large businesses issue and receive many source documents on a daily basis. What do the businesses do with these documents after they have recorded the transactions? How long do you think that they have to keep them on file? Why?

11. Which of the following filing systems would be used for the source documents discussed in this chapter: numeric, alphabetic, or by date?

12. A business buys a property with an office building located on it. The purchase price is $450 000; $100 000 is to be paid in cash, with the balance covered by a mortgage. What two asset accounts will be increased due to the transaction? Why must the purchase price be separated into two accounts? How will the business decide on the amount to be put in each account?

13. As a creditor of a business, would you prefer the creditors' claims or the owner's claim on the business to be larger? Why?

Organizing

Prepare an organizer that will show the following information:
(a) the three types of accounts that we have studied to date;
(b) a definition of the three types of accounts;
(c) the rules for increasing and decreasing the three types of accounts.

Applications

1. The general ledger of Milks' Decks and Play Structures, given in Figure 2-20, shows the entries for a number of transactions. Starting with July 2, for each date given find the corresponding debit and credit and
   (a) complete an analysis chart with columns for Account Changed, Type of Account, Increase/Decrease, Debit/Credit, and Amount;
   (b) give a verbal description of the transaction;
   (c) indicate the source document for the transaction.

2. The balance sheet for Comet Appliance Services, owned by R. Nilan, is given in Figure 2-21, along with transactions for the first part of October.
   (a) Open the general ledger for Comet Appliance Services, using the accounts and balances given on the balance sheet, and supplying appropriate account numbers.
   (b) Record the October transactions in the ledger.
   (c) Calculate the balance of the accounts after entering the last of the transactions for October 10.
   (d) Take off a formal trial balance as at October 10.

Transactions

Oct. 1 Cash Receipt Slip #493: Received $2 300 from the owner, Ross Nilan, as an investment.

2 Purchase Invoice #492/Cheque Copy #49: Purchased a new truck from Rowan's Chev Olds Ltd., paid $5 000 down. Borrowed the balance of $12 200 from Canada West Trust Co.

FIGURE 2-20

GENERAL LEDGER

Cash			100	Accounts Receivable			110	Supplies			120
dr.		cr.		dr.		cr.		dr.		cr.	
July 1	8 000	July 4	16 000	July 1	2 400	July 3	200	July 1	1 400		
2	16 000	5	300					7	200		
3	200	7	200								
6	3 000	8	900								
		9	300								

Equipment			130	Truck			140	Accounts Payable			200
dr.		cr.		dr.		cr.		dr.		cr.	
July 1	2 000			July 4	16 000			July 5	300	July 1	1 140
8	900							9	300		

Bank Loan			210	D. Milks, Capital			300
dr.		cr.		dr.		cr.	
		July 2	16 000			July 1	12 660
						6	3 000

FIGURE 2-21

Comet Appliance Services
Balance Sheet
as at September 30, 19--

Assets		Liabilities	
Cash	$ 9 480	Accounts Payable	$ 4 200
Accounts Receivable	3 900	Canada West Trust Co. Loan	5 980
Office Supplies	845	Mortgage Payable	22 080
Land	33 500	Total Liabilities	32 260
Building	72 709		
Truck	14 970		
Furniture & Fixtures	13 600	**Owner's Equity**	
Repair Equipment	8 320	R. Nilan, Capital	125 064
		Total Liabilities and	
Total Assets	**$157 324**	**Owner's Equity**	**$157 324**

3 Purchase Invoice #94-332: Purchased a new tool kit, with tools, on account from Sears Canada Inc., $2 796.

4 Voucher #16: The owner took a $500 typewriter for his personal use.

4 Cash Receipt Slip #494: Received $120 on account from R. Bergin.

4 Cheque Copy #50: Paid $300 on the trust company loan.

5 Purchase Invoice #99887: Purchased a new office desk on account from Danish Furniture Ltd., $1 200.

7 Cheque Copy #51: Paid $420 on account to Sears Canada Inc.

9 Cash Receipt Slip #495: Received $750 on account from Boston Pizza.

9 Cash Receipt Slip #496: Received $650 on account from Foothills College.

10 Purchase Invoice #A331: Purchased $90 worth of office supplies on account from Western Stationery for the new desk.

10 Cheque Copy #52: Made the monthly mortgage payment, $900.

10 Cash Receipt Slip #497: Had a piece of vacant land beside the building severed, and sold the new lot for $18 000.

Applications — Comprehensive
1. Transactions to the balance sheet

The trial balance for W. Merritt, Architects, is given in Figure 2-22.

(a) Open the ledger for W. Merritt, Architects, supplying the account numbers, and using the accounts and balances given on the trial balance.

(b) Record the March transactions in the ledger.

(c) Calculate the balance of the accounts as at March 10.

(d) Take off a formal trial balance as at March 10.

(e) Prepare a balance sheet from the new trial balance.

FIGURE 2-22

W. Merritt, Architects
Trial Balance
February 28, 19--

	Debit	Credit
Cash	$ 12 362	
N. Mazpolis	14 652	
C. Taylor	6 842	
Drafting Supplies	2 539	
Office Supplies	320	
Land	52 090	
Building	89 455	
Furniture & Fixtures	3 921	
Computer Equipment	0	
Accounts Payable		$ 9 428
Mortgage Payable		74 870
W. Merritt, Capital		97 883
	$182 181	$182 181

Mar. 1 Cheque Copy #49: Made the $820 monthly payment on the mortgage.
2 Cash Receipt Slip #93: Received $940 on account from N. Mazpolis.
3 Cheque Copy #50: Paid $1 020 on account to Office Overload.
4 Purchase Invoice #49: Purchased $540 worth of drafting supplies on account from Stationery in Motion.
5 Cash Receipt Slip #94: Received $1 500 from the owner as an additional investment.
6 Purchase Invoice #99-33: Purchased 6 new drafting tables from Global Office Furniture for $3 600. Paid $1 600 by Cheque Copy #51, and the balance is due in 30 days.
7 Cheque Copy #52: Paid $500 on account to Superior Janitorial Services.
8 Cash Receipt Slip #95: Received $300 from C. Taylor.
9 Purchase Invoice #627: Purchased a fax machine on account from Blitz Electronics for $5 000. Opened a new account, Office Equipment, to record the item.
10 Purchase Invoice #964: Purchased a computer on account from ComputerLand for $14 000.
10 Purchase Invoice #101: Purchased CAD/CAM software, $1 500, on account from World of Software. Opened a new account, Computer Software, to record the item.

2. Source documents to the balance sheet
A trial balance is given in Figure 2-23.
(a) Open a ledger for the business, supply the account numbers, and enter the data from the trial balance.
(b) Enter the transactions from Figures 2-24 to 2-36 into the ledger.
(c) Calculate the ledger account balances, and take off a formal trial balance.
(d) Prepare a balance sheet.

FIGURE 2-23

Tex Shouldice, Auctioneer
Trial Balance
May 31, 19-6

	Debit	Credit
Cash	$ 25 693	
Accounts Receivable	4 390	
Office Supplies	534	
Land	42 000	
Building	78 400	
Office Equipment	3 260	
Accounts Payable		$ 2 900
Short-Term Loan		8 400
Mortgage Payable		21 000
Taxes Payable		1 100
T. Shouldice, Capital		120 877
	$154 277	$154 277

FIGURE 2-24

555-9814 No. 22

Shouldice Auctioneers
33 West Winds Drive, Mississauga, ON M4R 4M4

Date: June 1, 19-6

Received from: W. Vaillancourt, Trustees
Amount: Nine hundred and forty-two —————— xx/100
On Account: ✔   Other: _____
Cash: $ 942 xx   Chq.: _____   Chq. ref.: _____
Received by: T. Shouldice

FIGURE 2-25

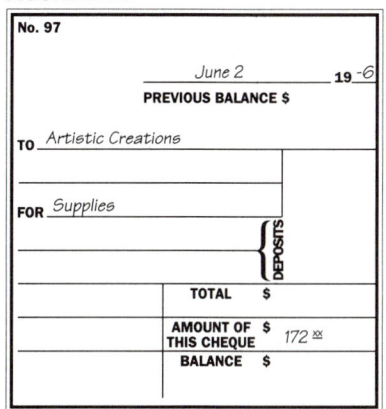

No. 97
June 2, 19-6
PREVIOUS BALANCE $
TO Artistic Creations
FOR Supplies
TOTAL $
AMOUNT OF THIS CHEQUE $ 172 xx
BALANCE $

FIGURE 2-26

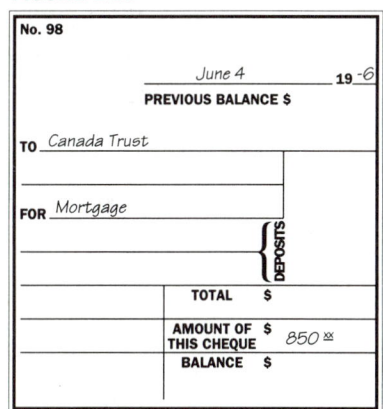

No. 98
June 4, 19-6
PREVIOUS BALANCE $
TO Canada Trust
FOR Mortgage
TOTAL $
AMOUNT OF THIS CHEQUE $ 850 xx
BALANCE $

FIGURE 2-27

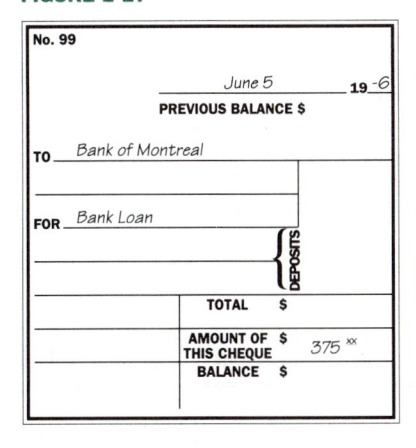

No. 99
June 5, 19-6
PREVIOUS BALANCE $
TO Bank of Montreal
FOR Bank Loan
TOTAL $
AMOUNT OF THIS CHEQUE $ 375 xx
BALANCE $

FIGURE 2-28

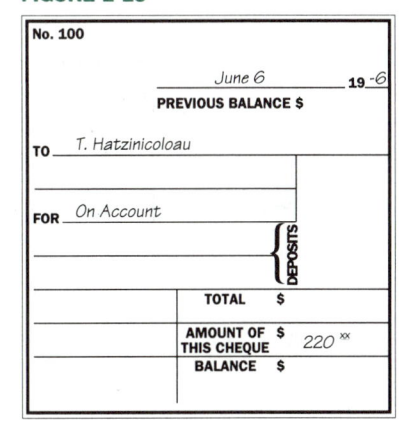

No. 100
June 6, 19-6
PREVIOUS BALANCE $
TO T. Hatzinicoloau
FOR On Account
TOTAL $
AMOUNT OF THIS CHEQUE $ 220 xx
BALANCE $

FIGURE 2-29

INVOICE 443	**Brantford Electronic Suppliers**		Date: 06/06/-6
	44 Wendover Road, Brantford, ON N5R 3F5		
	555-7781		
SOLD TO:	Shouldice Auctioneers		
	33 West Winds Drive		
	Mississauga, ON M4R 4M4		RECEIVED JUN 09 19-6

Your Order No.:553	Terms: July 1		Shipped Via: Local Transport	
Quantity	Item		Unit Price	Amount
1	#499-224 Telephone Answering Machine		$1 240 –	$1 240 –
		TOTAL		$1 240 –

FIGURE 2-30

INVOICE 98-553			Date: 06/06/-6
	Mississauga Computer Rental and Sales		
	22 Westminster Avenue		
	Mississauga, ON M4V 3Y7		
SOLD TO:	Shouldice Auctioneers		
	33 West Winds Drive		
	Mississauga, ON M4R 4M4		RECEIVED JUN 07 19-6

Your Order No.:473	Terms.: 10 days		Shipped Via: Purolator	
Quantity	Item		Unit Price	Amount
1	MAC SE with 80 meg hard drive		$8 380 –	$8 380 –
		TOTAL		$8 380 –

FIGURE 2-31

```
555-9814                                      No. 23

              Shouldice Auctioneers
         33 West Winds Drive, Mississauga, ON  M4R 4M4


                                    Date: June 7, 19-6


Received from: M. Abarca
Amount: One hundred and sixteen ———————————— xx/100
On Account: ✔          Other: _____
Cash: $ 116 xx    Chq.: _____    Chq. ref.: _____
Received by: T. Shouldice
```

FIGURE 2-32

```
MEMO # 272

DATE: 06/09/-6


DESCRIPTION: Received a fax machine, valued at $3 200, from T. Shouldice
             as an investment.



ACCOUNTS: Office Equipment / T. Shouldice, Capital


COMPLETED BY: V. Arness
```

FIGURE 2-33

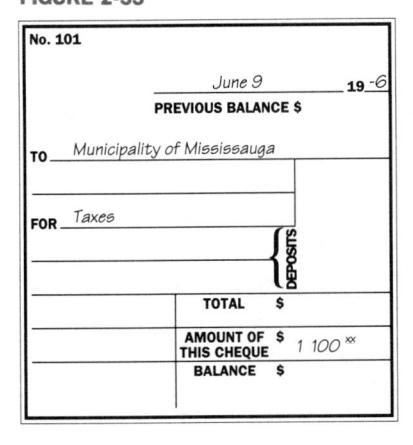

```
No. 101
                    June 9        19 -6
              PREVIOUS BALANCE $
TO   Municipality of Mississauga

FOR  Taxes


                    TOTAL       $
              AMOUNT OF  $
              THIS CHEQUE   1 100 xx
              BALANCE    $
```

FIGURE 2-34

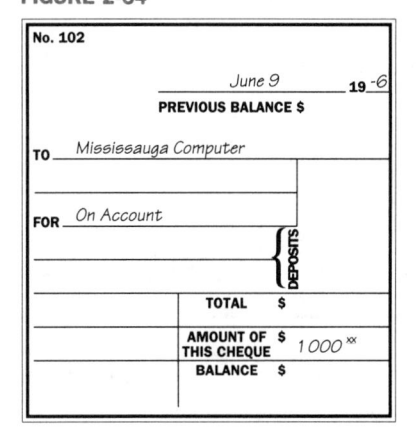

```
No. 102
                    June 9        19 -6
              PREVIOUS BALANCE $
TO   Mississauga Computer

FOR  On Account


                    TOTAL       $
              AMOUNT OF  $
              THIS CHEQUE   1 000 xx
              BALANCE    $
```

FIGURE 2-35

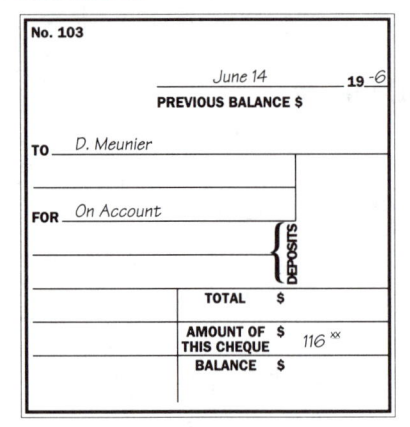

```
No. 103
                    June 14        19 -6
              PREVIOUS BALANCE $

TO   D. Meunier

FOR  On Account

                                  DEPOSITS
                  TOTAL      $
                  AMOUNT OF  $
                  THIS CHEQUE    116 xx
                  BALANCE    $
```

FIGURE 2-36

```
MEMO # 273

DATE:  06/14/-6

DESCRIPTION:  Received $300 worth of fax paper from T. Shouldice
              as an investment.

ACCOUNTS:  Office Supplies / T. Shouldice, Capital

COMPLETED BY:  V. Arness
```

Focussing — Trial Balance

The following trial balance was prepared by a clerk for Williams Graphics Studio:

Williams Graphics Studio
Trial Balance
November 30, 19–8

Tina Williams, Capital		$ 98 990
Bank Loan	$ 5 400	
Cash		300
Equipment		12 400
John Norton (a debtor)	600	
Investments	12 900	
Office Supplies		150
Mortgage Payable		72 000
Office Decor Ltd. (a creditor)		9 450
Devin D'Aoust (a debtor)		100
Williams Enterprises Ltd. (a creditor)	490	
Land	78 000	
Building	$ 96 000	
	$193 390	$193 390

(a) Why should the accountant question the accuracy of the books?

(b) Which accounts should the accountant examine to ensure that they are correct? State why they should be examined.

Evaluate and Assess — Chart of Accounts

Bob Edwards was establishing an accounting system for his employer, Manale's Appliance Services. The firm provides both in-store and house-calls repair service for all types of appliances. When establishing the chart of accounts, Bob made the following decisions:

(a) All claims on debtors would be recorded in individual accounts rather than having one Accounts Receivable account. Bob estimated that there would be up to 200 debtors at any one time, but only one charge item per year for most debtors.

(b) All supplies, both office and repair, would be recorded in one account called Supplies.

(c) All equipment, both office and repair, would be recorded in one account called Equipment.

(d) Land and Building would be recorded in one account called Land and Building.

(e) Accounts Payable, for which there would be up to ten different creditors, would be recorded in separate accounts.

Comment on each of the above decisions that Bob Edwards has made concerning the establishment of his chart of accounts.

Synthesize and Conclude

1. Source Documents
Cindy Mammoletti, a student taking accounting, was hired to assist in the pro shop at the West Winds Golf Course. As part of her duties, she was to do the bookkeeping. When she started the job in May, the club had already been open for three weeks. The owner had put all the source documents in a pile. He had made deposits of the cash whenever it was convenient to get to the bank, and had taken money from the cash register for personal and business use. He did not make use of vouchers; he sometimes wrote notes on a piece of paper.
(a) Criticize the accounting system of the owner.
(b) Propose improvements in the system.

2. An Entrepreneur Buying a Business
Sandy Chung is considering the purchase of Yet Another Video Store from Peter Winston. Peter has operated the business as a sideline to his other businesses, and has decided to sell. Sandy has saved money from her job, and also recently won $80 000 in a lottery. She has total funds available of $122 000. Currently she works as an employee at a management consulting office which pays her $48 000 per year. She would have to quit her current job, or take a leave of absence for at least a year, if she were to buy the video store. Peter is asking $200 000 for the business. He states that it has an annual profit of $70 000.
(a) Prepare eight questions that Sandy should ask Peter concerning the business based on the balance sheet in Figure 2-37.
(b) Prepare five other questions that Sandy should ask Peter concerning the business.
(c) Why would Peter be asking more than his capital in the business as a purchase price?
(d) What immediate expenses will Sandy have when she takes over the business?
(e) Prepare a list of reasons why Sandy (i) should buy the business, and (ii) should not buy the business.

FIGURE 2-37

Yet Another Video Store
Balance Sheet
as at November 30, 19–8

Assets		Liabilities	
Cash	$ 22 900	Accounts Payable	$ 9 820
Accounts Receivable	1 370	Short-Term Loans	25 400
Supplies	690	Mortgage Payable	124 000
Videos	120 000	Total Liabilities	159 220
Land	80 000		
Building	60 000		
Popcorn Machine	1 200	**Owner's Equity**	
Video Equipment	32 900	P. Winston, Capital	159 840
		Total Liabilities and	
Total Assets	**$319 060**	**Owner's Equity**	**$319 060**

ACCOUNTING AT WORK

David Rattray
Assistant Auditor General

David Rattray holds the position of Assistant Auditor General responsible for the portfolio that includes National Defence, Justice, Solicitor General, Energy, Mines and Resources, major capital projects and materials management. His job is to support the Auditor General of Canada who provides members of Parliament with useful information about how money is spent and the kinds of results that have been achieved.

Rattray has moved very quickly in his career. He graduated from high school at 16 and finished a Commerce degree by the time he was 20. For the next ten years he worked in a variety of positions, including controller for a business and part-time university lecturer. These positions gave him a breadth of experience that has since proved useful. Eventually Rattray joined the Auditor General's Office as a student-in-accounts. In order to move up the ladder within the organization, he enrolled in the Certified General Accountant program and graduated in 1974. Since then, Rattray has held a number of posts within the Auditor General's Office, with increasingly greater responsibilities.

The workload for someone in Rattray's position is huge. One strategy that he uses to cope with the demands is to separate work and home. "When I'm at home I try to put the office as far from my mind as possible. On the other hand, I try very hard not to bring personal matters to the office. You can't cope well with stress if you blur work and relaxation time."

Rattray's success has not made him complacent or reluctant to change. He willingly takes leadership roles within the organization and searches for directions for the future. "My own feeling is that we should push forward," he says. "I think we should take risks, but I think we should know where it is we want to go." Rattray combines leadership ability, management skills, and accounting knowledge in the right amounts to be very successful in his field.

Assume you are the head of a hiring committee. Using the above career information and the ad on the following page, prepare an advertisement for an auditor to work in your firm.

Bombardier Inc.

Bombardier Inc., a Canadian corporation with an international focus, is engaged in the development, manufacture, and sale of equipment and products related to the transportation and aerospace industries.

Internal Auditor

Candidates are being sought to fill positions in our corporate internal audit department situated in Ville St. Laurent.

Reporting to the Director of Internal Auditing, you will be responsible for the planning and execution of financial as well as systems and operational audits. This position represents an excellent opportunity to start a dynamic career at Bombardier Inc.

You should be a chartered accountant with two to three years of experience in public practice. Computer audit experience is an asset. The position requires good analytical skills, diplomacy, and the ability to communicate in both French and English. Out of town travel requirements should not exceed 30%.

Please send your résumé to:

Johanne St-Amand
Organizational Development
Bombardier Inc.
800 René-Lévesque Blvd. West
Suite 1700
Montreal, Quebec H3B 1Y8

We offer equal employment opportunities.

Business Career Skills

1. Report Writing

Winnie Cheung was hired to do an audit of the Barnabe Athletic Club in Montreal. The Club sold memberships for various time periods, and also collected cash from walk-in customers. During her audit, Winnie noticed the following irregularities:

(1) In order to save money, the printed source documents (cash receipt slips, sales invoices, vouchers) were not prenumbered. The cheques printed by the bank were prenumbered.

(2) One of the front desk clerks, Pierre, appeared to be stealing money. When he was on duty, cash receipts were far below those received by other clerks who worked the same hours on other days. On observing Pierre's shift on two consecutive days, proof was obtained that he was not filling out cash sales slips. Instead, he pocketed the money paid by some walk-in customers.

Prepare a report to the owner, Marcel Barnabe, which
(a) outlines the problems which exist in the accounting system and
(b) suggests how the stealing by Pierre should be dealt with.

2. Decision Making — The Accountant as a Supervisor

Wendy Saunders is the accounting controller in a large accounting department that includes five secretaries, each of whom uses an electric typewriter. The firm has budgeted so that two new word processors can be purchased in the current year. These will replace the electric typewriters for two of the secretaries. Additional word processors will not be purchased for three or four years. The new equipment will greatly ease the stress and reduce the workload on the users as compared to the old typewriters. The firm also has budgeted to train only two secretaries on the necessary software.

Prepare a memo to your immediate supervisor indicating which secretaries will receive the new word processors. In your memo you are to give the rationale for your decisions. State any assumptions upon which you base your decision.

COMPUTER ACCOUNTING
CREATING A SPREADSHEET TEMPLATE (MODEL)

For a small business, one important feature of a spreadsheet program is its ability to set up a **source document form**, which can be saved and then quickly called up when needed. This **model**, or **template**, is a spreadsheet that has all of the constant information and formulas entered into it to make it ready for use in a number of different transactions. Invoices, remittance slips, and special purchase forms are a few examples.

We'll use an **invoice** as an example. When a retail business purchases assets on account from a manufacturer or supplier, the business form **(source document)** that the retailer receives is called a **purchase invoice**. The seller would call this document a **sales invoice**. As the following sample shows, the purchase/sales invoice states what items the business has purchased, the quantity of each item shipped, what they

FIGURE 2-38 AN INVOICE MADE WITH A SPREADSHEET

```
WESTCOAST COMPUTERS LTD                 SOLD TO:  Dr. L. Ng
Hardware/Software Suppliers                       43 Park St
1876 Lonsdale Avenue                              Richmond, BC
North Vancouver, BC                               V6X 1T4
V6M 3B6
(604) 555-7845                          INVOICE NO. S459

DATE:  1988 09 05                       TERMS:    30 Days

                                        UNIT
QUANTITY           ITEM                 PRICE            AMOUNT

   1         IBM Model 30-286 includes  $2 999.00     $2 999.00
             VGA Monitor and 45 MB Hard
             Drive

   1         Panasonic Laser Printer     2 200.00      2 200.00


                                        TOTAL         $5 199.00
```

cost both individually and in the quantity purchased, when payment is due, and other relevant data.

In the above example, Dr. Ng has purchased a computer system for use in his dental office. In this invoice, a formula is used to calculate the amount the items cost (quantity is multiplied by the unit price). Another formula calculates the final total (each amount is added to arrive at the final total).

One of the valuable features of the **electronic spreadsheet** is that you can change the data values and produce new results instantly without time-consuming manual calculations. Thus, once a source document has been formulated, it can be called up on the screen when needed, new data can be entered, and then a **hard copy** can be printed.

Exercises

1. Use your spreadsheet program to custom design a sales invoice for Gulf of Georgia Sea Products Ltd.

Format:

(1) Enter an exact copy of the invoice model shown in Figure 2-39. Ensure that you enter the material at the correct ROW and COLUMN locations. Remember, the invoice must print on 8.5-inch wide paper.

(2) Format the Price column to be fixed to two decimal places.

(3) Format the Amount column to dollars to two decimal places.

Formulas:

(1) When formulas are entered onto a spreadsheet model, they *must* be entered at the location where the answer is to be displayed.

(2) Amount = Quantity × Price

(3) Use the SUM function to calculate PLEASE PAY THIS AMOUNT.

FIGURE 2-39

```
GULF OF GEORGIA SEA PRODUCTS LTD.
2255 Commissioner Street
Vancouver, BC      V6A 2C9


SOLD TO: _____     INVOICE NO: _____
         _____     INVOICE DATE: _____
         _____     TERMS:  30 days
```

QTY (lbs)	DESCRIPTION	F	Z	CODE	PRICE	AMOUNT
	Red Spring - large					
	Red Spring - medium					
	Red Spring - small					
	White Spring - large					
	White Spring - med.					
	White Spring - small					
	Smoked Salmon					
	Offal					
	Other					
				PLEASE PAY THIS AMOUNT		

COPY

Model Test:
(1) Before using your model, test it with some sample data to ensure that it works as you wish. Enter the following data into the first three lines of the Qty and Price columns to see if your invoice model calculates the correct figures.

QTY (lbs)	PRICE
456	1.51
123	2.39
42	6.56

The please pay this amount line should be showing $1258.05.

(2) When your model calculates the correct answer, erase the numbers you have just inserted for the test and SAVE the template (model).

2. Use your spreadsheet program to create a source document for each of the following business situations.

(a) The coach of your school's basketball team has approached you to design and print a game cash report form that will record total tickets sold, total cash in drawer, change fund, and determine any cash overage or shortage. Customize the form by including your school name and signature lines for the ticket seller and teacher/sponsor.

Test your spreadsheet model with the following data:

Starting ticket number 2345
Ending ticket number 2950
Each ticket has a base price of $3

Cash in drawer:
610 one-dollar bills   20 quarters
300 two-dollar bills   20 dimes
50 five-dollar bills
35 ten-dollar bills
10 twenty-dollar bills

Change fund $200

(b) Pacific Rim Travel, located at 567 Burrard Street, Vancouver, BC, V5Y 3P8, has engaged you to design a sales invoice to be used in their office to record cash and credit sales. The form should prominently display the name of the business, provide space for entering customer detail, and feature columns with headings for recording the number of items sold (e.g., airline tickets), a description of the item sold (e.g., round-trip ticket on Air Canada Vancouver-Toronto), the dollar amount of item sold, and the total value of the sale. Think of other details that might be added to the invoice to make it more useful in recording all sales transactions. Print a copy of your proposed source document.

(c) Phil Singer, owner of Scottsdale Automotive Centre, has just purchased a new computer system for his automobile repair business. One function he wishes to computerize is the present tedious and time-consuming task of preparing monthly billing statements to customers. His present billing statement is shown in Figure 2-40. Use your spreadsheet program to prepare a suitable billing statement to include the above information and the appropriate formulas.

FIGURE 2-40

```
SCOTTSDALE AUTOMOTIVE CENTRE
   5646 Scott Road, Surrey, B.C.   V5F 1D5
   Telephone:  555-1256

Complete Auto Service    Professional Mechanics
```

Customer Name	Res. Phone No.	Bus. Phone No.
	Invoice Date	Invoice No.
	Make / Year	Model
	Serial Number	Motor Number
	Transmission No.	Distance
	Licence No.	

Cust. No.   Purchase Order No.

```
                                    Total Parts  :
                                    Sales Tax    :
                                    Sub Total    :
                                    Labour       :
                                    Total Invoice:
```

This company does not assume any responsibility whatever for vehicles or equipment left for repairs, storage or other purposes, or for articles left in same.

CHAPTER THREE

Analyzing Transactions Related to the Income Statement

LEARNING OBJECTIVES

At the end of this chapter you should be able to
- prepare an income statement;
- describe the significance of the income statement;
- analyze transactions involving the income statement;
- recognize transactions that affect the owner's drawings account;
- compare the terms comparative statements and condensed statements;
- prepare an income statement from a trial balance;
- load a spreadsheet program and use it to format an income statement template;
- use the spreadsheet template to enter revenues and expenses and automatically calculate the net income or loss;
- use the spreadsheet program to make forecasts or answer "what-if" questions.

LANGUAGE OF ACCOUNTING

You will see the following terms in this chapter:
comparative statements
condensed statements
drawings
economic resources
expenses
fiscal period
forecasts
income statement
matching
net income
revenue
revenue recognition
"what-if" questions

3.1 The Income Statement

One of Vijay Marshall's main concerns, after operating his business for a number of months, was whether he was earning a profit. Vijay needed to know how much revenue the business was generating and what his expenses were, so that he could make decisions that would improve the profitability of the business. He knew that if he did not make a profit he would not be able to stay in business for long. How would Vijay calculate the profit for his business?

For Vijay to calculate his profit, a second financial statement, the income statement, must be prepared. It is called an income statement, rather than a profit and loss statement, because the accounting profession prefers the word income. In addition, the meaning of "profit" varies from profession to profession. An **income statement** is a financial statement that lists the revenue and expenses for a given period of time and shows the net income or net loss of a business. Net income is the amount of gain that the business has from its transactions; net loss is the result when expenses exceed revenue. The income statement is usually made on a monthly basis, so that management will be able to make decisions that will increase the net income in future months. Quarterly statements are usually published by those firms that make their statements available to the public.

> **Income statement:** a financial statement that shows the revenue and expenses, and shows the net income or net loss of a business, for a given period of time.

Revenue

When Algor Computer Services started business, it installed computer networks and repaired certain brands. A little later, it also provided seminars on software. The source of revenue was the money collected from the customers at the time of giving the service, or from the claims (accounts receivable) on those who did not pay immediately. Thus, **revenue** is an increase in assets resulting from the sale of a good or a service. As we will study in Chapter 9, a good is the product that the business sells; it does not include items used in the business, such as office supplies. In Algor's case, when the business was small, only a service was being sold.

> **Revenue:** an increase in assets resulting from the sale of a good or a service.

Revenue:
Business gains assets (Cash, Accounts Receivable)	from	— providing a service or — selling a good

Revenue increases owner's equity. The Revenue account is referred to as an "equity account" because it increases the owner's claim on the business. Whenever a service is provided, an asset increases, and the owner's equity increases:

Assets	= Liabilities + Owner's Equity
(Cash and Accounts Receivable)	(Owner's claim increases from revenue)

Revenue is a good indicator of the success and growth of a business. If revenue is increasing, a business is usually healthy. A business cannot operate if it does not have a steady inflow of cash, for then it cannot pay its liabilities as they become due, and, if it is a merchandising business, it cannot buy goods for resale.

Revenue has been defined as the increase in assets resulting from the sale of a good or a service. All increases in assets are not caused by revenue: only increases coming from the sale of goods or services are. For instance, if the owner invests cash in the business, the cash gained is not revenue even though the transaction increases owner's equity. A sample transaction and T-account entries follow.

May 16   Cash Receipt Slip #33-0045: Received $500 from the owner as an additional investment.

GENERAL LEDGER

Cash		100	V. Marshall, Capital		300
dr.	cr.		dr.	cr.	
May 16 500				May 16 500	

Similarly, if unused supplies in the business were sold for cash, the entry for that transaction would be:

May 16 Cash Receipt Slip #33-0046: Received $300 from the sale of unused office supplies at cost price.

GENERAL LEDGER

Cash		100	Office Supplies		150
dr.	cr.		dr.	cr.	
May 16 300				May 16 300	

You should note that revenue is not recognized in either of these two examples, because the transactions do not represent a sale of a good or a service for the business.

Expenses

In order to provide the computer services it markets, Algor incurs a number of expenses. The business has to buy gas and oil for the automobile, pay for the utilities at the office, and pay wages. Some expenses are more directly related to the process of obtaining revenue than others. For example, Hasbro, which is the largest toy company in the United States, spent $7 million in one year for advertising its doll, Maxie. Maxie is one of the newest rivals to the Barbie doll in the $500 million fashion doll market. Thus, an **expense** is the cost of goods and services used in the process of obtaining revenue.

Expense: *the cost of goods and services used in the process of obtaining revenue.*

Expenses decrease owner's equity. In the accounting equation, Assets = Liabilities + Owner's Equity, expenses are referred to as "equity accounts." They are equity accounts because they decrease the owner's claim on the business.

Expenses have been defined as the cost of goods and services used in the process of obtaining revenue. All expenditures, however, are not expenses, since expenditures are also made to acquire assets or pay liabilities. For example, to buy office supplies for cash, the following entry would be made:

May 16 Cheque Copy #96: Paid $400 for the purchase of supplies.

GENERAL LEDGER

Office Supplies		150	Cash		100
dr.	cr.		dr.	cr.	
May 16 400				May 16 400	

The owner's equity in the business has not changed, for the business has merely exchanged one asset for another. One should note, however, that the supplies are going to be used. Similarly, in the payment of a liability, the equity of the business does not change.

THE FACTS SPEAK...

Revenue for 1989
Nestlé, $37.76 billion
McDonald's, $6.41 billion
Nintendo, $2.27 billion

May 16   Cheque Copy #97: Paid $359 on account to Westmore Office Cleaning.

GENERAL LEDGER

Accounts Payable	200		Cash		100
dr.	cr.		dr.	cr.	
May 16 359				May 16 359	

Net Income and Net Loss

Net income: the difference when revenue exceeds expenses.

When revenue exceeds expenses, the difference is referred to as **net income**. Net income increases the owner's claim on the business. It is one of the main reasons a person wants to own a business. If a business had revenue of $12 000 from the sale of goods and services, and paid expenses of $7 500 in order to earn the revenue, its net income would be calculated as follows:

Revenue	–	Expenses	=	Net Income
$12 000	–	$7 500	=	$4 500

There may be times in the life of a business, however, when expenses are larger than revenue. In this situation, a **net loss** occurs, and the claim of the owner on the business is decreased.

Net loss: the difference when expenses exceed revenue.

Revenue	–	Expenses	=	Net Loss
$10 000	–	$11 500	=	($1 500)

(The brackets indicate a loss.)

The Time-Period Principle

Accounting period or fiscal period: the time covered by an income statement.

In order to report on a business's net income or net loss, an income statement is prepared. The income statement measures the net income or net loss for a period of time called the **accounting period**, or **fiscal period**. A business might prepare an income statement for a period of a month, a quarter of a year, a half-year, or a year. If prepared for a year, the time period is referred to as the "**accounting year**," or "**fiscal year**." This one-year time period need not follow the calendar year and end on December 31. Indeed, for most businesses, the year end will occur during a slow business period, for a number of procedures must be

Accounting year or **fiscal year:** the twelve-month business year chosen by the business.

Time-period principle: the definition and consistent use of the same period of time for the accounting period.

completed in order to prepare the financial reports of the business. At Algor Computer Services, Vijay has found that May is a slow business period, so May 31 is used as the fiscal year end. An income statement must also be filed with the business's income tax.

The **time-period principle** requires the definition and consistent use of the same period of time for the accounting period. A business compares net income figures from period to period, for this is one of the indicators of the health of a business. If the time period for which an income statement is prepared were to change, it would be difficult to make these comparisons. A valid comparison could not be made between the earnings for 25 days, and those for 31 days, or those for 10 months and those for 12 months.

Steps in Preparing an Income Statement

An income statement for Algor Computer Services is shown below.

FIGURE 3-1 AN INCOME STATEMENT FOR ALGOR, SHOWING THE NET INCOME

Algor Computer Services
Income Statement
for the three months ended August 31, 1987

Revenue		
Computer Services	$98 432	
Software Lessons	43 200	$141 632
Expenses		
Wages	$73 240	
Bank	758	
Advertising	5 693	
Utilities	6 784	
Automobile	4 569	
Miscellaneous	147	91 191
Net Income		$ 50 441

THE FACTS SPEAK...

Various expenses for selected firms for 1989
Hasbro, $7 million to advertise the doll Maxie
McDonald's, interest expense, $306.9 million
McDonald's, payroll, $1 075.8 million

THE FACTS SPEAK...

Net income for 1989
Nestlé, $1.897 billion
McDonald's, $742.8 million
Nintendo, $541 million

For purposes of consistency, the format of the income statement is important. The steps in preparing the statement are as follows:

1. The centred heading again answers the three questions:

   who? (Algor Computer Services)
   what? (Income Statement)
   when? (for the three months ending August 31, 1987)

   There is an important difference in the date shown on an income statement compared to the date shown on a balance sheet. The balance sheet shows the financial position at one point in time; for the next business day, the balances of many accounts on the balance sheet would change. The date on the income statement, on the other hand, must show the length of the fiscal period. If the business reported that it had a net income of $28 150, it would not be very meaningful unless the user of the information knew whether it took a month, quarter, half-year, or year to earn it.

2. The Revenue section lists the various sources of revenue with the most important one usually appearing first. (The sources of revenue may be indented in order to set them off from the heading.) The total revenue is extended to the right-hand column. It may appear as in Figure 3-1, or as follows:
   (a) if there is only one source of revenue;

FIGURE 3-2 THE REVENUE SECTION WHEN THERE IS ONLY ONE SOURCE OF REVENUE

Revenue
Fees Earned $632 493

(b) when a separate total line is used.

FIGURE 3-3 THE REVENUE SECTION WHEN THERE IS MORE THAN ONE SOURCE OF REVENUE, AND A SEPARATE TOTAL LINE IS USED

Revenue
Computer Services $98 432
Software Lessons   43 200
   Total Revenue $141 632

3. The Expenses section lists various expenses in the order in which they appear in the general ledger. They could be arranged in alphabetical order, or from largest to smallest, or from most to least important. The total expenses are then extended to the right-hand column, either on the same line as the last expense, as shown in Figure 3-1, or on a separate line. The separate line is labelled "Total Expenses," as shown below.

FIGURE 3-4 THE EXPENSE SECTION WITH A SEPARATE TOTAL LINE FOR EXPENSES

Expenses		
Wages	$73 240	
Bank	758	
Advertising	5 693	
Utilities	6 784	
Automobile	4 569	
Miscellaneous	147	
Total Expenses		91 191
Net Income		$50 441

4. The Net Income or Net Loss is then calculated. If Revenue exceeds Expenses, a Net Income results. If Expenses exceed Revenue, a Net Loss results. A double rule is made below the final total, indicating that the work is complete and correct.

Uses for the Net Income

One of the objectives of a business is to have as high a net income as possible. This net income can be used for two purposes. First, the owner has a claim on it, and can therefore remove it from the business in the form of assets. For example, if the business has a net income of $10 000, the owner can remove that amount, or more or less, in the form of cash. However, there may not be that amount in cash, for sales may have been on account, or cash may have been used to buy other assets. The purchase of other assets is the second use of net income. The owner may decide not to remove assets from the business for personal use, but rather to leave them in the business for its expansion.

Uses of the Income Statement

The income statement provides very important information about the business. There is debate, however, as to whether the information provided on it is more important than the information provided on the balance sheet. Is the net income of the business more significant than

Comparative statements: show the accounting information for a number of fiscal periods.

Condensed statements: show the essential accounting information in summarized form.

what the business owns, or what it is worth? The balance sheet shows the growth of the business since its beginning, for it is an accumulation of the account balances. The income statement, on the other hand, shows only the performance for the accounting period indicated in its heading. However, when it is compared to statements of previous years, the income statement can be as valuable as the balance sheet for showing the growth of the firm. For this reason, businesses usually also show the income statement comparisons for a number of years in their annual report. These statements are therefore called **comparative statements**. In order to compare income statements from various years, businesses frequently reduce the information on the statement in order to show only the essential information. The removal of such information results in a **condensed statement**. The condensed comparative income statement for Algor Computer Services for the quarters ending August 31, and November 30, 1987 is shown below.

FIGURE 3-5 CONDENSED COMPARATIVE INCOME STATEMENT FOR TWO CONSECUTIVE QUARTERS

Algor Computer Services
Condensed Comparative Income Statement
for the Three Months Ended

	August 31, 1987	November 30, 1987
Revenue	$141 632	$172 349
Expenses	91 191	132 540
Net Income	$ 50 441	$ 39 809

An income statement is used extensively in order to make business decisions. A decrease in net income over that of previous years is cause for concern, as is a net loss. In analyzing the statement, one can focus on revenue and on expenses in order to change the net income trend of the business.

Great use is also made of the income statement by people outside of the business. If a business wants to obtain a loan from a lending institution, an income statement will have to be provided. Revenue Canada (the federal government department responsible for income tax) requires that a business prepare an income statement and file it with an income tax return. Also, investors who want to become part owners of a business will partly base their decision on information found in the income statement.

LESSON REVIEW

1. Why is the term "profit" not used by accountants?
2. What is the purpose of the income statement?
3. Define revenue. Using a store that you have recently visited as an example, state what its source of revenue would be.
4. What type of account is revenue? Why?
5. "All inflows of assets are not recorded as revenue." Explain this statement.
6. Define expense. Using a store that you have recently visited as an example, state five expenses that it would have.
7. What type of account are expenses? Why?
8. "A payment of cash does not necessarily mean that an expense has been incurred." Explain this statement.
9. Give the equations for calculating net income and net loss.
10. What is the time-period principle? Why is it important that it be followed?
11. Summarize the four steps followed in the preparation of an income statement.
12. What two uses can be made of net income?
13. Why is the net income or net loss figure significant to a business?
14. Compare comparative income statements to condensed income statements.

LESSON APPLICATIONS

15. Classify each of the following accounts as asset, liability, owner's equity, revenue, or expense.

    (a) Bank Loan
    (b) Utilities
    (c) Accounts Payable
    (d) Building
    (e) Salaries
    (f) Fees Income
    (g) Advertising
    (h) S. Smith, Capital
    (i) Commissions Earned
    (j) Accounts Receivable

16. Calculate the net income or net loss for each of the following situations:

   (a) Revenue $ 50 000   Expenses $ 22 000
   (b) Revenue $120 000   Expenses $124 450
   (c) Revenue $ 31 000   Expenses $ 37 070
   (d) Revenue $329 900   Expenses $287 200

17. Paul Chahal is a dentist. Indicate which of the following transactions represent an earning of revenue, and state why. Review the definition of revenue before you begin.
   (a) Received $1 000 from the owner as an additional investment.
   (b) Received $120 from N. Singh on account.
   (c) Completed tooth fillings for M. Williamson, $85 on account.
   (d) Completed X-rays for Verla Anderson, $45 cash.
   (e) Sold an old computer for $850 cash.
   (f) Borrowed $4 000 from the bank.

18. For Paul Chahal's dentistry practice, indicate which of the following transactions represent the incurring of an expense, and state why.
   (a) Paid the hydro bill which was received today, $150.
   (b) Purchased dental supplies from Capital Dental Specialties on account, $900.
   (c) Paid $400 to the owner for his personal use.
   (d) Paid $300 to reduce the bank loan.
   (e) Bought an office desk, $900 cash.
   (f) Paid $90 interest on the bank loan.
   (g) Paid $300 on account to Capital Dental Specialties.
   (h) Paid weekly wages to the employees, $1 400.

19. Prepare an income statement for the month ended October 31, 19–9, using the following information. The business is Rebecca's Athletic Installations.
   Installation Fees $49 800; Auto Expense $7 400; Rent Expense $10 000; Wages Expense $16 000; Office Expense $2 000; Miscellaneous Expense $1 500.

20. Ian Dumanski owns Dumanski's Auto Body Repairs. Prepare an income statement for the month ended October 31, 19–7, by taking the necessary information from the following selected ledger account balances.
   Cash $8 900; Repair Revenue $7 200; Utilities Expense $450; Bank Loan $3 000; Accounts Receivable $2 000; Advertising Expense $300; I. Dumanski, Capital $8 000; Rent Expense $1 000; Truck $18 000; Accounts Payable $1 400; Miscellaneous Expense $320; Wages Expense $2 200; Marketable Securities $5 300; Office Supplies $1 100.

3.2 Transactions Involving Income Statement Accounts

*S*ince *revenue and expenses have an impact on owner's equity, thought was given to putting all these items into the V. Marshall, Capital account. Revenue would be recorded as an increase in the V. Marshall, Capital account, and expenses as decreases. What is the disadvantage of this procedure?*

It is necessary for the business to keep a record of revenue and expenses in order that the income statement can be prepared. Transactions influencing these two items could be recorded in the Capital account: after all, revenue increases owner's equity, and expenses decrease owner's equity. However, when an income statement is prepared, it will be necessary to separate everything in the Capital account into different categories: revenue, owner's investment, expenses, and owner's withdrawals. It is much easier to make that classification as the transactions occur. For that reason, separate ledger accounts are opened for all revenue and expense items.

FIGURE 3-6 THE CAPITAL ACCOUNT IS DIVIDED INTO REVENUE AND EXPENSE ACCOUNTS

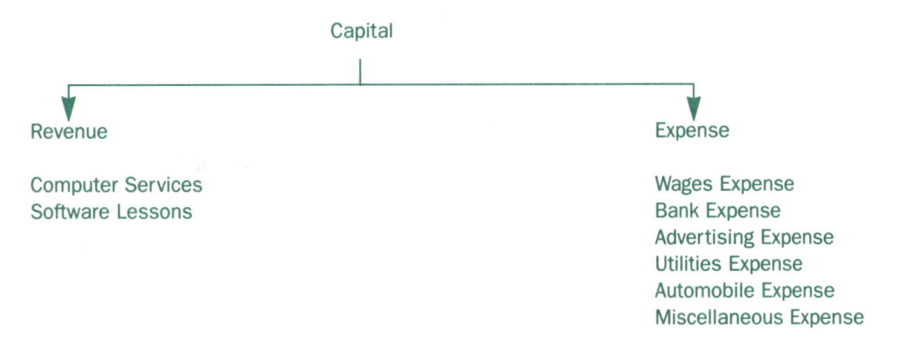

```
                        Capital
                          |
          ┌───────────────┴───────────────┐
          ▼                               ▼
       Revenue                         Expense

   Computer Services               Wages Expense
   Software Lessons                Bank Expense
                                   Advertising Expense
                                   Utilities Expense
                                   Automobile Expense
                                   Miscellaneous Expense
```

The ledger accounts will be found on the statement in the same order in which they are found in the general ledger. The Chart of Accounts used by Algor is shown in Chapter 2 on pages 58 and 59.

When analyzing transactions involving income statement accounts, the same principles are followed as for balance sheet accounts. Consider yourself to be the business, and imagine what actually took place. Structure your analysis to fit the four questions you ask yourself in analyzing a transaction:

1. What accounts change?

2. What type of account are they?

3. Does each account increase or decrease?

4. Should the amount be entered on the debit or credit side of the account?

Revenue Transactions

For each item found in the Revenue section of the income statement, an account is found in the general ledger. Algor Computer Services has two revenue accounts to reflect the two main sources of revenue for the business: Computer Services and Software Lessons. A revenue account is named according to the type of business. An accountant, a lawyer, or a doctor might have an account called Fees Earned; a real estate salesperson, Commissions Earned; a store selling merchandise, Sales.

In order to recognize revenue, a sale of a good or service must be made. A source document called a Sales Invoice is used for a sale on account, and a Cash Sales Slip is used for a cash sale. These two documents were described in Chapter 2, with the other main source documents.

Transaction 1
April 2   Sales Invoice #55-0237: Algor Computer Services performed computer services for Weston Courier Services, $500.

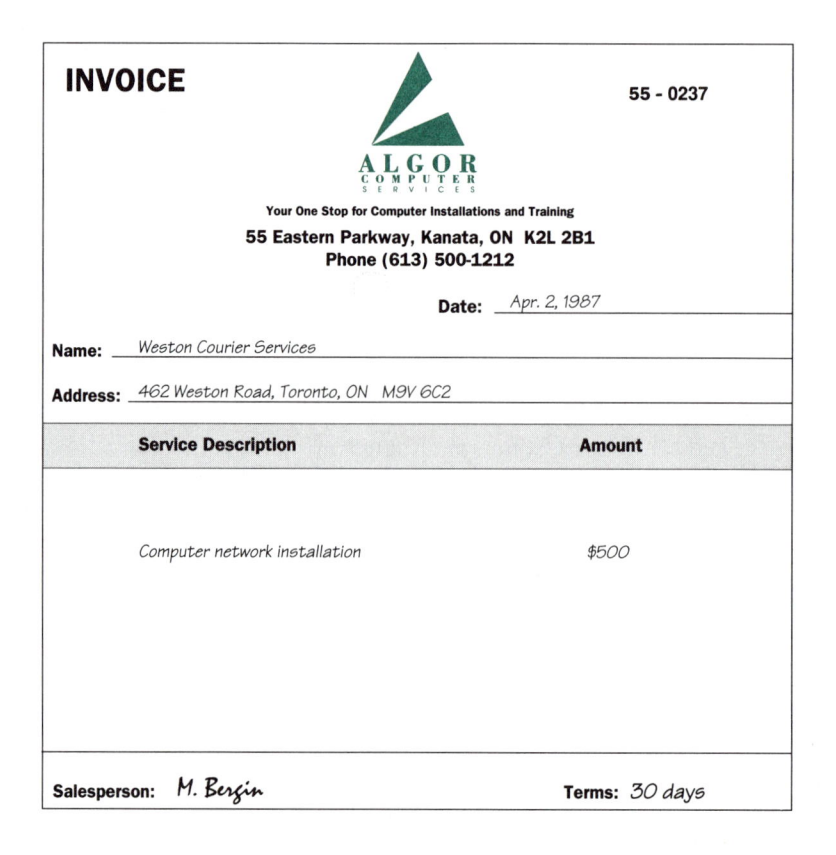

INVOICE   55 - 0237

ALGOR
COMPUTER
SERVICES

Your One Stop for Computer Installations and Training
55 Eastern Parkway, Kanata, ON K2L 2B1
Phone (613) 500-1212

Date: Apr. 2, 1987

Name: Weston Courier Services

Address: 462 Weston Road, Toronto, ON M9V 6C2

Service Description	Amount
Computer network installation	$500

Salesperson: M. Bergin   **Terms:** 30 days

- A Sales Invoice, or bill, was issued for the service provided, so we know that it was on account. By this transaction the business gained a claim on Weston Courier Services. The asset, Accounts Receivable, has increased, so a debit entry is made.
- The business provided a service, so revenue was earned. The revenue account for Algor is Computer Services. It will be credited. Why? Revenue increases the owner's claim on the business, so Owner's Equity must increase.

As we noted in Chapter 2, in order to increase Owner's Equity, a credit entry is made. However, for information purposes, revenue items are now recorded in separate accounts.

ACCOUNT CHANGED	TYPE OF ACCOUNT	INCREASE/ DECREASE	DEBIT/ CREDIT	AMOUNT
Accounts Receivable	Asset	Increase	Debit	$500
Computer Services	Revenue	Increase	Credit	$500

GENERAL LEDGER

```
   Accounts Receivable      120            Computer Services       400
        dr.        |        cr.                   dr.       |       cr.
   Apr. 2   500   |                                         | Apr. 2   500
```

In order to increase a revenue account, a credit entry is made. That is because revenue increases the owner's equity in the business. To decrease a revenue account, a debit entry is made. More information will be provided later on decreasing a revenue account.

```
              Revenue
         dr.      |      cr.
       decrease   |   increase
```

The double-entry accounting principle that, for every transaction, total debits must equal total credits was again followed for the above transaction. You should also note that the fundamental accounting equation still applies:

Assets	= Liabilities + Owner's Equity
(Accounts Receivable increases.)	(The Computer Services revenue account increases; revenue is an increase in Owner's Equity.)

Transaction 2

May 2   Cash Receipt Slip #33-0317: Received $500 on account from Weston Courier Services.

- Because the business received cash, the Cash account is debited $500.
- The business lost its $500 claim on Weston Courier Services, so Accounts Receivable is credited $500. The revenue account is not credited, because revenue is recognized when the service is given, not when the cash from it is received.

ACCOUNT CHANGED	TYPE OF ACCOUNT	INCREASE/ DECREASE	DEBIT/ CREDIT	AMOUNT
Cash	Asset	Increase	Debit	$500
Accounts Receivable	Asset	Decrease	Credit	$500

GENERAL LEDGER

Cash		100	Accounts Receivable		120
dr.	cr.		dr.	cr.	
May 2 500				May 2 500	

Transaction 3

May 2   Cash Sales Slip #99-0619: Algor Computer Services provided software lessons for Manesh Parikesh and received $80 in cash.

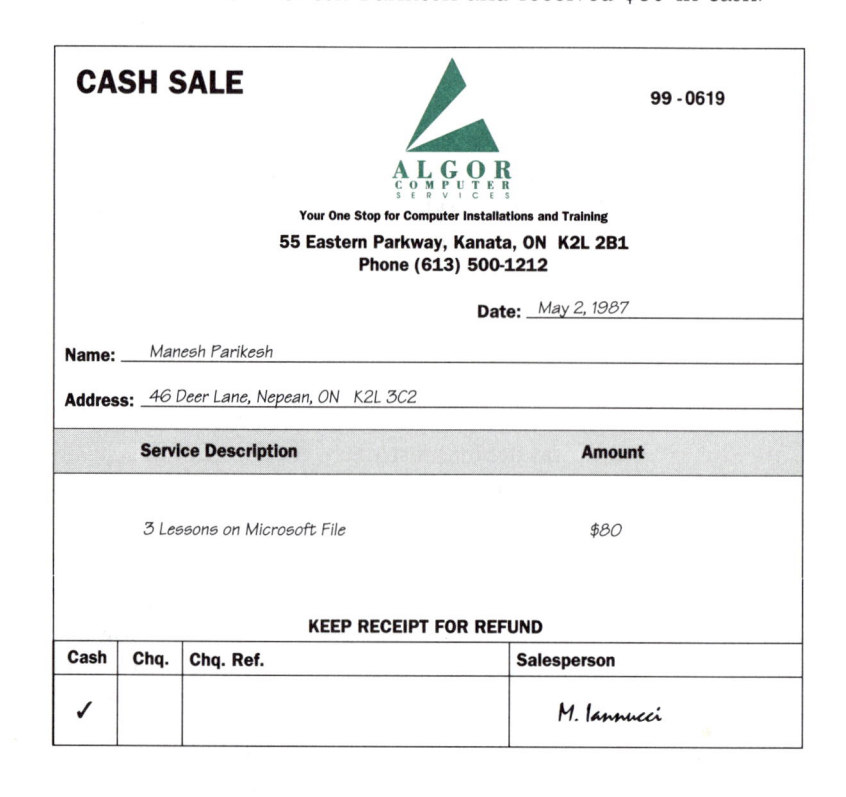

CASH SALE   99-0619

ALGOR COMPUTER SERVICES

Your One Stop for Computer Installations and Training

55 Eastern Parkway, Kanata, ON   K2L 2B1
Phone (613) 500-1212

Date: _May 2, 1987_

Name: _Manesh Parikesh_

Address: _46 Deer Lane, Nepean, ON   K2L 3C2_

Service Description	Amount
3 Lessons on Microsoft File	$80

KEEP RECEIPT FOR REFUND

Cash	Chq.	Chq. Ref.	Salesperson
✓			M. Iannucci

The person giving the lessons received the cash from Manesh, and gave him a copy of the Cash Sales Slip. At the end of the day the instructor turns the Cash Sales Slips over to the accountant for recording. The cash collected from customers is given to the person responsible for making deposits, usually the treasurer.
- Cash was gained by the business, so the Cash asset account increases: a debit is made.
- The business provided a service, so the Software Lessons revenue account increases. In order to increase the revenue account, a credit is made.

ACCOUNT CHANGED	TYPE OF ACCOUNT	INCREASE/ DECREASE	DEBIT/ CREDIT	AMOUNT
Cash	Asset	Increase	Debit	$80
Software Lessons	Revenue	Increase	Credit	$80

GENERAL LEDGER

Cash		100	Software Lessons		410
dr.	cr.		dr.	cr.	
May 2 80				May 2 80	

Expense Transactions

There is an account in the general ledger for each item found in the expense section of the income statement. When designing the accounting system, the accountant will decide what information is needed. For example, all utility items could be put into one account called Utilities Expense, or they could each be put into separate accounts: Electricity Expense, Water Expense, and Telephone Expense.

Transaction 4
May 15   Cheque Copy #284: The monthly radio advertising is paid, $1 000.
- The radio advertising is a cost of earning revenue, and is therefore an expense. Remember that *anything* used in order to earn revenue is an expense. As indicated earlier, expenses cause a decrease in Owner's Equity. Advertising Expense is therefore debited.
- Cash went out of the business, so the asset Cash is decreased.

ACCOUNT CHANGED	TYPE OF ACCOUNT	INCREASE/ DECREASE	DEBIT/ CREDIT	AMOUNT
Advertising Expense	Expense	Increase	Debit	$1 000
Cash	Asset	Decrease	Credit	$1 000

GENERAL LEDGER

Advertising Expense 660		Cash 100	
dr.	cr.	dr.	cr.
May 15 1 000			May 15 1 000

In order to increase an expense account, a debit entry is made. To decrease an expense account, a credit entry is made. More information will be provided later on decreasing an expense account.

Expense	
dr.	cr.
increase	decrease

Transaction 5

May 16   Cheque Copy #285: The electricity bill is received from the electric company, $200. The electricity bill is really a purchase invoice, but because the electricity has already been used and the bill will be paid immediately, it is not recorded first as an account payable. If it were to be paid in the future, it would first be recorded in Accounts Payable.

- Electricity is an expense, because it is a cost of earning revenue. The expense account Utilities Expense is debited, because it represents a decrease in owner's equity.
- Cash went out of the business, so the asset Cash decreases.

ACCOUNT CHANGED	TYPE OF ACCOUNT	INCREASE/ DECREASE	DEBIT/ CREDIT	AMOUNT
Utilities Expense	Expense	Increase	Debit	$200
Cash	Asset	Decrease	Credit	$200

GENERAL LEDGER

Utilities Expense 670		Cash 100	
dr.	cr.	dr.	cr.
May 16 200			May 16 200

Transaction 6

May 16   Purchase Invoice #89: Received a bill from the *Nepean Clarion* for advertising, $50. The bill does not have to be paid for 15 days.

- Advertising is an expense because it is a cost of earning revenue. The Advertising account is debited because it represents a decrease in owner's equity.
- Since payment will be made in the future, the liability Accounts Payable is increased.

ACCOUNT CHANGED	TYPE OF ACCOUNT	INCREASE/ DECREASE	DEBIT/ CREDIT	AMOUNT
Advertising Expense	Expense	Increase	Debit	$50
Accounts Payable	Liability	Increase	Credit	$50

GENERAL LEDGER

```
Advertising Expense        660        Accounts Payable        200
      dr.         |         cr.             dr.         |         cr.
May 16    50      |                                     | May 16    50
```

Revenue and Expense Related to Time Periods

Revenue recognition principle: *revenue must be recognized in the period in which it is earned.*

It is important to note that revenue is recognized in the period in which it is earned, and not the period in which payment is received from the customer. This is referred to as the **revenue recognition principle**. For example, if a firm provides a service during the current year, an invoice should be completed and sent to the customer during the current year. An entry should be made from the source document to reflect that the revenue was earned during the current fiscal year. In the following example, Algor Computer Services completed a computer installation during the last week of the current fiscal year. Payment, however, was not received for two weeks. Since the invoice was sent on the last day of the current year, revenue of $3 000 was recognized during the current year.

```
                              Year
                              End
May 25–31         May 31        |    June 14
Services          Invoice sent  |    Cash received
performed         to customer   |    from customer
```

The entry on May 31, made from the source document, recognizes that the revenue was earned during the current fiscal period.

GENERAL LEDGER

```
Accounts Receivable        120        Computer Services        400
      dr.         |         cr.             dr.         |         cr.
May 31    3 000   |                                     | May 31    3 000
```

The revenue recognition principle gains more significance when one examines the accounting plight of a manufacturer of a submarine. Suppose the submarine takes three years to make. When is the revenue recognized? If it is only recognized in the final year of building, the two previous years will not show any revenue. For this reason, the manufacturer will invoice the purchaser at intervals.

> **Matching principle:** expenses must be recorded in the same period as the revenue they helped to earn.

Expenses must similarly be recorded in the period in which they are used to earn revenue, and not when paid for. This is referred to as the **matching principle**. Imagine the manufacturer of the previously mentioned submarine recording all the revenue in the third year, but recording the expenses as they are incurred. The comparative income statements would show a very distorted picture.

A problem arises, as noted earlier, in respect of what should be classified as an expense, and what should be classified as an asset. For example, suppose that a business buys office supplies. Should they be recorded as something that the business owns, an asset, or something that the business is going to use to earn revenue, an expense? For the time being, we will record items that have already been used, such as utilities, as an expense. Items that will be used in the time period after they are purchased, such as office supplies, will be recorded as an asset. We will examine how some assets are converted to expenses as they are used, in Chapter 7.

3.3 The Owner's Drawings Account

The owner has a claim on the assets of the business. At any time, the owner can remove assets from the business for his or her personal use. Can he/she remove all of the assets? Theoretically yes, but, if the owner actually did so, the business would not be able to operate. Moreover, creditors would be reluctant to loan money to the business. Remember, in a proprietorship, the owner is personally liable for the debts of the business.

> **Drawings account:** used to record the value of the business assets that the owner withdraws or uses personally.

The owner is in business to make a profit. This profit, which we refer to as net income, can either be left in the business to expand it, or the owner can take it from the business. Obviously, the owner needs a source of income to live on, so some of the assets will be removed and represent a salary for the owner. In order to keep a record of the owner's withdrawals, a separate account called **Drawings**, is maintained.

Transaction 7
June 4 Cheque Copy #297: Issued a $500 cheque to the owner for his personal use.

ACCOUNT CHANGED	TYPE OF ACCOUNT	INCREASE/ DECREASE	DEBIT/ CREDIT	AMOUNT
V. Marshall, Drawings	Contra-equity	Increase	Debit	$500
Cash	Asset	Decrease	Credit	$500

GENERAL LEDGER

V. Marshall, Drawings	310	Cash	100
dr.	cr.	dr.	cr.
June 4 500			June 4 500

- Because it reduces the owner's equity, the Drawings account referred to as a "contra-equity" account. The word contra me __ opposite. Thus its balance will be opposite to that of Capital: it will increase on the debit side, and decrease on the credit side.

Drawings	
dr.	cr.
increase	decrease

- Since cash was paid out of the business, a credit is made to Cash. The business can pay a salary to the owner, but for income tax purposes it cannot be recorded as an expense. For that reason, all payments to the owner are recorded as Drawings. Also recorded as Drawings are:
  (a) withdrawal of assets for the owner's personal use;
  (b) spending of business funds for the owner's personal use.

  For example, if the owner were to use business funds for repairs to his personal car, the entry would be a debit to V. Marshall, Drawings, and a credit to Cash.

Summary of Rules for Debit and Credit

We have now studied the main types of accounts for a service business. The types of balances for the accounts are summarized below:

FIGURE 3-7 BALANCE SHEET ACCOUNTS SHOWING THE SIDE OF THE T-ACCOUNT ON WHICH THEY INCREASE AND DECREASE

Balance Sheet Accounts

Asset		Liability		Capital		Drawings	
dr.	cr.	dr.	cr.	dr.	cr.	dr.	cr.
increase	decrease	decrease	increase	decrease	increase	increase	decrease

FIGURE 3-8 INCOME STATEMENT ACCOUNTS SHOWING THE SIDE OF THE T-ACCOUNT ON WHICH THEY INCREASE AND DECREASE

Income Statement Accounts

Revenue		Expense	
dr.	cr.	dr.	cr.
decrease	increase	increase	decrease

The increase side of the account is also the side that indicates the normal type of balance. The reason for the type of balance is as follows:

Type of Account	Type of Balance	Reason for Type of Balance
Assets	Debit	Assets are found on the left side of the fundamental accounting equation, and so when entered in T-accounts they are put on the debit (left) side.
Liabilities	Credit	Liabilities are found on the right side of the fundamental accounting equation, and so when entered in T-accounts they are put on the credit (right) side.
Owner's Equity	Credit	Capital (the main equity account) is on the right side of the fundamental accounting equation, and so when entered in T-accounts it is put on the credit (right) side. Drawings decreases owner's equity, so it has a debit balance.
Revenue	Credit	Revenue increases owner's equity, and to increase owner's equity a credit entry is made.
Expenses	Debit	Expenses decrease owner's equity, and to decrease owner's equity a debit entry is made.

LESSON REVIEW

21. Why is the main owner's equity account, Capital, separated into capital, drawings, revenue, and expense accounts?

22. What determines the name(s) that will be used for Revenue accounts?

23. What two source documents may indicate that revenue has been earned?

24. State the type of balance that a revenue account has, and why it has that type of balance.

25. What determines the names of expense accounts?

26. What two source documents may indicate that an expense has been incurred?

27. State the type of balance that an expense account has, and why it has that type of balance.

28. What determines the time period in which revenue and expenses should be recorded?

29. Describe the relationship between the revenue recognition principle and the matching principle.

30. Describe three types of transactions for which the Drawings account is used.

Lesson Applications

31. Rosa Tremblay operates her own law firm, specializing in family law. Some of the accounts Rosa uses are: Cash; Accounts Receivable; Office Supplies; Office Equipment; Accounts Payable; R. Tremblay, Capital; Case Preparation Fees; Rent Expense; Utilities Expense; Donations Expense; Photocopy Expense; Wages Expense; Miscellaneous Expense. For each of the following transactions, complete the analysis using a method similar to that used in the text.

    e.g., Cheque Copy #43: Paid monthly rent, $400.

ACCOUNT CHANGED	TYPE OF ACCOUNT	INCREASE/ DECREASE	DEBIT/ CREDIT	AMOUNT
Rent Expense	Expense	Increase	Debit	$400
Cash	Asset	Decrease	Credit	$400

    (1) Cheque Copy #44: Paid $400 to the United Appeal as a donation.
    (2) Voucher #3: Received $2 000 from the owner as an additional investment.
    (3) Cash Sales Slip #88: Prepared a case file for V. Armstrong, for $200 cash.
    (4) Cheque Copy #45: Paid $350 to Mike Wilbrod, the legal assistant, for weekly wages.
    (5) Cash Receipt Slip #94: Received $780 on account from Diane Milne.
    (6) Purchase Invoice #8288: Purchased office supplies worth $300 on account from Weston Stationers.
    (7) Cash Sales Slip #89: Prepared documents for a sale of a home for Diane Chipper, $700.
    (8) Cheque Copy #46: Paid the monthly telephone bill, $98.
    (9) Cheque Copy #47: Paid $390 for rental of the photocopier.
    (10) Purchase Invoice #95-983: Purchased a new fax machine, $7 000, on account.

32. Nancy Samson is the owner of Penticton Air Service, an air service mapping and delivery business. Some of the accounts that Nancy uses in her business are:
    Cash; Accounts Receivable; Office Supplies; Aircraft; Accounts Payable; Bank Loan; Mortgage Payable; N. Samson, Capital; Mapping Services; Delivery Services; Rent Expense; Aircraft Expense; Wages Expense; Utilities Expense; Miscellaneous Expense. Using the analysis format given in Question 31 above, analyze the following transactions:

(1) Voucher #48: Received $3 000 from the owner as an investment.
(2) Cheque Copy #684: Paid the monthly rent, $1 200.
(3) Purchase Invoice #49: Purchased $200 worth of oil for the aircraft on account from Shell Canada Ltd.
(4) Cash Sales Slip #138: Received $350 for mapping services provided to the City of Penticton.
(5) Cash Receipt Slip #312: Received $250 on account from Eastern Map Supplies.
(6) Cheque Copy #685: Paid the monthly telephone bill, $320.
(7) Cheque Copy #686: Paid the Penticton Herald $150 for advertising when the invoice was received.
(8) Cheque Copy #687: Paid Elizabeth Kilfeather, the pilot, $900 for weekly wages.
(9) Purchase Invoice #98-787: Purchased a new supply of source documents on account from Crane Printers, $300.
(10) Cash Sales Slip #139: Received $200 cash for delivery services.

33. C. Takahashi is president and owner of Flin Flon Auto Wash. Some of the accounts that he uses in his business are:

Cash	Mortgage Payable
Office Supplies	C. Takahashi, Capital
Auto Cleaning Supplies	C. Takahashi, Drawings
Investments	Auto Cleaning Revenue
Cleaning Equipment	Utility Expense
Automobile	Wages Expense
Building	Advertising Expense
Land	Auto Expense
Accounts Payable	Promotions Expense
Trust Company Loan	Miscellaneous Expense

Using the format given in Question 31, analyze the transactions below.
(1) Cheque Copy #49: Owner withdrew $500 for his personal use.
(2) Cash Sales Slips #523 to #592: $650 in cash sales for the day.
(3) Cheque Copy #50: Paid $470 to Canadian Cleaning Products for car cleaning supplies.
(4) Purchase Invoice #422: Purchased new cleaning brushes on account from Modern Cleaners Ltd. for the cleaning equipment, $2 000.
(5) Purchase Invoice #33: Owe $320 to Granof Printers for printing free car wash tickets to be given to customers.
(6) Voucher #489: The owner took $17 worth of cleaning supplies for his personal use.
(7) Cheque Copy #51: Paid Pastel Interior Design Ltd. $500 on the owner's behalf for consultation on the interior of his home.

(8) Cheque Copy #52: Paid $1 020 to the employees for weekly wages.
(9) Cheque Copy #53: Paid $980 on the mortgage.
(10) Cheque Copy #54: Paid $650 on the trust company loan.
(11) Purchase Invoice #444: Had a tune-up done on the business's auto, $329.
(12) Cheque Copy #55: Purchased $5 000 worth of investments.

3.4 Month-End Procedures

Taking off a trial balance involves listing all accounts in the ledger, along with their debit or credit balances. The accounts on the trial balance will be in the same order as those in the ledger: assets, liabilities, capital, drawings, revenue, and expenses. The debit column and credit column are added to ensure that total debits equal total credits. The trial balance for Algor Computer Services is shown below:

Algor Computer Services
Trial Balance
November 30, 1989

	Debit	Credit
Cash	$113 240	
Marketable Securities	8 700	
Accounts Receivable	43 250	
Office Supplies	1 238	
Land	124 600	
Building	228 000	
Office Equipment	14 500	
Computer Equipment	53 950	
Automobile	12 500	
Accounts Payable		$ 28 560
Short-Term Loans		12 480
Mortgage Payable		204 500
V. Marshall, Capital		318 497
V. Marshall, Drawings	14 500	
Computer Services		98 432
Software Lessons		43 200
Wages Expense	73 240	
Bank Expense	758	
Advertising Expense	5 693	
Utilities Expense	6 784	
Automobile Expense	4 569	
Miscellaneous Expense	147	
	$705 669	$705 669

Once it is proven by the trial balance that the general ledger is in balance, the trial balance is used to prepare the financial statements. The income statement is prepared first, because the net income or net loss amount is needed to prepare the owner's equity section of the balance sheet. Note that the income statement can be easily made from the trial balance, because the income statement accounts are the last ones on the trial balance.

FIGURE 3-9 THE NET INCOME IS TRANSFERRED TO THE OWNER'S EQUITY SECTION OF THE BALANCE SHEET

Financial Statements

Income Statement	Balance Sheet
Revenue	Assets = Liabilities
− Expenses	+
Net Income ─────────────▶	Owner's Equity

> **Report form balance sheet:** a balance sheet with the assets listed above the liabilities and capital.

The balance sheet is then prepared, since the net income figure is now available. The balance sheet in Figure 3-11 has a different format from that shown in Chapter 1. Instead of being in the T-account format, it has the assets listed above the liabilities and capital. This format is known as the **report form balance sheet**. Assets are equal to liabilities plus capital, no matter which format is used. The owner's equity section is different, however, for it must recognize the effect of the net income or net loss, and drawings. These changes are discussed below.

The Owner's Equity Section of a Balance Sheet

The owner's equity section of the balance sheet will now be different from that studied in Chapter 1, for the Capital must be increased by a net income, and decreased by Drawings and a net loss, if there is one.

FIGURE 3-10 OWNER'S EQUITY IS INCREASED BY A NET INCOME AND DECREASED BY A NET LOSS AND DRAWINGS

Owner's Equity	
Increased by	Decreased by
Net income	Net loss
	Drawings

The three possibilities that can result are shown in Figures 3-12, 3-13 and 3-14.

The May owner's equity section (Figure 3-12) shows a net income with Drawings. The net income of $3 000 makes owner's equity increase, but the Drawings of $1 000 makes owner's equity decrease. The net increase in owner's equity is $2 000.

FIGURE 3-11

Algor Computer Services
Balance Sheet
as at November 30, 1989

Assets

Cash	$113 240	
Marketable Securities	8 700	
Accounts Receivable	43 250	
Office Supplies	1 238	
Land	124 600	
Building	228 000	
Office Equipment	14 500	
Computer Equipment	53 950	
Automobile	12 500	
Total Assets		$599 978

Liabilities

Accounts Payable	$ 28 560	
Short-Term Loans	12 480	
Mortgage Payable	204 500	
Total Liabilities		$245 540

Owner's Equity

V. Marshall, Capital, May 31, 1989		$318 497
Net Income	$50 441	
Less: Drawings	14 500	
Increase in Capital		35 941
V. Marshall, Capital, November 30, 1989		354 438
Total Liabilities and Owner's Equity		$599 978

FIGURE 3-12 OWNER'S EQUITY WHERE NET INCOME IS LARGER THAN DRAWINGS

Algor Computer Services
Partial Balance Sheet
as at May 31, 1987

Owner's Equity

V. Marshall, Capital, April 30, 1987		$234 500
Net Income	$3 000	
Less: Drawings	1 000	
Increase in Capital		2 000
V. Marshall, Capital, May 31, 1987		$236 500

The June beginning Capital is the May ending Capital. At the end of June, the owner's equity section (Figure 3-13) shows a net income with Drawings. However, in this case Drawings are larger than the net income. The net income of $4 500 increases owner's equity, but the Drawings of $5 000 decrease owner's equity. The net effect is a decrease in owner's equity of $500.

FIGURE 3-13 OWNER'S EQUITY WHERE DRAWINGS ARE LARGER THAN THE NET INCOME

Algor Computer Services
Partial Balance Sheet
as at June 30, 1987

Owner's Equity

V. Marshall, Capital, May 31, 1987		$236 500
Drawings	$5 000	
Less: Net Income	4 500	
Decrease in Capital		500
V. Marshall, Capital, June 30, 1987		$236 000

The July owner's equity section (Figure 3-14) shows a net loss with Drawings. The net loss of $4 000 decreases owner's equity, and the Drawings of $1 000 also decrease owner's equity. The net effect is a decrease in owner's equity of $5 000.

FIGURE 3-14 OWNER'S EQUITY WHERE THERE IS A NET LOSS AND DRAWINGS

Algor Computer Services
Partial Balance Sheet
as at July 31, 1987

Owner's Equity

V. Marshall, Capital, June 30, 1987		$236 000
Net Loss	$4 000	
Add: Drawings	1 000	
Decrease in Capital		5 000
V. Marshall, Capital, July 31, 1987		$231 000

LESSON REVIEW

34. In what order are the accounts arranged in the general ledger? In what order should the accounts be listed on the trial balance?
35. In what order are the financial statements prepared? Why?
36. In what ways is a report form balance sheet different from an account or T-form balance sheet?
37. Why has the owner's equity section of the balance sheet changed from the format used in Chapters 1 and 2?
38. What three possibilities exist for the owner's equity section of the balance sheet?

LESSON APPLICATIONS

39. Complete the following chart, showing the new Capital for the end of the year:

	Opening Capital	Net Income/ (Loss)	Drawings	Capital Increase/ (Decrease)	Ending Capital
(a)	$45 000	$ 5 500	$ 4 000	$?	$?
(b)	92 000	(6 900)	3 500	?	?
(c)	77 500	12 800	15 100	?	?
(d)	43 090	24 300	7 980	?	?
(e)	99 400	(3 200)	9 820	?	?

40. Complete the following chart by calculating the items indicated by a question mark.

	Opening Capital	Net Income/ (Loss)	Drawings	Ending Capital
(a)	$?	$ 5 900	$ 4 000	$87 000
(b)	55 900	(17 500)	?	34 590
(c)	66 750	21 300	9 000	?
(d)	41 990	?	12 000	87 800

41. The following financial data is for Hochkevich's Appliance Services, owned by S. Hochkevich. Prepare the owner's equity section of the balance sheet for each of the three consecutive months. The Capital as at May 31, 19–2, was $147 400.

	Net Income (Loss)	Drawings
June	$34 800	$ 7 000
July	12 300	14 540
August	(6 290)	3 900

42. The following financial data is for Athletic Installations, owned by C. Landreaux. Prepare the owner's equity section of the balance sheet for each of the three consecutive months. The Capital as at November 30, 19--, was $59 590.

	Net Income (Loss)	Drawings
December	($14 300)	$6 000
January	38 900	3 500
February	24 940	4 600

43. The following trial balance is for Martino's Paving Services. Using the account balances, prepare an income statement, for the month, and a report form balance sheet.

Martino's Paving Services
Trial Balance
July 31, 19--

	Debit	Credit
Cash	$ 26 900	
Accounts Receivable	84 320	
Supplies	1 120	
Land	94 000	
Building	73 200	
Equipment	43 870	
Trucks	87 300	
Accounts Payable		$ 21 900
Bank Loan		34 200
Mortgage Payable		95 600
J. Martino, Capital		235 050
J. Martino, Drawings	9 200	
Paving Revenue		88 400
Wages Expense	27 630	
Utilities Expense	2 420	
Truck Expense	16 700	
Miscellaneous Expense	8 490	
	$475 150	$475 150

CHAPTER REVIEW AND SKILL DEVELOPMENT

Accounting Principles and Concepts
- An **income statement** is prepared to calculate the net income or net loss for a fiscal period.
- **Revenue** is an increase in assets from the sale of a good or service.
- An **expense** is the cost of goods and services used in obtaining revenue.
- The **time-period principle** is the definition and consistent use of the same period of time for the accounting period.
- **Revenue** accounts have credit balances and **expense** accounts have debit balances. The rules for the types of balances were derived from the effect of these accounts on owner's equity: revenue increases owner's equity, expenses decrease owner's equity.
- The **revenue recognition principle** states that revenue is recognized in the period in which it is earned.
- The **matching principle** states that expenses are recorded in the time period in which the corresponding revenue was earned.
- The **Drawings** account is used to record the use of business assets for the personal benefit of the owner.
- The net income (or loss) and drawings are combined on the owner's equity section of the balance sheet.

Knowing the Terms
For each of the following statements, indicate the term being defined.
(a) The account used to record the withdrawal of assets by the owner.
(b) The definition and consistent use of the same length of time for the accounting period.
(c) The inflow of assets from the sale of goods and services.
(d) A balance sheet with the assets listed above the liabilities and owner's equity.
(e) An income statement showing only essential financial information.
(f) Cost of goods and services used in the process of generating revenue.
(g) The difference between revenue and expenses when expenses are larger than revenue.
(h) A financial statement which shows the revenue and expenses, and shows the net income or net loss of a business, for a given period of time.
(i) The time period covered by an income statement.
(j) The difference between revenue and expenses, when revenue exceeds expenses.

Food for Thought
1. A junior accountant records expenses in the wrong account on many occasions. She says that it does not matter, because the item has still been recorded as an expense. Comment on her view.
2. Net income for a business was $12 000. The business's owner's equity increases from $43 500 to $46 500. How is this possible?
3. An accounting clerk decides that he will not take off a trial balance at the end of the month. The reasons for not doing so are that he is too busy, and since it is not the end of a quarter when the firm normally prepares its financial statements, there is no need to do so. What difficulties might result because of the clerk's decision?
4. If a business were to use T-accounts, and record 20 000 transactions during the

month, what difficulties might result (a) during the month, and (b) at the end of the month?

5. An accountant records a $5 000 additional investment by the owner as a debit to Cash and a credit to Revenue.
   (a) How should the investment be recorded?
   (b) By comparing this accountant's entry to the correct entry, detail the effect on (i) the income statement, and (ii) the balance sheet.

6. An accountant records a $500 withdrawal by the owner for personal use as a debit to Salaries Expense and a credit to Cash.
   (a) How should the withdrawal be recorded?
   (b) By comparing this accountant's entry to the correct entry, detail the effect on (i) the income statement, and (ii) the balance sheet.

7. In setting up a ledger, the accounts could be arranged in a number of ways.
   (a) In what three ways could they be arranged?
   (b) What is the advantage of having them in the order indicated in the text?

8. The balance sheet can be described as a snapshot of a business, and the income statement as a film of a period of time. Explain this statement.

9. Accountants frequently refer to "the bottom line." What does it mean?

10. The account J. Swettenham, Capital had a balance of $130 000 at the end of year 1, and $159 000 at the end of year 2. Drawings for year 2 were $58 000. Calculate the net income or net loss for year 2.

Locate and Record

Find in the business section of a newspaper, or in financial reports, the financial information for any five businesses. Prepare an organizer to show the financial information given for the businesses.

Organizing — Increasing and Decreasing Accounts

Prepare an organizer that compares for each of the five types of accounts that we have studied the side on which it increases and decreases.

Applications

1. The general ledger for C. Stratton Surveyors, shown in Figure 3-15, has transactions recorded for the month of March. The debit and credit for each transaction is numbered. For each transaction, you are to complete the chart, and give a description of the transaction. The first one has been done for you in Figure 3-16.

2. Mary Knox operates a figure skating school, called West End Figure Skating Club. Mary charges her students a fee and in turn rents ice time from the City of St. Boniface. In the general ledger are the accounts shown in Figure 3-17, with balances as shown on December 1. Note that some accounts do not have balances since it is the beginning of the month and no revenue has been earned, expenses incurred, or withdrawals made.

   (a) Open a general ledger for the accounts using appropriate account numbers, and enter the balances where appropriate.
   (b) Enter the transactions for the month of December in the ledger.
   (c) Balance the ledger, and prepare a formal trial balance.
   (d) Prepare an income statement and a report form balance sheet.

FIGURE 3-15

GENERAL LEDGER

Cash		100
dr.	cr.	
Bal. 41 500	③ 1 200	
① 1 500	④ 200	
② 350	⑤ 700	
	⑦ 380	
	⑧ 800	
	⑨ 750	
	⑩ 180	

Accounts Receivable		101
dr.	cr.	
Bal. 16 200	⑥ 900	

Surveying Supplies		102
dr.	cr.	
Bal. 400		

Survey Equipment		103
dr.	cr.	
Bal. 12 800		
④ 200		

Automobile		104
dr.	cr.	
Bal. 32 000		

Accounts Payable		200
dr.	cr.	
⑤ 700	Bal. 3 200	

Short-Term Loans		201
dr.	cr.	
	Bal. 16 000	

C. Stratton, Capital		300
dr.	cr.	
	Bal. 83 700	
	① 1 500	

C. Stratton, Drawings		301
dr.	cr.	
⑧ 800		

Survey Fees		400
dr.	cr.	
	② 350	
	⑥ 900	

Rent Expense		500
dr.	cr.	
③ 1 200		

Wages Expense		501
dr.	cr.	
⑨ 750		

Automobile Expense		502
dr.	cr.	
⑦ 380		

Utilities Expense		503
dr.	cr.	
⑩ 180		

FIGURE 3-16

	Source Document	Account Changed	Type of Account	Increase/ Decrease	Debit/ Credit
(1)	Memo	Cash	Asset	Increase	Debit
		C. Stratton, Capital	Owner's Equity	Increase	Credit
	Owner, C. Stratton, invested an additional $1 500 into the business.				

FIGURE 3-17

Cash	$4 800	Lesson Fees	
Accounts Receivable	4 200	Advertising Expense	
Office Supplies	260	Telephone Expense	
Office Equipment	1 440	Ice Rental Expense	
Accounts Payable	900	Assistants' Wages	
M. Knox, Capital	9 800	Miscellaneous Expense	
M. Knox, Drawings			

Dec. 1 Cash Sales Slips #89 to #128: Sold 40 monthly memberships at $120 each.
1 Cash Receipt Slip #24: Received $190 from M. Weston on account.
4 Cheque Copy #84: Paid $900 to the City of St. Boniface as payment for two weeks' ice rental.
9 Cheque Copy #85: Paid $128 to Axiom Printers for advertising circulars.
12 Cheque Copy #86: Paid $24 for a skate-sharpening ticket for 12 skate sharpenings for Mary's (the owner) skates.
15 Cheque Copy #87: Paid $900 to the City of St Boniface as payment for two weeks' ice rental.
19 Cheque Copy #88: Paid $32 to the local grocery store for items for the Christmas skating party.
19 Cheque Copy #89: Paid the monthly telephone bill, $24.
19 Cheque Copy #90: Paid the assistants' wages for the month, $480.
19 Cheque Copy #91: Purchased office supplies, $90.
20 Cheque Copy #92: Paid $220 on account to A & B Sports Store.
20 Purchase Invoice #992: Purchased a word processor and printer on account for the business, $2 200.
20 Purchase Invoice #078: Purchased paper and ribbon supplies for the printer, and disks for the computer on account, $87.
21 Cheque Copy #93: Paid $1 200 to Mary for her personal use.

Applications — Comprehensive

Kinnaird's Book Binders is owned by Winston Kinnaird. The firm repairs books for libraries and schools, and also binds new books. The general ledger accounts for the firm and their respective balances on June 1 are given in Figure 3-18.

(a) Open a general ledger for the accounts using appropriate account numbers, and enter the balances where appropriate.

(b) Enter the transactions for the month of June in the ledger.

FIGURE 3-18

Cash	$22 000	Binding Revenue
Accounts Receivable	19 750	Delivery Expense
Binding Supplies	9 000	Advertising Expense
Office Supplies	730	Wages Expense
Land	93 400	Utilities Expense
Building	85 300	Donations Expense
Binding Equipment	41 500	Miscellaneous Expense
Truck	13 200	
Accounts Payable	9 700	
Bank Loan	36 430	
Mortgage Payable	85 200	
W. Kinnaird, Capital	153 550	
W. Kinnaird, Drawings		

(c) Balance the ledger, and prepare a formal trial balance.

(d) Prepare an income statement and a report form balance sheet.

June 1 Cheque Copy #543: Made the monthly mortgage payment, $1 100.

1 Cheque Copy #544: Made the monthly bank loan payment, $900.

2 Cash Receipt Slip #4598: Received $900 on account from the Carleton Board of Education.

4 Sales Invoice #93: Repaired $4 500 worth of books on account for the Ottawa Separate School Board.

5 Cheque Copy #545: Paid the employees their biweekly wages, $1 200.

7 Cheque Copy #546: Paid $460 on account to Shell Canada Ltd. for gas and oil for the delivery truck.

9 Cheque Copy #547: Gave $150 to the United Appeal.

14 Cheque Copy #548: Paid $900 to the owner, which was his biweekly withdrawal.

15 Cheque Copy #549: Paid $500 to the Ottawa Minor Hockey Association as sponsorship for one tyke hockey team.

16 Sales Invoice #94: Book repairs for $2 700 were completed on account for the Nepean Library.

17 Voucher #42: The owner took $50 worth of office supplies for his personal use.

19 Purchase Invoice #991: Purchased a laminator on account for $2 200.

19 Cheque Copy #550: Paid the employees their biweekly wages, $1 200.

22 Purchase Invoice #A243: Purchased $2 300 worth of book binding tape on account from Renfrew Tape Ltd.

22 Cheque Copy #551: Paid $45 for an advertisement in the *Nepean Clarion*.

24 Cheque Copy #552: Paid $230 to Renaud Office Suppliers for binding glue.

26 Sales Invoice #95: Book repairs of $2 900 were completed on account for the Carleton Roman Catholic School Board.

28 Purchase Invoice #922/Cheque Copy #553: Purchased a new gluing machine. The machine cost $4 200; $2 200 was paid in cash, with the balance owing on account.

28 Cheque Copy #554: Paid $900 to the owner for his personal use.

29 Cheque Copy #555: Paid $395 to Nepean PUC for utilities expenses.

29 Cheque Copy #556: Paid $400 to *The Citizen* for advertising.

Focussing

1. Income Statement Preparation

The following income statement has a number of errors in it.

Income Statement Velasquez Renovations June 30, 19–9	
Income	
Cash	$ 45 900
Renovation Services	193 200
Owner's Investment	12 500
Expenses	
Utilities Expense	1 200
Owner's Withdrawals	5 600
Salaries Expense	48 905
Accounts Payable	17 400
Rent Expense	32 900
Loan Payments	6 430
Miscellaneous Expense	1 325
NET PROFIT	$137 840

(a) Prepare a numbered list of errors; for each error indicate what has been done incorrectly. You should be able to find at least nine errors.
(b) Calculate the correct net income.

2. Trial Balance

The following unrelated errors have been made in the recording of transactions. Indicate whether the trial balance will balance after each of the transactions, and if not, why not. Also, indicate how the error might later come to the attention of the business.
(a) A $400 cash purchase of office supplies was recorded as a debit to Office Supplies, $40 and a credit to Cash, $40.
(b) $500 cash received on account from Jennifer Zeitz was recorded as a debit to Cash, $500 and a credit to Accounts Payable, $500.
(c) A $900 purchase of office furniture on account was recorded as a debit to Office Supplies, $900 and a credit to Accounts Payable, $900.
(d) A $200 telephone expense payment was recorded as a debit to Utilities Expense, $20 and a credit to Cash, $200.
(e) A $300 payment on the bank loan was recorded as a debit to Bank Loan, $300 and a debit to Cash, $300.

Evaluate and Assess — Income Growth

The Mountain View Video Centre has been in operation for five years. Over the first four years its net income steadily increased. In the fifth year, its net income decreased substantially. The income statement for the current year is shown in Figure 3-19, as well as net income figures for the five-year period. In addition, the industry averages for that same year, as found in *Small Business Profiles* published by Statistics Canada, are also given.
(a) Calculate the percentage decrease in net income for Mountain View Video Centre from 19–5 to 19–6.
(b) Calculate the net income to revenue percentages for Mountain View Video Centre and the industry.
(c) Compare the income statement for Mountain View Video Centre to that for the industry and state reasons for Mountain View's low net income percentage.
(d) Mountain View Video Centre wishes to increase its revenue to $125 000 in the 19–7 year. Calculate the percent increase from 19–6 that this figure represents.
(e) Mountain View Video Centre also wishes to reach a net income percentage of 9% for 19–7. Based on this goal, what percentage and what dollar amount must the expenses be?
(f) Based on the above calculations, what decisions could Mountain View Video Centre make concerning its expenses?

Synthesize and Conclude

1. Recording Transactions in Proper Period

The controller for Deschamps-Kostiuk Business Consultants is concerned that the net income for the current year is going to be significantly lower than that of the previous year. The business is concerned about this prospect, for it is entering negotiations with a bank for a large loan. The controller believes that a better net income will result if:
(i) $35 600 of current expenses are not recorded until the following year; the invoices from suppliers will be set aside for recording in the following year;
(ii) $234 000 of consulting jobs that are partially completed could be recorded as being completed in the current year, and the revenue recognized during the current year. The invoices could be dated this year, but not sent to the customers until the jobs are completed.

He therefore instructs you, the junior accountant, to make entries that will accommodate his plan.

FIGURE 3-19

Mountain View Video Centre

	19–6	19–5	19–4	19–3	19–2
Net Income	$6 400	$16 400	$15 500	$12 350	$9 330

For the Year Ended 19–6
Income Statement

	Mountain View Video Centre	Industry Average
Revenue		
Video and Equipment Rentals	$117 830	$104 532
Total Revenue	$117 830	$104 532
Expenses		
Occupancy (repairs, utilities, rent)	48 320	37 527
Personnel	32 950	17 039
Financial (interest and professional fees)	8 790	6 899
Other	21 370	33 032
Total Expenses	111 430	94 497
Net Income	$ 6 400	$ 10 035

The Video and Audio-visual Equipment Rental Industry

	Total Industry Averages	Businesses Reporting a Net Income	Businesses Reporting a Net Loss
Number of businesses in sample	313	231	82
Average sales	$104 532	$111 450	$ 89 121
Average expenses	94 903	91 785	99 697
Average net profit (loss)	9 629	19 665	(10 576)

(a) State the GAAPs that would be violated if these decisions were carried out.
(b) State the effect of the decisions on the current year's net income.
(c) What action should you take concerning the controller's instructions?

2. Economic Effects on Net Income

The following net income has been earned by the Richmond Furniture Co. Ltd. for the years shown:

19–0	$984 200
19–9	$902 100
19–8	$877 300
19–7	$873 000
19–6	$870 000

The business makes 50 percent of its sales in Canada, and 50 percent of its sales in the United States. Indicate what effect each of the following events might have on the future revenue of the business:

(a) The provincial government eliminates the provincial sales tax on furniture made in the province.
(b) The United States imposes a ten percent tariff (tax) on all furniture imported from Canada due to unfair subsidies being paid by the government to Canadian producers.
(c) The value of the Canadian dollar goes down in relation to the US dollar.
(d) The inflation rate in Canada for the year is eight percent; in the US the rate is five percent.
(e) The federal government introduces a program to pay one-half the wages for one year for all new employees. The maximum subsidy is $3 per hour.
(f) A new firm establishes itself in the province. This firm uses plastics to make furniture.
(g) The federal government imposes an additional three cents per litre tax on gasoline. The firm ships its products in its own trucks.

ACCOUNTING AT WORK

There are three professional accounting designations that one can obtain in Canada. The designations are awarded by each of the following bodies, with the designations shown in brackets: the Institute of Chartered Accountants (C.A.), the Society of Management Accountants (C.M.A.), and the Canadian Certified General Accountants' Association (C.G.A.). Each of these designations will be examined in this and the next two chapters.

Chartered Accountants

Chartered accountants have the educational requirements to hold many jobs in business. In Chapter 2, the advertisement for Bombardier Inc. required that the person be a chartered accountant.

The following are requirements that must be met in order to become a C.A.:
- obtain a university degree; certain courses are required, and can either be part of the degree, or taken separately;

- obtain employment in an office designated for the training of C.A. students, normally for three years;
- complete a one-week staff training program while working in the designated training office;
- pass (or receive exemption from) the School of Accountancy admission examinations;
- successfully complete the School of Accountancy;
- pass the national Uniform Final Examination.

The following career profile for Bob McLeod describes the job of one chartered accountant.

Bob McLeod
Chartered Accountant

Bob McLeod thinks the impression many people have of chartered accountants is inaccurate. C.A.s are not just bookkeepers; they are financial advisors, tax planners, and business managers. They must have a broad knowledge of their companies if they are to do their jobs effectively.

McLeod works as controller in a branch plant of a large Canadian corporation. His responsibilities include preparing annual budgets and monthly financial statements, and managing day-to-day financial transactions like accounts payable and sales invoicing. He reports to the plant manager: reporting to him are an accountant and several clerks.

After graduating with a Bachelor of Arts degree with a major in mathematics, McLeod took a position as an articling student in an accounting firm. Here he audited the firm's clients, prepared tax returns and the like. On-the-job training was provided by the firm. In addition, McLeod did the necessary course work to prepare for the C.A. exams. Two years after getting the C.A. designation he moved to his present company. Since then, he has moved through a variety of positions, including assistant to the manager, chief accountant, tax officer and, lately, controller.

McLeod takes advantage of professional development courses that are offered by professional associations and academic institutions. "I particularly stay in touch with what is happening with taxes," he says. "This is an area that is changing all the time and I need to know how the changes will influence my company." Also, he stays up-to-date on business uses of computers and on management techniques, as these improve his effectiveness in his position.

The challenges of running the financial functions of a plant, and the confidence that success brings, keep McLeod satisfied with his career choice. He values the opportunities that the C.A. designation has allowed him to pursue.

Using the ads below, answer the following questions:
(a) Describe the activities of each of the C.A. positions.
(b) What skills other than accounting are required for each position?
(c) What salary range could an experienced chartered accountant expect?

TD

Chartered Accountants

Moving ahead in our Finance & Control Division

where people make the difference

CA's at TD can bank on unending challenge in a highly motivated, forward thinking environment. The positions currently available in our Financial Controls Department are no exception. As a Financial Controls Analyst, you will provide support for the growth in the Treasury and Investment Banking, International, Domestic, and Corporate business areas of the bank.

For those professionals interested in further developing their financial and management skills in a progressive, energetic environment, this is the ideal opportunity. Joining a team involved with the research and development of accounting and financial policies, you will also assist other teams in the development and implementation of financial systems and controls for purposes of regulatory and management reporting.

These are diversified, demanding positions that require sound communication skills and well developed analytical abilities. Ideally you are a CA with 1-3 years' experience after designation and possess an excellent mathematical aptitude.

Because of the nature of these opportunities, your career at TD can take different paths. Excellent remuneration and career prospects await qualified individuals looking to join a people-oriented organization committed to employment equity. Interested candidates are invited to send a resume, in confidence to: **Peter D. McAdam, Manager, Corporate Human Resources Division, P.O. Box 1, Toronto Dominion Centre, Toronto, Ontario M5K 1A2**

Director of Accounting

With the installation of online Accounting and Corporate Reporting Financial Systems, including Accounts Payable and Purchasing, almost complete, your major focus in this key role will be to improve the integrity of the information within the financial systems.
Reporting directly to the Commissioner of Finance and heading a staff of 40, you will also be responsible for further developing the related "feeder systems" into an online mode and ensuring secure interface with the core financial systems. With significant changes occurring in Pensions, Benefits Management and Corporate Reporting as well as Accounting Standards, you must be able to respond professionally as they happen. Among your key objectives will be improving service to user departments, user support and training procedures as well as custom reporting and response.

Success in this prominent post requires membership in a recognized professional accounting body such as C.A., C.M.A., C.G.A. or C.F.P.A. and preferably, a relevant degree. You possess strong management and interpersonal skills gained through progressively responsible management experience within a large finance function.

Additionally, you bring extensive experience in development, implementation and use of advanced computerized accounting systems and control procedures; a thorough understanding of accounting and reporting principles and current standards, including those of Regulatory and Provincial Bodies. Finally, you must demonstrate proven leadership ability to direct a professionally-oriented staff and participate as an integral part of the department's Senior Mangement Team as well as sound people skills to tactfully deal with elected and senior appointed officials.

Salary for this position will be $61,649.00–$72,595.00 per annum, accompanied by an attractive benefits package.

For prompt and confidential consideration, please forward your resume, to: **Commissioner of Human Resources, P.O. Box 40, Station "A", Hamilton, Ontario L8N 3A2 Fax: (416) 526-2650**

An equal opportunity employer. We promote a non-smoking environment. Resumes submitted should not include discriminatory reference.

Business Career Skills

1. Goal Setting

One of the most important activities in a business is to establish its goals for the year. Studies show that many businesses fail because they did not establish goals — they had no direction. A well-known saying states: "People who plan seldom fail; people who fail seldom plan." Management will analyze the performance of the business during the current year, making use of the data that is provided by the accounting department. Using a variety of information it will then try to establish realistic goals. The goals may be short-term, medium-term, or long-term.

A goal is a condition or situation that you want to experience at some future date. For example, a business could establish a goal of increasing revenue by six percent during the next fiscal year. Various activities will then be established in order to reach the goal.

In establishing and attaining goals, one could use the following procedure:

(1) Brainstorm to obtain a list of wishes, both realistic and dreams.
   e.g., Business goals:
      to become the largest cookie shop in Canada
      to increase sales by five percent
      to decrease utility expenses by four percent
      Personal goals:
      to increase my average in the first term by five percent over last year's final average

(2) Rank your wishes from those most desired to those least desired.

(3) Using the wishes, define goals as accurately and completely as possible.
   e.g., to decrease utility expenses by four percent by the end of the fiscal year

(4) For each goal, establish the activities that will have to be carried out to attain the goal.
   e.g., analysis of current use of utilities
      consultation with experts in the field of heating, air conditioning, and lighting
      employee awareness program to decrease unnecessary use and waste of utilities

(5) Eliminate those goals that are unattainable, either because the activities cannot be carried out, or they are unreasonable; such goals may become long-term goals.
   e.g., to become the largest cookie shop in Canada

(6) Establish time guidelines for each activity that is a part of the final goals.

(7) Keep the goals in a prominent place, so that reference can frequently be made to them.

Instructions:
(a) Make a list of information that you would want if you were about to establish the one-year goals for a financial business specializing in loans. Assume that the business operates within your province only.
(b) Label three pieces of paper, one for Short-Term Goals (this year), one for Medium-Term Goals (the next five years), and one for Long-Term Goals. On each of the three pages, establish your personal goals, using the steps above.

2. Report Writing — Income Statement Analysis

The income statement and balance sheet for Drohan's Motor Boat Services are given in Figure 3-20. The owner, Sandeep Drohan, feels that the business could perform substantially better if it had some new ideas.

FIGURE 3-19

Drohan's Motor Boat Services
Income Statement
for the year ended October 31, 19–2

Revenue
Motor Boat Repairs		$196 400	
Boat Repairs		47 900	$244 300

Expenses
Wages		108 000	
Utilities		22 400	
Rent		16 000	
Repair		44 800	
Miscellaneous		5 600	196 800
			$ 47 500

Drohan's Motor Boat Services
Balance Sheet
as at October 31, 19–2

Assets		Liabilities	
Cash	$ 42 500	Accounts Payable	$ 26 700
Accounts Receivable	95 300	Short-Term Loan	22 300
Repair Supplies	57 920	Total Liabilities	49 000
Office Supplies	1 290		
Equipment	42 300	**Owner's Equity**	
Truck	14 390	S. Drohan, Capital	204 700
		Total Liabilities and	
Total Assets	**$253 700**	Owner's Equity	**$253 700**

His objective is to increase net income. The business rents space at two marinas. At each marina there is a clerk and two repair persons. The focus of the business is the repair of small engines, with some time devoted to repairs to damaged boats. Most damaged boats are taken to other businesses for repairs, mainly because Drohan's does not have the space that would be required to repair them. The business is open for eight months; the employees collect Unemployment Insurance while they are out of work.

To rent additional space the business would have to pay $500 per month at each location. Sandeep estimates increased revenue of $2 000 per month at each location. One repair person would have to be hired, and his time shared between the two locations. The person would be paid $18 000 for the eight months. The business would have to buy extra repair equipment in the amount of $2 000. Repair expenses are estimated at $1 000 for the eight months.

The marina is owned by the members who pay a membership fee. Also located at the marina is a restaurant.

(a) Brainstorm in groups to develop ways of increasing Drohan's Motor Boat Services' net income. Your brainstorming should include an analysis of each account on the income statement.
(b) Individually, write a business report to the owner with recommendations that should improve the business's net income.

COMPUTER ACCOUNTING
USING A SPREADSHEET TO ANALYZE ACCOUNTING DATA

The most powerful feature of the electronic spreadsheet is that it enables the computer to make **instant calculations** once you enter values and formulas. That means you can make corrections in one value and the spreadsheet will instantly recalculate all other values related to the one you changed. With an electronic spreadsheet, therefore, you can make **forecasts** very easily. For forecasting you ask **"what if" questions**, such as "What if we give our hourly rated employees an 8 percent raise?" To see what effect this would have on other figures, such as net income, you would not have to do anything except change the wages expense value on the spreadsheet and it would automatically show the new total.

This is the feature that makes electronic spreadsheets so useful to businesses. It allows people to see the effects of a transaction, such as a wage increase, before the transaction actually takes place. It helps the management of a company avoid problems and reach the best decisions about possible ways to generate profits and manage the **economic resources** of the company.

Exercises

1. Load your spreadsheet program into your computer and use a selected problem, or problems, from this chapter to prepare an income statement. Use the following plan to develop your income statement model.

   Column Widths:
   (1) Set the column width for the column containing the list of sources of revenue and expenses to 35.
   (2) Set a column width of 12 for the amount columns.

   Formulas:
   (1) Use the SUM function where applicable.
   (2) Calculation of Net Income/Loss = Revenue − Expenses

FIGURE 3-21

```
                        Name of Business
                        Income Statement
                          Date line                      Formulas
        Revenue:
                                                0
                                                0
                                               ___
        Total Revenue                                 0      1

        Expenses:
                                                0
                                                0
                                                0
                                                0
                                                0
                                                0
                                                0
                                               ___
        Total Expenses                                0      2
        Net Income/Loss                               0
                                                    ====     3
```

2. As the new manager of the school basketball team you are responsible for generating revenue at games. Your revenue goal this year is to take in $900 per game. Prior to the season you must estimate attendance and set ticket prices. Revenue from ticket sales is supplemented by refreshment sales at the concession stand. You have found from past records and discussions with your predecessor that, on average, each fan spends approximately $2.50 on refreshments.

   Use your spreadsheet program to set up a template to show the following worksheet labels: School Basketball Team Name; Admission Price; Expected Fans; Ticket Sales Revenue; Refreshment Sales Revenue; Total Revenue.

   Start with the following assumptions: (i) $2.00 cost per ticket; (ii) 150 fans expected.
   (a) What formula will calculate Ticket Sales Revenue? (Enter it onto the spreadsheet.)
   (b) What formula will calculate Refreshment Sales Revenue? (Enter it onto the spreadsheet.)
   (c) What formula will calculate Total Revenue? (Enter it onto the spreadsheet.)
   (d) How much income is generated using the current assumptions?
   (e) How many more fans would it take to reach your $900 goal?
   (Hint: Move the cursor to the data entry cell for Expected Fans and change your data. Watch the other cells change too!)
   (f) Now, change your Expected Fans figure to 225. What would you have to charge fans to reach your $900 goal?
   (g) As you are aware from your studies in this chapter, revenue does not mean net profit (net income). Expenses would have to be itemized and totalled and then subtracted from total revenue to arrive at net income. Can you think of any expense(s) applicable to this exercise that you would have to calculate?
   (h) Assuming that expenses are approximately 40 percent of total sales, modify your worksheet to enter this data and calculate the estimated net income. What is the net income if the expenses are 55 percent? 60 percent?

CHAPTER FOUR

The General Journal

LEARNING OBJECTIVES

At the end of this chapter you should be able to
- describe the need for a journal;
- journalize transactions;
- describe the running-balance ledger account;
- post from a general journal to a general ledger;
- recognize types of errors from using a trial balance;
- correct errors in a general journal and general ledger;
- outline the accounting cycle;
- use an accounting software program to set up and access accounting data files;
- enter transactions into the computer system;
- display or print accounting transactions from the computer system;
- display or print a trial balance.

LANGUAGE OF ACCOUNTING

You will see the following terms in this chapter:
accounting cycle
accounting software
audit trail
bankruptcy
chart of accounts
computerized accounting package
forwarding
general journal
general ledger
module
insolvent
journalizing
post
slide error
transposition error

4.1 The General Journal

The accountant for Algor Computer Services was required to find a particular transaction that had occurred on June 7. Jennifer Zeitz questioned the amount Algor claimed she owed. Jennifer believed that she had paid $150 on June 7, but she did not have her cash receipt. It was therefore necessary for the accountant to find the business's copy of the cash receipt slip, or search through the general ledger for an entry of $150 on June 7. In either case, it could be a time-consuming chore.

This type of search could result in hours of work in a business that has thousands of transactions a day. What system could be developed so that the debit and credit entries for any particular transaction are easily identified?

Journal: *a book in which transactions are first entered.*

Book of original entry: *an alternate name for a journal.*

Journalizing: *the process of entering a transaction in a journal.*

Journal entry: *the debit and credit entries for any one transaction.*

General journal: *a journal used to record all types of transactions.*

The purpose of a general ledger is to provide the balances for individual accounts. As previously illustrated, it is frequently necessary to locate the debit and credit parts of a particular transaction. To fulfil this need, a journal is used.

A **journal** is the book in which transactions are first entered from the source documents. For this reason, a journal is sometimes referred to as a **book of original entry**. The process of entering the transaction is called **journalizing**. A **journal entry** is the complete entry for a transaction. Thus, we say that "a transaction has been journalized."

Source Document ⟶ Journal

In some very small businesses, all of the transactions can be recorded into one journal. For this reason the journal is called a **"general" journal**. In other businesses, different journals are established according to the needs of the business and the volume of transactions. A business with a large number of sales on account in a day would find it convenient to open a journal in which only sales on account are recorded. These specialized journals will be studied in Chapter 11.

Two-Column General Journal

The two-column general journal is the simplest of journals. It has two money columns: one for debits, and one for credits. Accountants follow a consistent format when journalizing. This format is illustrated in the general journal shown in Figure 4-1.

Transactions

June 15   Memo #1: Received $15 000 cash and office equipment worth $3 422, from V. Marshall as an initial investment.
     23   Sales Invoice #55-0001: Network installation at Optima Investment Brokerage, $6 000.
     27   Sales Invoice #55-0002: Repair job at UIC, $693.
     29   Cheque Copy #1: Paid $500 to the owner for his personal use.
     29   Cheque Copy #2: Paid $401 to J.H. Yeo on account.
July 2   Cheque Copy #3: Paid the monthly rent, $450.
      4   Purchase Invoice #972: Purchased office supplies on account from Willson Stationery, $335.

FIGURE 4-1

GENERAL JOURNAL

PAGE 1

DATE 1985		PARTICULARS	PR	DEBIT	CREDIT
June	15	Cash		15000 —	
		Office Equipment		3422 —	
		V. Marshall, Capital			18422 —
		Memo #1			
	23	Accounts Receivable		6000 —	
		Computer Services			6000 —
		Sales Invoice #55-0001, Optima			
		Investment Brokerage			
	27	Accounts Receivable		693 —	
		Computer Services			693 —
		Sales Invoice #55-0002, UIC			
	29	V. Marshall, Drawings		500 —	
		Cash			500 —
		Cheque Copy #1			
	29	Accounts Payable		401 —	
		Cash			401 —
		Cheque Copy #2, J.H. Yeo			
July	2	Rent Expense		450 —	
		Cash			450 —
		Cheque Copy #3, monthly rent			
	4	Office Supplies		335 —	
		Accounts Payable			335 —
		Purchase Invoice #972, Willson Stationery			

Rules for Journalizing in a General Journal

For journal entries, the same steps for analyzing a transaction take place as were introduced in Chapter 2. For every transaction total debits must still equal total credits. Notice how the following rules for journalizing transactions relate to the journal in Figure 4-1.

1. The year is entered at the top of the page, followed by the month and day. The year and the month are *not* repeated on the page, but, if a new month or a new calendar year begins, that is indicated. The date used is the one on the source document for those issued by the business, and the receipt date for those source documents received by the business.

2. The name of the account that is debited for the transaction is *always* written first, at the extreme left side next to the date column, under the heading Particulars. The amount is written on the same line in the left-hand (debit) money column.

3. The name of the account that is credited for the transaction is written on the next line and is always indented so that it is easily distinguished from the debit entry. The amount is written on the same line in the right-hand (credit) money column.

    The principle of double-entry accounting is still being followed: debits must equal credits for every transaction.

4. An explanation may be given for the transaction. In some cases the explanation may take many lines; in other cases it may be only a few words. When a number is given for a source document, that frequently is all that is needed for the explanation.

5. A blank line is left between entries.

6. The first entry in a journal is referred to as the **opening entry**. This entry usually records the initial investment by the owner of the business. The first entry shown on June 15 in Figure 4-1 is the opening entry for Algor Computer Services.

7. A journal entry with more than one debit and/or credit is referred to as a **compound entry**. In Figure 4-1 the opening entry is a compound entry. The debits are all placed before the credits.

8. The account names used match those found in the chart of accounts. Thus, one would not write "paid in cash," or "cheque issued" opposite the debit or credit entry; the name of the appropriate account, in this case, is Cash.

9. Each source document is initialled and dated after the transaction has been journalized.

Opening entry: the owner's initial investment to start the business.

Compound entry: a journal entry with more than one debit and/or credit.

To summarize, every journal entry consists of
- the date
- the debit account(s) and amount(s)
- the credit account(s) and amount(s)
- the explanation of the entry.

Advantages of the General Journal

There are a number of advantages to using a general journal:

1. The complete transaction is kept together. If it becomes necessary to refer to an entry, it is easily located by its date, and both the debit and credit are together. It is then unnecessary to look through the ledger for all of the parts of the entry.

2. There is an explanation provided. The source document for an entry is usually filed, and is not easily accessible. A brief explanation of the entry will answer most questions.

3. The possibility of error is reduced. Frequently, when transactions are entered directly into a ledger, a debit or a credit may be left out inadvertently if other work interrupts. Such an error in a journal is easily noticed, for the two items are side by side.

4. All transactions are recorded in chronological order (by order of date). Any transaction can quickly be found if the date is known.

5. The journal is a proof of events. If the source documents were destroyed by fire, the journal would serve as evidence of the life of the business. For this reason, businesses usually store their **books of account**, the journal and the ledger, in fire-proof or fire-retardant safes after working hours.

Books of account: include the journal and the ledger.

"Start? Start what? I thought you said you hired me to take care of the books."

HERMAN copyright (1980) Jim Unger. Reprinted with permission of Universal Press Syndicate. All rights reserved.

Lesson Review

1. Where are all transactions first entered?
2. What is a journal? What is an alternate name?
3. What is the main reason for using a journal?
4. Describe the process of journalizing.
5. Why is the name "general" given to the general journal?
6. What rules are followed in order to distinguish the debits from the credits in a two-column general journal?
7. Explain how the double-entry accounting system relates to a journal.
8. Why are explanations included in journal entries?
9. Distinguish between an opening entry and a compound entry.
10. Summarize the five advantages of having a general journal.

Lesson Applications

11. (a) Journalize the following transactions for Charlottetown Student Painters. The firm paints houses during the summer months, and all sales are on a cash basis. It is owned by Krista Warlick. The accounts used by the firm are as follows:

    Cash
    Paint Supplies
    Paint Equipment
    Office Furniture
    Accounts Payable
    Bank Loan
    K. Warlick, Capital
    K. Warlick, Drawings

    Painting Revenue
    Advertising Expense
    Rent Expense
    Utilities Expense
    Van Rental Expense
    Miscellaneous Expense

    Transactions

    May 1   Memo #1: Received $2 000 cash, $400 in paint supplies, and $720 in paint equipment as the initial investment by the owner.

         1   Cheque Copy #1: Paid $120 to the Charlottetown *Guardian and Patriot* for advertising.

         1   Cheque Copy #2: Paid $300 rent to Campeau Real Estate Enterprises.

         2   Cheque Copy #3: Paid $240 for posters to post at the University of PEI to advertise for student painters.

3 Cash Sales Slip #1: Received $450 for painting the exterior of a house.
3 Cheque Copy #4: Purchased painting supplies, $900.
3 Purchase Invoice #5589: Purchased a new ladder from Canada Tire, $120.
6 Purchase Invoice #971: Purchased a used desk for the office from Westtown Used Furniture, $210.
6 Cash Sales Slip #2: Received $720 for painting a house.
7 Cheque Copy #5: Paid for the weekly van rental, $220.

(b) What are two ways of describing the first entry?
(c) For the journalizing done above, check that each of the rules given in the text for journalizing has been followed.

12. Journalize the following transactions for Malhotra's Formal Wear Rental. The accounts used by the firm are as follows:

Cash	N. Malhotra, Drawings
Accounts Receivable	Formal Wear Rentals
Formal Wear	Rent Expense
Furniture and Fixtures	Advertising Expense
Accounts Payable	Utilities Expense
N. Malhotra, Capital	Miscellaneous Expense

Transactions

Oct. 20 Cash Sales Slips #112–#126: Cash rentals for the day amounted to $840.
20 Cheque Copy #189: Paid $250 on account to Tuxedo Manufacturers Ltd.
20 Sales Invoices issued: #432 to R. Rapallo for $800; #433 to L. Iannucci for $790.
21 Cash Sales Slips #127–#149: Cash rentals for the day amounted to $730.
21 Sales Invoices issued: #434 to G. Kovacs for $400; #435 to K. Chari for $650; #436 to N. Sernas for $550; #437 to J. Wong for $700.
21 Cheque Copy #190: Paid $120 to the *Calgary Herald* for advertising.
21 Cheque Copy #191: Paid $600 to the owner, N. Malhotra.
21 Cash Receipt Slip #99: Received $480 on account from N. Pralow.
21 Purchase Invoice #B645: Purchased $3 400 worth of ladies' formal wear from Tuxedo Manufacturers Ltd.

13. You are given the completed journal in Figure 4-2 for Webster's Translation Service. Several errors have been made in the journalizing process. Describe each error. You should be able to find at least eight errors.

FIGURE 4-2

GENERAL JOURNAL

PAGE 114

DATE 19—		PARTICULARS	PR	DEBIT	CREDIT
Mar.	31	Cash		450 —	
		Accounts Receivable			450 —
		Cash Receipt Slip #203			
Mar.	31	Supplies		50 —	
		Accounts Payable			50 —
	31	Translation Services Revenue			300 —
		Accounts Receivable		300 —	
		Sales Invoice #940			
	1	Office Equipment		1000 —	
		Owed to Shawn Voisey			1000 —
		Bought a new office desk on account			

14. Journalize the following transactions for Fantinic's Business Services, a firm that provides accounting and inventory services for businesses. The accounts used by the firm are: Cash; Accounts Receivable; Furniture and Fixtures; Automobile; Accounts Payable; R. Fantinic, Capital; R. Fantinic, Drawings; Fees Earned; Rental Expense; Advertising Expense; Automobile Expense; Wages Expense; Utilities Expense; Miscellaneous Expense.

Transactions

Feb. 11 Voucher #61: Received $800 as an additional investment from the owner, Robert Fantinic.
    11 Cash Sales Slips #444–#445: Cash sales for the day were $900.
    11 Sales Invoice #876: For services provided to City Metal Fabrication, $1 720.
    11 Cash Receipt Slip #126: Received $780 on account from Lloyd's Photography.
    11 Cheque Copy #105: Paid the weekly wages, $650.
    11 Voucher #62: The owner took home furniture valued at $300.
    12 Cheque Copy #106: Paid $440 to the Nepean *Clarion* for advertising.
    12 Cheque Copy #107: Paid $398 to Reid's Service Station for repairs to the owner's personal car.
    12 Cash Sales Slips #446–#448: Cash sales for the day were $1 190.

4.2 Posting to Running-Balance Ledger Accounts

All transactions at Algor Computer Services were entered from the source documents to the general journal. The accountant for Algor Computer Services was asked by the owner to prepare a summary of expenses related to the use of the automobile. If only the journal was available, the accountant would have to examine every entry in it in order to find those that applied to the automobile. The account balance could then be calculated. Is there a better way of maintaining a record of what automobile expenses have been incurred?

Even though all source documents are first recorded in a journal, it is necessary to have the balances on hand for all of the accounts. To find the balance for an account by going through the journal page by page is a very time-consuming process. Account balances are needed on a day-to-day basis, and therefore must be maintained in an organized fashion. To obtain the account balances, all transactions are transferred, or **posted**, from the journal to the general ledger. It is therefore necessary that two books be kept: a journal, which has a record of transactions by date, and a ledger, which has a record of all changes in individual accounts.

> **Posting:** the transferring of information, usually from the journal to the ledger.

Source Document ⟶ Journal ⟶ General Ledger

Up to this point the T-account has been used as the ledger account. This form of the account is used to facilitate understanding of the concepts of debit and credit balances. In reality, most businesses doing manual accounting use a running-balance form of the ledger account. The Cash account in both the T-account format and the running-balance format is shown below.

FIGURE 4-3

GENERAL LEDGER

```
                      100
dr.           cr.
1  2 300  Sept. 2  200
2    660       4    50
3    400           250
4    320
   3 680
```

GENERAL LEDGER

ACCOUNT						NO	
DATE		PARTICULARS	PR	DEBIT	CREDIT	DR/CR	BALANCE
1986							
Sept.	1		J49	2 300 –		DR	2 300 –
	2		J49		200 –	DR	2 100 –
	2		J50	660 –		DR	2 760 –
	3		J51	400 –		DR	3 160 –
	4		J52		50 –	DR	3 110 –
	4		J52	320 –		DR	3 430 –

The running-balance ledger account has a number of advantages as compared to the T-account. First, all entries are in chronological order. Second, the source of the information is found in the PR (posting reference) column, which is discussed below. Finally, the amount of the balance and the type of balance are available after every entry. The account in Figure 4-3 had a debit balance of $2 300 on September 1. On September 2 a credit amount of $200 was entered. The balance column was updated to show the new debit balance of $2 100. Also on September 2 a debit amount of $660 was entered. The balance column was again updated to show the new debit balance of $2 760. It is important to note that the Dr./Cr. column indicates the type of balance, and *not* whether a debit or credit amount was entered. One knows whether a debit or credit amount was entered by observing which column the amount was placed in, and not by reference to the Dr./Cr. column.

From the Journal to the Ledger

The posting of an October journal entry for Algor Computer Services is shown below.

FIGURE 4-4 POSTING FROM THE GENERAL JOURNAL TO THE GENERAL LEDGER ACCOUNTS

GENERAL JOURNAL

PAGE 84

DATE 1986		PARTICULARS	PR	DEBIT	CREDIT
Oct.	1	Cash	100	200 —	
		Computer Services	400		200 —
		Cash Sales Slip #99-0394			

GENERAL LEDGER

ACCOUNT Cash   NO 100

DATE 1986		PARTICULARS	PR	DEBIT	CREDIT	DR CR	BALANCE
Oct.	1	Forwarded	✔			DR	32 250 —
	1		J84	200 —		DR	32 450 —

GENERAL LEDGER

ACCOUNT Computer Services   NO 400

DATE 1986		PARTICULARS	PR	DEBIT	CREDIT	DR CR	BALANCE
Oct.	1		J84		200 —	CR	200 —

Since posting is the manual transfer of many amounts, errors can easily occur. A procedure should be developed in order to reduce the chance of error; the steps shown below should be followed in order. The posting is done *line-by-line* from the journal, and *not* by doing all the Cash entries, then all the Supplies entries, etc.

Step 1 Locate the account in the general ledger. Reference to the Chart of Accounts at the front of the ledger may be required if the person doing the posting is not familiar with the account names and numbers.

Step 2 Enter the date. The date should be the same date as that shown in the general journal, *not* the date on which the posting is made to the account. Therefore, even though this journal entry was posted a day later, on October 2, when the accountant had time to do the postings, the date in the journal is entered in the general ledger account.

Step 3 Complete the Particulars column where necessary. This column is used infrequently in the general ledger. For now, it can be left blank.

Step 4 Enter the source from which the information is being taken into the PR column of the ledger. PR stands for posting reference. In this case, J84 is entered, indicating that the information was located on page 84 of the general journal. The J indicates General Journal. Some businesses use G or GJ instead.

Step 5 Calculate the new balance, and enter the amount in the Balance column. This form of ledger is called a running-balance account because the balance is always on hand. The Cash account had a balance of $32 250 at the beginning of the month, which is increased by the $200. The Computer Services account had a nil balance, since the $200 service was the first one performed that month. A new balance is calculated after each posting. The Dr./Cr. column is then completed to indicate the type of balance: Dr., Cr., or ∅ for debit balance, credit balance, and nil balance respectively. In our example, the Cash account has a debit balance since it is an asset account, and the Computer Services account has a credit balance since it is a revenue account. *The Dr./Cr. column does not indicate whether a debit or credit amount was entered in the account, for that is known by reference to the column in which the amount is entered.*

Step 6 In the journal, the account number to which the amount was posted is entered in the PR column. In our example $200 was posted to account 100, Cash, and $200 was posted to account 400, Computer Services. Entering the account number in the PR column of the general journal is always done last, for it indicates that the posting has been completed. If this step was done first, problems could occur. For example, if the accountant entered the account number in the PR column of the general journal first, and then someone interrupted, the accountant might assume that the posting was completed. This is a good example of why one should develop a system when posting.

Audit trail: the result of procedures that allow the tracing of data back to the source document.

The Audit Trail

The PR column in the journal and the ledger serves a valuable cross-reference purpose. All entries in the journal can be traced to their appropriate account in the ledger. More important, all entries in the ledger can be traced back to a journal entry. In turn, the explanation of the journal entry provides information indicating what source document was used to record the transaction. A number of problems are therefore solved in relation to our example of trying to calculate the balance of the Automobile Expense account. The balance is available in the general ledger in an account called Automobile Expense. As well, should there be a question about any of the amounts incurred, the accountant can refer back to the original source documents to try and resolve it.

Whenever there is an audit of a firm's books, a random check is made of transactions. The auditor should be able to find the trail of information: from a report back to the source document. Tracing the accounting steps back to the source document is done to ensure that the journalizing and posting of transactions is being carried out accurately. It would be impossible for the auditor to check every transaction: only a random sample is checked.

Uses of the Particulars Column

Two uses of the Particulars column of general ledger accounts can now be discussed. First, the column is used to indicate the first amount entered in an account. Therefore, when the opening entry for the business is posted from the journal to the ledger, each account that is opened will have the words "Opening Balance" written in the Particulars column. Similarly, when other accounts are opened as the business grows, Opening Balance should be written at the top of the Particulars column, as shown below.

FIGURE 4-5 A LEDGER ACCOUNT SHOWING THE OPENING BALANCE NOTATION IN THE PARTICULARS COLUMN

GENERAL LEDGER

ACCOUNT Cash   NO 100

DATE 1985		PARTICULARS	PR	DEBIT	CREDIT	DR CR	BALANCE
June	15	Opening Balance	J1	15 000 –		DR	15 000 –

Another use for the Particulars column occurs when a ledger page is filled. The information on the last line of the page is then forwarded to the top of the next page. The forwarding process is carried out as follows:

On the full page:

Enter "Forwarded" in the Particulars column on the last line.

FIGURE 4-6 A COMPLETED LEDGER PAGE, SHOWING FORWARDING NOTATION ON THE LAST LINE

GENERAL LEDGER

ACCOUNT Cash						NO 100	
DATE 1985		PARTICULARS	PR	DEBIT	CREDIT	DR CR	BALANCE
June	15	Opening Balance	J1	15 000 –		DR	15 000 –
	29		J1		500 –	DR	14 500 –
	27	Fowarded	J3	125 –		DR	13 330 –

On the new page:

1. Enter the account name and number.

2. Enter the year, and then enter the month and day of the last entry on the first line.

3. Enter "Forwarded" in the Particulars column, put a ✔ in the PR column, and enter the type of balance and the amount of the balance. Do not enter anything in the Debit or Credit columns.

FIGURE 4-7 A LEDGER PAGE SHOWING AN AMOUNT FORWARDED FROM THE PREVIOUS FULL PAGE

GENERAL LEDGER

ACCOUNT Cash						NO 100	
DATE 1985		PARTICULARS	PR	DEBIT	CREDIT	DR CR	BALANCE
July	27	Forwarded	✔			DR	13 330 –

LESSON REVIEW

15. Where are all source documents first entered?
16. Describe the differences between a T-account and a running-balance ledger account.
17. What are three advantages of the running-balance ledger account as compared to a T-account?
18. In a running-balance ledger account
    (a) how does one know that the amount entered was a debit?
    (b) how does one know that the balance is a debit or a credit?
19. Describe the process of posting.
20. What should be the last step in the posting process? Why?
21. What is the audit trail?
22. Describe two uses of the Particulars column of a general ledger account.

LESSON APPLICATIONS

23. The following running-balance ledger account for Cash is not complete. Using your copy of the account, complete the Dr./Cr. column, and the Balance column.

GENERAL LEDGER

ACCOUNT Cash   NO 100

DATE 19-4		PARTICULARS	PR	DEBIT	CREDIT	DR/CR	BALANCE
Dec.	4	Opening Balance	J44	4320 —		DR	
	4		J44		120 —		
	5		J46	1205 —			
	5		J47	320 —			
	5		J47		592 —		
	6		J48	220 —			
	7		J49		40 —		

24. The running-balance ledger account for Accounts Payable, shown in Figure 4-8, is full. Using the information found on the last line and a new ledger page, show how the balance should be forwarded.

FIGURE 4-8

GENERAL LEDGER

ACCOUNT Accounts Payable						NO 200
DATE 19-3	PARTICULARS	PR	DEBIT	CREDIT	DR CR	BALANCE
Mar. 26		J93	100 —		CR	776 —
27		J93	50 —		CR	726 —

25. The following running-balance ledger account for Accounts Receivable is not correct. List the errors, and state why each is an error.

GENERAL LEDGER

ACCOUNT Accounts Receivable						NO 110
DATE 19-9	PARTICULARS	PR	DEBIT	CREDIT	DR CR	BALANCE
May 4		J83	4320 —		DR	4320 —
6		J85		150 —	CR	4470 —
7		J86	980 —		DR	5450 —
8		J88		120 —	CR	5330 —

26. Summer Playhouse Theatre was started by Winnie DeRocher. The chart of accounts is as follows:

Cash	Theatre Revenue
Subscriptions Receivable	Program Revenue
Supplies	Advertising Expense
Costumes	Rent Expense
Office Equipment	Utilities Expense
Production Equipment	Wages Expense
Accounts Payable	Printing Expense
Short-Term Loan	Miscellaneous Expense
W. DeRocher, Capital	
W. DeRocher, Drawings	

(a) Journalize the transactions for June.
(b) Open a general ledger using the account names given. Establish an appropriate numbering system.
(c) Post to the ledger.

Transactions

June 1 Memo #1: Received $5 000 cash and $2 490 worth of costumes from the owner as the initial investment in the business. (Remember to apply the double-entry principle to this transaction!)

1 Cheque Copy #1: Paid $300 to the *Kingston Whig-Standard* for advertising.

1 Cheque Copy #2: Paid $975 for new costumes for the production of *Anne of Green Gables*.

2 Sales Invoice #1: Sold $4 300 in subscriptions on account to Kingston Cultural Society.

2 Memo #2: Short-term loan of $4 800 from Atlantic Trust.

4 Cheque Copy #3: Paid Bell Canada $145 for the installation of telephones.

5 Cheque Copy #4: Paid $50 to the owner for her personal use.

5 Cheque Copy #5: Paid $1 320 to Fort Henry Printing Ltd. for printing of tickets.

5 Cheque Copy #6: Paid $350 in wages to the office clerk.

8 Cheque Copy #7: Paid $450 for rental of rehearsal hall.

8 Sales Invoice #2: Sold $3 900 in subscriptions on account to Kingston Promotions.

9 Cash Receipt Slip #1: Sold $430 worth of advertising space on the program.

9 Cheque Copy #8: Purchased a telephone answering system, $620, from Electronics World.

10 Purchase Invoice #32-928: Purchased advertising flyers from Fort Henry Printing Ltd., $920.

10 Cash Receipt Slip #2: Sold $520 worth of advertising space on the program.

11 Cheque Copy #9: Paid $200 on account to Fort Henry Printing Ltd.

27. The following is the chart of accounts for Landry Citywide Movers, a firm owned by Terry Landry.

100 Cash
101 Accounts Receivable
102 Furniture and Fixtures
103 Moving Equipment
108 Truck
110 Computer Equipment
115 Computer Software
201 Accounts Payable
202 Bank Loan

301 T. Landry, Capital
302 T. Landry, Drawings
401 Moving Fees
501 Advertising Expense
502 Rent Expense
503 Utilities Expense
504 Wages Expense
505 Truck Expense
506 Miscellaneous Expense

Journalize and post the following transactions.

Transactions

May 1 Memo #1: Received the following from the owner to begin the business: Cash, $22 000; Moving Equipment, $6 780; Truck, $42 000; Bank Loan, $8 000. (Remember to apply the double-entry principle to this transaction!)
1 Cheque Copy #1: Paid for the monthly rental of the office. $870.
1 Cheque Copy #2: Paid $180 to CJOR in Vancouver for advertising.
1 Cheque Copy #3: Paid $200 for the installation of a telephone system.
1 Sales Invoice #1: Moved Tasty Donut Shop to a new location, $900.
3 Cash Sales Slip #1: Moved a piano for an elderly couple, $340.
4 Purchase Invoice #476: Purchased an office desk from Newtown Office Equipment, $420.
5 Cheque Copy #4: Paid $84 for gas for the truck.
7 Purchase Invoice #A879: Purchased a computer and printer for $5 000 and software for $1 500 in order to operate an accounting package from Computer Innovations, total $6 500.
10 Sales Invoice #2: Moved a branch of the Royal Bank of Canada to a new location, $3 200.
11 Cash Receipt Slip #1: Received $500 on account from the Royal Bank.
14 Cash Sales Slip #2: Moved a couple to a new residence, $840.
14 Cash Receipt Slip #2: Received $300 on account from Tasty Donut Shop.
14 Cheque Copy #5: Paid the semi-monthly wages, $900.
14 Cheque Copy #6: Paid the balance owing to Newtown Office Equipment.
14 Cheque Copy #7: Paid Neighbour's Petro-Canada $78 for gas for the truck.
14 Memo #2: Owner makes an additional investment: office chairs and a filing cabinet worth $850, and a computer work centre worth $450.
15 Memo #3: Moved Marge Landry, Terry's mother, across town at no charge. The two movers were paid $140 each, and it cost $35 for the gasoline. In addition, the men got a parking ticket for $78, because they left the truck in a fire zone. (Hint: Think of this as work done for Terry.)

4.3 The Trial Balance Revisited

One of the most important tasks in the accounting process is to take off a trial balance and make sure that it balances. The accountant must balance the books at month end, or else any errors will be carried forward. What happens if the trial balance does not balance? If the proper procedure is followed, finding the error is easier.

Steps in Correcting a Trial Balance

Step 1 Re-add the trial balance in the opposite direction from that first used. Add the following column of numbers on a separate piece of paper:

$$\begin{array}{r} 46 \\ 32 \\ 27 \\ \underline{54} \end{array}$$

Which digit did you start with: the 6 of the 46 at the top of the column, or the 4 of the 54 at the bottom of the column? Some people start at the top of the column, others at the bottom. You probably do it the same way on most occasions. If you start at the top of the columns when adding, when there is an error re-add starting at the bottom. If you start at the bottom of the columns, when there is an error re-add starting at the top. The different combinations of numbers may lead you to your error.

Step 2 Check that the account balances have been correctly transferred from the general ledger to the trial balance.

Step 3 Take the difference between the debit and credit totals, and *examine the difference*. The difference will frequently indicate what type of error has occurred. Examining the difference allows us to use the five shortcut techniques described below.

(a) If there is only one digit in the difference that is not a zero, then it is probable that a calculation error has occurred. This would be indicated by differences such as $0.04, $0.30, $3.00, $60.00, $800.00, and $2 000.00. The only column that is wrong is the one with the digit other than zero in it. Where has the calculation error occurred? If it is not found on the trial balance, it is likely that it was made in the ledger. The accountant would have to check the balance calculations in each of the accounts. More information will be given on that process later.

(b) If the difference is evenly divisible by nine, then a **transposition error** may have occurred. A transposition error means that digits have been reversed. The journal entry in Figure 4-9 has been made for a cash receipt slip in the amount of $6 420.

Transposition error: *this error results when the digits in a number are reversed.*

FIGURE 4-9 A GENERAL JOURNAL ENTRY SHOWING A TRANSPOSITION ERROR

GENERAL JOURNAL

PAGE 34

DATE 1986		PARTICULARS	PR	DEBIT	CREDIT
May	24	Cash		6 420 —	
		Accounts Receivable			6 240 —
		Cash Receipt Slip #33-0113			

Did you notice the transposition error that was made? The amount of $6 420 was entered as a debit, but the 2 and the 4 were reversed in the credit, giving $6 240. If the numbers are posted incorrectly, then the trial balance will not balance. If this was the only error, the debits on the trial balance would be $180 higher than the credits. Divide the difference by nine — it divides evenly, so a transposition error may have occurred.

A transposition error frequently occurs when numbers are being posted. To find the error, the accountant would have to check all postings from the journal to the ledger and the transferring of the balances from the general ledger to the trial balance. However, knowing the type of error gives a focus to the search.

Slide error: this error results from the incorrect placement of the decimal.

(c) If the difference is evenly divisible by nine, a **slide error** may have occurred. A slide error results from the incorrect placement of the decimal. Assume that the following journal entry is made:

GENERAL JOURNAL

PAGE 34

DATE 1986		PARTICULARS	PR	DEBIT	CREDIT
May	25	Cash		6 000 —	
		Accounts Receivable			6 000 —
		Cash Receipt Slip #33-0119			

When posting, the accountant enters the amounts as follows:
            debit to Cash   6 000
            credit to Accounts Receivable   600

If this is the only error, the difference between the debits and credits will be $5 400, a figure which is evenly divisible by nine. A transposition error may have occurred, or a slide error may have occurred. The slide error, like the transposition error, usually occurs when transferring numbers. When examining the journal and ledger, the accountant can look for numbers which could lead to this type of error — numbers which have several zeros in them.

(d) A common error made in posting is to put the entry on the wrong side of the account. To find this type of error, *divide the difference* between the debit and credit totals on the trial balance by two, and look for that number in the ledger. Assume that the following journal entry is made:

GENERAL JOURNAL

PAGE 34

DATE 1986		PARTICULARS	PR	DEBIT	CREDIT
May	26	Accounts Payable		423 –	
		Cash			423 –
		Cheque Copy #133			

When posting, however, the accountant inadvertently writes both amounts as credits. If this is the only error, the credit side of the trial balance will be $846 higher than the debit side.

    credit to Accounts Payable 423
    credit to Cash 423

Divide the difference between the debit total and the credit total by 2: 846 ÷ 2 = 423. Look for that amount in the journal. By checking the two postings, the error should be found.

Remember that if the difference between the debit and credit totals is an odd number, it cannot be this type of error, because odd numbers are not evenly divisible by two.

(e) Another common posting error is leaving out a debit or a credit completely. If the proper posting procedure is followed, such an error should not occur. Assume that the following journal entry has been made:

GENERAL JOURNAL

PAGE 34

DATE 1986		PARTICULARS	PR	DEBIT	CREDIT
May	26	Bank Loan		580 –	
		Cash			580 –
		Monthly payment made on the bank loan.			

When posting, the accountant forgets to post the credit. The debit side of the trial balance will therefore be $580 higher than the credit side. By examining the journal for the amount of $580, the accountant should be able to find the location of the error very quickly.

Step 4 If the error is not located using those three steps, retrace the steps taken prior to taking the trial balance. First, recalculate the balances of the general ledger accounts. The easiest way to do this is to check the final balances by obtaining the debit and credit total for each account. If this is done manually, put pin-totals or pencil footings at the bottom of the entry.

FIGURE 4-10 GENERAL LEDGER ACCOUNT SHOWING PIN-TOTALS OR PENCIL FOOTINGS

GENERAL LEDGER

ACCOUNT Cash   **NO** 100

DATE 1988		PARTICULARS	PR	DEBIT	CREDIT	DR CR	BALANCE
Jan.	2		J133	2900 –		DR	2900 –
	2		J135		200 –	DR	3100 –
	3		J137	920 –		DR	4020 –
	4		J137	500 –		DR	4420 –
	4		J138		80 –	DR	4340 –
	4		J139	805 –		DR	5145 –
				5125 –	280 –		

Using a calculator, each debit can be entered as a +, and each credit as a −. Taking a total will give the account balance. However, a better method when using the calculator is to take a subtotal after each entry. In this way, the specific line on which the error is located will be easily identified. Most electronic calculators automatically show the subtotal.

Step 5 The next step is to determine that the posting was done correctly. This process will obviously be time-consuming. As each item is checked, put a mark beside both the amount in the journal and the amount in the ledger. In this way, the same amount in the journal or the ledger will not be used twice. When you are finished, examine the journal and ledger to see if there are any amounts without a mark beside them. That should be the source of the error.

Step 6 If the error still has not been found, the journal should be checked to ensure that debits equal credits for each transaction.

Step 7 If all the work has been rechecked and the error has still not been found, the material should be set aside. Come back to it at a later date.

Summary of Correcting Procedures

1. Re-add the trial balance in the opposite direction.
2. Check the transfer of balances from the general ledger to the trial balance.
3. Take the difference between the debit and credit totals, and apply the five shortcut techniques.
4. Recalculate the account balances.
5. Check the posting from the journal to the ledger.
6. Check the journalizing to ensure that debits equal credits for every transaction.

Correcting Errors in the General Ledger

One of the most frustrating occurrences in locating errors is to find that the error was the first amount in the account, making all subsequent balances for the account incorrect. Does this mean that, when doing the accounting by hand, all the balances have to be changed? What if another error is found in the same account? There won't be space to change all the balances, especially if they have been done in ink. The following technique shows a much easier method of making the correction.

In the account shown in Figure 4-10, the pencil footings are shown, and they have a difference of $4 845. The balance showing in the account is $5 145. Obviously an error has occurred. A check shows that there are errors on the second and fourth lines.

FIGURE 4-11 GENERAL LEDGER ACCOUNT SHOWING CORRECTIONS FOR TWO DATES

GENERAL LEDGER

ACCOUNT Cash							NO 100	
DATE 1988		PARTICULARS	PR	DEBIT	CREDIT	DR/CR	BALANCE	
Jan.	2		J133	2 900 -		DR	2 900 -	
	2	Corrected on Jan. 5/88	J135		200 -	DR	3 100 -	
	3		J137	920 -		DR	4 020 -	
	4	Corrected on Jan. 5/88	J137	500 -		DR	4 420 -	
	4		J138		80 -	DR	4 340 -	
	4		J139	805 -		DR	5 145 -	
	5	Correction for Jan. 2				DR	4 745 -	
	5	Correction for Jan. 4				DR	4 845 -	
				5 125 -	280 -			

Rather than change all the balances in the Balance column, a two-step procedure is used in manual accounting. First, in the Particulars column of the line on which the error occurred, a notation is made stating that the error has been corrected and giving the date of the correction. This is to eliminate the possibility of someone correcting the error a second time. Secondly, a correction is made to correct the balance column. It is not necessary to correct all the account balances, for it is only the final balance that is entered on the trial balance. The corrected ledger account will then look like Figure 4-11.

Correcting Errors in the General Journal

If an error has been made in the general journal, the correcting procedure depends upon whether the entry has been posted.

(a) If the entry has *not* been posted, the correction can be made to the original entry by crossing it out with a ruler, and writing in the correct account name and/or amount. (See Figure 4-12.)

May 10   Cash Receipt Slip #33-0092: Received $430 on account from M. Nanjappa.

FIGURE 4-12 CORRECTION OF A JOURNAL ENTRY THAT HAS NOT BEEN POSTED

GENERAL JOURNAL

PAGE 34

DATE 1986		PARTICULARS	PR	DEBIT	CREDIT
May	10	Cash		430 —	
		~~Accounts Payable~~ Accounts Receivable			430 —
		Cash Receipt Slip #33-0092, M. Nanjappa			

An alternate procedure to the above is to cancel the original entry by making a journal entry reversing the original debits and credits, and then preparing a correct new journal entry.

(b) If the journal entry has been posted, a correcting entry is required because the ledger is also incorrect. When the correcting journal entry is posted, the ledger will then also be corrected.

May 10   Cash Sales Slip #99-0242: Received $250 in cash for software lessons.

FIGURE 4-13 CORRECTION OF A JOURNAL ENTRY THAT HAS BEEN POSTED

GENERAL JOURNAL

PAGE 34

DATE 1986		PARTICULARS	PR	DEBIT	CREDIT
May	10	Accounts Receivable	120	250 —	
		Cash	100		250 —
		Cash Sales Slip #99-0242			

On May 17 the error is detected. The entry should have been a debit to Cash and a credit to Software Lessons. The first step is to note at the original entry that the error has been corrected, and the date of the correction. (The blank line between journal entries can be used if there is not enough room.) This is to prevent someone from correcting the error a second time, later, not knowing that it has been corrected.

FIGURE 4-14 NOTATION SHOWING DATE ON WHICH ENTRY WAS CORRECTED

GENERAL JOURNAL

PAGE 34

DATE 1986		PARTICULARS	PR	DEBIT	CREDIT
May	10	Accounts Receivable	120	250 —	
		Cash	100		250 —
		Cash Sales Slip #99-0242			
		*Corrected on May 17/86			

The next step is to make the correcting entry.

FIGURE 4-15 CORRECTING ENTRY FOR MAY 10

GENERAL JOURNAL

PAGE 34

DATE 1986		PARTICULARS	PR	DEBIT	CREDIT
May	17	Cash		500 —	
		Software Lessons			250 —
		Accounts Receivable			250 —
		Correction of error on May 10,			
		Cash Sales Slip #99-0242			

Examine Figure 4-15. Notice that Cash is debited $500: $250 is to cancel the incorrect credit posting, and $250 is to enter the original correct amount as a debit. The $250 credit to Software Lessons is to enter the original correct amount in that account. The $250 credit to Accounts Receivable is to cancel the incorrect debit to that account.

Again, in order to correct the error it is possible to use two entries: one to cancel the incorrect entry, and one to make the correct entry.

The Accounting Cycle

The same accounting steps are carried out in each fiscal year. For this reason, the steps are referred to as the **accounting cycle**. You have now learned some of the steps in the accounting cycle. More will be added in later chapters. To date, the cycle is as shown below. The time during the fiscal period when the steps are done is also shown, on the assumption that the firm prepares quarterly statements. The source of the information needed to complete each step is shown in the final column.

Accounting cycle: the accounting steps carried out in a fiscal year.

ACCOUNTING CYCLE FOR QUARTERLY STATEMENTS

Step	When Done	Source of Information
Journalize	During the month	Source documents
Post	During the month	General journal
Trial Balance	Month end	General ledger
Income Statement	End of fiscal period	Trial balance
Balance Sheet	End of fiscal period	Trial balance

LESSON REVIEW

28. Why is it important that the general ledger balance at the end of each month?

29. What should be the first step in correcting a trial balance?

30. Why is it important to closely examine the difference between the debits and credits of a trial balance that does not balance?

31. Distinguish between a transposition error and a slide error.

32. A $500 amount is put on the credit side of an account instead of on the debit side. What amount must be put on the debit side in order to correct the error? Explain your answer.

33. Describe the correcting process for errors made in a general journal.

34. What must be noted concerning errors made in journal entries before they are corrected? Why?

35. Summarize the steps in the accounting cycle that we have studied to date.

LESSON APPLICATIONS

36. The following numbers indicate the difference between the debit total and the credit total for various trial balances. After examining each number and applying the shortcut techniques, indicate the most probable type of error and provide reasons for your opinion.
    (a) $4 000.00 (b) $354.23 (c) $4 988.07
    (d) $114.33 (e) $242.22

37. The following numbers indicate the difference between the debit total and the credit total for various trial balances. After examining each number and applying the shortcut techniques, indicate the most probable type of error and provide reasons for your opinion.
    (a) $453.27 (b) $0.01 (c) $360.00
    (d) $700.00 (e) $45.00

38. On May 23 it was found that the following general ledger account had been balanced incorrectly. Using your copy of the account, find the errors, and follow proper correction procedures.

GENERAL LEDGER

ACCOUNT Accounts Receivable   **NO** 121

DATE 19-4		PARTICULARS	PR	DEBIT	CREDIT	DR/CR	BALANCE
May	19		J33	4570 —		DR	4570 —
	19		J35		125 —	DR	4455 —
	20		J36	340 —		DR	4795 —
	20		J36	553 —		DR	5338 —
	21		J37		64 —	DR	5274 —

39. On March 20 it was found that the following general ledger account had been balanced incorrectly. Using your copy of the account, find the errors, and follow proper correction procedures.

GENERAL LEDGER

ACCOUNT Accounts Payable   **NO** 321

DATE 19-4		PARTICULARS	PR	DEBIT	CREDIT	DR/CR	BALANCE
Mar.	14		J79		4658 —	CR	4658 —
	15		J79		125 —	CR	4783 —
	15		J80	125 —		CR	4663 —
	16		J81	319 —		CR	4340 —
	17		J82		537 —	CR	4877 —

Chapter 4: The General Journal

40. On July 28 it was found that some of the following transactions had been entered into the general journal incorrectly. Using your copy of the journal, find the errors, and follow proper correction procedures.

July 21   Cash Receipt Slip #32: Received $400 on account from N. Bartholomew.
22   Purchase Invoice #44: Purchased a $900 fax machine from The Fax Connection.
23   Cheque Copy #87: Paid the owner $750 for personal use.
24   Sales Invoice #98: Performed an accounting service on account for Delcor Farms, $200.
25   Voucher #21: The owner invested an automobile in the business, $14 500.
26   Cheque Copy #88: Paid the monthly rent, $1 200.

GENERAL JOURNAL

PAGE 39

DATE 19-2		PARTICULARS	PR	DEBIT	CREDIT
July	21	Cash	100	400 –	
		Accounts Receivable	120		400 –
		N. Bartholomew, Cash Receipt Slip #32			
	22	Accounts Payable	200	900 –	
		Office Equipment	140		900 –
		Fax machine, Purchase Invoice #44			
	23	S. Tanchuk, Drawings	320	75 –	
		Cash	100		750 –
		Personal use, Cheque Copy #87			
	24	Accounts Payable	210	200 –	
		Fees Income	400		200 –
		Accounting service, Sales Invoice #98			
	25	Automobile	150	14 500 –	
		S. Tanchuk, Capital	300		14 500 –
		Investment, Voucher #21			
	26	Rent Expense		2 100 –	
		Cash			1 200 –
		One month, Cheque Copy #88			

41. On May 23 it was found that some of the following transactions had been entered into the general journal incorrectly. Using your copy of the journal, find the errors, and follow proper correction procedures.

May 16 Voucher #54: Received $5 000 from the owner as an additional investment.
 17 Cheque Copy #38: Paid the weekly wages, $3 200.
 18 Sales Invoice #229: Performed management services for J. Crosier, $470.
 19 Purchase Invoice #24: Auto repairs on account, $193, from Ted's Garage.
 20 Purchase Invoice #22: Purchased $34 000 worth of new computers from Dell Computers.
 21 Cheque Copy #39: Paid $1 200 on account to D. Matte.

FIGURE 4-16

GENERAL JOURNAL

PAGE 113

DATE 19-2		PARTICULARS	PR	DEBIT	CREDIT
May	16	Cash	100	5 000 —	
		M. Chipper, Capital	300		5 000 —
		Owner investment, Voucher #54			
	17	Wages Expense	590	3 200 —	
		Cash	100		2 300 —
		Weekly wages, Cheque Copy #38			
	18	Accounts Payable	200	470 —	
		Fees Earned	400		470 —
		J. Crosier, Sales Invoice #229			
	19	Automobile Expense	550	139 —	
		Accounts Payable	210		193 —
		Maintenance, Purchase Invoice #24			
	20	Office Equipment	140	34 000 —	
		Accounts Payable	210		3 400 —
		Computer equipment, Purchase Invoice #22			
	21	Accounts Receivable	120	1 200 —	
		Cash			1 200 —
		D. Matte, Cheque Copy #39			

CHAPTER REVIEW AND SKILL DEVELOPMENT

Accounting Principles and Concepts

- **Source documents** are all first entered into a journal.

- **Posting** is the transferring of information. This transfer is usually done from the journal to the ledger.

- An **audit trail** allows a person to trace the steps back to the original source document.

- The **correction of errors** is an important step in the accounting process.

- A **trial balance** is prepared at frequent intervals (monthly) to check the accuracy of the journalizing and posting.

- The **accounting cycle** refers to the accounting steps taken during the accounting year.

Knowing the Terms

For each of the following statements, indicate the term being defined.
(a) A book of accounts.
(b) The first entry in a journal, to start the business.
(c) To put the decimal in the wrong place in a number.
(d) The process of entering a transaction in a journal.
(e) The book of original entry.
(f) A journal entry with more than one debit and/or credit.
(g) The reversal of digits in a number.
(h) The first entry in any account.
(i) Book in which transactions are recorded from the source document.
(j) The result of procedures that allows the tracing of data back to the source document.

Food for Thought

1. A bookkeeper did not believe it was important that the debit be placed first when journalizing. He suggested that putting the credit first would make no difference, since both the debit amount and the credit amount will be posted. Criticize his viewpoint.

2. The accountant of a large business has decided to put off journalizing and posting of source documents for a number of days. What problems might this cause?

3. An accountant decides to complete the posting process by posting all the cash items first, then all the accounts receivable and so on. What advantage is there to this procedure? What disadvantage is there?

4. Some accountants merely use a check mark in the journal to indicate that an amount has been posted. What is the disadvantage to this method of cross-referencing? Others put a check mark in the ledger. What is the disadvantage to this method of cross-referencing?

5. An accountant posted data from the journal to the ledger, and then went back and entered all the account numbers in the journal at once. Criticize this procedure.

6. Two bookkeepers worked at an appliance repair service, where they rotated performing the accounting tasks. The auditor found many errors in the journalizing. What procedure should have been followed in order to know which person was responsible for which errors?

7. A bookkeeper did not think that it was overly important to be accurate in journalizing and posting. She stated that if the difference between the debit and credit totals on a trial balance was small, she would ignore it. If the difference was large, she would spend time looking for it. Criticize her viewpoint.

8. A firm that prepared quarterly statements only took off trial balances every quarter. Criticize this procedure.

9. After studying the first four chapters of accounting, a student remarked that the most important skill learned so far is the ability to analyze transactions. Explain why this is true.

10. A customer returns to the store with a copy of her sales invoice. The date and invoice number, however, have been torn off. Explain how the accountant should proceed in order to find the trail back to the original source document on file in the business.

Organizing

1. We have studied four steps in the accounting cycle. Draw a circular diagram to illustrate the steps in the cycle. Draw a picture at each step of the cycle to illustrate the process carried out, and label each of the steps.

2. Summarize the steps that are to be followed in the correction of a trial balance.

FIGURE 4-17

GENERAL JOURNAL
PAGE 295

DATE 19—		PARTICULARS	PR	DEBIT	CREDIT
July	22	Cash		4500 90	
		Janitorial Services			4500 90
	23	Office Equipment		2540 80	
		Accounts Payable			2540 80
	24	Rent Expense		1850 —	
		Cash			1850 —
	25	Accounts Receivable		980 —	
		Janitorial Services			980 —
	25	Computer Equipment		4600 —	
		K. Stockwell, Capital			4600 —
	26	Cash		7690 —	
		Accounts Receivable			7690 —
	28	K. Stockwell, Drawings		4500 —	
		Cash			4500 —

Applications

1. Figure 4-17 is a partially completed journal for Lethbridge Janitorial Service, owned by K. Stockwell. For each transaction, you are to
   (a) indicate the source document that would have provided the information for the entry, and
   (b) give a brief description of the entry.

2. Derry's Office Temporaries of Saskatoon is a firm started by Paul Derry. It provides short-term office help. The accounts established by the firm are as follows:

100 Cash	400 Placement Income
110 Accounts Receivable	500 Training Expense
120 Supplies	510 Utilities Expense
130 Equipment	520 Rent Expense
140 Automobile	530 Advertising Expense
200 Accounts Payable	540 Courier Expense
220 Bank Loan	550 Miscellaneous Expense
300 P. Derry, Capital	
310 P. Derry, Drawings	

   (a) Journalize the transactions below. Note that source documents are not indicated.
   (b) Post to the general ledger.
   (c) Take off a formal trial balance on October 31.

Transactions

Oct. 1 Received $15 000 cash and $21 000 worth of word processors as an investment by the owner.
   1 Paid the monthly rent expense, $1 400.
   2 Paid $975 to CFQC for advertising.
   2 Paid legal fees for establishment of the firm, $350.
   3 Purchased a municipal licence for operating the business, $120.
   4 Borrowed $27 900 from the bank.
   5 Purchased $18 000 worth of word processors on account from Superior Office Technology.
   8 Purchased an automobile, $18 900, from Buchwald Motors Ltd. A cash payment of $4 000 was made, with the balance borrowed from the bank.
   9 Paid the teachers who train the temporaries, $1 400.
   10 Purchased accounting forms on account, $890, from Stationery in Motion.
   10 Received $2 400 cash from Johnson's Tax Services for use of temporaries.
   11 Negotiated a $1 000 reduction in the price of the automobile through the owner of the dealership.
   12 Purchased a $4 500 fax machine on account from Data Max Corp.
   16 Paid the teachers who train the temporaries, $1 400.
   20 Paid $320 in courier fees.
   21 Received $1 980 as a fee for use of temporaries.
   25 Paid $300 on the bank loan.
   26 Purchased $4 300 worth of computer tables on account from Global Office Outfitters.
   28 Paid $220 for installation of the telephone.
   31 Paid $400 to the owner for personal use.
   31 Paid the teachers who train the temporaries, $1 400.

3. The trial balance in Figure 4-18 was prepared for Gambhir's Management Consultants. Using the information provided in the T-accounts,
   (a) find the errors on the trial balance;
   (b) number the error and explain the type of error;
   (c) prepare a corrected trial balance.
   Assume that the information given in the T-accounts is correct, and that any T-accounts not given are correct.

FIGURE 4-18

Gambhir's Management Consultants
Trial Balance
October 31, 19-4

	Debit	Credit
Cash	$ 21 060.86	
Martin Barton	1 608.00	
D.E. Reid		622.61
D.C. Smyth		199.88
Supplies	4 776.11	
Land	1 600.00	
Building	62 000.00	
Furniture	4 766.21	
Carlyle Equipment Ltd.		1 200.00
D. Smith		116.16
D.E. Smythe		247.23
Bank Loan		12 000.00
Mortgage Payable		26 000.00
T. Gambhir, Capital		56 987.29
Fees Earned		32 000.00
Wages Expense	14 500.00	
General Expense	1 200.00	
	$111 711.06	$129 173.29

GENERAL LEDGER

Cash		100
dr.	cr.	
6 462.61	4 268.31	
2 666.56		
16 300.00		

Martin Barton		110
dr.	cr.	
1 680.00		

D.E. Reid		111
dr.	cr.	
622.16		

D.C. Smyth		112
dr.	cr.	
1 998.80		

Supplies		120
dr.	cr.	
4 776.11		

Land		130
dr.	cr.	
16 000.00		

Building		140
dr.	cr.	
62 000.00		

Furniture		150
dr.	cr.	
4 666.21		

Carlyle Equipment Ltd.		200
dr.	cr.	
	12 000.00	

D. Smith		201
dr.	cr.	
	247.16	

D.E. Smythe		202
dr.	cr.	
	116.23	

D. Reade		203
dr.	cr.	
	62.46	

Bank Loan		210
dr.	cr.	
	1 200.00	

Mortgage Payable		220
dr.	cr.	
	26 000.00	

T. Gambhir, Capital		300
dr.	cr.	
	56 978.29	

Applications — Comprehensive
The Accounting Cycle to Date
The Nordic Kennels is starting business, and will board dogs, as well as groom them. The accounts for the firm are as follows:

Cash	V. Divincenzo, Capital
Accounts Receivable	V. Divincenzo, Drawings
Office Supplies	Kennel Fees
Kennels	Advertising Expense
Automobile	Utility Expense
Building	Wages Expense
Land	Automobile Expense
Accounts Payable	Cleaning Expense
Bank Loan	Miscellaneous Expense
Mortgage Payable	

(a) Open a ledger using the chart of accounts and provide appropriate account numbers.
(b) Journalize each of the following transactions.
(c) Post to the ledger.
(d) Prepare a formal trial balance.
(e) Prepare an income statement for the two weeks ending June 14.
(f) Prepare a balance sheet as at June 14.

Transactions

June 1 Cash Receipt Slip #1: Received $48 000 from the owner as an initial investment.

1 Voucher #1: Purchased an existing kennel operation for $120 000. The land was valued at $40 000, the kennels at $20 000, and the building at $60 000. A $90 000 mortgage was arranged, and the balance was paid in cash. Cheque Copy #1.

2 Cheque Copy #2: Paid $320 for advertising in the *Vancouver Province*.

2 Cheque Copy #3: Paid $430 for an opening day reception.

5 Cash Sales Slips #1-#5: Cash sales for the day were $420.

5 Purchase Invoice #299-2: Purchased a new truck from Keon Auto Sales Ltd., paying $4 000 cash; financed the balance of $7 000 over two years with the bank.

6 Sales Invoice #1: Sale on account was $1 200 to Civic Security Services.

6 Cash Sales Slips #6-#14: Cash sales for the day were $769.

7 Purchase Invoice #554: Purchased $427 worth of office supplies on account from Willson Stationers Ltd.

9 Sales Invoice #2: Sale on account was $997 to Shalomar Show Dogs.

9 Cheque Copy #4: Weekly wages were $320.

10 Cheque Copy #5: Paid $228 to B.C. Telephone for installation of the telephone.

10 Cheque Copy #6: Paid $427 on account to Willson Stationers Ltd.

10 Cash Sales Slips #15-#24: Cash sales were $1 745.

14 Sales Invoice #3: Sale on account was $2 300 to Province of British Columbia.

14 Cheque Copy #7: Paid $400 on the bank loan.

14 Cheque Copy #8: Made the first mortgage payment, $900.

14 Cheque Copy #9: Paid $320 to the *Vancouver Province* for advertising.

14 Cheque Copy #10: Paid $12 to send a package by Arrowspeed Courier.

14 Cheque Copy #11: Paid $1 305 for a car telephone from Radio Shack.

14 Cheque Copy #12: Paid $140 for legal fees to start the business.

Focussing — The Trial Balance

The following unrelated errors were made by a bookkeeper while journalizing and posting some transactions. For each error, indicate
(a) the amount of the difference, if any, that will result between the debits and credits on a trial balance;
(b) the shortcut method that could be used to find the error.
  (i) A purchase invoice in the amount of $500 for the purchase of equipment was recorded as a debit to Supplies, $500, and a credit to Accounts Payable, $500.
  (ii) A cash receipt of $300 was recorded as a debit to Cash, $300, and a credit to Accounts Payable, $300.
  (iii) A sales invoice of $250 was recorded as a debit to Accounts Receivable, $250, and a credit to Fees Earned, $520.
  (iv) A voucher for a payment to the owner of $4 000 for personal use was recorded as a debit to P. Ivay, Drawings, $400, and a credit to Cash, $4 000.
  (v) A $200 cheque issued to Leong's Camera Shop on account was recorded as a debit to Accounts Payable, $200, and a debit to Cash, $200.

Evaluate and Assess — The Books of Account

Linda Stachuk, the bookkeeper for a small engine repair shop, had taken several accounting courses while in high school. Her employer, Walter Worden, relied completely on Linda's knowledge of accounting for he had no previous experience in the area.

When she started at her position, Linda was able to keep up with her tasks. However, as the business grew, she found it was more difficult to complete the tasks that were part of her job. To save time, Linda decided to enter transactions from source documents directly into the general ledger. She would *not* use a journal. For reference purposes, she would enter the number of the source document in the Particulars column of the ledger accounts affected by a transaction. She could, therefore, refer back to the source document if there was any problem concerning the transaction. She also would enter the account numbers to which the transaction was posted in the top right-hand corner of the source document. She did this to ensure that she made a posting to the account(s) that should be debited and to the account(s) that should be credited.

Evaluate the system used by Linda. Does it provide the necessary components of an accounting system as we have studied it to date?

Synthesize and Conclude

Statistics indicate that in the late 1980s over forty-four percent of all working Canadians were employed in enterprises small enough to be managed by the owner. On average, these companies employed 5.5 workers, and one out of five firms had no employees except the owner or owners. Two out of three paid workers in such operations were classified as general and unskilled or clerical workers.
(a) What types of businesses would be small firms? What types of businesses would not lend themselves to being small firms?
(b) Why are small businesses such an important part of any nation's economy?
(c) Why would most of the employees in a small business be classified as general and unskilled or clerical workers?
(d) Many small businesses are not able to afford their own bookkeeper or accountant. How do these businesses complete the bookkeeping and accounting functions?

Accounting At Work

Chris Earle
Certified Management Accountant

Chris Earle holds the position of Manager, Cost Distribution with Alberta Government Telephone (AGT). As a management accountant he works to ensure that AGT's resources are managed creatively, competitively, and profitably. One aspect of his job is to determine what part of the company's revenue must be paid to other companies. This is necessary because those calls that originate in Alberta and go to other parts of the country use the equipment of other phone companies. The revenue that AGT collects has to be shared with those companies.

A second aspect of Earle's job is the setting up of a management information system. This will allow managers within the company to make decisions about products or services that look like they have potential. "The system is very results oriented," said Earle. "It allows us to better predict the impact of changes we make." The third part of his job is to set up a reporting system that satisfies the federal government's regulations for the telecommunications industry.

The experiences that Earle had in the telecommunications industry prepared him for his three challenges. After he graduated from university with a commerce degree, he explored several career opportunities and eventually chose management accounting with a firm that manufactured electronic components and telecommunications equipment. As part of his job he had to work towards a professional accounting designation, and he chose the Certified Management Accountant (C.M.A.) program. As he completed his courses and gained experience in the fast-growing company, his personal marketability improved. Over the years he moved to other companies in the telecommunications field, each time taking positions that expanded his depth of experience or gave him additional skills. He moved to AGT because changes in government regulations allowed many new players into the telecommunications field. "Competition has increased tremendously," Earle explained. "There are real opportunities for aggressive companies, and people. I've made sure that I have the right balance of training and experience to move into top jobs."

One of the key skills of a management accountant is to be proactive — to make changes happen instead of responding to change. To Earle, this means that managers have to be flexible, able to apply concepts and principles when the rules are unclear. "That," said Earle, "is the mark of a good management accountant."

(a) What is C.M.A.? What are the three main aspects of Chris's job?
(b) Why does one's personal marketability increase?
(c) What advantage is there to gaining experience in a number of different work environments, as Chris did?
(d) What does it mean to be "proactive"?

There are two types of accountants: public accountants, and management accountants. Our study of a chartered accountant in the previous chapter was of a public accountant, for he or she offers a service to the public, primarily in the areas of auditing and taxation. A management accountant is one who deals with financial information to improve the profitability of a business. These accountants are therefore involved in management.

To enter the C.M.A. program, a university degree is required. The C.M.A. program is taken under the direction of the Society of Management Accountants. The following are the requirements to complete the program, as of 1991.

- completion of a professional accreditation examination, Part I; this examination is to ensure that all candidates have the necessary knowledge base required for entry into the C.M.A. Professional Program;

- a Professional Program, which consists of
  (a) management and professionalism studies, consisting of independent study, group sessions of 8 to 10 hours in length, and weekend residential sessions.
  (b) a professional accreditation examination, Part II.
  (c) practical experience of at least 24 months within a management accounting environment that must be approved and monitored by the Society.

The advertisement on page 171 is for a person who possibly has a C.M.A. designation.

(a) What firm is the position with?
(b) Indicate which of the responsibilities require supervisory skills.
(c) What skills other than accounting are required for the position?

We have an immediate opening for a

SENIOR ACCOUNTANT

RESPONSIBILITIES
- supervises a staff of two accounting clerks
- prepares and analyzes financial statements for outlet and administration centres
- analyzes balance sheet accounts
- controls banking
- attends and controls physical inventories at corporate locations as required
- assists with preparation of annual plan data

REQUIREMENTS
- enrolment in Level 4 C.G.A./C.M.A. program and completion of at least two Level 4 courses
- three years' accounting experience plus one year supervisory experience
- working knowledge of Lotus 1-2-3 and dBase III
- excellent organizational, supervisory, and problem-solving skills
- strong analytical skills with ability to work under pressure and meet deadlines

CONDITIONS
- full compensation and benefits package
- based in our Ottawa office

Qualified candidates should submit their résumés in confidence to:

Human Resource Department
Starks International
50 Fasken Dr.
Rexdale, ON
M9W 1L5

The addresses for limited companies can be obtained from a number of sources. The products which they sell may have the address on them. There may be a local office in your area, so the company will be listed in the telephone book. The *Financial Post* publishes a directory that may be available in your school or local library.

Keep the annual report for information purposes.

2. Communication — Listening Skills

Listening is an important communication skill.

(a) In groups, brainstorm to obtain a list of characteristics that make a good listener.

(b) The controller of a business indicated to Mark that he needed to work on his listening skills, because many of the instructions given to him were not followed. In groups, brainstorm strategies by which Mark could improve his listening skills.

3. Problem Solving: Employee Supervision

Lori Hansen is the accountant for Juneja's Paint Supplies. She is in charge of a department of five junior accountants. Martino, one of the male junior accountants, is continually talking with Ramona, a female employee of the firm. He frequently leaves his work station in order to talk with her. Martino keeps asking her out, and makes reference to her dress and figure. Ramona has finally complained to Hansen that she finds Martino's conversations harassing.

Both Martino and Ramona have worked for the firm for six years. In both cases their work has been excellent.

(a) In groups, brainstorm to develop ways in which Hansen could handle the problem.

(b) Prepare a memo to Martino indicating the nature of the problem, and what action the firm intends to take concerning it.

Business Career Skills

1. Communication — The Business Letter

Prepare a diagram to show the various parts of a business letter. Ensure that your format is correct. Write a letter to a business requesting a copy of its most recent annual report.

COMPUTER ACCOUNTING
NO BUSINESS THAT CAN AFFORD A PERSONAL COMPUTER SHOULD BE PREPARING ACCOUNTS MANUALLY.

Businesses and organizations that are still keeping their accounting books manually now find the time has come to take the plunge and convert to a **computerized accounting package**. However, caution should be exercised! Accounting packages are not like word processors and spreadsheets.

First of all, accounting packages are larger and more complicated, and, consequently, more expensive than the simple applications packages. Because of this complexity, accounting packages are often sold in a number of modules: general ledger, accounts receivable, accounts payable, and so on. Another difference is that your accounting software deals with the lifeblood of a business. A problem with a word processor or a spreadsheet will probably cause inconvenience and frustration; a problem with your accounting software could mean chaos.

Choosing accounting software, then, is a big step for any business, and along with choosing the software comes the necessity of very carefully planning the system that accounting personnel will set up with it.

The thing a computer does best is crunching numbers. So it's no wonder that one of the primary uses of the machines has been in accounting — which is, after all, mainly a matter of numbers. Choosing an accounting software package, as has been stated earlier, is a very important decision. Not only does it concern one of the most vital aspects of any business, but it also deals with a piece of software that people in the organization will be spending a lot of time with. It is, therefore, important that the selected software be easy to use, yet powerful enough to meet the needs of the business.

The accounting software now on the market can be divided into several levels, although it is difficult to know just where to draw the category lines. There are, for example, very simple programs suitable for very small businesses and one-person professional offices, or even home use. There are personal computer accounting packages developed specifically for business, which vary in price and power. And finally, there are extremely sophisticated, powerful systems that still require mainframe computers to run them.

Your first exposure to an accounting exercise utilizing an accounting software package will involve using the **general ledger module** only.

Exercises

LINDA SCHUMAN, DDS

INSTRUCTIONAL OBJECTIVES
You have completed the study of the individual topics involved in the first four steps of the accounting cycle using a manual accounting system (analyzing source documents, journalizing, posting, and preparing a trial balance). You are now ready to learn how this process is handled on a microcomputer system.

Upon completion of this exercise, you will be able to:

1. Load your accounting software into the computer.

2. Set up and access accounting data files for a sole proprietorship, service-oriented business.

3. Enter transactions into a computer using the general ledger module of the accounting program.

4. Display or print accounting transactions.

5. Print a trial balance.

6. Exit the accounting software program.

INFORMATION ABOUT THE BUSINESS ENTERPRISE

Linda Schuman, DDS, recently graduated from the UBC Dental School and decided to establish her practice in Richmond, BC, a suburb south of Vancouver. She located suitable office space at 900 Park Place, Richmond, BC V3Z 1X4. She has engaged you to set up and perform the accounting functions for her new dental practice, using a microcomputer and accounting software suitable for her professional practice.

SOLUTION

Your first step will be to make a list of accounts to form a preliminary chart of accounts. HINT: Think of the account titles that a dental practice would probably use in recording transactions common to this form of business operation. Have your chart of accounts approved by your teacher before proceeding.

Now record the company name and other data before making your program ready for journalizing. NOTE: These steps will vary according to the software package being used.

After journalizing the first month's transactions assigned to you by your teacher, you will print your general journal and a trial balance to determine if your journalizing is correct. Once your journalizing is correct, you will then print out all the ledger accounts and submit all printouts or complete an audit test.

Outlined below are steps to be followed in completing this exercise if you are using *ACCPAC Bedford Integrated Accounting* software. If you are using another software package, your teacher will give further instructions on how to proceed.

LESSON 1 — GETTING STARTED

The accounting application software you will be using is called *ACCPAC Bedford Integrated Accounting* (Educational Version). It is published by Computer Associates, Vancouver, BC. Other accounting software available includes *ACCPAC, DAC-Accounting*, and *BPI*.

Before the IBM (or compatible) microcomputer can be used, you must load the operating system. The brand name of the operating system you are going to use could be called MS-DOS or PC-DOS; MS-DOS is published by Microsoft Corporation and PC-DOS is published by International Business Machines (IBM).

The operating system will wake up your computer equipment and then wait for you to tell it what you would like to do with the computer.

To load the operating system, use the procedure outlined below:

1. Put the operating system diskette in drive A.

2. Turn on your computer system's printer, monitor, and system unit.

3. Your computer will do a check on itself and then load the operating system from the operating system diskette that you put in drive A.

4. The operating system may ask for the current date; if it does, key in the date using this format: mm-dd-yy

5. The operating system may then ask for the current time; if it does, key in the time in this format: hh:mm

6. You know that the operating system is finished loading when the last line on your monitor is the operating system prompt:

A > ←———————— Operating System Prompt

LESSON 2 — DATA DISKETTE PREPARATION

(Skip this lesson if your data diskette has already been formatted.)

Diskettes come from a computer retailer unprepared to accept data. So that you can store information on the data diskette you are going to use, it must be FORMATTED.

1. Ensure your operating system diskette is in drive A.

2. Put your data diskette in drive B.

3. After the operating system prompt, key in the command for formatting a data diskette:

   A>**format b:/v**   press [**ENTER**]

   You will now see a message on your screen: Insert new diskette for drive B: and strike [**ENTER**] when ready.
   Ensure that your data diskette is in drive B and then press [**ENTER**].

4. The computer will begin to format the data diskette that you have in drive B. The light on disk drive B will remain on until the formatting process is complete.

5. Soon you will be told the format is complete and you will be asked for a volume label. Key in your last name (no longer than 11 characters) and then press [**ENTER**].

6. You will be asked if you wish to format another diskette; key in **n** and press [**ENTER**].

LESSON 3 — CREATING A FILE DIRECTORY ON YOUR DATA DISKETTE

Since you will use your data diskette for more than one exercise, you will need to use file directories to help *Bedford* locate the different electronic company files. In this lesson you are going to create a file directory for Linda Schuman, DDS.

1. Make sure your data diskette is in drive B.

2. After the operating system prompt, key in the command for creating a directory (md) and then key in the name you wish to give the file, e.g., the first letter of each name of the business:

   A>**md b:\lsm**   press [**ENTER**]

3. Now list the files and file directories on your data diskette to ensure you created the file directory for Linda Schuman:

   A>**dir b:**   press [**ENTER**]

LESSON 4 — LOADING *BEDFORD*

You are now ready to load the *ACCPAC Bedford Integrated Accounting* program. Follow the procedure outlined below.

1. Remove the operating system diskette from drive A and replace it with the *Bedford* program diskette.

2. Ensure that your data diskette is in drive B.

3. Immediately after the operating system prompt, issue the command to load *Bedford*:

   A>**bedford**   press [**ENTER**]

4. *Bedford* will load and wait for the name of the file directory where you wish to store the electronic company files:

   Company: ....d:\[path]

5. Key in the name you gave the file directory on your data diskette where the electronic company files will be stored for Linda Schuman:

   Key In **b:\lsm**   press [**ENTER**]

6. *Bedford* will then ask if you wish to create a set of company files in the lsm file directory. Press [**ENTER**] to confirm.

NOTE: With the educational version of *Bedford*, you cannot use the current date. For that reason, you will use the date provided by your teacher.

You will be prompted to key in three dates.

Start	**0901yy**	press [**ENTER**]
Conversion	**0901yy**	press [**ENTER**]
Finish	**0930yy**	press [**ENTER**]

As this is a new business, the **Start** and **Conversion** dates are one and the same.

You will then be presented with the *Bedford* main menu:

FIGURE 4-19 THE *BEDFORD* MAIN MENU

LESSON 6 — EXITING *BEDFORD*

Another important step is to learn how to exit a program.

Exit *Bedford* by doing the following:

1. Move the block cursor over the **SYSTEM** module by using the [**RIGHT ARROW**] key.

2. Choose the **SYSTEM** module by pressing [**DOWN ARROW**].

3. [**DOWN ARROW**] to the **Finish**.

4. Choose the **Finish** command by pressing [**RIGHT ARROW**]. Your work is automatically saved and then you leave the program. The A> appears on your screen.

LESSON 5 — SAVING YOUR WORK

You are *now* going to learn how to save your work, since saving it is very important.

1. Move the block cursor over the **SYSTEM** module by using the [**RIGHT ARROW**] key.

2. Choose the **SYSTEM** module by pressing [**DOWN ARROW**].

3. [**DOWN ARROW**] to the **Save** command.

4. Choose the **Save** command by pressing [**RIGHT ARROW**].

It is a good practice to save your work every ten minutes.

To get back up to the main menu, press [**LEFT ARROW**]. By continuing to press [**LEFT ARROW**] you can return to the original cursor position.

LESSON 7 — LOADING *BEDFORD* AND PREPARING THE GENERAL LEDGER MODULE

1. Load the operating system.

2. Place the *Bedford* diskette in drive A and your data diskette in drive B.

3. Activate the *Bedford* program as follows:

   A>**bedford**   press [**ENTER**]

4. Enter the company name as follows:

   Company: **b:\lsm** . . . .[d:\]
   Press [**ENTER**]

5. Enter the using date provided by your teacher.

6. You should then see the *Bedford* main menu shown in Figure 4-19.

7. Now record the name and address of the company that you will be entering accounting data for:

   Linda Schuman, DDS
   900 Park Place
   Richmond, BC
   V3Z 1X4

The name and address are entered under **SYSTEM, Default, Module, System**:

1. Use the [**RIGHT ARROW**] to put the block cursor over **SYSTEM** and press [**DOWN ARROW**].

2. Press [**DOWN ARROW**] to **Default**, and press [**RIGHT ARROW**].

3. Press [**RIGHT ARROW**] at **Module**.

4. Press [**DOWN ARROW**] to **System**, and then press [**RIGHT ARROW**].

5. Press [**RIGHT ARROW**] again to enter the **Company** information.

   Key In: **Linda Schuman, DDS**
   Press [**ENTER**]

   Note that the capitals are inserted for the first letters of the name automatically.

6. Press [**DOWN ARROW**] to **Street**, and then press [**RIGHT ARROW**].

   Key In: **900 Park Place**
   Press [**ENTER**]

7. Press [**DOWN ARROW**] to **City**, and then press [**RIGHT ARROW**].

   Key In: **Richmond**
   Press [**ENTER**]

8. Press [**DOWN ARROW**] to **Province**, and then press [**RIGHT ARROW**].

   Key In: **British Columbia**
   Press [**ENTER**]

9. Press [**DOWN ARROW**] to **Postal Code**, and then press [**RIGHT ARROW**].

   Key In: **V3Z1X4**
   Press [**ENTER**]

10. Press [**LEFT ARROW**] and then [**UP ARROW**] to **General**. Press [**RIGHT ARROW**] and then [**DOWN ARROW**] to **Ready**. Set **Ready** to **Yes**.

11. Press [**LEFT ARROW**] three times and move the cursor to **Save**. Press [**RIGHT ARROW**] to save this data. Press [**LEFT ARROW**] to return to the main *Bedford* menu.

Because you will only be using the general ledger module, and because this is a single proprietorship, you must immediately tell *Bedford* what account number and name you are going to use for the Capital account.

The name and account number of the Capital account for this business is Linda Schuman, Capital: 301.

1. Move the block cursor so it is over the **GENERAL** module.

2. Press [**DOWN ARROW**], and then press [**RIGHT ARROW**] to choose **Ledger**.

3. Press [**DOWN ARROW**], then press [**RIGHT ARROW**] to choose **Insert**.

4. Choose **Account** by pressing [**RIGHT ARROW**].

   Key In: **Linda Schuman, Capital**
   Press [**ENTER**]

5. Press [**RIGHT ARROW**] at **Number**.

   Key In: **301**

6. The cursor automatically goes to **Type**. You are presented with five choices H, L, R, S, T.

   Key In: **R**

7. The cursor automatically goes to **Suppress**.

   Key In: **N**

8. Press [**LEFT ARROW**] to make entry. Press [**LEFT ARROW**] twice to return to main menu.

9. Change the integration account
   (a) Choose **SYSTEM, Integrate, General**.
   (b) Press [**RIGHT ARROW**] to choose **RetEar   356**
   (c) Key In: **301**
   (d) Press [**LEFT ARROW**]

LESSON 8 — PREPARING FOR GENERAL LEDGER OPERATION

This lesson explains how the program handles the structure and composition of financial documents; how to organize your financial records so that they may be entered into the general ledger; and how to modify, insert, or delete accounts in the general ledger.

Bedford provides the user with a full list of general ledger accounts each time a new set of company files is created. These accounts may subsequently be modified or deleted. Other accounts may also be added.

There are several stages to organizing your general ledger records. For this exercise, the first stage is to lay out Linda Schuman's balance sheet and income statement in a prescribed format. The second is to classify each item on the financial statements according to its account type as defined by one of six letters, so that the program knows the purpose of each account. The third is to assign a number to each of the accounts to be printed on the financial statements, so that the program knows in what order to print them. The fourth is to identify which accounts will always be printed on the financial statements, and which accounts you will suppress if they have a zero balance.

Refer now to the chart of accounts that you prepared earlier and enter each account's details into a ledger account. Your teacher may give additional instructions for you to follow or have you complete this step on your own if you are familiar with the software.

MODIFYING, INSERTING, OR DELETING ACCOUNTS

TO DELETE A LEDGER ACCOUNT
(a) Choose **GENERAL Ledger**.
(b) Press [**RIGHT ARROW**] and [**DOWN ARROW**] to **Delete**, then press [**RIGHT ARROW**].
(c) Key in the account number.
(d) You will be asked if you are sure you wish to delete this ledger account. Press [**ENTER**] to confirm.

TO MODIFY A LEDGER ACCOUNT
(a) Choose **GENERAL, Ledger, Modify**.
(b) Key in the account number. The current information related to that account number appears on your screen.
(c) Key in the new account name; press [**ENTER**].
(d) [**DOWN ARROW**] to **number**; press [**RIGHT ARROW**].
(e) Key in the new account number.
(f) Press [**LEFT ARROW**].

TO INSERT A LEDGER ACCOUNT
(a) Choose **GENERAL, Ledger, Insert**.
(b) Key in the account name; press [**ENTER**].
(c) Key in the account number.
(d) Key in **R** or **L**. (L should be selected if data will have a subtotal taken.)
(e) Key in **Y** or **N** beside **Suppress**. (Y should be selected if you do not want zero-balance accounts to show on your printed statements.)
(f) Press [**LEFT ARROW**].

LESSON 9 — MAKING THE GENERAL LEDGER MODULE READY

Before the *Bedford* system can be made ready, the program checks to see that all sections in the chart of accounts begin with an H and end with a T. All L-type accounts must be followed by an S. Any historical data (from the current trial balance) must now be entered. Since this is a new business there is no historical data to be entered; account balances are nil. When the module is set to

Ready, the word history no longer appears and journal entries can be made.

1. Move the cursor to **SYSTEM** and press **[DOWN ARROW]**.
2. Press **[DOWN ARROW]** to **Default** and press **[RIGHT ARROW]**.
3. Press **[RIGHT ARROW]** with the cursor on **Module**.
4. Press **[RIGHT ARROW]** with the cursor on **General**.
5. Be certain the start and finish dates of your company's fiscal period are correct. To make changes open any of those fields by pressing **[RIGHT ARROW]** when the highlighted cursor is opposite the field. Move the cursor beside **Ready**. Press **[RIGHT ARROW]** to set the system to **Ready**.
   ```
   Start         0901yy
   Conversion    0901yy
   Finish        0930yy
   Ready         Yes
   ```
6. Press **[LEFT ARROW]** four times to return to the main menu.

LESSON 10 — JOURNALIZING TRANSACTIONS

You are now ready to learn how to journalize transactions with *Bedford*. We will start with Transaction 1. Normally transaction data would be entered from source documents or data entry sheets. For this exercise you will assume that each transaction has been recorded on the appropriate source document.

Transaction 1
Memo #1: On September 1, Linda Schuman opened a current account at the Royal Bank in Richmond and deposited $20 000, which represented her initial investment in her dental practice. The amount was a graduation gift from her parents.

If we were going to journalize this transaction manually it would look like Figure 4-20. This is how you enter the transaction for Memo #1 into *Bedford*.

1. Ensure the block cursor is over **GENERAL**.
2. Choose **GENERAL** by pressing **[DOWN ARROW]**.
3. Press **[DOWN ARROW]** to **Journal**.
4. Choose **Journal** by pressing **[RIGHT ARROW]**.
5. You will be presented with a set of fields:

   ```
   Comment........................
   Source
   Date
   Account
    Amount
   Project
    Amount
   ```

6. Key in the transaction:
   (a) Comment Field

   Key In: **initial investment of the owner**
   Press **[ENTER]**

FIGURE 4-20

GENERAL JOURNAL

PAGE 1

DATE 19—		PARTICULARS	PR	DEBIT	CREDIT
Sept.	1	Cash	101	20 000 —	
		Linda Schuman, Capital	301		20 000 —
		To record the initial investment of Linda			
		Schuman in her dental practice.			

Bedford will format the comment.

(b) Source Document Field

Key In: **m1**
Press [**ENTER**]

Bedford will format the source document entry.

(c) Transaction Date Entry

Key In: **0901yy**
Press [**ENTER**]

Bedford will format the date entry.

(d) Enter the debit part of the transaction.

A list of the accounts will appear on the right side of the screen.

Key In: **101**
Press [**ENTER**]

Bedford will display the name of the account you choose.

Key In: **20000**
Press [**ENTER**]

Bedford will format the amount.

Notice that the screen immediately clears information from Account and Amount and the cursor returns to Account.

Bedford will be waiting for the rest of the transaction. Notice that you were not asked for information for the last two entry lines because the **JOBCOST** module has not been activated.

```
Comment    Initial Investment
           Of The Owner
Source     M1
Date       09-01-yy
Account    ...
 Amount
Project
 Amount
```

(e) Enter the credit part of the transaction.

A list of the accounts will appear on the right side of the screen.

Key In: **301**
Press [**ENTER**]

Bedford will display the account you choose and what it feels should be the credit part of the transaction.

```
Comment    Initial Investment
           Of The Owner
Source     M1
Date       09-01-yy
Account    Linda Schuman, Capital
 Amount    .........[20,000.00]
Project
 Amount
```

Press [**SHIFT**] and [**ENTER**] at the same time to accept the **20,000.00** figure.

Bedford will format the amount.

Bedford will be waiting for you to add to the transaction:

```
Comment    Initial Investment
           Of The Owner
Source     M1
Date       09-01-yy
Account
 Amount
Project
 Amount
```

IMPORTANT: At this point, press the function key, [**F2**], to review the transaction. If it is incorrect, press [**ESC**] to cancel the transaction and begin over. If it is correct, press [**F2**] again and continue with the next instruction.

(f) Finish and save the transaction.

Bedford is still waiting for you to add to the transaction at this point.

```
Comment     Initial Investment
            Of The Owner
Source      M1
Date        09-01-yy
Account
 Amount
Project
 Amount
```

Since you are finished with this transaction, press [**ENTER**].

YOU MUST NOW SAVE THE TRANSACTION; press [**LEFT ARROW**].

NOTE: The only way to save a transaction to the memory of the computer is by pressing [**LEFT ARROW**]; if you press [**RIGHT ARROW**] you will cancel the transaction you just completed. If you press [**ESC**] the transaction will also be cancelled. So remember, TO SAVE A TRANSACTION YOU MUST USE [**LEFT ARROW**].

NOTE: If you have inadvertently recorded the transaction incorrectly, you must record a REVERSING ENTRY to correct the error in the accounting records.

(g) Save your work on your data diskette.

Save your work on the diskette with **SYSTEM Save**.

Transaction 2

Purchase Invoice 8764: On September 1, Linda purchased an IBM microcomputer system and computer supplies for the dental practice from Computer Electronics Ltd.; computer equipment $4 800; computer paper and ribbons for the printer $500; total price $5 300. Terms n/30.

Often transactions consist of one or more debits and credits. Purchase Invoice 8764 tells us that office equipment for $4 800 and office supplies for $500 were purchased on account.

Figure 4-21 shows how to record the transaction manually.

This is how you would enter the transaction for Purchase Invoice 8764 into *Bedford*.

1. Ensure the block cursor is over **GENERAL**.
2. Choose **GENERAL Journal**.
3. You will be presented with a set of fields.

```
Comment......................
Source
Date
Account
 Amount
Project
 Amount
```

FIGURE 4-21

GENERAL JOURNAL

PAGE 1

DATE 1985		PARTICULARS	PR	DEBIT	CREDIT
Sept.	1	Office Equipment	141	4 800 —	
		Office Supplies	111	500 —	
		A/P Computer Electronics	202		5 300 —
		Purchase Invoice 8764; IBM microcomputer			
		system and supplies			

4. Key in the transaction as follows:
   (a) Comment, Source, Date, Account and first debit

   ```
   Comment     IBM Microcomputer
               System
   Source      P8764
   Date        09-01-yy
   Account     Office Equipment
   Amount      4800
   Project
   Amount
   ```

   (b) Enter the account number of the second debit part of the transaction.

   Key In: **111**
   Press [**ENTER**]

   Bedford will display the name of the account you choose.

   Next, enter the amount to be debited to that account.

   Key In: **500**
   Press [**ENTER**]

   ```
   Comment     IBM Microcomputer
               System
   Source      P8764
   Date        09-01-yy
   Account     Office Supplies
   Amount      500
   Project
   Amount
   ```

   (c) Enter the account number of the credit part of the transaction.

   Key In: **202**
   Press [**ENTER**]

   The *Bedford* screen now appears as follows:

   ```
   Comment     IBM Microcomputer
               System
   Source      P8764
   Date        09-01-yy
   Account     A/P Computer
               Electronics
   Amount      .........[5,300.00]
   Project
   Amount
   ```

   Press [**SHIFT**] and [**ENTER**] at the same time to accept the **5,300.00** figure.

   (d) Check and then save the transaction.
   To check the transaction, press [**F2**].
   If you need to cancel the transaction, press [**ESC**], otherwise press [**F2**].
   Finish the transaction by pressing [**ENTER**]. Save the transaction by pressing [**LEFT ARROW**].

Journalize the remaining transactions for the month. Use the following for coding the source documents:

    Cheque is coded **CH**
    Purchase Invoice is coded **P**
    Remittance Slip is coded **RS**
    Memo is coded **M**
    Billing Statement is coded **BS**
    Form is coded **F**
    Cash Receipt Slip is coded **CRS**

Remember to save your work to your data diskette every 10 to 15 minutes using **SYSTEM Save**.

Sept. 1 Cheque No. 101: Paid the month's rent to FarWest Realty, $1 000 for office space.
    2 Memo 2: Borrowed $25 000 from the bank. The money was borrowed on a demand note basis and deposited in the firm's current account.
    3 Cheque No. 102: Paid $100 for liability insurance to Great West Insurance Company.

4	Cheque No. 103: Sent a $400 cheque to Landsdowne Motors for the monthly payment on Linda Schuman's car. (This payment must be charged to her Drawings account.)	20	Cash Receipt Slip 1: Received a cheque from CU & C Health Services in payment of the fees submitted on September 15.
4	Cheque No. 104: Purchased dental supplies for the office, $800.	22	Cheque No. 109: Linda Schuman withdrew $1 500 for her personal use.
5	Purchase Invoice A3456/Cheque No. 105: Purchased furniture for the office at a cost of $12 000. Paid $3 000 cash and the remainder was financed over one year to Focus Two Interiors.	23	Cheque No. 110: Paid the amount owing to the *Richmond Times* for the invoice received on September 16.
		26	Cheque No. 111: Paid BC Hydro & Power Authority the utility bill received today, $210.
7	Purchase Invoice 4589/Cheque No. 106: Purchased dental equipment from Regency Dental Equipment for $18 500. A down payment of $6 500 was made with the balance to be paid in six monthly instalments.	28	Billing Statements 001 to 003: Statements were mailed to the following patients for amounts not covered by their dental plans; terms n/30. B. Harveson $175; E. Jones $60; J. Leroux $55.
		30	Cheque No. 112: Made the monthly payment to Regency Dental Equipment.
15	Form 113378: Patient fees submitted to CU & C Health Services for the first week of operation were $2 475. (You will have to insert a new account in your ledger called CU & C Health Services Receivable.)	30	Cheque No. 113: Paid BC Telephone Company for the telephone bill received today, $45.
		30	Form 113379: Patient fees submitted to CU & C Health Services for two weeks, $3 890.
15	Cheque Nos. 107 and 108: Paid the semi-monthly office salaries for the dental hygenist and receptionist, $950 each. Both persons were employed for one week.	30	Cheque Nos. 114 and 115: Paid the semi-monthly office salaries for the dental hygenist and office receptionist, $1 900 each.

LESSON 11 — DISPLAYING THE GENERAL JOURNAL

Bedford allows you to view journal transactions on the screen with a **Display** command, or to print a hard copy using the **Print** command.

16	Purchase Invoice A345: From the *Richmond Times* newspaper for advertising the opening of the dental practice, $350; terms n/30.
17	Purchase Invoice 45897: Purchased office supplies on account, $420, from Miller's Office Supplies; terms n/30.

To use the command to view the general journal entries:

1. Choose **GENERAL, Display, Journal, General**.

2. Enter the dates of the entries you wish to review: (In this case we will print the month's journal entries.)
   Start   **0901yy**
   Finish   **0930yy**

3. Use the [**DOWN ARROW**] key to view more transactions. Use the [**UP ARROW**] key to review previous transactions. [**ESC**] returns you to your sub-menu.

LESSON 12 — PRINTING A HARD COPY OF THE GENERAL JOURNAL

1. Check to see that the printer is ready.

2. Choose **GENERAL, Print, Journal, General**.

3. Enter the dates for which you wish journal entries printed.
   Start   **0901yy**
   Finish   **0930yy**

4. Print the hard copy by choosing **Print** with [**RIGHT ARROW**].

LESSON 13 — PRINTING A HARD COPY OF THE GENERAL LEDGER

1. Check to see that the printer is ready.

2. Choose **GENERAL, Print, Ledger, General**.

3. Enter the dates for which you wish the ledger entries printed.
   Start   **0901yy**
   Finish   **0930yy**

   Select **Accounts** . . . . . . [all] by pressing [**SHIFT**] and [**ENTER**] at the same time.

4. Print the hard copy by choosing **Print** with the [**RIGHT ARROW**].

LESSON 14 — PRINTING THE TRIAL BALANCE

1. Check to see that the printer is ready.

2. To print the trial balance:
   (a) Choose **GENERAL, Print, Trial**.
   (b) Enter the date: **0930yy**
   (c) Print by choosing **Print**.

3. Check with your teacher that the trial balance is correct before proceeding to the next lesson.

Optional Exercise
LESSON 15 — PRINTING FINANCIAL REPORTS

Before you print the financial reports, you must review your general journal transactions and trial balance with your teacher.

1. To print the income statement:
   (a) Choose **GENERAL, Print, Income**.
   (b) Enter the dates of the beginning and end of the accounting cycle:
       Start   **0901yy**
       Finish   **0930yy**
   (c) Print by choosing **Print** with the [**RIGHT ARROW**].

2. To print the balance sheet:
   (a) Choose **GENERAL, Print, Balance**.
   (b) Enter the date: **0930yy**
   (c) Print by choosing **Print** with the [**RIGHT ARROW**].

YOU WILL NOW USE YOUR PRINTOUTS TO COMPLETE AN AUDIT TEST OF THE ACCURACY OF THE ACCOUNTING RECORDS FOR THE BUSINESS.

CHAPTER FIVE

The Worksheet

LEARNING OBJECTIVES

At the end of this chapter you should be able to
- prepare a worksheet;
- locate errors on a worksheet;
- prepare an income statement from a worksheet;
- prepare a classified balance sheet from a worksheet;
- prepare comparative financial statements;
- calculate working capital and current ratio;
- analyze financial statements;
- outline the accounting cycle as studied to date;
- use a spreadsheet program to design and complete a six-column worksheet;
- use a spreadsheet program to design a classified income statement and balance sheet.

LANGUAGE OF ACCOUNTING

You will see the following terms in this chapter:
current assets
current liabilities
current ratio
extending
fixed assets
long-term liabilities
microcomputer systems
software
working capital
worksheet

5.1 The Worksheet

Algor Computer Services wanted to know the results of its operations on a monthly basis so that it could react to them. It would then make business decisions which, hopefully, would improve its net income and its overall financial position. When Vijay Marshall became an entrepreneur, he knew that one of the keys to success in business was continued growth. The purpose of having monthly information was to make changes before any small problems developed into large ones.

Although the production of month-end reports could be done informally, more formal reports were required on a quarterly basis. Algor Computer Services needed a method of preparing the reports so that they could then be published with an accurate and attractive format.

Worksheet: an informal preparation of the financial statements.

In order to organize the data for the preparation of financial statements, a worksheet is prepared. The **worksheet** is an informal preparation of the financial statements. Since it is done at the end of the month, the steps in the accounting cycle will now include:

Journalize → Post → Trial Balance → Worksheet → Financial Statements

Financial statements are required on a monthly basis in order that management can make adjustments to the operation of the business. To wait until the end of a quarter or the end of a year to examine the financial data may cause losses or a lower net income than might otherwise be achieved. In some businesses, the worksheet serves as the financial statements for information required more frequently than at the end of a quarter. Businesses that make their statements available to the public usually publish quarterly statements, with a formal annual

FIGURE 5-1 FORMAT FOR PREPARATION OF A WORKSHEET

WORKSHEET

Algor Computer Services — FOR THE _Month_ ENDED _Aug. 31_ 19 _88_

	ACCOUNTS	ACCT. NO.	TRIAL BALANCE DR	TRIAL BALANCE CR	INCOME STATEMENT DR	INCOME STATEMENT CR	BALANCE SHEET DR	BALANCE SHEET CR	
1	Cash	100	97843 –						1
2	Accounts Receivable	120	37901 –						2
3	Office Supplies	150	1239 –						3
4	Land	160	124600 –						4
5	Building	170	228000 –						5
6	Office Equipment	175	11300 –						6
7	Computer Equipment	180	48800 –						7
8	Automobile	190	12500 –						8
9	Accounts Payable	200		24503 –					9
10	Short-Term Loans	210		17302 –					10
11	Mortgage Payable	220		248000 –					11
12	V. Marshall, Capital	300		267078 –					12
13	V. Marshall, Drawings	310	2500 –						13
14	Computer Services	400		13052 –					14
15	Software Lessons	410		8433 –					15
16	Wages Expense	600	10909 –						16
17	Bank Expense	650	121 –						17
18	Advertising Expense	660	963 –						18
19	Utilities Expense	670	1007 –						19
20	Automobile Expense	680	664 –						20
21	Miscellaneous Expense	760	21 –						21
22			578368 –	578368 –					22
23									23

report prepared at fiscal year end. Month end is a busy time for an accountant, for the ledger must be balanced, the worksheet prepared, and the statements made.

Since the worksheet is an informal preparation of the statements, it is usually done in pencil. The format of the worksheet shown in Figure 5-1 accommodates the preparation of the income statement and the balance sheet.

Steps in Preparing a Worksheet

The steps followed to prepare a worksheet are as follows:

1. The three-line heading is the same as that found on the income statement, answering the questions Who?, What?, When? The length of the accounting period is indicated in the date.

2. The trial balance is listed. In some businesses, a separate trial balance is not prepared, for it is entered directly onto the worksheet using the account balances in the general ledger. In either case, the trial balance should be added to ensure its accuracy. The remaining steps in the preparation of a worksheet should not be followed until the trial balance is correct.

3. The balances for each of the accounts are extended to the columns for the financial statement on which they are found. Extending means to transfer horizontally. (See Figure 5-2.) The extending process should be started with the account first shown on the trial balance, which is usually Cash, and continued down the page.

> "Extending means to transfer horizontally."

FIGURE 5-2 ALL ACCOUNTS ARE EXTENDED TO THE COLUMN SHOWING THE STATEMENT ON WHICH THEY BELONG

WORKSHEET

Algor Computer Services — FOR THE _____ ENDED _____ 19___

	ACCOUNTS	ACCT. NO.	TRIAL BALANCE DR	TRIAL BALANCE CR	INCOME STATEMENT DR	INCOME STATEMENT CR	BALANCE SHEET DR	BALANCE SHEET CR	
1	Assets		xxx				→ xxx		1
2	Liabilities			xxx				→ xxx	2
3	Capital			xxx				→ xxx	3
4	Drawings		xxx				→ xxx		4
5	Revenue			xxx		→ xxx			5
6	Expenses		xxx		→ xxx				6
7									7
8									8

It should *not* be done by extending all the income statement account balances, and then all the balance sheet account balances.

4. The amount columns of the income statement and balance sheet are totalled. (See Figure 5-3.)

5. The net income is calculated by taking the difference between the revenue (total of the credit column of the income statement) and the expenses (total of the debit column of the income statement). To prove the calculation, the difference is added to the smaller amount (the debit side) so that the debit column and credit column for the income statement should be equal.

6. The net income figure is transferred to the Balance Sheet columns and put on the credit side, for it increases the owner's equity. The debit and credit columns of the balance sheet are then added to see if they are equal. If they are not, an error has occurred. When balanced, all final totals should be double ruled.

FIGURE 5-3 A COMPLETED WORKSHEET

WORKSHEET

Algor Computer Services FOR THE __Month__ ENDED __Aug. 31__ 19 __88__

#	ACCOUNTS	ACCT. NO.	TRIAL BALANCE DR	TRIAL BALANCE CR	INCOME STATEMENT DR	INCOME STATEMENT CR	BALANCE SHEET DR	BALANCE SHEET CR
1	Cash	100	9 843 –				9 843 –	
2	Accounts Receivable	120	37 901 –				37 901 –	
3	Office Supplies	150	1 239 –				1 239 –	
4	Land	160	124 600 –				124 600 –	
5	Building	170	228 000 –				228 000 –	
6	Office Equipment	175	11 300 –				11 300 –	
7	Computer Equipment	180	48 800 –				48 800 –	
8	Automobile	190	12 500 –				12 500 –	
9	Accounts Payable	200		24 503 –				24 503 –
10	Short-Term Loans	210		17 302 –				17 302 –
11	Mortgage Payable	220		248 000 –				248 000 –
12	V. Marshall, Capital	300		267 078 –				267 078 –
13	V. Marshall, Drawings	310	2 500 –				2 500 –	
14	Computer Services	400		13 052 –		13 052 –		
15	Software Lessons	410		8 433 –		8 433 –		
16	Wages Expense	600	10 909 –		10 909 –			
17	Bank Expense	650	121 –		121 –			
18	Advertising Expense	660	963 –		963 –			
19	Utilities Expense	670	1 007 –		1 007 –			
20	Automobile Expense	680	664 –		664 –			
21	Miscellaneous Expense	760	21 –		21 –			
22			578 368 –	578 368 –	13 685 –	21 485 –	564 683 –	556 883 –
23	Net Income				7 800 –			7 800 –
24					21 485 –	21 485 –	564 683 –	564 683 –

Completing a Worksheet When There Is a Net Loss

The steps in completing a worksheet that shows a net loss are basically the same as those where there is a net income. Steps 5 and 6 are altered slightly:

5. The net loss is calculated by taking the difference between the expenses column (total of the debit column of the income statement) and the revenue column (total of the credit column of the income statement). To prove the calculation, the net loss figure is added to the smaller amount (the credit side in this case) so that the debit column and credit column should be equal.

6. The net loss figure is transferred to the balance sheet and put on the debit side, for it decreases the owner's equity. The debit and credit columns of the balance sheet are then added to see if they are equal. Remember, all final totals should be double ruled.

The procedure for carrying out steps five and six in a loss situation is illustrated in Figure 5-4.

FIGURE 5-4 TECHNIQUE FOR COMPLETING A WORKSHEET WITH A NET LOSS

WORKSHEET

Algor Computer Services — FOR THE Month ENDED Dec. 31 19 88

ACCOUNTS	ACCT. NO.	TRIAL BALANCE DR	TRIAL BALANCE CR	INCOME STATEMENT DR	INCOME STATEMENT CR	BALANCE SHEET DR	BALANCE SHEET CR
		107 2 1 0 —	107 2 1 0 —	39 6 7 0 —	37 2 0 0 —	67 5 4 0 —	70 0 1 0 —
Net Loss					2 4 7 0 —	2 4 7 0 —	
				39 6 7 0 —	39 6 7 0 —	70 0 1 0 —	70 0 1 0 —

Self-Balancing Nature of the Worksheet

An accountant knows that a worksheet is correct when the debits equal the credits in the Balance Sheet column. Why does this occur? In Chapter 4 you learned how to expand the Capital account into separate Revenue, Expense, and Drawings accounts. By transferring the difference between revenue and expenses back onto the balance sheet (either as net income or net loss), the revenue and expense accounts are transferred back to the capital account. A more detailed examination of how this procedure is formally completed by the preparation of closing entries will be carried out in Chapter 8.

Locating Errors on the Worksheet

To find a single error on a worksheet, first calculate the difference between the total debits and total credits on the balance sheet.

FIGURE 5-5 CALCULATE THE DIFFERENCE BETWEEN THE TOTAL DEBITS AND TOTAL CREDITS IN THE BALANCE SHEET COLUMNS WHEN STARTING TO LOOK FOR AN ERROR

Algor Computer Services

WORKSHEET FOR THE Month ENDED Oct. 31 19 85

	ACCOUNTS	ACCT. NO.	TRIAL BALANCE DR	TRIAL BALANCE CR	INCOME STATEMENT DR	INCOME STATEMENT CR	BALANCE SHEET DR	BALANCE SHEET CR	
20			90 400 –	90 400 –	24 600 –	46 700 –	65 800 –	43 400 –	20
21	Net Income				22 100 –			22 100 –	21
22					46 700 –	46 700 –	65 800 –	65 500 –	22
23									23
24									24
25							Calculate		25
26							the		26
27							difference		27

Then follow the steps described in Chapter 4 for locating a single error on a trial balance. Once again, if there are several errors they will be more difficult to find. The steps are as follows:

(a) look for the amount of the difference on the trial balance — it may not have been extended;
(b) divide the difference by two — a debit may have been extended as a credit or vice versa (a common error on a worksheet);
(c) divide the difference by 9 — if it divides evenly a transposition or slide error may have occurred;
(d) a difference with only one digit not a zero, as in the example in Figure 5-5, indicates that a calculation error (usually adding in this case) may have occurred.

Lesson Review

1. When and why is a worksheet prepared?
2. What date is used on the heading of the worksheet?
3. What is extending? In what order is it done on the worksheet?
4. How is the net income or net loss calculated on a worksheet?
5. (a) To which column is the net income transferred on the balance sheet? Why?
   (b) To which column is the net loss transferred on the balance sheet? Why?
6. How does the accountant know that an error has occurred on a worksheet? Summarize the four common types of errors that may have occurred, giving an example of each.
7. One of the first tests to find an error on a worksheet should be to divide the difference between the debit total and the credit total of the balance sheet by two, and look for that amount. Why should it be one of the first tests?

Lesson Applications

8. Given the trial balance in Figure 5-6, prepare a worksheet for the month of April, providing suitable account numbers. The trial balance total has been omitted intentionally; total it on your worksheet to ensure that it is correct.

FIGURE 5-6

W. Kennedy, Psychologist
Trial Balance
April 30, 19–2

	Debit	Credit
Cash	$ 4 390	
Marketable Securities	3 000	
Accounts Receivable	11 965	
Office Supplies	740	
Office Equipment	9 320	
Automobile	17 900	
Accounts Payable		$ 2 400
W. Kennedy, Capital		34 170
W. Kennedy, Drawings	2 500	
Fees Income		19 200
Automobile Expense	740	
Rent Expense	2 400	
Utilities Expense	320	
Salaries Expense	2 270	
Miscellaneous Expense	225	
	?	?

9. Complete the following partial worksheets.
   (a)

WORKSHEET

Winthrop Automobile Repairs — FOR THE Month ENDED May 31, 19 -4

ACCOUNTS	ACCT. NO.	TRIAL BALANCE DR	TRIAL BALANCE CR	INCOME STATEMENT DR	INCOME STATEMENT CR	BALANCE SHEET DR	BALANCE SHEET CR
		239 050 –	239 050 –	92 205 –	128 005 –	146 845 –	111 045 –

(b)

WORKSHEET

Churchill Falls Veterinary Centre — FOR THE Month ENDED April 30, 19 -1

ACCOUNTS	ACCT. NO.	TRIAL BALANCE DR	TRIAL BALANCE CR	INCOME STATEMENT DR	INCOME STATEMENT CR	BALANCE SHEET DR	BALANCE SHEET CR
		98 725 –	98 725 –	32 980 –	36 540 –	65 745 –	62 185 –

10. Given the following trial balance, prepare a worksheet for the month of November, providing suitable account numbers. The trial balance total has been omitted intentionally; total it on your worksheet to ensure that it is correct.

Didi's Visual Arts Studio
Trial Balance
November 30, 19-8

	Debit	Credit
Cash	$12 350	
Accounts Receivable	4 670	
Office Supplies	230	
Art Supplies	6 700	
Furniture & Equipment	22 340	
Automobile	14 500	
Accounts Payable		$ 5 640
D. Snider, Capital		36 800
D. Snider, Drawings	2 490	
Fees Income		46 670
Automobile Expense	240	
Rent Expense	1 600	
Utilities Expense	830	
Salaries Expense	6 435	
Supplies Expense	16 400	
Miscellaneous Expense	325	
	?	?

11. In preparing a worksheet, the following unrelated errors were made. For each error, indicate the effect that it will have on (i) the income statement, and (ii) the balance sheet on the worksheet.
    (a) Cash was recorded as $4 500 instead of $45 000 on the trial balance.
    (b) Wages Expense, $6 900, was extended to the debit column of the balance sheet.
    (c) C. Gorchynski, Drawings, $4 500, was extended to the debit column of the income statement.
    (d) Accounts Payable, $2 450, was extended as $2 540 to the credit column of the balance sheet.
    (e) Fees Earned, $56 700, was extended to the credit column of the balance sheet.

12. Given the trial balance in Figure 5-7, prepare a worksheet for the month of May, providing suitable account numbers. The trial balance total has been omitted intentionally; total it on your worksheet to ensure that it is correct.

FIGURE 5-7

Trenton Dog Studio
Trial Balance
May 31, 19–7

	Debit	Credit
Cash	$ 4 350	
Accounts Receivable	3 615	
Office Supplies	140	
Furniture & Fixtures	4 560	
Land	85 000	
Building	45 600	
Van	14 500	
Accounts Payable		$ 1 450
Bank Loan		9 670
Mortgage Payable		94 500
T. Gooch, Capital		57 165
T. Gooch, Drawings	2 350	
Fees Income		14 350
Van Expense	1 245	
Utilities Expense	980	
Salaries Expense	13 400	
Interest Expense	150	
Miscellaneous Expense	1 245	
	?	?

5.2 Preparing Financial Statements from the Worksheet

Once the worksheet is completed, the preparation of the financial statements can be done quickly and accurately, because all the information pertaining to a specific statement is found on the worksheet in the appropriate columns.

The Income Statement

The heading on the income statement is the same as that on the worksheet, for it indicates the length of the financial period. The balances for the revenue accounts are found in the credit column of the income statement on the worksheet. The balances for the expense accounts are found in the debit column of the income statement on the worksheet. Note that on statement paper the columns are not debit and credit columns! Total revenue and expenses do not need to be calculated when preparing the statement: they are available as totals on the worksheet. Similarly the net income or net loss does not have to be calculated: the amount can merely be copied from the worksheet.

FIGURE 5-8 AN INCOME STATEMENT PREPARED FROM THE WORKSHEET

Algor Computer Services
Income Statement
for the month ended August 31, 1988

Revenue		
Computer Services	$13 052	
Software Lessons	8 433	$21 485
Expenses		
Wages	$10 909	
Bank	121	
Advertising	963	
Utilities	1 007	
Automobile	664	
Miscellaneous	21	13 685
Net Income		$ 7 800

The Classified Balance Sheet

The classified balance sheet divides assets and liabilities into various classes. The purpose of this format is to provide management with more information in order to make better business decisions.

Assets

Current assets: assets that will be used up or converted to cash within one year.

Assets are divided into current assets and fixed assets. **Current assets** are those that will be used up or converted to cash within one year. The asset Cash is therefore listed first, since it is already in the form of cash. Accounts receivable are current assets, for in most businesses they will be collected within thirty days. Assets that will be used up within a year, such as supplies, are also recorded as current assets. Remember, current assets are recorded in the *order* in which they will be converted to cash or used, that is, in the order of liquidity.

Fixed assets: assets that will not be converted to cash or used up within a year.

Fixed assets are those that will not be converted to cash or used up within a year. They are listed in reverse order of liquidity with the longest lasting asset listed first. Fixed assets include land, buildings, equipment, and automobiles.

Liabilities

Current liabilities: liabilities that are due within one year.

To parallel the division of assets, liabilities are divided into current and long-term liabilities. **Current liabilities** are those that will be paid within a year, such as accounts payable. The portion of a loan or a mortgage that is to be paid within the current year will also be included as a short-term liability. For reporting purposes, all short-term liabilities

Long-term liabilities: *liabilities that are not due within one year.*

are sometimes grouped into one category, Current Liabilities, rather than being listed separately.

Long-term liabilities include the portion of liabilities that will not be paid within one year, most commonly loans and mortgages. As with the short-term liabilities, for reporting purposes they are frequently grouped into one category, Long-Term Liabilities.

FIGURE 5-9 A CLASSIFIED BALANCE SHEET PREPARED FROM THE WORKSHEET

Algor Computer Services
Balance Sheet
as at August 31, 1988

Assets

Current Assets
Cash	$ 97 843	
Accounts Receivable	37 901	
Office Supplies	1 239	$136 983

Fixed Assets
Land	124 600	
Building	228 000	
Office Equipment	11 300	
Computer Equipment	48 800	
Automobile	12 500	425 200
Total Assets		$562 183

Liabilities and Owner's Equity

Current Liabilities
Accounts Payable	$ 24 503	
Short-Term Loans	17 302	$ 41 805

Long-Term Liabilities
Mortgage Payable		248 000
Total Liabilities		289 805

Owner's Equity
V. Marshall, Capital, August 1, 1988		267 078	
Net Income	$7 800		
Less: Drawings	2 500		
Net Increase in Capital		5 300	
V. Marshall, Capital, August 31, 1988			272 378
Total Liabilities and Owner's Equity			$562 183

All the data for preparing the balance sheet from the worksheet is found in the Balance Sheet columns. Moreover, the accounts should already be in the proper order to classify the balance sheet, because the accounts are found in the proper order in the general ledger. When preparing the Owner's Equity section of the balance sheet, the information is found in the Balance Sheet section of the worksheet, as shown in Figure 5-10.

FIGURE 5-10 THE DATA TO COMPLETE THE OWNER'S EQUITY SECTION OF THE BALANCE SHEET IS FOUND IN ORDER IN THE BALANCE SHEET COLUMNS ON THE WORKSHEET

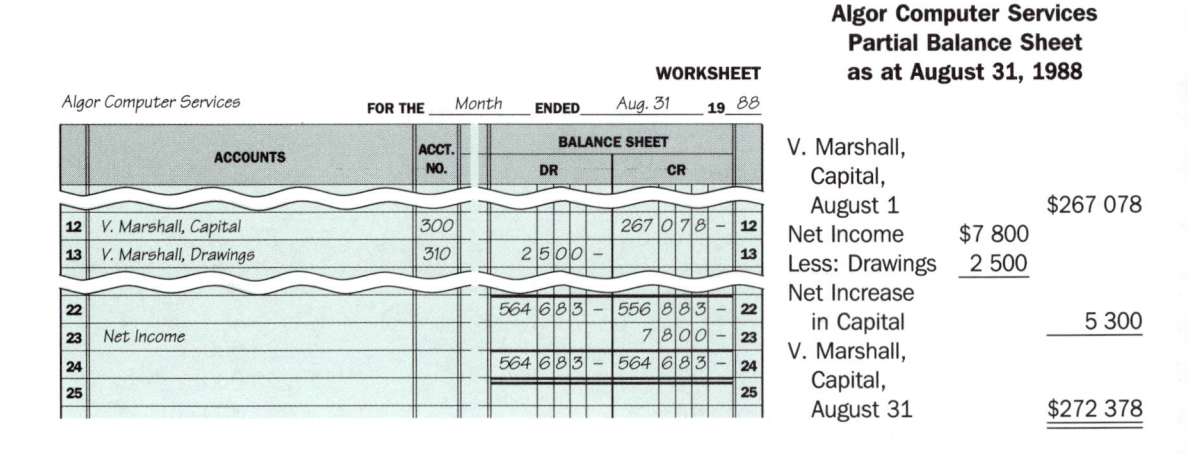

Algor Computer Services — WORKSHEET — FOR THE Month ENDED Aug. 31, 19 88

	ACCOUNTS	ACCT. NO.	BALANCE SHEET DR	BALANCE SHEET CR
12	V. Marshall, Capital	300		267 078 —
13	V. Marshall, Drawings	310	2 500 —	
22			564 683 —	556 883 —
23	Net Income			7 800 —
24			564 683 —	564 683 —
25				

Algor Computer Services
Partial Balance Sheet
as at August 31, 1988

V. Marshall,
Capital,
August 1 $267 078
Net Income $7 800
Less: Drawings   2 500
Net Increase
 in Capital   5 300
V. Marshall,
Capital,
August 31 $272 378

LESSON REVIEW

13. Where is all the information for the preparation of the income statement found on the worksheet?

14. Where is all the information for the preparation of the balance sheet found on the worksheet?

15. What is a classified balance sheet? Why are balance sheets classified?

16. Distinguish between a current asset and a fixed asset.

17. (a) List the current assets in your classroom.
    (b) List the fixed assets in your classroom.

18. Distinguish between a current liability and a long-term liability.

19. Describe the treatment given to a mortgage that is payable over the next five years when preparing a classified balance sheet.

Lesson Applications

20. (a) Indicate whether each of the following are current assets, fixed assets, current liabilities, or long-term liabilities.
    - (i) marketable securities
    - (ii) accounts receivable
    - (iii) office equipment
    - (iv) mortgage payable (12 years)
    - (v) building
    - (vi) a one-year bank loan
    - (vii) cash in the bank
    - (viii) a Canada Savings Bond
    - (ix) accounts payable
    - (x) a 20-year-old car

    (b) List the current assets in part (a) in their order of liquidity.
    (c) List the fixed assets and the current liabilities in the order in which they should appear on a balance sheet.

21. Using the following worksheet, prepare an income statement and a classified balance sheet.

WORKSHEET

North Gower Flying School — FOR THE Month ENDED Aug. 31, 19-4

	ACCOUNTS	ACCT. NO.	TRIAL BALANCE DR	TRIAL BALANCE CR	INCOME STATEMENT DR	INCOME STATEMENT CR	BALANCE SHEET DR	BALANCE SHEET CR
1	Cash		4250-				4250-	
2	Accounts Receivable		1620-				1620-	
3	Supplies		115-				115-	
4	Aircraft		234500-				234500-	
5	Equipment		12340-				12340-	
6	Accounts Payable			1235-				1235-
7	Short-Term Loan			3920-				3920-
8	Long-Term Loan			115200-				115200-
9	D. Wong, Capital			125760-				125760-
10	D. Wong, Drawings		2350-				2350-	
11	Course Fees			45670-		45670-		
12	Wages Expense		28760-		28760-			
13	Interest Expense		150-		150-			
14	Advertising Expense		420-		420-			
15	Utilities Expense		1230-		1230-			
16	Rent Expense		2350-		2350-			
17	Gas Expense		3560-		3560-			
18	Miscellaneous Expense		140-		140-			
19			291785-	291785-	36610-	45670-	255175-	246115-
20	Net Income				9060-			9060-
21					45670-	45670-	255175-	255175-

22. Prepare the income statement and classified balance sheet from the worksheet completed for
    (a) W. Kennedy, Psychologist in Question 8 on page 190.
    (b) Didi's Visual Arts Studio in Question 10 on page 192.

5.3 Working Capital and Current Ratio

The purpose of financial statements and of classifying the balance sheet is to provide management with data in order to make business decisions. An analysis of the statements is carried out in order to make the decisions. Two calculations made when interpreting the information on the balance sheet are the amount of working capital and the current ratio. Both are made in order to determine the solvency of a business. A business is solvent if it is able to pay its debts as they become due, and insolvent if not able to do so.

Working Capital

Working capital is the excess of current assets over current liabilities:

$$\text{Working capital} = \text{Current assets} - \text{Current liabilities}$$

The calculation for Algor Computer Services for the balance sheet shown in Figure 5-9 (page 195) is as follows:

$$\text{Working capital} = \$136\,983 - \$41\,805$$
$$= \$95\,178$$

> **Working capital:** the excess of current assets over current liabilities.

The amount of working capital is an indicator of the short-term financial strength of a business. Algor's working capital level indicates that the firm will have no financial difficulty, for there are more than enough current assets to cover current liabilities in the short term. However, a business can have current assets amounting to much more than current liabilities, but still not be able to pay its debts as they become due. This may occur when accounts receivable represent the majority of the current assets, and the firm cannot collect them for various reasons.

A business may also not be able to meet its debt obligations because it has invested too heavily in fixed assets. If a business cannot remain solvent, it may be forced to close, or be forced into bankruptcy by its creditors. A favourable working capital level is especially important to a merchandising business, for it needs to stock its shelves with merchandise for sale. If it is not meeting its payments, a supplier will be reluctant to extend credit to the firm. Working capital is further discussed in Chapter 14.

Current Ratio

> **Current ratio:** the ratio of current assets to current liabilities.

The **current ratio** is another indicator of the short-term debt-paying ability of the business. It is calculated by dividing the current assets by the current liabilities.

$$\text{Current ratio} = \frac{\text{Current assets}}{\text{Current liabilities}}$$

The current ratio for Algor Computer Services for the balance sheet shown in Figure 5-9 is as follows:

$$\text{Current ratio} = \frac{\$136\,983}{\$41\,805}$$

$$= 3.3 : 1$$

This indicates that there are $3.30 in current assets for every $1 in current liabilities. A favourable current ratio is generally considered to be approximately 2:1 to 3:1, while a current ratio of 1:1 is not considered to be favourable. When current assets are close in value to current liabilities, there is no surplus of liquid assets available to meet emergencies, or to take advantage of business opportunities that may arise. Furthermore, note that all current liabilities are payable in cash, but current assets such as office supplies will not be converted to cash in order to pay the liabilities. On the other hand, a current ratio of 4:1 or higher is usually not beneficial to a business, for the return on investments is usually higher if funds are invested in long-term securities, or used for expansion of the business. The current ratio for Algor Computer Services appears to be favourable. Current ratio is further discussed in Chapter 14.

5.4 Comparative Financial Statements

"*Comparative statements are statements that show financial data for more than one fiscal period.*"

The financial statements are useful for providing information about the current fiscal year. The data from the current fiscal year is also compared to the same data for previous fiscal periods. It is this comparison that allows the business to determine whether it is improving its net income position and its financial position in general. As well, the comparison of individual items on the statements for consecutive years indicates specific areas where there can be, or has been, improvement. In order to make a more valid comparison, comparative statements also usually show the percentage change from the previous year. The preparation of comparative income statements and balance sheets is discussed here.

Comparative Income Statements

The comparative income statement for 1988 and 1989 for Algor Computer Services is shown in Figure 5-11.

The third column shows the dollar increase or decrease from 1988 to 1989, and the fourth column shows the percentage change. In order to calculate the percentage change in any item from one year to the next the following equation is used:

$$\% \text{ change} = \frac{\text{Value in Year 2} - \text{Value in Year 1}}{\text{Value in Year 1}} \times 100$$

FIGURE 5-11

Algor Computer Services
Comparative Income Statement
for the years ended May 31, 1988 and 1989

	1989	1988	Increase or Decrease	% Change
Revenue				
Computer Services	$180 700	$156 619	$24 081	15.4
Software Lessons	131 140	101 200	29 940	29.6
Total Revenue	311 840	257 819	54 021	21.0
Expenses				
Wages	161 260	130 908	30 352	23.2
Bank	1 668	1 456	212	14.6
Advertising	12 525	11 556	969	8.4
Utilities	14 925	12 079	2 846	23.6
Automobile	10 052	7 970	2 082	26.1
Miscellaneous	350	250	100	40.0
Total Expenses	200 780	164 219	36 561	22.3
Net Income	$111 060	$ 93 600	$17 460	18.7

For example, for Algor Computer Services, the percentage change in Net Income from 1988 to 1989 is calculated as follows:

$$\frac{\text{Net Income 1989} - \text{Net Income 1988}}{\text{Net Income for 1988}} \times 100$$

$$= \frac{\$111\ 060 - \$93\ 600}{\$93\ 600} \times 100$$

$$= 18.7\%$$

The net income for Algor Computer Services therefore increased by 18.7% from 1988 to 1989. Had Algor experienced a decrease instead, a careful analysis of the income statement would have to be made in order to find the cause. As well, management would engage in the preparation of new goals in order to overcome the decline in net income.

Comparative Balance Sheets

The comparative balance sheet for the years 1988 and 1989 for Algor Computer Services is shown in Figure 5-12. The dollar increase or decrease is shown in the third column, and the percentage increase or decrease is shown in the fourth column.

The two main financial statements, the income statement and the balance sheet, cannot be considered in isolation of one another. If accounts receivable (on the balance sheet) have increased significantly

FIGURE 5-12

Algor Computer Services
Comparative Balance Sheet
as at May 31, 1988 and 1989

	1989	1988	Increase or Decrease	% Change
Assets				
Current Assets				
Cash	$113 240	$ 97 843	$ 15 397	15.7
Marketable Securities	8 700	0	8 700	—
Accounts Receivable	43 250	37 901	5 349	14.1
Office Supplies	1 238	1 239	−1	−0.1
	166 428	136 983	29 445	21.5
Fixed Assets				
Land	124 600	124 600	0	0
Building	228 000	228 000	0	0
Office Equipment	12 950	11 300	1 650	14.6
Computer Equipment	55 500	48 800	6 700	13.7
Automobile	12 500	12 500	0	0
Total Assets	$599 978	$562 183	$ 37 795	6.7
Liabilities and Owner's Equity				
Current Liabilities				
Accounts Payable	$ 28 560	$ 24 503	$ 4 057	16.6
Short-Term Loans	12 480	17 302	−4 822	−27.9
	41 040	41 805	−765	−1.8
Long-Term Liabilities				
Mortgage Payable	204 500	248 000	−43 500	−17.5
Total Liabilities	245 540	289 805	−44 265	−15.3
Owner's Equity				
V. Marshall, Capital, June 1	272 378	203 778	68 600	33.7
Add: Net Income	111 060	93 600	17 460	18.7
	383 438	297 378	86 060	28.9
Less: Drawings	29 000	25 000	4 000	16.0
V. Marshall, Capital, May 31	354 438	272 378	82 060	30.1
Total Liabilities and Owner's Equity	$599 978	$562 183	$ 37 795	6.7

but there has been no significant increase in revenue (on the income statement), then management should be concerned. Similarly, if the owner has increased his or her investment (on the balance sheet) in the business, the revenue (on the income statement) should be higher. This should be the result because the business had more assets in order to pursue business opportunities such as opening another store, or buying more merchandise to sell. Otherwise the owner could have placed the money in other investments, such as bonds, and increased his or her income that way.

The Accounting Cycle

The accounting cycle has been expanded in this chapter in order to include the worksheet. The cycle is now as follows:

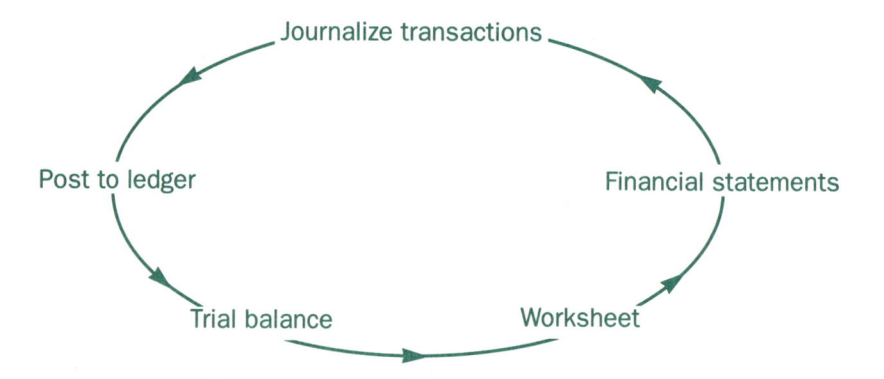

Journalize transactions → Financial statements → Worksheet → Trial balance → Post to ledger → Journalize transactions

LESSON REVIEW

23. What is the formula for calculating working capital?

24. What does the working capital indicate?

25. What is the formula for calculating the current ratio?

26. Indicate whether the following are good or poor current ratios. Justify your decision.
    (a) 4:1
    (b) 1:1
    (c) 10:1
    (d) 2:1

27. What is the benefit of preparing comparative financial statements?

28. Why are percentages shown when preparing comparative financial statements?

29. Why should the income statement and the balance sheet not be examined in isolation of one another?

30. Outline the accounting cycle as we have studied it to date.

Lesson Applications

31. Calculate the working capital, given the following data.
    (a) Current assets $117 930, current liabilities $84 905.
    (b) Current assets $3 560 800, current liabilities $2 980 450.
    (c) Current assets $53 480, current liabilities $54 300.

32. Calculate the current ratio for (a) to (c) in Question 31.

33. The following financial data is provided for Mortimore Computer Services.

Current assets	$196 400
Fixed assets	187 700
Current liabilities	124 700
Long-term liabilities	122 900

    (a) Calculate the working capital for the year. Comment on whether it is satisfactory, giving reasons for your position.
    (b) Calculate the current ratio for the year. Comment on whether it is satisfactory, giving reasons for your position.

34. (a) Calculate the working capital and current ratio for W. Kennedy, Psychologist and Didi's Visual Arts Studio. The balance sheets were completed in Question 22 on page 197.
    (b) Comment on the working capital and current ratio of the above two businesses.

35. Given the following data, prepare a comparative income statement for Dobson Engineering Consultants for the years 19–2 and 19–3. The year end is June 30. Complete columns to show the amount of increase or decrease, and the percentage change for each item.

	19–3	19–2
Consulting Fees	$883 285	$792 405
Wages Expense	524 090	506 350
Utilities Expense	23 400	22 500
Advertising Expense	35 600	30 990
Rent Expense	204 000	191 400
Professional Fees Expense	3 400	3 100
General Expense	11 350	9 870

36. Given the following data, and using that generated in Question 35, prepare a comparative balance sheet for Dobson Engineering Consultants for the years 19–2 and 19–3. Complete columns to show the amount of increase or decrease, and the percentage change for each item.

	19–3	19–2
Cash	$ 23 002	$ 14 435
Accounts Receivable	12 232	1 946
Office Supplies	4 397	2 439
Land	44 500	44 500
Building	104 900	104 900
Office Equipment	11 600	9 200
Automobile	18 400	13 400
Accounts Payable	2 430	3 890
Short-Term Loan	3 600	14 500
Mortgage Payable	92 900	122 774
P. Dobson, Capital, July 1	49 056	31 261
P. Dobson, Drawings	10 400	9 800

37. The following condensed income statement is for the telecommunications operations of the British Columbia Telephone Company for the years 1986 and 1987.

British Columbia Telephone Company
Income Statement — Telecommunications Operations

	1987	1986
	(millions)	
Telecommunications Revenue	$1 438.6	$1 340.5
Telecommunications Expenses	1 010.6	954.8
Earnings from Telecommunications operations	$ 428.0	$ 385.7

(a) Calculate the dollar increase or decrease in each item.
(b) Calculate the percentage increase or decrease in each item.
(c) Comment on the trend of the net income for the business in relation to the revenue.

CHAPTER REVIEW AND SKILL DEVELOPMENT

Accounting Principles and Concepts
- **Worksheets** are completed as an informal preparation of the financial statements.
- **Classified balance sheets** are made in order to provide more information with which to analyze the business activities.
- **Current assets** are listed in order of liquidity; **fixed assets** are listed in order of length of life, with the longest lasting listed first.
- **Analysis of the financial statements** is made in order to improve the net income and/or the financial position of the business.
- **Comparative financial statements** are made to show dollar and percentage changes from one fiscal period to another.

Knowing the Terms
For each of the following statements, indicate the term being defined.
(a) Assets that will be converted to cash or used up within one year.
(b) Statements comparing data for two or more years.
(c) An informal preparation of the financial statements.
(d) The difference between current assets and current liabilities.
(e) Statements that show only the totals for major categories.
(f) Assets that will be used for more than one year.
(g) Liabilities that will be paid within one year.
(h) To transfer horizontally.
(i) Liabilities that will not be paid within one year.
(j) The ratio of current assets to current liabilities.

Food for Thought
1. An accountant believed that he could prepare the financial statements directly from the accounts in the general ledger. What are the disadvantages of this procedure?

2. If the Drawings account is extended incorrectly from the Trial Balance to the Income Statement debit column, the worksheet will still balance. Explain why this can occur.

3. Don Zimmer did not grasp the concept of double-entry accounting very well. He decided that the accounts in the general ledger for his business should be in the order of those with debit balances and then those with credit balances. What problems will this cause Don when he posts and when he prepares the worksheet?

4. Martin Zundra completed his worksheet and financial statements, which indicated a net income. In examining his work, he noticed that the total of the debit side of the Balance Sheet column on the worksheet was not equal to the total assets shown on the balance sheet. Martin thought that they should be equal. Should the amounts be the same? Explain to Martin why they should or should not be the same.

5. Winnifred had completed her worksheet and it did not balance. She then took the difference between the debit total and the credit total of the Balance Sheet columns. Her friend Neetu told her to divide the difference by two, and to look for that amount on the trial balance. Why

did Neetu tell Winnifred to follow that procedure? Explain why the difference is divided by two.

6. The accounts receivable for a business increase from 40 percent to 70 percent of total sales. What problems could this cause for the business?

7. The long-term loans for a business change from being 20 percent of total liabilities to 45 percent of total liabilities. What problems could this present for the business in the future?

8. A user of a particular balance sheet notes to the accountant that the current assets have decreased substantially. The accountant states that it is not a problem, because the fixed assets have increased substantially. Criticize the accountant's viewpoint.

9. A user of a particular income statement notices that the increase in wages expense is ten percent for a year, yet the number of employees did not increase. How can the user determine whether a ten percent increase is reasonable?

10. A student indicates that it is a waste of time to calculate the percentage change on a comparative income statement. Indicate the advantages of having the percentage in addition to the dollar amount.

Organizing

We have now studied five steps in the accounting cycle. Prepare an organizer with the following column headings:

Step   Definition   Purpose

Applications

1. Given the following trial balance,
   (a) prepare a worksheet for the month of August, providing suitable account numbers;
   (b) prepare an income statement;
   (c) prepare a classified balance sheet.

C. Ramsay, Home Consultant
Trial Balance
August 31, 19–8

	Debit	Credit
Cash	$11 400	
Accounts Receivable	7 400	
Office Supplies	1 428	
Land	78 000	
Building	76 000	
Computer Equipment	12 490	
Automobile	13 209	
Accounts Payable		$11 087
Short-Term Loan		4 796
Long-Term Loan		19 184
Mortgage Payable		98 760
C. Ramsay, Capital		50 308
C. Ramsay, Drawings	1 800	
Consultation Fees		28 550
Automobile Expense	980	
Utilities Expense	842	
Salaries Expense	7 980	
Interest Expense	172	
Miscellaneous Expense	984	
	?	?

2. The worksheets on page 207 have only the total section shown. They did not balance when they were completed. For each, indicate the most probable type of error that has occurred.

a)

WORKSHEET

P. Martin, Painter

FOR THE _Month_ ENDED _Nov. 30_ 19_-4_

ACCOUNTS	ACCT. NO.	TRIAL BALANCE DR	TRIAL BALANCE CR	INCOME STATEMENT DR	INCOME STATEMENT CR	BALANCE SHEET DR	BALANCE SHEET CR	
		4 206 16 –	4 206 16 –	6 200 –	9 100 –	35 861 6 –	32 061 6 –	18
Net Income				2 900 –			2 900 –	19
				9 100 –	9 100 –	35 861 6 –	34 961 6 –	20

b)

WORKSHEET

Kennedy, Dentist

FOR THE _Six Months_ ENDED _June 30_ 19_-8_

ACCOUNTS	ACCT. NO.	TRIAL BALANCE DR	TRIAL BALANCE CR	INCOME STATEMENT DR	INCOME STATEMENT CR	BALANCE SHEET DR	BALANCE SHEET CR	
		117 320 –	117 320 –	4 104 0 –	3 922 1 –	7 628 0 –	8 709 9 –	21
Net Loss					1 819 –	1 819 –		22
				4 104 0 –	4 104 0 –	7 809 9 –	8 709 9 –	23

c)

WORKSHEET

Denis Cousineau, Puppeteer

FOR THE _Quarter_ ENDED _March 31_ 19_-8_

ACCOUNTS	ACCT. NO.	TRIAL BALANCE DR	TRIAL BALANCE CR	INCOME STATEMENT DR	INCOME STATEMENT CR	BALANCE SHEET DR	BALANCE SHEET CR	
		2 749 7 –	2 749 7 –	4 607 –	5 827 –	2 289 0 –	2 057 8 –	21
Net Income				1 220 –			1 220 –	22
				5 827 –	5 827 –	2 289 0 –	2 179 8 –	23

Applications — Comprehensive:
The Accounting Cycle to Date

Byron Quast owns Quast Dry Cleaners. The firm rents space at six shopping centres, but all the accounting is done at the head office.

(a) Open a general ledger, using the accounts shown on the trial balance in Figure 5-13. March 31 is the end of the first month of the fiscal year. Use a numbering system similar to that used by Algor.

(b) Journalize and post the transactions. Notice that source document information has not been provided.

(c) Take off a formal trial balance.

(d) Prepare a worksheet.

(e) Prepare an income statement.

(f) Prepare a classified balance sheet.

(g) Calculate the working capital and current ratio.

(h) Prepare a brief report to the owner outlining the current financial position of the business.

FIGURE 5-13

Quast Dry Cleaners
Trial Balance
March 31, 19-7

	Debit	Credit
Cash	$53 652	
Accounts Receivable	9 870	
Office Supplies	900	
Cleaning Supplies	12 350	
Equipment	34 508	
Vans	93 490	
Accounts Payable		$ 5 370
Short-Term Loan		12 469
Trust Company Loan (Long-Term Loan)		112 221
B. Quast, Capital		71 793
B. Quast, Drawings	4 800	
Cleaning Revenue		98 740
Advertising Expense	2 820	
Donations Expense	2 300	
Office Cleaning Expense	9 400	
Rent Expense	18 400	
Utilities Expense	18 408	
Van Expense	8 905	
Wages Expense	29 080	
Interest Expense	1 040	
General Expense	670	
	?	?

Transactions

Apr. 3 Owner invested an additional $4 300.
3 Purchased $4 200 worth of cleaning supplies on account from Eastern Dry Cleaning Suppliers Ltd.
3 Paid $3 070 for rent.
4 Paid the electricity expense, $12 435.
5 Donated $250 to the Swift Current Canadians for their hockey banquet.
5 Paid the weekly wages, $6 462.
6 Paid $450 for radio advertising.
7 Paid $1 400 on account to Eastern Dry Cleaning Suppliers Ltd.
7 Received $480 on account from Cara Caterers.
7 Cleaning services sold on account to Cara Caterers for the week were $430, and for cash were $25 904.
10 Paid $1 309 for gas and tune-ups for the vans.
11 Paid $1 400 for television ads.
12 Purchased postage stamps, $45.
12 Paid the weekly wages, $6 462.
12 Received $220 on account from Cara Caterers.
13 Signed a contract to perform the cleaning for the new Best Eastern Hotel, $2 300 per month.
14 Paid the owner $45 for office supplies that he purchased with his own funds.
14 Cleaning services sold on account to Cara Caterers for the week were $430, and for cash were $22 804.
17 Paid $4 800 on the Trust Company Loan. (Interest of $935 is included.)
18 Paid $140 to the local municipality for renewal of the business licence.
19 Paid the weekly wages, $6 462.
20 Cleaning services sold on account to Cara Caterers for the week were $430, and for cash were $27 211.
20 Paid $4 500 for a fax machine.
21 Paid $132 for dryer repairs.
22 Purchased $1 390 worth of cleaning supplies on account.
24 Paid a $225 fee for the owner to attend a business conference.
25 Paid $1 982 on account to Dow Chemicals.
26 Paid the weekly wages, $6 462.
27 Cleaning services sold on account to Cara Caterers for the week were $430, and for cash were $29 222.
27 Paid $280 for window repairs.
27 Received $1 200 from the local hockey team for cleaning uniforms.
28 Paid $3 200 to the owner for his personal use.
28 Paid $940 for monthly office cleaning.

Focussing — The Worksheet

Given the completed worksheet for J. Crosier in Figure 5-14:
(a) state why you should immediately know that it is not correct;
(b) state the errors that have been made in its preparation, and indicate why each is an error. You should find at least ten errors.

Evaluate and Assess — Statement Analysis

The following data (in $ thousands) is from an annual report of Teleglobe Canada, a federal Crown agency created by the *Teleglobe Canada Act*. As Canada's international telecommunications carrier, it transmits communications via satellites and submarine cable to other countries.

Current Assets	$191 459
Fixed Assets	300 718
Current Liabilities	
Accounts Payable	89 427
Income Tax Payable	13 406
Portion of Long-Term Debt due within one year	9 371
Total Current Liabilities	112 204
Long-Term Debt	50 363

(a) Calculate the working capital for Teleglobe Canada. Comment on the firm's ability to meet its current debt obligations.
(b) Calculate Teleglobe's current ratio and comment on its adequacy.
(c) The current liabilities figure includes an amount for the portion of long-term debt due within one year. Why is this amount for long-term debt listed as a current liability?

FIGURE 5-14

WORKSHEET

J. Crosier, Systems Analyst — FOR THE _____ ENDED Dec. 31, 19 −9

	ACCOUNTS	ACCT. NO.	TRIAL BALANCE DR	TRIAL BALANCE CR	INCOME STATEMENT DR	INCOME STATEMENT CR	BALANCE SHEET DR	BALANCE SHEET CR	
1	Cash		9 800 −				9 800 −		1
2	Accounts Receivable		16 000 −			16 000 −			2
3	Supplies		470 −				470 −		3
4	Office Equipment		7 600 −				7 600 −		4
5	Computer Equipment		18 400 −				18 400 −		5
6	Automobile		18 040 −				18 004 −		6
7	Accounts Payable			3 200 −				3 200 −	7
8	Short-Term Loan			7 320 −				7 320 −	8
9	J. Crosier, Capital			32 480 −		32 480 −			9
10	J. Crosier, Drawings		4 000 −		4 000 −				10
11	Consultant's Fees			39 820 −		39 820 −			11
12	Rent Expense		1 400 −		1 400 −				12
13	Salaries Expense		3 200 −		3 200 −				13
14	Utilities Expense		780 −		780 −				14
15	Cellular Phone Expense		390 −		390 −				15
16	Advertising Expense		1 600 −		1 600 −				16
17	Miscellaneous Expense		1 140 −		1 140 −				17
18					12 510 −	88 300 −	54 274 −	10 520 −	18
19						75 790 −		75 790 −	19
20					12 510 −	12 510 −	54 274 −	86 310 −	20
21									21

Synthesize and Conclude

The accountant for the Lethbridge Laser hockey team gave the owner the financial statements for the year. The owner examined the statements, and made the following comments:
(a) "The net income was $15 000 higher this year than last, so the cash should have also increased by $15 000;
(b) The net income was $15 000 higher this year than last, so the total assets should have also increased by $15 000;
(c) There is a net income, and therefore the liabilities should have decreased."

Explain the fallacy in each of the owner's statements.

ACCOUNTING AT WORK

Shirley Reilly
Certified General Accountant

As controller of a firm that buys and sells seeds to 57 countries around the world, Shirley Reilly puts her accounting training to good use. The Certified General Accountant (C.G.A.) designation qualified her for the position that includes such duties as preparing monthly financial statements and annual budgets, supervising commercial invoicing, training staff, and in general, supervising the corporate cash flow. "My background in computers certainly has come in handy," she said. "Computers are now essential if you are going to be effective in accounting."

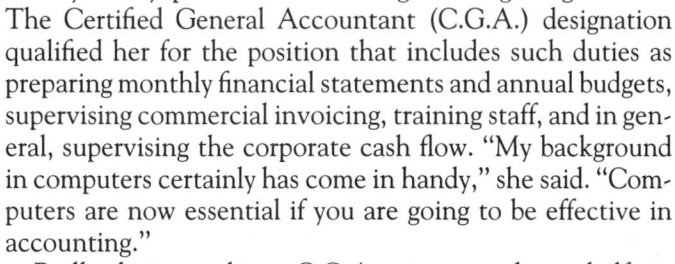

Reilly began taking C.G.A. courses about halfway through her career. Prior to this she had been a manager for a telecommunications company, but had left that position to work in her husband's business, a job that sparked her strong interest in accounting. First she took accounting courses at a technical college, but soon turned to the C.G.A. program. Related job experience is an important component of the C.G.A. program and Reilly worked in progressively more responsible positions in several firms as she completed the courses. With the C.G.A. program behind her, she took her present position as controller.

Reilly has reached the highest position she can get in the seed company. Because it is a family-owned business, the top positions are held by family members. "It's different working in a family business," she explained. "While there is less office politics going on, the staff must always consider the goals and personalities of the owners." Reilly finds the job very rewarding, with tremendous scope for people eager to try new challenges.

For Reilly, accounting has been a marvellous career. She maintains that people who are good at their jobs can go many places, right to the upper levels of management. "I'm only sorry I didn't get into accounting right out of high school," she said. "These last few years have been fun."

The Certified General Accountants' Association, the third in our study of public accountants, prepares its graduates for positions in financial management. The graduates find positions in public practice accounting, the government and public service, and industry and commerce.

The minimum educational requirement for enrolment in the C.G.A. program is graduation from a secondary school; university and college graduates may qualify for exemptions.

To graduate a person must successfully complete 17 courses, which are offered by the Association. A minimum of two years of practical experience is also required, which is done at the same time the courses are taken. Students must also provide proof of successful completion of an approved business communications course prior to the end of their second academic year of enrolment.

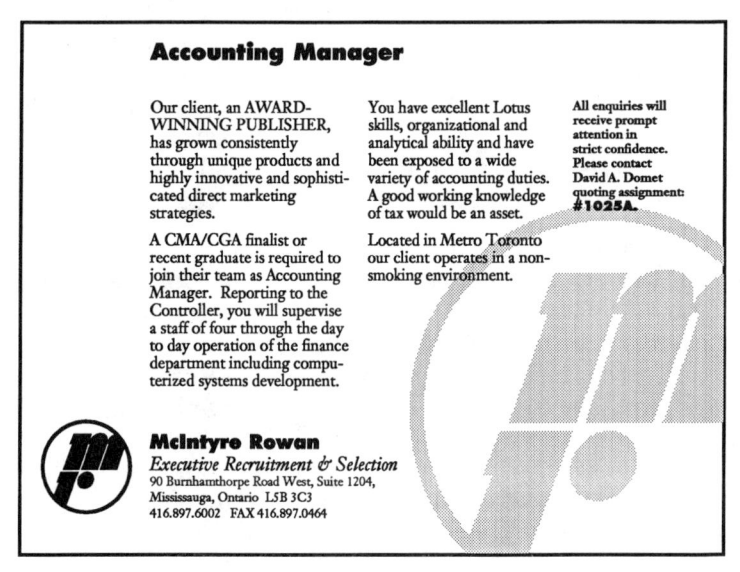

Accounting Manager

Our client, an AWARD-WINNING PUBLISHER, has grown consistently through unique products and highly innovative and sophisticated direct marketing strategies.

A CMA/CGA finalist or recent graduate is required to join their team as Accounting Manager. Reporting to the Controller, you will supervise a staff of four through the day to day operation of the finance department including computerized systems development.

You have excellent Lotus skills, organizational and analytical ability and have been exposed to a wide variety of accounting duties. A good working knowledge of tax would be an asset.

Located in Metro Toronto our client operates in a non-smoking environment.

All enquiries will receive prompt attention in strict confidence. Please contact David A. Domet quoting assignment: **#1025A.**

McIntyre Rowan
Executive Recruitment & Selection
90 Burnhamthorpe Road West, Suite 1204,
Mississauga, Ontario L5B 3C3
416.897.6002   FAX 416.897.0464

1. McIntyre Rowan is a management and executive selection firm. It finds management-level employees for its clients. Why would a business hire a personnel selection firm to find and recommend a person for a position in the business?

2. What skills do you think are required by Shirley Reilly or the person who will be successful in obtaining the Accounting Manager position?

Business Career Skills

1. Leadership Skills

One of the most important roles that an accountant may have to fulfil is that of a leader. Many accountants become controllers, partners in an accounting firm, or heads of departments. In these positions, they are supposed to serve in the role of a coach. As coaches, they are to facilitate the attainment by each of the team members of those of their individual goals that are in conformity with the business's goals. To be the best coach possible, the accountant must demonstrate good leadership skills.

(a) In groups, brainstorm to obtain a list of skills that a good leader should have.
(b) Individually, rank the list of skills that the group obtained, from most important to least important.
(c) In the original groups, obtain a consensus ranking of the skills that the group listed.
(d) Compare your group's ranking with those of the other groups.

2. Problem Solving — The Cost of Time

The following is a digest of a news report.

Fact: 80% of employees steal from their employers! What are they stealing? Time, the most precious commodity of the business. Studies indicate that over $15 billion per year is stolen in Canada. Time theft includes:
- arriving at work late
- leaving early
- taking extended lunches or coffee breaks
- deliberately slowing the pace of work to create overtime opportunities
- reading on company time
- spending too much time associating with co-workers
- making excessive personal telephone calls
- taking care of personal chores on company time

In addition, employee pilferage, embezzlement, insurance fraud, vandalism, kick-backs, arson and other recognized crimes against Canadian business are estimated to total no more than $5 billion.

Assume that, as supervisor of the accounting department, you have been asked to establish a company policy on lateness and absenteeism that is designed to overcome the previously stated problems. The business employs seventy-two people, who all are paid an hourly wage. They are currently required to punch a time clock when arriving and leaving. The firm's annual wage cost is $2 994 000. In groups,

(a) brainstorm to come up with the reasons that people steal time from their employers;
(b) brainstorm to develop a policy for lateness for the firm;
(c) brainstorm to develop a policy for absenteeism for the firm.

On your own prepare a report to your supervisor outlining the policy that you recommend.

3. Communication and Careers

Using one of the business periodicals in the library, or another acceptable source, research the career of any Canadian business person. Write a short paper of a minimum of 500 words. Your paper should focus on
(a) the career history of the person;
(b) education that assisted the person's career;
(c) the roles that the person carries out in their current position;
(d) major entrepreneurial decisions that the person has made in order to be successful.

COMPUTER ACCOUNTING
SPREADSHEETS REVISITED

In a recent article in a leading financial publication, it was stated that about 25 percent of all Canadian firms with sales of less than $5 million now have a computer, and many others are contemplating such a purchase in the near future. Also, during the past decade, bargain-wise owner-managers have stepped up their demands for top quality accounting services. Almost any operation that involves the storage of data or a repetitious handling of that data can be computerized, if it is justifiable economically.

It now makes sense for a small firm to buy its own computer when:

1. The business support systems no longer provide management with the information needed to run the operation.

2. The company is struggling to grow and could increase revenue significantly by, say, mailing invoices and statements to all customers monthly, or by offering special sales promotions through the mail.

3. The owner feels the service provided by the business is not competitive enough, but does not have the analytical tools readily available to help with financial planning.

It is possible to use **microcomputer systems** for virtually every phase of accounting operations. The most common computer application is the processing of large masses of accounting data relating to routine repetitive operations, such as recording sales, maintaining inventory records, preparing payroll, and posting to ledger accounts.

However, the main reason for computerizing the accounting function is that it expands the ability of the accounting system to generate information. A computerized accounting system provides management with control over the day-to-day operations of the business. Reports can be prepared for almost any information that management desires, as long as the data is first brought into the system. Common reporting areas are inventory control, accounts payable, balance sheet, income statement, and marketing analysis.

The programs and operating system that make the computer perform various functions, such as journalizing and posting, are generally referred to as **software**. For this and the previously mentioned applications, a firm would purchase one of the many integrated accounting packages that are available, as well as a suitable spreadsheet program.

Along with word processing programs, spreadsheets and databases are by far the best-selling categories of software available for microcomputers today.

Exercises

1. Use your spreadsheet program to design and complete a six-column worksheet similar to the model in Figure 5-15.

   Format:
   Use the underscore key (_) or hyphen key (-) for drawing horizontal lines and the equals sign (=) for double ruling.

FIGURE 5-15

	A	B	C	D	E	F	G	H	I
1				Name of company					Formulas
2				Worksheet					
3				Date					
4									
5			Acct	Trial Balance		Income Statement		Balance Sheet	
6	Account Title		No.	Debit	Credit	Debit	Credit	Debit	Credit
7									
8									1
9									2
10									3
11									4
12									5
13									6
14									7
15									8
16									9
17									10
18									
19									11
20									12

Column Widths:
(i) A total of 8 columns is needed for this worksheet (A to H).
(ii) The Account Title column should be set at 25.
(iii) Set a column width of 4 for the Acct. No. column.

Formulas:
Use the SUM function for calculating amount column totals (C through H).

You must enter data values for only the Trial Balance columns. For the other amount columns formulas must be used to move or calculate the data. See Figure 5-15.

Prepare a worksheet for the Jazzercise Fitness Centre from the trial balance in Figure 5-16 for the month ended July 31.

2. Load your spreadsheet program into your computer, and use a completed worksheet exercise to design a classified income statement and a classified balance sheet in report form or account form for a service business.

FIGURE 5-16

Jazzercise Fitness Centre Trial Balance July 31, 19--		
	Debit	**Credit**
Cash	$12 800	
AR/Barb Asseltine	40	
AR/Lori Davidson	120	
AR/Maureen Fong	80	
AR/Judy Torelli	240	
AR/Cynthia Zuvich	360	
Supplies	680	
Equipment	4 890	
Furniture	2 588	
Bank Loan Payable		$12 000
AP/CanFit		2 000
AP/Office Outfitters		560
AP/Ideal Office Supplies		230
AP/RobScon Advertising		650
J. De Silva, Capital		6 984
J. De Silva, Drawings	1 800	
Membership Fees		3 400
Casual Fees		1 760
Salaries Expense	1 400	
Rent Expense	1 800	
Advertising Expense	650	
Loan Interest Expense	80	
Miscellaneous Expense	56	
	$27 584	$27 584

Format:
(i) Double underline all column totals where appropriate.
(ii) Centre titles in the statements where applicable.

Formulas:
(i) Use the SUM function where applicable.
(ii) Net Income/Loss = Revenue − Expenses
(iii) Net Change In Capital = Beginning Capital + Net Income (or minus Net Loss) − Withdrawals by Owner

Column Widths:
(a) Income Statement
   (i) Set the column width containing the Revenue and Expense account titles to 50.
   (ii) Set a column width for each of the two amount columns to 12.
(b) Balance Sheet
Report Form
   (i) Set the column width containing the section headings and account titles to 50.
   (ii) Set a column width of 12 for each of the amount columns.
Account Form
   (i) The Assets and Liabilities/Owner's Equity columns should each be set at 25.
   (ii) Set a column width of 12 for each of the amount columns.

Project 1 — THE ACCOUNTING CYCLE

This project includes the steps in the accounting cycle that have been studied to date. Remember that your trial balance must balance before you proceed to complete the remainder of the accounting cycle. If it does not balance, use proper error location procedures and follow proper correction procedures.

Tai's Real Estate Services specializes in renting suitable properties to foreign firms that wish to do business in Canada. In some cases Tai's Real Estate Services rents space from other firms, which it in turn rents to its clients; in other cases it owns the property it rents to clients. Tai's business plan indicates that it focusses on advertising its services in Pacific Rim countries. Its headquarters is in Vancouver, but it operates offices in all the provincial capitals.

The trial balance for the firm, as at July 31, 19– –, is shown in Figure A.

(a) Enter the balances for the accounts in a general ledger.
(b) Journalize the following transactions on page 48 of the general journal and post to the general ledger.

Aug. 3 Cash Receipt Slip #91-214: Received cash on account from Far East Trading, $25 900.
Sales Invoice #922: To Bank of Hong Kong, $80 800.
Cheque Copy #473: $4 806 for the monthly payment on the bank loan, which includes $506 for interest.
Cheque Copy #474: To Zenith Real Estate Holdings, $49 000 for rental of offices in provincial capitals.
Cheque Copy #475: To Royal Trust, $33 800 for monthly mortgage payment, including interest of $27 600.
Cheque Copy #476: $2 000 to Lincoln Paper Products on account.
Purchase Invoice #25-444: From Wilton Office Outfitters, $12 900 for office equipment.

FIGURE A

Tai's Real Estate Services
Trial Balance
July 31, 19--

Acc. No.	Account	Debit	Credit
100	Cash	$ 83 200	
105	Accounts Receivable	142 640	
110	Supplies	8 490	
115	Land	950 000	
120	Building	930 700	
125	Furniture & Equipment	75 000	
130	Computer Equipment	42 800	
135	Automobiles	84 208	
205	Bank Loan (Current)		$ 54 902
210	Accounts Payable		24 090
215	Mortgage Payable		932 070
300	V. Tai, Capital		1 305 976
305	V. Tai, Drawings		
400	Real Estate Services		
500	Advertising Expense		
502	Bank Charges		
505	Travel Expense		
510	Salaries and Commissions Expense		
515	Rent Expense		
520	Utilities Expense		
525	Courier Expense		
530	Telephone Expense		
535	Interest Expense		
540	Automobile Expense		
545	General Expense		
		$2 317 038	$2 317 038

10 Cash Receipt Slip #91-215: $84 500 received on account from Singh and Wong Inc.
Sales Invoice #923: To Singapore Textiles, $34 900.
Cheque Copy #477: $8 000 to Southam News for newspaper advertising.
Cheque Copy #478: $17 500 to Japan TV for advertising.
Cheque Copy #479: $47 800 to employees for biweekly salaries and commissions.
Cheque Copy #480: $3 600 to the owner for personal use.
Purchase Invoice #44-333: From Carling Motors Ltd., $17 800 for a new automobile. Deposit $4 000, balance in 2 weeks.
Purchase Invoice #402-91: From Air Canada, $14 300 for travel.
Purchase Invoice #2261: From Far East Press, $11 400 for advertising in various Pacific Rim trade magazines.
17 Cash Receipt Slip #91-216: $88 700 received on account from Philippine Export Corp.
Sales Invoice #924: To Indian Trade Commission, $43 980.
Cheque Copy #481: $17 650 to BC Power Authority for hydro.
Memo #41: The owner paid $8 000 to the bank to reduce the business's bank loan.
Purchase Invoice #993: From Lincoln Paper Products, $4 300 for supplies.
Sales Invoice #925: To Vietnamese Trading Corp., $52 700.
Cheque Copy #483: $16 000 on account to Computer Innovations.
24 Cash Receipt Slip #91-217: $75 900 received on account from Thai Shippers.
Sales Invoice #926: To South Korean Enterprises, $34 800.
Cheque Copy #484: $1 503 to Purolator for monthly courier charges.
Cheque Copy #485: $1 783 to Loomis Courier Service for monthly courier charges.
Sales Invoice #927: To Bombay House, $8 640.
Cheque Copy #486: $14 300, on account to Air Canada.
Sales Invoice #928: Lahore Connections billed $24 390.
Cheque Copy #487: $12 900 to Wilton Office Outfitters, on account.

Cheque Copy #488: $44 800 to employees for biweekly salaries and commissions.
Cheque Copy #489: $3 600 to the owner for personal use.
Purchase Invoice #699: $4 833, from Shell Canada Ltd. for automobile gas and servicing.
Memo #42: The owner took $184 of supplies home for his personal use.

31 Cash Receipt Slip #91-218: $35 780 received on account from Yang Trading Co.
Sales Invoice #929: To Indonesian Textiles Ltd., $42 300.
Purchase Invoice #00979: From Morton Cleaning Services, $21 400 for cleaning services.
Cheque Copy #490: $21 302 to BC Tel for monthly telephone expense.
Purchase Invoice #401: From Jan Yung Travel Services, $29 329 for airline travel for the month.

(c) Prepare a trial balance as at August 31.

(d) Prepare a worksheet, and from it the financial statements for the month.

(e) Calculate the working capital and the current ratio, and prepare a brief report on the financial position of the business.

CHAPTER SIX

Special Transactions

LEARNING OBJECTIVES

At the end of this chapter you should be able to
- describe the relationship between a financial institution and a business;
- describe the circumstances under which a financial institution or a business would issue a debit or credit memo;
- journalize transactions involving debit memos and credit memos;
- describe the federal goods and services tax, and the provincial retail sales tax system;
- journalize transactions involving sales taxes;
- journalize transactions that involve financial institution credit cards;
- compare a credit card, a debit card, and a prepaid card;
- use a spreadsheet program to help solve special accounting problems.

LANGUAGE OF ACCOUNTING

You will see the following terms in this chapter:
aged list of accounts payable
ageing of the accounts receivable
contra accounts
credit bureau
credit memo
debit card
debit memo
goods and services tax
input tax credit
prepaid card
printout
sales draft

6.1 Debit and Credit Memos

When Algor Computer Services opened an account at the local bank, it was entitled to use the services of the financial system. In exchange for the services, Algor paid a fee. It was obvious to Algor's management that it would be impossible to operate without having a bank account and using the bank's services. Following good business practice, the treasurer would deposit all cash receipts on a daily basis, including cheques received from customers. Algor wanted the bank to collect payment on these cheques from the financial institution on which they were written by the customer. Similarly, Algor wanted to make most payments by cheque. It wanted its bank to honour these cheques when they were presented for payment.

There were many other bank services that Algor would be able to take advantage of in its business operations. It could arrange for a loan or a line of credit. A line of credit would allow Algor to make purchases even if funds for payment were not available in its bank account. The bank would advance funds up to the amount agreed on in the line of credit. For payments made in a foreign currency, the bank would make the necessary currency available. One of the more important services was the mailing to Algor of a statement each month showing all changes in its bank account. Included with the statement were all the cheques cashed on the account during the month. These cheques served as a receipt of payment for Algor.

> "A business has a claim on a financial institution for amounts on deposit."

The relationship between a business and its financial institution for accounting purposes varies, depending on the transaction that occurs. When the business makes a deposit of daily receipts, it owns a claim on the financial institution for that amount. The deposit is therefore recorded as the asset Cash. Remember that money on deposit was included in our definition of cash. In the bank's books, however, the deposit represents a liability, for it owes the amount to the depositor.

Deposit made by Algor Computer Services

Algor	Bank
Deposits receipts, and *owns* a claim on the bank for the amount deposited.	Receives deposit, and *owes* the amount deposited, on demand, to Algor.

> "A business lists a financial institution as a creditor for loans received."

However, when Algor Computer Services obtains a short-term loan from the bank, the opposite relationship exists.

Loan obtained by Algor Computer Services from a Bank

Algor	Bank
Borrows money, and *owes* the amount borrowed to the bank. A debit is made to Cash, and a credit is made to Short-Term Loans.	Lends the money to Algor, and *owns* a claim on Algor for the amount loaned.

The agreement with the bank, signed by Algor Computer Services when it opened its account, specified that the bank could deduct amounts from Algor's account for specified reasons. For example, the bank could deduct from Algor's account its monthly service charge, and payments due on a bank loan. Similarly, it could add amounts, such as interest on investments. In order to notify Algor of these changes, debit memos and credit memos are used.

Financial Institution Debit Memos

Debit memos issued by financial institutions inform the customer that money has been taken from the customer's account. The institution would remove money from a business's account for the following reasons:
- payment due on a loan
- bank service charges
- correction of previous errors

NSF cheque: *a cheque issued by a person who does not have funds in his or her account equal to the amount of the cheque.*

- an **NSF cheque**: NSF stands for non-sufficient funds. In this case Algor Computer Services deposits a cheque from one of its customers, increasing the business's bank account. However, when it is found that the cheque is of no value because the customer has no funds in his or her account to cover the cheque, the bank takes the money out of Algor's account. It immediately notifies Algor Computer Services that the cheque is NSF by sending a debit memo. It is then up to Algor Computer Services to collect the amount of the worthless cheque from the customer.

FIGURE 6-1 A BANK DEBIT MEMO ISSUED TO ALGOR COMPUTER SERVICES

THE ROYAL BANK OF CANADA
Oct. 26, 19 90
Account Number: 6 2 5 - 0 4 0 - 8 7 0
Particulars: Non-sufficient funds – Shannon Fagan

Algor Computer Services
55 Eastern Parkway
Kanata, ON
K2L 2B1

MADE UP BY: R.C.
CHECKED BY: T.L.
TOTAL: 900 —
PLUS CHARGES: 20 —
TOTAL: 920 —

"A debit memo received from a financial institution reduces the business's claim on the institution."

Again, one should note that the form is called a *debit memo* because the financial institution issued the document. The entry in the institution's books would be a debit to reduce the institution's liability to the business. However, the entry in the business's books will show a decrease in the bank balance (that is, a credit to the Cash account). The entry for the bank debit memo received by Algor Computer Services is shown below.

Oct. 26 Bank Debit Memo: The debit memo is for $920. A $900 NSF cheque was returned to Algor Computer Services by the bank; it had originally been deposited by Algor Computer Services after being received from a customer, Shannon Fagan, on account. The bank charged $20 for its cost in processing and returning the cheque.

GENERAL JOURNAL

PAGE 391

DATE 1990		PARTICULARS	PR	DEBIT	CREDIT
Oct.	26	Accounts Receivable	120	900 —	
		Bank Expense	650	20 —	
		Cash	100		920 —
		NSF cheque of Shannon Fagan			

GENERAL LEDGER

Accounts Receivable 120	Bank Expense 650	Cash 100
dr. / cr.	dr. / cr.	dr. / cr.
Oct. 26 900	Oct. 26 20	Oct. 26 920

The explanation for the entry is as follows:
- A debit is made to Accounts Receivable for $900 because Algor Computer Services has regained its claim on Shannon Fagan. The original cheque issued to Algor by Fagan had no value.
- A debit is made to Bank Expense to record the $20 NSF charge.
- The bank took the $900 out of Algor Computer Services' account, because the cheque was returned by Shannon Fagan's bank. As well, Algor's bank took $20 for its services in connection with the NSF cheque. To decrease the asset Cash, a credit is made.

In some businesses, the cost of the NSF cheque to the business is passed on directly to the customer, for it is the customer who issued the NSF cheque. In such a case the entry would be as follows:

GENERAL JOURNAL

PAGE 391

DATE 1990		PARTICULARS	PR	DEBIT	CREDIT
Oct.	26	Accounts Receivable	120	920 —	
		Cash	100		920 —
		NSF cheque of Shannon Fagan			

GENERAL LEDGER

Accounts Receivable 120	Cash 100
dr. / cr.	dr. / cr.
Oct. 26 920	Oct. 26 920

In many cases, it is not necessary for a financial institution to immediately inform a customer of changes that it has made to the customer's account. A service charge for the month is an example. In these situations, the bank notifies the customer of the changes on the bank statement which is sent to the customer each month. This procedure is examined in Chapter 12.

Financial Institution Credit Memos

> "A credit memo received from a financial institution increases the business's claim on the institution."

Credit memos issued by financial institutions inform the business that money has been added to its account. The institution could add money to a business's account for a variety of reasons:
- deposit of interest on savings accounts or investments
- deposit of a loan to the business
- collection of an account receivable for the business
- correction of a previous error

FIGURE 6-2 A BANK CREDIT MEMO RECEIVED BY ALGOR COMPUTER SERVICES

```
THE ROYAL BANK                                              Oct. 24    19 90
OF CANADA
C/A PCA S/A   ACCOUNT NUMBER   TRAN CODE   DATE OF DEPOSIT   AMT. OF DEPOSIT   ☐ ERROR BRINGING   ☐ CHEQUE NOT
                               SEE REVERSE                     TOTAL FORWARD      LISTED
 ✓   6 2 5 1 — 1 0 4 0 1 — 1 8 5 1 3    ☐ ERROR           ☐ U.S. LISTED AS   LISTED AS         CORRECT
                                          SUBTR./ADDIT.     CDN./CDN. AS U.S.   $                $
                            PARTICULARS                                       AMOUNT/ADJUSTMENT
Short-Term Loan

                                                       TOTAL
              Algor Computer Services      MADE UP      OF         5 000   —
                                             BY       FORMS
              55 Eastern Parkway            RJ       ATTACHED
                                                      SUB-
              Kanata, ON                              TOTAL
                                          CHECKED    LESS
              K2L 2B1                        BY      CHARGES
                                            MB       TOTAL      5 000   —
```

The above document, issued by a bank, is called a credit memo, because according to the bank's books, more money is owed to the business. To record this liability to the business, a credit is made in the bank's books. However, we are doing the business's books, so the entry in Algor Computer Services' books to account for credit memos received from the bank would be as follows:

Example 1
Oct. 24   Bank Credit Memo: Algor Computer Services borrowed $5 000 from the bank.

GENERAL JOURNAL

PAGE 390

DATE 1990		PARTICULARS	PR	DEBIT	CREDIT
Oct.	24	Cash	100	5 000 —	
		Short-Term Loans	210		5 000 —
		One-year loan; 9% interest; monthly payments of $437			

GENERAL LEDGER

Cash	100	Short-Term Loans	210
dr.	cr.	dr.	cr.
Oct. 24 5 000			Oct. 24 5 000

The explanation for the entry is as follows:
- To increase the balance in the bank by $5 000, a debit to the asset account Cash is made.
- The short-term loan is a liability and to increase the liability a credit is made to Short-Term Loans.

THE FACTS SPEAK...

Canadian chartered banks had 72 802 business loans outstanding at the end of 1988.

Example 2

Oct. 25 Bank Credit Memo: The bank deposited $490 in interest from marketable securities held by Algor Computer Services.

GENERAL JOURNAL

PAGE 391

DATE 1990		PARTICULARS	PR	DEBIT	CREDIT
Oct.	25	Cash	100	490 –	
		Bank Interest	440		490 –
		Interest from securities			

GENERAL LEDGER

Cash	100		Bank Interest	440
dr.	cr.		dr.	cr.
Oct. 25 490				Oct. 25 490

The explanation for the entry is as follows:
- To increase the balance in the bank account by $490, a debit is made to the asset account Cash.
- The revenue account Bank Interest increases because there was an increase in an asset caused by providing a service (a loan from Algor Computer Services to the issuer of the marketable securities). To increase a revenue account a credit is made.

Business Debit and Credit Memos

When Algor Computer Services started business, it purchased a number of items that had to be returned to suppliers. In some cases the items were damaged; in other cases the wrong item was delivered. The bookkeeper at Algor communicated with the supplier in order to arrange for either a reduction in the price or a return of the item. Similarly, some of Algor's customers wanted a reduction in the amount they owed, or a refund of the money they had paid. In some cases the computer services had not been correctly completed; in other cases, people who registered for computer software lessons had been unable to attend. In some instances, the amount of the invoice was incorrect, and had to be either increased or decreased.

It soon became obvious to the bookkeeper at Algor Computer Services that source documents had to be designed to handle these situations.

Businesses also rely on debit and credit memos to communicate information. Memos received by Algor from suppliers communicate information

THE FACTS SPEAK...

Canadian chartered banks had 8 581 loans valued at over $50 million each outstanding at the end of 1988.

> "Debit invoices, debit notes, and debit advices are synonymous with debit memos."

> "Credit invoices, credit notes, and credit advices are synonymous with credit memos."

> "Debit memos received by a company increase the accounts payable."

about amounts owing. Memos issued to Algor's customers communicate information about claims that Algor has on them.

Business Debit and Credit Memos Received

Businesses receive debit and credit memos that indicate changes made to their account by the supplier. Alternate names for debit memos are debit invoices, debit notes, and debit advices; alternate names for credit memos are credit invoices, credit notes, and credit advices.

A debit memo received by Algor increases the amount it owes to the supplier (an account payable to Algor). When a debit memo is issued by a supplier, it makes a debit entry to its Accounts Receivable account to increase the claim on Algor. There are a number of reasons that the supplier would send Algor a notice indicating that the amount owing by Algor has increased:

- the supplier undercharged Algor on a previous invoice due to an error
- the quantity shipped was more than was indicated on the original invoice

The entry to record a debit memo in Algor's books is:

Oct. 31 Debit Memo #46 received: From Dumachel Lumber Ltd., $79 due to error made on Purchase Invoice #593.

GENERAL JOURNAL

PAGE 396

DATE 1990		PARTICULARS	PR	DEBIT	CREDIT
Oct.	31	Office Equipment	175	79 —	
		Accounts Payable	200		79 —
		Error on Purchase Invoice #593, Dumachel Lumber Ltd.,			
		Debit Memo #46			

GENERAL LEDGER

Office Equipment	175	Accounts Payable	200
dr.	cr.	dr.	cr.
Oct. 31 79			Oct. 31 79

FIGURE 6-3 A DEBIT MEMO RECEIVED BY ALGOR FROM DUMACHEL LUMBER LTD.

```
                                                    DEBIT MEMORANDUM
                                                          #46
                    DUMACHEL LUMBER LTD.
                           47 Warrington Road
                           Nepean, ON  K2B 4R3
                              (613) 555-9382

                                       Date:  Oct. 31, 1990

    Name:    Algor Computer Services
    Address: 55 Eastern Parkway, Kanata, ON  K2L 2B1

         Reason for Charge                    Amount

         Error on Purchase Invoice #593       $79.00




    Authorized by:  T. Dumachel
```

The explanation for the entry is as follows:
- The amount of the original invoice was too low, so a debit is made to Office Equipment to increase that asset by the amount of the error.
- A credit is made to Accounts Payable to increase the amount outstanding.

> *Credit memos received by a business reduce the accounts payable.*

Credit memos received decrease the amount owing to suppliers. The document is issued by the supplier, who has made a credit entry to reduce its claim on the business. Suppliers send credit memos for a variety of reasons:
- overcharge on original invoice due to an error
- service performed below expectations and price reduced
- assets returned (only service businesses have been studied to date; entries for merchandise returned will be examined in Chapter 9)

FIGURE 6-4 A CREDIT MEMO RECEIVED BY ALGOR FROM WESTWAY WINDOW CLEANERS LTD.

CREDIT INVOICE   No. 334

WESTWAY WINDOW CLEANERS LTD.

99 Carlisle Avenue West
Nepean, ON K2B 3F4

Date: Oct. 31, 1990

Name: Algor Computer Services

Address: 55 Eastern Parkway, Kanata, ON K2L 2B1

Reason for Refund	Amount
Incomplete job - Purchase Invoice #358	$50.00

Authorized by: T. Peazel

The following illustrates the entry required for a credit memo received by Algor Computer Services:

Oct. 31   Credit Memo #334 received: From Westway Window Cleaners Ltd., $50 reduction on Purchase Invoice #358 due to incomplete job.

GENERAL JOURNAL

PAGE 396

DATE 1990		PARTICULARS	PR	DEBIT	CREDIT
Oct.	31	Accounts Payable	200	50 —	
		Miscellaneous Expense	760		50 —
		Reduction on Purchase Invoice #358; Credit Memo #334			
		from Westway Window Cleaners Ltd.			

GENERAL LEDGER

Accounts Payable	200		Miscellaneous Expense	760
dr.	cr.		dr.	cr.
Oct. 31 50				Oct. 31 50

The explanation for the entry is as follows:
- The amount owing to Westway Window Cleaners Ltd. is reduced because it was an incomplete job. To reduce the liability, a debit is made to Accounts Payable.

- The cost of window cleaning is reduced, so a credit is made to Miscellaneous Expense, which had been debited at the time of the original transaction.

Business Debit and Credit Memos Issued

> "Debit memos issued by a business increase accounts receivable."

Algor Computer Services issues debit and credit memos to its customers (accounts receivable) for the same reasons that Algor Computer Services receives them from its suppliers. However, from the accounting point of view, one must remember that

> "Credit memos issued by a business decrease accounts receivable."

(a) debit memos issued by Algor Computer Services increase Algor's claims on its customers (a debit to an asset account increases that asset).

(b) credit memos issued by Algor Computer Services decrease Algor's claims on its customers (a credit to an asset account decreases that asset).

The following entries illustrate transactions that occur from the issuing of debit and credit memos:

Debit Memo Issued

Nov. 1   Debit Memo #11-0022 issued: To Connie Belsher, $23 due to undercharge on Sales Invoice #55-6633.

FIGURE 6-5 DEBIT MEMO ISSUED BY ALGOR COMPUTER SERVICES TO CONNIE BELSHER

DEBIT MEMO		11 - 0022
	ALGOR COMPUTER SERVICES	
	Your One Stop for Computer Installations and Training	
	55 Eastern Parkway, Kanata, ON K2L 2B1	
	Phone (613) 500-1212	
	Date:	November 1, 1990
Name:	Connie Belsher	
Address:	32 Majestic Drive, Nepean, ON K3B 4V3	
Reason for Charge		**Amount**
Error on Sales Invoice #55-6633, undercharged for lessons		$23.00
Authorized by:	V. Marshall	

GENERAL JOURNAL

PAGE 398

DATE 1990		PARTICULARS	PR	DEBIT	CREDIT
Nov.	1	Accounts Receivable	120	23 —	
		Software Lessons	410		23 —
		Error on Sales Invoice #55-6633; Debit Memo #11-0022			

GENERAL LEDGER

Accounts Receivable	120
dr.	cr.
Nov. 1 23	

Software Lessons	410
dr.	cr.
	Nov. 1 23

The explanation for the entry is as follows:
- Since Connie Belsher was undercharged on Sales Invoice #55-6633, the business increases its claim on her by making a debit to the asset Accounts Receivable.
- The increase in the asset is caused by providing a service, which means an increase (credit) to the revenue account Software Lessons.

Credit Memo Issued

Nov. 2   Credit Memo #77-0076 issued: To Shaun Port, $90 to reduce Sales Invoice #55-6712 as all computer network services were not completed.

FIGURE 6-6 A CREDIT MEMO ISSUED BY ALGOR COMPUTER SERVICES TO SHAUN PORT

CREDIT MEMO   77 - 0076

ALGOR
COMPUTER
SERVICES

Your One Stop for Computer Installations and Training
55 Eastern Parkway, Kanata, ON   K2L 2B1
Phone (613) 500-1212

Date: _November 2, 1990_

Name: _Shaun Port_

Address: _22 Vermont Drive, Ottawa, ON   K6F 2D4_

Reason for Refund	Amount
Sales Invoice #55-6712, Computer Network Services	$90.00

Authorized by: _V. Marshall_

GENERAL JOURNAL

PAGE 399

DATE 1990		PARTICULARS	PR	DEBIT	CREDIT
Nov.	2	Computer Services	400	90 –	
		Accounts Receivable	120		90 –
		Refund on Sales Invoice #55-6712; Credit Memo #77-0076			
		issued to Shaun Port			

GENERAL LEDGER

Computer Services		400	Accounts Receivable		120
dr.		cr.	dr.		cr.
Nov. 2	90			Nov. 2	90

The explanation for the entry is as follows:
- The revenue account must be decreased because the $90 was not earned, and to decrease a revenue account a debit is made.
- Since the services provided to Shaun Port were not completed, the business's claim on him has been reduced by $90, so Accounts Receivable must be credited.

Some businesses use a separate Refund account to maintain better internal control over the dollar value of refunds. That Refund account would be a contra-revenue account, for it recognizes that the business has had to refund some of the revenue received. An example of an entry to a contra-revenue account for a refund is illustrated below.

> *"A contra-revenue account recognizes a decrease in an asset due to the cancellation of a sale of a good or a service."*

Nov. 2 Credit Memo #77-0077 issued: To V. Lindquist, $120 to reduce Sales Invoice #55-6715; Lindquist was unable to complete software lessons.

GENERAL JOURNAL

PAGE 399

DATE 1990		PARTICULARS	PR	DEBIT	CREDIT
Nov.	2	Refunds	415	120 –	
		Accounts Receivable	120		120 –
		Refund on Sales Invoice #55-6715; Credit Memo #77-0077			
		issued to V. Lindquist			

GENERAL LEDGER

Refunds		415	Accounts Receivable		120
dr.		cr.	dr.		cr.
Nov. 2	120			Nov. 2	120

The explanation for the entry is as follows:
- A debit is made to Refunds, a contra-revenue account, because the inflow of assets from the sale of services has decreased.
- A credit is made to Accounts Receivable, to decrease the claim on V. Lindquist.

To exercise even more internal control, a separate account could be used for Service Refunds and Software Lessons Refunds. If the more specific contra-revenue account Service Refunds is used, it is deducted from the revenue account Computer Services on the income statement, to give a net figure. A similar treatment occurs for Software Lessons. Algor, however, uses one refund account for both items.

FIGURE 6-7 INCOME STATEMENT SHOWING PRESENTATION OF A CONTRA-REVENUE ACCOUNT

Algor Computer Services
Partial Income Statement
for the month ended October 31, 1990

Revenue		
Computer Services	$98 500	
Software Lessons	19 400	117 900
Less: Refunds		5 400
Total Revenue		$112 500

If refunds are significantly higher in certain fiscal periods, management should examine the reasons and institute policies to control the amount.

Source Document Summary

The major source documents used by a business have now been studied. Figure 6-8 summarizes the six main source documents studied in Chapter 2 along with those studied in this chapter. It is very important that you be able to correctly journalize transactions from these source documents. If an error is made in journalizing, all the steps in the accounting cycle that follow journalizing will have incorrect data.

FIGURE 6-8 THE SOURCE DOCUMENTS THAT ARE COMMONLY USED IN A BUSINESS

Summary of Source Documents

Purchase Invoice	Financial Institution — Debit Memo
Cheque Copy or Stub	Credit Memo
Sales Invoice	Business Debit Memo — Received
Cash Receipt Slip	Issued
Cash Sales Slip	Business Credit Memo — Received
Memo or Voucher	Issued

Chapter 6: Special Transactions

LESSON REVIEW

1. In general, why do financial institutions issue debit and credit memos?

2. Give four reasons why a financial institution would increase the balance of a business's account. What document informs the business that this has been done?

3. Give four reasons why a financial institution would reduce the balance of a business's account. What document informs the business that this has been done?

4. In general, why would a business receive debit and credit memos from other businesses?

5. Why do businesses issue debit memos?

6. Why do businesses issue credit memos?

7. The relationship between the bank and a customer with money on deposit is frequently described as "the opposite sides of the same coin." Describe this relationship.

LESSON APPLICATIONS

8. Refer to the source document below to answer the following questions.
   (a) What type of source document is it?
   (b) Who issued the source document?
   (c) Why was this document issued?
   (d) Who received the document?
   (e) Give the journal entry to record the document in the books of the recipient. The NSF charge will not be absorbed by the company.

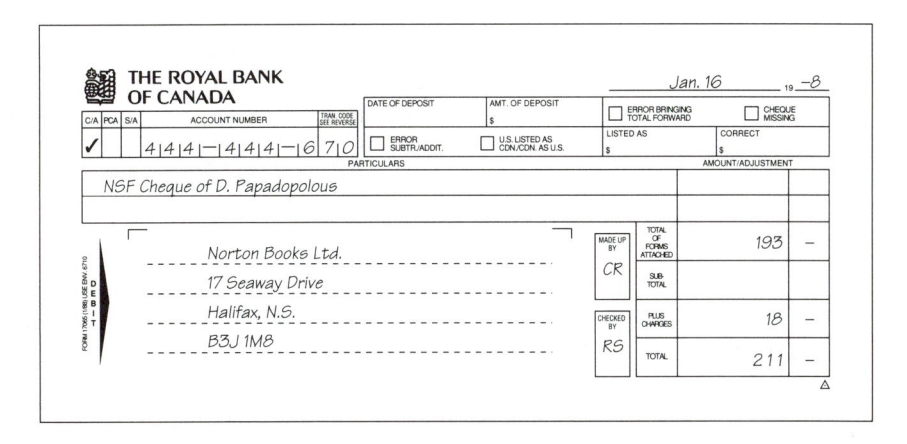

THE ROYAL BANK OF CANADA					Jan. 16	19 –8
C/A PCA S/A	ACCOUNT NUMBER	TRAN. CODE SEE REVERSE	DATE OF DEPOSIT	AMT. OF DEPOSIT $	☐ ERROR BRINGING TOTAL FORWARD	☐ CHEQUE MISSING
✓	4|4|4|–|4|4|4|–|6|7|0		☐ ERROR SUBTR./ADDIT.	☐ U.S. LISTED AS CDN./CDN. AS U.S.	LISTED AS $	CORRECT $
	PARTICULARS				AMOUNT/ADJUSTMENT	
NSF Cheque of D. Papadopolous						
	Norton Books Ltd.			MADE UP BY CR	TOTAL OF FORMS ATTACHED	193 –
	17 Seaway Drive				SUB-TOTAL	
	Halifax, N.S.			CHECKED BY RS	PLUS CHARGES	18 –
	B3J 1M8				TOTAL	211 –

9. Refer to the source document below to answer the following questions.
   (a) What type of source document is it?
   (b) Who issued the source document?
   (c) Why was this document issued?
   (d) Who received the document?
   (e) Give the journal entry to record the document in the books of the recipient.

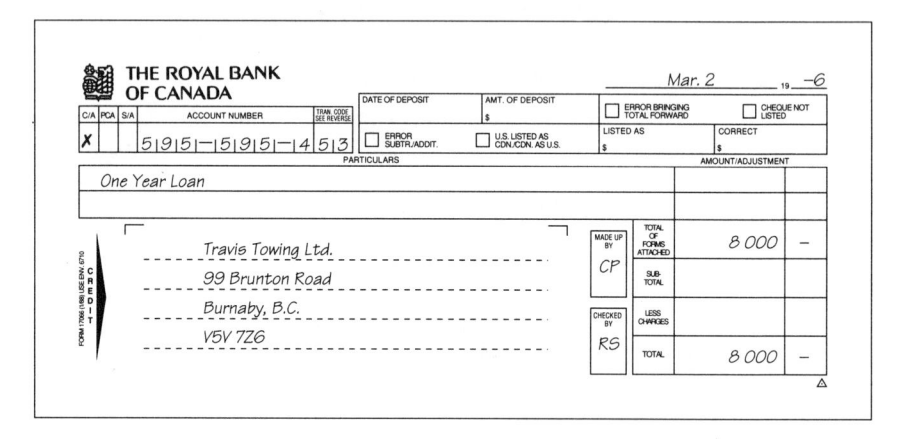

```
THE ROYAL BANK                                      Mar. 2      19 -6
OF CANADA
                DATE OF DEPOSIT    AMT. OF DEPOSIT
C/A PCA S/A  ACCOUNT NUMBER  TRAN. CODE           ☐ ERROR BRINGING    ☐ CHEQUE NOT
                             SEE REVERSE            TOTAL FORWARD       LISTED
 X   5195-15195-1453  ☐ ERROR      ☐ U.S. LISTED AS   LISTED AS          CORRECT
                       SUBTR./ADDIT.  CDN./CDN. AS U.S.  $               $
                        PARTICULARS                              AMOUNT/ADJUSTMENT
  One Year Loan

                                                    TOTAL
                                          MADE UP   OF FORMS       8 000  —
         Travis Towing Ltd.                BY       ATTACHED
                                          CP
         99 Brunton Road                            SUB-
                                                    TOTAL
         Burnaby, B.C.                    CHECKED   LESS
                                            BY     CHARGES
         V5V 7Z6                           RS
                                                    TOTAL          8 000  —
```

10. Journalize the following transactions. Choose appropriate account names.

   Dec. 4 Bank Debit Memo: $42 for service charges for month of November.
         5 Bank Debit Memo: $75 including charge for NSF cheque deposited on November 29; it was received on account on that date from Arthur Ault.
            Note: NSF charge is $18. It is company policy not to absorb this charge.
        11 Bank Credit Memo: Borrowed $7 000 from the bank.
        12 Bank Debit Memo: $125 including charge for NSF cheque deposited on December 6; it was received on account on that date from Wendy Marshall.
        19 Bank Debit Memo: $24 to correct error on loan interest; previous amount deducted was insufficient.

11. Refer to the source document in Figure 6-9 to answer the following questions.
   (a) Who issued the document?
   (b) Who received the document?
   (c) What is the document? Why was it issued?
   (d) What effect does it have on the books of the issuer?
   (e) Assuming that you are the accountant for Wendover Accounting Services, prepare a journal entry for the source document.

FIGURE 6-9

```
┌─────────────────────────────────────────────────────────────┐
│  Moribund Printers Ltd.              CREDIT MEMORANDUM      │
│                                             #330           │
│  33 Clearview Road                                          │
│  Oakville, ON   K3B 4V9                                     │
│  (416) 555-0001                                             │
│                                                             │
│                                    Date:  June 11, 19-4     │
│                                                             │
│  Name:    Wendover Accounting Services                      │
│  Address: 88 Trenton Blvd., Delta, BC  V4B 3R5              │
│                                                             │
│  ┌──────────────────────────────────────┬────────────────┐  │
│  │ Reason for Adjustment                │ Amount         │  │
│  ├──────────────────────────────────────┼────────────────┤  │
│  │ Invoice #449                         │                │  │
│  │ Additional copies were to be         │   $320.00      │  │
│  │ provided free of charge              │                │  │
│  └──────────────────────────────────────┴────────────────┘  │
│                                                             │
│  Authorized by:  K. Hyde                                    │
└─────────────────────────────────────────────────────────────┘
```

12. Refer to the source document below to answer the following questions.
    (a) Who issued the document?
    (b) Who received the document?
    (c) What is the document? Why was it issued?
    (d) What effect does it have on the books of the issuer?
    (e) Assuming that you are the accountant for Wendover Accounting Services, prepare a journal entry for the source document.

```
┌─────────────────────────────────────────────────────────────┐
│  Modern Office Supplies Ltd.         DEBIT MEMORANDUM       │
│                                             M226           │
│  76 Pacific Court, Unit 12                                  │
│  Delta, BC   V4B 2C2                                        │
│  (604) 555-9901                                             │
│                                                             │
│                                    Date:  05/24/-4          │
│                                                             │
│  Name:    Wendover Accounting Services                      │
│  Address: 88 Trenton Blvd., Delta, BC  V4B 3R5              │
│                                                             │
│  ┌──────────────────────────────────────┬────────────────┐  │
│  │ Reason for Charge                    │ Amount         │  │
│  ├──────────────────────────────────────┼────────────────┤  │
│  │ Error on Invoice #440, for           │   $420.00      │  │
│  │ office desks                         │                │  │
│  │                                      │                │  │
│  │                              TOTAL   │   $420.00      │  │
│  └──────────────────────────────────────┴────────────────┘  │
│                                                             │
│  Authorization:  E. Ludanyi                                 │
└─────────────────────────────────────────────────────────────┘
```

13. Journalize each of the following transactions. Choose appropriate account names.

    Nov. 14 Purchase Invoice #883: From Independent Computer Supplies Ltd. for computer supplies, $210.

    17 Credit Memo #44 received: From Independent Computer Supplies Ltd., $72 for computer supplies returned.

    18 Purchase Invoice #92: From Regina Computer Equipment Ltd., $2 498 for computer equipment.

    21 Debit Memo #18 received: From Regina Computer Equipment Ltd., $122 for undercharge on Invoice #92.

    22 Bank Debit Memo: $76.50 including charge for NSF cheque deposited on November 16; it was received on account on that date from D. Mortimore.
    Note: NSF charge is $20. It is company policy not to absorb this charge.

    23 Bank Credit Memo: $3 000 bank loan.

14. Refer to the source document below to answer the following questions.
    (a) Who issued the document?
    (b) Who received the document?
    (c) What is the document? Why was it issued?
    (d) What effect does it have on the books of the receiver?
    (e) Assuming that you are the accountant for Northern Plumbing Services, prepare a journal entry for the source document.

Northern Plumbing Services

44 Waskigan Lane
Sudbury, ON L3V 4N8
(705) 555-5555

Date: _Aug. 31, 19–9_

Name: _Nickel Co-operative_

Address: _912 Harvey Crescent, Sudbury, ON L4V 4V5_

Reason for Credit	Amount
Error on Invoice #12–338	$1 230.00
TOTAL CREDIT to your account	$1 230.00

Authorization: _L. Bigcanoe_

CREDIT MEMORANDUM #671

15. Using the source document below, answer the following questions.
    (a) Who issued the document?
    (b) Who received the document?
    (c) What is the document? Why was it issued?
    (d) What effect does it have on the books of the receiver?
    (e) Assuming that you are the accountant for Northern Plumbing Services, prepare a journal entry for the source document.

Northern Plumbing Services

44 Waskigan Lane
Sudbury, ON L3V 4N8
(705) 555-5555

Date: _Aug. 27, 19-9_

Name: _Sudbury High School_

Address: _33 Deavy Street, Sudbury, ON L4M 3N8_

Reason for Charge	Amount
Price on Invoice #92-997 to be established on receipt of invoice from our supplier	$924.00
Please Pay	$924.00

Authorization: _L. Bigcanoe_

DEBIT MEMORANDUM #0229

---

16. Journalize the following transactions. Choose appropriate account names.

    Nov. 14 Sales Invoice #834: $245 for legal service performed for Tracy Bartoli.

    17 Credit Memo #15 issued: To Tracy Bartoli, $25 overcharge on Sales Invoice #834.

    19 Sales Invoice #835: $25 for legal service performed for B. Kennedy.

    22 Debit Memo #41 issued: To B. Kennedy, $15 for error on Sales Invoice #835.

    24 Bank Debit Memo: $94.50 including charge for NSF cheque deposited on November 6; the cheque was received on account on that date from Peter Lewe. Note: NSF charge is $16. It is company policy not to absorb this charge.

    30 Bank Debit Memo: $27.80 for service charges.

    30 Bank Credit Memo: $500 for interest on savings.

6.2 Sales Tax

"Provincial governments, except Alberta, levy a retail sales tax (PST)."

The provincial governments (except for Alberta) have passed legislation that allows them to collect a retail sales tax. The provincial retail sales tax system has been in place for a number of years. The rates of the retail sales tax in the various provinces are shown in Figure 6-10.

"The federal government levies a 7 percent goods and services tax (GST)."

The federal government instituted a goods and services tax of 7 percent in 1991. It replaces the manufacturers' sales tax, which was a 13.5 percent tax imposed on goods manufactured in Canada.

FIGURE 6-10 RETAIL SALES TAX BY PROVINCE, AS OF JUNE, 1990

Alberta	0%	Nova Scotia	10%
British Columbia	6	Ontario	8
Manitoba	7	Prince Edward Island	10
New Brunswick	11	Quebec	9
Newfoundland	12	Saskatchewan	7

(Neither the Yukon nor the Northwest Territories apply a territory retail sales tax.)

The Federal Goods and Services Tax (GST)

"The GST is referred to as a value-added tax."

The goods and services tax applies to most goods and services. It is referred to as a value-added tax, because the government only receives tax on the increase in the value of the good at each stage of its distribution. The following example illustrates this process. After a desk is made, the manufacturer collects from the wholesaler, to whom it is sold, a 7 percent tax on the $500 wholesale selling price of the desk, which is $35. The amount of this tax is remitted to the federal government. The wholesaler receives an input tax credit for the $35. An **input tax credit** is a credit given to a seller of goods or services for the GST that was paid on purchases. Assume the wholesaler sells the desk to the retailer for $800 plus $56 GST. The wholesaler collects $56 in GST, but received a $35 credit for the amount paid to the manufacturer. Thus, the wholesaler remits only $21 GST to the federal government. This figure represents 7 percent of the $300 increase in value of the desk. When the retailer sells the desk to the consumer for $1 200, $84 GST is charged. The retailer, who received a $56 input tax credit for the GST that was paid when the desk was bought, remits the difference between the $56 paid and the $84 collected, or $28, to the federal government. This represents a 7 percent tax on the $400 value added to the desk by the retailer, who bought the desk at $800 and sold it for $1 200. In effect then, the total GST on the article is paid by the consumer, who pays $84 GST to the retailer on the final selling price of $1 200.

Input tax credit: a credit given to a seller of goods or services for the GST that was paid on purchases.

FIGURE 6-11 THE FEDERAL GOODS AND SERVICES TAX IS LEVIED AT EACH STEP IN THE DISTRIBUTION PROCESS

Manufacturer	**Wholesaler**	**Retailer**	**Consumer**
Sells desk for $500 + $35 tax	Sells desk for $800 + $56 tax	Sells desk for $1 200 + $84 tax	Pays total of $84 of tax
	Wholesaler keeps $35 (input tax credit) of tax collected	Retailer keeps $56 (input tax credit) of tax collected	
Tax paid to federal government $35	$21	$28	

Total taxes paid to federal government = $35 + $21 + $28 = $84

> *Goods and services may be classified as taxable, tax-free, or tax-exempt for the purposes of the GST.*

Tax-free (or zero-rated) items: basic groceries, prescription drugs, and medical devices.

Tax-exempt items: health and dental care, educational services, day-care services, legal aid services, residential rents, financial services, and municipal transit and passenger ferries.

Not all goods and services are taxed by the federal government under the GST. Goods and services are classified as taxable, tax-free, and tax-exempt. **Tax-free** (or zero-rated) items include basic groceries, prescription drugs, and medical devices. For these items, the seller does not charge GST. The sellers will still be able to claim input tax credits for any tax paid on purchases used in making the tax-free goods or services. Thus, the items will be tax-free. **Tax-exempt** items include health and dental care, educational services (Algor is not a recognized educational institution for GST purposes), day-care services, legal aid services, residential rents, financial services, and municipal transit and passenger ferries. For these items, the seller does not charge GST. However, sellers will not be able to claim input tax credits on the items required for the purpose of making the exempt good or service. A dentist will not charge a customer GST for goods and services given, and similarly cannot claim an input tax credit on tax that was paid for any of the goods or services used in the treatment. It is assumed that the dentist would price his or her own goods and services to include the GST that was paid when they were purchased.

Businesses whose gross revenue is less than $30 000 may also exempt themselves from collecting the GST. However, they cannot claim payments of the GST on goods and services that they buy as an input tax credit.

The following journal entries illustrate the bookkeeping concepts related to the collection of the GST from sales, and the remittance of it to the federal government. The first example relates to the purchase of goods and services.

May 5   Purchase Invoice #934: From Wesley Office Supplies, $400 for office supplies, $28 GST.

GENERAL JOURNAL

PAGE 438

DATE 1991		PARTICULARS	PR	DEBIT	CREDIT
May	5	Office Supplies	150	400 —	
		GST Recoverable	135	28 —	
		Accounts Payable	200		428 —
		Purchase Invoice #934, Wesley Office Supplies			

GST Recoverable: the asset account used to record the GST input credit.

The explanation for the entry is as follows:
- A debit is made to Office Supplies to increase that asset.
- A debit is made to GST Recoverable for the input tax credit, the claim that Algor Computer Services has on the federal government for the amount of GST that was paid on the office supplies. Because the office supplies will be used by Algor Computer Services as it provides its services, the firm has a claim on the federal government for an input tax credit.
- A credit is made to Accounts Payable to reflect the liability to Wesley Office Supplies.

GENERAL LEDGER

Office Supplies		150
dr.		cr.
May 5 400		

GST Recoverable		135
dr.		cr.
May 5 28		

Accounts Payable		200
dr.		cr.
		May 5 428

When a sale is made by Algor Computer Services, the firm must collect the 7 percent GST from the customer.

May 5   Sales Invoice #55-7446: To Brendan Butler, $500 plus $35 GST, for software lessons.

GENERAL JOURNAL

PAGE 438

DATE 1991		PARTICULARS	PR	DEBIT	CREDIT
May	5	Accounts Receivable	120	535 —	
		Software Lessons	410		500 —
		GST Payable	230		35 —
		Sales Invoice #55-7446, Brendan Butler			

THE FACTS SPEAK...

Revenue from the GST is expected to be over $23 billion per year.

GENERAL LEDGER

Accounts Receivable 120		Software Lessons 410		GST Payable 230	
dr.	cr.	dr.	cr.	dr.	cr.
May 5 535			May 5 500		May 5 35

The explanation for the entry is as follows:
- A debit is made to Accounts Receivable to increase that asset, which represents a claim on Brendan Butler.
- A credit is made to the revenue account Software Lessons, which represents an increase in the inflow of assets from the sale of services.
- A credit is made to GST Payable, which represents an increase in Algor's liability to the federal government.

Businesses are required to remit to the federal government the difference between the GST Recoverable account and the GST Payable account at different times, depending on their annual sales. Firms that have annual sales greater than $6 million are required to file a GST return on a monthly basis. Firms with less than $6 million in sales may file quarterly, or annually if sales are less than $500 000. If filing on an annual basis, remittance of the tax must be made quarterly. The entry required for payment of the GST is shown below.

May 31   Cheque Copy #683: $2 390 in GST, which was the difference between GST Recoverable ($6 400) and GST Payable ($8 790).

GENERAL JOURNAL

PAGE 452

DATE 1991		PARTICULARS	PR	DEBIT	CREDIT
May	31	GST Payable	230	8 790 —	
		GST Recoverable	135		6 400 —
		Cash	100		2 390 —
		Cheque Copy #683, payment of GST			

GENERAL LEDGER

GST Payable	230		GST Recoverable	135		Cash	100
dr.	cr.		dr.	cr.		dr.	cr.
May 31 8 790	Balance as of		Balance as of	May 31 6 400			May 31 2 390
	May 31 8 790		May 31 6 400				
	0		0				

The explanation for the entry is as follows:
- A debit of $8 790 is made to GST Payable to reduce the balance of the account to nil.
- A credit of $6 400 is made to GST Recoverable to cancel the claim on the federal government for input tax credits.
- A credit of $2 390 is made to Cash to represent the decrease in that asset. An amount equal to the difference between the GST Payable and the GST Recoverable was paid to the federal government.

Provincial Retail Sales Tax

The nine provinces that levy a retail sales tax follow rules that are similar to those of the federal goods and services tax. The provincial sales taxes (PST) basically apply to goods and some services. At the time of writing, the federal government wanted the provinces to join its tax system, so that there would be one tax on the same goods and services. The revenue would then be split between the two levels of government. Such a universal tax would reduce the confusion for consumers and for businesses keeping track of taxes that apply at different rates and to different goods and services. Each province exempts certain goods from the retail sales tax. Some goods and services have a different rate applied to them, such as liquor, and hotel and motel accommodations. Some services are taxed, such as movies, repair services, and telephones.

For goods that will be resold, one should remember that the provincial retail sales tax is only paid by the final consumer. This differs from the GST, which is collected at each stage of the distribution process. Therefore a business pays the retail sales tax on taxable goods that it is not going to resell, and does not pay the tax on taxable goods that it will resell. A business that buys goods that will be resold provides the seller with a sales tax exemption number as proof that the tax does not have to be paid. The exemption number is obtained from the retail sales tax branch of the provincial government. The seller indicates on the invoice that the goods are sales tax exempt.

It is the responsibility of the business that sells the good to the "final"

> "A business pays the provincial retail sales tax on items that it is not going to resell."

consumer to collect the tax and remit it to the government. The term final consumer is debatable, for a person who buys a new car pays sales tax, and, in some provinces, so does the person who buys it when it is a used car. In order to be able to legally collect the tax, a business obtains a retail sales tax vendor's permit or licence. The business then collects the tax from customers each time a sale is made, and remits it to the government the following month.

There are generally three circumstances under which the sales tax does not have to be collected by the retailer:
(a) the good or service is tax-exempt;
(b) the good is going to be resold;
(c) the good is going to be used as part of another good in the manufacturing process.

> "Provincial retail sales taxes do not apply to all goods and services."

The following entries illustrate the collection and payment of the provincial retail sales tax. In the provinces of British Columbia, Saskatchewan, Manitoba, and Ontario, the retail sales tax is calculated as a percentage of the base price only. In the provinces of New Brunswick, Nova Scotia, Prince Edward Island, and Newfoundland, the retail sales tax is calculated as a percentage of the base price plus GST. Thus, one is paying a tax on a tax. At the time of writing, only Quebec has merged its provincial sales tax with the GST. In cases such as this, the province grants an input tax credit to businesses in the same way the federal government does. For Algor Computer Services the provincial retail tax rate will be 8 percent. This tax is calculated on the base price only.

May 11   Purchase Invoice #349: From Computer Suppliers of Canada, for computer supplies which are to be used in the business: supplies, $900; GST, $63; and PST, $72.

GENERAL JOURNAL

PAGE 444

DATE 1991		PARTICULARS	PR	DEBIT	CREDIT
May	11	Computer Supplies	155	972 —	
		GST Recoverable	135	63 —	
		Accounts Payable	200		1 035 —
		Purchase Invoice #349 from Computer Suppliers			
		of Canada			

GENERAL LEDGER

Computer Supplies		155
dr.		cr.
May 11 972		

GST Recoverable		135
dr.		cr.
May 11 63		

Accounts Payable		200
dr.		cr.
	May 11	1 035

The explanation for the entry is as follows:
- A debit is made to Computer Supplies to increase the amount of that asset. Note that since Algor Computer Services is the final consumer, the amount of the provincial sales tax is included in the cost of the asset.
- A debit is made to increase the asset GST Recoverable, since the goods are going to be used in the production of goods and services by Algor Computer Services. The firm therefore has a claim on the federal government for an input tax credit.
- A credit is made to Accounts Payable to increase the liability to Computer Suppliers of Canada.

Collecting Provincial Retail Sales Tax

An entry is made to record the retailer's liability for the provincial sales tax each time a sale is made. The following entry for cash sales of computer services by Algor records the liability to the provincial government for taxes collected.

June 4   Cash Sales Slips #99-7444 to #99-7446: $690 for cash sales; sales, $600; GST, $42; PST, $48.

GENERAL JOURNAL

PAGE 456

DATE 1991		PARTICULARS	PR	DEBIT	CREDIT
June	4	Cash	100	690 —	
		Computer Services	400		600 —
		GST Payable	230		42 —
		PST Payable	240		48 —
		Cash Sales Slips #99-7444 to #99-7446			

GENERAL LEDGER

Cash	100	Computer Services	400
dr.	cr.	dr.	cr.
June 4 690			June 4 600

GST Payable	230	PST Payable	240
dr.	cr.	dr.	cr.
	June 4 42		June 4 48

The explanation for the entry is as follows:
- A debit is made to Cash to increase that asset.
- A credit is made to Computer Services to increase that revenue account, for there is an increase in assets due to the sale of a service.
- A credit is made to GST Payable to increase the liability to the federal government for the goods and services tax collected from the sales.

- A credit is made to PST Payable to increase the liability to the provincial government for the provincial retail sales tax collected from the sales. The rate used in the example is 8 percent.

Remitting Provincial Retail Sales Tax

When the amounts for PST Payable are posted to the ledger account, it will show the accumulated sales tax collected for the month. Because the tax has been collected by Algor Computer Services, it represents a liability to the provincial government for it must be paid the following month. The PST Payable account is, therefore, a current liability. Algor Computer Services must remit to the provincial government sometime during July, the amount of sales tax collected in June. The date varies from province to province. The total collected in June was $9 254.

In some provinces, the retailer is permitted to keep part of the sales tax collected as a commission. This commission is paid to compensate the retailer for the labour and record keeping costs involved in collecting the tax. The amount may be a percentage of the tax collected, but there may be a maximum amount per year. For example, in Ontario the maximum amount of commission per year is $1 500. When the sales tax is remitted, the amount of the commission is deducted from the payment. The journal entry below shows Algor's sales tax submission for the month of June taking sales tax commission into account.

July 15   Cheque Copy #714: Paid $8 976.38 to the provincial treasurer. June sales tax collected amounted to $9 254.00. A commission of 3% was earned.

> "The Provincial Sales Tax Payable account is a liability to the provincial government."

> "A sales tax commission is a fee paid to the retailer for fulfilling the service of a tax-collector. This is not the primary source of revenue for a business, but it is a form of revenue nonetheless."

GENERAL JOURNAL

PAGE 493

DATE 1991		PARTICULARS	PR	DEBIT	CREDIT
July	15	PST Payable	240	9 254 —	
		Cash	100		8 976 38
		Sales Tax Commission	460		277 62
		Cheque Copy #714 to the Provincial Treasurer for sales tax			
		collected in June, less 3% commission			

GENERAL LEDGER

PST Payable		240
dr.	cr.	
July 15 9 254.00	Balance as of June 30 9 254.00	
	0	

Cash		100
dr.	cr.	
	July 15 8 976.38	

Sales Tax Commission		460
dr.	cr.	
	July 15 277.62	

The explanation for the entry is as follows:
- A debit is made to PST Payable to record the reduction in the liability to the provincial government.
- A credit is made to Cash to record the reduction in that asset. The amount sent is calculated as follows:
PST collected − Commission earned = Amount owing
- A credit is made to Sales Tax Commission to record the increase in an asset from the sale of a service. Sales Tax Commission is therefore a revenue account. The service in this case is acting as a tax collector for the provincial government.

LESSON REVIEW

17. Distinguish between the sales taxes collected by the federal and the provincial governments.

18. Which province does not have a retail sales tax?

19. Compare the manufacturers' sales tax to the GST.

20. Distinguish among taxable, tax-free, and tax-exempt goods under the GST.

21. Why is the GST referred to as a value-added tax?

22. What does the GST Recoverable account represent?

23. Comment on the following statement: "All items sold are subject to provincial sales tax."

24. What responsibilities does a retailer have concerning retail sales tax?

25. Under what three circumstances is retail sales tax not collected when goods are sold?

26. Why does the retailer receive a commission under some sales tax laws?

LESSON APPLICATIONS

Please note that for the following questions GST is 7 percent.

27. Journalize each of the following transactions for an elevator installation firm. Select appropriate account names. Assume that there is no provincial sales tax.

June 20 Sales Invoice #0339: To Highrise Developments Ltd., $172 plus GST.
  20 Cash Sales Slip #2227: Cash sale, $572 plus GST.
  21 Sales Invoice #0340: To Terrace Investments Ltd., $2 391 plus GST.
  21 Cash Sales Slip #2228: Cash sale, $2 195 plus GST.

28. Journalize each of the following transactions for an outdoor advertising firm. Select appropriate account names. Assume that there is no provincial sales tax.
   Nov. 14 Sales Invoice #94-922: To Pepsi-Cola Ltd., $22 300 plus GST, for outdoor advertising.
     14 Cash Sales Slips #94-229 to #94-232: Cash sales for the day, $4 572 plus GST.
     15 Sales Invoice #94-923: To Procter & Gamble, $16 539 plus GST.
     15 Cash Sales Slips #94-233 to #94-236: Cash sales for the day, $6 743 plus GST.
     15 Cheque Copy #94-739: $27 844 to the Receiver General of Canada for GST collected in October. The GST Payable was $39 462, and the GST Recoverable was $11 618.

29. Journalize each of the following transactions for a landscaping firm. Select appropriate account names. Assume that the GST and a provincial retail sales tax of 8 percent apply for each sale. The provincial retail sales tax is to be applied to the base price only.
   Sept. 12 Sales Invoice #528: To Windermere Estates, $4 902 for landscaping.
     12 Cash Sales Slip #33: Cash sale, $1 325.
     15 Sales Invoice #529: To Victoria Trust, $7 653.
     15 Cash Sales Slip #34: Cash sale, $780.
     15 Cheque Copy #727: $19 488 to the Receiver General of Canada for GST collected in August. The GST Payable was $28 423, and the GST Recoverable was $8 935.
     15 Cheque Copy #728: $23 831.04 to the Provincial Treasurer for provincial sales tax collected in August.

30. Journalize each of the following transactions for a management consulting firm. Select appropriate account names. Assume that a GST and a provincial retail sales tax of 6 percent apply to each sale. The provincial retail sales tax should be applied to the base price of the sale, and not include the GST.
   Nov. 13 Sales Invoice #7744: To Victoria Realty, $3 200.
     13 Cash Sales Slip #996: Cash sale, $670.
     15 Sales Invoice #7745: To Wong's Food Services, $1 400.
     15 Cash Sales Slip #997: Cash sale, $320.

15   Cheque Copy #83: $11 394 to the Receiver General of Canada for GST collected in October. The GST Payable was $17 220, and the GST Recoverable was $5 826.

15   Cheque Copy #84: $9 766.29 to the Provincial Treasurer for provincial retail sales tax collected in October; $292.99 was the commission deducted before the cheque was issued.

31. Journalize each of the following transactions for a cartoon film producer. Select appropriate account names. Assume that the GST and an 8 percent provincial retail sales tax apply to each sale. The provincial tax is to be applied to the base price plus the GST.

Dec. 12   Sales Invoice #44: To Bodin Television Acquisitions, $78 900 for television showing of cartoons.

12   Cash Sales Slip #63: Cash sale for video rental, $120.

15   Sales Invoice #45: To Beauchamp Broadcasting Company, $98 400 for television showing of cartoons.

15   Cash Sales Slip #64: Cash sale for video rentals, $930.

15   Cheque Copy #65: $82 476 to the Receiver General of Canada for GST collected in November. The amount of the GST Payable was $137 420, and the amount of the GST Recoverable was $54 944.

15   Cheque Copy #66: $99 356.36 to the Provincial Treasurer for retail sales tax collected in November; a $1 500 commission was deducted from the amount owing before the cheque was issued.

6.3 Credit Cards, Debit Cards, and Prepaid Cards

It is estimated that there are over 20 million financial institution credit cards in Canada. That does not include the large number issued by gas companies, airlines, and department stores. Very clearly, in this age of "plastic," many customers make their purchases through the use of a credit card.

> "Purchase by use of a credit card allows the buyer to pay at a later date."

When buying goods or services by using a credit card, the card issuer is giving the buyer additional time to pay for them. If payment is not made within a specified time, interest charges are added. The credit card may be one issued by the business itself, as is done by many major department stores such as Eaton's and oil companies such as Shell Canada Ltd. Other cards, such as VISA, MasterCard, or American Express are issued by a financial institution. Cards issued by a business are intended for use only when buying from the card-issuing company, whereas bank credit cards are meant for more widespread use.

The future holds out the possibility for even more use of "plastic" for our daily transactions. Consumer tests are being conducted on the use of debit cards. Prepaid cards are already being used to some degree

THE FACTS SPEAK...

There are more than 500 million credit card transactions in Canada every year.

in Canada, and extensively in Japan. It is forecast that by the year 2010 there will be little reason for one to carry cash. Credit cards, debit cards, and prepaid cards are discussed below.

Credit Cards

The obvious advantage to a business of accepting a credit card is that sales are increased. Consumers may be happy to have a credit card for any of the following reasons:
- they can carry less cash
- they can take advantage of sales and specials
- they can purchase necessities when carrying no cash
- they receive a record of all transactions, because the issuing business or financial institution sends all cardholders a monthly record of charges and payments on the card
- they have use of the card issuer's funds for up to thirty days before payment of the account is due

Consumers may not want a credit card, for
- they must pay a high rate of interest on amounts not paid shortly after receipt of the monthly statement (It is usually cheaper to obtain a bank loan to pay an overdue account.)
- they may not be able to control their spending, and fall susceptible to impulse buying
- they may not be able to meet monthly payment requirements

The advantages to a business in accepting a credit card go beyond increased sales. Businesses issuing their own credit cards
- do not have to count and handle as much cash
- have a record of customers; advertisements can subsequently be sent to them
- have a record of the value and number of purchases by individual customers; discounts can be offered to high volume customers to encourage them to stay loyal
- receive interest on overdue accounts (This amount would be earned by the bank for bank credit cards. The interest rate varies from 16 percent to 30 percent on outstanding balances.)

There are also some disadvantages to a business issuing their own credit cards. They
- can result in some of the customers not paying the amount due
- may result in a poor cash flow, for accounts receivable are not being collected
- increase the cost of goods and services, for the operation of a credit card system is a cost to the business

THE FACTS SPEAK...

The interest charges collected from credit cards exceed $1 billion in Canada every year.

Credit Department of a Business

When a customer wishes to obtain a retailer's credit card or open an account, he or she is sent to the credit department. Here the customer will complete a credit application that provides the retailer with information on which to decide whether credit should be extended. The credit department considers the credit application, and does a credit check before extending credit. The main points examined on the application are as follows:

(a) capital — does the person own assets of value, such as a house and car?
(b) stability — does the person keep a job, and live in one place?
(c) income — can the person afford monthly payments on a credit card?
(d) credit management — does the person understand his or her credit position, and manage it properly?

The credit department will contact the local credit bureau or a national credit rating institution such as Dun & Bradstreet in order to run a credit check on the applicant.

Credit Bureaus

> "A credit bureau collects information on people who buy on credit, and provides the information to credit grantors."

A credit bureau is an agency that provides information to credit grantors about people who apply for credit. In order to do business, such bureaus must register with the provincial government. A credit grantor is a business that offers credit to its customers. Businesses that use the credit bureau

(a) agree to provide the bureau with information on their credit customers; and
(b) obtain information from the bureau on credit applicants.

A file is maintained by the bureau on each person whose name is referred to it by the grantors. When a person makes an application for credit, the credit department of that business contacts the credit bureau in order to determine the applicant's credit history. The business identifies itself by business name and a code, and identifies the consumer being investigated by name, address, age, and place of employment. This procedure protects both the consumer and the business against misuse by unauthorized individuals.

The credit bureau is able to provide the credit grantor with information obtained from other credit grantors, or from public sources such as newspapers. The information supplied by other credit grantors usually includes that which is shown on their credit application. As well, the bureau will have information on where credit was used, the amount of credit granted, and past due amounts. A service charge is paid by the business to the credit bureau each time information is requested.

Due to consumer fears about improper use of information on file at credit bureaus, governments have passed legislation outlining the use to which the information can be put. Some of the important clauses relating to this legislation in British Columbia are outlined below, and they are consistent with the legislation of other provinces.

FIGURE 6-12 BC CREDIT BUREAU LEGISLATION

Explanation by consumer

15. A person may deliver to a reporting agency, in writing of not more than 100 words, an explanation, or additional information, about the circumstances surrounding any item of information referring to him in his file, and the reporting agency shall maintain the explanation or additional information in the file accompanying the item and include it in any report given containing the item.
1973-139-15.

Correction of errors

16. (1) Where the consumer disputes the accuracy and completeness of any information referring to him in his file in a reporting agency, he may file a statement of protest, in writing of not more than 100 words, with the reporting agency.

(2) Where a statement of protest is filed, the reporting agency shall use its best endeavours to confirm or complete the information and shall correct, supplement or delete the information in accordance with good practice.

(3) Where a reporting agency corrects, supplements or deletes information under subsection (2), the reporting agency shall, unless otherwise requested by the consumer, furnish notification of the correction, supplement or deletion to every person to whom a report based on the unamended file was given within one year before the correction, supplement or deletion is made.
1973-139-16.

Based on the information obtained from the credit bureau, and using its own guidelines for granting credit, the business decides whether to grant credit. A limit may also be placed on the amount that can be charged. As the customer shows his or her reliability in making payments, that limit may be increased.

The Facts Speak...

There are more than 20 million VISA and MasterCards issued in Canada.

Financial Institution Credit Cards

The introduction of financial institution credit cards and computer funds transfers has greatly changed the use of retail credit. Many businesses have completely abandoned offering their own credit system and rely exclusively on the financial institution credit cards.

Currently the major bank credit cards in Canada are MasterCard, VISA, and American Express. As indicated earlier, consumers make extensive use of these cards.

From the consumer's perspective, there are additional advantages to holding a financial institution's credit card as opposed to other credit cards:

- the cards are accepted in most retail outlets
- the holder can obtain cash advances up to a predetermined limit
- fewer cards need to be obtained and carried
- the cards are accepted in foreign countries

Algor Computer Services decided to join the VISA credit card system. When doing so, it realized that the advantages were as follows:

- Algor receives its money for the credit sale on the day of the transaction. At the end of the day it deposits the sales drafts (the documents on which the sales are recorded) with the bank, and the cash is credited to Algor's account. It is then the card issuer's responsibility to collect from the user.
- Algor does not have to operate its own credit card system, for it

"A sales draft is the document on which a financial institution credit card sale is recorded."

FIGURE 6-13 A SALES DRAFT FOR VISA

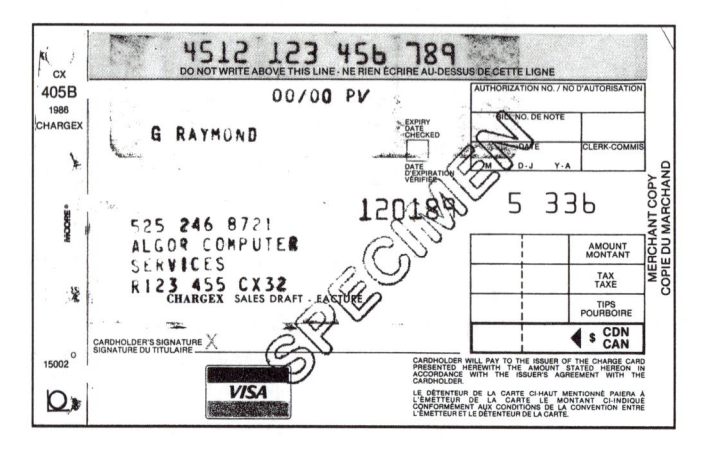

relies completely on VISA. It does not have to check out the reliability of prospective credit card customers.
- Algor does not have to concern itself with collection of payments from these customers. The financial institutions in the VISA system guarantee payment to the store in most cases.
- Algor may even increase its sales because many people have financial institution credit cards.

The disadvantage to Algor Computer Services of joining a financial institution credit card system is that it must pay a percentage of its sales as a fee to the bank. This discount is to compensate the institutions for the tasks involved in collecting the accounts: keeping records, collecting the accounts, issuing statements, issuing lists of lost and cancelled cards to businesses, and compensation for bad debts. The discount rate varies, as shown in the following chart for VISA:

FIGURE 6-14 A VISA DISCOUNT SCHEDULE

ROYAL BANK

VISA MERCHANT DISCOUNT SCHEDULE

* Average Monthly Volume		Average Draft Size			
		Under $30.00	$30.00 to $49.99	$50.00 to $99.99	$100.00 and Over
		%	%	%	%
$ 1-	$ 999	5.50	4.50	3.50	3.25
1,000-	2,499	4.75	4.00	3.25	2.75
2,500-	4,999	4.50	3.75	3.00	2.75
5,000-	12,499	4.25	3.50	2.75	2.50
12,500-	19,999	4.00	3.25	2.50	2.25
20,000-	29,999	3.75	3.00	2.25	2.25
30,000-	49,999	3.50	2.75	2.25	2.00
50,000-	74,999	3.25	2.75	2.00	2.00
75,000-	149,999	3.00	2.50	2.00	2.00
150,000-	299,999	2.50	2.25	2.00	2.00
300,000-	and over	2.00	2.00	2.00	2.00

The financial institution that issued the card also recovers its costs in other ways:

1. cardholders are charged transaction fees and interest on overdue balances;

2. businesses pay an annual fee;

3. businesses pay a fee for use of imprinters.

THE FACTS SPEAK...

There are over 710 000 merchants that accept VISA and/or MasterCard in Canada.

THE FACTS SPEAK...

Losses to fraud for VISA and MasterCard totalled $19.18 million in 1989.

Accounting Procedure for Financial Institution Credit Cards

When customers make a purchase from Algor Computer Services using their credit card, the procedure is as follows:

1. The clerk checks the card to ensure that
   (a) it has not expired (the expiry date is on the card);
   (b) it is valid; a Card Recovery Bulletin of lost, stolen, and cancelled cards is given to Algor by the bank. Algor is supposed to recover any cards listed on this bulletin.

   Some businesses now have point-of-sale terminals that connect them directly to the credit card centre. In this case the expiry date and the validity of the credit card are automatically checked. A check is also made to ensure that the holder has not exceeded his or her credit limit.

2. Credit approval is obtained: the store has a floor limit, for which the clerk can process the sale without authorization. If the amount of the sale is above the floor limit of the store, the clerk must obtain authorization from VISA. The authorization may be obtained by phone, or through a point-of-sale terminal.

3. A sales draft is completed; it is run through an imprint machine that copies the customer's name and credit card number, the business's name and number, and the date onto the draft.

4. The customer signs the draft; the signature is checked against that on the back of the card.

5. The customer is given one copy of the draft and two are kept for the business. One copy will be given to the bank when a deposit is made.

> "A Merchant Sales Recap is a summary for deposit of total VISA sales for the day."

The sales drafts are kept until the end of the day, when a Merchant Sales Recap (Figure 6-15) is completed. A copy of this summary, along with one copy of each sales draft, is included with the daily deposit.

An entry is required for the deposit of the sales drafts. It is not necessary to record separate entries for each sales draft because the business does not need to know to whom the sale was made. It is the responsibility of VISA to collect the amounts from the individual customers. When deposited, the bank credits the business's account with the total of the drafts. Thus, the business receives its money immediately. The following is the required journal entry, assuming a discount rate of 2 percent:

FIGURE 6-15 MERCHANT SALES RECAP USED BY RETAILERS WHO ACCEPT VISA CREDIT CARDS

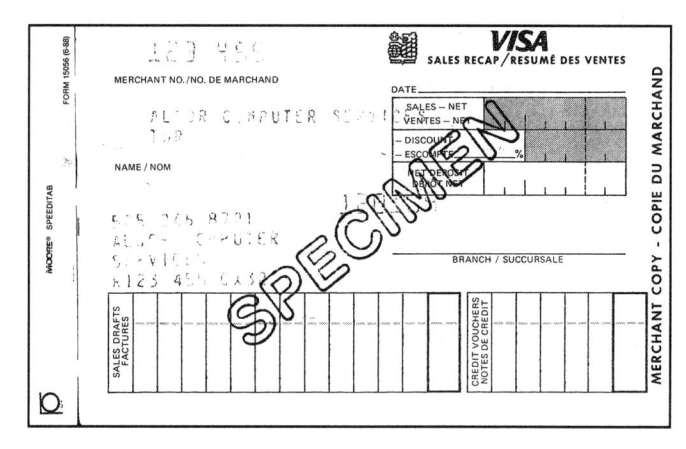

May 24   VISA Merchant Sales Recap for the day, $2 690.79, and the discount expense is $54.91. The sales were made as follows: Computer Services $1 820, Software Lessons $610, GST $170.10, and PST $145.60.

GENERAL JOURNAL

PAGE 442

DATE 1991		PARTICULARS	PR	DEBIT	CREDIT
May	24	Cash	100	2 690 79	
		VISA Discount Expense	655	54 91	
		Computer Services	400		1 820 —
		Software Lessons	410		610 —
		GST Payable	230		170 10
		PST Payable	240		145 60
		VISA Merchant Sales Recap			

GENERAL LEDGER

Cash 100
dr. | cr.
May 24   2 690.79 |

VISA Discount Expense 655
dr. | cr.
May 24   54.91 |

Computer Services 400
dr. | cr.
| May 24   1 820.00

Software Lessons 410
dr. | cr.
| May 24   610.00

GST Payable 230
dr. | cr.
| May 24   170.10

PST Payable 240
dr. | cr.
| May 24   145.60

> "A business pays a credit card issuer a percentage of its sales each month."

The explanation for the entry is as follows:
- A debit is made to Cash to increase that asset. The business makes a deposit to its account for the amount of VISA sales made on that day minus the VISA discount.
- A debit is made to VISA Discount Expense to record the discount that is charged to Algor Computer Services as a member of the VISA system. It is 2 percent of the sales, including taxes.
- A credit is made to the revenue accounts, for there has been an increase in the asset Cash from providing a service. (Separate revenue accounts could be used so that the VISA sales could be separated from the cash sales. In that case they would be called VISA Computer Services and VISA Software Lessons.)
- A credit is made to GST Payable in order to record the liability to the federal government for the tax collected on the sales.
- A credit is made to PST Payable in order to record the liability to the provincial government for the 8 percent tax collected (in Ontario) on the computer services. There is no provincial retail sales tax on the software lessons.

Debit Cards

> "Debit cards are used to buy now and to pay directly from one's bank account."

Debit cards were introduced in some Canadian markets in the late 1980s as a consumer test. They are intended to be used along with credit cards. Credit cards are used to buy now and pay later: debit cards are used to buy now and pay now. A business that accepts a debit card receives the cash immediately. The money is transferred in one of two ways. The cash may be transferred directly from the customer's bank account to the business's through a point-of-sale terminal. In this case, the customer provides the store with an identifying card that the terminal reads. Some consumers are leery of this method, as they fear that someone may remove money from their account without their knowledge. Another method of using a debit card is to allow the customer to have direct access to their account. This is done through an instant payment machine located at the business. The customer uses an identifying card, and receives from the machine vouchers in denominations up to $40. The customer then pays for the purchase with vouchers and receives any change due.

There are advantages to a business of accepting debit cards:
- cash is received immediately
- paper handling is reduced since cheques are eliminated
- there is no possibility of receiving NSF cheques.

The advantage of the debit card to the consumer is questionable. For those who don't want to take advantage of the interest-free grace period provided by using a credit card, the debit card eliminates the need to carry cash or write a cheque. It also allows the consumer who wants to pay cash to engage in impulse shopping, and have access to cash for emergencies.

The accounting entry to record a sale and the receipt of cash from a customer using a debit card is the same as for any cash sale: a debit to Cash, a credit to the revenue account, and a credit to the respective sales taxes that apply. Again, for internal control purposes, a business may want to establish separate revenue accounts in order to have a record of the volume of sales made through accepting debit cards. The amount would also be recorded on the business's monthly bank statement.

Prepaid Cards

> "Prepaid cards are paid for in advance of being used."

Another type of plastic card that is coming into use is the prepaid card, sometimes also called a cash card. For a prepaid card, the customer pays in advance for a card, such as a McDonald's card. For example, a person could make a $50 payment, and the amount is encoded on a card. Each time a purchase is made at McDonald's, the amount of the purchase is deducted from the total on the card. The point-of-sale terminal also indicates the balance on the card. If the amount is low, the customer may increase the balance by paying the cashier to increase the amount. Such cards are especially handy in situations where the person makes frequent purchases, or small amount purchases, such as at vending machines, highway tolls, and photocopy machines.

The advantages of the prepaid card to a business are the same as for a debit card. The cards also serve as an advertising medium, for each business issues it own cards. Prepaid cards are extensively used in Japan at the time of writing, and to some degree in Canada. The accounting procedure for these cards will be examined in Chapter 8.

FIGURE 6-16 A CASH CARD USED FOR PHOTOCOPYING

```
┌─────────────────────────────────────────┐
│         Carleton University             │
│         Ottawa, Canada K1S 5B6          │
│                                         │
│         CASH CARD        N°  131        │
│      INSERT THIS SIDE UP                │
│                                         │
│    Not Responsible For Lost Or Damaged Cards │
└─────────────────────────────────────────┘
```

Lesson Review

32. What are the two types of credit cards?
33. What are the advantages to the holder of having a credit card?
34. What are the disadvantages to the holder of having a credit card?
35. What are the advantages and disadvantages to a store of accepting credit cards?
36. What are the four most significant items in a credit check?
37. What is a credit bureau? How is it financed?
38. What information does a credit bureau have about credit users? Where does it get the information?
39. What rights does the consumer have concerning information stored at the credit bureau?
40. What are the three major bank credit cards?
41. What are the advantages of holding a bank credit card as compared to other credit cards?
42. What are the advantages to a business of accepting a bank credit card for payment of sales?
43. What is the major disadvantage to a business of accepting a bank credit card for payment of sales?
44. Give the purpose of each of the following:
    (a) store limit
    (b) sales draft
    (c) merchant sales recap
45. How does the bank recover its costs of operating a credit card system?
46. Describe how payments can be made using a debit card.
47. State the advantages and disadvantages to a consumer of using a debit card.
48. State the advantages and disadvantages to a business of accepting payment through use of a debit card.
49. What is a prepaid card? For what type of purchases are they convenient?

LESSON APPLICATIONS

50. Journalize each of the following transactions for Calgary Entertainment Services. Assume there is GST (7%), but no PST. The firm accepts VISA and MasterCard, and the discount rate is 3%.
    Dec. 14 VISA Sales: $2 240 plus GST.
    14 MasterCard Sales: $1 340 plus GST.
    15 VISA Sales: $3 943 plus GST.
    15 MasterCard Sales: $4 529 plus GST.
    15 Cash Sales Slips #491-#496: $2 781 plus GST.
    15 Cheque Copy #833: $5 922 to Receiver General of Canada for GST collected for the month of November. The GST Payable was $14 961, and the GST Recoverable was $9 039.

51. Journalize each of the following transactions for London Cablevision Services. The firm accepts both VISA and MasterCard, and their discount rate is 2%. Assume the GST (7%) and a PST of 8% apply to all services. The PST is calculated on the base price only.
    Feb. 12 VISA Sales: $465 plus taxes.
    12 MasterCard Sales: $643 plus taxes.
    12 Cash Sales Slips #592-#605: $1 453 plus taxes.
    12 Cash Receipt Slip #918: $930 received on account from The Jet Set Hotel.
    15 VISA Sales: $758 plus taxes.
    15 MasterCard Sales: $329 plus taxes.
    15 Cash Sales Slips #606-#634: $1 893 plus taxes.
    15 Cheque Copy #112: $9 533 to Receiver General of Canada for GST collected during the month of January. The GST Payable was $14 016.31, and the GST Recoverable was $4 483.31.
    15 Cheque Copy #113: $16 018.64 to the Provincial Treasurer for retail sales tax collected during the month of January.

CHAPTER REVIEW AND SKILL DEVELOPMENT

Accounting Principles and Concepts

- **A transaction between a business and a financial institution has opposite effects** on each other's books.

- **Businesses act as tax collectors** for the provincial and federal governments.

- **Credit cards, debit cards, and prepaid cards** are accepted by businesses in order to increase revenue.

- **Credit bureaus** provide information to businesses concerning credit applicants.

Knowing the Terms

For each of the following statements, indicate the term being defined.

(a) Document issued by a financial institution to indicate that it has withdrawn money from a customer's account.
(b) Maximum amount authorized by a bank in any single credit card transaction without the business obtaining authorization from the bank.
(c) Publication listing cardholder numbers on credit cards which the bank wishes the business to recover.
(d) Document issued by a business reducing its claim on a customer on a previous transaction.
(e) Fee paid by a business to the bank based on credit card drafts deposited.
(f) Document issued by a bank indicating that it has increased the amount in a customer's account.
(g) Card that transfers money from the user's account to the business's account.
(h) Document issued by a business to indicate that it has increased its claim on a customer on a previous transaction.
(i) Card on which the balance is decreased each time a transaction occurs.
(j) Source document used to record acceptance of VISA for payment on a sale.

Food for Thought

1. Lisa Hayden started as a bookkeeper for Dinardo Campsite. When purchase invoices arrived at the business, she added eight percent provincial retail sales tax to the amount. For example, an invoice for a $4 000 purchase of equipment was entered in the journal as follows: debit Equipment $4 320, credit Accounts Payable $4 000, and credit Sales Tax Payable $320. Comment on Lisa's handling of purchase invoices.

2. A provincial government decides to eliminate the sales tax on automobiles for a six-month period. What would be the purpose and probable effect of this economic policy?

3. The agreement between a bank and a merchant in respect of the merchant's use of VISA states that the "Bank may refuse to credit the account of the Merchant with or may charge back to the Merchant the total amount of any sales draft in any of the following circumstances: . . .". Indicate at least five circumstances under which the bank would not accept a sales draft that has been completed by the merchant.

4. The clerk responsible for closing the cash at night states that there is no need to deposit the VISA sales drafts each day. She indicates that they can be collected for a week and then deposited. Give reasons why they should be deposited immediately.

5. The federal government imposed the federal goods and services tax in 1991. Most cash terminals, of which there were estimated to be 50 000 in Canada, were not able to calculate a tax on top of another tax. In order to do so, a computer chip had to be replaced, at a cost of $200 to $500 per machine. As well, computer programs had to be adjusted. Businesses had to pay the costs of adapting the equipment. Should the federal government be allowed to impose a tax collecting requirement that results in businesses having to make major expenditures in order to comply?

6. There is a substantial cost to a business to comply with the requirement of collecting and remitting the GST to the federal government. Businesses will not be compensated for these costs. Should they be compensated from government revenue? Why or why not?

Organizing

Prepare a list of the 12 basic source documents issued or received by a business. Give an example of a transaction in which the source document would be issued. Also give the debit and credit for the transaction. The first one has been done for you.

Source Document: Purchase Invoice
Transaction: Purchased a computer, $5 000 plus taxes, from Central Computer Ltd. on account.
Debit: Equipment, GST Recoverable
Credit: Accounts Payable

Applications

1. Give the journal entry for each of the following transactions for the Fort Vermilion Motel Ltd. Assume that the motel operates its own credit system. Add the GST (7 percent) to sales, and calculate an 8 percent provincial sales tax on the base price only. Choose appropriate account names.

Oct. 13 Cash Sales Slip #879: Room rental for three nights, $180 plus taxes.
   13 Sales Invoice #1293: Room rental to Minima International for four nights, $240 plus taxes.
   13 Bank Credit Memo: $2 500 bank loan.
   14 Cash Sales Slip #880: Room rental for two nights, $120 plus taxes.
   14 Sales Invoice #1294: Room rental to Dr. A. Ferlisi for two nights, $120 plus taxes.
   14 Bank Debit Memo: For $122 including charge for NSF cheque received from M. Zuro on October 9. Note: NSF charge is $18. It is company policy not to absorb this charge.
   15 Cheque Copy #83: $839 to the Provincial Treasurer for retail sales tax for the month of September.
   15 Sales Invoice #1295: Room rental to National Airlines for three nights, $180 plus taxes.
   15 Cash Receipt Slip #422: Received $180 on account from J. Seth Ltd.
   15 Cash Sales Slip #881: Room rental for four nights, $240 plus taxes.
   16 Purchase Invoice #440: $480 plus GST, from Poy & Cheung, Lawyers, for consultation.
   16 Cheque Copy #84: Paid the owner, W. Scrivener, $490 for personal use.
   16 Cash Sales Slip #882: Room rental for five nights, $300 plus taxes.
   16 Cheque Copy #85: Paid $850 to the Receiver General of Canada for GST for the previous month. The GST Payable was $1 240, and the GST Recoverable was $390.
   16 Purchase Invoice #991: From Canso Furniture Ltd., $900 plus taxes for an office desk.

2. Journalize each of the following transactions for Naddaffi's Tailor & Clothing Repairs. Naddaffi's offers its own credit to customers, and also accepts VISA, which applies a discount rate of 4 percent. Choose appropriate account names. Add the GST (7 percent) and a provincial sales tax of 6 percent on the base price only.

May 12 Cash Receipt Slip #488: $220 received on account from V. Patenaude.
   12 Sales Invoice #712: To T. Ohmayer, $72 plus taxes.
   12 Cheque Copy #76: $125 plus GST paid to Professional Bookkeeping Services for bookkeeping.
   13 VISA Sales Drafts: $320 plus taxes.
   13 Bank Debit Memo: $42 including charge for NSF cheque received from L. Brazeau. Note: NSF charge is $16. It is company policy not to absorb this charge.
   14 Credit Invoice #49 received: From Boutilier's Store Furniture, $120 plus taxes for return of equipment.

14 Purchase Invoice #822: From Boutilier's Store Furniture, $1 780 plus taxes for a new sewing machine.
14 Bank Credit Memo: For bank loan to improve storefront, $2 000.
15 Cheque Copy #77: $1 702 to the Provincial Treasurer for sales tax for the month of April; commission of $34.04 had been deducted.
15 Debit Memo #22 issued: To T. Ohmayer, $12 plus taxes, for error on Sales Invoice #712.
15 VISA Sales Drafts: $739 plus taxes.
15 Cheque Copy #78: To P. Brodersen, $700 for wages.
15 Cheque Copy #79: To C. Naddaffi, owner, $250 for personal use.

Applications — Comprehensive
Journalize to Financial Statements
Victoria Fax and Photocopy Rental rents office equipment to businesses. It also has a fleet of vans that contain photocopy and fax machines that can be driven to a place of business and operated from the van. The firm accepts MasterCard, which applies a discount rate of 3 percent. Apply the GST (7 percent), and a provincial retail sales tax of 6 percent to the base price only.

(a) Open a ledger with the following accounts, supplying appropriate account numbers, and enter the balances as shown. Cash $45 630; Accounts Receivable $12 829; GST Recoverable; Supplies $9 453; Fax Equipment $27 822; Photocopy Equipment $83 403; Vans $93 650; Accounts Payable $12 300; PST Payable; GST Payable; Short-Term Loan $29 800; Long-Term Loan $164 300; M. Poy, Capital $66 387; M. Poy, Drawings; Rental Revenue; Fax and Copy Revenue; Fax and Copy Refunds; Rent Expense; Wages Expense; Van Expense; Advertising Expense; Utilities Expense; Equipment Repairs Expense; MasterCard Discount Expense; General Expense.

(b) Journalize the transactions below. Note that source documents have not been indicated.

(c) Complete the steps in the accounting cycle to the completion of the financial statements.

(d) Prepare a brief report on the financial position of the business.

Transactions
Sept. 19 Received $12 000 as an additional investment from the owner.
19 Fax and photocopy revenue for the day, $6 459 plus taxes.
19 Paid $530 on the short-term loan.
19 Paid rent, $2 340 plus GST.
19 Refund given to J.D. Summers' account for poor quality photocopies, $123 plus taxes.
20 Paid $378 plus taxes for repair of fax equipment.
20 Received $900 on account, F. Mai.
20 MasterCard sales drafts for equipment rental deposited, $3 560 plus taxes.
20 Rented an additional MasterCard imprinter, $120 plus taxes.
20 Paid the weekly wages, $2 451.
21 Fax and photocopy sales on account, $12 309 plus taxes.
21 The owner withdrew supplies for personal use, $120 plus taxes.
22 Deposited machine rental revenue, $9 602 plus taxes.
22 Paid for decorating of the office, $560 plus taxes.
23 Paid monthly heating bill, $429 plus taxes.
23 Paid $450 to the owner for personal use.
23 MasterCard sales drafts deposited, $5 029 plus taxes: rental revenue

of $4 000, and fax and photocopy revenue of $1 029.
26 Paid $750 plus GST to CFXC for advertising.
26 Machine rental on account, $5 380 plus taxes.
26 MasterCard drafts deposited for fax and photocopy sales, $2 410 plus taxes.
27 Paid the weekly wages, $2 451.
27 Fax and photocopy revenue for the day, $6 459 plus taxes.
28 Refund (cheque) given for poor quality photocopies, $83 plus taxes.
28 Paid $439 plus taxes for repair of photocopy equipment.
28 Received $333 on account, J. Ng.
28 MasterCard drafts for equipment rental deposited, $2 918 plus taxes.
29 Fax and photocopy sales on account, $12 309 plus taxes.
29 Paid $792 plus taxes for repairs to the owner's personal car.
29 Paid $142 plus taxes for telephone usage.
30 Machine rental on account, $9 819 plus taxes.

Focussing

1. The Business-Financial Institution Relationship

For each of the following transactions, prepare the journal entry that would be made
(a) in the business's books
(b) in the trust company's books.
Choose appropriate account names.

May 23 The trust company notified the business that $620 was deducted from the business's account for a $600 NSF cheque that the business had deposited. The cheque had been given to the business by V. Tarawal. The trust company had included a $20 service charge. The business passes such charges along to the issuer of the cheque.

24 The trust company issued a credit memo to the business, confirming that a $43 500 loan had been deposited in the business's account.

25 The business deposited $53 670 in MasterCard sales drafts which includes provincial sales tax of 6 percent and the GST (7 percent). The PST is not levied on the GST. The MasterCard discount rate is 2 percent.

31 The trust company withdrew $450, including taxes as above, from the business's account as a rental fee for MasterCard imprint machines used by the business.

31 The trust company withdrew $932 from the business's account as monthly payment for the loan.

31 The trust company charged the business $89.50 from the business's account as a monthly service charge.

2. Contra-accounts

Each of the following accounts is a contra-account. Indicate in each case:
(a) why the account is referred to as a contra-account;
(b) the type of balance which the account would normally have;
(c) the placement of the account on the financial statements.
   (i) Drawings
   (ii) Service Refunds

Evaluate and Assess

Western Bicycle Revival is a firm with sales averaging $2.5 million per year. Approximately 40 percent of the sales are on credit. The firm operates its own credit system. On average it takes the firm 30 days to collect the accounts. At any one time there are up to $80 000 of accounts receivable outstanding, of which $10 000 are overdue. The firm adds 2 percent per month onto outstanding accounts. It estimates that the cost to operate its own credit system is $12 000 per year.

Western Bicycle Revival is considering joining the VISA system. It believes that it could attain sufficient sales that it would have a discount of 2 percent.

1. What is the cost to Western Bicycle Revival of operating its own credit system?
2. What incentives could Western Bicycle Revival offer its credit customers to encourage them to pay their balances quickly?
3. What costs are referred to when Western Bicycle Revival indicates that it costs $12 000 to operate its credit system?
4. What advantages are there to Western Bicycle Revival in offering its own credit card to customers? What are the disadvantages?
5. What are the advantages and disadvantages to Western Bicycle Revival in joining the VISA system?
6. Should Western Bicycle Revival join the VISA system? Defend your decision.

Synthesize and Conclude
Fraud

Deborah Lane was charged with four counts under section 320(1)(a) of the Criminal Code of Canada, that she did by false pretence and with intent to defraud, obtain goods from Sears Limited by means of four worthless cheques. She made out four cheques on Saturday, December 17th in order to obtain merchandise. The cheques were subsequently dishonored when presented to her bank on December 22nd.

Deborah's estranged husband had promised that he would deposit to the credit of her account, or give to her, the sum of $200, on or before Monday, December 19th. She indicated that she had no reason to believe that her husband would lie to her. Upon that expectation she made out the cheques to Sears.

(a) What do the following terms mean: false pretence, fraud, and dishonored?
(b) It is a criminal offence to write a cheque, knowing that there are not sufficient funds in the account to cover the cheque. Should Deborah be found innocent or guilty based on the facts given?

ACCOUNTING AT WORK

Raffaella Frescura
Collection Officer

Raffaella sees potential in a collection officer's work to exercise both accounting skills and managerial talent. With a variety of responsibilities to be faced in her daily work, she makes many decisions that bring those skills to bear to influence her company's bottom line.

Essential to her flexibility and ability to make those important choices is Raffaella's solid background in the principles of credit and accounting, combined with a knowledge of financial statements and an understanding of the different methods of monitoring and evaluating accounts receivable.

Raffaella gained this background through a combination of on-the-job training and formal education. To begin she completed Accounting 1 and 2 courses, and then got a job as an Internal Audit Supervisor. The familiarity she gained with her company's financial policies and procedures helped her move up to Senior Accounts Payable Supervisor. She then moved to a new firm, where she began as an Intermediate Collection Analyst and progressed to her current position. Along the way she completed two of the requisite four years of the MCI (Member of Credit Institute) course, which brought her up to date in such subjects as financial statements, law, and economics.

Raffaella hopes these qualifications will help her move to a position of greater influence over management decisions. She enjoys working with her staff, and providing training opportunities and contact with upper management. For the time being, however, she sees her primary goal as ensuring a sound credit policy, while providing good service to the customers with whom she deals. "A good collector must wear several hats," Raffaella says, "as police, to ensure there are no delinquencies; as customer service representative, because we have close contact with the customers; and as part of a sales team, to better understand the customers' needs."

Besides providing many different opportunities, a collection officer's job is satisfying in that it makes a direct contribution to the company's performance. As Raffaella points out, "A sale is not a sale until it's collected." So, a collection officer has the chance to influence the company's bottom line and also its policies, by exercising management skills and contributing to decision making. Accounting skills and initiative applied in the field of credit management can lead to a lot of opportunities.

Collection Officer

Major retailer requires a resourceful professional capable of contributing to our future success by answering all customer inquiries in an effort to ensure full account payment.

Key responsibilities include authorizing credit on current orders, collecting accounts by correspondence or phone, and expediting claim resolution. Challenges are geared for a high-initiative individual with a background that includes 3-5 years of commercial credit experience, preferably gained in a computer or retailing environment. The successful applicant must possess the following characteristics:

- Self-starter
- Detail-oriented
- Work with minimal supervision
- Excellent organizational skills

This position offers an attractive salary/benefits package as well as a supportive work environment and opportunity for professional development. To apply, please phone Ms. L. Lam at (604) 555-1713.

1. What educational background does Raffaella Frescura require in order to be a collection officer?
2. What is MCI? What did it offer Raffaella?
3. What are the two contrasting tasks that a collection officer carries out?
4. List six skills that a good collection officer should have.

Business Career Skills

1. Communication — Business operation
Meetings! Meetings! Meetings!

In a business, it is frequently necessary to have meetings in order to operate efficiently. Studies estimate that one third of most meetings are not productive, and that meetings are a very expensive method of communication. A meeting of executives in a business is very costly. A meeting of ten executives earning $100 an hour costs the firm $1 000 per hour. Also lost, however, is the work that they could have been accomplishing if they were not at the meeting.

You are to assume that a meeting is required of all the people in the accounting department. There are three purposes of the meeting:

1. to distribute and discuss the current year's financial reports
2. to establish new policies for evaluating employees
3. to plan the staff golf day in June

In groups, carry out the following tasks:
(a) Prepare a proper agenda for the meeting; make up anything that you think is required; assume that the agenda is to be sent one week in advance of the meeting to those required to attend.
(b) Brainstorm to develop a list of at least ten items that make a meeting successful; rank the items from one to ten.
(c) Brainstorm to develop a list of at least ten items that make a meeting unproductive.

2. Communication — Credit Granting
For this exercise you are to consider yourself to be the credit department of a large retailer. Your job description indicates that you are to have the final decision in the granting of credit.

In groups:
(a) brainstorm to generate a list of information that you would obtain from a customer who is applying for credit;
(b) brainstorm to generate a list of items that you would consider when granting credit;
(c) rank the list developed in (b) in order of highest priority item to lowest.

3. Communication — Letter Writing
On your own, write a business letter to a prospective credit customer. You are to inform the customer that his credit application has been refused because of a poor credit payment record at other businesses. All other items that you think are necessary may be made up by you.

COMPUTER ACCOUNTING
AND NOW... THE COMPUTERIZED RESTAURANT

Trevor and Linda James finished their meal at the new Seven Seas Floating Restaurant, a converted and refurbished freighter that had for many years plied the coastal waters of Newfoundland. Trevor asked for the bill. An elegant folder arrived and inside was . . . a grocery-type cash register tape?

The waiter explained that this was something customers would probably see more of. Of course, he admitted, the fancy bills customers were used to were more pleasing to the eye, but with the new bills customers could see a neat list of what they had ordered — instead of trying to match up items and prices.

Trevor had to admit it was true. The new bill described food and drink items so clearly that it was a welcome change from the more usual restaurant checks, both handwritten and computerized. On those, it was often impossible to match up the waiter's or waitress's handwriting with the amounts billed, if you could even decipher the abbreviations.

This new computerized system is also impressive behind the scenes. The waiter or waitress rings in your order by number. As a double check, a screen displays each item in words. That order is immediately printed out in the appropriate area of the restaurant — a drink order will show up on the computer in the bar, a salad order on the computer in the cold kitchen, and so on. This information also registers in the office so management can tell at any time how many bottles of wine or seafood specials have been ordered.

There are also codes for no butter, no rice, medium rare, and other special requests.

One waiter opens the order for a particular table and only he can ring in subsequent orders. Thus, the waiter owes the house everything he rings in on that table's bill and he must collect the payment to balance off. The waiter can also ask for a **printout** of the bill at any time to check the order. So that each item can be adequately described, there is room for 14 characters per line in addition to space used to indicate quantity and price.

The waiter added that the bill would eventually have the restaurant's logo and be a little fancier so that it wouldn't look quite so much like a cash register tape.

This is another example of business finding new, productive applications for the computer. The bill for Trevor and Linda appears below.

```
              GUEST CHECK
    SERVER 9 TABLE 4/ 1 TIME 20:04
         1 DLY FEATURE   11.00
         2 BTL WN        17.50
         1 SOUP DU JOUR   3.25
         1 SALAD BAR      6.75
         1 DLY FEATURE    9.75
            TOTAL        48.25
            GST           3.38
            TAX           6.20
         GRAND TOTAL     57.83
      THE SEVEN SEAS FLOATING
            RESTAURANT
         FOOD            30.75
         BEVERAGE        17.50
    91-12-14  3 GUESTS  NUMBER  9
```

Exercises

1. Jim Boyd owns a cattle feed lot business in Carstairs, Alberta. He has just hired you to help him with the day-to-day accounting and also to undertake some special projects using his newly acquired microcomputer system. One immediate problem that he has outlined for you is that he is continually receiving reminders about unpaid bills, and he has no idea of how much he owes and how much is overdue. Use your spreadsheet program to prepare an aged list of accounts payable as at July 31 from the following source documents that you have assembled. You might use the plan in Figure 6-17 for developing your spreadsheet model.

FIGURE 6-17

	A	B	C	D	E	F	G	H
1			Name of Business					Formulas
2			Aged List of Accounts Payable					
3			Date line					
4								
5	Account	Invoice	Invoice	Current	1-30	31-60	Over	
6	Name	Amount	Date		Days	Days	90 Days	
7								
8								
9								
10								
11								
12								
13								
14								
15								
16								
17								
18	Totals							1,2,3,4
19								
20								

List of Invoices Received

Name	Date		Amount	Paid	– Date
Vandervalen Hay Sales	Mar	25	$ 890	$450	Apr 28
CanWest Feed Supplies	Mar	30	600	300	Apr 30
Toppick Feed and Farm Supply	Apr	2	276		
Vandervalen Hay Sales	Apr	27	2 300		
Agro Chemicals	May	12	1 400	300	Jul 12
Harry White's Meat Brokerage	May	17	5 490	900	Jun 20
Great Plains Equipment Co.	Jun	16	3 320		
CanWest Feed Supplies	Jun	30	3 320		
Glenbriar Transport Co.	Jul	6	1 587		
Harry White's Meat Brokerage	Jul	27	1 800		

2. Jake McTavish owns a janitorial service in Charlottetown, Prince Edward Island. He has hired you to help him with the day-to-day accounting and to help him get caught up with clients whose accounts are long overdue. He is experiencing serious cash flow problems and his bank is pressing him to straighten out this problem immediately. Jake's accounts receivable accounts follow.

Use your spreadsheet program to prepare an accounts receivable ageing report as of June 30. You might use the plan in Figure 6-18 for your spreadsheet model.

List of Accounts Receivable

A/R Baytree Business Centre			104
Date	Debit	Credit	Balance
Jan 1	2 000		2 000
Feb 28		1 500	500
Apr 15	700		1 200

A/R International Office			105
Date	Debit	Credit	Balance
Jan 1	1 000		1 000
Feb 15	7 000		8 000
Mar 15	1 500		9 500
Apr 15		5 000	4 500
May 15		2 000	2 500

A/R Morco Investment Properties			106
Date	Debit	Credit	Balance
Mar 10	3 200		3 200
Apr 15	5 000		8 200
May 10		3 200	5 000
Jun 10		1 000	6 000
Jun 20		4 000	2 000

A/R Tri K Services			107
Date	Debit	Credit	Balance
May 15	800		800
May 30		800	—
Jun 20	3 000		3 000

FIGURE 6-18

	A	B	C	D	E	F	G	H
1				Name of Business				Formulas
2				Accounts Receivable Ageing Report				
3				Date line				
4								
5	Customer	Invoice	Current	Over 30	Over 60	Over 90	Total	
6	Name	Date	Billing	Days	Days	Days	Due	
7			0.00	0.00	0.00	0.00	0.00	1
8			0.00	0.00	0.00	0.00	0.00	2
9			0.00	0.00	0.00	0.00	0.00	3
10			0.00	0.00	0.00	0.00	0.00	4
11			0.00	0.00	0.00	0.00	0.00	5
12			0.00	0.00	0.00	0.00	0.00	6
13			0.00	0.00	0.00	0.00	0.00	7
14			0.00	0.00	0.00	0.00	0.00	8
15			0.00	0.00	0.00	0.00	0.00	9
16			0.00	0.00	0.00	0.00	0.00	10
17								
18			0.00	0.00	0.00	0.00	0.00	11,12,13,14,15
19								
20								

CHAPTER SEVEN

End-of-Period Procedures — 1

LEARNING OBJECTIVES

At the end of this chapter you should be able to
- describe the purpose of adjusting entries;
- describe the matching principle;
- prepare adjusting entries;
- prepare financial statements from an eight-column worksheet;
- enter adjusting entries into the computer system;
- use the computer to print updated financial reports.

LANGUAGE OF ACCOUNTING

You will see the following terms in this chapter:
accumulated depreciation
computer accounting module
contra-asset
declining-balance depreciation
depreciation
"garbage in, garbage out"
integrated accounting system
matching
materiality
premium
prepaid expenses
straight-line depreciation

7.1 Adjusting Entries for Prepaid Expenses

At the end of the fiscal year, Algor Computer Services prepared its financial statements. When doing so, the accountant realized that the dollar values of a number of assets were either incorrect or not realistic. For example, supplies had been purchased and recorded at their cost price, following the cost principle. However, many of the supplies had been used up, and therefore the dollar value in the account did not match the value of the supplies on hand. The automobile was shown at cost price, but it had been used for the year and was not worth the amount shown. Similarly, the building and various insurance policies were not worth the amount shown on the balance sheet. In order to make the balance sheet dollar amounts more realistic, and to recognize that items had been used up in the process of earning revenue, a technique was needed to adjust the amounts.

"Adjusting entries are made at the end of a fiscal year to update the accounts of an entity."

In order to have financial statements that are accurate and realistic, the process of making adjusting entries was developed. Adjusting entries are prepared at the end of the fiscal period. The accounting cycle with the inclusion of adjusting entries is shown in Figure 7-1.

FIGURE 7-1 ACCOUNTING CYCLE FOR ALGOR COMPUTER SERVICES

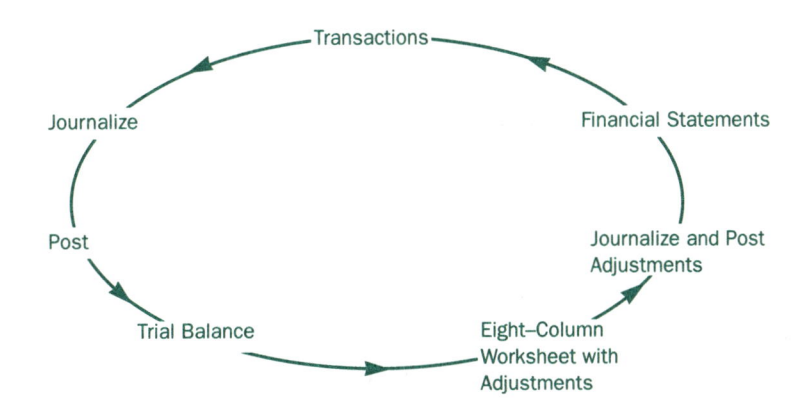

```
                    Transactions
        Journalize              Financial Statements

        Post                    Journalize and Post
                                Adjustments
            Trial Balance   Eight–Column
                            Worksheet with
                            Adjustments
```

There are basically four types of adjusting entries:

(1) adjustments for prepaid expenses and fixed assets

(2) adjustments for prepaid revenue

(3) adjustments for unrecorded expenses

(4) adjustments for unrecorded revenue

The first of these adjustments will be discussed in this chapter. The last three will be discussed in Chapter 8.

Adjustments for Prepaid Expenses

Prepaid expenses: items recorded as assets in the financial period they are purchased, and converted to expenses in later financial periods as they are used.

Prepaid expenses, or recorded costs, are items that are recorded as assets when purchased because the business owns them. For example, Algor records supplies as an asset when they are purchased. However, some of these assets are going to be used during more than one accounting year. We've learned that items used in the normal operation of the business are called expenses. Thus, though the purchase of supplies is originally recognized as an asset, it is in reality a prepaid expense. In each accounting period that benefits from use of the asset, an adjusting entry is made to transfer an appropriate amount from the asset account to an expense account. Prepaid insurance and prepaid rent are also referred to as prepaid expenses.

FIGURE 7-2 PREPAID EXPENSES ARE FIRST RECORDED AS ASSETS, BUT ARE CONVERTED TO AN EXPENSE AS THEY ARE USED

| Supplies purchased in 1990 | Supplies used in 1990, 1991, 1992, etc. |
| Recorded as an asset | Converted to an expense as used |

For some prepaid expenses such as supplies, the exact dollar amount of the asset that has been used can be determined. In other cases, the value of the asset that was used must be estimated, using some consistent method. It is important that the measurement for the adjustment be accurate, for in some businesses, the dollar amount of prepaid expenses can be extremely high.

The Matching Principle

Why aren't prepaid expenses, such as supplies, recorded as expenses when they are purchased? Because recording them as expenses would violate the matching principle. The **matching principle** states that expenses must be matched with the revenue earned through the use of those expenses. For instance, pens, paper, and photocopier and fax supplies purchased in the current year may be used during that year, but some of these may be left over for use in subsequent years. Supplies that were used during the current year were used as part of the process of earning revenue for that year. The cost of these expenses should therefore be deducted from the current year's revenue to arrive at the net income. However, the supplies that were purchased during the current year but not used should not be recorded as an expense of the current year. They should only be recorded as an expense in the year in which they are used. To record the purchase of all supplies as an expense of the current year results in a lower income than that which was truly earned. In the following example, a business bought $10 000 worth of supplies in Year 1; none was bought in Year 2. By following the matching principle, and assuming an even rate of use over the years, the cost of the supplies has been spread equally over their two-year life as follows:

Matching principle: expenses must be matched with the revenue earned through the use of those expenses.

FIGURE 7-3 MATCHING ALLOWS THE AMOUNT OF THE PREPAID EXPENSES THAT HAVE EXPIRED TO BE MATCHED WITH THE CORRESPONDING REVENUE

	YEAR 1		YEAR 2	
Revenue		$75 000		$80 000
Expenses				
Supplies	$ 5 000		$ 5 000	
Other	40 000	45 000	42 000	47 000
Net Income		$30 000		$33 000

If matching was not followed, and the cost of the supplies was recorded as an expense in the year in which they were purchased, the income statement would appear as in Figure 7-4.

THE FACTS SPEAK...

Prepaid expenses (approximate) for selected Canadian businesses, December 31, 1989, in $ millions.

Bell Canada Enterprises (BCE)	$463.0
McDonald's Corporation	78.0
Canadian Tire Corporation, Ltd.	12.5
Dominion Textile Inc.	11.9

FIGURE 7-4 IF MATCHING IS NOT FOLLOWED, THE AMOUNT OF THE PREPAID EXPENSES THAT HAVE EXPIRED ARE NOT MATCHED WITH THE CORRESPONDING REVENUE

	YEAR 1		YEAR 2	
Revenue		$75 000		$80 000
Expenses				
Supplies	$10 000		$ 0	
Other	40 000	50 000	42 000	42 000
Net Income		$25 000		$38 000

An examination of Figures 7-3 and 7-4 shows the effect the matching principle has on net income. When the matching principle is not followed, the total cost of the supplies is recorded as an expense in Year 1. As a result, the net income is lower in the first year, but higher in subsequent years. By not following the matching principle, the income statement does not reflect what has actually occurred in the business: the supplies were used in each of the years to assist in the earning of revenue. Therefore, a share of the cost of the original expenditure should be charged against the revenue of each year. The net income will then more realistically reflect the true operations of the business each year.

An adjusting entry is not made as the items are used because it would be very time consuming to make an entry every time a supply, such as a piece of paper, is used. Once a year, accountants make formal adjusting entries to record the use of these prepaid expenses. For interim statements, informal adjustments using estimates are entered on the worksheet.

> "For interim statements, informal adjustments using estimates are entered on a worksheet."

Adjusting for Supplies

When supplies are purchased, an entry is made to record them as a current asset:

Jan. 19 Purchase Invoice #249: Purchased supplies, $546.30 plus GST of $38.24 and PST of $43.70, from Martineau Office Supplies.

GENERAL JOURNAL

PAGE 411

DATE 1991		PARTICULARS	PR	DEBIT	CREDIT
Jan.	19	Office Supplies	150	590 —	
		GST Recoverable	135	38 24	
		Accounts Payable	200		628 24
		Purchase Invoice #249, Martineau Office Supplies			

At the time of purchase:

Office Supplies ─────────────────────→ recorded as an ASSET

Because a portion of the supplies will be available for use in the next accounting period, they are a prepaid expense. Subsequent purchases of supplies during the fiscal year will be shown as follows in T-account form:

GENERAL LEDGER

Office Supplies		150
dr.		cr.
Jan. 19	590	
Mar. 15	300	
May 3	94	

Year-End Adjustment for Supplies Used

At May 31, Algor Computer Services' year end, the Office Supplies account shows a balance of $984. However, many of the supplies have been used during the year, so the business no longer owns them. In order to calculate the value of the supplies used, an inventory must be taken. **To take an inventory** means to count and price the supplies on hand. As well, for inventory purposes, someone working in the supply room of the business may have kept a running record, by hand or by computer, of supplies purchased and supplies issued. The year-end inventory count would be compared to these records to ensure that the value assigned to the inventory is correct. The inventory count of Algor's supplies shows $250 on hand. To calculate the quantity used the following formula is used:

To take an inventory: to count and price the items on hand.

Supplies used = Balance of supplies account before adjustments
                − Inventory of supplies
         = $984 − $250
         = $734

The adjusting entry is then made:

DATE 1991		PARTICULARS	PR	DEBIT	CREDIT
May	31	Office Supplies Expense	730	734 —	
		Office Supplies	150		734 —
		To record office supplies used during the year			

GENERAL JOURNAL
PAGE 452

The explanation for the adjusting entry is as follows:
- The debit to Office Supplies Expense shows the value of the supplies used during the year, $734, which follows the matching principle. These supplies were used in the process of earning revenue.
- The credit to Office Supplies reduces the value of the asset account from the $984 purchased to the actual amount of supplies on hand at year end, $250.

Office Supplies used ⟶ recorded as an EXPENSE

The effect of these entries on the general ledger accounts after posting is shown below:

GENERAL LEDGER

Office Supplies	150		Office Supplies Expense	730
dr.	cr.		dr.	cr.
Jan. 19 590	May 31 734		May 31 734	
Mar. 15 300				
May 3 94				

The balance of the Office Supplies account, $250, will be carried over until the next year as a prepaid expense, and will be matched against the revenue from that year if they are used.

Adjusting for Insurance

Insurance policies are frequently purchased to cover a year, and in some cases longer periods of time. The amount that is paid for insurance coverage is called the **premium**. Algor Computer Services purchases insurance on its building and equipment as protection against fire and theft. It also carries **liability insurance**, in case any of its customers are injured when on the business's premises, or as a result of work that Algor has done for them.

When the insurance policy is purchased, the following entry is made:

March 1   Purchase Invoice #633: Purchased a one-year policy for property insurance from Dominion Insurance Ltd., $1 200.

Premium: the amount paid for insurance coverage.

Liability insurance: protects a business from the costs of having persons injured on their property, or as a result of using their product or services.

GENERAL JOURNAL

PAGE 425

DATE 1991		PARTICULARS	PR	DEBIT	CREDIT
March	1	Prepaid Insurance	140	1200 —	
		Accounts Payable	200		1200 —
		Purchase Invoice #633, one year's property insurance			
		from Dominion Insurance Ltd.			

The account Prepaid Insurance is an asset, for the business now owns property insurance. If the business were to close, it would be able to get a refund for a portion of the premium paid. Since the policy is going to expire over the ensuing months, it is referred to as a prepaid expense.

Year-End Adjustment for Insurance

As time passes the policy expires and becomes worth less and less. An adjustment to reflect the reduction in the value of the insurance policy is made at the fiscal year end with the other adjustments. As three months have passed since the one-year policy was purchased on March 1, one-quarter of the policy term has been used. The firm no longer owns a policy valued at $1 200, so the asset value must be adjusted.

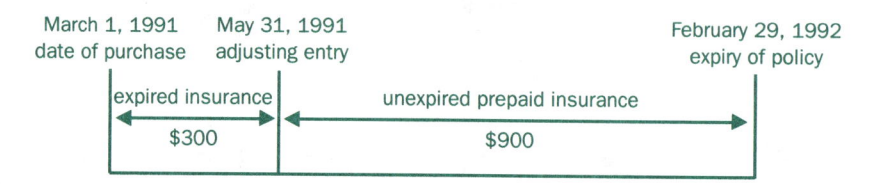

```
March 1, 1991      May 31, 1991                              February 29, 1992
date of purchase   adjusting entry                           expiry of policy

   | expired insurance |   unexpired prepaid insurance      |
              $300                      $900
```

The adjusting entry to reflect the insurance expense is:

GENERAL JOURNAL

PAGE 452

DATE 1991		PARTICULARS	PR	DEBIT	CREDIT
May	31	Insurance Expense	720	300 —	
		Prepaid Insurance	140		300 —
		To record use of one-quarter of insurance policy			

The explanation for the adjusting entry is as follows:
- The debit to Insurance Expense reflects the amount of the policy that expired during the current year, $300. The matching principle has, therefore, been followed, as the expense applicable to the current year has been recorded in the current year.
- The credit to Prepaid Insurance reduces the balance of the asset account to $900 to reflect the value of the policy owned at the beginning of the fiscal year.

The effect of the entries on the general ledger accounts after posting is shown below:

GENERAL LEDGER

Prepaid Insurance		140		Insurance Expense		720
dr.	cr.			dr.	cr.	
Mar. 1 1 200	May 31 300			May 31 300		

Prepaid Rent

"Prepaid Rent is a current asset."

Businesses that rent premises may pay the rental fee for a number of months at one time. The business owns a prepaid lease, which is an asset, the value of which will decrease as it is used. Should the firm no longer wish to use the premises, it could sublease the property to someone else. Payment of the rent in advance results in a prepaid expense. The entry to record payment of the rent is as follows:

December 1   Cheque Copy #588: $5 136 for rental space for one year.

GENERAL JOURNAL

PAGE 404

DATE 1990		PARTICULARS	PR	DEBIT	CREDIT
Dec.	1	Prepaid Rent	145	4 800 —	
		GST Recoverable	135	336 —	
		Cash	100		5 136 —
		Cheque Copy #588, rental of warehouse space for one year			

Year-End Adjustment for Rent

The account Prepaid Rent is a current asset, for the business owns a claim to use the rented warehouse for one year. It is considered a prepaid expense because the rental was paid in advance. As the warehouse is used, the prepaid rent is converted to an expense.

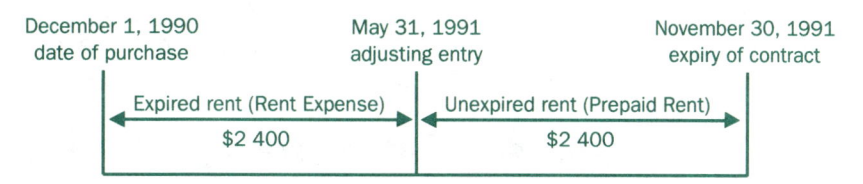

December 1, 1990   May 31, 1991   November 30, 1991
date of purchase   adjusting entry   expiry of contract

⟵ Expired rent (Rent Expense) ⟶ ⟵ Unexpired rent (Prepaid Rent) ⟶
            $2 400 $2 400

The following adjusting entry is made on May 31:

GENERAL JOURNAL

PAGE 452

DATE 1991		PARTICULARS	PR	DEBIT	CREDIT
May	31	Rent Expense	675	2 400 —	
		Prepaid Rent	145		2 400 —
		To record use of warehouse space for one-half of a year			

The explanation for the adjusting entry is as follows:
- The debit to Rent Expense recognizes expiration of one-half of the prepaid expense, $2 400. The warehouse was used to assist the business in earning revenue. The matching principle has therefore been followed.
- The credit to Prepaid Rent reduces the value of the asset from the balance of $4 800 on December 1 to the value at the end of the current fiscal year, $2 400.

The effect of these entries on the general ledger accounts after posting is shown below:

GENERAL LEDGER

Prepaid Rent			145	Rent Expense			675
dr.		cr.		dr.		cr.	
Dec. 1	4 800	May 31	2 400	May 31	2 400		

LESSON REVIEW

1. What are prepaid expenses? What else are they sometimes called?

2. Give three examples of prepaid expenses.

3. Can the amount of the adjusting entry required for prepaid expenses always be exactly determined? Explain.

4. What generally accepted accounting principle is being followed when an adjusting entry is made?

5. Why are adjusting entries for a prepaid expense not made as the item is used?

6. How is the value of supplies on hand at year end determined?

7. Give the debit and credit for each of the following.
   (a) the purchase of supplies, and the year-end adjustment
   (b) the purchase of insurance, and the year-end adjustment
   (c) the prepayment of rent, and the year-end adjustment

LESSON APPLICATIONS

8. The T-account for the current asset Supplies is shown below.

GENERAL LEDGER

Supplies			
dr.		cr.	
Jan. 28	1 400		
Feb. 18	700		
May 23	240		
Aug. 27	1 930		

At the end of the fiscal year, December 31, an inventory of supplies was taken, showing $372 worth of supplies on hand. Answer the following questions concerning the Supplies account.
   (a) What is the total amount of supplies purchased during the year?
   (b) When reference is made to supplies, what terminology is used to reflect the fact that they will be used over a period of time after they are purchased?
   (c) What is the amount of Supplies Expense for the fiscal year?
   (d) What should the balance in the Supplies account be at the end of the fiscal year? Why?
   (e) When is the Supplies account changed to show the new balance?
   (f) Prepare the adjusting entry to record the supplies that were used.
   (g) What should the amount for Supplies Expense be on the income statement prepared at the end of the fiscal period?
   (h) What should the amount for Supplies be on the balance sheet prepared at the end of the fiscal period?
   (i) Give two reasons why an adjusting entry was necessary.

9. A firm purchased a one-year insurance policy on October 1 for $1 800. The fiscal year ends on December 31.
   (a) Prepare the entry to record the purchase of the insurance on October 1.
   (b) What term is used to reflect the fact that it will be used over a period of time after it is purchased?
   (c) What is the amount of Insurance Expense for the fiscal year?
   (d) What should the balance in the Prepaid Insurance account be at the end of the fiscal year? Why?
   (e) When is the Prepaid Insurance account changed to show the year-end balance?
   (f) Prepare the adjusting entry to record the insurance that was used.
   (g) What should the amount for Insurance Expense be on the income statement prepared at the end of the fiscal period?
   (h) What should the amount for Prepaid Insurance be on the balance sheet prepared at the end of the fiscal period?
   (i) Give two reasons why an adjusting entry was necessary.

10. A firm prepays its rent every six months. The payment of $5 400 plus GST is made on March 1 and September 1. The fiscal year ends on December 31.
    (a) Prepare the entry to record the payment of the rent on September 1.
    (b) What is the amount of Rent Expense for the fiscal year?
    (c) What should the balance in the Prepaid Rent account be at the end of the fiscal year? Why?
    (d) When is the Prepaid Rent account changed to show the year-end balance?

(e) Prepare the adjusting entry to record the prepaid rent that was used.
(f) What should the amount for Rent Expense be on the income statement prepared at the end of the fiscal period?
(g) What should the amount for Prepaid Rent be on the balance sheet prepared at the end of the fiscal period?

11. The T-accounts for Supplies, Prepaid Rent, and Prepaid Insurance are shown below as at March 1.

GENERAL LEDGER

Supplies	160	Prepaid Rent	140	Prepaid Insurance	135
dr.	cr.	dr.	cr.	dr.	cr.
March 1 680		March 1 2 700		March 1 2 400	

Inventories taken at the end of March show
(a) supplies on hand, $317
(b) prepaid rent not used, $1 800
(c) prepaid insurance not used, $1 600
Prepare adjusting entries for the month of March for each of the above.

12. Prepare adjusting entries for the period ending on October 31, 19–4. Assume that the last adjusting entries were made on October 31 of the previous year.
    (a) Supplies on hand November 1, 19–3, $720; supplies purchased since November 1, $2 280; supplies on hand at the end of October, 19–4, $479.
    (b) A 12-month insurance policy was purchased August 1, 19–4 for $3 600.
    (c) The yearly rent of $6 408 was paid on July 1, 19–4.

7.2 Depreciation of Fixed Assets

When Algor Computer Services purchased an automobile, it was to be used in the operation of the business. When the employees went to a client's office to work, they went in the automobile, and the equipment was carried in the automobile. The automobile was, therefore, used to earn revenue. However, it was recorded as an asset when it was purchased. The entry to record the purchase of the automobile is as follows:

June 1   Cheque Copy #689: $13 310.18 to Myers Motors, for purchase of an automobile.

GENERAL JOURNAL

PAGE 453

DATE 1991		PARTICULARS	PR	DEBIT	CREDIT
June	1	Automobile	190	12 500 –	
		GST Recoverable	135	8 10 18	
		Cash	100		13 310 18
		Cheque Copy #689, purchased auto from Myers Motors			

"*Depreciation is the decrease in value of a fixed asset, due to wear, tear, and obsolescence.*"

"*The depreciation entry is the systematic allocation of the cost of an asset to an expense account over its useful life.*"

Year-End Adjustment

Each year the value of the automobile will decrease due to depreciation, which results from wear, tear, and obsolescence. In order to acknowledge the use of the automobile to earn revenue during a fiscal period, Algor Computer Services' accountant will make an adjusting entry at the end of the period. This adjusting entry is a systematic allocation, to an expense account, of the cost of the asset (in this case, an automobile) over its useful lifetime.

The accountant for Algor made the following adjusting entry at the end of Year 1:

GENERAL JOURNAL

PAGE 590

DATE 1992		PARTICULARS	PR	DEBIT	CREDIT
May	31	Depreciation Expense: Automobile	710	3 500 –	
		Accumulated Depreciation: Automobile	191		3 500 –
		To record depreciation of auto for one year			

How was the amount $3 500 established? Algor's accountant estimated that the automobile was going to last three years, and at that time would have a salvage, or resale, value of $2 000. Since the car happened to be purchased at the start of the fiscal year, the depreciation for the first year is calculated as follows (using the straight-line method, which will be discussed later):

$$\text{Depreciation per year} = \frac{\text{Cost} - \text{Salvage value}}{\text{Estimated life of the asset in years}}$$

$$= \frac{\$12\,500 - \$2\,000}{3}$$

$$= \$3\,500$$

The explanation for the adjusting entry is as follows:
- The debit to Depreciation Expense: Automobile records the expense (for one year) of using the automobile to earn revenue, and therefore follows the matching principle.
- The credit to Accumulated Depreciation: Automobile records the

Accumulated Depreciation: Automobile: a contra-asset account.

Contra-asset accounts: accounts that will reduce the value of another asset when they are combined on the balance sheet.

allocation of part of the cost of the automobile to this particular accounting period. **Accumulated Depreciation: Automobile** is a contra-asset account, or a negative asset. **Contra-asset accounts** are accounts that will reduce the value of another asset when they are combined on the balance sheet. Accumulated Depreciation: Automobile will be combined with the Automobile account on the balance sheet, as shown later.

The effect of these journal entries on the general ledger accounts is shown below:

GENERAL LEDGER

Automobile		190
dr.	cr.	
June 1 (1991) 12 500		

Accumulated Depreciation: Automobile		191
dr.	cr.	
	May 31 (1992) 3 500	

Depreciation Expense: Automobile		710
dr.	cr.	
May 31 (1992) 3 500		

Why not make a credit to Automobile instead of to the new account Accumulated Depreciation: Automobile? By using a separate account to record the accumulated depreciation from year to year the balance sheet will show both the cost price of the automobile and the accumulated depreciation. The accumulated depreciation is that portion of the original cost which has been allocated as an expense.

Algor Computer Services
Partial Balance Sheet
as at May 31, 1992

Fixed Assets

Automobile	$12 500	
Less: Accumulated Depreciation	3 500	$ 9 000

Accumulated Depreciation: Automobile is a contra-asset, or negative asset account. Although it is found in the fixed asset section of a balance sheet it has a credit balance, and it is combined with the Automobile account to show the net value of the automobile. The balance sheet presents the original cost of the automobile, $12 500, the accumulated depreciation, $3 500, and the net book value of the automobile, $9 000. **Net book value** is the undepreciated cost of a fixed asset, and is calculated as follows:

Net book value: the undepreciated cost of a fixed asset.

$$\text{Net Book Value} = \text{Cost} - \text{Accumulated Depreciation}$$

The $9 000 is the asset value recorded on the books, and is not

Net Book Value:
Cost − Accumulated Depreciation

necessarily the same as the market value, should Algor try to sell the automobile. Alternate names for net book value are carrying value and undepreciated capital cost.

At the end of Year 2, another entry will be made to record the depreciation for that year.

GENERAL JOURNAL

PAGE 701

DATE 1993		PARTICULARS	PR	DEBIT	CREDIT
May	31	Depreciation Expense: Automobile	710	3 500 —	
		Accumulated Depreciation: Automobile	191		3 500 —
		To record depreciation of auto for one year			

The general ledger accounts related to the depreciation of the automobile will appear as follows after two years of depreciation:

GENERAL LEDGER

Automobile	190		Accumulated Depreciation: Automobile	191
dr.	cr.		dr.	cr.
June 1 (1991) 12 500				May 31 (1992) 3 500
				May 31 (1993) 3 500

The balance sheet after two years of depreciation will appear as follows:

Algor Computer Services
Partial Balance Sheet
as at May 31, 1993

Fixed Assets
Automobile $12 500
Less: Accumulated Depreciation   7 000 $ 5 500

THE FACTS SPEAK...

Depreciation of fixed assets for McDonald's Corporation, and BCE (Bell Canada Enterprises).

1989	McDonald's Corporation	BCE
Property, plant and equipment	$9.8 billion	$26.9 billion
Less: Accumulated Depreciation	2.1	9.7
Net book value	$7.7 billion	$17.2 billion

Effects of Depreciation

The effect of making an adjusting entry to the Automobile account to record the depreciation of the vehicle at the end of the fiscal year is to spread the cost of the automobile over its useful life.

Cost of Automobile	Allocation of Cost to Expense			
	Year 1	Year 2	Year 3	Salvage
$12 500	$3 500	$3 500	$3 500	$2 000

Algor Computer Services' condensed, comparative income statement for the three years that the automobile was used will appear as follows:

FIGURE 7-5 COMPARATIVE INCOME STATEMENT SHOWING THE EFFECT OF DEPRECIATION

Algor Computer Services
Comparative Income Statement
for the years ending May 31, 1992, 1993, and 1994

	1992		1993		1994	
Revenue		$380 000		$398 000		$449 000
Expenses						
Depreciation Expense:						
Automobile	$ 3 500		$ 3 500		$ 3 500	
Other	292 400		315 700		337 200	
Total Expenses		295 900		319 200		340 700
Net Income		$ 84 100		$ 78 800		$108 300

The cost price of the automobile has been spread over the three years that it was used to earn revenue. Obviously, the effect on each year's net income is different than if the matching principle had not been followed, and the automobile had been recorded as an expense in the year that it was purchased.

The effect on the balance sheet of the annual depreciation of the automobile is shown in Figure 7-6.

Depreciation is recorded for all fixed assets except land. Thus, there will be separate accounts for depreciation expense and accumulated depreciation of equipment, building and so on. Land does not depreciate; indeed, its value usually increases. It is not customary for increases in the value of this asset to be recorded for one reason: it is difficult to get an objective value for land. Furthermore, following the going concern assumption discussed in Chapter 1, the land is necessary for the operation of the business.

FIGURE 7-6 COMPARATIVE PARTIAL BALANCE SHEET SHOWING THE EFFECT OF DEPRECIATION

Algor Computer Services
Comparative Partial Balance Sheet
as at May 31, 1992 to May 31, 1994

	1992		1993		1994	
Cost	12 500		12 500		12 500	
Accumulated Depreciation	3 500	9 000	7 000	5 500	10 500	2 000

The effect of spreading the cost of a fixed asset over many years may also be beneficial to a business for tax purposes. Instead of having a deductible expense only in the year that the fixed asset was purchased, the deduction can be spread over the life of the asset.

Calculating Depreciation

There are a variety of methods of calculating depreciation. It is not possible to estimate the exact amount of a fixed asset that should be depreciated. One reason is that the fixed asset might last longer than expected. Another reason is that it is nearly impossible to estimate exactly by how much the asset has depreciated — how many more items it will produce, or how many more kilometres it will go. The financial statements would not truly reflect annual operating costs, however, if accountants waited until the end of the asset's life to determine the amount of depreciation to allocate to each year's financial statements. Thus, an estimate is made when the asset is purchased.

Three methods of estimating depreciation are:
- straight-line
- declining-balance
- capital cost allowance

Straight-Line Depreciation

The easiest way to calculate depreciation is using the straight-line method, which determines the annual amount of depreciation by taking into account the estimated useful life of the fixed asset. A survey of annual reports of Canadian businesses will show that this method is frequently used. The following statement from Alberta Government Telephones (AGT) describes their system of calculating depreciation:

> (c) Depreciation
>
> Depreciation is provided on a straight-line basis using rates determined by a continuing program of engineering studies, calculated to allocate to operations the cost of groups of property with equal service lives over the estimated useful lives of the groups.
>
> When depreciable telephone property is retired for reasons of exhausted service capacity, obsolescence, loss or destruction, the original cost of such property, adjusted by any disposal proceeds and costs of removal, is charged to accumulated depreciation.

The formula used to calculate depreciation for one year using this method is:

$$\frac{\text{Cost} - \text{Salvage value}}{\text{Estimated life of the asset in years}}$$

To show the calculation for depreciating assets for Algor Computer Services, lets assume the following purchase.

Jan. 1 Purchase Invoice #34-91 from Modern Business Furniture Ltd. Purchased office furniture, $15 000, estimated life 10 years, salvage value estimated to be $2 000.

Straight-line depreciation: *an equal portion of the cost of the fixed asset is allocated to an expense based on the estimated life of the asset.*

The calculation for one year, using straight-line depreciation, is as follows:

$$= \frac{\text{Cost} - \text{Salvage value}}{\text{Estimated life of the asset in years}}$$

$$= \frac{\$15\,000 - \$2\,000}{10}$$

$$= \$1\,300$$

The depreciation for each of the ten years using the straight-line method will be the same amount, $1 300. This method of calculating depreciation is referred to as the straight-line method, because if the value depreciated each year was put on a graph it would result in a straight line on the graph. (See Figure 7-7.)

If a fixed asset is purchased part way through a fiscal year, the calculation of the amount for the adjusting entry will have to reflect this fact. For example, a $15 000 computer purchased on August 1 by a business using December 31 as its year end will have to be depreciated for only five months. Assuming a three-year life, with a salvage value of $2 000, the calculation will then be:

Straight-line depreciation for five months

$$\frac{\text{Original cost} - \text{Salvage value}}{\text{Estimated life of the asset in months}} \times 5$$

$$= \frac{\$15\,000 - \$2\,000}{36} \times 5$$

$$= \$1\,805.56$$

However, at the end of the *next* fiscal year, the adjustment would be for a full year of depreciation.

FIGURE 7-7 A GRAPH SHOWING STRAIGHT-LINE DEPRECIATION OVER THE USEFUL LIFE OF THE ASSET

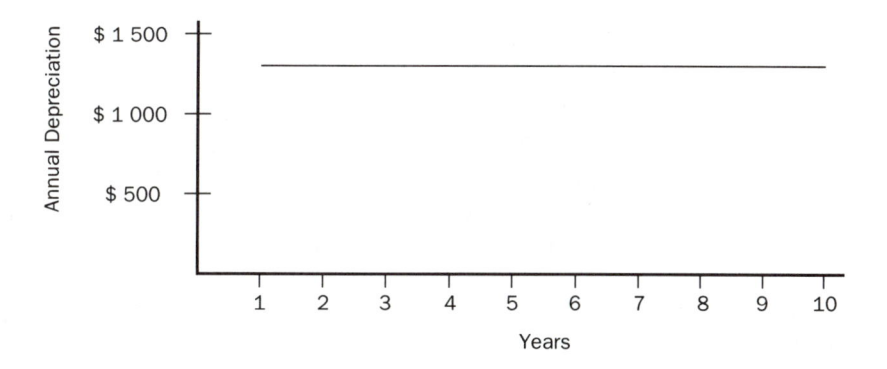

Declining-Balance Depreciation

"Declining-balance method of depreciation is based on applying a fixed percentage to the net book value of the fixed asset."

The declining-balance method of calculating depreciation reflects the fact that new items provide greater and more efficient service than they do as they get older. If the benefits provided by the asset in the early years of its life are greater, then the matching principle requires that more of the cost be allocated to depreciation expense in the early years. In calculating depreciation by this method, a fixed percentage is applied to the net book value of the fixed asset. The fixed percentage should be chosen so that the matching principle is best fulfilled.

Let us apply the declining-balance method of depreciation to the same office furniture purchase used to illustrate the straight-line method. Assume that the business chose a rate of 10 percent. Note that the salvage value is ignored when using the declining-balance method. Should the fixed asset be kept for many years, it would not be depreciated below the salvage value.

Year 1
Jan. 1   Purchase Invoice #34-91 from Modern Business Furniture Ltd. Purchased office furniture, $15 000.

Declining-balance method of calculating depreciation
= Net Book Value × Rate
= $15 000 × 0.10
= $1 500

The original cost was $15 000. Since this is the first year that the office furniture has been used, no previous depreciation has been recorded, so its net book value is still $15 000. The accumulated depreciation at the end of the first year will be $1 500. The net book value at the end of Year 1 will be $13 500.
(Remember: Net Book Value = Cost − Accumulated Depreciation)

Year 2
Declining-balance method of calculating depreciation
= Net Book Value × Rate
= $13 500 × 0.10
= $1 350

The accumulated depreciation at the end of the second year will be $2 850 ($1 500 + $1 350). The net book value at the end of Year 2 will be $12 150 ($15 000 − $2 850). The amount of depreciation will decrease each year using the declining-balance method. It gets its name from the fact that the net book value declines each year.

FIGURE 7-8 A GRAPH SHOWING DECLINING-BALANCE DEPRECIATION OVER THE USEFUL LIFE OF THE ASSET

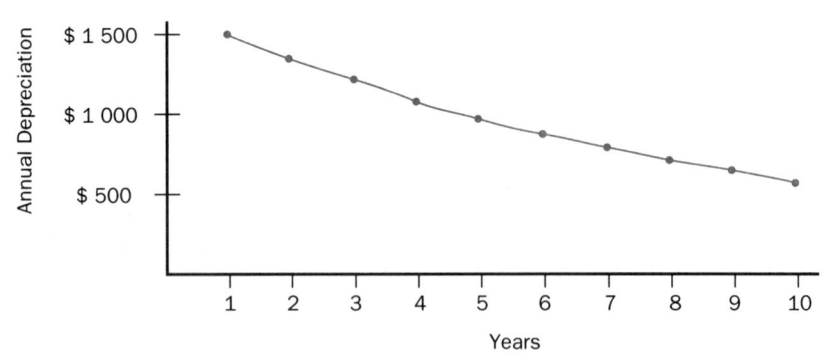

Capital Cost Allowance

"*Capital cost allowance is the term used for depreciation for income tax purposes.*"

The capital cost allowance method of calculating depreciation is required under the *Income Tax Act*. The method of calculation is similar to the one used for the declining-balance method, but the rate applied to each asset is specified under the *Income Tax Act*. There are over forty classes of items, ranging from unmanned telecommunication spacecraft designed to orbit above the earth (40 percent), to chinaware and cutlery (100 percent). The classes and rates needed for this text are shown in Figure 7-9.

FIGURE 7-9 CAPITAL COST ALLOWANCE RATES FOR INCOME TAX PURPOSES

Classes and Rates for Capital Cost Allowance		
Class	Fixed asset	Rate per year
3	Buildings	5%
8	Equipment	20%
10	Automobiles	30%
10	Computer Equipment	30%

In the first year that a fixed asset is owned, the *Income Tax Act* specifies that only one half of the amount of the depreciation can be claimed for tax purposes. Thus, the calculation for the first year is as follows, assuming that office equipment was purchased in the amount of $12 000.

$$\text{Capital Cost Allowance} = \frac{\text{Cost} \times \text{Rate}}{2}$$
$$= \frac{\$12\,000 \times 0.20}{2}$$
$$= \$1\,200$$

In the subsequent year, the following calculation would be made to determine the capital cost allowance:

Capital Cost Allowance
= (Cost − Accumulated Depreciation) × Rate
= ($12 000 − $1 200) × 0.20
= $2 160

Which Method of Depreciation to Choose

According to the matching principle, a business should choose the method that best matches fixed asset costs with revenue. A business could, therefore, use one method for calculating depreciation for its own books, and another for its income tax return, where the rate is specified by the *Income Tax Act*. In reality, many businesses adopt the capital cost allowance method for both rather than calculating two amounts: one for tax purposes and another for internal accounting purposes. The justification for doing so is the fact that depreciation is only a valuation, and not an exact calculation. Moreover, the calculation of depreciation is based on the cost of a fixed asset expressed in dollars that may be a number of years old, but it is being matched against revenue expressed in current dollars.

Irrespective of which method of calculating depreciation is used, the full disclosure principle requires that the method be disclosed either on the balance sheet, or in a note. The *CICA Handbook* also specifies that the fixed assets should be disclosed by major category, with accumulated depreciation deducted from each. In recent years, it has become common for firms to disclose on the balance sheet the major categories of fixed assets, with only one figure for accumulated depreciation, or to put a net figure on the balance sheet for fixed assets, with individual fixed assets and corresponding accumulated depreciation shown in notes.

Principle of Materiality

> **Principle of materiality:** an item is material if there is a reasonable expectation that knowledge of it would influence the decisions of users of financial statements.

The principle of materiality involves the consideration of what is relevant in the preparation of the financial statements. Accountants consider transactions and events to be material, or important, if they have an effect on the financial statements. This principle is especially important when preparing adjusting entries. Theoretically, the purchase of any item that is going to contribute to the revenue earning process in more than one fiscal period should be recorded as an asset, and depreciated. Yet, will the purchase of a pair of scissors, and the recording of it as a depreciable asset, measurably affect the financial statements? It is doubtful that it will, so the purchase will probably be recorded as an expense according to the principle of materiality. The **principle of materiality** states that an item is material if there is a reasonable expectation that knowledge of it would influence the decisions of users of financial statements.

> **Conservatism:** an accountant, when deciding between two equally defensible alternatives, will choose the one that results in the lower net income in the current period.

Businesses will apply the principle differently, for what is material in one business may not be material in another. Businesses will make decisions on whether an item will be recorded as an asset or an expense based on the value and nature of the item purchased. For example, a business may decide that any equipment that costs $500 or more will be recorded in the Equipment account, and equipment under $500 will be recorded in an expense account. When establishing these policies, conservatism is followed. **Conservatism** means that an accountant, when deciding between two equally defensible alternatives, will choose the one that results in the lower net income in the current period. Such a policy should neither bring results that overstate nor understate the facts.

Accrual Basis of Accounting

The use of adjusting entries is a component of the accrual basis of accounting, as opposed to the cash basis. The cash basis of accounting would require that expenses be recorded as expenses when the cash is paid for them. The accrual basis requires that the matching principle be followed: revenue for a fiscal year should be offset with all expenses incurred in earning that revenue. Adjustments for expenses should therefore be recorded during the accounting period in which those expenses helped to earn revenue.

LESSON REVIEW

13. What is depreciation? What items depreciate?
14. Give the debit and credit entry for each of the following:
    (a) the purchase of an automobile for cash
    (b) the adjustment to record depreciation at year end
15. What type of account is each of the following? Explain why.
    (a) Automobile
    (b) Accumulated Depreciation: Automobile
    (c) Depreciation Expense: Automobile
16. What is net book value? How is it calculated?
17. What is the accounting effect of an adjusting entry for depreciation?
18. Why can the amount of depreciation not be calculated exactly?
19. What are two methods of calculating depreciation? Give the formula for each.
20. Which method of depreciation is required by Revenue Canada?
21. Describe the influence that the principle of materiality has on the recording of the purchase of an item.
22. State how conservatism applies to decisions that accountants must make.
23. Outline how adjusting entries correspond to the accrual basis of accounting.

LESSON APPLICATIONS

24. Warner's Skate Sharpening purchased a new sharpener for $5 700 on January 1, 19–3. The sharpener is expected to last three years and the firm uses straight-line depreciation. It is expected that the machine will have no salvage value at the end of three years.
    (a) Prepare the adjusting entry for the December 31 fiscal year end.
    (b) Prepare a partial balance sheet to illustrate how accounts related to the sharpener will appear on December 31.
    (c) What type of account is Accumulated Depreciation: Sharpener? Why?
25. The Kenora Animal Hospital purchased a truck for $14 500 on April 1, 19–1. The business expected to use the truck for three years at the end of which it was estimated the salvage value would be $2 500. Use the straight-line method of depreciation.

(a) Prepare the adjusting entry for the fiscal year ending December 31, 19–1.
(b) Prepare a partial balance sheet to illustrate how accounts related to the truck will appear on December 31, 19–1.
(c) What type of account is Accumulated Depreciation: Truck? Why?
(d) What will the total amount of depreciation be at the end of 19–2?

26. Gibson's Chimney Sweep purchases a truck valued at $26 000. It is estimated that the truck will last four years with a salvage value of $2 000. The business uses the straight-line method of depreciation. Assume the truck is purchased at the beginning of Year 1.
    (a) Make a chart with the headings shown below. Complete the chart for each of the four years that the firm will own the truck.

YEAR	UNDEPRECIATED COST AT BEGINNING OF YEAR	DEPRECIATION FOR THE YEAR	ACCUMULATED DEPRECIATION AT END OF YEAR	UNDEPRECIATED COST AT END OF YEAR
1				

(b) Prepare partial balance sheets for years three and four showing the accounts related to the truck.

27. Superior Insurance Agency purchases a computer valued at $14 500. The business uses the declining-balance method of depreciation, with a rate of 30 percent per year.
    (a) Make a chart with the headings shown below. Complete the chart for the four years that it is estimated the firm will own the computer.

YEAR	UNDEPRECIATED COST AT BEGINNING OF YEAR	DEPRECIATION FOR THE YEAR	ACCUMULATED DEPRECIATION AT END OF YEAR	UNDEPRECIATED COST AT END OF YEAR
1				

(b) Prepare partial balance sheets for years three and four showing the accounts related to the computer.

7.3 The Eight-Column Worksheet

Although we have taken a look at adjusting entries in general journal form in the previous sections, they should actually be entered on a worksheet *before* they are journalized. Two special columns are added to the worksheet in order to accommodate this extra preparation. The order of completing the adjusting entries at the end of the fiscal cycle is as follows:

> "An eight-column worksheet is used to record adjustments."

FIGURE 7-10 STEPS IN COMPLETING THE ADJUSTMENTS AT THE END OF A FISCAL PERIOD

(1) Worksheet, including adjustments
(2) Journalize and Post Adjusting Entries
(3) Financial Statements

In order to examine the preparation of adjustments on the worksheet, we will look at selected information related to Algor Computer Services on May 31, 1992, the end of the fiscal year. Several adjustments are listed below and are shown on the worksheet in Figure 7-11.

Prepaid Insurance expired, $600;
Office Supplies on hand, $890;
Computer Supplies on hand, $2 700;
Depreciation using the declining-balance method.

For the purpose of illustration, the adjustments are placed on the worksheet in the way they would be at the end of the first fiscal year. In subsequent years, the Accumulated Depreciation accounts are shifted up on the worksheet to follow the asset account to which they belong.

Preparing the Worksheet

The first two steps in preparing an eight-column worksheet are the same as those for a six-column worksheet. They are illustrated on the worksheet in Figure 7-11.

Step 1 Enter the heading including the name of the firm.
Step 2 Enter the trial balance.

The next step is the significant change on the eight-column worksheet:

> "Footnotes are entered on the worksheet to explain each of the adjusting entries."

Step 3 Enter the adjustments, ensuring that debits equal credits for each adjustment. Each adjustment has a letter beside it to match the debit and credit, and also to match the corresponding footnotes, which will explain the adjustment. Note the footnotes that are found at the bottom of the worksheet. Total and rule the adjustments columns to prove that they balance.

FIGURE 7-11 COMPLETED WORKSHEET SHOWING ADJUSTMENTS

WORKSHEET

Algor Computer Services — FOR THE _year_ ENDED _May 31_ 19 _92_

#	ACCOUNTS	ACCT. NO.	TRIAL BALANCE DR	TRIAL BALANCE CR	ADJUSTMENTS DR	ADJUSTMENTS CR	INCOME STATEMENT DR	INCOME STATEMENT CR	BALANCE SHEET DR	BALANCE SHEET CR	#
1	Cash	100	4900 00						4900 00		1
2	Accounts Receivable	120	500 00						500 00		2
3	GST Recoverable	135	140 00						140 00		3
4	Prepaid Insurance	140	180 00			a) 600 —			120 00		4
5	Office Supplies	150	146 00			b) 570 —			89 00		5
6	Computer Supplies	155	490 00			c) 2200 —			270 00		6
7	Land	160	12460 00						12460 00		7
8	Building	170	22800 00						22800 00		8
9	Office Equipment	175	1450 00						1450 00		9
10	Computer Equipment	180	5960 00						5960 00		10
11	Automobile	190	1250 00						1250 00		11
12	Accounts Payable	200		1450 3 —						1450 3 —	12
13	Mortgage Payable	220		24800 00						24800 00	13
14	GST Payable	230		146 00						146 00	14
15	PST Payable	240		172 00						172 00	15
16	V. Marshall, Capital	300		22247 7 —						22247 7 —	16
17	V. Marshall, Drawings	310	2800 00						2800 00		17
18	Computer Services	400		28200 00				28200 00			18
19	Software Lessons	410		980 00				980 00			19
20	Refunds	415	220 00				220 00				20
21	Wages Expense	600	18460 00				18460 00				21
22	VISA Discount Expense	655	720 00				720 00				22
23	Advertising Expense	660	4460 00				4460 00				23
24	Utilities Expense	670	3240 00				3240 00				24
25	Automobile Expense	680	440 00				440 00				25
26	Miscellaneous Expense	760	170 00				170 00				26
27			86816 0 —	86816 0 —							27
28	Insurance Expense	720			a) 600 —		600 —				28
29	Office Supplies Expense	730			b) 570 —		570 —				29
30	Computer Supplies Expense	740			c) 2200 —		2200 —				30
31	Depreciation Expense: Building	690			d) 11400 —		11400 —				31
32	Accumulated Dep'n: Building	171				d) 11400 —				11400 —	32
33	Depreciation Expense: Off. Equip.	700			e) 1450 —		1450 —				33
34	Accumulated Dep'n: Off. Equip.	176				e) 1450 —				1450 —	34
35	Depreciation Expense: Comp. Equip.	705			f) 17880 —		17880 —				35
36	Accumulated Dep'n: Comp. Equip.	181				f) 17880 —				17880 —	36
37	Depreciation Expense: Auto	710			g) 3750 —		3750 —				37
38	Accumulated Dep'n: Auto	191				g) 3750 —				3750 —	38
39					37850 —	37850 —	330250 —	380000 —	572390 —	522640 —	39
40	a) Insurance expired, $600.						49750 —			49750 —	40
41	b) Office supplies used, $570.						380000 —	380000 —	572390 —	572390 —	41
42	c) Computer supplies used, $2 200.										42
43	d) Building depreciation, 0.05 x $228 000.										43
44	e) Office equipment depreciation, 0.10 x $14 500.										44
45	f) Computer equipment depreciation, 0.30 x $59 600.										45
46	g) Automobile depreciation, 0.30 x $ 12 500.										46
47											47

Prepaid Insurance

Algor Computer Services had $1 800 of Prepaid Insurance, and of that amount it is found that $600 has expired. To record this adjustment on the worksheet, the letter a) is put beside each item, and

- a debit is made to Insurance Expense, which appears below the trial balance total. The amount is $600.

- a credit is made to Prepaid Insurance in the amount of $600, to reduce the balance of that account.

Office Supplies

The office supplies on hand after taking an inventory total $890. The balance of the account as shown on the trial balance is $1 460. This balance represents the supplies on hand at the beginning of the year, plus any purchases of supplies during the year. In order to establish the value of the supplies used, subtract the amount on hand from the balance of the account:

Balance of supplies account	$1 460
Supplies inventory	890
Supplies used	$ 570

The adjusting entry should be:
a debit to Office Supplies Expense	$570
a credit to Office Supplies	$570

To enter this adjustment on the worksheet:
- Office Supplies Expense is added below the trial balance total because it does not appear on the trial balance. It is debited $570 in the adjustments column. The matching principle has therefore been followed: the revenue earned has been matched with the supplies expense incurred in order to earn that revenue.
- Office Supplies is credited $570 in the adjustments column to reduce the balance of that account.

The letter b) is put beside each item, and a footnote is added to explain that adjustment. A similar adjustment is made for Computer Supplies: a debit is made to Computer Supplies Expense for $2 200, and a credit of $2 200 is made to Computer Supplies. The letter c) is put beside each item.

Building

The building owned by the business is used to earn revenue. The expenses related to it must be matched with the corresponding revenue. Therefore, an adjusting entry is made to record the depreciation expense. Using the rate of 5 percent and the declining-balance method, the depreciation for the year is equal to 0.05 × $228 000, or $11 400. The adjusting entry to record the depreciation is entered as follows:

a debit to Depreciation Expense: Building	$11 400
a credit to Accumulated Depreciation: Building	$11 400

To enter this adjustment on the worksheet:
- A debit is made to Depreciation Expense: Building, which must be added to the list of accounts below the trial balance total line. The debit to the expense account follows the matching process.

- A credit is made to Accumulated Depreciation: Building, which is a contra-asset account. Because the account would not previously have been used, it must also be added below the trial balance total line. In subsequent years, it will be listed after the Building account on the trial balance. The amount of the credit indicates the allocation of that portion of the cost of the building to the time period in which it was used. It also indicates the estimated reduction in the value of the building for the year.

A d) is entered beside each of the above entries, to correspond to the footnote.

Equipment

The equipment owned by the business is used during the accounting period to earn revenue. Algor Computer Services has decided to divide it into two categories: Office Equipment, and Computer Equipment. Office equipment is depreciated at a rate of 10 percent per year using the declining-balance method, and Computer Equipment at a rate of 30 percent. The depreciation on the Office Equipment for the first year is therefore $1 450.

The entry to record this should be:
    a debit to Depreciation Expense: Office Equipment $1 450
    a credit to Accumulated Depreciation: Office Equipment $1 450

To record this adjustment on the worksheet:
- Depreciation Expense: Office Equipment is not found on the trial balance, so it too must be added to the list at the bottom of the trial balance. The debit of $1 450 is entered to show the estimated amount by which the equipment has depreciated. The matching principle has therefore been followed: the revenue earned has been matched with the equipment expense incurred in order to earn that revenue.
- Accumulated Depreciation: Office Equipment is also not found on the trial balance, so it must be added to the list at the bottom of the trial balance as well. The credit of $1 450 to this contra account indicates the portion of the cost of the equipment that has been allocated as an expense for the fiscal period. It also indicates the estimated reduction in the value of the office equipment.

The letter e) is put beside each of the above, and a footnote is written at the bottom of the worksheet.

A similar entry is made to show the depreciation of the computer equipment. However, the rate of depreciation is higher (30%), for the rapid change in technology makes the machines obsolete quickly. An entry is made to debit Depreciation Expense: Computer Equipment and to credit Accumulated Depreciation: Computer Equipment in the amount of $17 880. The letter f) is put beside each of the items.

Automobile

The automobile is used by Algor to transport computer service personnel to the various sites in order to carry out the necessary services. Therefore, the expense of operating the automobile (as shown in the Automobile Expense account) as well as the cost of the automobile itself, must be matched with the corresponding revenue it helps to earn. The cost of the automobile is spread over the years that it is used and that expense is recorded as Depreciation Expense: Automobile.

Algor Computer Services depreciates its automobile at the rate of 30 percent per year using the declining-balance method. The cost of the automobile was $12 500. The depreciation at the end of the first year is therefore $12 500 × 0.30, or $3 750.

The entry to record this should be:
    a debit to Depreciation Expense: Automobile $3 750
    a credit to Accumulated Depreciation: Automobile $3 750

To record this adjustment on the worksheet:
- The account Depreciation Expense: Automobile is not found on the trial balance, so it must be added to the list of new accounts below the trial balance. The debit of $3 750 shows the estimated amount the automobile has depreciated this year, and indicates that it was used to earn revenue. Matching has taken place.
- The account Accumulated Depreciation: Automobile is similarly not found on the trial balance and must be added to the list. The account must therefore be added at the bottom of the trial balance. The credit of $3 750 to this contra account indicates the estimated reduction in the value of the automobile. In future years this account will not have to be added to the trial balance, for it will have a balance carried forward from previous years.

The letter g) is put beside each of the above, and a footnote is written at the bottom of the worksheet.

The Accumulated Depreciation: Automobile account is similar to the Accumulated Depreciation: Office Equipment account; it will not be found on the trial balance until the depreciation is accumulating.

Step 4 The remaining procedures, once the adjustments have been entered on the worksheet and totalled, are the same as for the six-column worksheet. The amounts should therefore be extended to their proper statements. The amount in the trial balance column must be changed by the amount in the adjustments column: be careful to note whether it increases or decreases the amount.

Step 5 Total the four remaining columns.

Step 6 Calculate the amount of the net income or net loss, and add it to the smaller amount to prove the calculation.

Step 7 Transfer the net income or net loss to the balance sheet and total the balance sheet. Double rule the final totals.

A Ten-Column Worksheet?

> "A ten-column worksheet may be used to show adjustments, with the extra two columns for an adjusted trial balance."

Some accountants prefer to use a ten-column worksheet instead of an eight-column worksheet. The extra two columns are for an adjusted trial balance. The adjusted trial balance combines the figures from the trial balance and the adjustments columns. It can then be proven that total debits are equal to total credits before the extensions are made to the appropriate financial statement columns. The use of the ten-column worksheet, therefore, reduces the possibility of making an error when extending amounts to the financial statement columns. The column headings would appear as follows on a ten-column worksheet:

TRIAL BALANCE		ADJUSTMENTS		ADJUSTED TRIAL BALANCE		INCOME STATEMENT		BALANCE SHEET	
Dr.	Cr.	Dr.	Cr.	Dr.	Cr.	Dr.	Cr.	Dr.	Cr.

Using the Worksheet

Once the eight-column worksheet has been completed, the information is used to prepare financial statements. The income statement is prepared using all account balances found in the Income Statement col-

FIGURE 7-12 INCOME STATEMENT PREPARED FROM EIGHT-COLUMN WORKSHEET

Algor Computer Services		
Income Statement		
for the year ended May 31, 1992		
Revenue:		
Computer Services	282 00 -	
Software Lessons	98 00 -	380 00 -
Less: Refunds		2 20 -
Net Revenue		377 80 -
Expenses:		
Wages	184 60 -	
VISA Discount	72 00 -	
Advertising	44 60 -	
Utilities	32 40 -	
Automobile	4 40 -	
Miscellaneous	17 00 -	
Insurance	6 00 -	
Office Supplies	5 70 -	
Computer Supplies	22 00 -	
Depreciation Expense: Building	11 40 -	
Depreciation Expense: Office Equipment	14 50 -	
Depreciation Expense: Computer Equipment	17 88 -	
Depreciation Expense: Automobile	37 50 -	
Total Expenses		328 05 -
Net Income		49 75 -

umns, including the expenses recorded by the adjusting entries. The net income, or net loss, is used in the preparation of the owner's equity section of the balance sheet.

The balance sheet is prepared from the Balance Sheet columns of the worksheet. Note how the assets that have corresponding contra-asset accounts are shown. The fixed asset is listed, with the accumulated depreciation shown, as well as the net book value.

FIGURE 7-13 BALANCE SHEET PREPARED FROM EIGHT-COLUMN WORKSHEET

Algor Computer Services			
Balance Sheet			
as at May 31, 1992			
Assets			
Current Assets:			
Cash		49 00 –	
Accounts Receivable		50 00 –	
GST Recoverable		1 4 00 –	
Prepaid Insurance		1 2 00 –	
Office Supplies		8 90 –	
Computer Supplies		2 7 00 –	
Total Current Assets			105 1 90 –
Fixed Assets:			
Land		124 6 00 –	
Building	228 00 –		
Less: Accumulated Depreciation	11 4 00 –	216 6 00 –	
Office Equipment	14 5 00 –		
Less: Accumulated Depreciation	1 4 50 –	13 0 50 –	
Computer Equipment	59 6 00 –		
Less: Accumulated Depreciation	17 8 80 –	41 7 20 –	
Automobile	12 5 00 –		
Less: Accumulated Depreciation	3 7 50 –	8 7 50 –	
Total Fixed Assets			404 7 20 –
Total Assets			509 9 10 –
Liabilities and Owner's Equity			
Current Liabilities:			
Accounts Payable		14 5 03 –	
GST Payable		1 4 60 –	
PST Payable		1 7 20 –	
Total Current Liabilities			17 6 83 –
Long-Term Liabilities:			
Mortgage Payable			248 0 00 –
Owner's Equity:			
V. Marshall, Capital, June 1, 1991		222 4 77 –	
Net Income	49 7 50 –		
Less: Drawings	28 0 00 –		
Increase in Capital		21 7 50 –	
V. Marshall, Capital, May 31, 1992			244 2 27 –
Total Liabilities and Owner's Equity			509 9 10 –

Journalizing and Posting the Adjusting Entries

Although the adjusting entries are first entered on the worksheet, that does not change the account balances found in the ledger. The entries, therefore, must be copied from the worksheet into the journal, and from there, posted to the ledger. One of the advantages of labelling the adjustments with letters is the easy identification of the debit and credit for each entry. The explanation for each journal entry can be found in the footnotes on the worksheet.

The journal entries to record the adjusting entries illustrated on the worksheet in Figure 7-11 are shown in general journal form below:

FIGURE 7-14 JOURNALIZED ADJUSTING ENTRIES

GENERAL JOURNAL

PAGE 590

DATE 1992		PARTICULARS	PR	DEBIT	CREDIT
		Adjusting Entries			
May	31	Insurance Expense		600 —	
		Prepaid Insurance			600 —
		To record insurance expired during the year			
	31	Office Supplies Expense		570 —	
		Office Supplies			570 —
		To record office supplies used during the year			
	31	Computer Supplies Expense		2 200 —	
		Computer Supplies			2 200 —
		To record computer supplies used during the year			
	31	Depreciation Expense: Building		11 400 —	
		Accumulated Depreciation: Building			11 400 —
		To record depreciation for one year			
	31	Depreciation Expense: Office Equipment		1 450 —	
		Accumulated Depreciation: Office Equipment			1 450 —
		To record depreciation for one year			
	31	Depreciation Expense: Computer Equipment		17 880 —	
		Accumulated Depreciation: Computer Equipment			17 880 —
		To record depreciation for one year			
	31	Depreciation Expense: Automobile		3 750 —	
		Accumulated Depreciation: Automobile			3 750 —
		To record depreciation for one year			

Lesson Review

28. Where are adjusting entries first entered? Why?
29. Give two reasons why a letter is put before the debit and credit of an adjusting entry on a worksheet.
30. The account Accumulated Depreciation: Office Equipment will not be found on a worksheet trial balance the first year that office equipment is owned. Why not?
31. Where is the information for the preparation of formal financial statements found?
32. Other than the trial balance columns, each set of columns on the worksheet is used for preparing something. What is each used for?

Lesson Applications

33. The Burnaby Real Estate Company has completed its first year of operation, and is about to adjust its accounts at the end of the calendar year. The trial balance taken at that time is given below. Complete an eight-column worksheet, using the other data provided.

Burnaby Real Estate Company
Trial Balance
December 31, 19–2

100	Cash	$ 5 080	
110	Accounts Receivable	3 280	
115	GST Recoverable	400	
120	Prepaid Insurance	1 400	
130	Office Supplies	984	
140	Office Equipment	12 840	
150	Automobile	15 600	
200	Accounts Payable		$ 3 290
210	Short-Term Loan		5 800
220	GST Payable		670
300	E. Schieman, Capital		45 263
310	E. Schieman, Drawings	22 900	
400	Sales Commissions Earned		96 000
500	Rent Expense	27 000	
510	Wages Expense	41 800	
520	Advertising Expense	6 000	
530	Interest Expense	1 080	
540	Automobile Expense	6 049	
550	Utilities Expense	4 590	
595	General Expense	2 020	
		$151 023	$151 023

Other data:
Unexpired insurance is $485.
The office supplies on hand are worth $320.
Equipment is depreciated using the straight-line method; estimated life five years, with a salvage value of $300.
Automobile is depreciated using the straight-line method; estimated life four years, with a salvage value of $1 600.

34. The Western Canada Video Company makes advertising videos for firms that then mail them to prospective customers. It adjusts its accounts on a yearly basis at the end of June. Complete an eight-column worksheet using the trial balance and other data provided.

Western Canada Video Company
Trial Balance
June 30, 19–6

100	Cash	$ 72 109	
110	Accounts Receivable	84 470	
115	GST Recoverable	200	
120	Prepaid Rent	18 000	
130	Prepaid Insurance	1 200	
140	Office Supplies	403	
150	Video Equipment	64 095	
151	Accumulated Depreciation: Video Equipment		$ 16 450
160	Truck	18 200	
161	Accumulated Depreciation: Truck		4 000
200	Accounts Payable		7 901
210	Long-Term Bank Loan		32 900
220	GST Payable		1 200
300	E. Swerhun, Capital		163 156
310	E. Swerhun, Drawings	22 900	
400	Video Filming Commissions		175 300
500	Wages Expense	92 340	
505	Advertising Expense	2 180	
510	Truck Expense	6 700	
515	Utilities Expense	3 290	
520	Interest Expense	3 400	
550	General Expense	11 420	
		$400 907	$400 907

Other data:
Rent for the year was prepaid on January 1, for $1 000 per month.
Unexpired insurance is $400.
The office supplies on hand are $80.
Depreciation is based on the declining-balance method with the following rates:
   Video Equipment   30 percent
   Truck   30 percent

CHAPTER REVIEW AND SKILL DEVELOPMENT

Accounting Principles and Concepts

- **Prepaid expenses** are items that are recorded as assets when purchased because the business owns them.

- The **matching principle** states that expenses must be matched with the revenue that was earned through the use of those expenses.

- **Year-end adjustments** are required to match expenses with the corresponding revenue.

- **Depreciation** is caused by wear, tear, and obsolescence.

- **Depreciation** is the allocation of the cost of a fixed asset to the fiscal period in which it was used to earn revenue.

- **Straight-line depreciation** means that the fixed asset depreciates the same amount each year.

- **Declining-balance depreciation** means that a fixed rate is applied to the net book value of the fixed asset.

- **Capital cost allowance** is the income tax term used for depreciation.

- The **principle of materiality** states that an item is material if there is a reasonable expectation that knowledge of it would influence the decisions of users of financial statements.

- **Conservatism** requires that, when judgements are made, the option that produces a lower net income for the current period should be selected.

- **Accrual basis accounting** is carried out by the use of adjusting entries in order to offset revenue with all expenses incurred in earning that revenue.

- **Worksheets** are used to assist in the preparation of the adjusting entries and financial statements.

Knowing the Terms

For each of the following statements, indicate the term being defined.
(a) Account that shows total depreciation for an item for previous years.
(b) Amount paid for insurance.
(c) Asset that will be used during the current and future fiscal periods.
(d) Method of calculating depreciation that results in the same amount being deducted from revenue each year.
(e) Decrease in value of a fixed asset due to wear, tear, and obsolescence.
(f) Worksheet used to record adjustments.
(g) To match revenue with expenses incurred in order to earn that revenue.
(h) Method of calculating depreciation that results in large amounts of depreciation in early years.

Food for Thought

1. At what point in the life of a truck will the balance of Depreciation Expense: Truck be equal to the balance of Accumulated Depreciation: Truck? Why?

2. When preparing the worksheet at the end of the first year of owning an automobile, Accumulated Depreciation: Automobile was not found with the trial balance accounts. Why?

3. Why would Prepaid Insurance have a $5 000 balance when an insurance policy with a $5 000 premium was purchased eight months ago?

4. Why is there a Supplies Expense account and a Supplies account?

5. Warner Chemical Supplies purchased $250 worth of office supplies that were going to be used during the current fiscal period. Should the purchase be recorded as a debit to Supplies Expense, or a debit to Supplies? Justify your decision.

6. Some people look upon fixed assets as being the same as prepaid expenses. In what way can that viewpoint be justified?

7. A firm purchases an $18 000 automobile, which it depreciates at 30 percent per year, based on rates for capital cost allowance for income tax purposes. The firm, however, for its own books decides to base the depreciation on the number of kilometres travelled. The firm estimates that the automobile will be kept until it travels 120 000 kilometres. Assuming that it travels 28 000 kilometres the first year, what should the amount of depreciation be for that year?

8. Depreciation is referred to as a valuation. Why?

9. When examining a balance sheet, a user noted that the firm only presented the net book value for fixed assets. What is not shown by this figure?

10. Explain cost price, net book value, and market value for a fixed asset.

Locate and Record

Using the annual report for the firm that you wrote to in Chapter 4, complete a brief report on the following, where possible:

1. Using the balance sheet, report on
   (a) the prepaid expenses;
   (b) the fixed assets, including accumulated depreciation and net book value;
   (c) the depreciation policies.

2. Using the income statement, report on
   (a) the depreciation expense;
   (b) the selling and administrative expenses, which include prepaid expenses.

Organizing

Summarize the two types of entries that were illustrated in this chapter, adjustments for prepaid expenses and for depreciation, by
(a) preparing a sample transaction for the purchase of the prepaid expense and fixed asset;
(b) preparing the journal entries for the purchases;
(c) preparing the journal entry for the adjusting entries, using sample amounts;
(d) describing the types of accounts that were used in your adjusting entries.

Applications

1. The legal firm of Watson & Watson prepares adjustments on a monthly basis. Prepare the adjusting entries required at the end of May for each of the following:
   (a) Supplies on hand at beginning of month, $870. Supplies inventory at end of month, $445.
   (b) Liability insurance cost $4 800 for a six-month policy.
   (c) Rent for the three months ending May 31 was $1 500.
   (d) Office equipment cost $16 000. The declining-balance method is used, with a depreciation rate of 20 percent. The net book value at the end of April was $12 400.
   (e) Furniture and fixtures cost $27 000. The declining-balance method is used with a rate of 20 percent. The net book value at April 30 was $16 980.

2. Westbury Enterprises is an environmental consulting firm. It prepares adjusting entries on a yearly basis. Using Figure 7-15 and the other data given:
   (a) prepare an eight-column worksheet
   (b) journalize the adjusting entries
   (c) prepare the financial statements

FIGURE 7-15

Westbury Enterprises
Trial Balance
December 31, 19–4

100	Cash	$ 41 474	
110	Accounts Receivable	153 980	
115	GST Recoverable	400	
120	Office Supplies	4 589	
130	Land	153 400	
140	Building	340 800	
141	Accumulated Depreciation: Building		$106 000
150	Furniture and Fixtures	27 540	
151	Accumulated Depreciation: Furniture and Fixtures		6 440
160	Computer Equipment	15 860	
170	Automobile	18 400	
171	Accumulated Depreciation: Automobile		6 400
200	Accounts Payable		32 961
210	Short-Term Loan		20 900
220	Mortgage Payable		132 000
230	GST Payable		1 680
300	P. Scobie, Capital		411 720
310	P. Scobie, Drawings	16 000	
400	Consultation Fees		240 900
500	Automobile Expense	9 750	
510	Utilities Expense	21 658	
520	Wages Expense	140 920	
530	Advertising Expense	6 980	
590	Miscellaneous Expense	7 250	
		$959 001	$959 001

Other data:
Office supplies on hand are $750.
Depreciation is based on the declining-balance method. Rates are

Automobile	30 percent
Building	5 percent
Computer Equipment	30 percent
Furniture and Fixtures	20 percent

Applications — Comprehensive

The Edmonton Computer School is owned by Gord Michon. The business began operation on January 1 in a rented premise. The chart of accounts is as follows:

100 Cash
101 Accounts Receivable
103 Prepaid Rent
104 Prepaid Insurance
105 Prepaid Repairs
106 Supplies
110 Computer Equipment
111 Acc. Dep.: Computer Equipment
112 Furniture and Equipment
113 Acc. Dep.: Furniture and Equipment
201 Accounts Payable
210 Short-Term Loan
220 Long-Term Loan
300 G. Michon, Capital

301 G. Michon, Drawings
401 Tuition Fees
501 Advertising Expense
502 Utilities Expense
503 Teaching Wages Expense
504 Rent Expense
505 Software Expense
506 Interest Expense
507 Insurance Expense
508 Repairs Expense
509 Miscellaneous Expense
510 Dep. Exp.: Computer Equipment
511 Dep. Exp.: Furniture and Equipment

(a) Open a ledger for the computer school.
(b) Journalize the transactions for January. (Source documents have not been indicated.) The lessons are tax exempt, i.e., GST is not collected on them. Hence, there is no input tax credit available for the purchases by the school, even though GST is paid. There is no PST, and GST has already been included in the amounts shown.
(c) Post to the general ledger.
(d) Prepare a trial balance on January 31, entering it directly onto the worksheet.
(e) Complete the worksheet, using the other data.
(f) Journalize and post the adjusting entries.
(g) Prepare the financial statements.
(h) Calculate the working capital and current ratio for the school. Comment on the solvency of the business.

Transactions

Jan. 2 Received a $38 000 investment from the owner.
  2 Obtained a five-year loan from the Royal Bank of Canada, $40 000.
  2 Purchased $36 000 worth of computer equipment, for cash.
  2 Paid three month's rent, $2 300 per month.
  2 Purchased a one-year insurance policy, $2 940.
  3 Received tuition fees of $2 800 for the month.
  3 Enrolled 10 students at $200 each for a one-month computer course; equal payment to be received at mid-month and month end.
  3 Paid $4 200 for computer repair contract for the year.
  4 Purchased an office desk, chair and telephone answering machine, $1 720 on account from Remeny's Office Outfitters.
  4 Purchased $7 490 worth of software programs and diskettes.
  4 Purchased computer supplies, $2 305.
  5 Paid $250 to the *Edmonton Journal* for advertising.
  5 Signed a contract to buy $7 000 worth of computers in March.
  8 Received $1 870 for tuition fees for the balance of the month.
  8 Purchased $350 worth of computer paper on account from Foothills Computer Supplies.
  9 Paid the employees their weekly wages, $950.
  10 Purchased a NEC printer, $3 700 from Western Computer Suppliers Ltd., paying $2 000 cash and owing the balance on account.
  15 Hired a new part-time employee; expected additional expense of $200 per week.
  15 Received mid-month payment from students owing on account.
  16 Paid the weekly wages, $1 150.
  16 Received $850 tuition fees for a two-week course.
  16 Made the semi-monthly payment of the loan, $800 plus interest of $153.
  16 Purchased $240 worth of computer paper.
  17 Paid $300 on account to Western Computer Suppliers Ltd.
  17 Paid $1 000 to the owner for personal use.

20 Paid $720 for computer software.
20 Paid $537 for advertising brochure for direct mailing.
22 Paid $47 for postage on advertising brochure.
22 Paid $35 for printing of certificates to be given to course graduates.
23 Paid the weekly wages, $1 350.
29 Paid $700 on account to Western Computer Suppliers Ltd.
30 Paid the telephone bill for the month, $564.
30 Paid the employees their weekly wages, $1 350.
30 Paid $800 to the owner for his personal use.
31 Received balance owing on account from students.
31 Made the semi-monthly payment on the bank loan, $800 plus interest of $152.
31 Paid the monthly electricity bill, $730.

Other data:
Supplies, on hand $2 300
One month prepaid rent expired.
One month prepaid insurance expired.
One month of prepaid repairs expired.
Declining-balance method of depreciation used. Rates are:
    Computer Equipment   30 percent
    Office Equipment   20 percent

Focussing
Analysis of Effects of Adjustments
You are given the trial balance and income statement found in Figures 7-16 and 7-17. Using the data contained in these documents, prepare a balance sheet for the firm.

FIGURE 7-16

Zenith Furniture Restoration
Trial Balance
May 31, 19–8

Cash	$ 24 005	
Accounts Receivable	11 428	
GST Recoverable	360	
Supplies	2 691	
Prepaid Insurance	3 600	
Prepaid Advertising	2 000	
Equipment	23 546	
Accumulated Depreciation: Equipment		$ 2 800
Van	14 900	
Accumulated Depreciation: Van		4 900
Accounts Payable		12 320
GST Payable		1 200
V. Dunlop, Capital		56 162
V. Dunlop, Drawings	14 000	
Restoration Fees		78 520
Van Expense	2 489	
Wages Expense	35 370	
Rent Expense	18 000	
Utilities Expense	2 543	
Miscellaneous Expense	970	
	$155 902	$155 902

FIGURE 7-17

Zenith Furniture Restoration
Income Statement
For the Year Ended May 31, 19–8

Revenue:		
Restoration Fees		$78 520
Expenses:		
Van	$ 2 489	
Wages	35 370	
Advertising	900	
Rent	18 000	
Insurance	2 300	
Utilities	2 543	
Miscellaneous	970	
Supplies	1 436	
Depreciation Expense: Equipment	2 075	
Depreciation Expense: Van	3 000	69 083
Net Income		$ 9 437

Evaluate and Assess

1. Effect of Not Making Adjusting Entries

At the end of the year for Westgate Curtain Cleaning and Repairs, due to a change in accountants, adjusting entries were not made in relation to the following data.

Trial Balance:
   Office Supplies $ 980
   Prepaid Insurance $4 800

Office supplies on hand were $520, and unexpired insurance was $800.
The net income is $54 090, and the total assets are $162 593.

(a) What effect will the errors have on the income statement for the current year? What is the corrected net income?
(b) What effect will the errors have on the balance sheet for the current year? What is the corrected total for assets?
(c) When might the errors come to the new accountant's attention?
(d) What effect will the errors have on the income statement and the balance sheet for the next year if the errors are not detected?
(e) What GAAP has not been followed?

2. Errors on a Worksheet

The following independent errors are made on separate worksheets. For each error, assuming that there is a net income,
(i) indicate whether the debit or credit side of the balance sheet column will be too large because of the error, and by what amount;
(ii) indicate the amount of the difference between the debit and credit sides of the balance sheet column.

(a) A $400 debit to Office Supplies Expense was recorded as a credit.
(b) A $900 credit to Accumulated Depreciation: Automobile was recorded as a debit.
(c) A $750 debit to Depreciation Expense: Equipment was recorded as a credit.
(d) The net income of $550 is extended to

the debit column of the balance sheet.
(e) A $12 000 debit to Drawings is extended to the debit column of the income statement.

Synthesize and Conclude

1. Dawn McElligott is owner of McElligott's Motors. She has asked her accountant to prepare a brief for her addressing the following issues, since she did not fully understand the firm's financial statements.
   (a) Why did the Depreciation Expense: Equipment account have a balance different from the Accumulated Depreciation: Equipment account?
   (b) Why did the Accumulated Depreciation: Equipment account not have a balance when the trial balance was prepared at the end of the first fiscal year, yet have a balance on the final balance sheet?
   (c) Why is there an account called Prepaid Insurance when the policy was paid for eight months ago?
   (d) Why is there a Supplies Expense account and a Supplies account?

2. The Martin Art Studio purchased a $50 000 computer system to maintain its inventory, payroll, and other accounting tasks. The owner, Mario Martin, asks you, the accountant, to prepare a report on the following so that a decision can be made by management as to what depreciation method should be followed. Prepare the report for him, indicating the advantages and disadvantages of each possibility.
   (a) Can the computer system be recorded as an expense and written off against income tax in its first year?
   (b) What is the rate of depreciation for income tax purposes? Can the business use one rate for income tax purposes and another for its own books?
   (c) The firm forecasts net income before depreciation of computer equipment in the future years to be as follows:

1991	1992	1993	1994	1995
$173 000	$175 000	$180 000	$200 000	$220 000

   Based on the above forecast, what is the effect on the net income of depreciation calculated using the straight-line and declining-balance methods?
   (d) What procedure do you recommend?

ACCOUNTING AT WORK

Delores Lawrence
Entrepreneur

Delores Lawrence saw an unfilled need in health care services and took the opportunity to establish her own business. She now directs Nursing and Home Health Care Inc., a company that provides full-time, part-time, and temporary nursing services to hospitals, clinics, doctors, and individuals. Her staff includes over 1 600 nurses and nursing assistants. "It hasn't been easy," she points out. "There are days when I put in 16 hours at the office and go home exhausted. But, the success has been worth the long hours."

Lawrence began her career with a nursing degree. Her first jobs were in large hospitals where she rose through the ranks to become the nursing co-ordinator. Along the way, she also completed a degree in business administration. In her management positions in hospitals, she faced the difficult task of finding and training nursing staff. She realized that a private company could play a key role in dealing with the problem. That lead her to start her company.

One aspect that has contributed to Lawrence's success is the training she provides to her staff. "What I try to do is to improve the quality of service my people deliver to our clients," she says. Continued training and skill development are very much a part of Lawrence's personal outlook on life. She continues to take courses and to up-date her management techniques and communication skills. Courses are selected to help her meet specific business needs.

Accounting has played a major role in Lawrence's life, right from the time she took the subject in high school. While she retains an accounting firm to handle the day-to-day functions of her business, she uses accounting skills to plan and to provide effective leadership for her staff. She is convinced that these skills will serve her well as she expands her business to keep pace with the increasing demands for it.

When asked what it takes to be successful in business, Lawrence replied: "You've got to have a goal, something that you like and want to do. Then, be the best that you possibly can be. That's the secret to success."

Answer the following questions concerning the above career profile.

1. What is an entrepreneur?
2. What is a degree in business administration?
3. What is the main reason for Lawrence's success? Why is it so important?
4. What aspects of accounting that we have studied to date would be most important for Lawrence to be aware of?
5. What does Lawrence say is the secret to success? Do you agree? Explain.

Business Career Skills

1. Communication Skills

In Chapter 4 we looked at listening skills, one part of effective communication. Another aspect of effective communication is the ability to speak effectively. Business people are constantly speaking with fellow employees individually, in small groups, and in large groups. As well, they spend a good deal of time speaking with people outside the business.

(a) In groups, brainstorm to develop a list of characteristics of a good speech.
(b) In groups, brainstorm to develop a list of characteristics of a poor speech.
(c) Your teacher will provide you with a list of topics for a speech. From it, select one, and give a short speech on it to the class.

2. Time Management

There is a saying that "when you want a job well done, find a busy person to do it." Why is that true? It is usually true because the busy person has developed the skills required to maximize use of his or her time. Time is an irreplaceable item. Those skilled in time management have learned to establish goals, to develop time schedules to accommodate those goals, to delegate, and even to say no when appropriate. As well, they have learned certain time saving skills that are useful in handling day-to-day chores. For each of the situations below, suggest at least two methods that could be used to save time.

(a) William Groleau is business manager of a large accounting office. During the day he is required to make and receive numerous phone calls. When he makes a phone call, he asks for the person he is calling. If the person is not there, Groleau leaves his number, and asks that he be called back. When the person calls back, Groleau is frequently busy, or out of the office. The person calling then leaves Groleau a message, and telephone tag begins. Groleau also insists that his secretary pass all incoming calls for him directly to him, no matter who is in his office at the time. Groleau then spends time talking on the phone while the person in his office is left to wait.

(b) Karen Pettifer is the office manager for a large accounting firm. Each day, Karen must open between fifty and one hundred letters. As well, she receives memos from each of the partners in the firm, directing that certain things be done. At the beginning of the day, Karen reads each of the memos, puts them in a pile, and usually goes for a coffee. By then, the mail has arrived, and Karen opens each letter, reads it, and puts the letters in a pile. She then sifts through the pile to find those letters that she has to direct to other people, and puts them in the respective mail slots of each partner. Next, she finds those letters that she has to attend to immediately and takes the necessary action. The remaining letters that she has to act upon are left on her desk until she finds time to deal with them.

3. Personal Time Management

On a sheet of paper, write
(a) one goal that you wish to achieve in the next day
(b) one goal that you wish to achieve in the next week, such as an assignment for school.

Using a weekly calendar, with the days broken down into time segments for school, after school, and evenings, indicate when you intend to fulfill each of the two goals that you chose. Tell a friend what the two goals are, and when you intend to complete them. Put the calendar in a conspicuous place so that you can refer to it at the end of the week. Use a similar calendar for subsequent weeks, and always enter your short-term goals on the calendar. For subsequent weeks, enter your short-term goals on a calendar at a specific time period.

COMPUTER ACCOUNTING
ADJUSTMENTS AND THE COMPUTER

An **integrated accounting system** provides a separate program or module to handle each of the major accounting functions. These **computer accounting modules**, in many cases, mirror manual accounting departments such as accounts receivable, accounts payable, and payroll.

In an integrated system, the general ledger

module is a control point into which all other accounting information is transferred. It can be used either as a stand-alone unit into which data is entered directly, or as a consolidator of information gathered by more specialized modules. The general ledger takes this information and transforms it into the financial statements and management reports that have become so vital to business.

Accounting systems tend to be unique to a particular business or type of business. Finding the right package for a certain company entails comparing the accounting requirements of the firm with the features and operating philosophy of each accounting package under consideration.

Regardless of the software selected, or the enhancements or add-ons available to a certain accounting package, the critical procedure of adjusting certain accounts at period-end is still performed through the general ledger module, and still requires the manual preparation and entry of data transactions. It is still the responsibility of someone in the organization to determine the required adjustments and give authorization for their subsequent entry into the computer system. The old adage "**garbage-in, garbage-out**" still applies: even when the use of computerized accounting systems produces sophisticated reports in a fraction of the time it takes to produce similar reports manually, only reliable data produces reliable financial reports.

Exercise

Linda Schuman has just completed her first month of operations as a practising dentist. She has taken her accounting records and financial statements to Donaldson and Griffiths Chartered Accountants for advice.

After examining the business documents, John Griffiths has advised Linda that the financial statements are not technically correct. He has stated that several of the accounts in the firm's ledger do not show proper end-of-period balances, which are required for the preparation of the financial statements, even though all transactions have been recorded correctly. He has explained that several account balances are incorrect for statement purposes, not because of error but because of the expiration of costs due to the passage of time. He has given as an example, Dental Supplies, which shows a balance of $800 on the trial balance and on the balance sheet, yet a physical inventory of the supplies shows only $300 worth on hand. Thus $500 has been used up and hence, has become an expense. Likewise, a portion of the office supplies has been used, and the furniture, office equipment, and dental equipment have begun to wear out and thus depreciate.

Obviously then, the end-of-period balances for these accounts simply do not reflect the proper amounts to be shown on the financial statements. The balances for these and several other accounts must be adjusted to show proper amounts for the September 30 financial statements.

Linda has asked you to prepare and enter the adjusting entries from details provided by the accounting firm. Call up the company files for Linda Schuman, DDS, which you completed in Chapter 4, and make the adjustments using the information below:

Inventory as at September 30
   Dental Supplies, $300
   Office Supplies, $500
Depreciation
   Furniture 20% per annum
   Dental Equipment 20% per annum
   Office Equipment 20% per annum
Interest on the bank loan of 12% per annum is payable monthly and due by the 10th of the following month.

Print updated financial statements.

CHAPTER EIGHT

End-of-Period Procedures — 2

LEARNING OBJECTIVES

At the end of this chapter you should be able to
- prepare adjustments for unrecorded expenses;
- prepare adjustments for unearned revenue;
- prepare adjustments for unrecorded revenue;
- describe the matching principle as it relates to all adjusting entries;
- prepare a worksheet with adjustments;
- prepare closing entries;
- use a computer accounting program to close the accounts.

LANGUAGE OF ACCOUNTING

You will see the following terms in this chapter:
accrual method of accounting
"books" of the business
closing entries
demand loan
matching principle
principal
temporary accounts
unearned revenue
unrecorded expenses
unrecorded revenue

In this chapter the accounting cycle will be completed. Adjustments for prepaid expenses were examined in Chapter 7. In this chapter, other necessary year-end adjustments will be examined. As well, closing entries are introduced. They are necessary in order to prepare the books for the next fiscal period.

By the end of this chapter, the complete accounting cycle will have been studied. The steps in the cycle are as follows:

FIGURE 8-1 THE COMPLETE ACCOUNTING CYCLE

Daily: Journalize and Post Transactions

End-of-period: Worksheet
Financial Statements: Income Statement
                                  Balance Sheet
Adjust and Close the Books: Journalize and Post
Post-Closing Trial Balance

8.1 Adjustments for Unrecorded Expenses

Unrecorded expenses: *expenses that have not been recorded by the end of the fiscal year, but have been incurred. The liability from them will be paid in future fiscal periods.*

Accrued liabilities: *liabilities that have been incurred during an accounting period for which payment is due in a future period.*

In Chapter 7 prepaid expenses were examined: assets that were bought for use by the business were recorded as assets (recorded costs) and then converted to expenses as they expired. In many businesses another situation arises: not all expenses will have been recorded by the year end, so it becomes necessary to calculate the amount of these expenses and to record them. The recording of these expenses will also follow the matching principle, for they were incurred in order to earn revenue. These items are referred to as **unrecorded expenses**: expenses that have not been recorded by the end of the fiscal year, but have been incurred. The liability resulting from them will be paid in future fiscal periods, and is referred to as an **accrued liability**. Rather than list the different accrued liabilities separately, they are usually lumped together on a balance sheet.

If the cash basis of accounting was followed, these items would not be recorded until the liabilities were paid. However, under the accrual method of accounting, the items must be recognized in the year in which they occurred.

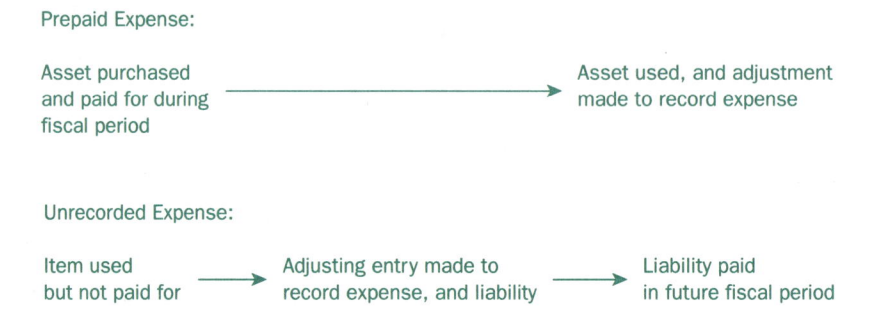

Prepaid Expense:

Asset purchased and paid for during fiscal period ⟶ Asset used, and adjustment made to record expense

Unrecorded Expense:

Item used but not paid for ⟶ Adjusting entry made to record expense, and liability ⟶ Liability paid in future fiscal period

Interest Payable

Principal: *the amount of the loan.*

Term: *the length of time of the loan.*

Demand loans: *loans that the lending institution can call at any time.*

In the course of business activities, Algor Computer Services borrows money from financial institutions. The purpose of the borrowing is to allow Algor to buy more servicing equipment, and therefore to create possibilities for increased revenue. The amount borrowed is the **principal**, and the duration of the loan is the **term**. Loans from lending institutions require either regular payments, such as monthly, or repayment in a lump sum. Some loans are **demand loans**. They are callable by the lending institution at any time, on demand. The cost of borrowing money is the **interest** that is added to the payments. Algor Computer Services has also borrowed money to buy its building and the land on which it is located. This loan, referred to as a mortgage, also requires payments of part of the principal plus interest on a monthly basis.

THE FACTS SPEAK...

Accrued liabilities, December 31, 1989
IBM	$5 780 million
Canadian Tire Corporation, Limited	149 million
Maritime Tel & Tel	23 million

Interest: the cost of borrowing money.

An adjusting entry is required for interest if the payment of interest does not coincide exactly with the year end.

May 16	May 31	June 16
Loan received →	Fiscal year end Adjusting entry required for 15 days of interest expense →	Interest payment due

This adjustment will reflect that the borrowed money is a cost to the business, and it must be allocated to the period in which the revenue from use of the money was earned. Therefore, the cost of using the money must be recorded as an expense. The following illustrates the entry required when the loan is received:

May 16   Bank Credit Memo: Borrowed $30 000 from the bank. Interest is 10 percent per annum, and the term is five years. Monthly payments of interest are required.

GENERAL JOURNAL

PAGE 580

DATE 1992		PARTICULARS	PR	DEBIT	CREDIT
May	16	Cash		30 000 —	
		Long-Term Loan			30 000 —
		Loan from Royal Bank of Canada:			
		interest rate, 10%; term, 5 years; monthly payments			
		on interest required			

Formula to calculate simple interest:
Interest = Prt.

Because payment of interest is made monthly, the first interest payment will be required June 16. However, an adjusting entry must be made on May 31, the fiscal year end, to reflect the allocation of the cost of the money (interest) from May 16 to May 31, for the purpose of earning revenue. To calculate **simple interest**, the formula is

$$\text{Interest} = \text{Principle} \times \text{rate} \times \text{time}$$

The amount owing for interest as at May 31 will therefore be

$$\begin{aligned}\text{Interest} &= Prt \\ &= \$30\ 000 \times 0.10 \times 15/365 \\ &= \$123.29\end{aligned}$$

The adjusting entry to record the interest will be as follows:

GENERAL JOURNAL

PAGE 590

DATE 1992		PARTICULARS	PR	DEBIT	CREDIT
May	31	Interest Expense	651	123 29	
		Interest Payable	215		123 29
		To adjust for interest expense on bank loan;			
		30 000 x 0.10 x 15/365			

GENERAL LEDGER

```
    Interest Expense        651          Interest Payable         215
         dr.         |       cr.              dr.        |       cr.
    May 31   123.29  |                                   | May 31   123.29
```

The explanation for the entry is as follows:
- The debit to Interest Expense follows the matching principle. The cost of borrowing the money for the fifteen days is matched with the revenue earned from using the money during that time period.
- The credit to Interest Payable indicates the amount owing to the bank for interest on the loan. It will be paid on June 16 when the monthly payment is due. Interest Payable is listed as a current liability on the balance sheet. Some businesses use the term Accrued Interest Payable. The word "accrued" means that it has grown in the past.

On June 16, when the interest payment due on that date is made, the following entry will be made:

June 16   Bank Debit Memo: $254.79 for interest on loan.

GENERAL JOURNAL

PAGE 598

DATE 1992		PARTICULARS	PR	DEBIT	CREDIT
June	16	Interest Expense	651	131 50	
		Interest Payable	215	123 29	
		Cash	100		254 79
		To record monthly interest payment;			
		30 000 x 0.10 x 31/365			

GENERAL LEDGER

```
  Interest Expense    651        Interest Payable          215         Cash                    100
       dr.       |    cr.             dr.       |       cr.              dr.       |     cr.
  June 16  131.50|               June 16 123.29 | May 31  123.29                    | June 16  254.79
```

The Facts Speak...

Interest accrued as at December 31, 1989
- BCE — $291 million
- McDonald's Corporation — 128 million
- SaskTel — 22 million

The explanation for the entry is as follows:
- The debit to Interest Expense records the cost of using the money for the 16 days from June 1 to June 16, which follows the matching process.
- The debit to Interest Payable records the cancelling of the amount owing for the period May 16 to May 31.
- The credit to Cash records the reduction in the asset cash and payment of the interest due.

Adjusting For Wages

Employees' paydays do not necessarily coincide with the fiscal year end. Therefore, an adjusting entry is required to allocate the cost of wages that were incurred in order to earn revenue for the days between the last payday and the fiscal year end.

For purposes of illustration, assume that Algor pays its employees up-to-date every Friday, but the fiscal year end occurs on a Thursday. Also assume that the wage cost per 5-day week is $5 000, or $1 000 per day. The cost of labour for the Monday, Tuesday, Wednesday, and Thursday, the four days before the fiscal year end, will not have been recorded. An adjusting entry for employee wages will be required.

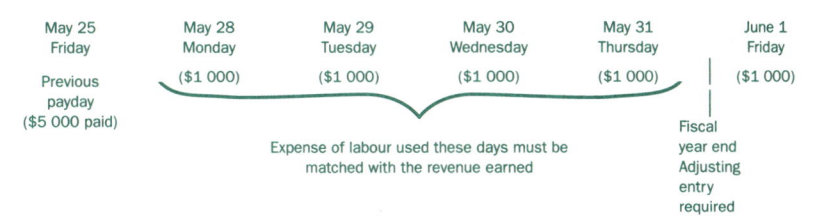

May 25 Friday	May 28 Monday	May 29 Tuesday	May 30 Wednesday	May 31 Thursday	June 1 Friday
Previous payday ($5 000 paid)	($1 000)	($1 000)	($1 000)	($1 000) Fiscal year end Adjusting entry required	($1 000)

Expense of labour used these days must be matched with the revenue earned

The adjusting entry will appear as follows:

GENERAL JOURNAL

PAGE 590

DATE 1992		PARTICULARS	PR	DEBIT	CREDIT
May	31	Wages Expense	600	4 000 —	
		Wages Payable	205		4 000 —
		To record wages expense for four days before year end			

GENERAL LEDGER

Wages Expense	600	Wages Payable	205
dr.	cr.	dr.	cr.
May 31 4 000			May 31 4 000

The explanation for the entry is as follows:
- The debit to Wages Expense records the use of labour to earn revenue from Monday to Thursday. The matching principle has, therefore, been adhered to.
- The credit to Wages Payable shows the amount due to employees for the four days of work prior to the fiscal year end. The amount will be paid on the Friday payday. Wages Payable is recorded as a current liability on the balance sheet. Some businesses use the term Accrued Wages or Accrued Payroll Payable.

The entry to record payment of the employees on the Friday will be as follows:

June 1   Cheque Copy #897: Weekly payment of employees, $5 000.

GENERAL JOURNAL

PAGE 590

DATE 1992		PARTICULARS	PR	DEBIT	CREDIT
June	1	Wages Expense	600	1 000 —	
		Wages Payable	205	4 000 —	
		Cash	100		5 000 —
		To record weekly payment of employee wages			

GENERAL LEDGER

Wages Expense	600	Wages Payable	205	Cash	100
dr.	cr.	dr.	cr.	dr.	cr.
June 1 1 000		June 1 4 000	May 31 4 000		June 1 5 000

The explanation for the entry is as follows:
- The debit to Wages Expense records the use of labour for the Friday, the one day in the new fiscal period.
- The debit to Wages Payable records the cancellation of the liability recorded in the previous fiscal period.
- The credit to Cash records the payment of the wages and the reduction of the asset cash.

There are many other expenses that could be recognized at the end of the financial period. However, according to the principle of materiality, not all of these expenses are recognized. For example, the amount of telephone expense, and other utility expenses, would usually not be adjusted to match the corresponding revenue. In cases such as this, it should also be recognized that the amount of the expense is fairly constant from month to month, so that not adjusting for it will not affect the judgement of a reasonably knowledgeable user of the financial data. Each business would have to establish policies to recognize the consistent recording of adjustments, taking into consideration the principle of materiality.

LESSON REVIEW

1. What are unrecorded expenses? Give two examples.
2. Why are unrecorded expenses referred to as accrued liabilities?
3. (a) Give the formula to calculate simple interest.
   (b) Calculate the simple interest for each of the following:
      (i) $12 000, for one year at 7 percent
      (ii) $23 000, for 3 months at 8 percent
      (iii) $48 000, for 6 months at 9 percent
      (iv) $37 000, for 121 days at 11 percent
4. Why must an adjusting entry be made to record interest owing at year end?
5. Why must an adjusting entry be made to record wages owing at year end?
6. How does the principle of materiality affect the making of adjustments for unrecorded expenses?

LESSON APPLICATIONS

7. Viewbrook Insurance is a firm that sells insurance policies for a variety of insurers. At the end of the fiscal year it prepared adjusting entries to record the following items:
   (a) supplies used
   (b) prepaid insurance expired
   (c) depreciation on automobile
   (d) depreciation on office equipment
   (e) wages expense accrued during the year
   (f) interest expense accrued during the year

   For each of the above, indicate their effect upon the financial statements by completing the chart on the next page. Indicate with a "+" any items that would increase, and a "−" any items that would decrease, and "nil" for no effect. The first adjusting entry has been done for you.

| | Income Statement ||| Balance Sheet |||
Adjusting Entry	Revenue	Expenses	Net Income	Assets	Liabilities	Owner's Equity
(a)	nil	+	−	−	nil	−

8. The Lethbridge Air Advertising Company borrowed $20 000 on demand on August 1 from the Toronto Dominion Bank in order to make a down payment on an aircraft. The interest was payable every two months, and was at a rate of 11 percent per annum. The firm adjusts its books at month end.
   (a) Prepare the journal entry to record the loan.
   (b) Calculate the amount of interest owing at the end of August.
   (c) Prepare the August 31 adjusting entry for the interest owing.
   (d) Prepare the entry required to pay the interest at the end of September.
   (e) What type of account is Interest Payable? Why is it that type of account?
   (f) Why is an adjusting entry required on August 31?

9. The Camrose Dress Shop borrowed $5 000 from the Royal Bank of Canada on April 15 in order to finance the purchase of new equipment. Payments of $500 on the principal, plus interest, were payable in monthly instalments. The interest rate was 12 percent per annum. The dress shop adjusts its books on a monthly basis.
   (a) Prepare the journal entry to record the loan.
   (b) Calculate the amount of interest owing at the end of April.
   (c) Prepare the adjusting entry required on April 30 for the interest owing.
   (d) Prepare the entry required to pay the interest and principal on May 15.
   (e) What type of account is Interest Expense? Why?

10. The Martin Answering Company pays its employees weekly, on Friday. The payroll is $45 000 per week. January 31 falls on a Wednesday. The business adjusts its books on a monthly basis.
    (a) Record the adjusting entry required on January 31.
    (b) Record the payment of the employees on Friday, February 2.
    (c) What type of account is Wages Payable? Why?
    (d) Why is an adjusting entry required on January 31?

11. The legal firm of Dublinski, Parker and Rote pays its employees biweekly. The biweekly payroll is $24 000. The last payday was Friday, November 23. The firm adjusts its books on a monthly basis.
    (a) Record the adjusting entry required on November 30.
    (b) Record payment of the employees on Friday, December 7.
    (c) What type of account is Wages Expense? Why?

8.2 Adjustments for Unearned Revenue and Unrecorded Revenue

In many businesses, it is necessary to recognize unearned revenue and unrecorded revenue at the end of the fiscal period. Each of these will be examined in turn.

Adjustments for Unearned Revenue

> **Unearned revenue:** payments are received for services to be rendered in future accounting periods.

Unearned revenue adjustments are necessary in those businesses that collect in advance for services to be rendered to customers in future accounting periods. An example of such a business is one that sells prepaid cards to clients (see Chapter 6). Other businesses that have unearned revenue include repair firms that sell warranties, legal firms that are engaged under a retainer fee, airlines that have advance bookings, and athletic clubs that sell yearly memberships. The revenue that each of these firms earns must be allocated to the fiscal period in which it was actually earned.

Assume that an athletic club sells one-year memberships. Fifty annual memberships are sold on November 1 at a special rate of $480 each. The total cash received is $25 680. The entry to record the receipt of cash and the sale of the memberships is:

Nov. 1   Cash Sales Slips #458-#507: Receipts for one-year memberships, $24 000 plus GST, $1 680.

GENERAL JOURNAL
PAGE 111

DATE 1991		PARTICULARS	PR	DEBIT	CREDIT
Nov.	1	Cash	100	25 680 —	
		GST Payable	220	1 680 —	
		Unearned Membership Fees	230		24 000 —
		To record sale of fifty memberships @ $480 each			

GENERAL LEDGER

Cash	100		GST Payable	220		Unearned Membership Fees	230
dr.	cr.		dr.	cr.		dr.	cr.
Nov. 1 25 680				Nov. 1 1 680			Nov. 1 24 000

THE FACTS SPEAK...

Unearned revenue as at December 31, 1989
  IBM $1 365 million
  AGT   43.5 million
  Southam Inc.   32.9 million

> "Unearned items are recorded as a liability."

The explanation for the entry is as follows:
- The debit to Cash records the receipt of the membership fees.
- The credit to GST Payable recognizes the increase in that liability.
- The credit to Unearned Membership Fees indicates that although the fees have been received, they have not been earned. They therefore cannot be recorded as revenue. They will be earned over the next twelve months, during which time the athletic club has an obligation to render the services. Unearned Membership Fees is a current liability, for the business owes to the new members twelve months of club activities.

On December 31, the fiscal year end, an adjusting entry is required to recognize the portion of unearned revenue that has now been earned.

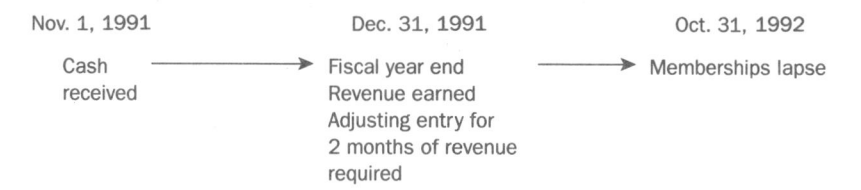

Nov. 1, 1991	Dec. 31, 1991	Oct. 31, 1992
Cash received	→ Fiscal year end Revenue earned Adjusting entry for 2 months of revenue required	→ Memberships lapse

The adjusting entry will therefore be:

GENERAL JOURNAL

PAGE 128

DATE 1991		PARTICULARS	PR	DEBIT	CREDIT
Dec.	31	Unearned Membership Fees	230	4 000 —	
		Membership Fees Earned	400		4 000 —
		To record earning of two months of the			
		twelve-month memberships			

GENERAL LEDGER

Unearned Membership Fees 230		Membership Fees Earned 400	
dr.	cr.	dr.	cr.
Dec. 31 4 000	Nov. 1 24 000		Dec. 31 4 000

The explanation for the entry is as follows:
- The debit to Unearned Membership Fees recognizes that the club no longer owes these two months of club usage to the members. The current liability is therefore reduced. The new balance in the Unearned Membership Fees account of $20 000 indicates that ten months of club facility usage is still owing to the members.
- The credit to the revenue account Membership Fees Earned records that two months of the fees have been earned and can be declared as revenue for the fiscal period.

Adjustments for Unrecorded Revenue

> **Unrecorded revenue:** a service is provided in advance of billing the client.

Unrecorded revenue results when a firm has provided a service in advance of billing the client. For example, a real estate firm may contract with a client to manage their property, and not bill the client until some future period. Similarly, a lawyer may represent a client in a legal matter that goes on over many months. In both of these cases, there must be an adjustment at the end of a fiscal period to recognize the unrecorded revenue from the performing of the service. In this case, the client will be billed in a future fiscal period.

Assume that on December 1 a real estate firm enters into a one-year contract with P. Ziebart to manage a rental property. The fee is to be $300 per month, with payment to be received every two months. On December 1, when the contract is agreed to, no transaction has occurred. On December 31, the fiscal year end, the real estate firm has earned one month of the fee. Although the fee has not been received, the revenue must be recognized.

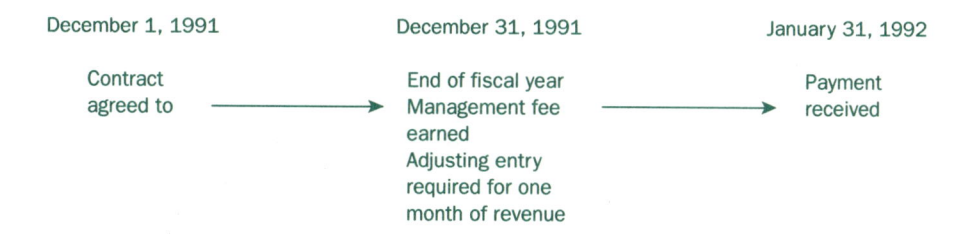

December 1, 1991	December 31, 1991	January 31, 1992
Contract agreed to →	End of fiscal year Management fee earned Adjusting entry required for one month of revenue →	Payment received

The adjusting entry required on December 31 is as follows:

GENERAL JOURNAL

PAGE 62

DATE 1991		PARTICULARS	PR	DEBIT	CREDIT
Dec.	31	Management Fees Receivable	155	300 —	
		Management Fees Earned	400		300 —
		To record one month's revenue earned from Ziebart			
		property management agreement			

GENERAL LEDGER

Management Fees Receivable 155		Management Fees Earned 400	
dr.	cr.	dr.	cr.
Dec. 31 300			Dec. 31 300

The explanation for the entry is as follows:
- The debit to Management Fees Receivable recognizes the claim that the real estate firm has on the client, Ziebart, for management services rendered.
- The credit to Management Fees Earned recognizes that one month's management fees have been earned under the Ziebart contract.

On January 31, payment is received from Ziebart for the two months of services which the real estate firm has rendered. On that date, the following entry is made:

Cash Receipt Slip #402: Received $642 from P. Ziebart for management services from December 1 to January 31.

GENERAL JOURNAL

PAGE 74

DATE 1992		PARTICULARS	PR	DEBIT	CREDIT
Jan.	31	Cash	100	642 —	
		GST Payable	230		42 —
		Management Fees Receivable	155		300 —
		Management Fees Earned	400		300 —
		Cash Receipt Slip #402, Ziebart fee for December			
		and January			

GENERAL LEDGER

Cash		100		GST Payable		230
dr.	cr.			dr.	cr.	
Jan. 31 642					Jan. 31 42	

Management Fees Receivable		155		Management Fees Earned		400
dr.	cr.			dr.	cr.	
Dec. 31 300	Jan. 31 300				Jan. 31 300	

The explanation for the entry is as follows:
- The debit to Cash recognizes the increase in that asset.
- The credit to GST Payable recognizes the increase in that liability.
- The credit to Management Fees Receivable cancels the $300 claim on P. Ziebart for the management period December 1 to December 31.
- The credit to Management Fees Earned recognizes the revenue earned for the management period January 1 to January 31.

LESSON REVIEW

12. What is unearned revenue?
13. Give examples of businesses in your area that would have unearned revenue.
14. What type of account is Unearned Revenue? Why?
15. When is an adjustment for the unearned revenue made?
16. What is unrecorded revenue?
17. Give examples of businesses in your area that would have unrecorded revenue.
18. What accounts are debited and credited to recognize the recording of unrecorded revenue? Why?

LESSON APPLICATIONS

19. Viewbrook Insurance sells insurance policies for a variety of insurers. At the end of the fiscal year it prepared adjusting entries to record the following items:
    (a) earning of unearned revenue
    (b) recording of unrecorded revenue
    For each of the above, indicate their effect upon the financial statements by completing the following chart. Indicate with a "+" any items that would increase, and a "−" any items that would decrease, and "nil" for no effect.

Adjusting Entry	Income Statement			Balance Sheet		
	Revenue	Expenses	Net Income	Assets	Liabilities	Owner's Equity

20. The Canada Sports Magazine sold yearly subscriptions for $60 plus 7 percent GST, and issued monthly magazines. Eighty-five subscriptions were sold in October, its first month.
    (a) Record the entry for the sale of the subscriptions. Use an account called Unearned Subscriptions.
    (b) Record the earned revenue at the end of October.
    (c) What type of account is Unearned Subscriptions? Why?
    (d) What type of account did you use to record the subscriptions earned?

21. The Terrace Hockey Team sells season tickets at $230 (plus 7 percent GST) a seat for adults, and $125 (plus GST) a seat for children and senior citizens. When the season started on November

3, 400 adult tickets, 120 child tickets and 30 senior citizen tickets were sold. The team has 20 home games.
   (a) Prepare an entry on November 3 to record receipt of the ticket revenue from season subscribers.
   (b) Prepare an entry to record the revenue earned at the end of November. The team had played 4 home games.
   (c) Prepare an entry to record the revenue earned at the end of December after 3 more home games had been played.

22. Prepare adjusting entries on May 31 for each of the following:
   (a) Pay is biweekly. Wages owing but not recorded for the week ending May 31 are $3 500.
   (b) Interest owing on the bank loan as at May 31 is $740.
   (c) $24 000 of the Unearned Ticket Admissions has been earned as at May 31.

23. Prepare journal entries for the following selected transactions for the month of March for Flin Flon Travel Services. Use the account names given below:
   Cash, Interest Payable, Bank Loan, Wages Payable, Unearned Ticket Revenue, Earned Ticket Revenue, Interest Expense, Wages Expense.
   Mar. 1 Borrowed $4 000 from the Bank of Nova Scotia; interest payable monthly at 11 percent per annum.
   7 Received $3 000 as deposits for flights.
   10 Paid employees their biweekly wages, $1 100.
   18 Received $2 500 as deposits for flights.
   24 Paid employees their biweekly wages, $1 100.
   31 Adjusting entries required for the following:
      — one week's wages owing
      — $1 700 of flight deposits had been earned
      — interest owing on bank loan

24. The trial balance for Bastion Small Engine Centre is shown in Figure 8-2.
   (a) Enter the trial balance on an eight-column worksheet, assigning the appropriate account numbers.
   (b) Using the other data, complete the worksheet for the month of April.
   (c) Journalize the adjusting entries.

   Other Data:
   (1) Inventory at month end shows the following on hand:
      Office Supplies $117; Repair Supplies $2 120.
   (2) The prepaid rent is for three months, April 1 to June 30.
   (3) Unexpired insurance, $250.
   (4) Depreciation on equipment and truck is by income tax rates.
   (5) Wages owing and payable at month end are $980.
   (6) Warranties worth $2 200 have expired, and therefore have been earned.

(7) Interest at the rate of 8 percent per annum is owing on the bank loan for the month.

FIGURE 8-2

Bastion Small Engine Centre
Trial Balance
April 30, 19--

Cash	$ 7 700	
GST Recoverable	229	
Office Supplies	882	
Repair Supplies	3 444	
Prepaid Rent	2 400	
Prepaid Insurance	600	
Equipment	18 290	
Accumulated Depreciation: Equipment		$ 2 700
Truck	16 000	
Accumulated Depreciation: Truck		4 000
Accounts Payable		2 980
Bank Loan		3 490
GST Payable		1 459
Unearned Warranties		18 700
R. Bastion, Capital		5 160
R. Bastion, Drawings	2 300	
Engine Repairs		22 000
Advertising Expense	832	
Wages Expense	3 240	
Rent Expense	2 400	
Truck Expense	753	
Utilities Expense	988	
General Expense	431	
	$60 489	$60 489

25. The trial balance for the Calgary Bow Islanders baseball team is shown in Figure 8-3.
    (a) Enter the trial balance on an eight-column worksheet, assigning the appropriate account numbers.
    (b) Prepare the adjusting entries for the month using the other data.
    (c) Complete the worksheet.
    (d) Answer the questions that follow.

    Other Data:
    (1) Inventory at month end shows the following on hand:
        Office Supplies $144; Baseball Supplies $6 390.
    (2) The prepaid rent is for six months, May 1 to October 31.
    (3) Unexpired insurance, $1 000.
    (4) Depreciation on furniture and truck is by the straight-line method. The furniture is estimated to last 4 years with no

salvage value; the truck is estimated to last four years with a salvage value of $2 000.
(5) Wages owing and payable at month end are $350.
(6) $570 of the unearned season tickets have been earned.
(7) Interest of $18 is owing on the bank loan.

FIGURE 8-3

Calgary Bow Islanders Baseball Team
Trial Balance
May 31, 19--

Cash	$ 9 010	
GST Recoverable	388	
Office Supplies	481	
Baseball Supplies	7 640	
Prepaid Rent	1 800	
Prepaid Insurance	1 200	
Furniture & Fixtures	3 400	
Truck	14 000	
Accumulated Depreciation: Truck		$ 3 500
Accounts Payable		1 233
Bank Loan		2 500
GST Payable		2 087
Unearned Season Tickets		22 500
L. Tarswell, Capital		9 170
L. Tarswell, Drawings	1 500	
Ticket Revenue		7 320
Wages Expense	3 349	
Utilities Expense	1 432	
Bus Travel Expense	2 940	
Truck Expense	900	
General Expense	270	
	$48 310	$48 310

Questions:
(i) What type of account is Unearned Season Tickets?
(ii) What type of account is Baseball Supplies? Why is it not changed every time supplies are used?
(iii) What type of account is Prepaid Insurance? Why is it also called a prepaid asset? Why is an adjustment required for it?
(iv) What type of account is Accumulated Depreciation: Truck?
(v) What effect does the adjusting entry to record the earning of season ticket revenue have on the income statement and balance sheet respectively?
(vi) The Accumulated Depreciation: Furniture and Fixtures account showed no balance as of May 31. What does this indicate about the furniture and fixtures?

8.3 Closing Entries and the Post-Closing Trial Balance

In Chapter 3 the main equity account, Capital, was divided into Capital, Drawings, Revenue, and Expense accounts. The purpose of this division was to obtain more information in order to prepare an income statement, and to know the amount of the owner's drawings.

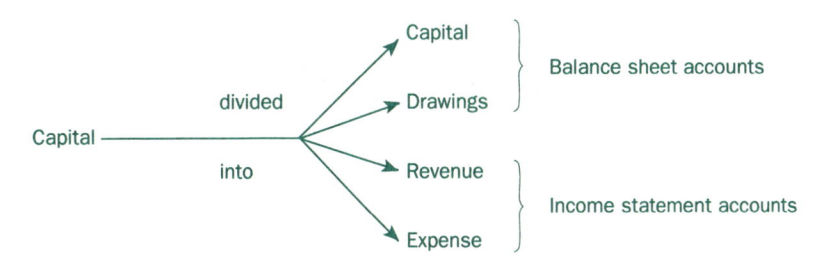

```
                         → Capital   ⎫
                                     ⎬ Balance sheet accounts
              divided    → Drawings  ⎭
Capital ─────
              into       → Revenue   ⎫
                                     ⎬ Income statement accounts
                         → Expense   ⎭
```

In order to know the amount of the drawings, revenue, and expenses for the year, it is necessary to start each year with those accounts having a nil balance. The business can then measure the drawings, revenue, and expenses for the year in question. In order to bring the accounts to a nil balance, they are closed. Because they are closed at the end of the fiscal period, they are referred to as **temporary accounts**. There are four separate closing entries, as follows:

Temporary accounts: *accounts that are closed at the end of a fiscal period.*

1. to close temporary accounts with a credit balance (for now, these consist of revenue accounts);

2. to close temporary accounts with a debit balance (for now, these consist of expense accounts, and contra-revenue accounts);

3. to close the net income or net loss into Capital;

4. to close the Drawings account into Capital.

Income Summary

Income Summary: *an account used to combine the temporary accounts before closing the net income or net loss into Capital.*

The **Income Summary** account is used to combine the temporary accounts before closing the net income or net loss into Capital. These temporary accounts are the revenue and expense accounts. The balance of the Income Summary account, which represents the net income or net loss, is then transferred to the Capital account.

```
Revenue  ─────┐
              ├──→ closed into Income Summary
Expenses ─────┘              │
                             ↓
Drawings ─────────→ closed into Capital
```

Where is the information for the closing entries found? The balances of the accounts to be closed can be found in a number of places:
(a) the general ledger
(b) the income statement and the balance sheet
(c) the worksheet

It is easiest to do the closing entries from the information found on the worksheet since the required information is concisely shown, mainly in the Income Statement columns.

Closing Entries for a Net Income Situation

The four closing entries for Algor Computer Services done from the partial worksheet shown in Figure 8-4 for the year ended May 31, 1992 are shown below.

1. The closing entry for the temporary accounts with a credit balance is shown below. The accounts with a credit balance that are to be closed are found on the credit side of the Income Statement columns of the worksheet.

GENERAL JOURNAL

PAGE 590

DATE 1992		PARTICULARS	PR	DEBIT	CREDIT
May	31	Computer Services	400	282 000 —	
		Software Lessons	410	98 000 —	
		Income Summary	320		380 000 —
		To close temporary accounts with a credit balance			

GENERAL LEDGER

Computer Services	400
dr.	cr.
May 31 282 000	June 1 to
	May 31 282 000

Software Lessons	410
dr.	cr.
May 31 98 000	June 1 to
	May 31 98 000

Income Summary	320
dr.	cr.
	May 31 380 000

> "The first closing entry is to close temporary accounts with a credit balance into Income Summary."

The explanation for the entry is as follows:
- The debits to the temporary accounts with credit balances, Computer Services and Software Lessons, mean that when these entries are posted to the ledger the two revenue accounts will each have a nil balance. The total amount of the revenue has been transferred to the credit side of the Income Summary account. Note that the temporary accounts with a credit balance at the end of the year can be found on the credit side of the Income Statement columns of the worksheet.

FIGURE 8-4

PARTIAL WORKSHEET

Algor Computer Services — FOR THE Year ENDED May 31, 19 92

	ACCOUNTS	ACCT. NO.	TRIAL BALANCE DR	TRIAL BALANCE CR	INCOME STATEMENT DR	INCOME STATEMENT CR
1	Cash	100	49 000 –			
2	Accounts Receivable	120	50 000 –			
3	GST Recoverable	135	1 400 –			
4	Prepaid Insurance	140	1 800 –			
5	Office Supplies	150	1 460 –			
6	Computer Supplies	155	4 900 –			
7	Land	160	124 600 –			
8	Building	170	228 000 –			
9	Office Equipment	175	14 500 –			
10	Computer Equipment	180	59 600 –			
11	Automobile	190	12 500 –			
12	Accounts Payable	200		14 503 –		
13	Mortgage Payable	220		248 000 –		
14	GST Payable	230		1 460 –		
15	PST Payable	240		1 720 –		
16	V. Marshall, Capital	300		222 477 –		
17	V. Marshall, Drawings	310	28 000 –			
18	Computer Services	400		282 000 –		282 000 –
19	Software Lessons	410		98 000 –		98 000 –
20	Refunds	415	2 200 –		2 200 –	
21	Wages Expense	600	184 600 –		184 600 –	
22	VISA Discount Expense	655	7 200 –		7 200 –	
23	Advertising Expense	660	44 600 –		44 600 –	
24	Utilities Expense	670	32 400 –		32 400 –	
25	Automobile Expense	680	4 400 –		4 400 –	
26	Miscellaneous Expense	760	17 000 –		17 000 –	
27			868 160 –	868 160 –		
28	Insurance Expense	720			600 –	
29	Office Supplies Expense	730			570 –	
30	Computer Supplies Expense	740			2 200 –	
31	Depreciation Expense: Building	690			11 400 –	
32	Accumulated Dep'n: Building	171				
33	Depreciation Expense: Off. Equip.	700			1 450 –	
34	Accumulated Dep'n: Off. Equip.	176				
35	Depreciation Expense: Comp. Equip.	705			17 880 –	
36	Accumulated Dep'n: Comp. Equip.	181				
37	Depreciation Expense: Auto	710			3 750 –	
38	Accumulated Dep'n: Auto	191				
39					330 250 –	380 000 –
40	a) Insurance expired, $600.				49 750 –	
41	b) Office supplies used, $570.				380 000 –	380 000 –
42	c) Computer supplies used, $2 200.					
43	d) Building depreciation, 0.05 × $228 000.					
44	e) Office equipment depreciation, 0.10 × $14 500.					
45	f) Computer equipment depreciation, 0.30 × $59 600.					
46	g) Automobile depreciation, 0.30 × $12 500.					

- The credit to the Income Summary account means that this account balance is now equal to the total of the temporary accounts with a credit balance.

2. The closing entry for the temporary accounts with a debit balance is shown here. The accounts with a debit balance that are to be

closed are found on the debit side of the Income Statement columns of the worksheet.

GENERAL JOURNAL

PAGE 590

DATE 1992		PARTICULARS	PR	DEBIT	CREDIT
May	31	Income Summary	320	330 250 —	
		Refunds	415		2 200 —
		Wages Expense	600		184 600 —
		VISA Discount Expense	655		7 200 —
		Advertising Expense	660		44 600 —
		Utilities Expense	670		32 400 —
		Automobile Expense	680		4 400 —
		Miscellaneous Expense	760		17 000 —
		Insurance Expense	720		600 —
		Office Supplies Expense	730		570 —
		Computer Supplies Expense	740		2 200 —
		Depreciation Expense: Building	690		11 400 —
		Depreciation Expense: Office Equipment	700		1 450 —
		Depreciation Expense: Computer Equipment	705		17 880 —
		Depreciation Expense: Automobile	710		3 750 —
		To close temporary accounts with a debit balance			

"The second closing entry is to close temporary accounts with a debit balance into Income Summary."

The explanation for the entry is as follows:
- The debit to Income Summary transfers the total of the temporary accounts with a debit balance to this account. Note that the amount of the temporary accounts with a debit balance for the year can be found in the debit column of the Income Statement on the worksheet.
- The credit to the individual expenses will result in each of the expense accounts having a nil balance when the journal entries have been posted.

The balance of the Income Summary account will be equal to the net income once the first two closing entries have been posted. This is because the balance is the difference between the total revenue (credit side of the account) and the total expenses and contra-revenue accounts (debit side of the account).

GENERAL LEDGER

Income Summary   320

dr.	cr.
May 31 330 250	May 31 380 000
Total of temporary accounts with a debit balance	Total of temporary accounts with a credit balance

Refunds   415

dr.	cr.
2 200	May 31 2 200
Refunds to May 31	Closing entry

Wages Expense   600

dr.	cr.
184 600	May 31 184 600
Wages to May 31	Closing entry

VISA Discount Expense   655

dr.	cr.
7 200	May 31 7 200
Discount Expense to May 31	Closing entry

Advertising Expense   660

dr.	cr.
44 600	May 31 44 600
Advertising Expense to May 31	Closing entry

Utilities Expense   670

dr.	cr.
32 400	May 31 32 400
Utilities Expense to May 31	Closing entry

Automobile Expense   680

dr.	cr.
4 400	May 31 4 400
Auto Expense to May 31	Closing entry

Dep'n. Expense: Building   690

dr.	cr.
11 400	May 31 11 400
Depreciation to May 31	Closing entry

Dep'n. Expense: Office Equipment   700

dr.	cr.
1 450	May 31 1 450
Depreciation to May 31	Closing entry

Dep'n. Expense: Computer Equipment   705

dr.	cr.
17 880	May 31 17 880
Depreciation to May 31	Closing entry

Dep'n. Expense: Automobile   710

dr.	cr.
3 750	May 31 3 750
Depreciation to May 31	Closing entry

Insurance Expense   720

dr.	cr.
600	May 31 600
Insurance Expense to May 31	Closing entry

Office Supplies Expense   730

dr.	cr.
570	May 31 570
Office Supplies Expense to May 31	Closing entry

Computer Supplies Expense   740

dr.	cr.
2 200	May 31 2 200
Computer Supplies Expense to May 31	Closing entry

Miscellaneous Expense   760

dr.	cr.
17 000	May 31 17 000
Miscellaneous Expense to May 31	Closing entry

3. The third closing entry, which transfers the net income to the owner's capital account, can now be completed. The owner's claim on the business increases by an amount equal to the net income of the business. The amount of the net income can be found on the worksheet. It is also equal to the balance of the Income Summary account after the first two closing entries have been completed. This third closing entry will also, therefore, close the Income Summary account.

GENERAL JOURNAL

PAGE 590

DATE 1992		PARTICULARS	PR	DEBIT	CREDIT
May	31	Income Summary	320	49 750 —	
		V. Marshall, Capital	300		49 750 —
		To close net income for the year into the Capital account			

GENERAL LEDGER

Income Summary		320		V. Marshall, Capital		300
dr.		cr.		dr.		cr.
May 31 330 250		May 31 380 000				June 1 222 477
49 750						May 31 49 750

The explanation for the entry is as follows:
- A debit is made to Income Summary to bring the balance of that account to nil. Note that this account is only used at the end of the fiscal year for closing entries. In this situation, because it has a credit balance, a debit must be made to close it. The amount of the balance before closing, and the debit required to close the account, is equal to the net income for the year. Note that the balance of the Income Summary account is now nil.
- A credit is made to V. Marshall, Capital, in order to transfer the net income for the year to the owner's capital account. Note that the balance of the Capital account increases by the amount of the net income.

> "The third closing entry is to close the Income Summary account into Capital."

4. The fourth closing entry is to close the Drawings into the Capital account.

GENERAL JOURNAL

PAGE 590

DATE 1992		PARTICULARS	PR	DEBIT	CREDIT
May	31	V. Marshall, Capital	300	28 000 —	
		V. Marshall, Drawings	310		28 000 —
		To close Drawings into Capital			

GENERAL LEDGER

V. Marshall, Capital	300
dr.	cr.
May 31 28 000	June 1 222 477
	May 31 49 750

V. Marshall, Drawings	310
dr.	cr.
28 000	May 31 28 000
Drawings for the year	Closing entry

"The fourth closing entry is to close Drawings into Capital."

The explanation for the entry is as follows:
- The debit to V. Marshall, Capital decreases the owner's claim on the business by an amount equal to the drawings for the year. Remember that every personal withdrawal of assets from the business causes a decrease in owner's equity.
- The credit to V. Marshall, Drawings when posted will result in the Drawings account having a nil balance in order that the amount of Drawings can easily be calculated during the next period.

Closing Entries for a Net Loss Situation

The first, second, and fourth closing entries when there is a loss situation are exactly the same. The third closing entry will be different, however. Let us assume that the year has ended for Algor with a net loss of $8 600, which represents total revenue for the year, $139 400, less the total expenses for the year, $148 000. After the first and second closing entries have been journalized and posted, the Income Summary account will appear as follows:

GENERAL LEDGER

Income Summary	320
dr.	cr.
May 31 148 000	May 31 139 400
Total expenses for the year	Total revenue for the year

The balance of the account is a debit, $8 600, which represents the amount of the net loss for the year. In order to close the Income Summary account, and to reduce the owner's capital account by the amount of the net loss, the following entry is made:

GENERAL JOURNAL

PAGE 590

DATE 1992		PARTICULARS	PR	DEBIT	CREDIT
May	31	V. Marshall, Capital	300	8 600 —	
		Income Summary	320		8 600 —
		To close the Income Summary account, and to reduce the Capital by the net loss			

GENERAL LEDGER

V. Marshall, Capital		300
dr.	cr.	
May 31 8 600		

Income Summary		320
dr.	cr.	
Total expenses for the year 148 000	Total revenue for the year 139 400 May 31 8 600	

Closing Entries: Summary

There are usually four closing entries for a proprietorship, which are for the following purposes:

1. close temporary accounts with a credit balance and transfer balances into Income Summary;
2. close temporary accounts with a debit balance and transfer balances into Income Summary;
3. close the Income Summary account into Capital;
4. close the Drawings account into Capital.

Posting the Closing Entries and Ruling the Accounts

Once the closing entries have been journalized and posted, the temporary accounts will have a nil balance. In order to show where the new period begins, the date and money columns of the closed accounts are double **ruled**. An example of a ruled temporary account is shown below. All other temporary accounts will be similarly ruled. Remember that the asset and liability accounts have not been affected by the closing entries, for those amounts are still owned and owed respectively. Thus, they are not double ruled. Nor is the Capital account double ruled, because its balance also carries over into the next fiscal period.

Ruled accounts: these accounts indicate that the temporary accounts were closed at the end of the fiscal year.

FIGURE 8-5 EXAMPLE OF A RULED RUNNING-BALANCE LEDGER ACCOUNT

GENERAL LEDGER

ACCOUNT Depreciation Expense: Building					NO 690	
DATE 1992	PARTICULARS	PR	DEBIT	CREDIT	DR CR	BALANCE
May 31		J590	11 400 —		Dr	11 400 —
31		J590		11 400 —	—	0

Post-Closing Trial Balance

Post-closing trial balance: a trial balance prepared to prove that the ledger balances before beginning the next fiscal period.

The last step in the accounting cycle is to prepare the **post-closing trial balance**, which proves that the ledger balances before beginning the next fiscal period. If this step is omitted, the errors of one year will be carried forward to the next year. The post-closing trial balance for Algor

Computer Services is shown in Figure 8-6. Note that it contains only asset, liability, and capital accounts, for the other accounts have been closed.

FIGURE 8-6 A POST-CLOSING TRIAL BALANCE FOR ALGOR COMPUTER SERVICES

Algor Computer Services
Post-Closing Trial Balance
May 31, 1992

Cash	$ 49 000	
Accounts Receivable	50 000	
GST Recoverable	1 400	
Prepaid Insurance	1 200	
Office Supplies	890	
Computer Supplies	2 700	
Land	124 600	
Building	228 000	
Accumulated Depreciation: Building		$ 11 400
Office Equipment	14 500	
Accumulated Depreciation: Office Equipment		1 450
Computer Equipment	59 600	
Accumulated Depreciation: Computer Equipment		17 880
Automobile	12 500	
Accumulated Depreciation: Automobile		3 750
Accounts Payable		14 503
GST Payable		1 460
PST Payable		1 720
Mortgage Payable		248 000
V. Marshall, Capital		244 227
	$544 390	$544 390

LESSON REVIEW

26. When are closing entries made? How many are there?

27. Why are closing entries made?

28. What are the possible sources of information for closing entries? Which is easiest to use?

29. Which accounts are closed?

30. Which accounts are not closed? Why are they not closed?

31. Why is the Income Summary account called a temporary account?

32. What is the purpose of the post-closing trial balance?

LESSON APPLICATIONS

33. Using the data from the following partial worksheet, prepare the closing entries.

PARTIAL WORKSHEET

FOR THE _Year_ ENDED _May 31_ 19 _-2_

	ACCOUNTS	ACCT. NO.	TRIAL BALANCE DR	TRIAL BALANCE CR	INCOME STATEMENT DR	INCOME STATEMENT CR	
1	Cash	100	17 000 —				1
2	Accounts Receivable	110	13 710 —				2
3	Allowance for Doubtful Acc.	115		800 —			3
4	GST Recoverable	117	290				4
5	Office Supplies	120	1 200 —				5
6	Equipment	150	11 200 —				6
7	Accum. Dep'n.: Equipment	155		4 000 —			7
8	Accounts Payable	200		11 000 —			8
9	GST Payable	210		800 —			9
10	G. Seguin, Capital	300		10 200 —			10
11	G. Seguin, Drawings	310	20 000 —				11
12	Revenue from Fees	400		146 000 —		146 000 —	12
13	Wages Expense	500	68 000 —		68 000 —		13
14	Utilities Expense	510	17 500 —		17 500 —		14
15	Bank Expense	520	900 —		900 —		15
16	Auto Rental Expense	530	12 000 —		12 000 —		16
17	Advertising Expense	540	9 000 —		9 000 —		17
18	Miscellaneous Expense	580	2 000 —		2 000 —		18
19			172 800 —	172 800 —			19
20	Supplies Expense	550			780 —		20
21	Dep'n. Expense: Equipment	560			640 —		21
22	Bad Debts Expense	570			700 —		22
23					111 520 —	146 000 —	23
24	Net Income				34 480 —		24
25					146 000 —	146 000 —	25
26							26

34. Van's Window Wash is owned and operated by Jon Vanderhinden.
    (a) Open a ledger for Van's Window Wash, providing appropriate account numbers and using the following account balances: Cash, $4 560.90; Accounts Receivable, $11 771.00; GST Recoverable, $575.00; Supplies, $2 340.10; Equipment, $12 450.85; Accumulated Depreciation: Equipment, $2 589.00; Trucks, $29 684.00; Accumulated Depreciation: Trucks, $12 340.00; Accounts Payable, $11 329.00; GST Payable, $2 000.00; J. Vanderhinden, Capital, $32 826.15; J. Vanderhinden, Drawings, $4 500.00; Cleaning Revenue, $28 790.00; Depreciation Expense: Equipment, $780.80; Depreciation Expense: Trucks, $8 598.00; Cleaning Expense, $2 349.00; Wages Expense, $6 392.80; Rent Expense, $2 300.00; Office Expense, $2 340.90; Miscellaneous Expense, $1 230.80.
    (b) Journalize the closing entries for the month of March, using page 72 of the journal.
    (c) Post the closing entries, and rule the closed accounts.
    (d) Prepare a post-closing trial balance.

35. Using the data from the following partial worksheet, prepare the closing entries.

PARTIAL WORKSHEET

FOR THE _Year_ ENDED _Nov. 30_ 19 _90_

	ACCOUNTS	ACCT. NO.	TRIAL BALANCE DR	TRIAL BALANCE CR	INCOME STATEMENT DR	INCOME STATEMENT CR	
1	Cash	100	26 710 –				1
2	Accounts Receivable	110	16 000 –				2
3	Allowance For Doubtful Acc.	120		1 000 –			3
4	GST Recoverable	125	350 –				4
5	Supplies	130	2 470 –				5
6	Equipment	140	61 050 –				6
7	Accum. Dep'n.: Equipment	150		18 300 –			7
8	Accounts Payable	200		36 595 –			8
9	GST Payable	210		1 025 –			9
10	D. McCutcheon, Capital	300		100 720 –			10
11	D. McCutcheon, Drawings	310	32 000 –				11
12	Service Fees	400		146 300 –		146 300 –	12
13	Advertising Expense	500	22 000 –		22 000 –		13
14	Communication Expense	510	9 000 –		9 000 –		14
15	Auto Rental Expense	520	17 600 –		17 600 –		15
16	Utilities Expense	530	16 400 –		16 400 –		16
17	Wages Expense	540	97 600 –		97 600 –		17
18	Miscellaneous Expense	580	2 760 –		2 760 –		18
19			303 940 –	303 940 –			19
20	Bad Debts Expense	550			900 –		20
21	Supplies Expense	560			1 720 –		21
22	Dep'n. Expense: Equipment	570			4 275 –		22
23					172 255 –	146 300 –	23
24	Net Loss					25 955 –	24
25					172 255 –	172 255 –	25
26							26

CHAPTER REVIEW AND SKILL DEVELOPMENT

Accounting Principles and Concepts

- **Adjusting entries** are required for unrecorded expenses, unearned revenue, and unrecorded revenue.

- **Eight- or ten-column worksheets** are used to prepare the adjusting entries, and as a rough preparation of the financial statements.

- **Closing entries** are required to close all temporary accounts to a nil balance, and to update the Capital account.

- A **post-closing trial balance** is prepared to ensure that the general ledger balances before commencing the next fiscal period.

Knowing the Terms

For each of the following statements, indicate the term being defined.
(a) Revenue that has been earned during the fiscal period but has not been recorded prior to the end of the period.
(b) Advance payments for expenses, of which the unused portion appears on the balance sheet as an asset.
(c) Expenses that have accumulated, but are unrecorded and unpaid at the end of the fiscal period.
(d) The sequence of accounting procedures performed during an accounting period.
(e) An account used only for closing entries.
(f) An obligation to render services or deliver goods in the future because of receipt of advance payments.

(g) An eight-column sheet used for rough preparation of the adjusting entries and the financial statements.
(h) Accounts that are closed at the end of the fiscal year.
(i) Trial balance prepared to ensure that the general ledger balances before starting a new fiscal year.
(j) Principle that states that the revenue earned during an accounting period is offset with the expenses incurred in generating this revenue.

Food for Thought

1. An accounting student questioned the value of making adjustments, and indicated that the adjustments for the current year will probably be balanced by the same amounts in the following year. Comment on the student's views.

2. An invoice arrived dated May 24 from the electricity company, indicating that a firm owed $2 300 for electricity used since the last billing, which was on March 24. The firm's year end is April 30. No adjustment was made for electricity on April 30. On what basis can the decision not to make an adjustment be justified? On what basis could this policy of the firm be changed?

3. Many items that are accrued liabilities are lumped together on the balance sheet for reporting purposes. On what basis can this decision be justified?

4. The Facts Speak at the beginning of the chapter indicates that accrued liabilities for IBM were $5 780 million. Give the journal entry to record this liability, assuming that it is all interest expense. What would be the effect on (a) the income statement, and (b) the balance sheet, if the adjustment for these liabilities had not been made?

5. Air Canada had $4 million in unearned revenue at the end of a recent fiscal year. What does the unearned revenue represent? What type of account is it? If the cash basis of accounting had been followed by Air Canada when the ticket was sold to the customer, what would the entry have been? What was the entry under the accrual basis of accounting?

6. A firm that performs services in advance of billings must have a system in place that allows it to calculate the value of services rendered at the end of a fiscal year. How would a lawyer keep track of the billings to be made for clients so that the revenue earned at the end of the fiscal year can be calculated?

7. If a lawyer did not make an adjustment for unrecorded revenue at the end of the fiscal year, what would be the basis for his or her accounting system? What GAAP would this procedure violate?

8. When preparing closing entries, an accountant can look in a number of places to see if the balance of the Income Summary account being closed into Capital is correct. On what items does this balance of the Income Summary account appear?

9. When preparing closing entries for a business in which there were 14 different expense accounts, a student made a debit to Income Summary, and a credit to Expenses. Criticize the entry.

10. An airline offers to its customers a frequent flyer service. How will the airline record the liability to the customers for all the points that the firm has awarded?

Locate and Record

Using the annual report that you obtained from your request in Chapter 4, prepare a

report summarizing the following items concerning adjusting entries.
(a) The adjusting entries that would have been made by the business.
(b) The effect of the adjusting entries on the net income of the business.
(c) Accounting policies which influence the adjusting entries that the business makes each fiscal period.

Organizing

1. Adjusting Entries

We have now studied four types of adjusting entries. For each of the four, complete the following:
(a) State the type of adjustment.
(b) Give an example of the adjustment.
(c) Describe why the adjustment is required, referring to the matching principle.
(d) State the effect upon the following year's net income if the adjusting entry is not made.

2. Closing Entries

We have studied four closing entries. For each of the four, complete the following:
(a) Describe the purpose of the adjustment.
(b) Describe the accounts that will be affected.
(c) State the effect upon the following year's net income if the closing entry is not made.

Applications

The trial balance for Westboro Outdoor Advertising is shown in Figure 8-7. The fiscal period is one month.
(a) Enter the trial balance on an eight-column worksheet providing appropriate account numbers.
(b) Using the other data, complete the worksheet.
(c) Journalize the adjusting entries.
(d) Journalize the closing entries.

FIGURE 8-7

Westboro Outdoor Advertising Trial Balance July 31, 1993		
Cash	$ 38 600	
GST Recoverable	1 270	
Office Supplies	3 450	
Prepaid Rent	12 900	
Prepaid Insurance	2 700	
Equipment	29 800	
Accumulated Depreciation: Equipment		$ 12 890
Truck	23 400	
Accumulated Depreciation: Truck		7 020
Billboards	94 800	
Accumulated Depreciation: Billboards		18 490
Accounts Payable		11 400
Unearned Advertising Revenue		7 420
Bank Loan		8 200
GST Payable		2 100
P. Wanamaker, Capital		138 072
P. Wanamaker, Drawings	4 800	
Advertising Revenue		22 600
Wages Expense	11 220	
Truck Expense	2 197	
Utilities Expense	1 765	
Miscellaneous Expense	1 290	
	$228 192	$228 192

Other Data:
(1) Inventory at month end shows Office Supplies, $2 900.
(2) The prepaid rent is for four months; 1 month has expired.

(3) Unexpired insurance, $2 200.
(4) Depreciation rates are as given in the text for capital cost allowance; billboards depreciation rate is 35 percent.
(5) Wages owing and payable at month end are $1 200.
(6) $3 400 of the unearned advertising revenue has been earned.
(7) Interest at the rate of 10 percent per annum is owing for the month on the bank loan.

Applications — Comprehensive

Wilbert Westbury decided, after years of working as a fireman, to start his own lawn maintenance firm. At the end of his second year in business the trial balance for the firm is as shown in Figure 8-8.

Other Data:
(1) Inventories at year end show Office Supplies, $112; Chemical Supplies, $1 100.
(2) Unexpired insurance, $200.
(3) Depreciation rates are as given in the text for capital cost allowance.
(4) Interest owing is as follows: bank loan, $1 450; mortgage interest, $1 270.
(5) Wages owing and payable at year end are nil; salaries owing and payable at month end are $2 000.
(6) The unearned fees have all been earned.

(a) Open ledger accounts providing appropriate account numbers, and enter the balances from the trial balance.
(b) Enter the trial balance on an eight-column worksheet, and complete the worksheet using the Other Data.
(c) Journalize the adjusting entries, and post to the general ledger.
(d) Journalize the closing entries, and post to the general ledger.
(e) Double rule the ledger accounts that are closed.

FIGURE 8-8

The Westbury Weeder
Trial Balance
November 30, 1991

Cash	$ 28 564	
GST Recoverable	400	
Prepaid Insurance	1 400	
Office Supplies	420	
Chemical Supplies	12 300	
Equipment	7 640	
Accumulated Depreciation: Equipment		$ 982
Trucks	70 936	
Accumulated Depreciation: Trucks		19 305
Building	84 200	
Accumulated Depreciation: Building		16 840
Land	88 400	
Accounts Payable		2 390
Bank Loan		14 500
Mortgage Payable		124 800
GST Payable		2 200
Unearned Fees		30 000
W. Westbury, Capital		74 204
W. Westbury, Drawings	7 200	
Spray Application Revenue		102 670
Wages Expense	24 380	
Salaries Expense	32 900	
Truck Expense	7 902	
Mortgage Interest Expense	13 970	
Utilities Expense	6 499	
Miscellaneous Expense	780	
	$387 891	$387 891

(f) Prepare an income statement and a classified balance sheet.
(g) Prepare a post-closing trial balance.
(h) Calculate the working capital and current ratio.
(i) Comment on Wilbert's ability as an entrepreneur after two years in business, based on the facts available.

Focussing
The Eight-Column Worksheet
In preparing an eight-column worksheet for Rutschkowski Scrapyard, the following errors were made:
(a) Unexpired Insurance on the trial balance was $1 500, and had an adjustment of $400. It was extended to the balance sheet as $1 900.
(b) Depreciation Expense: Equipment of $4 300 was extended to the credit side of the income statement columns.
(c) Salaries Payable, $1 300, and Accrued Interest Payable, $900, were extended to the credit side of the income statement columns.
(d) J. Rutschkowski, Drawings, $9 000, was extended to the debit side of the income statement columns.
(e) An adjustment to indicate a decrease of office supplies in the amount of $250 was omitted.

The net income which resulted on the worksheet was $73 400. Calculate the correct net income.

Evaluate and Assess
The following errors were made when adjusting entries were prepared at the firm of Doolittle and Doolittle:
(a) The balance of the Supplies account was $2 480 before adjustments. The inventory of supplies showed $560 on hand. An adjustment was made for $1 720.
(b) The balance of the Unearned Fees account was $32 450 before adjustments. Of this amount, $21 400 was earned as of the end of the current fiscal year. An adjusting entry was made for $11 400.
(c) The balance of the Prepaid Insurance account was $1 230 before adjustments. One-third of the policy had expired during the current fiscal year. The adjustment was made for $140.

For each of the above adjustments, describe the effect upon the current year's income statement and balance sheet.

Synthesize and Conclude
Martin McCaffrey was interested in buying the Macho Fitness Studio from Andrea Taylor. Andrea presented the financial statements in Figure 8-9 to Martin as evidence of the excellent financial condition of the business.

Andrea and Martin discuss a price. Andrea's asking price is $235 000, and as evidence of the reasonableness of it, she indicates that the owner's equity is more than that amount. Also, there are no liabilities according to Andrea. She further discloses to Martin that the membership initiations are for five-year memberships. On average, one-fifth of the initiations have expired. The membership fees are an annual fee. On average, three-quarters of the fees have expired. The advertising revenue is derived from advertisements for sportswear that appear in the fitness studio.

Prepare a report to Martin, indicating your views on whether he should purchase the business for the asking price. Include in your report an income statement that truly reflects the revenue, expenses, and net income (loss) for the year.

FIGURE 8-9

Macho Fitness Studio
Income Statement
for the year ended June 30, 19–8

Revenue:
Advertising Revenue		$ 4 350	
Membership Fees		124 500	
Membership Initiation		228 000	
Total Revenue			$356 850

Expenses:
Advertising		16 000	
Wages		112 450	
Utilities		36 900	
Rent		120 000	
Miscellaneous		4 800	
Total Expenses			290 150
Net Income			$ 66 700

Macho Fitness Studio
Balance Sheet
as at June 30, 19–8

Assets:
Cash		$200 000	
Equipment	$50 000		
Accumulated Depreciation	12 500	37 500	
Total Assets			$237 500

Owner's Equity
A. Taylor, Capital			$237 500

Accounting At Work

Asim Siddiqui
Public Accountant

Asim Siddiqui operates his own public accounting firm, providing services to small and medium-sized businesses. Among his clients are owners of restaurants, dry cleaners, construction companies, body shops, real estate firms, and manufacturers. He prepares financial reports for his clients, advises them on taxation, and conducts audits on their operations. Because Asim has concentrated on businesses of a particular size, he feels he can offer better service since he understands their problems better than other accounting firms might.

Asim graduated from York University with a Bachelor of Business Administration (BBA) degree and started in an accounting firm as a student-in-accounts. He spent three years in this training position, gradually gaining experience in dealing with problems. At the same time, he took the courses and wrote the exams leading to the Chartered Accountant (CA) designation. By the time he completed the final CA exams, he had a strong theoretical knowledge of accounting as well as a solid practical skill. Asim spent several years working for the federal government in the Office of the Auditor General, and in the taxation department before going to work for a large petrochemical company. Over the next several years he worked in his spare time as a public accountant, gradually building up a list of clients. Eventually he went into business full-time, setting up the firm he runs today.

"Accounting is the language of business," Asim maintains. "A report should tell a story to the reader." It is the task of accountants to compile the information, interpret and summarize it, and communicate the findings to clients. Business people can then use the information to make decisions and plan for the future. "Employers shouldn't make the mistake of hiring untrained people to do their accounting," said Asim. "The results of poor accounting practices are not immediately apparent; they will only be felt later through poor profits, bad decisions, and tax problems."

Asim is very optimistic about the future of the profession. He sees that business in general is getting more complicated, with new and different tax laws and trading conditions, and heavier financial obligations. Business people will need well-trained and knowledgeable accountants to help them make the best possible choices.

1. What is a public accountant?
2. Why would small businesses rely on the services of a public accountant?
3. What areas of accounting would a public accountant have to be aware of?
4. In what ways is Asim an entrepreneur?

Business Career Skills

1. Employee Performance Appraisal

In recent years, appraisal of employee performance on the job has become a greater concern for businesses. Increased employee productivity is an objective of all businesses, especially in this era of increased global competition.

(a) In groups, brainstorm to develop a list of job factors that you think an employee should be appraised on. Assume that the person is employed as an accounting clerk.

(b) Individually, rank the list that you have created from most important to least important.

(c) In groups, compare your individual rankings. Then, come to a consensus on a group ranking.

2. Résumé

The following advertisement appeared in a local newspaper. In order to respond to the advertisement, a person must prepare a letter of application and a résumé.

A résumé is usually prepared first, and should be an account of one's experience and qualifications. It should include the writer's name, address, education, work experience, and other items required by the job advertisement, such as skills and abilities. Personal information may also be included, such as hobbies, physical condition, and birth date, though they are no longer required under human rights legislation. A list of references is usually provided. Prepare a résumé for the following advertisement.

Accounting Clerk

Part-time position for high school student who has completed one year of accounting studies. Work time is to include one evening, Saturdays, and the summer. The successful candidate will be self-motivated, able to get along with fellow workers, and have good communication skills. Pay will be based on experience. Applicants should send a résumé to

Algor Computer Services
55 Eastern Parkway
Kanata, ON
K2L 2B1

---

3. The Letter of Application

The letter of application should do more than state that you are interested in the position and would like an interview. It should: (1) get the reader's attention, (2) state your purpose, (3) possibly give a brief summation of your selling points, and (4) ask for an interview. Prepare a letter of application to accompany the résumé prepared for the advertisement shown above, using proper business letter form.

COMPUTER ACCOUNTING
THE POWER OF ACCOUNTING SOFTWARE, OR WHAT A TYPICAL COMPUTER ACCOUNTING PROGRAM CAN DO FOR YOU AT THE END OF THE ACCOUNTING YEAR

For a firm using a manual accounting system, you have learned that the closing entries must be made by a series of compound entries — usually four for a single proprietorship. These are:

1. Close all revenue accounts to the Income Summary account.
2. Close all expense accounts to the Income Summary account.
3. Close the Income Summary account to the Capital account.
4. Close the Drawings account to the Capital account.

The procedure is dramatically different when one uses a computerized accounting software package. If we use *ACCPAC Bedford Integrated Accounting* as a typical example, the procedure would be as follows:

1. Enter whatever adjusting entries are necessary to make the year's income statement fairly represent the company's net income/loss for the year. In other words, ensure that the Matching Principle has been followed as required by the **accrual method of accounting**. Included in this process would be the closing of the Drawings account to the Capital account.

2. Print whatever reports the company requires for internal and external use, and then make and store a backup copy of the Company's files. THIS IS IMPORTANT!

3. When you now load the Company's files and enter a USING date, which is the start of the new accounting year, the program will prompt you that, if you press **RETURN** to proceed, the program will close revenue and expense account balances into the Capital account if it is a single proprietorship, or into Retained Earnings if it is a limited company. Before proceeding to this step, it is important that you make backup copies of the Company files so that if needed you can make extra year-end adjusting entries on the backup disk and enter the same adjusting entries to the Capital or Retained Earnings account instead of revenue and expense accounts using the data disk for the new accounting year. Also you will have a complete record of all the accounting entries for the year just ended.

4. When you press **RETURN**, the year-end closing journal entry will be made. The program will then start a new income statement for the year just entered. It will also advance the **START** date of the company's accounting year to the day following the current **FINISH** date, and reset the **FINISH** date to 12 months from the new **START** date.

You can readily see that the time-consuming and laborious job of journalizing and then posting the closing entries is eliminated, replaced by a few key strokes and the speed and power of the computer. In addition, the "books" of the business are now ready for the new accounting year.

Exercise

Call up the Linda Schuman problem (Chapters 4 and 7). Before "closing" the revenue and expense accounts transfer the balance in the Drawings account to the Capital account. Now use the power of your accounting software program to "close the accounts." Print a trial balance for November 1 and submit it to your teacher.

CHAPTER NINE

The Merchandising Business

LEARNING OBJECTIVES

At the end of this chapter you should be able to
- distinguish between a periodic inventory system and a perpetual inventory system;
- prepare journal entries for the purchase and payment cycle for a merchandising business that uses a periodic inventory system;
- prepare journal entries for the sales and collection cycle for a merchandising business that uses a periodic inventory system;
- prepare an adjusting entry for doubtful accounts;
- calculate the Cost of Goods Sold;
- complete the accounting cycle for a business that uses a periodic inventory system;
- prepare journal entries for a merchandising business that uses a perpetual inventory system;
- complete the accounting cycle for a business that uses a perpetual inventory system;
- set up and access accounting data files for a merchandising business using the periodic inventory system;
- enter transactions for a merchandising business into the computer system;
- display and print accounting transactions and reports;
- use a spreadsheet program to design and complete a ten-column worksheet for a merchandising business using a periodic/perpetual inventory system;
- use a spreadsheet program to design an income statement and balance sheet for a merchandising business.

LANGUAGE OF ACCOUNTING

You will see the following terms in this chapter:
ageing of accounts receivable
allowance for doubtful accounts
contra-cost account
cost account
cost of goods sold
gross profit/gross margin
inventory control
inventory turnover
merchandise inventory
periodic inventory
perpetual inventory
stock card

Merchandising businesses: *businesses that sell goods, or merchandise.*

To date we have studied only service businesses. This chapter begins the study of **merchandising businesses**, which sell goods, or merchandise. Merchandising businesses can either be wholesalers or retailers. Wholesalers buy goods directly from a manufacturer or producer, and sell them to a retailer. The retailer buys goods from either the manufacturer/producer or the wholesaler and sells them to the final consumer.

CHANNELS OF DISTRIBUTION FOR GOODS

MANUFACTURER ⟶ WHOLESALER ⟶ RETAILER ⟶ CONSUMER

MANUFACTURER ⟶ RETAILER ⟶ CONSUMER

MANUFACTURER ⟶ CONSUMER

Algor Computer Services started out as a service business, repairing computers and providing software lessons. At the outset, Vijay did not think that he could raise enough capital to also stock and sell computer networks. The firm was successful in its service role, and, as a result, was able to finance the addition of merchandise. It became, therefore, a seller of both goods and services.

When Algor Computer Services began selling goods, it had to decide on the type of inventory system it would use. An inventory system is a record of the goods on hand available for sale. The firm had a choice of two inventory systems: a perpetual inventory system, or a periodic inventory system. Since the choice of inventory system would have an impact on the accounting system, a great deal of time was put into the decision-making process. The accounting firm setting up Algor Computer Services' accounting system indicated the following about the two types of systems.

FIGURE 9-1 RECOMMENDATIONS OF THE SYSTEMS ANALYST CONCERNING SELECTION OF AN INVENTORY METHOD AT ALGOR COMPUTER SERVICES

Page 7: Algor Computer Services
Accounting System Proposal, June, 1992

INVENTORY SYSTEMS

The choice of an inventory system influences the accounting entries required, as well as the financial reports of the business. The inventory system can be one of two types: a periodic system or a perpetual system. The two are briefly described below.

Periodic inventory system: *a physical inventory is usually taken once a year at the end of the fiscal period.*

1. *Periodic System:* A periodic system implies that a physical inventory will be taken periodically, usually once a year at the end of the fiscal year. A physical inventory consists of counting and pricing all merchandise on hand. It is necessary to take the inventory at the end of the fiscal period in order to find the value of merchandise on hand. Because the business owns this merchandise, it will be listed as a current asset on the balance sheet. Since

the inventory would only be taken once a year, the actual value of the goods on hand will only be known at the end of the period. Thus the name periodic. The firm could take a physical inventory more often, but it is a costly and time-consuming process.

The advantage of this system is that detailed records of changes in inventory are not required. However, the disadvantages of the system are significant. The major disadvantage is that the quantity of any one item on hand at a particular time is not known unless one goes to the shelf and counts the goods. It is, therefore, difficult to be certain that adequate quantities of items are on hand to satisfy customer demand. Since it usually takes time to receive goods from suppliers, shortages of goods may result. This could cause prospective customers to take their business elsewhere.

Perpetual inventory system: a continuous record of all merchandise on hand.

2. *Perpetual System*: A perpetual inventory system requires the keeping of inventory records on a day-to-day basis. This system is especially adaptable to the accounting software system that we recommend for your business. The perpetual inventory record is maintained on stock cards that will be produced by your computer for each item. A sample stock card is shown below.

When goods are purchased by the business, an entry is made on the stock record card to show an increase of goods on hand. When goods are sold a record is made on the stock card to show a decrease of goods on hand. The quantity of goods on hand is therefore available at any time.

Since this is the system that we recommend for your business. . .

FIGURE 9-2 A SAMPLE STOCK CARD USED TO MAINTAIN A PERPETUAL INVENTORY

Algor Computer Services — Stock Record

Stock Item: _____ Stock Number: _____

Supplier: _____

Address: _____
_____

Telephone: (___) _____

Supplier Order Number: _____ Usual Terms: _____

Minimum Quantity: _____ Maximum Quantity: _____

Unit Cost Price: _____

Other Order Information: _____

Date	Quantity Ordered	Received	Quantity Sold	Adjustment	Balance

Algor Computer Services could therefore choose between using a perpetual or a periodic inventory system. Periodic inventory systems are used by firms that do not use computers to maintain records of their inventories, and by firms that have a large number of small items available for sale. Perpetual inventory systems are used by firms that use computers to maintain records of their inventories, and by firms that have a small number of large items available for sale. We will look at the accounting procedures required of a firm using the periodic system first, and then those followed by a firm using a perpetual system.

9.1 Purchase Transactions for a Merchandising Business Using a Periodic Inventory System

New accounts are needed to record the transactions of a merchandising business. The business buys items for the purpose of resale, which a service business does not. Merchandising businesses usually have more returns of goods than a service business has refunds of fees. As well, additional accounts are used to record costs to the business of getting goods on the shelf ready for sale. The new accounts related to purchases are:
- Purchases
- Freight-in
- Purchases Returns and Allowances
- Purchases Discounts

Purchases

Purchases: *an account used to record the purchase of merchandise.*

The cost of merchandise purchased from suppliers is recorded in an account called **Purchases**. While terms of the purchase may call for a cash payment, purchases of merchandise are more commonly made on account. The purchase cycle consists of the purchase of the merchandise, the establishment of an account payable, and the resulting payment. It is obviously in the firm's best interest to delay the payment as long as possible. In this way it may be able to sell the item and receive the cash in order to make payment to the supplier.

FIGURE 9-3 THE PURCHASE AND PAYMENT CYCLE

1.	2.	3.
Purchase of merchandise	Record the account payable	Payment to supplier

→ Time

> "A cost account is any account that shows expenditures on merchandise in order to make the goods available for sale."

The Purchases account is a cost account. A cost account is any account that shows expenditures on merchandise in order to make the goods available for sale. Its balance indicates the accumulated cost of merchandise purchased during the year. It does not indicate whether the goods have been sold or are still on hand. The account has a debit balance because it reduces net income, so, in turn, it reduces owner's equity. Some businesses use only one Purchases account, while others have several so that each type of merchandise purchased can be separately recorded.

The following entry records a cash purchase of merchandise:

Oct. 2   Cheque Copy #969: $19 474 to Apple Computers; $18 200 for computers plus GST of $1 274.

GENERAL JOURNAL

PAGE 624

DATE 1992		PARTICULARS	PR	DEBIT	CREDIT
Oct.	2	Purchases	500	18 200 –	
		GST Recoverable	135	1 274 –	
		Cash	100		19 474 –
		Cheque Copy #969, Apple Computers			

GENERAL LEDGER

Purchases		500
dr.		cr.
Oct. 2 18 200		

GST Recoverable		135
dr.		cr.
Oct. 2 1 274		

Cash		100
dr.		cr.
		Oct. 2 19 474

The explanation for the entry is as follows:
- A debit is made to Purchases to record the cost of purchasing the merchandise.
- A debit is made to GST Recoverable, to represent the input tax credit.
- A credit is made to Cash to reduce that asset, reflecting the fact that payment was made.

Most purchases are made on account due to the distances that many goods must travel and to the amount of cash involved. For example, it would be difficult to pay cash for goods imported from another country. As well, businesses prefer to buy on account because it gives them an opportunity to inspect the goods, and also an opportunity to sell them before having to pay for them. An entry to record the purchase of merchandise on account is shown below.

Oct. 2 Purchase Invoice #939: From NEC for $19 688; $18 400 for monitors plus $1 288 GST.

GENERAL JOURNAL

PAGE 624

DATE 1992		PARTICULARS	PR	DEBIT	CREDIT
Oct.	2	Purchases	500	18 400 —	
		GST Recoverable	135	1 288 —	
		Accounts Payable	200		19 688 —
		Purchase Invoice #939, NEC monitors			

GENERAL LEDGER

Purchases	500		GST Recoverable	135		Accounts Payable	200
dr.	cr.		dr.	cr.		dr.	cr.
Oct. 2 18 400			Oct. 2 1 288				Oct. 2 19 688

The explanation for the entry is as follows:
- A debit is made to Purchases to record the cost of purchasing the merchandise.
- A debit is made to GST Recoverable, to represent the input tax credit.
- A credit is made to Accounts Payable to record the claim on Algor Computer Services given to the supplier.

According to the recognition of cost principle, the cost of the purchase is recognized at the time of the purchase, not at the time of the payment. Note that the Purchases account is only used to record the purchase of merchandise. It is *not* used to record the purchase of items that will not be sold by the business, such as office supplies and office equipment. Purchases of these items will result in a debit to their respective accounts.

Freight-in

Freight-in, or Transportation-in, is the account used to record the cost of transporting merchandise into the business. The purchase invoice indicates whether the supplier or purchaser will have to pay for the cost of shipping the merchandise. The invoice may use the term "F.O.B.," which means "free on board" and will read either:

Freight-in: *a cost account that shows the cost of shipping of merchandise only.*

F.O.B. shipping point: the purchaser pays shipping costs from that particular shipping point.

F.O.B. destination: the supplier pays the shipping costs.

F.O.B. shipping point (The purchaser pays shipping costs from that particular shipping point.)

F.O.B. destination (The supplier pays the shipping costs. Even though the supplier assumes the shipping costs, shipping has usually been included in the price of the goods.)

When goods are sent F.O.B. shipping point, a special bookkeeping entry is required to record shipping costs. However, when goods are sent F.O.B. destination, a separate entry is not required because the cost is included in the price paid for the goods.

Freight-in is a cost account, in that it increases the cost of obtaining the merchandise. It has a debit balance because it reduces owner's equity. The entry to record freight-in is as follows:

Oct. 2   Purchase Invoice #429C: From Smith Courier Service Ltd., $130.54; $122.00 for transportation of merchandise and $8.54 for GST.

GENERAL JOURNAL

PAGE 624

DATE 1992		PARTICULARS	PR	DEBIT	CREDIT
Oct.	2	Freight-in	510	122 –	
		GST Recoverable	135	8 54	
		Accounts Payable	200		130 54
		Purchase Invoice #429C, Smith Courier Service Ltd.			

GENERAL LEDGER

Freight-in	510	GST Recoverable	135	Accounts Payable	200
dr.	cr.	dr.	cr.	dr.	cr.
Oct. 2 122.00		Oct. 2 8.54			Oct. 2 130.54

The explanation for the entry is as follows:
- A debit is made to Freight-in, the cost account, to show the increase in the cost of the goods purchased.
- A debit is made to GST Recoverable, which represents the input tax credit.
- A credit is made to Accounts Payable to record the claim on Algor Computer Services that was given to Smith Courier Service Ltd.

Additional accounts could be opened in order to record other costs incurred in getting the merchandise to the business. Such accounts could include import duties and insurance on goods-in-transit.

When transportation costs are incurred for items other than merchandise, the cost of the transportation should be recorded in the appropriate asset account. Thus, if a purchase invoice is received for the transportation of the new fax machine to Algor Computer Services, the debit should be to Office Equipment, not to Freight-in.

Oct. 2 Cheque Copy #972: $18.19 to City Wide Delivery; $17.00 for transportation of new fax machine and GST of $1.19.

GENERAL JOURNAL

PAGE 624

DATE 1992		PARTICULARS	PR	DEBIT	CREDIT
Oct.	2	Office Equipment		17 —	
		GST Recoverable		1 19	
		Cash			18 19
		Cheque Copy #972, City Wide Delivery			

Purchases Returns and Allowances

When Algor Computer Services receives merchandise that is either damaged, or the wrong model, or the wrong size, it contacts the supplier concerning a purchase return or an allowance. If the supplier grants a return, the merchandise is sent back, and a credit memo is received from the supplier. Because of the high cost of transportation, however, the supplier and Algor Computer Services may agree on an allowance rather than a return. Algor Computer Services will then purchase the merchandise, but the supplier will reduce the price. Algor Computer Services wants a reduction because it may not be able to sell the wrong or damaged item as quickly as the one that was ordered, or for the same price as an undamaged one.

The cost of returns and allowances is very significant for some businesses. The auto industry regularly has recalls of its products, and the cost of the recall must be offset against the revenue from the original sale.

Purchases Returns and Allowances is the account used to record a purchase return or allowance for merchandise. It is referred to as a contra-cost account, for it reduces the total cost of purchases. It will be combined with the Purchases account on the income statement, as shown later in the chapter. It has a credit balance because by reducing the cost of purchases, it is increasing the equity of the business.

Purchases Returns and Allowances: the account used to record the returns or allowances for merchandise.

THE FACTS SPEAK...

In 1989 there were 536 258 vehicles recalled in Canada for adjustments.

The source document for returns and allowances is a credit memo. The following entry records an allowance:

Oct. 12   Received Credit Memo #328: $197.95 from Epson Canada Limited; $185.00 allowance granted on Purchase Invoice #440 of Oct. 4 (wrong model) and GST of $12.95.

GENERAL JOURNAL

PAGE 626

DATE 1992		PARTICULARS	PR	DEBIT	CREDIT
Oct.	12	Accounts Payable	200	197 95	
		Purchases Returns and Allowances	520		185 —
		GST Recoverable	135		12 95
		Credit Memo #328, Epson Canada Limited			

GENERAL LEDGER

Accounts Payable 200		Purchases Returns and Allowances 520		GST Recoverable 135	
dr.	cr.	dr.	cr.	dr.	cr.
Oct. 12 197.95			Oct. 12 185.00		Oct. 12 12.95

The explanation for the entry is as follows:
- A debit is made to Accounts Payable, a liability, to reduce the amount owing by $197.95. This reflects an adjustment to the GST owing on the purchase as well as the price of the item itself, which was adjusted by $185.
- A credit is made to Purchases Returns and Allowances to show that the amount of purchases has been reduced by $185.
- A credit is made to GST Recoverable. Because the credit memo reduced the purchase price, there must be an accompanying reduction in GST Recoverable.

Some businesses combine the Purchases Returns and Allowances account with the Purchases account. Each time a purchase is returned or an allowance is received, a credit is made to the Purchases account. The disadvantage of this procedure is that the total value of the returns and allowances for a fiscal period is not known. The business will therefore not have good internal control over returns and allowances. When a separate account is used to record returns and allowances, the total value will be known and steps can be taken to correct the problem if it is a large amount.

When items other than merchandise are returned, the Purchases Returns and Allowances account should not be used. If the fax machine mentioned previously was returned, the credit would be to Office Equipment, for it is that asset account which has been reduced.

Purchases Discounts

In order to encourage their customers to pay amounts owing quickly, suppliers offer cash discounts. The terms of sale stated on the invoice indicate the due date for payment of the invoice, and the discount allowed if the payment is made within a specified time. Business policies differ as to the cutoff date for discounts: some require payment in hand by the due date, while others will accept items postmarked on the due date as being eligible for discounts. It should be noted that there is no discount allowed on GST owed to the government. Therefore, discounts on purchases of goods for resale will only be calculated on the base price. For example, for an invoice received by Algor with the terms 2/10, n/30, the supplier will give a 2 percent discount on the base amount if Algor pays within 10 days of the invoice date (postmark accepted). If Algor does not take advantage of the discount the net (n) amount is due in thirty days. Some other common discount terms are as follows:

Terms	Payment Due
1/10, n/60	1 percent discount if paid within 10 days, net amount due in 60 days
EOM	at the end of the month
COD	when goods are delivered
Receipt of invoice	when invoice is received
10 EOM	on the tenth day following the end of the month
net 30	30 days from the invoice date

Purchases Discounts: *the account used to record the reduction in the amount paid caused by paying within a given time.*

Purchases Discounts is a contra-cost account because it reduces the cost of purchases. It has a credit balance because by reducing the cost of purchases it is increasing the equity of the business. It will be combined with the Purchases account on the income statement. Some businesses prefer the name "Discount off Purchases" or "Discounts Earned" instead of Purchases Discounts.

Oct. 2   Purchase Invoice #939: From NEC for $19 688; $18 400 for monitors plus $1 288 GST.

GENERAL JOURNAL

PAGE 624

DATE 1992		PARTICULARS	PR	DEBIT	CREDIT
Oct.	2	Purchases	500	18 400 —	
		GST Recoverable	135	1 288 —	
		Accounts Payable	200		19 688 —
		Purchase Invoice # 939, NEC monitors			

Consider the above October 2 purchase on account by Algor Computer Services of monitors from NEC. The purchase price was $18 400, plus GST of $1 288, giving a total purchase invoice of $19 688. If the terms of sale were 2/10, n/30 (and postmarked payment was acceptable) and Algor Computer Services took full advantage of the discount, the entry to record payment would be as follows:

Oct. 12   Cheque Copy #983: To NEC, $19 320 for payment of Purchase Invoice #939 for $19 688 less discount of $368.

GENERAL JOURNAL

PAGE 626

DATE 1992		PARTICULARS	PR	DEBIT	CREDIT
Oct.	12	Accounts Payable	200	19 688 —	
		Purchases Discounts	525		368 —
		Cash	100		19 320 —
		Cheque Copy #983, NEC Purchase Invoice #939			

GENERAL LEDGER

Accounts Payable		200		Purchases Discounts		525		Cash		100
dr.		cr.		dr.		cr.		dr.		cr.
Oct. 12 19 688		Oct. 2 19 688				Oct. 12 368				Oct. 12 19 320

The explanation for the entry is as follows:
- A debit is made to Accounts Payable for the total amount of the purchase invoice to show that the full liability has been met, even though the full amount owing was not paid.
- A credit is made to Purchases Discounts to recognize the reduced amount owing because Algor has taken advantage of the terms offered. Purchases Discounts has a credit balance because it increases owner's equity.
- A credit is made to Cash to reduce that asset. The cash amount is equal to the purchase invoice amount of $19 688 less the discount of $368.

It is to Algor Computer Services' advantage to take all discounts when offered. In most cases, it would cost less for the firm to borrow the money from the bank to pay on the discount date (if it does not have enough cash to do so), than the amount of money to be lost if the discount is not taken. The loan from the bank could then be paid back at the end of the thirty days at a savings to the firm.

In the previous example, Algor Computer Services received a discount of $368. If Algor Computer Services did not have sufficient funds on hand to pay the invoice on the discount date, it could borrow the money from the bank on the 10th day in order to take full advantage of the discount. It would then pay the bank loan on the 30th day (the day that it would have had to pay the invoice because of the n/30), thus having borrowed the money for a total of 20 days. Assuming an interest rate of 10% on the loan, the cost of borrowing the money would be

$$\begin{aligned} \text{Interest} &= \text{Principal} \times \text{rate} \times \text{time} \\ &= \$19\,320 \times 10\% \times 20/365 \\ &= \$105.86 \end{aligned}$$

The firm received a $368.00 discount but paid interest of $105.86 to the bank. The net gain to Algor Computer Services is $262.14.

When a credit invoice is received from a supplier for a purchase return or allowance, the discount date is usually extended from the date of the credit invoice. If a purchase invoice is dated October 10 with terms of 2/10, n/30 and a subsequent credit invoice is received dated October 18, the ten days begin on October 18. The discount date becomes October 28.

October 10   Purchase Invoice received
October 18   Credit Invoice received
October 28   New discount date, 10 days after credit invoice

LESSON REVIEW

1. What is a merchandising business?
2. Name some merchandising businesses in your area.
3. Distinguish between a periodic inventory and a perpetual inventory.
4. What is a physical inventory? How often is one usually taken?
5. What does the balance of the Purchases account show? What does it not show?

6. What steps comprise the purchase cycle?
7. A business purchases office supplies for its own use. What account will be debited?
8. What advantages are there to purchasing on account instead of paying cash?
9. Distinguish between F.O.B. destination and F.O.B. shipping point.
10. Where can a purchase return be recorded if it is not recorded in Purchases Returns and Allowances? What is the disadvantage of recording the return this way?
11. What account should be credited when office equipment is returned?
12. What is the purpose of offering a cash discount?
13. For each of the following, indicate the type of account and why it is that type of account.
    (a) Purchases   (c) Purchases Returns and Allowances
    (b) Freight-in   (d) Purchases Discounts
14. For each of the following, indicate the type of balance the account normally has and why it has that type of balance.
    (a) Purchases   (c) Purchases Returns and Allowances
    (b) Freight-in   (d) Purchases Discounts

LESSON APPLICATIONS

Note that GST of 7 percent is already included in all items in this section. Also, all discounts apply to the base price.

15. Journalize the following transactions for Kanata Furniture Ltd. The source document for all transactions is a Purchase Invoice.
    Nov. 4   #793 from Capital Home Furniture Ltd., $4 200 for merchandise; terms 1/10, n/30.
         5   #492 from Willson Office Supplies Ltd., $220 for office supplies; terms n/30. The amount includes PST of 8 percent calculated on the base price.
         5   #933A from Modern Furniture Ltd., $800 for merchandise; terms 2/10, n/30.
         6   #1427 from Capital Home Furniture Ltd., $3 895 for merchandise; terms 2/10, n/30.
         7   #811 from Martin's Transport Ltd., $278 for transportation of merchandise to our business.

8   #814 from Modern Furniture Ltd., $1 498 for merchandise; terms 2/10, n/30.

16. Journalize each of the following transactions for Westway Auto Parts Ltd. Use a Purchases Returns and Allowances account where necessary.

Jan. 7   Purchase Invoice #248: From Master Auto Parts Ltd., $459 for merchandise; terms 2/10, n/30.
    7   Purchase Invoice #9494: From Willnot Auto Glass Ltd., $1 408 for merchandise; terms 2/10, n/30.
    8   Purchase Invoice #33: From Delaney Office Supplies Ltd., $428 for accounting supplies; terms n/30. The amount includes PST of 6 percent calculated on the base price.
    9   Purchase Invoice #883: From Quick Transport Ltd., $172 for transportation on incoming merchandise.
    9   Credit Memo #938 received: From Master Auto Parts Ltd., $459 for merchandise shown on Purchase Invoice #248 returned.
    10 Purchase Invoice #838: From Zesty Radiator Supplies Ltd., $1 042 for merchandise; terms 2/10, n/30.
    10 Purchase Invoice #9294: From Quick Transport Ltd., $221 for transportation on incoming merchandise; terms n/30.
    10 Credit Memo #499 received: From Willnot Auto Glass Ltd., $206 for allowance on Purchase Invoice #9494.

17. Complete the columns headed Discount Date and Amount Payable, assuming that the discount is taken and payments postmarked on the due date are eligible for discount.

	Purchase Invoice			Discount Date	Amount Payable
	Amount	Date	Terms		
(a)	$1 080.00	March 3	2/10, n/30		
(b)	550.50	March 10	EOM		
(c)	9 040.70	March 12	1/10, n/30		
(d)	8 020.50	March 24	2/10, n/30		
(e)	990.00	March 18	10 EOM		

18. Journalize each of the following transactions for Lover's Computer Centre. The source documents are all cheque copies.

Nov. 3   #688 for $756.00; on account to Merritt Computer Supplies for merchandise, Purchase Invoice #433, $770.40, less discount of $14.40.
    4   #689 for $1 498.00; monthly rent.
    4   #690 for $1 362.90; on account to Destiny Office Furniture for merchandise, Purchase Invoice #909, $1 388.86, less discount of $25.96.

5 #691 for $766.50; on account to Lincoln Computers for merchandise, Purchase Invoice #2366, $781.10, less discount of 2%.
6 #692 for $287.00; monthly hydro expense.
6 #693 for $1 007.00; on account to Merritt Computer Supplies for merchandise, Purchase Invoice #587, $1 016.50, less discount of 1%.
9 #694 for $2 457.00; on account to Lincoln Computers for merchandise, Purchase Invoice #2399, $2 503.80, less discount of $46.80.

19. Prepare journal entries to record payment of the purchase invoices received in Question 15. Assume that the discount is always taken, and that payment is made on the last date possible to take advantage of the discount. Where no discount is provided, date the payment thirty days after the invoice date.

20. (a) Set up the following T-accounts for Sandy's Casual Wear and enter the two balances given.
      101 Cash $14 339.00
      140 GST Recoverable
      202 Accounts Payable   6 391.00
      502 Purchases
      503 Freight-in
      504 Purchases Returns and Allowances
      505 Purchases Discounts
      615 Advertising Expense

(b) Journalize and post the following transactions.
July 4 Purchase Invoices:
#444 from Stateside Fashions, $2 503.80 for merchandise; terms 2/10, n/30.
#838 from Modern Fashions, $856.00 for merchandise; terms 2/10, n/30.
4 Credit Memo #215 received: From Waterton Fashions Ltd., $254.00 plus GST of $17.78 for allowance on Purchase Invoice #726; damaged shipment of merchandise.
5 Cheque Copy #491: $299.60 to *Vancouver Sun* for advertising.
5 Cheque Copy #492: $1 785.00 to Waterton Fashions Ltd., for Purchase Invoice #218, $1 819.00, less discount of $34.00.
8 Purchase Invoice #288: From Palisser Transport, $245.03 for transportation on incoming merchandise; n/30.
9 Credit Memo #212 received: From Stateside Fashions, $160.00 plus GST of $11.20 on Purchase Invoice #444 as some items were the incorrect size.

11 Cheque Copy #493: $189.00 to Palisser Transport, on account.
14 Cheque Copy #494: $840.00 to Modern Fashions, for Purchase Invoice #838, $856.00, less discount of $16.00.
16 Purchase Invoice #411: From Palisser Transport, $176.55 for transportation on incoming merchandise; n/30.
19 Cheque Copy #495: $2 289.00 on account to Stateside Fashions for Purchase Invoice #444, $2 503.80, less Credit Memo #212, $171.20, less discount of $43.60.

21. (a) Calculate the amount lost to the firm by *not* taking advantage of the following discounts.

Invoice Total	Terms	Amount Lost
$4 250.00	2/10, n/30	
1 350.00	1/10, n/60	
9 445.00	3/10, n/60	

(b) Calculate the amount gained by a firm that borrows from a lending institution to pay the following invoices. Assume payments postmarked by the tenth day are eligible for discount.

Invoice Total	Terms	Loan Rate	Amount Gained
$3 490.00	2/10, n/30	10%	
2 325.00	1/10, n/30	12%	
875.00	1/10, n/60	11.5%	
1 450.00	2/10, n/60	11%	

9.2 Sales Transactions for a Merchandising Business Using a Periodic Inventory System

Sales

The new accounts used by merchandising businesses for recording items related to sales parallel those used for purchases. They are
- Sales
- Delivery Expense
- Sales Returns and Allowances
- Sales Discounts

The sales and collection cycle consists of the sale, establishing the account receivable if the sale is made on account, and the subsequent collection of cash. Obviously, a business would want to make the sales and collection cycle as short as possible, for the rapid collection of the accounts receivable means that the money can be used either to reduce liabilities or to purchase more merchandise.

FIGURE 9-4 THE SALES AND COLLECTION CYCLE

```
      1.                    2.                      3.

   Sale made         Account receivable       Collection of cash
                       is recorded              from customer
   ─────────────────────────────────────────────────────────────▶  Time
```

Sales: *the revenue account used to record the sale of merchandise.*

The revenue account used to record the sale of merchandise is **Sales**. The sale of a good results in the inflow of an asset, in the form of either cash or an account receivable. Revenue accounts increase owner's equity, so they have a credit balance. This account is similar to Algor Computer Services' accounts for Computer Services and Software Lessons, which were the only revenue accounts used before the firm started to sell goods.

The sale of goods and services must also be increased by 7 percent, the amount of the goods and services tax (GST). Exempt from the GST are the following items: basic groceries, tutoring, and financial services.

Except in Alberta, provincial sales tax is added to the sale price for most merchandise. Each province has its own list of merchandise that is exempt from taxation. The elimination of the provincial sales tax on a particular item is meant to assist that industry, for more people will buy the good if there is no tax on it. Some tax exemptions are introduced to assist certain groups of people, such as those with small children, for the tax is frequently eliminated on their clothing.

As noted in Chapter 6, in British Columbia, Saskatchewan, Manitoba, and Ontario, the provincial sales tax is calculated as a percentage of the base price, excluding the GST. New Brunswick, Nova Scotia, Prince Edward Island, and Newfoundland include the GST when calculating the provincial sales tax. Quebec has merged its provincial sales tax with the GST.

Sales of merchandise are made for cash and on account. For cash sales, the source document will be either a cash sales slip, or a cash register summary. For sales on account, the source document will be a sales invoice.

THE FACTS SPEAK...

Sales revenue for the year ending December 31, 1989

IBM	$41 586 million
Shell Canada Ltd.	4 844 million
Hudson's Bay Company	1 859 million

Oct. 2 Sales Invoice #55-0592: To Gary Thom for $977.50, sale of $850.00 plus GST of $59.50 and PST of $68.00, for a printer.

GENERAL JOURNAL

PAGE 624

DATE 1992		PARTICULARS	PR	DEBIT	CREDIT
Oct.	2	Accounts Receivable	120	977 50	
		Sales	420		850 —
		GST Payable	230		59 50
		PST Payable	240		68 —
		Sales Invoice #55-0592, Gary Thom			

GENERAL LEDGER

Accounts Receivable	120
dr.	cr.
Oct. 2 977.50	

Sales	420
dr.	cr.
	Oct. 2 850.00

GST Payable	230
dr.	cr.
	Oct. 2 59.50

PST Payable	240
dr.	cr.
	Oct. 2 68.00

The explanation for the entry is as follows:
- A debit is made to Accounts Receivable to increase that asset, since the business now has a claim on Gary Thom.
- A credit is made to Sales to record the increase in revenue. There has been an inflow of an asset, an account receivable, from the sale of a good. Revenue accounts increase on the credit side because they increase owner's equity.
- A credit is made to GST Payable to record that liability. The federal government has a claim on the business due to the collection of the goods and services tax. The liability will be paid at a later date.
- A credit is made to PST Payable to record that liability. The provincial government has a claim on the business because Algor collects the sales tax. The liability will be paid at a later date.

Sales of items other than merchandise are not recorded in the Sales account. If Algor Computer Services decides to sell one of its old office desks, it will make a debit to Cash for the amount received, and credits to Office Equipment, GST Payable, and PST Payable. If the credit is not made to the Office Equipment account, the account will continue to include the undepreciated value of the desk in its debit balance, which indicates that the business still owns it.

It should also be noted that a withdrawal of merchandise from the business by the owner is not recorded by a credit to Sales. If the owner has taken the item for personal use, it is no longer available for sale to customers. Since the Purchases account is used to record the cost of goods purchased for sale to customers, the cost of the item must be removed from the Purchases account. Note that the owner's Drawings account is also charged for the amount of the sales taxes that must be paid on the withdrawal. The entry to record such a withdrawal is as follows:

GENERAL JOURNAL

PAGE 624

DATE 1992		PARTICULARS	PR	DEBIT	CREDIT
Oct.	2	V. Marshall, Drawings		212 75	
		Purchases			185 —
		GST Payable			12 95
		PST Payable			14 80
		Memo #489, to record withdrawal of merchandise			
		by owner			

Delivery Expense

Delivery Expense: the expense account used to record the cost of delivery of items to customers.

Businesses may hire a firm to handle deliveries for them. The expense of delivering items is recorded in an account called **Delivery Expense**. It is an expense account because it is something used in the normal operation of the business. The entry to record a delivery expense is shown below.

Oct. 2 Cheque Copy #973: Paid $211.86 to City Wide Delivery, $198.00 for delivery of sales for the week plus GST of $13.86.

GENERAL JOURNAL

PAGE 624

DATE 1992		PARTICULARS	PR	DEBIT	CREDIT
Oct.	2	Delivery Expense	685	198 —	
		GST Recoverable	135	13 86	
		Cash	100		211 86
		Cheque Copy #973, City Wide Delivery			

GENERAL LEDGER

Delivery Expense	685	GST Recoverable	135	Cash	100
dr.	cr.	dr.	cr.	dr.	cr.
Oct. 2 198.00		Oct. 2 13.86			Oct. 2 211.86

The explanation for the entry is as follows:
- A debit is made to Delivery Expense to record the expense of delivering merchandise to customers. Delivery Expense reduces owner's equity and therefore a debit entry is made.
- A debit to GST Recoverable is recorded because Algor receives an input tax credit.
- A credit to Cash records the reduction of that asset.

Sales Returns and Allowances

Frequently, for a variety of reasons, a customer will return a good or ask for an allowance. The policy of businesses concerning returns varies: some firms advertise that customer satisfaction is guaranteed or the money is refunded. Others will only give a credit note for use in the store to buy something else. Finally, some do not allow any returns, and all sales are considered final.

The contra-revenue account used to record returns or allowances on sales is **Sales Returns and Allowances**. It is termed a contra-revenue account because it cancels the inflow of assets from the sale of a good. It has a debit balance because it reduces equity. Sales returns and allowances may be in the form of a cash refund, for which the source document would be a cash refund slip or a cheque. If the return or allowance is on account, a credit memo would be issued to the customer.

Since many sales are made on account, it is more common that a return or allowance reduces the balance of Accounts Receivable. A business will not give a cash refund if the original sale was made on account. If it were to do so, a person could buy a good on account and return it the next day for cash. Since statements showing the transactions on a customer's account are only sent out monthly, the customer would then have use of the business's money until the due date on the statement. The entry to show a return is shown below.

> **Sales Returns and Allowances:** the contra-revenue account used to record returns of or allowances on sales.

Oct. 8   Issued Credit Memo #188: To Gary Thom, $977.50, for return of printer, Sales Invoice #55-0592, $850.00, GST Payable $59.50, PST Payable $68.00.

GENERAL JOURNAL

PAGE 625

DATE 1992		PARTICULARS	PR	DEBIT	CREDIT
Oct.	8	Sales Returns and Allowances	425	850 —	
		GST Payable	230	59 50	
		PST Payable	240	68 —	
		Accounts Receivable	120		977 50
		Credit Memo #188, return by Gary Thom on Sales			
		Invoice #55-0592			

GENERAL LEDGER

Sales Returns and Allowances	425		GST Payable	230
dr.	cr.		dr.	cr.
Oct. 8 850.00			Oct. 8 59.50	

PST Payable	240		Accounts Receivable	120
dr.	cr.		dr.	cr.
Oct. 8 68.00				Oct. 8 977.50

The explanation for the entry is as follows:
- A debit is made to Sales Returns and Allowances to show that the revenue received from the sale of goods has been refunded via the credit memo.
- A debit is made to GST Payable and to PST Payable because the claim that the governments had on the business for sales taxes has been cancelled.
- Accounts Receivable is credited in order to reduce that asset.

The balance of the Sales Returns and Allowances account will be deducted from the balance of the Sales account on the income statement, as illustrated later. Some businesses prefer to make a debit to the Sales account for returns and allowances rather than have a separate account. The advantage of having a separate account is that the amount of returns and allowances is evident to management, and not hidden in the balance of the sales account. Internal control is better served by having a separate account, for management should take action if a large balance or sudden increase occurs in the Sales Returns and Allowances account. A large number of returns may indicate a number of problems: the products sold may be of poor quality, the sales people may be doing a poor job at the time of the sale, or the return policy may be too liberal.

Sales Discounts

When a sale on account is made by a retailer, a discount may be offered to encourage quick payment. Such discounts are not offered as frequently on sales to the final consumer as they are to wholesalers and retailers by manufacturers. Firms that do offer the discount may offer a different percentage to certain customers, based on the dollar volume of sales made to them. The amount is usually negotiated between the seller and the customer. It should be noted that there is no discount allowed on GST or PST owed to governments. Therefore, sales discounts will all be calculated on the base price only.

The account used to record the discount is called **Sales Discounts**, or Discount on Sales, or Discounts Allowed. Businesses that do not offer such a discount will, of course, not have this account. The Sales Discounts account is a contra-revenue account for it reduces the inflow

Sales Discounts: the contra-revenue account used to record the reduction of the claim on a customer, due to receipt of the payment within a specified time.

of assets from the sale of a good or service. Because of this, it will be deducted from the Sales account on the income statement.

The entries required for a sale on account and a sales discount are shown below.

Oct. 3   Sales Invoice #55-0593: $517.50, sale of merchandise on account to V. Logan; sale of $450.00, GST $31.50, PST $36.00; terms 2/10, n/30.

GENERAL JOURNAL

PAGE 624

DATE 1992		PARTICULARS	PR	DEBIT	CREDIT
Oct.	3	Accounts Receivable	120	517 50	
		Sales	420		450 —
		GST Payable	230		31 50
		PST Payable	240		36 —
		Sales Invoice #55-0593, V. Logan			

GENERAL LEDGER

Accounts Receivable 120		Sales 420
dr.	cr.	dr. cr.
Oct. 3 517.50		Oct. 3 450.00

GST Payable 230		PST Payable 240
dr.	cr.	dr. cr.
	Oct. 3 31.50	Oct. 3 36.00

If Logan pays by October 13, she is entitled to a 2 percent discount.

Oct. 12   Cash Receipt Slip #33-6730: Received $508.50 from V. Logan on account for Sales Invoice #55-0593 for $517.50 less discount of $9.00.

GENERAL JOURNAL

PAGE 626

DATE 1992		PARTICULARS	PR	DEBIT	CREDIT
Oct.	12	Cash	100	508 50	
		Sales Discounts	430	9 —	
		Accounts Receivable	120		517 50
		Cash Receipt Slip #33-6730, V. Logan for Sales			
		Invoice #55-0593 less discount			

GENERAL LEDGER

Cash 100		Sales Discounts 430		Accounts Receivable 120
dr.	cr.	dr.	cr.	dr. cr.
Oct. 12 508.50		Oct. 12 9.00		Oct. 3 517.50 Oct. 12 517.50

Note that in the T-accounts, which show the entry posted, the claim on V. Logan has been reduced to nil.

The explanation for the entry is as follows:
- A debit is made to Cash to increase that asset.
- A debit is made to Sales Discounts to record the reduction of the inflow of the asset cash, which reduces revenue. **Note:** the sales discount is calculated on the price of the goods excluding taxes.
- A credit is made to Accounts Receivable in order to reduce that asset. Note that the claim on V. Logan has been reduced by the total of the original sales invoice.

Taking a Discount After the Discount Date

Sometimes the business may receive payment from the customer after the discount date, but the customer has already taken the discount amount off his or her cheque. The business then has the right to accept the cheque as full payment, or to require the customer to pay the balance. The entry to record payment if Logan had taken the discount but was not entitled to it would be:

Oct. 14   Cash Receipt Slip #33-6730: Received $508.50 on account from V. Logan in payment of Sales Invoice #55-0593 for $517.50. Logan was not entitled to the discount.

GENERAL JOURNAL

PAGE 627

DATE 1992		PARTICULARS	PR	DEBIT	CREDIT
Oct.	14	Cash	100	508 50	
		Accounts Receivable	120		508 50
		Cash Receipt Slip #33-6730, V. Logan on account,			
		discount not allowed			

When the above entry is posted to Logan's account, the balance will show that the business still has a claim on her for the discount that she took. She will notice that the discount of $9.00 was not allowed when she receives her monthly statement from Algor Computer Services.

GENERAL LEDGER

Cash		100		Accounts Receivable		120
dr.		cr.		dr.		cr.
Oct. 14 508.50				Oct. 3 517.50		Oct. 14 508.50

Sales Discount Combined with a Sales Return or Allowance

When a customer is allowed a sales return or allowance, the amount owing will be equal to the amount of the original invoice less the return or allowance. A sale of $520 (not taking PST and GST into account) with an allowance of $200 leaves a net amount owing of $320. For discount purposes, and assuming a 2/10, n/30 offer of terms, the percentage will be calculated on the $320. The discount date is adjusted to 10 days from the date of the credit memo, recognizing the return or allowance.

Oct. 13   Cash Receipt Slip #33-6742: Received $361.60 on account from S. Szabo in payment of Sales Invoice #511 for $598.00 (sale of $520.00, GST of $36.40, and PST of $41.60), less Credit Memo #93 (return of $200.00, GST of $14.00, and PST of $16.00). A discount of $6.40 had been taken.

GENERAL JOURNAL

PAGE 626

DATE 1992		PARTICULARS	PR	DEBIT	CREDIT
Oct.	13	Cash	100	361 60	
		Sales Discounts	430	6 40	
		Accounts Receivable	120		368 —
		Cash Receipt Slip #33-6742, from S. Szabo			

GENERAL LEDGER

Cash		100	Sales Discounts		430	Accounts Receivable			120
dr.		cr.	dr.		cr.	dr.		cr.	
Oct. 13 361.60			Oct. 13 6.40			Oct. 5 598.00		Oct. 7 230.00	
								13 368.00	

Bad Debts Allowance

The last step in the sales and collection cycle, the collection of cash from the customer, does not always occur. The customer may have "**skipped**", which means that he or she has left without paying their account, and cannot be traced. Also, the customer may have had to declare bankruptcy, due to their inability to pay their debts. If it is known for certain that there will not be a collection of an account receivable, it is declared a bad debt, and written off.

In order to follow the matching principle, an adjusting entry is prepared at the end of the fiscal period to match the expense of the

A skip: *a person who cannot be traced in order to collect an account.*

Net accounts receivable: the difference between the balances of Accounts Receivable and Allowance for Doubtful Accounts.

estimated bad debts for the period with the corresponding revenue. An account called **Allowance for Doubtful Accounts** is used as an estimate of the bad debts that may result from the accounts receivable. This account is combined with Accounts Receivable on the balance sheet, with the difference between the two called the **net accounts receivable**. The presentation of the two accounts on the balance sheet is shown below.

FIGURE 9-5 A PARTIAL BALANCE SHEET FOR ALGOR COMPUTER SERVICES, SHOWING THE PRESENTATION OF ALLOWANCE FOR DOUBTFUL ACCOUNTS

Algor Computer Services
Partial Balance Sheet
as at May 31, 1993

Current Assets
Accounts Receivable   53 800
Less: Allowance for Doubtful Accounts   6 000   47 800

Allowance for Doubtful Accounts: a contra-asset account showing the estimated amount of accounts receivable that will not be collected.

Allowance for Doubtful Accounts is a contra-asset account, for it reduces the value of the asset Accounts Receivable. The figure $47 800 is the net realizable value. On many balance sheets, Allowance for Doubtful Accounts will not be shown separately, but rather combined with Accounts Receivable, to show only the net realizable value. This procedure is followed because the dollar amount of the bad debts is usually insignificant. However, should the amount have made a significant impact on the financial results of the fiscal period, it should either be shown on the balance sheet, or in footnotes to the balance sheet.

Estimating Bad Debts

Since the allowance for bad debts must be estimated, a consistent method must be followed in order to determine the amount from one fiscal year to the next. There are basically two methods that are followed: the income statement method, and the balance sheet method. It should be noted that each method of calculation yields a different figure for possible bad debts.

"*The income statement method of estimating the allowance for bad debts uses a percentage of the net sales.*"

(a) The income statement method assumes that a certain percentage of net sales will result in bad debts. At the end of the fiscal period, this percentage is applied, and an adjusting entry is made. To arrive at net sales, sales returns and allowances, and sales discounts must be subtracted from sales. For example, a firm that has net sales of $300 000 may estimate that 2 percent of those sales will not be collectable.

Therefore, the firm estimates that $6 000 worth of bad debts will result from sales of the current year. The reason for calling it the income statement method is that the calculation is based on figures found on the income statement. An adjusting entry is then made, as follows:

GENERAL JOURNAL

PAGE 701

DATE 1993		PARTICULARS	PR	DEBIT	CREDIT
May	31	Bad Debts Expense	715	6 000 —	
		Allowance for Doubtful Accounts	125		6 000 —
		To record estimate of bad debts for the year, 2 percent			
		of net sales			

GENERAL LEDGER

Bad Debts Expense	715	Allowance for Doubtful Accounts	125
dr.	cr.	dr.	cr.
May 31 6 000			balance remaining from previous year 400
			May 31 6 000

The explanation for the entry is as follows:
- A debit is made to Bad Debts Expense to follow the matching principle; the expense will be matched with the corresponding revenue from the sales made during the current fiscal period.
- A credit is made to Allowance for Doubtful Accounts to increase that contra-asset. The balance of $400 remains from the previous year, and is not considered when calculating the allowance. The Allowance for Doubtful Accounts will have a balance of $6 400 to start the next fiscal period.

In order to determine the percentage that should be used in the calculation, a business would examine its bad debts experience in previous years. As well, industry averages can be obtained from Statistics Canada or from collection agencies.

"*The balance sheet method of estimating bad debts uses an ageing of the accounts receivable.*"

(b) The balance sheet method uses an ageing of accounts receivable in order to estimate the bad debts. The method gets its name from the fact that Accounts Receivable is found on the balance sheet. In order to calculate the amount of the adjusting entry, a two step process is followed: the accounts receivable are aged, and then a percentage for the bad debts is applied to each age category.

FIGURE 9-6 AGEING OF ACCOUNTS RECEIVABLE FOR ALGOR COMPUTER SERVICES

Ageing of Accounts Receivable
May 31, 1993

Customer	Total	Not Yet Due	Number of Days Past Due			
			1-30	31-60	61-90	Over 90
Carling Real Estate	$ 23 400	$12 200	$10 400	$ 800		
Devonshire	4 300	2 800	700			$ 800
Martineau	12 400	12 400				
Sambino	10 300	6 300		2 000	$2 000	
Others	87 700	63 400	11 300	6 500	4 600	1 900
	$138 100	$97 100	$22 400	$9 300	$6 600	$2 700

The percentage applied to each category represents the estimated percentage of the outstanding receivables that will not be collected.

FIGURE 9-7 CALCULATION OF ALLOWANCE FOR DOUBTFUL ACCOUNTS, USING THE AGEING OF ACCOUNTS RECEIVABLE (BALANCE SHEET) METHOD

Calculation of Uncollectable Amounts
May 31, 1993

	Accounts Receivable	Estimated Loss	Uncollectable Amount
Not yet due	$ 97 100	1.5%	$1 456.50
1-30 days	22 400	3.0	672.00
31-60 days	9 300	5.0	465.00
61-90 days	6 600	10.0	660.00
Over 90 days	2 700	35.0	945.00
	$138 100		$4 198.50

Once the amount of the uncollectable receivables has been determined, the amount of the adjusting entry must be determined. Using the balance sheet method (or ageing of accounts receivable method), it is necessary to consider the balance in Allowance for Doubtful Accounts. The reason for this is that the ageing method includes all accounts receivable, even those from previous periods. Therefore, if the business wants the Allowance for Doubtful Accounts account to have a credit balance of $4 198.50, and it has a credit balance before the adjustment of $400, then the adjusting entry amount should be $3 798.50. The calculation and adjusting entry are illustrated below.

If a credit balance of	$ 400.00 (cr.)	is already in the account
Adjusting entry required	3 798.50 (cr.)	to bring the account to the desired balance
Resulting (desired) balance of Allowance for Doubtful Accounts	$4 198.50 (cr.)	

The journal entry would then be:

GENERAL JOURNAL

PAGE 701

DATE 1993		PARTICULARS	PR	DEBIT	CREDIT
May	31	Bad Debts Expense	715	3 798 50	
		Allowance for Doubtful Accounts	125		3 798 50
		To record estimate of bad debts for the year			

GENERAL LEDGER

Bad Debts Expense	715		Allowance for Doubtful Accounts	125
dr.	cr.		dr.	cr.
May 31 3 798.50				balance remaining from previous year 400.00
				May 31 3 798.50

The explanation for the entry is as follows:
- A debit is made to Bad Debts Expense to follow the matching principle; the expense will be matched with the corresponding revenue from the sales during the current fiscal period.
- A credit is made to Allowance for Doubtful Accounts to increase that contra-asset. The balance of $400 remains from the previous year, and is not considered when calculating the allowance. However, it is considered when calculating the adjustment for the current year. The Allowance for Doubtful Accounts will have a balance of $4 198.50 to start the next fiscal period.

If, instead, the Allowance for Doubtful Accounts account has a debit balance, the adjusting entry must be for more than the estimated uncollectables in order that the account will have a credit balance. The following illustrates the calculation and adjusting entry that would have been required if there had been a debit balance of $600 in Allowance for Doubtful Accounts and the desired balance was still $4 198.50.

If a debit balance of	$ 600.00 (dr.)	is already in the account
Adjusting entry required	4 798.50 (cr.)	to bring the account to the desired balance
Resulting (desired) balance of Allowance for Doubtful Accounts	$4 198.50 (cr.)	

GENERAL JOURNAL

PAGE 701

DATE 1993		PARTICULARS	PR	DEBIT	CREDIT
May	31	Bad Debts Expense	715	4 798 50	
		Allowance for Doubtful Accounts	125		4 798 50
		To record estimate of bad debts for the year			

GENERAL LEDGER

Bad Debts Expense	715
dr.	cr.
May 31 4 798.50	

Allowance for Doubtful Accounts	125
dr.	cr.
balance remaining from previous year 600.00	May 31 4 798.50

The explanation for the entry is as follows:
- A debit is made to Bad Debts Expense to follow the matching principle; the expense will be matched with the corresponding revenue from the sales during the current fiscal period.
- A credit is made to Allowance for Doubtful Accounts to increase that contra-asset. The debit balance of $600 remains from the previous year, and is not considered when calculating the allowance. However, it is considered when calculating the adjustment for the current year. The Allowance for Doubtful Accounts will have a balance of $4 198.50 to start the next fiscal period.

Writing off an Uncollectable

To write off: to cancel the claim on the customer by bringing the balance of that account receivable to nil.

During the subsequent year, accounts receivable will be written off against the allowance that was established. To **write off** means to cancel the claim on the customer by bringing the balance of that account receivable to nil. An account is not written off unless it is certain that it is uncollectable. The following example illustrates the entry required.

June 14 Memo #525: The account of W. Deka, in the amount of $250, was determined to be uncollectable.

GENERAL JOURNAL

PAGE 706

DATE 1993		PARTICULARS	PR	DEBIT	CREDIT
June	14	Allowance for Doubtful Accounts	125	250 —	
		Accounts Receivable	120		250 —
		To write off the account of W. Deka			

GENERAL LEDGER

Allowance for Doubtful Accounts	125
dr.	cr.
June 14 250.00	May 31 4 198.50

Accounts Receivable	120
dr.	cr.
Feb. 16 250.00	June 14 250.00

It is important to note that the net accounts receivable amount does not change, for both the Allowance for Doubtful Accounts and the Accounts Receivable have changed.

	Before write off	After write off
Accounts Receivable	$138 100.00	$137 850.00
Less Allowance for Doubtful Accounts	4 198.50	3 948.50
Net Accounts Receivable	$133 901.50	$133 901.50

Due to the fact that the Allowance for Doubtful Accounts is an estimate made at the end of the fiscal year, the number of uncollectables resulting during the next fiscal year may or may not match that estimate. If the uncollectables are overestimated, then the Allowance for Doubtful Accounts account will have a credit balance at the end of the following year. If the uncollectables are underestimated, then the Allowance for Doubtful Accounts account will have a debit balance at the end of the following year. This balance must be taken into account when making the adjusting entry at the end of the year, if the balance sheet method of estimating the uncollectables is being used.

Should an uncollectable account be found later to be collectable, the entry to write it off should be reversed. A separate entry would then be required to record the collection of the account receivable, by making a debit to Cash and a credit to Accounts Receivable.

July 30 Cash Receipt Slip #33-7654: W. Deka submitted a cheque for $250 to pay an account that had been written off June 14.

GENERAL JOURNAL

PAGE 728

DATE 1993		PARTICULARS	PR	DEBIT	CREDIT
July	30	Accounts Receivable	120	250 —	
		Allowance for Doubtful Accounts	125		250 —
		To reverse the entry of June 14			
	30	Cash	100	250 —	
		Accounts Receivable	120		250 —
		Cash Receipt Slip #33-7654, payment on account			
		from W. Deka			

GENERAL LEDGER

Accounts Receivable	120		Allowance for Doubtful Accounts	125		Cash	100
dr.	cr.		dr.	cr.		dr.	cr.
July 30 250	July 30 250			July 30 250		July 30 250	

The explanation for the first entry is as follows:
- A debit is made to Accounts Receivable to reverse the removal of W. Deka's account from the total accounts receivable, since payment on account has been received.
- A credit is made to Allowance for Doubtful Accounts to decrease that contra-asset.

The explanation for the second entry is as follows:
- A debit is made to Cash to record W. Deka's payment on account.
- A credit is made to Accounts Receivable to remove Algor's claim on W. Deka.

LESSON REVIEW

22. What account is used to record the sale of merchandise?

23. What are the steps in the sales cycle?

24. What assets usually flow into a business from the sale of merchandise?

25. Contrast Freight-in with Delivery Expense.

26. What policies can a firm use regarding sales returns?

27. What two methods can be used to record sales returns and allowances?

28. On what amount is the sales discount calculated?

29. How will customers know that they took a discount to which they were not entitled?

30. For each of the following, indicate the type of account and why it is that type of account.
    (a) Sales
    (b) Delivery Expense
    (c) Sales Returns and Allowances
    (d) Sales Discounts

31. For each of the following, indicate the type of balance that the account normally has, and why it has that type of balance.
    (a) Sales
    (b) Delivery Expense
    (c) Sales Returns and Allowances
    (d) Sales Discounts

32. What is the purpose of the Allowance for Doubtful Accounts account?

33. When is the balance for the Allowance for Doubtful Accounts account established?

34. What type of account is the Allowance for Doubtful Accounts? Why?

35. What are the two methods of calculating the allowance for doubtful accounts? Which one considers the year-end balance in the account? Why does it?

36. Describe the two steps in calculating the allowance for doubtful accounts using the balance sheet method.

37. What is the effect on the net value of accounts receivable of a write-off of a bad debt?

Lesson Applications

38. Calculate the goods and services tax (GST) using 7 percent and the provincial sales tax (PST) for each of the following sales. Use the sales tax percentage in your province. For British Columbia, Saskatchewan, Manitoba, and Ontario, calculate the provincial sales tax on the base price; for the other provinces, calculate the provincial sales tax on the base price plus the GST.

	Sale	**GST**	**PST**		**Sale**	**GST**	**PST**
(a)	$167.84			(e)	$1 993.07		
(b)	$11.24			(f)	$633.91		
(c)	$749.51			(g)	$1.16		
(d)	$66.94			(h)	$91.77		

39. Journalize the following transactions for Bayview Furniture Ltd. The source document for all transactions is a sales invoice. All sales are subject to the 7 percent GST and a 6 percent provincial sales tax on the base price.

   Nov. 4 #873 to D. Mehta, sale of $520, plus taxes.
        4 #874 to R. Wang, sale of $725, plus taxes.
        5 #875 to V. Bleeker, sale of unused office supplies, $120, plus taxes.
        5 #876 to E. Holuj, sale of $917, plus taxes.
        6 #877 to V. Szpakowski, sale of $1 320, plus taxes.

40. Journalize each of the following transactions for Westway Auto Parts Ltd. Use a Sales Returns and Allowances account where necessary. Calculate the taxes where indicated. Provincial sales tax is 8 percent applied to the base price. GST is 7 percent.

   Jan. 7 Sales Invoices:
           #183, to E. Tarnaske, sale of $29.50, plus taxes.
           #184, to T. Bennett, sale of $94.20, plus taxes.
           #185, to R. Blunt, sale of $173.00, plus taxes.
        7 Purchase Invoice #249: From City Wide Delivery for delivery of sales to customers, $325.00 plus GST.
        8 Sales Invoices:
           #186, to M. St. Aubin, sale of $93.00, plus taxes.
           #187, to N. Teng, sale of $422.80, plus taxes.
        8 Credit Memos:
           #26, issued to T. Bennett, $33.00 plus taxes for return on Sales Invoice #184.
           #27, issued to E. Tarnaske, $93.00 plus taxes on Sales Invoice #173.
       10 Memo #44: The owner, A. Westway, withdrew $68.00 worth of merchandise for personal use. (Don't forget to calculate the taxes she owes.)

41. (a) Set up the following T-accounts for Sandy's Casual Wear and enter the balance given for cash and accounts receivable.
   101 Cash, $14 339; 102 Accounts Receivable, $9 641; 120 GST Recoverable; 140 Office Supplies; 210 Accounts Payable; 250 GST Payable; 260 PST Payable; 400 Sales; 401 Sales Returns and Allowances; 402 Sales Discounts; 508 Delivery Expense.

(b) Journalize and post the following transactions, using page 23 of the General Journal. Calculate the taxes where indicated. Provincial sales tax is 7 percent, calculated on the base price; GST is 7 percent; terms on all sales invoices are 2/10, n/30.

Mar. 10 Sales Invoices:
#551 to C. Muscari, $324.00 plus taxes.
#552 to G. Newhouse, $219.00 plus taxes.

12 Sales Invoices:
#553 to L. Matheson, $227.00 plus taxes.
#554 to A. Burrows, $126.00 plus taxes.

12 Credit Memo #58, issued to C. Muscari, return of all the merchandise from Sales Invoice #551.

15 Sales Invoice #555, to R. Brugmans, $691.00 plus taxes.

15 Cash Refund #45: Refund of $117.00, plus taxes, to B. Morrow.

15 Cash Sales Slips #409 to #427: Sales of $2 439.00 plus taxes.

15 Purchase Invoice #83-134: From Alliance Delivery, $57.00 plus GST for deliveries to customers for the first half of the month.

16 Credit Memo #59: Issued to A. Burrows, allowance of $56.00, plus taxes on Sales Invoice #554.

18 Sales Invoice #556, to A. Coutts, $153.30 plus taxes.

20 Cash Receipt Slip #26: From G. Newhouse, total account reduction of $249.66 for Sales Invoice #552; discount of $4.38 on the sale, cash payment of $245.28.

21 Sales Invoice #557: Sale of unused office supplies to Prairie Travel, $142.00 plus taxes.

22 Cash Sales Slips #428 to #459: Sales of $3 893.00 plus taxes.

22 Sales Invoices:
#558 to C. Lakhani, $922.00 plus taxes.
#559 to K. Zoehner, $258.00 plus taxes.

26 Cash Receipt Slip #27: From A. Burrows, total account reduction of $79.80 for Sales Invoice #554; discount of $1.40 on the sale, cash payment of $78.40.

28 Cash Receipt Slip #28: From A. Coutts, total account reduction of $174.76 for Sales Invoice #556; discount of $3.07 on the sale, cash payment of $171.69.

31 Purchase Invoice #83-824: From Alliance Delivery, $122.00 plus GST for deliveries to customers for the last half of the month.

42. Prepare the adjusting entry that will be required for each of the following situations. Assume that the year-end balance in Allowance for Doubtful Accounts is a $450 credit.
   (a) Net sales are $456 000. Estimated uncollectables are 2 percent of net sales.
   (b) The ageing of accounts receivable indicates that the balance in Allowance for Doubtful Accounts should be $10 200.

43. Prepare the adjusting entry that will be required for each of the following situations. Assume that the year-end balance in Allowance for Doubtful Accounts is a $375 debit.
   (a) Net sales are $520 000. Estimated uncollectables are 1.5 percent of net sales.
   (b) The ageing of accounts receivable indicates that the balance in Allowance for Doubtful Accounts should be $8 200.

44. The following are the balances found in the respective accounts shown at the beginning of the fiscal year:
   Accounts Receivable $224 000
   Allowance for Doubtful Accounts   4 600
   During the year, the following events occurred. Prepare journal entries to record each of the events. Use the current date for your entries.
   (a) $4 800 of accounts receivable were written off.
   (b) An account for $115 that was previously written off was collected.
   (c) An ageing of the accounts receivable indicated that Allowance for Doubtful Accounts should have a balance of $5 350.

9.3 Completing the Accounting Cycle for a Merchandising Business Using a Periodic Inventory System

In order to prepare the financial statements for a merchandising business that follows a periodic inventory system, it is necessary to take a **physical inventory** of the goods on hand on the date for which the statements are prepared. The goods are first counted, and then the cost price is applied to each good to find the total dollar value of the inventory. This process is time consuming, and frequently requires that the business close for a day or that the inventory be taken on a non-business day. Part-time help is sometimes hired so

Physical inventory: a counting of the merchandise on hand.

The Facts Speak...

Merchandise inventory of goods available for sale, 1989 (in millions)
Imperial Oil Limited	$1 130
Sears Canada Inc.	807
Ford Motor Company of Canada, Limited	457

that the process can be completed quickly. The two steps involved are outlined below.

Counting the goods: Inventory counters are assigned to various areas of a business in order to count the merchandise on hand. Along with each counter is a person who records the information on an Inventory Record similar to the following:

FIGURE 9-8 AN INVENTORY RECORD, USED TO TAKE A PHYSICAL INVENTORY

Inventory Record

Page Number _____ of _____

Date _____ Location _____

Counter _____ Checked by _____

Supervisor _____

Bin/storage/location No. _____

Stock Number	Quantity	Price	Total

When the goods are counted, the quantity is entered on a prenumbered tag that is left with the merchandise so that it is not double counted. At the end of the inventory, the tags are collected and the numerical sequence is checked to ensure that no tags are missing.

Pricing inventory: For pricing the merchandise, the cost price, or some other objective cost, must be used. (The study of inventory pricing is left to more advanced accounting courses.) In some businesses the process of recording the cost price on an inventory record is simple, for the price already appears on the price tag in a coded form. The code is used so that customers will not know the cost price of the item.

Once the ending inventory is known, it will be entered on the income statement and the balance sheet as shown later.

The Income Statement for a Merchandising Business

The calculation of net income for a service business is different from the calculation of net income for a merchandising business. Not only does the merchandising business incur normal operating expenses, but it must also buy the merchandise. If Algor Computer Services were to calculate the net income on the sale of *one* of its computers, the following calculation would be made:

Revenue	$4 560
Cost of the computer	2 320
Gross Profit	$2 240
Expenses involved in the sale	935
Net Income	$1 305

The following calculation applies to the above:

Revenue
− Cost of Goods Sold
Gross Profit
− Expenses
Net Income

Let us examine the three sections, revenue, cost, and expenses, in the order in which they appear on the income statement.

Revenue

The revenue section of an income statement for Algor Computer Services shows the following accounts:
- Sales, which is an inflow of assets from the sale of goods, and Computer Services and Software Lessons, which are an inflow of assets from the sale of services. These are the revenue accounts.
- Sales Returns and Allowances, which is a reduction in the inflow of assets from the sale of goods, and Refunds which is a reduction in the inflow of assets from the sale of services. These are contra-revenue accounts.
- Sales Discounts, which is a reduction in the inflow of assets from the sale of goods. This is a contra-revenue account.

The following revenue section of an income statement shows these accounts in proper accounting form:

FIGURE 9-9 THE REVENUE SECTION OF AN INCOME STATEMENT FOR ALGOR COMPUTER SERVICES

Algor Computer Services
Income Statement
for the year ended May 31, 1993

Revenue:		
Computer Services		$312 400
Software Lessons		51 300
Sales		176 337
Gross Revenue		540 037
Less: Refunds	$2 140	
Sales Returns and Allowances	1 364	
Sales Discounts	2 267	5 771
Net Revenue		$534 266

Businesses frequently do not include the sales discounts or sales returns and allowances on their financial statements because their amounts are insignificant in relation to the sales. In such cases only the net figure is shown on the income statement.

FIGURE 9-10 THE INCOME STATEMENT FOR ALGOR COMPUTER SERVICES, SHOWING A CONSOLIDATED PRESENTATION OF REVENUE

Algor Computer Services
Income Statement
for the year ended May 31, 1993

Net Revenue $534 266

Cost of Goods Sold

It is important to realize that Algor Computer Services is concerned with matching the cost of goods sold during the current period with the revenue earned from the sale of merchandise. The cost of goods sold calculation can initially be best illustrated using units of merchandise. To find the *number* of units of computers sold, the following calculation is made by Algor Computer Services:

Started year with (opening inventory)	6 computers
Units purchased during the year	53 computers
Total units available for sale during the year	59 computers
Ended year with (ending inventory)	8 computers
Units sold during the year	51 computers

The previous example is done in units. Of course, on an income statement dollar figures are used. However, the example shows the basic outline to be used when calculating the cost of goods sold. The cost of goods sold section for Algor Computer Services is shown in Figure 9-11. Note how it corresponds to the previous example done in units.

FIGURE 9-11 THE COST OF GOODS SOLD SECTION OF AN INCOME STATEMENT FOR ALGOR COMPUTER SERVICES

Cost of Goods Sold:
Inventory, June 1, 1992	$ 89 600
Purchases	86 200
Cost of Goods Available for Sale	175 800
Less: Ending Inventory	87 200
Cost of Goods Sold	$ 88 600

In the previous section of this chapter, we learned that other accounts also influence the cost of goods sold. The calculation of net purchases must take into account Purchases Discounts and Purchases Returns and Allowances, both of which reduce the total cost of the purchases. On the other hand, Transportation-in increases the cost of purchases. It is therefore added to the net purchases to obtain the total cost of merchandise purchased, as shown below.

FIGURE 9-12 THE COST OF GOODS SOLD SECTION OF AN INCOME STATEMENT, INCLUDING OTHER COST AND CONTRA-COST ACCOUNTS

Cost of Goods Sold:
Inventory, June 1, 1992		$ 89 600
Purchases	$86 200	
Freight-in	1 939	
Gross Purchases	88 139	
Less: Purchases Returns and Allowances	500	
Purchases Discounts	468	
Net Purchases		87 171
Cost of Goods Available for Sale		176 771
Less: Ending Inventory		87 200
Cost of Goods Sold		$ 89 571

The matching principle, discussed in Chapter 7, which requires matching of expenses with corresponding revenue, is followed in the cost of goods sold section. The cost of goods sold includes only the cost of those goods sold during the current fiscal period.

Expenses

The expense section is the last to be entered on the income statement. Note the new account, Delivery Expense, which applies to merchandise delivered to customers. A completed income statement for Algor Computer Services appears in Figure 9-13. This type of Income Statement is referred to as a multi-step income statement, for each calculation is shown.

FIGURE 9-13 A COMPLETED MULTI-STEP INCOME STATEMENT FOR ALGOR COMPUTER SERVICES

Algor Computer Services
Income Statement
for the year ended May 31, 1993

Revenue:

Computer Services			$312 400.00
Software Lessons			51 300.00
Sales			176 337.00
Gross Revenue			540 037.00
Less: Refunds		$ 2 140.00	
Sales Returns and Allowances		1 364.00	
Sales Discounts		2 267.00	5 771.00
Net Revenue			534 266.00

Cost of Goods Sold:

Inventory, June 1, 1992		89 600.00	
Purchases	$86 200.00		
Freight-in	1 939.00		
Gross Purchases	88 139.00		
Less: Purchases Returns and Allowances	500.00		
Purchases Discounts	468.00		
Net Purchases		87 171.00	
Cost of Goods Available for Sale		176 771.00	
Less: Ending Inventory		87 200.00	
Cost of Goods Sold			89 571.00
Gross Profit			444 695.00

Expenses:

Wages	214 309.00	
Bank	368.00	
Interest	24 600.00	
VISA Discount	5 460.00	
Advertising	40 400.00	
Utilities	29 400.00	
Automobile	5 360.00	
Delivery	2 000.00	
Miscellaneous	1 436.00	
Bad Debts	1 200.00	
Depreciation Expense: Building	10 288.50	
Depreciation Expense: Office Equipment	275.50	
Depreciation Expense: Computer Equipment	6 703.20	
Depreciation Expense: Automobile	1 837.50	
Insurance	1 600.00	
Office Supplies	640.00	
Computer Supplies	2 160.00	
Total Expenses		348 037.70
Net Income		$ 96 657.30

Many businesses don't show the calculation of gross profit on their income statement, preferring instead to list Cost of Goods Sold with the other expenses. As well, other details such as sales returns and allowances and sales discounts are eliminated. In such cases, the income statement is referred to as a single-step income statement.

FIGURE 9-14 A COMPLETED SINGLE-STEP INCOME STATEMENT FOR ALGOR COMPUTER SERVICES

Algor Computer Services
Income Statement
for the year ended May 31, 1993

Revenue:		
Net Revenue		$534 266.00
Expenses:		
Cost of Goods Sold	$ 89 571.00	
Wages	214 309.00	
Bank	368.00	
Interest	24 600.00	
VISA Discount	5 460.00	
Advertising	40 400.00	
Utilities	29 400.00	
Automobile	5 360.00	
Delivery	2 000.00	
Miscellaneous	1 436.00	
Bad Debts	1 200.00	
Depreciation Expense: Building	10 288.50	
Depreciation Expense: Office Equipment	275.50	
Depreciation Expense: Computer Equipment	6 703.20	
Depreciation Expense: Automobile	1 837.50	
Insurance	1 600.00	
Office Supplies	640.00	
Computer Supplies	2 160.00	
Total Expenses		437 608.70
Net Income		$ 96 657.30

The Balance Sheet for a Merchandising Business

Since the *ending* merchandise inventory will be sold within a year, it is recorded as a current asset on the balance sheet. (See Figure 9-15.) It represents an unexpired cost for the business. The Merchandise Inventory account follows Accounts Receivable on the balance sheet; the accounts receivable are usually collected within thirty days while it may take longer than that to sell some of the inventory. Note the addition of the Allowance for Doubtful Accounts account, and Merchandise Inventory.

FIGURE 9-15 A COMPLETED BALANCE SHEET FOR ALGOR COMPUTER SERVICES

Algor Computer Services
Balance Sheet
as at May 31, 1993

Assets

Current Assets:			
Cash		$ 14 600.00	
Accounts Receivable	$ 42 700.00		
Less: Allowance for Doubtful Accounts	1 400.00	41 300.00	
Merchandise Inventory		87 200.00	
GST Recoverable		1 605.00	
Prepaid Insurance		200.00	
Office Supplies		125.00	
Computer Supplies		147.00	
Total Current Assets			$145 177.00
Fixed Assets:			
Land		124 600.00	
Building	228 000.00		
Less: Accumulated Depreciation	32 518.50	195 481.50	
Office Equipment	14 500.00		
Less: Accumulated Depreciation	12 020.50	2 479.50	
Computer Equipment	45 600.00		
Less: Accumulated Depreciation	29 959.20	15 640.80	
Automobile	12 500.00		
Less: Accumulated Depreciation	8 212.50	4 287.50	
Total Fixed Assets			342 489.30
Total Assets			$487 666.30

Liabilities and Owner's Equity

Current Liabilities:			
Accounts Payable		$ 27 205.00	
Short-Term Loans		14 612.00	
GST Payable		1 976.00	
PST Payable		2 368.00	
Total Current Liabilities			$ 46 161.00
Long-Term Liabilities:			
Mortgage Payable			236 500.00
Owner's Equity:			
Capital, June 1, 1992		149 148.00	
Net Income	$ 96 657.30		
Less: Drawings	40 800.00		
Increase in Capital		55 857.30	
Capital, May 31, 1993			205 005.30
Total Liabilities and Owner's Equity			$487 666.30

Other Steps in the Accounting Cycle

The accounting cycle for a merchandising business is the same as that followed for a service business. The steps are as follows:

During the Month	Journalize
	Post
End of Month	Trial balance
	Worksheet
	Financial statements
	Adjusting entries
	Closing entries
	Post-closing trial balance

As we have already examined journalizing, posting, and the financial statements, we will now examine the remainder of the cycle.

The Worksheet

The previous section outlined the changes in the financial statements for a merchandising business. The worksheet is the rough preparation of the financial statements. The focus in this section will be on the location of the new revenue and expense accounts on the worksheet. The worksheet for Algor Computer Services for the year ending May 31, 1993 is shown in Figure 9-16. The trial balance has been entered, and the adjustments and extensions have been completed. The following aspects concerning the extensions should be noted.

1. An adjustment must be made for the estimated uncollectable accounts. Allowance for Doubtful Accounts is a contra-asset, and as such it will be extended to the credit side of the Balance Sheet columns.

2. Sales is the name of the revenue account that records the sale of goods to customers. As such it increases owner's equity and has a credit balance. It is extended to the credit side of the Income Statement columns.

3. The two new accounts related to Sales (which are contra-revenue accounts), Sales Returns and Allowances and Sales Discounts, decrease owner's equity and have debit balances. They are extended to the debit side of the Income Statement columns.

4. Purchases is found in the cost of goods sold section of the income statement, and it reduces owner's equity. It therefore has a debit balance, and when extended to the Income Statement columns of the worksheet is also placed on the debit side. Similarly Freight-in increases cost, has a debit balance, and is extended to the debit side of the Income Statement columns.

FIGURE 9-16 A COMPLETED WORKSHEET FOR ALGOR COMPUTER SERVICES

WORKSHEET

Algor Computer Services

FOR THE __Year__ ENDED __May 31__ 19 9_

#	ACCOUNTS	ACCT. NO.	TRIAL BALANCE DR	TRIAL BALANCE CR	ADJUSTMENTS DR	ADJUSTMENTS CR	INCOME STATEMENT DR	INCOME STATEMENT CR	BALANCE SHEET DR	BALANCE SHEET CR
1	Cash	100	14 600 —						14 600 —	
2	Accounts Receivable	120	42 700 —						42 700 —	
3	Allowance For Doubtful Accounts	125		200 —		a) 1 200 —				1 400 —
4	Merchandise Inventory	130	89 600 —				89 600 —	87 200 —	87 200 —	
5	GST Recoverable	135	1 605 —						1 605 —	
6	Prepaid Insurance	140	1 800 —			b) 1 600 —			200 —	
7	Office Supplies	150	765 —			c) 640 —			125 —	
8	Computer Supplies	155	2 307 —			d) 2 160 —			147 —	
9	Land	160	124 600 —						124 600 —	
10	Building	170	228 000 —						228 000 —	
11	Accumulated Dep'n.: Building	171		22 230 —		e) 10 288 50				32 518 50
12	Office Equipment	175	14 500 —						14 500 —	
13	Accumulated Dep'n.: Off. Equip.	176		11 745 —		f) 275 50				12 020 50
14	Computer Equipment	180	45 600 —						45 600 —	
15	Accumulated Dep'n.: Comp. Equip.	181		23 256 —		g) 6 703 20				29 959 20
16	Automobile	190	12 500 —						12 500 —	
17	Accumulated Dep'n.: Automobile	191		6 375 —		h) 1 837 50				8 212 50
18	Accounts Payable	200		27 205 —						27 205 —
19	Short-Term Loans	210		14 612 —						14 612 —
20	Mortgage Payable	220		236 500 —						236 500 —
21	GST Payable	230		1 976 —						1 976 —
22	PST Payable	240		2 368 —						2 368 —
23	V. Marshall, Capital	300		149 148 —						149 148 —
24	V. Marshall, Drawings	310	40 800 —						40 800 —	
25	Computer Services	400		312 400 —				312 400 —		
26	Software Lessons	410		51 300 —				51 300 —		
27	Refunds	415	2 140 —				2 140 —			
28	Sales	420		176 337 —				176 337 —		
29	Sales Returns and Allowances	425	1 364 —				1 364 —			
30	Sales Discounts	430	2 267 —				2 267 —			
31	Purchases	500	86 200 —				86 200 —			
32	Freight-in	510	1 939 —				1 939 —			
33	Purchases Returns and Allowances	520		500 —				500 —		
34	Purchases Discounts	525		468 —				468 —		
35	Wages Expense	600	214 309 —				214 309 —			
36	Bank Expense	650	368 —				368 —			
37	Interest Expense	651	24 600 —				24 600 —			
38	VISA Discount Expense	655	5 460 —				5 460 —			
39	Advertising Expense	660	40 400 —				40 400 —			
40	Utilities Expense	670	29 400 —				29 400 —			
41	Automobile Expense	680	5 360 —				5 360 —			
42	Delivery Expense	685	2 000 —				2 000 —			
43	Miscellaneous Expense	760	1 436 —				1 436 —			
44			1036 620 —	1036 620 —						
45										
46	Bad Debts Expense	715			a) 1 200 —		1 200 —			
47	Dep'n. Expense: Building	690			e) 10 288 50		10 288 50			
48	Dep'n. Expense: Off. Equip.	700			f) 275 50		275 50			
49	Dep'n. Expense: Comp. Equip.	705			g) 6 703 20		6 703 20			
50	Dep'n. Expense: Automobile	710			h) 1 837 50		1 837 50			
51	Insurance Expense	720			b) 1 600 —		1 600 —			
52	Office Supplies Expense	730			c) 640 —		640 —			
53	Computer Supplies Expense	740			d) 2 160 —		2 160 —			
54					24 704 70	24 704 70	531 547 70	628 205 —	612 577 —	515 919 70
55	NET INCOME						96 657 30			96 657 30
56	a) Allowance estimate by ageing, $1 400						628 205 —	628 205 —	612 577 —	612 577 —
57	b) Insurance inventory, $200									
58	c) Office supplies inventory, $125									
59	d) Computer supplies inventory, $147									
60	e) Building (228 000 – 22 230) x 0.05									
61	f) Office (14 500 – 11 745) x 0.10									
62	g) Computer (45 600 – 23 256) x 0.30									
63	h) Auto (12 500 – 6 375) x 0.30									

5. The two new contra-cost accounts related to Purchases, Purchases Returns and Allowances and Purchases Discounts, increase owner's equity and therefore have credit balances. They are extended to the credit side of the Income Statement columns.

6. The Delivery Expense account reduces owner's equity and therefore has a debit balance. It is extended, like other expense accounts, to the debit side of the Income Statement columns.

7. When the cost of goods sold section is completed on the income statement, the following calculation is made:

$$\text{Cost of Goods Sold} = \text{Opening inventory} + \text{Purchases} - \text{Ending inventory}$$

When extending accounts on the worksheet, the balance for the opening inventory and the ending inventory must be located on the income statement so as to follow the above calculation.

"The opening inventory is extended to the debit side of the income statement."

The opening merchandise inventory is shown on the trial balance as being $89 600. It has not changed all year, for under the periodic inventory method the account balance represents the opening inventory and does not actually match the inventory on hand during the fiscal period. The balance is allowed to be incorrect during the year and is only changed at year end when a new inventory is taken. The opening inventory is added to purchases, and therefore must be put in the same column as purchases when extended on the worksheet. It is therefore extended to the debit side of the Income Statement columns.

"The ending inventory is entered on the credit side of the income statement and the debit side of the balance sheet."

8. The ending inventory is obtained by taking a physical inventory of the goods on hand at the end of the year. The ending inventory is subtracted from the total of opening inventory plus purchases on the cost of goods sold section of the income statement. Therefore, when extended on the worksheet it must be put on the credit side of the Income Statement columns, the side opposite to where the opening inventory and purchases are shown.

The ending inventory is the amount of goods on hand owned by the business, and, as such, is a current asset. It, therefore, must also be entered on the debit side of the Balance Sheet columns. Note that the ending inventory is located on two statements on the worksheet:
(a) the credit column of the Income Statement, and
(b) the debit column of the Balance Sheet.

In order to complete the worksheet, the columns are added and balanced. Then the net income, or net loss, is extended from the income statement to the balance sheet.

The Closing Entries

After the adjusting entries have been entered from the worksheet into the general journal and posted, the closing entries are completed. As with closing entries for a service business, it is easiest to make these closing entries by referring to the information on the worksheet. They could also be made by using the ledger accounts. The following four entries are made:

1. All the amounts in the debit column of the Income Statement are entered in the journal as credits, with the total being debited to Income Summary. The effect of this entry is to close all temporary (income statement) accounts with debit balances.

FIGURE 9-17 THE FIRST CLOSING ENTRY

GENERAL JOURNAL

PAGE 701

DATE 1993		PARTICULARS	PR	DEBIT	CREDIT
May	31	Income Summary		531 547 70	
		Merchandise Inventory			89 600 -
		Refunds			2 140 -
		Sales Returns and Allowances			1 364 -
		Sales Discounts			2 267 -
		Purchases			86 200 -
		Freight-in			1 939 -
		Wages Expense			214 309 -
		Bank Expense			368 -
		Interest Expense			24 600 -
		VISA Discount Expense			5 460 -
		Advertising Expense			40 400 -
		Utilities Expense			29 400 -
		Automobile Expense			5 360 -
		Delivery Expense			2 000 -
		Miscellaneous Expense			1 436 -
		Bad Debts Expense			1 200 -
		Depreciation Expense: Building			10 288 50
		Depreciation Expense: Office Equipment			2 755 50
		Depreciation Expense: Computer Equipment			6 703 20
		Depreciation Expense: Automobile			1 837 50
		Insurance Expense			1 600 -
		Office Supplies Expense			640 -
		Computer Supplies Expense			2 160 -
		To close temporary accounts that have a debit balance			

When this entry is posted, all the temporary accounts with debit balances will have nil balances. The new accounts — Purchases, Freight-in, Sales Returns and Allowances, Sales Discounts, and Delivery Expense — will all be closed by this entry. Note the effect that it has on the merchandise inventory account: the original balance is entered on the debit side of the Trial Balance columns and represents the opening inventory. The posting of the credit amount in the closing entry brings the account balance to nil.

GENERAL LEDGER

Merchandise Inventory			130
dr.		cr.	
June 1, 1992	89 600	May 31, 1993	89 600

2. All the amounts in the credit column of the Income Statement are entered in the journal as debits, with the total being credited to Income Summary. The effect of this entry is to close all temporary (income statement) accounts with credit balances.

FIGURE 9-18 THE SECOND CLOSING ENTRY

GENERAL JOURNAL

PAGE 701

DATE 1993		PARTICULARS	PR	DEBIT	CREDIT
May	31	Merchandise Inventory		87 200 —	
		Computer Services		312 400 —	
		Software Lessons		51 300 —	
		Sales		176 337 —	
		Purchases Returns and Allowances		500 —	
		Purchases Discounts		468 —	
		Income Summary			628 205 —
		To close temporary accounts with a credit balance			

When this entry is posted all the temporary accounts with credit balances will have nil balances. The new accounts — Sales, Purchases Returns and Allowances, and Purchases Discounts — are all closed by this entry. When the posting is made to Merchandise Inventory, it results in the account having a debit balance. The amount of the closing inventory has therefore been recorded in the accounts as a current asset. This is the amount that will be on the books for the Merchandise Inventory account through the next fiscal period.

FIGURE 9-19 THE MERCHANDISE INVENTORY ACCOUNT, SHOWING THE CLOSING ENTRIES

GENERAL LEDGER

Merchandise Inventory			130
dr.		cr.	
June 1, 1992	89 600	May 31, 1993	89 600
May 31, 1993	87 200		

3. The amount of the net income, shown by the balance in the Income Summary account and by the worksheet, is transferred to V. Marshall, Capital.

FIGURE 9-20 THE THIRD CLOSING ENTRY, ASSUMING A NET INCOME

GENERAL JOURNAL

PAGE 701

DATE 1993		PARTICULARS	PR	DEBIT	CREDIT
May	31	Income Summary		96 657 30	
		V. Marshall, Capital			96 657 30
		To close Income Summary into Capital			

4. The V. Marshall, Drawings account is closed into V. Marshall, Capital. This account is closed at each year end so that the amount represents the owner's drawings for the current fiscal year. The drawings for the year have reduced the owner's claim against the assets of the business.

FIGURE 9-21 THE FOURTH CLOSING ENTRY

GENERAL JOURNAL

PAGE 701

DATE 1993		PARTICULARS	PR	DEBIT	CREDIT
May	31	V. Marshall, Capital		40 800 —	
		V. Marshall, Drawings			40 800 —
		To close Drawings into Capital			

LESSON REVIEW

45. Why are physical inventories not taken on a monthly basis?

46. Briefly describe the two steps followed in taking an inventory.

47. Give the formula for calculation of net income for a merchandising business.

48. What accounts reduce the net amount of Sales? Why do some businesses not show these accounts on their income statement?

49. A business starts with 620 hockey sticks, buys 4 320 during the hockey season, and has 403 left at the end of the season. How many sticks did it sell during the year?

50. What accounts increase the cost of goods sold? What accounts decrease it?

Chapter 9: The Merchandising Business

51. How does the calculation of the cost of goods sold follow the matching principle?
52. Where is Merchandise Inventory recorded on the balance sheet? Why is it listed on the balance sheet?
53. Distinguish between a multi-step and a single-step income statement.
54. What are the steps in the accounting cycle for all businesses?
55. Indicate to which columns on the worksheet the following are extended, and why.
    (a) Purchases
    (b) Purchases Returns and Allowances
    (c) Purchases Discounts
    (d) Freight-in
    (e) Sales
    (f) Sales Returns and Allowances
    (g) Sales Discounts
    (h) Opening inventory
56. Where is the ending inventory entered on the worksheet? Why?
57. What balance will appear in the Merchandise Inventory account after the adjusting and closing entries have been made?

Lesson Applications

58. Complete the following inventory summary sheet for Red Deer Sporting Goods. The item number, description and quantity were copied from inventory tags. The unit cost has been obtained from invoices.

Red Deer Sporting Goods
Inventory Summary Sheet

Date: _May 31, 19-6_

Item #	Description	Quantity	Unit Cost	Cost of Inventory
744-1	Rackets, tennis	6	$79.50	
744-2	Rackets, tennis	2	98.05	
745-1	Balls, tennis	7	7.50	
746-1	Sweat tops	2	42.80	
746-2	Sweat tops	9	61.00	
746-3	Sweat tops	3	40.75	
747-1	Sweat bottoms	2	21.30	
747-2	Sweat bottoms	8	24.50	
747-3	Sweat bottoms	3	19.70	

Transfer from inventory tags done by: _RC_

Costing completed by: _PM_

59. The following T-account for Merchandise Inventory shows three entries after the closing entries for the year have been completed.
   (a) What does the January 1 debit entry for $40 000 represent, and where would it have been posted from?
   (b) What does the December 31 credit entry for $40 000 represent, and where would it have been posted from?
   (c) What does the December 31 debit entry for $46 000 represent, and where would it have been posted from?

GENERAL LEDGER

Merchandise Inventory

dr.		cr.	
Jan. 1	40 000	Dec. 31	40 000
Dec. 31	46 000		

60. Poltimore Building Supplies had sales of $345 820 in June. The cost of those goods was $220 355. Expenses for the month were $93 403.
   (a) Calculate the gross profit. Show your formula.
   (b) Calculate the net income. Show your formula.
   (c) Calculate the gross profit percentage. Show your formula.

61. West End Athletics had sales of $1 435 900 in 1990. The cost of those goods was $675 400. Expenses for the year were $429 200.
   (a) Calculate the gross profit. Show your formula.
   (b) Calculate the net income. Show your formula.
   (c) Calculate the gross profit percentage. Show your formula.

62. (a) Complete the heading and the revenue section of an income statement given the following data. The firm is Easy Stroke Painters, and the accounting period is the month of July.
   Sales $49 200
   Sales Discounts   738
   Sales Returns and Allowances   1 968
   (b) Calculate the percentage of sales which have been returned or given an allowance.

63. (a) Complete the heading and the revenue section of an income statement given the following data. The firm is Delta Pools, and the accounting period is the month of July. Note that Delta has an account to record merchandise revenue and a separate account for pool service revenue. Discounts are not offered on service revenue.
   Sales $134 560
   Pool Service Revenue   43 430

Sales Discounts   1 894
Sales Allowances   6 437
Service Refunds   127

(b) Calculate the percentage of sales that have been returned or given an allowance.

(c) What might Delta Pools do when preparing its income statement in order to be more concise but provide basically the same information?

64. For each of the following, prepare the Cost of Goods Sold section of the income statement. Prepare a proper heading, and make up business names.
    (a) For June: Opening inventory $53 508; Purchases $32 420; Ending inventory $49 302.
    (b) For August: Opening inventory $4 390; Purchases $3 298; Ending inventory $4 602.
    (c) For January: Opening inventory $19 388; Purchases $15 690; Freight-in $403; Ending inventory $18 977.

65. For each of the following, prepare the Cost of Goods Sold section of the income statement. Prepare a proper heading, and make up business names.
    (a) For December: Opening inventory $33 109; Purchases $24 398; Purchases Returns and Allowances $459; Purchases Discounts $876; Ending inventory $34 599.
    (b) For April: Opening inventory $9 430; Purchases $6 540; Purchases Returns and Allowances $75; Purchases Discounts $70; Ending inventory $8 423.
    (c) For September: Opening inventory $122 949; Purchases $96 420; Freight-in $1 552; Purchases Returns and Allowances $1 490; Purchases Discounts $1 235; Ending inventory $109 987.
    (d) For May: Opening inventory $73 459; Purchases $62 535; Freight-in $656; Purchases Returns and Allowances $1 143; Purchases Discounts $995; Ending inventory $72 424.

66. (a) Prepare a partial income statement to show gross profit for Di's Pottery Studio for the month of November.

    Sales $72 490
    Sales Returns and Allowances   1 345
    Opening Inventory   46 780
    Purchases   37 098
    Freight-in   142
    Purchases Returns and Allowances 972
    Purchases Discounts   231
    Ending Inventory   44 352

    (b) Calculate the gross profit percentage.

67. Prepare a complete income statement for Eastern Hardware Store for the month ending August 31 using any of the following information.

Cash	$ 24 294
Sales	182 957
Purchases Discounts	1 459
Wages Expense	17 900
Delivery Expense	1 234
Accounts Receivable	42 922
Sales Returns	3 693
Opening Inventory	217 402
Rent Expense	6 400
Ending Inventory	206 482
Purchases Returns	2 320
Utility Expense	3 758
Freight-in	920
Accounts Payable	11 392
Purchases	124 900
Miscellaneous Expense	2 391
C. Darnell, Drawings	42 000

68. The following data is for Westbury Book Suppliers for the month of October.
   (a) Enter the following balances in the trial balance of your worksheet providing appropriate account numbers.

Cash	$13 268
Accounts Receivable	25 359
GST Recoverable	1 795
Merchandise Inventory	118 900
Prepaid Insurance	2 400
Supplies	1 200
Furniture and Equipment	24 300
Accumulated Depreciation: Furniture and Equipment	6 200
Van	22 400
Accumulated Depreciation: Van	14 200
Accounts Payable	12 198
Bank Loan	36 700
GST Payable	2 912
J. Westbury, Capital	129 706
J. Westbury, Drawings	3 000
Sales	41 600
Sales Returns and Allowances	560
Purchases	22 400
Freight-in	550

Purchases Returns and Allowances	400
Purchases Discounts	600
Wages Expense	4 300
Bank Charges	18
Interest Expense	367
Rent Expense	2 200
Utilities Expense	900
Van Expense	200
Delivery Expense	225
Telephone Expense	110
Miscellaneous Expense	64

    (b) Enter the following adjustments, and complete the worksheet.

Supplies on hand	$ 500
Unexpired Insurance	1 800

        Depreciation rates: Furniture and Equipment, 10%,
                declining balance
                Van, 30%, declining balance

    (c) Prepare an income statement.
    (d) Prepare a classified balance sheet.

69. Using your completed worksheet for Westbury Book Suppliers in Question 68,
    (a) journalize and post the adjusting entries;
    (b) journalize and post the closing entries;
    (c) prepare a post-closing trial balance.

9.4 Accounting System for a Merchandising Business Using a Perpetual Inventory System

Many firms use a perpetual inventory system instead of a periodic system. The perpetual system lends itself to firms with a small number of large items for sale, such as cars and furniture. However, in recent years the introduction of computers as an inventory tool has allowed firms with a large number of small items for sale to switch to a perpetual inventory system. This change in inventory procedure has been facilitated by the use of scanners that read a code, such as the UPC bars, on each item.

    As we noted earlier in this chapter, a perpetual inventory is maintained on some form of stock cards, whether they be done by hand or by computer. There are advantages to using this system, as outlined on page 9 of the report made to Algor Computer Services by the firm recommending an accounting system for the firm.

> Page 9: Algor Computer Services
> Accounting System Proposal, June, 1992
>
> ### Advantages of the Perpetual Inventory System
>
> 1. The information on the stock card identifies all aspects of the product.
>
> 2. The minimum quantity is shown on the stock card. When the goods on hand reach this level, the person in charge of ordering should order enough goods so that the maximum are on hand. Following this procedure should prevent the firm from running short of the product, and therefore losing sales. The minimum can be adjusted through experience.
>
> 3. The maximum quantity, when compared with the minimum amount, shows the stockkeeper the quantity to order. This prevents the firm from overordering, which ties up its assets in stock that is not moving, and increases warehousing and insurance costs. As well, goods that sit in the stockroom may become obsolete.
>
> 4. Accurate statements can be prepared during the fiscal year, because the amount of inventory on hand can be determined from the stock cards at any time.

Journal Entries for a Perpetual Inventory System

The accounting entries required for the perpetual inventory system are different from those required for the periodic inventory system. Because the cost of the item being sold can be easily obtained from the stock card, the cost of goods sold can be recorded each time a sale is made. The following journal entries illustrate the accounting procedures required for the perpetual inventory system if it was used by Algor Computer Services. We will examine those entries related to the purchase and payment cycle first, and then those related to the sales and collection cycle. The Cost of Goods Sold account (number 500) would replace all the cost and contra-cost accounts.

Entries Related to the Purchase and Payment Cycle

The entries related to the purchase and payment cycle will illustrate that the Merchandise Inventory account is updated each time a purchase is made. The entry required for a purchase of merchandise is shown below.

Mar. 8 Purchase Invoice #449: $3 638, purchased a $3 400 computer from Sarnia Computers Ltd. on account; terms 2/10, n/30.

GENERAL JOURNAL

PAGE 682

DATE 1993		PARTICULARS	PR	DEBIT	CREDIT
Mar.	8	Merchandise Inventory	130	3 400 —	
		GST Recoverable	135	238 —	
		Accounts Payable	200		3 638 —
		Purchase Invoice #449, Sarnia Computers;			
		terms 2/10, n/30			

GENERAL LEDGER

Merchandise Inventory		130
dr.		cr.
Mar. 8 3 400		

GST Recoverable		135
dr.		cr.
Mar. 8 238		

Accounts Payable		200
dr.		cr.
		Mar. 8 3 638

The explanation for the entry is as follows:
- A debit is made to Merchandise Inventory to show the increase in the merchandise on hand. Merchandise Inventory is an asset, and to increase an asset account a debit is made.
- A debit is made to GST Recoverable, which represents the input tax credit.
- A credit is made to Accounts Payable to record the liability to Sarnia Computers Ltd.

The amount of inventory on hand has increased, and is shown immediately in the Merchandise Inventory account. All other transactions related to purchases are similarly reflected by a change in the Merchandise Inventory account. One of the advantages of the perpetual system is that the dollar value of merchandise on hand is always available. This allows the preparation of interim statements, where the Merchandise Inventory is required, to be more accurate. Therefore, there is no Purchases account under a perpetual inventory system.

"There is no Purchases account under a perpetual inventory system."

Purchases Returns and Allowances

When merchandise is returned to a supplier or an allowance is granted, a credit invoice will be received. The entry to record the credit invoice under the perpetual inventory system is as follows:

Mar. 11   Credit Memo #84 received: From Sarnia Computers Ltd., $160.50; $150.00 for allowance on Purchase Invoice #449 for damaged goods and $10.50 for GST.

GENERAL JOURNAL

PAGE 683

DATE 1993		PARTICULARS	PR	DEBIT	CREDIT
Mar.	11	Accounts Payable	200	160 50	
		GST Recoverable	135		10 50
		Merchandise Inventory	130		150 —
		Credit Memo #84, from Sarnia Computers Ltd.,			
		Purchase Invoice #449			

GENERAL LEDGER

Accounts Payable 200		GST Recoverable 135		Merchandise Inventory 130	
dr.	cr.	dr.	cr.	dr.	cr.
Mar. 11 160.50			Mar. 11 10.50		Mar. 11 150.00

The explanation for the entry is as follows:
- A debit to Accounts Payable reduces that liability.
- A credit to GST Recoverable reduces the input tax credit that can be claimed, for the original purchase has been reduced in cost.
- A credit to Merchandise Inventory reduces the value of merchandise inventory (the item was damaged when received), thus reducing the cost of the purchase.

Purchases Discounts

The balance of Merchandise Inventory is similarly reduced for a purchase discount. When Sarnia Computers Ltd. is paid the balance owing within the discount period, a discount of two percent is taken on the base price.

Mar. 21   Cheque Copy #192: Paid Sarnia Computers Ltd. $3 412.50; Purchase Invoice #449 for $3 638.00, less Credit Memo #84 for $160.50, less discount 2/10, n/30, $65.00.

GENERAL JOURNAL

PAGE 686

DATE 1993		PARTICULARS	PR	DEBIT	CREDIT
Mar.	21	Accounts Payable	200	3 477 50	
		Cash	100		3 412 50
		Merchandise Inventory	130		65 —
		Cheque Copy #192, Sarnia Computers Ltd.,			
		Purchase Invoice #449 less Credit			
		Memo #84 less discount			

GENERAL LEDGER

Accounts Payable		200	Cash		100	Merchandise Inventory		130
dr.	cr.		dr.	cr.		dr.	cr.	
Mar. 21 3 477.50				Mar. 21 3 412.50			Mar. 21 65.00	

The explanation for the entry is as follows:
- A debit is made to Accounts Payable to reduce that liability.
- A credit is made to Cash to reduce that asset.
- A credit is made to Merchandise Inventory to reduce that asset; the true cost of the merchandise has been reduced by the amount of the discount.

One should note that under the perpetual inventory system, there are no Purchases, Purchases Returns and Allowances, Purchases Discounts, or Transportation-in accounts, for all changes in the cost of the merchandise inventory are made directly to the Merchandise Inventory account. This may result in some loss of internal control, especially over returns and allowances. Alternative methods could be designed so that management knows what items are being returned to what suppliers. However, the fact that the dollar value of Merchandise Inventory is always available allows for a more accurate figure to be presented on interim statements.

Entries Related to the Sales and Collection Cycle

Each time a sale is made an additional entry is required when the perpetual inventory system is used. This entry updates a new account, Cost of Goods Sold. Rather than having to calculate the cost of goods sold, as was done on the income statement shown earlier for a business using the periodic inventory system, the value of the cost of goods sold will always be available under the perpetual system. This is possible because each time an item is sold, the cost can be readily found on the stock card. The following entries illustrate the procedure each time a sale is made. The first entry is the same as that required to record a sale under the periodic system.

Mar. 10   Sales Invoice #55-1099: Sale of a computer printer to M. Chang on account, $517.50; sale, $450.00; GST, $31.50; PST, $36.00. The stock card showed the cost of the goods to be $300.00.

GENERAL JOURNAL

PAGE 683

DATE 1993		PARTICULARS	PR	DEBIT	CREDIT
Mar.	10	Accounts Receivable		517 50	
		Sales			450 —
		GST Payable			31 50
		PST Payable			36 —
		Sales Invoice #55-1099, M. Chang			

However, another entry is required at this time to record the cost of goods sold and the resulting reduction in the inventory, for one computer printer has been sold. The entry is as follows:

GENERAL JOURNAL

PAGE 683

DATE 1993		PARTICULARS	PR	DEBIT	CREDIT
Mar.	10	Cost of Goods Sold	500	300 —	
		Merchandise Inventory	130		300 —
		To record the cost of Sales Invoice #55-1099			

GENERAL LEDGER

Cost of Goods Sold	500		Merchandise Inventory	130	
dr.		cr.	dr.		cr.
Mar. 10 300					Mar. 10 300

The explanation for the entry is as follows:
- A debit is made to Cost of Goods Sold to show the cost of the merchandise sold. This cost can easily be found by using the stock card, or if using a computer by using the inventory or UPC number. A debit is made because Cost of Goods Sold is an expense account, which reduces owner's equity.
- A credit is made to Merchandise Inventory to reduce that asset. Note that after every sale the Merchandise Inventory is updated by this entry, and therefore the business will always know the dollar value of its merchandise on hand.

One might ask why these same entries are not used by all businesses, and, therefore, why not abandon the periodic system? For a firm, such as a hardware store, that sells very small goods, it would obviously be very time-consuming to look up the cost of every item sold in order to make the necessary entry. It is therefore not feasible for such a firm to use the perpetual inventory system. It would, however, be feasible for a business selling small goods to use the system if the cost of the small items could be found quickly, for instance, by a computer reading the inventory number or UPC.

When merchandise is returned by a customer, it is also necessary to make two entries: one to record the return, the other to change the merchandise inventory on hand. The first entry is the same as for a return under a periodic system. The second entry is required to update Merchandise Inventory and Cost of Goods Sold.

Mar. 12 Credit Memo #77-0302 issued: To M. Paikin, $200 plus taxes, for return of software. Cost price to Algor Computer Services was $120.

GENERAL JOURNAL

PAGE 683

DATE 1993		PARTICULARS	PR	DEBIT	CREDIT
Mar.	12	Sales Returns and Allowances		200 —	
		GST Payable		14 —	
		PST Payable		16 —	
		Accounts Receivable			230 —
		Credit Memo #77-0302, M. Paikin			

GENERAL JOURNAL

PAGE 683

DATE 1993		PARTICULARS	PR	DEBIT	CREDIT
Mar.	12	Merchandise Inventory		120 —	
		Cost of Goods Sold			120 —
		Credit Memo #77-0302			

The explanation for the second entry is as follows:
- Merchandise Inventory must be increased by $120, for that is the cost price of the returned item which has been put back with the merchandise.
- Cost of Goods Sold is decreased by $120, for the sale has been cancelled.

Under the perpetual inventory system, a physical inventory still must be taken, usually once a year at the fiscal year end. The reason is that the stock card may not be correct due to a good being stolen, or to recording errors. When the value of the physical inventory is calculated, it is compared to the balance of the Merchandise Inventory account:

Balance of Merchandise Inventory = $35 900
Physical inventory = 35 450
Inventory shortage = 450

An entry must be made to correct the balance of the Merchandise Inventory account so that it corresponds to the physical inventory. That entry is as follows:

DATE 1993		PARTICULARS	PR	DEBIT	CREDIT
May	31	Inventory Shortage		450 —	
		Merchandise Inventory			450 —
		To adjust balance of Merchandise Inventory			
		to equal the physical inventory			

GENERAL JOURNAL
PAGE 701

The explanation for the entry is as follows:
- A debit is made to Inventory Shortage, an expense account.
- A credit is made to Merchandise Inventory to reduce that asset account by the amount of the inventory shortage.

Completing the Cycle for Perpetual Inventory Systems

The completion of the accounting cycle for a perpetual inventory system follows the same procedure as for a periodic inventory system. Therefore, all the steps from the preparation of the trial balance to the post-closing trial balance must be completed.

When preparing the worksheet, instead of having a number of accounts related to the cost of goods sold, there will only be one account called Cost of Goods Sold. This account will appear on the trial balance and will be extended to the debit side of the Income Statement columns, for the cost of goods sold reduces owner's equity. Also note that it is not necessary to make the same calculations with the Merchandise Inventory account as were carried out under the periodic inventory method. There are two reasons:

(1) The cost of goods sold was recorded each time a sale was made. It is, therefore, not necessary to make the calculation on the worksheet, or the income statement.

(2) The Merchandise Inventory shown on the trial balance is the ending inventory for it has been updated after each purchase and sale, and after the taking of an inventory. It must only be extended to the balance sheet as a current asset.

FIGURE 9-22 A PARTIAL WORKSHEET, SHOWING EXTENSION OF MERCHANDISE INVENTORY AND COST OF GOODS SOLD

WORKSHEET
FOR THE ___Year___ ENDED ___May 31___ 19 _93_

	ACCOUNTS	ACCT. NO.	TRIAL BALANCE DR	TRIAL BALANCE CR	ADJUSTMENTS DR	ADJUSTMENTS CR	INCOME STATEMENT DR	INCOME STATEMENT CR	BALANCE SHEET DR	BALANCE SHEET CR	
1	Cash	100	14 600 —						14 600 —		1
4	Merchandise Inventory	130	89 600 —						89 600 —		4
34	Cost of Goods Sold	500	89 571 —				89 571 —				34

Earlier it was noted that one of the advantages of the perpetual inventory system is that accurate financial statements can be made on a monthly basis, for an accurate Merchandise Inventory account balance is always available. A business can therefore react more quickly to changes in its financial status, and therefore improve its bottom line. Under the periodic inventory system it is possible to prepare monthly statements, but the merchandise inventory must be estimated. Inventory estimation is examined in advanced accounting courses.

When an income statement is made from the worksheet by a firm that uses the perpetual inventory system, the amount of the Cost of Goods Sold is listed as one of the expenses rather than in a separate section. The income statement for Algor is shown below.

FIGURE 9-23 A COMPLETED INCOME STATEMENT, ASSUMING A PERPETUAL INVENTORY SYSTEM

Algor Computer Services
Income Statement
for the year ended May 31, 1993

Revenue:

Computer Services			$312 400.00
Software Lessons			51 300.00
Sales			176 337.00
Gross Revenue			540 037.00
Less: Refunds		$ 2 140.00	
Sales Returns and Allowances		1 364.00	
Sales Discounts		2 267.00	5 771.00
Net Revenue			534 266.00

Expenses:

Cost of Goods Sold		89 571.00	
Wages		214 309.00	
Bank		368.00	
Interest		24 600.00	
VISA Discount		7 460.00	
Advertising		40 400.00	
Utilities		29 400.00	
Automobile		5 360.00	
Miscellaneous		1 436.00	
Bad Debts		1 200.00	
Depreciation Expense: Building		10 288.50	
Depreciation Expense: Office Equipment		275.50	
Depreciation Expense: Computer Equipment		6 703.20	
Depreciation Expense: Automobile		1 837.50	
Insurance		1 600.00	
Office Supplies		640.00	
Computer Supplies		2 160.00	
Total Expenses			437 608.70
Net Income			$ 96 657.30

Lesson Review

70. Describe a perpetual inventory system.

71. Why have many types of businesses changed to a perpetual inventory system in recent years?

72. On what are perpetual inventories maintained? When are they changed?

73. What are the main advantages of using a perpetual inventory system as compared to a periodic inventory system?

74. How often does the Merchandise Inventory account change under a perpetual inventory system?

75. Why must two entries be made each time a sale is made under the perpetual inventory system?

76. Why is it easy for a firm using a perpetual inventory system to record the cost of goods sold each time a sale is made?

77. Why must an inventory still be taken at the end of the year under the perpetual inventory system?

78. Why can more accurate financial statements be made during the year under the perpetual inventory system than under the periodic inventory system?

Lesson Applications

Unless otherwise indicated, taxes have been included in the final dollar figures given.

79. Prepare journal entries for each of the following transactions, assuming a perpetual inventory system and a GST of 7 percent. Provincial sales tax of 6 percent is applied to the base price only for non-merchandise purchases.
    Jan. 4 Purchase Invoice #400: $450 for merchandise on account from Ross Hardware Suppliers; terms 2/10, n/30.
    6 Purchase Invoice #992-91: $1 020 for merchandise on account from Renfrew Tape Ltd.; terms 2/10, n/30.
    7 Purchase Invoice #883: $729 for merchandise on account from Black & Decker; terms 2/10, n/30.
    9 Purchase Invoice #0912: $850 for office equipment on account from Modern Office Products Ltd.; terms n/30.
    10 Purchase Invoice #922: $902 for merchandise from Ross Hardware Suppliers Ltd.; terms 2/10, n/30.

80. Prepare journal entries for each of the following transactions, assuming a perpetual inventory system and a GST of 7 percent.

There is no provincial sales tax applied for non-merchandise purchases.

Mar. 17 Purchase Invoice #939: $724 for merchandise on account from Western Linens; terms 2/10, n/30.

18 Purchase Invoice #4233: $1 028 for merchandise on account from Fashion Importers; terms 1/10, n/30.

18 Purchase Invoice #393: $17 300 for merchandise on account from Worldwide Fabrics; terms 2/10, n/30.

20 Credit Memo #39 received: From Western Linens, $120 for allowance on Purchase Invoice #939.

26 Purchase Invoice #3219: $2 800 for fax machine; terms n/30.

26 Debit Memo #47 received: From Worldwide Fabrics, $72 for error on Purchase Invoice #393.

28 Cheque Copy #882: To Fashion Importers, $1 018.39 on account for Purchase Invoice #4233, $1 028.00, less discount.

81. Journalize each of the following transactions for Western Hardware Ltd. Assume that the business uses the perpetual inventory system. PST is 8 percent applied to the base price only for non-merchandise purchases, and GST is 7 percent.

Jan. 2 Purchase Invoice #229: From Canadian Tools Ltd., $917 for merchandise; terms 2/10, n/30.

4 Purchase Invoice #911: From Renfrew Tape Ltd., $217 for merchandise; n/30.

7 Purchase Invoice #915: From Modern Display Cabinets, $570 for display cabinets; terms 2/10, n/30.

7 Credit Memo #992-91 received: From Canadian Tools Ltd., $112 for allowance on Purchase Invoice #229.

17 Cheque Copy #80: $560.09 on account for Purchase Invoice #915 from Modern Display Cabinets, $570.00, less discount of $9.91.

17 Cheque Copy #81: $217 on account for Purchase Invoice #911 from Renfrew Tape Ltd.

17 Memo #102: The owner, Martin Weston, withdrew $59 worth of merchandise for personal use. (Remember to add on the taxes.)

82. Journalize each of the following transactions. Assume that the business uses a perpetual inventory system. All sales are net 30, and are subject to a GST of 7 percent and a PST of 6 percent both calculated on the base price only.

Jan. 3 Sales Invoices:

#244, to S. Doja, sale of $162 plus taxes. Cost of the merchandise is $94.

#245, to P. Basil, sale of $94 plus taxes. Cost of the merchandise is $53.

#246, to P. Whittaker, sale of $92.50 plus taxes. Cost of the merchandise is $61.

6 Credit Invoice #38 issued: To S. Doja, refund on Sales Invoice #244, $162 plus taxes. Cost of the merchandise is $94.

6 Cash Receipt Slip #612: $153 from C. Norton on account.

6 Debit Memo #18 issued: To P. Whittaker, $14 plus taxes for error on Sales Invoice #246. Cost of the merchandise is $8.75.

7 Cash Sales Slips #8882 to #8899: Sales of $1 022 plus taxes. Cost of the merchandise is $641.

9 Sales Invoices:

#247, to Duane Barker, sale of $113 plus taxes. Cost of the merchandise is $73.

#248, to Fera Aydal, sale of $77 plus taxes. Cost of the merchandise is $49.

10 Cash Sales Slips #8900 to #8913: Sales of $1 423 plus taxes. Cost of the merchandise is $903.50.

11 Credit Invoice #39 issued: To Duane Barker, refund on Sales Invoice #247; the sale was originally for $113 plus taxes. Cost of the merchandise is $73.

15 Cheque Copy #533: $1 734 to Provincial Treasurer for sales tax for December.

16 Cheque Copy #534: $1 517.25 to the Receiver General of Canada for GST for December. The GST Payable was $1 639.17 and the input tax credit was $121.92.

83. Journalize the following transactions. Assume that the business uses a perpetual inventory system. All purchases and sales are 2/10, n/30 and are subject to GST of 7 percent. All sales and non-merchandise purchases are also subject to PST of 8 percent calculated on the base price only.

Aug. 2 Sales Invoice #449: B. Sandhu, $173 plus taxes. Cost of the merchandise is $89.

2 Cheque Copy #63: For monthly rent, $1 326.80 (includes GST).

2 Cash Receipt Slip #922: From B. Norris, $800 on account.

4 Cash Sales Slips #53 to #94: Sales of $9 332 plus taxes. Cost of the merchandise is $5 392.

5 Purchase Invoice #338: $221 for office supplies from Sabourin Office Supplies Ltd.; terms n/30.

6 Purchase Invoice #82A: $8 829 for merchandise from Sanyo Ltd.
6 Sales Invoice #450: To D. Arrechi, $722 plus taxes. Cost of the merchandise is $369.
6 Debit Memo #72 issued: To B. Sandhu, $29 plus taxes, due to error on Sales Invoice #449. Cost of the merchandise is $16.
8 Sales Invoice #451: To V. Yazdani, $368 plus taxes. Cost of the merchandise is $191.
8 Credit Memo #22-92 received: $822 from Sanyo Ltd. for allowance on Purchase Invoice #82A.
9 Credit Memo #83 issued: To V. Yazdani, $18 plus taxes, for allowance on Sales Invoice #451. Cost of the merchandise is $10.50.
12 Sales Invoice #452: To V. Zitzelsberger, $586 plus taxes. Cost of the merchandise is $301.
12 Cash Sales Slips #95 to #125: Sales of $8 326 plus taxes. Cost of the merchandise is $4 723.
15 Cheque Copy #64: $2 639 for semi-monthly wages.
15 Cash Refund #25: $172 plus taxes. Cost of the merchandise is $81.
16 Cash Receipt Slip #923: From D. Arrechi, $815.86 for Sales Invoice #450, $830.30, less discount.
16 Cheque Copy #65: $7 857.34 to Sanyo Ltd., for Purchase Invoice #82A, $8 829, less Credit Memo #22-92, $822, less discount.
16 Cheque Copy #66: To the Receiver General of Canada, $13 509 for GST collected in July. The GST Payable was $13 896.20 and the tax input credit was $387.20.

84. (a) Enter the trial balance on page 414 on a worksheet, and provide suitable account numbers.
    (b) Complete the adjustments for the year using the following information:
    Supplies on hand $ 247.00
    Unexpired Insurance   900.50
    Inventory Shortage   1 290.00
    Depreciation rates: Building, 5%, declining balance
                        Computer equipment, 30%, declining balance
                        Automobile, 30%, declining balance
    (c) Complete the worksheet.
    (d) Prepare an income statement.
    (e) Complete a classified report form balance sheet.

BC Sporting Goods
Trial Balance
November 30, 19--

Cash	$ 11 529.05	
Accounts Receivable	35 893.01	
Merchandise Inventory	87 291.18	
GST Recoverable	900.00	
Prepaid Insurance	1 400.40	
Supplies	922.12	
Land	160 000.00	
Building	198 400.00	
Accumulated Depreciation: Building		$ 19 840.00
Computer Equipment	15 420.00	
Accumulated Depreciation: Computer Equipment		4 626.00
Automobile	15 600.00	
Accumulated Depreciation: Automobile		5 200.00
Accounts Payable		62 400.00
Bank Loan		37 600.50
Mortgage Payable		145 096.00
GST Payable		1 456.00
PST Payable		1 248.00
E. Needra, Capital		244 697.22
E. Needra, Drawings	36 700.00	
Sales		239 082.50
Sales Returns and Allowances	3 200.50	
Cost of Goods Sold	142 409.75	
Bank Charges	111.75	
Interest Expense	22 273.60	
Delivery Expense	902.40	
Miscellaneous Expense	1 092.39	
Wages Expense	27 200.07	
	$761 246.22	$761 246.22

CHAPTER REVIEW AND SKILL DEVELOPMENT

Accounting Principles and Concepts
- A **merchandising business** requires accounting procedures and entries that are different from a service business.

- A **periodic inventory system** means that Merchandise Inventory is adjusted only at the end of the fiscal year.

- A **perpetual inventory system** means that Merchandise Inventory is changed every time merchandise is received or sold.

- A **Cost of Goods Sold** must be calculated in order to obtain the amount of the net income or net loss.

- An **adjusting entry** is required in order to match the expenses due to bad debts with the corresponding revenue.

Knowing the Terms
For each of the following statements, indicate the term being defined.
(a) An inventory system maintained on stock cards.
(b) An account used to record increases in the cost of acquiring goods for sale.
(c) The procedure of dividing accounts receivable into categories according to how long they have been outstanding.
(d) Any record of merchandise on hand that is updated regularly.
(e) Account used to record the cost of transporting merchandise into the business.
(f) An account against which bad debts are written off.
(g) The result of net revenue less cost of goods sold.
(h) Any account used to record a reduction in the cost of getting merchandise available for sale.
(i) Method of calculating the allowance for bad debts using a percentage of net sales.
(j) Inventory system in which the Merchandise Inventory account is updated once a year through the closing entries.

Food for Thought
1. Most purchases by retailers are on account, not for cash. Why?

2. Purchase of an office desk is recorded in the Purchases account instead of the Office Equipment account. What will the effect be on
   (a) the balance sheet?
   (b) the income statement?

3. Transportation costs of $2 500 on a large piece of equipment are entered in the Freight-in account instead of in the Equipment account. What effect will this have on
   (a) the balance sheet?
   (b) the income statement?

4. A firm records all of its purchase returns as a credit to Purchases. What information will not be evident by looking at the balance of the Purchases account? Of what value is the information?

5. What will be the amount of saving if a firm borrows $4 200 at the bank to pay an invoice that had terms of 2/10, n/30? The interest rate on the loan is 11%.

6. A business must organize its invoices for Accounts Payable so that they can be paid on the last day in order to take advantage of discounts. In order to ensure that this is done, what should be done with the invoices after they have been recorded in the general journal on the day that they were received?

7. A firm records the sale of a computer, which was used by the business, by making a credit to Sales instead of to Office Equipment. What will the effect be on
   (a) the balance sheet?
   (b) the income statement?

8. A receiving clerk in a business told his friends that the store sells its goods at about twice the price it pays for them. He suggests that his friends shop elsewhere due to this 100 percent markup. What business costs are covered by this markup?

9. Why would a person who is analyzing the income statement for a business want a multi-step statement, that shows the gross profit?

10. What GAAP is being followed by making an adjustment for bad debts?

11. An accountant makes the following entry for the purchase of merchandise on account: debit to Merchandise Inventory, credit to Accounts Payable. Which system of inventory is used by the business?

12. A business wishes to change from a periodic inventory system to a perpetual inventory system. Describe the changes that would have to be made in the ledger to accommodate this change.

13. Criticize the following statement made by an accounting student: On a worksheet the opening inventory for the year goes on the debit side of the Trial Balance columns, and the credit side of the Income Statement columns. The closing inventory goes on the debit side of the Income Statement columns, and the debit side of the Balance Sheet columns.

Locate and Record

Using the Annual Report that you obtained in Chapter 4,
(a) indicate the value of the merchandise inventory that is on hand in the business according to the annual report, if it is a merchandising business or manufacturing business;
(b) calculate the percentage that the Merchandise Inventory account is of the total assets;
(c) calculate the percentage that the Merchandise Inventory account is of the Cash;
(d) calculate the percentage that the Merchandise Inventory account is of the Accounts Receivable;
(e) calculate the percentage that the Merchandise Inventory account is of the Sales;
(f) comment on the value of the Merchandise Inventory account as compared to each of the items calculated.

Organizing

1. Prepare a list of accounts that would be used in a merchandising business, but that would not be used in a service business. Assume a periodic inventory system. Indicate the type of balance that each of the accounts would normally have.

2. Prepare a list of accounts that would be used in a merchandising business, but that would not be used in a service business. Assume a perpetual inventory system. Indicate the type of balance that each of the accounts would normally have.

Applications

(a) Enter the trial balance in Figure 9-24 on a worksheet, and supply suitable account numbers.

(b) Complete the adjustments for the quarter ending January 31 using the following information:
   Supplies on hand $ 247.00
   Unexpired Insurance   380.00
   Inventory Shortage   1 240.00
   Depreciation rates: as per capital cost allowance

(c) Complete the worksheet.

(d) Prepare an income statement.

(e) Complete a classified report form balance sheet.

(f) Journalize the adjusting entries and the closing entries.

FIGURE 9-24

Argue's Craft Shop
Trial Balance
January 31, 19--

Account	Debit	Credit
Cash	$ 1 992.53	
Accounts Receivable	9 834.82	
Merchandise Inventory	23 366.99	
GST Recoverable	1 025.20	
Prepaid Insurance	960.00	
Supplies	832.19	
Office Equipment	12 690.00	
Accumulated Depreciation: Office Equipment		$ 1 280.50
Automobile	18 640.00	
Accumulated Depreciation: Automobile		4 490.00
Accounts Payable		9 583.74
Bank Loan		9 403.00
GST Payable		710.61
PST Payable		1 015.15
C. Argue, Capital		44 981.93
C. Argue, Drawings	6 000.00	
Sales		40 606.69
Sales Returns and Allowances	141.91	
Cost of Goods Sold	28 300.72	
Bank Charges	1 103.20	
Delivery Expense	159.80	
Miscellaneous Expense	178.36	
Rent Expense	3 200.00	
Wages Expense	3 645.90	
	$112 071.62	$112 071.62

Applications — Comprehensive

Unless otherwise indicated, taxes have been included in the final dollar figures given.

(a) Enter the trial balance shown in Figure 9-25 into running-balance ledger accounts.

(b) Journalize and post the following transactions. Assume that a periodic inventory system is used. PST of 10 percent is applied to the base price plus GST (7 percent).

(c) Take off a trial balance.

(d) Complete the worksheet for the month ending August 31 using the following adjusting information:
Merchandise inventory $24 200
Supplies on hand 370
Declining balance depreciation rates:
(Adjust for one month of depreciation.)
   Computer equipment, 30% per year;
   Office equipment, 20% per year;
   Automobile, 30% per year.
Interest on the bank loan is 10% per year. (Charge interest for the month.)

(e) Prepare the adjusting entries in general journal form and post to the general ledger.

(f) Prepare an income statement and a classified balance sheet.

(g) Prepare the closing entries in general journal form and post to the general ledger.

(h) Take off a post-closing trial balance.

Transactions

Aug. 1 Purchase Invoice #24932: From Holiday Cycles Ltd., $4 820 for merchandise; terms 2/10, n/30.

    1 Cheque Copy #493: To Barton's Real Estate, $2 490 plus GST for monthly rent.

    3 Cheque Copies:
#494 to C.C.M. Ltd., $4 867.29 for Purchase Invoice #231, $4 960, less discount of $92.71.
#495 to Nova Scotia Electric, for $187 plus GST for hydro expense.

    4 Sales Invoices:
#429 to M. Reklitis, $170 plus taxes.
#430 to A. Nesrallah, $320 plus taxes.

    4 Cash Sales Slips #892 to #914: Cash sales of $1 420 plus taxes.

    4 Cash Refund Slip #44: To G. Gray, $16 plus taxes.

    4 Memo #32: The owner withdrew $220 worth of merchandise for personal use. (Remember to calculate the taxes.)

    9 Purchase Invoice #553: From C.C.M. Ltd., $2 392 for merchandise; terms 2/10, n/30.

    9 Cheque Copies:
#496 to Metropolitan Life, $400 for insurance. (No taxes are applicable.)
#497 to Daytona Cycle Ltd., $2 240 on account.

    10 Bank Debit Memo: $23 for service charges.

    10 Sales Invoices:
#431 to C. Watanabe, $280 plus taxes.
#432 to J. Labrosse, $190 plus taxes.

    10 Credit Memo #48 received: From Holiday Cycles Ltd., $279 for allowance on Purchase Invoice #24932, due to damaged merchandise.

    14 Cash Sales Slips #915 to #963: Cash sales of $2 497 plus taxes.

    14 Credit Memo #92 issued: To C. Watanabe, refund on Sales Invoice #431, $280 plus taxes.

15 Purchase Invoice #883B: From the *Halifax Chronicle* for advertising, $247 plus GST. Terms n/30.
15 Credit Memo #22 received: From C.C.M. Ltd., $220 return on Purchase Invoice #553.
20 Purchase Invoice #88: From Daytona Bicycle Co., $3 290 for merchandise; terms 2/10, n/30.
20 Cheque Copy #498: To Holiday Cycles Ltd., $4 456.12 for Purchase Invoice #24932, $4 820, less Credit Memo #48, $279, less discount of $84.88.
23 Purchase Invoice #64: From Scotia Pride Transport, $84 for transportation on incoming merchandise.

FIGURE 9-25

Performance Bicycles of Halifax
Trial Balance
July 31, 19--

Acct	Account	Debit	Credit
100	Cash	$ 7 110	
101	Accounts Receivable	14 029	
102	Merchandise Inventory	29 200	
103	GST Recoverable	319	
104	Supplies	982	
105	Prepaid Insurance	840	
106	Computer Equipment	6 488	
107	Accumulated Depreciation: Computer Equipment		$ 4 924
108	Office Equipment	14 980	
109	Accumulated Depreciation: Office Equipment		11 240
110	Automobile	17 420	
111	Accumulated Depreciation: Automobile		12 480
201	Accounts Payable		19 200
202	Bank Loan		22 550
203	GST Payable		420
204	PST Payable		600
301	M. Terrett, Capital		22 954
302	M. Terrett, Drawings	3 000	
401	Sales		
402	Sales Returns and Allowances		
403	Sales Discounts		
501	Purchases		
502	Freight-in		
503	Purchases Returns and Allowances		
504	Purchases Discounts		
505	Advertising Expense		
506	Bank Charges		
507	Miscellaneous Expense		
508	Rent Expense		
509	Utilities Expense		
510	Delivery Expense		
		$94 368	$94 368

25 Cheque Copies:
    #499 to C.C.M. Ltd., $2 131.40 for Purchase Invoice #553, $2 392, less Credit Memo #22, $220, less discount of $40.60.
    #500 to Scotia Pride Transport, $53 for delivery of sales.
29 Purchase Invoice #644: From Office Furniture Products, $725 plus taxes for computer equipment.
30 Memo #33: A correcting entry was required. A $350 purchase of merchandise, on account, had been incorrectly debited to Office Equipment.

Focussing

1. Purchases Returns and Allowances

Barbara Cheung is owner of Skate Accessories, a store that caters to figure skaters. As her accountant, you notice that there has been a significant increase in purchases returns and allowances during the current busy season. The constant returns have caused her to lose sales. The returns have been for a variety of reasons.

(a) When designing the chart of accounts, what should be done in order to make the amount of purchases returns and allowances readily apparent.
(b) Prepare a list of five reasons why merchandise that has been purchased would have to be returned to the supplier.
(c) For each item in (b), indicate how the problem could be eliminated.

2. Comparing Periodic Inventory to Perpetual Inventory

For each of the following,
(a) indicate the source document that would provide the data for the accounting entry,
(b) give the accounting entry that would occur under the periodic inventory system, and
(c) give the accounting entry that would occur under the perpetual inventory system.

Use two columns similar to the following for the entries, so that a comparison can easily be made.

PERIODIC INVENTORY	PERPETUAL INVENTORY

(i) Purchased $5 000 of merchandise on account.
(ii) Paid $200 for transportation-in on merchandise.
(iii) Returned $750 worth of merchandise which was defective.
(iv) Paid $2 300 on account. A discount of $120 had been taken off the original amount owing.
(v) Sold $250 worth of merchandise on account. Cost of the merchandise was $160.
(vi) Paid $170 for delivery expense.
(vii) Paid $230 for return of merchandise. Cost of the merchandise was $140.
(viii) Received $500 on account. A discount of $12 had been taken off the original amount by the debtor.

Evaluate and Assess

It is estimated that Canadian retailers are losing $2 million a day to shoplifting, employee theft, and through clerical error. The term used to describe these losses is shrinkage. In 1988, this represented approximately 1.28 percent of total sales. Estimates show that over one half of the shrinkage is stolen by consumers, one quarter by employees, and the balance is due to clerical error.

Peter Viglasky owns a hardware store. He noticed that in the last few months there seemed to be an increase in merchandise theft, and he assumed that it was by customers.

(a) Which system of inventory would allow Peter to make "spot checks" in order

to confirm that merchandise was being stolen? Explain how this procedure would work.
(b) Would it be practical for Peter to maintain a perpetual inventory system using a manual accounting system? Justify your answer.
(c) What costs would there be for Peter in switching from a manual to a computer accounting system?
(d) As the accountant for Peter, recommend five steps that would reduce the chance of theft by customers.

Synthesize and Conclude

1. Accounting Errors

For each of the following errors, indicate
(a) what effect the error would have on the balance sheet;
(b) what effect the error would have on the income statement;
(c) when the error might be found;
(d) the journal entry required to correct the error.

(i) A $4 500 debit was made to Purchases, instead of to Office Equipment.
(ii) A $200 debit was made to Office Supplies, instead of to Sales Returns and Allowances.
(iii) A $700 debit was made to Merchandise Inventory, instead of to Purchases.
(iv) A $500 credit was made to Sales Returns and Allowances, instead of to Purchases Returns and Allowances.
(v) A $980 debit was made to Office Expense, instead of to Purchases.
(vi) A $2 400 adjustment for bad debts was omitted.

2. Effect of Errors

George Lamirande was hired as accountant for Great Western Hardware Ltd. In the first few days, purchase invoices were received for the following items:

Merchandise	$2 900
Office Supplies	424
Office Equipment	4 390
Transportation-in	120

George, in error, made a debit to Purchases for all of these items.
(a) Indicate the account that should have been debited for each of these items.
(b) Indicate the effect that the incorrect recording of these invoices by George will have on the income statement, and the balance sheet.

3. Departmental Income and Loss

When Mary Cosenzo started her sports shop, she was unsure of how she could calculate the net income/net loss of each department in the store. She wanted to be aware of these statistics so that she could increase the display area of the successful departments, and decrease the display area of the unsuccessful departments.
(a) In merchandising, it is assumed that 20 percent of the products carried provide 80 percent of the sales. Explain how this relates to what Mary wants to do.
(b) What costs are involved in having a product line that does not sell? Why might some slow-selling product lines have to be carried?
(c) Propose an accounting system that would provide Mary with the information that she wants.
(d) What can Mary do with the inventory of product lines that she no longer intends to carry?

Accounting At Work

Michael Iannou
Computer Analyst/Programmer

Michael Iannou works as a computer analyst/programmer helping to design database systems for various companies. He gained his expertise in systems analysis and design through a combination of formal education and on-the-job training. Michael believes that the work environment is the best place to learn about the newest developments in the area of computer science.

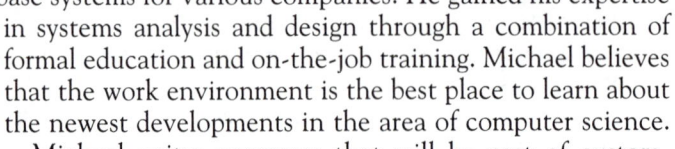

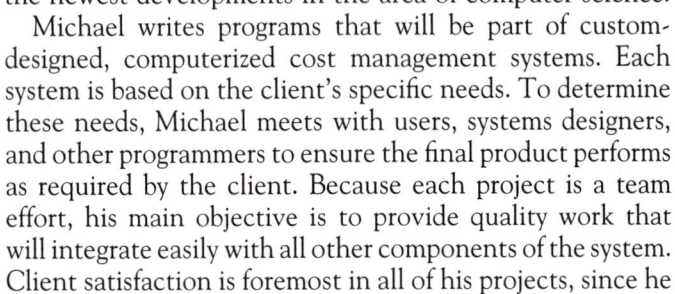

Michael writes programs that will be part of custom-designed, computerized cost management systems. Each system is based on the client's specific needs. To determine these needs, Michael meets with users, systems designers, and other programmers to ensure the final product performs as required by the client. Because each project is a team effort, his main objective is to provide quality work that will integrate easily with all other components of the system.

Client satisfaction is foremost in all of his projects, since he works on a contract basis: future clients are attracted by the success of past projects.

Michael graduated from secondary school in Australia, where he specialized in mathematics and science subjects. This was followed by four years of broad-based business studies courses. Because of his interest in computer subjects, he took specialized computer courses at certificate level on a part time basis while working. He learned that it is often more economical for smaller employers to train their own people rather than to bring in specialists. Consequently, Michael found that he was able to supplement his formal education with on-the-job computer experience.

Throughout his career he has acquired a number of special skills. He emphasizes those needed in the field of database management. "It's a relatively new technique of describing, storing, and processing different types of information . . . and the ability to use new software products that are based on this technology seems to be in strong demand." Michael contends that these specialized database design skills complement the understanding of organizational and systems analysis he brings to his work.

For now, Michael plans to expand his client base. He hopes that his current position will lead to work opportunities with clients having new and varied requirements for computer applications. He hopes to gain the freedom whereby he can select the sort of clients and the type of work he undertakes. Michael feels that computer science and its application is a dynamic and growing area and he thoroughly enjoys the challenges it presents him.

Programmer/Analyst
$33,592 - $36,946

Responsibilities: The Programmer/Analyst is responsible for providing technical and analytical skills, including analyzing business requirements and completing a systems analysis of user requests for computer system development. You will also develop computer applications and provide training to divisional users.

Education: The ideal candidate will have a degree in Computer Science or a comparable community college certificate along with 3 years of experience in systems design, programming, and systems maintenance. A thorough knowledge of all end-user tools, for both microcomputers and mainframes, is required, together with an enhanced reliability clearance and good English communications skills.

The Offer: An extremely competitive and attractive benefits package includes relocation expenses.

If you are interested in this position, please mail your résumé to Personnel Manager, Technodata International, P.O. Box 4621, Kitchener, ON, N3C 4J2.

1. Describe the job of a computer analyst/programmer.
2. What education and experience is necessary to be a computer programmer?
3. What skills, other than computer and accounting, are required for either of these positions?
4. What is the "benefits package" referred to in the advertisement?
5. What parts of his job does Michael Iannou enjoy?

Business Career Skills

Problem Solving

1. A sporting goods business's bad debts are 3 percent of sales. The owner thinks that this percentage is too high, and establishes a goal of 2 percent for the next fiscal period. The store carries a large variety of seasonal goods for popular sporting and recreation activities, including footwear. Sales for the last two years have averaged $1 430 000.
   In groups,
   (a) brainstorm to develop at least five reasons why sales returns result;
   (b) provide a possible solution for each of the reasons;
   (c) establish a return policy for the store, and justify each of the conditions in it.

2. In recent years, performance appraisal on the job has become a greater concern for businesses. Increased employee productivity is an objective of all businesses, especially in this era of increased global competition.

(a) In groups, brainstorm to develop a list of items that you think an employee should be appraised on.
(b) Individually, rank the list that you obtain from most important to least important.
(c) In groups, compare your individual rankings. Then, come to a consensus on a group ranking.

Communication

3. Many businesses have a procedure for bringing to the attention of customers the fact that their account is overdue. They have standard form letters which they send to clients who have been delinquent in paying their accounts. The wording of the letters varies, depending upon whether the account is overdue by 60, 90, or more than 90 days.
(a) Prepare a standard form letter that could be sent to clients whose accounts are 90 days overdue.
(b) Prepare a standard form letter that could be sent to clients whose accounts are more than 90 days overdue. This letter should indicate that legal action will be taken if the account is not paid within 10 days.

COMPUTER ACCOUNTING
INVENTORY CONTROL

One of the most obvious changes that we are now seeing is the vast proliferation of computers in the home and in small business. What started as a hobby or curiosity in the 1970s, has become an operational reality. In the coming years, the microcomputer will become an almost indispensable tool in every conceivable category of small business — from the gas station to the most elegant of restaurants. In the 1990s, any small operator who runs his or her business without some form of data or word processing will be severely hampered from a competitive standpoint. Not only will the cost of operating a non-computerized business rise rapidly, but the effective use of time, which is essential in a small business, will have a significant impact on the successful operation of the firm. Time, it is said, is the one commodity that we all possess equally — 24 hours per day, no more, no less. As the computer takes over more and more of the repetitive, time-consuming jobs in a small business, the manager or owner will be freer to devote more energy to planning, growth, and return on investment.

One area where the computer can be used for real savings in both time and money is inventory control. Outside of any fixed assets, such as real estate and equipment, inventory is where most of the investment in a business really is. The objective in respect of inventory is to stock only movable, saleable, profitable items, but never to run out of an item that customers might need.

Finding a computerized inventory control package that fits a particular business may require more research than that required to locate a general ledger program. The problem is to find the routine that most closely resembles the way a particular business operates. Both wholesale and retail firms have considerable sums tied up in the finished goods of others. Hospitality and tourism operations have unique inventory situations such as, the necessity to stock seasonal items, while service businesses may have limited inventory, or no inventory at all. If a firm has purchased a total accounting package that includes an inventory control module, they may or may not be able to make use of it. If they have to seek an inventory control package, they must be certain that they understand the nature of their own inventory system and needs.

Inventory control means a great deal more than just knowing how many of an item are on hand. The purchase of a good inventory control program may be one of the best investments a business makes, especially if the business buys goods for resale. It is not uncommon for medium-size retail stores to have between 15 000 and 25 000 different items in their inventory.

When considering inventory for resale, there are two measurements that are critical to the success of the business. The first is return on investment, which directly reflects the markup on the cost of items to the business. This is known as **gross profit** or **gross margin**. The second is **inventory turnover** — the number of times that an inventory level is replenished and then sold. Good inventory packages deal primarily with these aspects.

Exercises
1. WestCoast Interiors

Instructional Objectives
You have studied the steps involved in processing financial data for a merchandising firm using a manual accounting system. That system included a general journal and general ledger. You are now ready to learn how the periodic inventory system can be converted to a microcomputer system.

Upon completion of this exercise you will be able to:

1. Load your accounting software program, and set up and access accounting data files for a sole proprietorship merchandising business using the periodic inventory system.
2. Convert an existing manual accounting system to one using an integrated accounting software package.
3. Enter transactions into the computer using the general ledger module.
4. Display and print accounting transactions and reports.
5. Save your data entries and exit the accounting software program.

Steve Robens, the owner of WestCoast Interiors, a paint and decorating store located at 800 East Hastings Street, Vancouver, BC V3N 4C6, has been keeping his own accounting records since he started his business two years ago. Because he stocks many low-priced items for resale, Steve follows the periodic inventory method to determine the cost of goods sold for an accounting period.

At a recent Rotary luncheon, he listened to an interesting presentation from a computer consultant from a major public accounting firm on the advantages of computerizing accounting records. After much investigation, he has decided to purchase an IBM microcomputer system with the appropriate accounting software. He has engaged you to set up his computerized accounting system and input the accounting transactions for the first month following the conversion of the accounting records. This happens to be the start of his fiscal year, July 1.

Solution
You will use your data files disk to create a file directory for this company, if this is part of your accounting software requirements. After recording the company name and other data, you will need to prepare the module(s) you will require and also set up the Chart of Accounts to be used by the business.

After converting the account balances from the manual accounting records to the

FIGURE 9-26

Chart of Accounts

101 Cash	301 S. Robens, Capital
102 A/R Budget Decor	302 S. Robens, Drawings
103 A/R Deverill Painting	401 Sales
104 A/R Multicolour Painting	402 Sales Discounts
105 A/R Van-Rich Decorators	403 Sales Returns and Allowances
106 A/R West Coast Painting	501 Cost of Goods Sold
108 Merchandise Inventory	502 Purchases
110 GST Recoverable	503 Freight-in
112 Office Supplies	504 Purchases Discounts
116 Store Supplies	505 Purchases Returns and Allowances
130 Office Equipment	506 Store Supplies Expense
131 Acc. Dep. — Office Equipment	507 Salaries Expense
135 Store Equipment	508 Bank Charges
136 Acc. Dep. — Store Equipment	510 Advertising Expense
201 Bank Loan	511 Office Supplies Expense
202 A/P Canadian General Paint	512 Rent Expense
203 A/P Mohawk Finishing Supplies	513 Telephone Expense
204 A/P Tower Exclusive Paints	514 Cash Short and Over
205 A/P Your Finishing Warehouse	515 Miscellaneous Expense
206 GST Payable	516 Dep. Exp. — Office Equipment
207 PST Payable	517 Dep. Exp. — Store Equipment
208 Salaries Payable	

computerized files, you will journalize the transactions for the month of July. You will print or display your general journal and a trial balance to determine if your journalizing is correct. Once your journalizing is correct, you will then print out the general journal, all ledger accounts, the trial balance, and the financial statements.

As this business uses a periodic inventory system, a Cost of Goods Sold account is used and must be updated at the end of the month. This is necessary since most accounting software packages do not provide for the printing of a detailed cost of goods sold section as part of the income statement. The procedure to follow is given in detail at the end of the exercise.

Steve has provided you with the company's present chart of accounts (Figure 9-26). Use that as well as Figures 9-27, 9-28, and 9-29 to layout the financial statements, and to obtain the opening balances for the ledger accounts. Prepare the necessary module(s) in your accounting software package to process the accounting transactions for this business.

Journalizing the Transactions

Note: Assume unless otherwise indicated that GST (7%) has been applied to these transactions as required. Where PST (6%) has been applied, it is to the base price only. Terms of sales are 1/10, n/30. Remember that discounts are calculated on the base price only. There is no discount on GST.

July 1 Purchase Invoice #702: From Canadian General Paint for paint products, $880.00; terms 2/10, n/30.

1 Cash Receipt Slip #284: $588.50 from Deverill Painting in full payment of Sales Invoice #560. No discount taken.

1 Cash Receipt Slip #285: $428.00 from Budget Decor in full payment of Sales Invoice #559. No discount taken.

FIGURE 9-27

WestCoast Interiors
Income Statement
For the Month Ended June 30, 19--

Revenue:
Sales			$28 900
Sales Discounts		$ 560	
Sales Returns and Allowances		430	990
Net Sales			27 910

Cost of Goods Sold:
Inventory, June 1			$18 560
Purchases		$16 890	
Freight-in		240	
Cost of Delivered Goods		17 130	
Purchases Discounts	$200		
Purchases Returns and Allowances	210	410	
Net Purchases			16 720
Cost of Goods Available for Sale			35 280
Inventory, June 30			23 560
Cost of Goods Sold			11 720
Gross Profit on Sales			16 190

Expenses:
Store Supplies		$ 180
Salaries		3 255
Bank Charges		145
Advertising		750
Office Supplies		240
Rent		1 800
Telephone		120
Cash Short and Over		5
Miscellaneous		12
Dep. Exp. — Office Equipment		160
Dep. Exp. — Store Equipment		115
Total Expenses		6 782
Net Income		$ 9 408

1. Cash Receipt Slip #286: $212.11 from Multicolour Painting in full payment of Sales Invoice #561, $214.00, less the sales discount of $1.89.
1. Cheque Copy #238: $1 800.00 plus GST, to pay the store rent for July.
1. Sales Invoice #567: To Deverill Painting for merchandise sold, $760.00 plus taxes.
2. Cheque Copy #239: $113.00 (includes taxes) to Brenda Peters, the office clerk, to reimburse her for the purchase of office supplies from Premier Office Supplies Ltd. She submitted Purchase Invoice 5667 marked "Paid."
2. Cash Receipt Slip #287: $1 021.29 from Van-Rich Decorators in full payment of Sales Invoice #562, $1 030.41, less the sales discount of $9.12.
3. Cheque Copy #240: $450.00 to Mohawk Finishing Supplies in full payment of Purchase Invoice A380. No discount taken.
4. Cheque Copy #241: $1 177.57 to Canadian General Paint in full payment of Purchase Invoice S682, $1 200.00, less the purchase

FIGURE 9-28

WestCoast Interiors
Balance Sheet
as at June 30, 19--

Assets

Current Assets:			
Cash		$13 955.00	
Accounts Receivable:			
Budget Decor	$1 070.00		
Deverill Painting	588.50		
Multicolour Painting	1 498.00		
Van-Rich Decorators	1 514.05		
West Coast Painting	465.45	5 136.00	
Merchandise Inventory		23 560.00	
GST Recoverable		568.00	
Office Supplies		600.00	
Store Supplies		700.00	
Total Current Assets			$44 519.00
Fixed Assets:			
Office Equipment	$9 600.00		
Less: Accumulated Depreciation	4 000.00	5 600.00	
Store Equipment	6 900.00		
Less: Accumulated Depreciation	2 875.00	4 025.00	
Total Fixed Assets			9 625.00
Total Assets			$54 144.00

Liabilities

Current Liabilities:			
Bank Loan		$12 000.00	
Accounts Payable:			
Canadian General Paint	$1 200.00		
Mohawk Finishing Supplies	450.00		
Tower Exclusive Paints	810.00		
Your Finishing Warehouse	564.00	3 024.00	
GST Payable		2 023.00	
PST Payable		860.00	
Total Current Liabilities			$17 907.00
Owner's Equity:			
S. Robens, Capital		$29 829.00	
Add: Net Income		9 408.00	
		39 237.00	
Less: Withdrawals		3 000.00	
Total Owner's Equity			36 237.00
Total Liabilities and Owner's Equity			$54 144.00

discount of $22.43.
5 Purchase Invoice A402: Purchased decorating materials for $1 892.00 from Mohawk Finishing Supplies; terms 2/10, n/30.

5 Cash Receipt Slip #288: $636.32 from Budget Decor in full payment of Sales Invoice #563, $642.00, less the sales discount of $5.68.

FIGURE 9-29

```
                    WestCoast Interiors
                 Post-Closing Trial Balance
                       June 30, 19--
```

Cash	$13 955.00	
A/R Budget Decor	1 070.00	
A/R Deverill Painting	588.50	
A/R Multicolour Painting	1 498.00	
A/R Van-Rich Decorators	1 514.05	
A/R West Coast Painting	465.45	
Merchandise Inventory	23 560.00	
GST Recoverable	568.00	
Office Supplies	600.00	
Store Supplies	700.00	
Office Equipment	9 600.00	
Accumulated Depreciation — Office Equipment		$ 4 000.00
Store Equipment	6 900.00	
Accumulated Depreciation — Store Equipment		2 875.00
Bank Loan		12 000.00
A/P Canadian General Paint		1 200.00
A/P Mohawk Finishing Supplies		450.00
A/P Tower Exclusive Paints		810.00
A/P Your Finishing Warehouse		564.00
GST Payable		2 023.00
PST Payable		860.00
S. Robens, Capital		36 237.00
	$61 019.00	$61 019.00

5 Sales Invoice #568: To Budget Decor for merchandise sold, $200.00 plus taxes.

5 Cash Sales Slips #175-#189: Weekly cash sales of $2 410.00 plus taxes.

5 Cheque Copy #242: To Tower Exclusive Paints, in full payment of Purchase Invoice B69587, $810.00.

8 Cheque Copy #243: $172.00 plus GST to Western Canada Carriers, for freight bill on merchandise purchased from Mohawk Finishing Supplies.

8 Cash Receipt Slip #289: $1 272.64 from Multicolour Painting in full payment of Sales Invoice #564, $1 284.00, less the sales discount of $11.36.

8 Purchase Invoice B70423: From Tower Exclusive Paints for merchandise, $813.20; terms 2/10, n/30.

8 Credit Memorandum CM45: From Mohawk Finishing Supplies, $120.00, for damaged goods that were returned to them on Purchase Invoice A402.

8 Cheque Copy #244: $564.00 to Your Finishing Warehouse in full payment of Purchase Invoice 108695. No discount taken.

8 Cash Receipt Slip #290: $483.64 from Van-Rich Decorators in full payment of Sales Invoice #565.

9 Sales Invoice #569: To Van-Rich Decorators for merchandise sold for $650 plus taxes.

11 Sales Invoice #570: To West Coast Painting for merchandise sold for $320.00 plus taxes.

11 Cash Receipt Slip #291: From Deverill Painting, $851.20 in full payment of Sales Invoice #567, $858.80, less the sales discount of $7.60.

11 Cheque Copy #245: $863.55 to Canadian General Paint in full payment of Purchase Invoice #702, $880.00, less the purchase discount of $16.45.

12 Cash Sales Slips #190-#214: Weekly cash sales of $2 134.00 plus taxes.

15 Cheque Copy #246: To Provincial Treasurer for sales tax collected for the month of June, $860.00.

15 Cheque Copy #247: $1 455.00 to the Receiver General of Canada for GST collected in June. The GST Payable was $2 023.00 and the input tax credit was $568.00.

15 Cash Receipt Slip #292: From Budget Decor, $224.00 in full payment of Sales Invoice #568, $226.00, less the sales discount of $2.00.

15 Cheque Copy #248: $1 738.88 to Mohawk Finishing Supplies in full payment of Purchase Invoice A402, $1 892.00, less Credit Memorandum CM45, $120.00, less the purchase discount of $33.12.

16 Sales Invoice #571: To Multicolour Painting for merchandise sold, $642.00 plus taxes.

18 Cheque Copy #249: $798.00 to Tower Exclusive Paints in full payment of Purchase Invoice B70423, $813.20, less the purchase discount of $15.20.

19 Cash Receipt Slip #293: $728.00 from Van-Rich Decorators in full payment of Sales Invoice #569, $734.50, less the sales discount of $6.50.

19 Cash Sales Slips #215-#222: Weekly cash sales of $1 897.00 plus taxes.

22 Cash Receipt Slip #294: $465.45 from West Coast Painting in full payment of Sales Invoice #566.

22 Sales Invoice #572: To Budget Decor for merchandise sold for $740.00 plus taxes.

23 Cheque Copy #250: To the *Vancouver Sun* for $800.00 plus GST for advertisements.

26 Cash Sales Slips #223-#245: Weekly cash sales of $1 987.00 plus taxes.

26 Sales Invoice #573: To Deverill Painting for $1 328.00 plus taxes.

27 Sales Invoice #574: To Van-Rich Decorators for $856.00 plus taxes.

28 Cheque Copy #251: To BC Telephone Company for $136.30 plus taxes to pay the monthly telephone bill.

28 Purchase Invoice S867: From Canadian General Paint for paint products for $1 400.00; terms 2/10, n/30.

30 Cheque Copy #252: $3 000.00 to Steve Robens for his personal use.

30 Cheque Copy #253: To Super Computer Supplies, $680.25 (includes taxes), for computer forms and ribbons.

30 Cheque Copy #254: Record the salaries expense for the month, $3 400.00.

Before you enter any adjusting entries print a copy of the trial balance and have it checked by your teacher.

Month-End Activities

30 At the end of the business day, the closing merchandise inventory, as determined by a physical count, was $24 452.00. Since the business is using a periodic inventory system, the following entries must now be made in order to include cost of goods sold in the income statement.
   (a) Remove the beginning inventory by debiting Cost of Goods Sold and crediting Merchandise Inventory.
   (b) Transfer the account balances of Purchases, Freight-in, Purchases Discounts, and Purchases Returns and Allowances to Cost of Goods Sold.
   (c) Record the ending inventory by debiting Merchandise Inventory for $24 452.00 and crediting Cost of Goods Sold for the same amount.

30 Additional adjusting entries must be made from the following information ascertained from company records or inventory procedures:
   (a) Office Supplies on hand $395.
   (b) Store Supplies on hand $487.
   (c) The company depreciates both the office equipment and store equipment at a rate of 20% per year on the declining-balance basis.

Before printing any of the requested reports, display or print the adjusted trial balance and have it checked by your teacher.

Print a hard copy of the following or those requested by your teacher:

1. General Journal
2. General Ledger
3. Income Statement
4. Balance Sheet

Evaluation

You will now use your printouts to complete,

(a) an audit test of the accuracy of the accounting records of the business.

(b) analysis exercises.

2. Great North Suppliers I

Instructional Objective

To load and use your spreadsheet program to design and complete an eight-column worksheet for a merchandising business using a periodic inventory system. The trial balance appears in Figure 9-30. The data for the adjustments for the month are as follows:

(i) Accrued interest earned on the term deposit is calculated to be $140.00.

(ii) Provision for bad debts is based on a standard 5% of accounts receivable.

(iii) The value of the office supplies on hand is $1 100.00 and the value of store supplies is $413.00.

(iv) Office equipment was purchased 10 months ago and was estimated at that time to have a useful life of 4 years, and a salvage value of $400.00.

(v) Store equipment was completely replaced at the beginning of May of this year and was estimated at that time to have a useful life of 3 years, and a salvage value of $600.00.

(vi) A physical count of the goods on hand revealed a merchandise inventory of $12 235.00.

Formulas:

(i) Use the SUM function to calculate column totals.

(ii) Use the IF function (condition,x,y) to determine the net income/loss and its placement on the worksheet.

FIGURE 9-30

Great North Suppliers
Trial Balance
October 31, 19-4

101	Cash	$11 351.00	
102	Petty Cash	100.00	
103	Term Deposit — 90 Days	15 000.00	
104	Accounts Receivable	8 666.00	
105	GST Recoverable	326.00	
106	Allowance for Bad Debts		$ 126.00
108	Merchandise Inventory	14 452.00	
112	Office Supplies	1 305.00	
116	Store Supplies	722.00	
120	Office Equipment	9 400.00	
121	Accumulated Depreciation — Office Equipment		1 687.50
125	Store Equipment	6 936.00	
126	Accumulated Depreciation — Store Equipment		880.00
201	Demand Loan Payable		12 000.00
204	Accounts Payable		1 372.00
205	GST Payable		1 274.00
207	PST Payable		1 138.85
301	B. Faxton, Capital		42 962.00
302	B. Faxton, Drawings	3 000.00	
401	Sales		26 315.50
402	Sales Discounts	73.25	
403	Sales Returns and Allowances	230.00	
410	Interest Income		140.00
501	Purchases	9 430.00	
502	Freight-in	890.00	
503	Purchase Returns and Allowances		304.00
504	Salaries Expense	3 400.00	
505	Bank Charges	130.00	
506	Advertising Expense	800.00	
507	Office Expense	13.40	
508	Rent Expense	1 800.00	
509	Telephone Expense	136.20	
510	Cash Short and Over	11.00	
511	Miscellaneous Expense	28.00	
		$88 199.85	$88 199.85

(iii) You must enter data values for only the Trial Balance columns. For the other columns, formulas are required.

3. Great North Suppliers II

Instructional Objective

To use the completed worksheet exercise from Question 2 in conjunction with your spreadsheet program to design an income statement and balance sheet for the merchandise business.

Column Widths:

(i) Income Statement
  (a) Set the column width containing the Revenue, Cost of Goods Sold and Expense account titles to 40.
  (b) Set a global column width for the three amount columns to 12.

(ii) Balance Sheet
  Report Form
  (a) Set the column width containing the

section headings and account titles to 50.

(b) Set a column width of 12 for the amount columns.

Account Form

(a) The Assets and Liabilities/Owner's Equity columns should be set at 25.

(b) Set a column width of 12 for the amount columns.

Formulas:

(i) Use the SUM function where applicable.

(ii) Net Sales = Sales − (Sales Discounts + Sales Returns and Allowances)

(iii) Gross Profit on Sales = Net Sales − Cost of Goods Sold

(iv) Net Income/Loss = Gross Profit on Sales − Expenses

(v) Formulas will be needed for assets that have contra accounts.

Project 2 — THE ACCOUNTING CYCLE

Olympic Sporting Goods rents premises in the Outaouais Shopping Complex. The business has shown an increase in profits each year, focussing on the merchandising of seasonal sporting goods in team and racquet sports.

(a) Prepare a general ledger using the accounts and balances shown in Figure A.
(b) Journalize and post the transactions for October 27 to 31. (Assume that the transactions for the rest of the year have been journalized and posted, and are included in the account balances given.) Olympic Sporting Goods does not operate its own credit card system — its only accounts receivable are from NSF cheques, which the bank returns. It accepts MasterCard and VISA. The discount rate in both cases is 3 percent. The GST is 7 percent and the PST is 8 percent calculated on the base price. The firm's policy on returns is to issue a credit memo to be applied against outstanding account balances or used for a future purchase.

Oct. 27 Cash Sales Slips #732-#794: Sales $1 890 plus taxes.
Purchase Invoices:
#393, from Bauer Sporting Suppliers, $4 360 plus GST of $305.20 for merchandise.
#093-221, from Needhill Office Supplies, $680 plus GST of $44.07 for supplies.
Cheque Copies:
#429, $1 323 on account to Titan Hockey Equipment; a discount of $27 was taken.
#430, $2 300 plus GST to CJOH television, for advertising.
Credit Memo #400: From Northstar Skate Co., $2 300 plus GST for return of skates.
Credit Memo #783: Issued to Mothi Nanjappa, $138 plus taxes. Item was purchased on account.
Bank Credit Memo: $21 error on bank charges for previous month.
VISA and MasterCard Deposit Summary: Sales, $560 plus taxes less discount.

FIGURE A

No.	Account	Debit	Credit
100	Cash	$ 24 680	
101	Accounts Receivable	430	
105	Merchandise Inventory	96 490	
110	GST Recoverable	1 380	
115	Supplies	7 400	
120	Prepaid Rent	8 000	
125	Prepaid Insurance	2 400	
130	Furniture and Fixtures	140 000	
135	Acc. Dep.: Furn. & Fix.		$ 34 400
140	Van	24 600	
145	Acc. Dep.: Van		14 600
200	Accounts Payable		21 640
205	GST Payable		2 380
210	PST Payable		3 257
215	Bank Loan		72 880
300	K. Snider, Capital		143 336
310	K. Snider, Drawings	32 800	
320	Income Summary		
400	Sales		564 400
410	Sales Returns & Allowances	4 820	
500	Purchases	237 980	
510	Transportation-In	4 505	
520	Purchases Returns & Allowances		1 690
530	Purchases Discounts		4 603
600	Advertising Expense	22 025	
605	Bank Charges	375	
610	Cleaning Expense	14 600	
620	Dep. Exp.: Furn. & Fix.		
630	Dep. Exp.: Van		
640	Insurance Expense	12 400	
645	Interest Expense	7 300	
650	Light, Heat, Water Expense	17 300	
660	Miscellaneous Expense	9 080	
670	Rent Expense	44 000	
680	Repairs and Maintenance Expense	13 450	
690	Supplies Expense	16 022	
700	Telephone Expense	6 349	
710	Van Expense	7 800	
720	VISA & MasterCard Discount Expense	5 400	
730	Wages Expense	101 600	

28 Cash Sales Slips #795-#817: Sales, $1 680 plus taxes.
   Purchase Invoices:
      #43-801, from Yanovich Business Fixtures, $2 300 plus taxes for display cabinets.
      #944, from Modern Sportswear, $2 450 plus GST for merchandise.
   Cheque Copies:
      #431, $124 plus taxes to Acme Repair Services, for repairs to fixtures.
      #432, $200 plus GST to Tidy Maid, for cleaning of store.
      #433, $260 plus taxes to Bell Canada, for telephone expenses.
      #434, $250 to Outaouais Secondary School Students' Council, for advertising in the local yearbook. (GST exempt)
   Bank Debit Memo: $56 plus $15 service charge for NSF cheque from Carl Fraser. The service charge is passed on to the customer.
   VISA and MasterCard Deposit Summary: Sales, $1 200 plus taxes less discount.
   Memo #44: The owner took merchandise worth $120 plus taxes for personal use.
29 Cash Sales Slips: #818-#829: Sales, $240 plus taxes.
   Purchase Invoices:
      #13B, from Beeline Transport, $112 plus GST for transportation of display fixtures purchased from Yanovich Business Fixtures.
      #214, from Cantel, $900 plus taxes, for purchase of a cellular telephone.
      #887, from Tartan Swimwear, $820 plus GST for merchandise.
   Cheque Copies:
      #435, $500, to the owner for personal use.
      #436, $680, to the Receiver General for GST; GST Recoverable was $310.
      #437, $116, to Outaouais Water Services.
      #438, $456, to Northern Sportswear on account; a discount of $24 had been taken.
   Bank Debit Memo: $1 607, for payment on bank loan (interest $607 included).
   VISA and MasterCard Deposit Summary: Sales, $420 plus taxes less discount.
30 Cash Sales Slips #830-#851: Sales, $1 200 plus taxes.
   Purchase Invoices:
      #402, from Honest Auto, $350 plus taxes for van expenses.

#602, from Dolmy Football Equipment Ltd., $1 200 plus GST for merchandise.

Cheque Copies:
#439, $220 plus GST to Outaouais Power, for electricity.
#440, $62 plus GST to Canada Post, for postage stamps.

VISA and MasterCard Deposit Summary: Sales, $910 plus taxes less discount.

Memo #45: Error correction; a $48 debit to Telephone Expense earlier in the month should have been to Light, Heat, Water Expense.

31 Cash Sales Slips #852-#860: Sales, $408 plus taxes.

Cash Receipt Slip #181: $154 from K. Petch, on account for an NSF cheque.

Purchase Invoices:
#0338, from Bauer, $902 plus GST for merchandise.
#633, from Beeline Transport, $104 plus GST for transportation of merchandise.

Cheque Copies:
#441, $2 000 for weekly wages.
#442, $112 plus taxes to Joe's Garage, for repairs to the owner's personal car.
#443, $1 260 on account to Northern Sportswear; the original invoice was for $1 200 plus GST. A discount of 2 percent was taken.

Credit Memo #309: From Yanovich Business Fixtures, $300 plus taxes, on return of a display cabinet.

Credit Memo #784: Issued to T. Whyte, $35 plus taxes, for merchandise returned. Amount applied to outstanding account.

VISA and MasterCard Deposit Summary: Sales, $230 plus taxes less discount.

(c) Prepare a trial balance on an eight-column worksheet, for the year ending October 31.
(d) Complete the worksheet, using the following additional information:

Merchandise inventory, $98 405

Supplies on hand, $1 340

One month of the prepaid rent, in the amount of $4 000, had expired.

The insurance policy, purchased on August 1, was for six months.

Depreciation rates used are the capital cost allowance rates.
(e) Prepare the financial statements.
(f) Journalize and post the adjusting and closing entries.
(g) Prepare a post-closing trial balance.

CHAPTER TEN

Subsidiary Ledger Systems

LEARNING OBJECTIVES

At the end of this chapter you should be able to
- describe the design of a three-ledger system;
- describe the tasks carried out by the people involved in a subsidiary ledger system;
- complete the accounting tasks of an accounts payable clerk, accounts receivable clerk, and accounting supervisor;
- describe the process of batch journalizing;
- distinguish between direct and indirect posting;
- state and explain the need for, and advantages of, a subsidiary ledger system;
- use an accounting software program to convert an existing manual system to a microcomputer-based system;
- utilize the general ledger, accounts payable, and accounts receivable modules of the accounting software program in the conversion process.

LANGUAGE OF ACCOUNTING

You will see the following terms in this chapter:
batch journalizing
computer subsidiary modules
control account
direct posting
indirect posting
matching of documents
requisition
schedule of accounts
statement of account
subsidiary ledger
systems analysis and design

10.1 The Subsidiary Ledger System

As a business grows, its accounting system needs adjustments in order to keep up with the volume of transactions. One of the more significant changes in the business is in the number of suppliers and customers with whom it deals. Imagine the largest retail store in your area, and the number of items that it must obtain from suppliers. Most of these items are bought on account. Then, imagine the number of customers who buy goods on account. In a large metropolitan area, the sales on account for one department store could be in the hundreds of thousands of dollars a day.

Chapter 10: Subsidiary Ledger Systems

If one person was doing the journalizing and posting for a large store using a general journal and a general ledger, the job would never be completed because there would be too many transactions to record. A trial balance would take pages and pages if all the names of the suppliers and customers were listed. In order to efficiently provide information on individual suppliers and customers, a change in the accounting system that we have studied to date is needed.

> **Systems analysis and design:** the network of related procedures initiated to perform some major business activity.

To make necessary changes, a process called **systems analysis and design** first takes place. Systems analysis and design consists of the network of related procedures initiated to perform some major business activity. An accounting expert analyzes the accounting needs of the business and designs a system that should be used. He or she must take into consideration all the users of the accounting information so that the best available system can be implemented. In this chapter we will look at a system that has a general journal, and three ledgers: the general ledger, the accounts payable ledger, and the accounts receivable ledger. Such a system would only be used by a large business, at a stage when the accounting task became too large for one person to handle. In the next chapter, more elaborate systems that add different types of journals will be examined.

FIGURE 10-1 A SUBSIDIARY LEDGER SYSTEM

ACCOUNTING SYSTEMS

```
                    Source documents
                    /              \
           General journal      Subsidiary ledgers
                  |                    |
           General ledger              |
                    \                 /
                   End of month procedures
```

> **Subsidiary ledger:** an extra ledger containing accounts of one type.

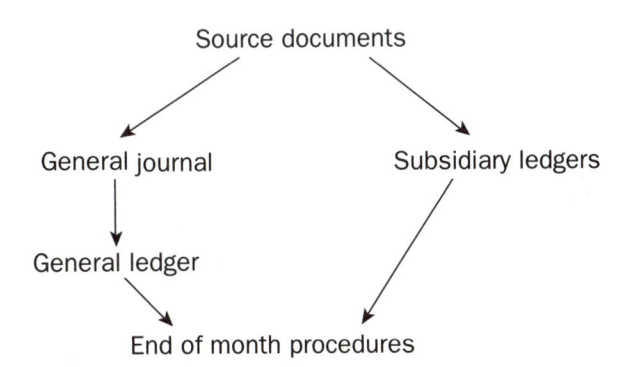

The criterion for setting up an accounts payable subsidiary ledger system or an accounts receivable subsidiary ledger system is that the number of suppliers providing credit and/or customers using credit has become so large that it is practical to establish additional ledgers to keep records of changes in their accounts. The word subsidiary means additional or extra. A **subsidiary ledger** is an extra ledger containing accounts of one type. These subsidiary ledgers are subordinate to the general ledger, and give more detail. Even when computer systems are used and one person can do the accounting alone, there may be so many suppliers from which the business buys on credit, or customers using credit, that it is practical to establish subsidiary ledgers.

In order to establish these ledgers, all of the individual accounts for suppliers that the business buys from on credit and customers that the business sells to on credit are put into separate ledgers. The accounts of the suppliers that the business buys from on credit are removed from the general ledger and put into a ledger called the accounts payable subsidiary ledger. The accounts of the customers that the business sells to on credit are removed from the general ledger and put into a ledger called the accounts receivable subsidiary ledger.

Once the supplier accounts and customer accounts are removed from the general ledger, the trial balance will no longer balance. Because the trial balance is one of the essential proofs in accounting, the new system must be organized so that the double-entry accounting principle still relates to the general ledger. For this reason, a **control account** is found in the general ledger, and its balance represents the total of all accounts in its related subsidiary ledger. The total of all the individual accounts payable is represented in the general ledger by one account called the Accounts Payable (control) account. Similarly, the total of the individual accounts receivable is represented in the general ledger by one account called the Accounts Receivable (control) account.

Control account: an account in the general ledger whose balance represents the total of all accounts in its related subsidiary ledger.

FIGURE 10-2 IN A SUBSIDIARY LEDGER SYSTEM, INDIVIDUAL CUSTOMER AND SUPPLIER ACCOUNTS ARE REMOVED FROM THE GENERAL LEDGER AND REPLACED BY CONTROL ACCOUNTS

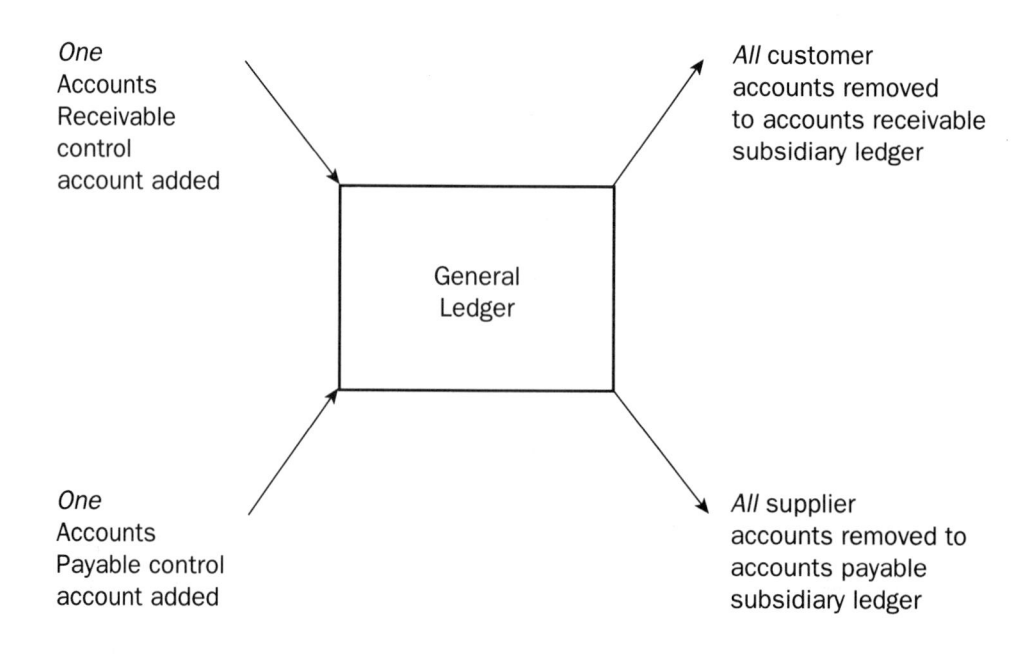

One Accounts Receivable control account added

All customer accounts removed to accounts receivable subsidiary ledger

General Ledger

One Accounts Payable control account added

All supplier accounts removed to accounts payable subsidiary ledger

There are now three ledgers: the general ledger, the accounts receivable ledger, and the accounts payable ledger. The task of entering transactions in each of the three ledgers and the general journal is divided among people in the accounting department. In some cases, the business may be so large that there are hundreds of people looking after accounts receivable. The people maintaining the two subsidiary ledgers are closely related to other departments: the accounts payable clerk to the purchasing department, and the accounts receivable clerk to the credit and sales departments. For the purposes of this text, we will assume that there are three people doing the accounting, with the following responsibilities:

FIGURE 10-3 TASKS PERFORMED BY PERSONNEL IN THE ACCOUNTING DEPARTMENT

Accounting Department

Accounting Supervisor	Accounts Payable Clerk	Accounts Receivable Clerk
(All source documents)	(Source documents related to accounts payable)	(Source documents related to accounts receivable)
Journalize		
Post	Post to the accounts payable subsidiary ledger	Post to the accounts receivable subsidiary ledger
Trial balance	Schedule of accounts payable	Schedule of accounts receivable
Worksheet		
Financial statements		
Journalize; post adjusting and closing entries		
Post-closing trial balance		

The job specifications related to each of these positions are described in detail in the sections that follow.

LESSON REVIEW

1. Why do businesses need to change their accounting systems as they grow?

2. What process is carried out in order to determine the accounting needs of a business?

3. (a) What does "subsidiary" mean?
   (b) What two subsidiary ledgers are used in this chapter?

4. What must physically be done in order to establish the subsidiary ledgers?

5. Describe the relationship between the Accounts Payable control account and the accounts payable ledger.

6. Describe the relationship between the Accounts Receivable control account and the accounts receivable ledger.

LESSON APPLICATIONS

7. The following trial balance as at November 30, 19-- is for the Frisky Trading Company. The firm has decided to establish a subsidiary ledger system for accounts payable and accounts receivable, using the information on the trial balance.

Frisky Trading Company
Trial Balance
November 30, 19--

No.	Account	Debit	Credit
100	Cash	$ 1 593.43	
110	R. Ambridge	242.50	
111	B. Kuntz	193.92	
112	F. Larimer	928.16	
113	D. Potvin	89.14	
114	S. Stanko	320.91	
120	GST Recoverable	400.00	
130	Supplies	934.05	
140	Equipment	28 248.00	
150	Automobile	18 200.00	
200	Bunton Merchandisers		$ 328.50
201	Kelly Building Cleaning		1 212.00
202	Parkinson's Supply Service		112.00
203	Palmer's Store Displays		721.45
220	Short-Term Loan		2 400.00
230	GST Payable		595.00
300	J. Parker, Capital		32 134.36
310	J. Parker, Drawings	2 800.00	
400	Revenue		34 000.00
500	Rent Expense	2 500.00	
510	Utilities Expense	800.00	
520	Wages Expense	14 000.00	
525	Interest Expense	120.55	
530	Miscellaneous Expense	132.65	
		$71 503.31	$71 503.31

(a) Set up the accounts payable ledger, using T-accounts.
(b) Set up the accounts receivable ledger, using T-accounts.
(c) Show the two new accounts that will appear in the general ledger, and enter the balances that should be in them.

10.2 The Purchasing Department and Accounts Payable

> **Purchasing procedure:** all the steps from the time that a good or service is wanted by a business, to the time that payment for the good or service has been completed.

The **purchasing procedure** includes all the steps from the time that a good or service is wanted by a business, to the time that payment for the good or service has been completed. The procedure varies from business to business. The purchasing department is usually responsible for approving purchases, finding suppliers, and ensuring that the goods arrive at their destination. The department may also be responsible for approving payment of purchase invoices. An accounts payable clerk may assist in this latter task. The clerk will record the liabilities arising from purchases, and the subsequent payment of those liabilities.

For discussion purposes, we will assume that the purchasing department carries out the first two steps in the purchasing procedure, as outlined below; the accounts payable clerk carries out steps three, four, and six; and the accounting supervisor carries out step five.

Purchasing Procedure

1. Checking purchase requisitions
2. Issuing purchase orders
3. Matching documents and approving payment
4. Making entries in the accounts payable ledger
5. Making entries in the general journal, and posting to the general ledger
6. Preparing a schedule of accounts payable

Each of these tasks is discussed in more detail.

> **Purchase requisition:** a request by someone in a business that goods or services be purchased by the business.

1. Checking Purchase Requisitions

An employee who wishes to purchase an article for the business needs to complete a **purchase requisition**, or request. Usually only certain persons have permission to order items for any one department.

FIGURE 10-4 A PURCHASE REQUISITION USED BY ALGOR COMPUTER SERVICES

```
                        Algor Computer Services
                        Purchase Requisition # 461

Department: ____Furniture_____  Date: __May 28, 1992__
Department Budget Number: ___ACF 242_____
Date Required By: ___June 15, 1992_____
Suggested Supplier: ___Modern Business Products Ltd._____
Address: ___790 Industrial Ave._____
         ___Ottawa ON  K1G 4H3_____
```

Quantity	Description	Unit Price	Total
2	high back swivel and tilt armchairs	170 –	340 –
	TOTAL		340 –

```
To be completed by Purchasing:
Approved by: ___D. Webster_____ Date: __May 31, 1992__
Purchase Order Number: ___91 – 773_____
Copy Returned to Department: ___✔_____
```

The requisition is sent to the purchasing department. The department checks to ensure that there are sufficient funds remaining in the department's budget, and it will find a supplier for the goods if one is not named on the requisition. In larger businesses, buyers are sent out by the firm to purchase merchandise and can do so under their own authority, without a requisition being required.

2. Issuing Purchase Orders

Purchase order: form sent to a supplier for the purchase of goods or services.

Once the requisition has been approved, a **purchase order** is sent to the supplier for the purchase of goods or services. The order should indicate the items wanted, the stock numbers if ordered from a catalogue, the price to be paid for the goods, and, possibly, a suggested method of transportation and terms of payment.

FIGURE 10-5 A PURCHASE ORDER SENT BY ALGOR COMPUTER SERVICES TO A SUPPLIER

```
                        Algor Computer Services
                           55 Eastern Parkway
                              Kanata, ON
    ALGOR                      K2L 2B1
    COMPUTER
    SERVICES             Order Number: 91-773

Order Date:  June 1, 1992          Date Required:  June 15, 1992
To: Modern Business Products Ltd.  Deliver to: Algor Computer Services
    790 Industrial Ave.                        55 Eastern Parkway
    Ottawa, ON  K1G 4H3                        Kanata, ON  K2L 2B1
```

Item	Quantity	Description of Goods or Services	Unit Price	Amount
642	2	high back swivel and tilt armchairs	170 —	340 —
			TOTAL	340 —

Note: 1. Terms Net 30 unless preauthorized.
       2. Order not valid unless signed by a buyer of Algor Computer Services.
       3. Price variances in excess of $50 must be approved by Algor Computer Services prior to shipment.

Dale Webster
Signature of Buyer

See Reverse for Tax Information.

Copies of the purchase order may be distributed as follows:
- to the supplier;
- to the department making the request, so that they know the goods have been ordered;
- to the receiving department, so that it is aware that the goods will arrive in the future, and necessary arrangements can be made for storage;
- to the purchasing department, so that matching of documents can take place.

3. Matching Documents and Approving Payment

The supplier will send the goods via a delivery system to the receiving department of the business. When the cartons are opened, there should be a packing slip inside. The **packing slip** indicates which goods should be in the carton. The slip looks exactly like an invoice, except that the cost prices are usually missing.

Packing slip: *form indicating the contents of a shipment.*

FIGURE 10-6 A PACKING SLIP, RECEIVED BY ALGOR COMPUTER SERVICES

Modern Business Products Ltd.
790 Industrial Ave.
Ottawa, ON K1G 4H3

Sales Order No. __4332__ Sales Order Date __June 8, 1992__
Customer No. __3187__ P.O. Number __91 - 773__
Sold To __Algor Computer Services__ Ship To __Algor Computer Services__
__55 Eastern Parkway__ __55 Eastern Parkway__
__Kanata, ON__ __Kanata, ON__
__K2L 2B1__ __K2L 2B1__

Terms __2/10, n/30__ Date Shipped __June 13, 1992__

Product No.	Quantity	Description	Unit Price		Ordered	B/O	Amount
642	2	high back swivel	170	–	2	nil	******
Delivery							******
						TOTAL	******

Filled by __Tom S.__ Checked by __JD__ Packed by __Fred K__
Delivery Charges __$ 20.00__ Number of Pieces __2__

This is a Packing Slip, Not an Invoice
See Reverse for Conditions

The receiving department compares the contents of the carton with the information on the packing slip. Discrepancies are noted on the slip. The slip is signed and dated, and sent to the accounts payable

Receiving report: a separate document which may be completed, indicating the contents of a shipment.

clerk. In some businesses, a separate document called a **receiving report** is completed. Once the paper work is completed, the receiving department notifies the department that ordered the goods that the order has arrived in the business.

The purchase invoice usually arrives by mail. The goods and the invoice are usually sent separately, so that if one is lost the other arrives. As well, management usually does not want employees in the receiving department to know the cost of purchases.

FIGURE 10-7 A PURCHASE INVOICE RECEIVED BY ALGOR COMPUTER SERVICES

Modern Business Products Ltd.
790 Industrial Ave.
Ottawa, ON K1G 4H3   #449

Sales Order No. __4332__   Sales Order Date __June 8, 1992__
Customer No. __3187__   P.O. Number __91 - 773__
Sold To __Algor Computer Services__   Ship To __Algor Computer Services__
         __55 Eastern Parkway__   __55 Eastern Parkway__
         __Kanata, ON__   __Kanata, ON__
         __K2L 2B1__   __K2L 2B1__

Terms __2/10 , n/30__   Date Shipped __June 13, 1992__

Product No.	Quantity	Description	Unit Price	Ordered	B/O	Amount
642	2	high back swivel	170 00	2	nil	320 00
Delivery						20 00
					GST	23 80
					PST	25 60
					TOTAL	389 40

Filled by __Tom S.__   Checked by __JD__   Packed by __Fred K__
Delivery Charges __$20.00__   Number of Pieces __2__

INVOICE
See Reverse for Conditions

Matching of documents: *the process of comparing the purchase order, the packing slip and/or the receiving report, and the purchase invoice.*

Accounts payable clerk: *the clerk responsible for updating the accounts payable subsidiary ledger, which shows amounts owing to suppliers.*

Direct posting: *the transferring of information directly from a source document to a subsidiary ledger.*

Accounting supervisor: *the person responsible for two books: the general journal, and the general ledger.*

Once the invoice and the copy of the receiving report or packing slip have been received by the accounts payable clerk, a process called document matching takes place. The three documents to be **matched** are the purchase order, the packing slip and/or the receiving report, and the purchase invoice. The items compared are

(a) purchase order and packing slip: shows that the goods ordered were the ones received;
(b) purchase order and purchase invoice: shows that the price offered was the price charged;
(c) packing slip and purchase invoice: shows that the goods that were received are the goods that the business is charged for.

4. Making Entries in the Accounts Payable Ledger

If the three documents match, the **accounts payable clerk** makes an entry in the accounts payable subsidiary ledger to record the liability to the supplier. The clerk's initials, and the date, are recorded on the purchase invoice to indicate that the entry was made in the subsidiary ledger. Note that instead of making an entry in the PR column, an entry has been made in the Particulars column to indicate the source of the information for the entry. Suppliers may be listed in the subsidiary ledger in alphabetical order, or in numerical order if they have been assigned an account number. This procedure of posting from a source document to a subsidiary ledger account is called **direct posting**.

ACCOUNTS PAYABLE SUBSIDIARY LEDGER

ACCOUNT	Modern Business Products Ltd.					NO	
DATE 1992		PARTICULARS	PR	DEBIT	CREDIT	DR/CR	BALANCE
June	22	Purchase Invoice #449			389 40	CR	389 40

5. Making Entries in the General Journal, and Posting to the General Ledger

The documents are then forwarded to the **accounting supervisor** who is responsible for making an entry in the general journal and posting that entry to the general ledger. (In some businesses, the accounts

GENERAL JOURNAL

PAGE 601

DATE 1992		PARTICULARS	PR	DEBIT	CREDIT
June	22	Office Equipment	175	365 60	
		GST Recoverable	135	23 80	
		Accounts Payable	200		389 40
		Purchase Invoice #449, Modern Business Products Ltd; terms 2/10, n/30			

payable clerk will have made a copy of the purchase invoice when it arrived, if the supplier didn't send multiple copies, and will have forwarded a copy to the accounting supervisor.)

It is this entry that keeps the control account in balance with the accounts payable subsidiary ledger, for the posting of the $389.40 credit to the control account matches the amount that was posted to Modern Business Products Ltd. in the subsidiary ledger.

GENERAL LEDGER

Office Equipment	175	GST Recoverable	135	Accounts Payable	200
dr.	cr.	dr.	cr.	dr.	cr.
June 22 365.60		June 22 23.80			June 22 389.40

Figure 10-8 summarizes the accounting procedures carried out by the accounts payable clerk and the accounting supervisor in processing the purchase invoice.

FIGURE 10-8 ACCOUNTING PROCEDURES FOR PROCESSING A PURCHASE INVOICE

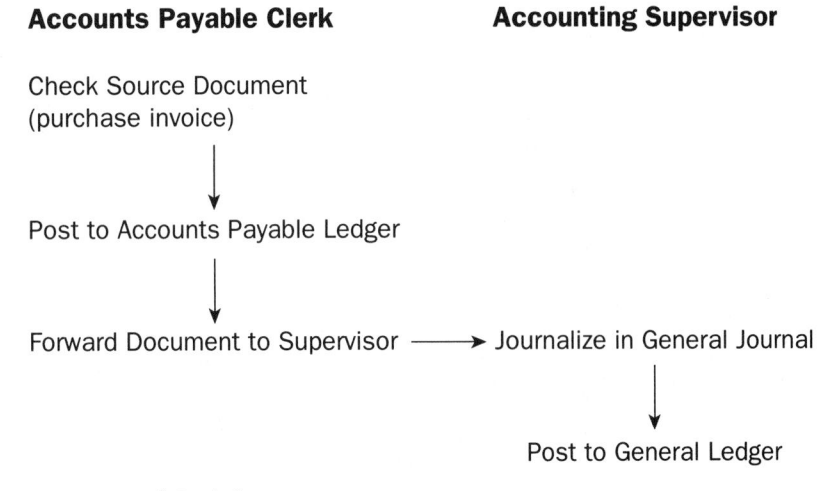

Accounts Payable Clerk

Check Source Document
(purchase invoice)
↓
Post to Accounts Payable Ledger
↓
Forward Document to Supervisor ⟶

Accounting Supervisor

Journalize in General Journal
↓
Post to General Ledger

Payment of Liabilities

Tickler file: *a system used to file purchase invoices by due date.*

The source documents may be filed by the accounting supervisor in a **tickler file**, which is a system used to file purchase invoices by due date. In this filing system, there is a section for each calendar day. For example, a purchase invoice with a discount date of October 10, with terms 2/10, n/30 should be filed under October 7 to ensure that it is mailed on time to obtain the discount. On any particular day, the accounts payable clerk removes the purchase invoices due on that day, has them approved for payment, prepares a cheque requisition, and forwards all the documents to the treasurer. The treasurer issues a cheque, and sends a cheque copy or a cheque stub to the accounts payable clerk for entry into the accounts payable ledger. The supplier's account will be debited to reduce the liability.

FIGURE 10-9 REDUCING THE LIABILITY IN THE SUBSIDIARY LEDGER

ACCOUNTS PAYABLE SUBSIDIARY LEDGER

ACCOUNT Modern Business Products Ltd.					NO	
DATE 1992	PARTICULARS	PR	DEBIT	CREDIT	DR/CR	BALANCE
June 22	Purchase Invoice #449			389 40	CR	389 40
29	Cheque Copy #313		389 40		—	0

The cheque copy is then forwarded to the accounting supervisor who makes an entry in the general journal and posts to the general ledger.

GENERAL JOURNAL

PAGE 603

DATE 1992	PARTICULARS	PR	DEBIT	CREDIT
June 29	Accounts Payable	200	389 40	
	Cash	100		389 40
	Cheque Copy #313, Modern Business Products Ltd. for			
	Purchase Invoice #449			

Again, this entry by the accounting supervisor keeps the control account in balance with the accounts payable ledger, for the posting of the $389.40 debit to the Accounts Payable control account matches the amount that was posted to Modern Business Products Ltd. in the subsidiary ledger.

GENERAL LEDGER

Accounts Payable	200	Cash	100
dr.	cr.	dr.	cr.
June 29 389.40	June 22 389.40		June 29 389.40

When the accounting supervisor is finished with the cheque copy, it is filed numerically. The purchase invoice that has been paid will be filed according to the supplier's name.

Figure 10-10 summarizes the accounting procedures carried out by the accounts payable clerk and the accounting supervisor in processing the cheque copy.

FIGURE 10-10 ACCOUNTING PROCEDURES FOR PROCESSING A CHEQUE COPY

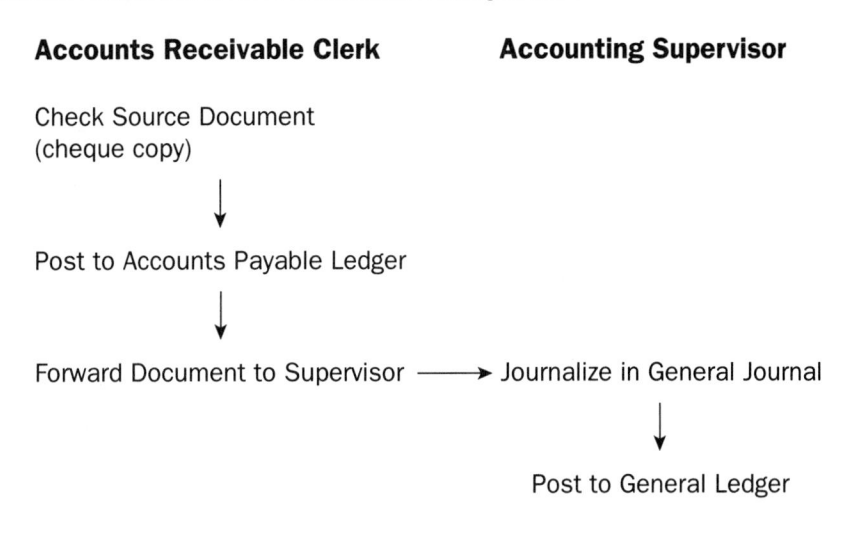

Accounts Receivable Clerk

Check Source Document
(cheque copy)
↓
Post to Accounts Payable Ledger
↓
Forward Document to Supervisor ⟶

Accounting Supervisor

Journalize in General Journal
↓
Post to General Ledger

6. Preparing a Schedule of Accounts Payable

Schedule of accounts payable: *a list of the suppliers and the amounts owing to them.*

The accounts payable clerk prepares a **schedule of accounts payable** at the end of the month. This schedule is a list of all the suppliers and the amounts owing to them. Note that the balances are usually all credit balances, for they are liabilities. It is possible, however, for an Accounts Payable account to have a debit balance. This can result from an overpayment, a return or allowance, or a correction of an error. Theoretically, accounts with debit balances should be listed as current assets. However, in practice such accounts, if they are not significant in amount, are combined with the accounts payable that have credit balances.

FIGURE 10-11 A SCHEDULE OF ACCOUNTS PAYABLE PREPARED AT MONTH END

Algor Computer Services
Schedule of Accounts Payable
June 30, 1992

	Credit
Apple Canada Inc.	$12 340
Baton Furniture Ltd.	2 071
Berkley Computer Suppliers	9 870
Kanata Insurance Brokers	(20)
Modern Building Cleaners Ltd.	923
Willson Office Supplies Ltd.	342
	$25 526

When the schedule of accounts payable is finished, how does the clerk know if the ledger is correct? The clerk forwards a copy of the schedule of accounts payable to the accounting supervisor. If the total of the schedule is equal to the balance of the Accounts Payable control account found in the general ledger, then it is assumed that the accounting is correct. If the amounts are not equal, then a check must be made by both the clerk and the accounting supervisor to find any errors.

Errors made in the accounts payable ledger are usually of two types:
- debit entries put on the credit side, or vice versa
- errors in calculating the balance

To check for the first type of error, the accounts payable clerk should look down the Particulars column of each supplier's account and check to see that the proper entry was made for the type of source document involved in the transaction. Purchase invoices and debit memos received result in credit entries; cheque copies and credit memos received result in debit entries. To check for the second type of error, the quick techniques for checking account balances outlined in Chapter 4 should be followed.

The accounting supervisor should check for errors in the general journal and general ledger, following the procedures outlined in Chapter 4.

Summary of the Accounts Payable Procedure

All source documents related to accounts payable must be given to the accounts payable clerk. These documents include the following:
- Purchase invoices
- Cheque copies
- Credit memos received
- Debit memos received
- Memos for unusual transactions

The key to understanding the accounts payable ledger is to remember that the accounts payable clerk only deals with source documents that relate to accounts payable. Every time the accounts payable clerk makes an entry to a supplier's account, the accounting supervisor must make a change in the Accounts Payable control account. When all the posting is completed at month end, the following should always be true:

Total of all supplier accounts in accounts payable ledger = Balance of Accounts Payable control account

Figure 10-12 is a summary of the flow of documents through the various departments of the business that deal with purchasing.

FIGURE 10-12 THE FLOW OF DOCUMENTS THROUGH DEPARTMENTS THAT DEAL WITH PURCHASING

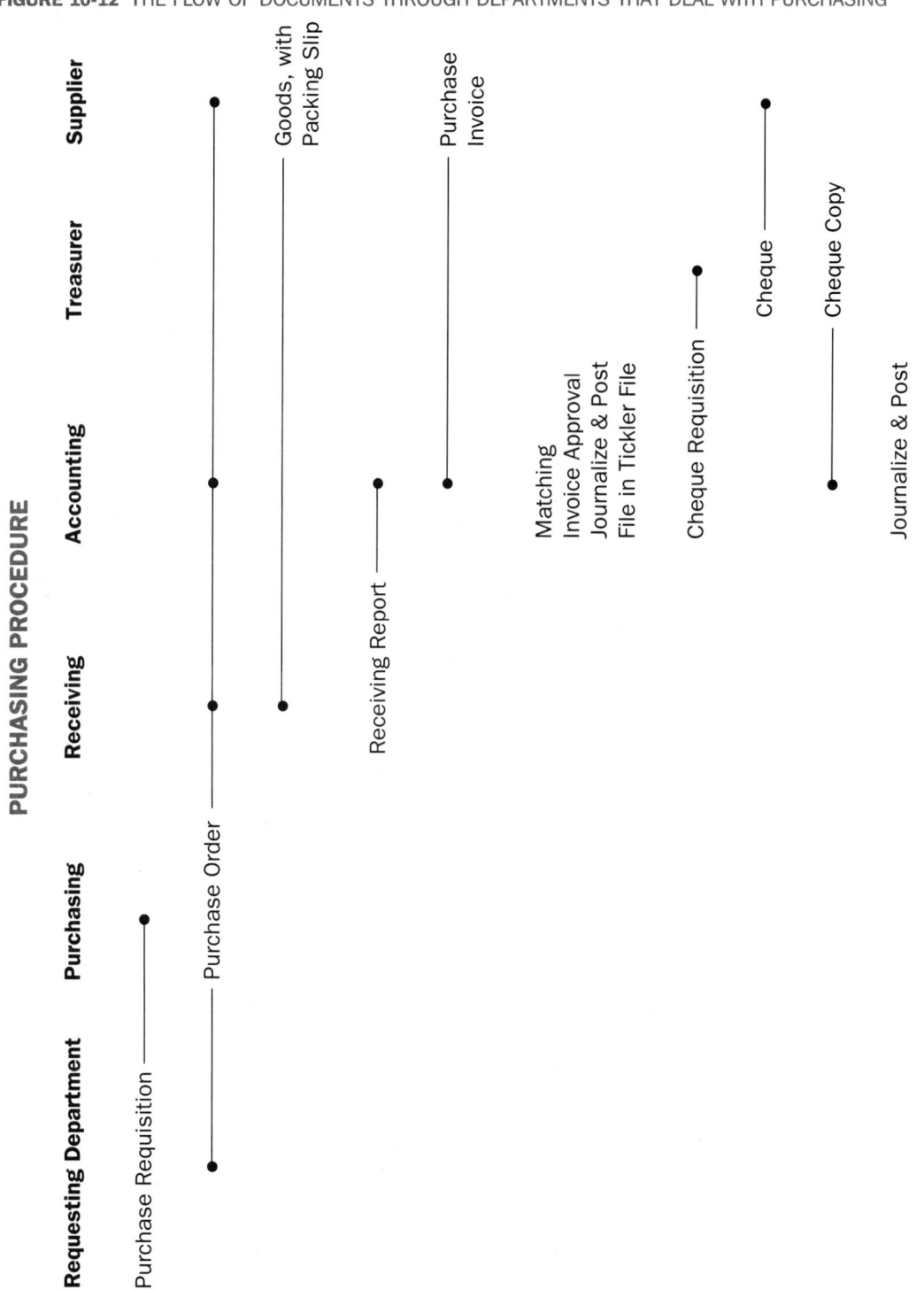

PURCHASING PROCEDURE

Requesting Department	Purchasing	Receiving	Accounting	Treasurer	Supplier
Purchase Requisition ———	●				
	——— Purchase Order ——————————————————————————→				●
		● ←————— Goods, with Packing Slip ———————————			●
		——— Receiving Report ———→ ●			
			● ←————— Purchase Invoice ———————————————		●
			Matching Invoice Approval Journalize & Post File in Tickler File		
			——— Cheque Requisition ———————→ ●		
				——— Cheque ——————————————→ ●	●
			● ←————— Cheque Copy ———————		
			Journalize & Post		

LESSON REVIEW

8. What is the relationship between the purchasing department and the accounts payable clerk?

9. Describe the first two steps in the purchasing process.

10. What departments in the business will receive a copy of the purchase invoice? State why each needs one.

11. What two documents does the business receive from the supplier? What is the purpose of each?

12. What three documents have to be matched? Why?

13. Describe the process of direct posting.

14. For a purchase of equipment on account, what entry does
    (a) the accounts payable clerk make?
    (b) the accounting supervisor make?

15. For a payment on account, what entry does
    (a) the accounts payable clerk make?
    (b) the accounting supervisor make?

16. (a) What is the main task carried out by the accounts payable clerk at month end?
    (b) How does the accounts payable clerk know if the work is correct?

17. In diagram form, show the movement of a purchase invoice through the business.

18. Distinguish between the theoretical and practical handling of accounts payable accounts with debit balances.

19. What are the two most common errors made in a subsidiary ledger? How does one check for each error?

20. What source documents are handled by the accounts payable clerk?

21. What cheque copies does the accounts payable clerk not handle?

22. What is the key relationship when trying to understand the accounts payable subsidiary ledger system?

LESSON APPLICATIONS

23. Marino Iannucci is an accounts payable clerk for Child's World. He has an accounts payable ledger with the following supplier accounts and the balances shown.

Gervais Business Supplies	$ 428.91
Houghton's Clothing Distributors	2 835.18
Saro's Clothiers	2 001.13
Westpoint Children's Wear	1 239.83

(a) Prepare an accounts payable ledger with an account for each of the suppliers, and enter the balances shown as of April 29.

(b) The following source documents were on Marino Iannucci's desk when he arrived at work on the morning of April 30. Enter them in the accounts payable ledger.

Purchase Invoice #152 from Saro's Clothiers, $820.00 plus GST of $57.40, for merchandise.

Purchase Invoice #493 from Westpoint Children's Wear, $325.00 plus GST of $22.75, for merchandise.

Purchase Invoice #494 from Westpoint Children's Wear, $732.00 plus GST of $51.24, for merchandise.

Purchase Invoice #915 from Gervais Business Supplies, $125.28 plus GST of $8.12, for accounting forms.

Purchase Invoice #14 from Houghton's Clothing Distributors, $491.00 plus GST of $34.37, for merchandise.

Credit Memo #19 from Gervais Business Supplies, $12.96 plus GST of $0.84, for computer ribbons returned to them.

Debit Memo #58 from Saro's Clothiers, $49.00 plus GST of $3.43, for error on Purchase Invoice of April 22, for merchandise.

24. In the afternoon, cheque copies arrived on Marino Iannucci's desk.
    (a) Using the same accounts payable accounts from Question 23, enter the cheque copies.
    Cheque Copy #58 to Gervais Business Supplies, $218.91 on account.
    Cheque Copy #59 to Houghton's Clothing Distributors, $1 535.18 on account.
    Cheque Copy #60 to Saro's Clothiers, $2 001.13 on account.
    Cheque Copy #61 to Westpoint Children's Wear, $417.90 on account.
    (b) Prepare a schedule of accounts payable for the end of April.

25. Each of the following source documents has been received from a supplier, and affects the accounts payable subsidiary ledger.
    (a) What is the first task that the accounts payable clerk will perform with each document?
    (b) When the clerk is finished with the document, what will be done with it?
    (c) Enter the transactions in an accounts payable ledger for City Clothiers. Assume that it is a new business, and open accounts for each supplier as needed. Add the 7% GST to all purchase invoices and debit and credit memos received. Apply 6% PST to the base price of all non-merchandise purchases as required.

Date	Source Document	#	Supplier	Explanation	Base Amount
May 3	Purchase Invoice	439	Norton Ltd.	Supplies	$ 129.08
4	Purchase Invoice	192	Weston	Merchandise	8 120.00
6	Credit Memo	19	Norton Ltd.	Supplies returned	18.00
8	Purchase Invoice	492	Norton Ltd.	Equipment	220.50
10	Purchase Invoice	824	Albion	Merchandise	2 405.12
10	Debit Memo	32	Weston	Error on May 4 purchase	87.45
13	Cheque Copy	4	Norton Ltd.	On account	125.52
14	Purchase Invoice	881	Albion	Merchandise	923.43
14	Cheque Copy	5	Weston	On account, less discount	8 781.97 164.15
15	Credit Memo	23	Weston	Merchandise returned	125.00
18	Cheque Copy	9	Norton Ltd.	On account	249.17
18	Purchase Invoice	253	Weston	Merchandise	3 420.03

(d) Prepare a schedule of accounts payable.

(e) In this business, the source documents are forwarded by the accounts payable clerk to the accounting supervisor. This saves the task of making copies of the source documents when they arrive in the business. Carry out the task of the accounting supervisor by entering the above source documents in general journal form, and posting them to the general ledger. The balance in the Cash account as of May 3 is $12 000.

26. John Kennedy & Sons operate a general store. The accounts payable ledger consists of the following suppliers and balances owing:

Ahuja News Co.	$ 239.14
Duncan Crafts Ltd.	722.91
S. Boriska Supplies	1 498.11
Veevers Importers Ltd.	2 914.20

When the accounts payable clerk arrived at work on November 1, all the source documents issued and received by John Kennedy & Sons were in a pile. She decided to separate them and begin work before the others arrived. From the following source documents, select those that she should take for entry in the accounts payable ledger, and enter them.

Sales Invoice #1772 to M. Gibson, $820.00 plus $57.40 GST and $65.60 PST, total $943.00.

Purchase Invoice #59 from S. Boriska Supplies, $369.90 plus $23.98 GST, for computer supplies on account.

Purchase Invoice #92 from Veevers Importers Ltd., $1 200.00 plus $84.00 GST, for merchandise.

Purchase Invoice #124 from Duncan Crafts Ltd., $750.00 plus $52.50 GST, for merchandise.

Sales Invoice #1773 to F. Carmasino, $284.00 plus $19.88 GST and $22.72 PST, total $326.60.

Cheque Copy #1 to Victoria Realty Ltd., $1 000.00 plus $70.00 GST, for rent for the month.

Cheque Copy #2 to Martin Delivery Service, $25.00 plus $1.75 GST for a total of $26.75, for transportation on Duncan Crafts Ltd. purchase.

Purchase Invoice #9112 from Ahuja News Co., $984.00 plus $68.88 GST, for merchandise.

Cash Receipt Slip #914 from K. Koops, $142.00 on account.

Credit Invoice #801 received from S. Boriska Supplies, $50.76 plus $3.29 GST, for return of merchandise.

Debit Memo #455 issued to D. Crosby, $41.00 plus $2.87 GST and $3.28 PST, for error on Sales Invoice #1423.

Cheque Copy #3 to Ahuja News Co., $234.36 including GST of $15.33 for Purchase Invoice #8931, less discount of $4.38.

Bank Debit Memo, $12 for service charges.

Cash Receipt Slip #915 from C. Laphen, $96 on account.

Debit Memo #28 received from S. Boriska Supplies, $53.00 plus $3.43 GST, for error on Purchase Invoice #59.

Credit Memo #68 issued to V. Arthur, $12.50 plus $0.88 GST and $1.00 PST, for goods returned.

10.3 The Credit Department and Accounts Receivable

In this "age of plastic," many merchandising businesses make the majority of their sales to those who use a credit card. One purchase of merchandise, such as swimsuits by a ladies wear store, will usually result in many sales to consumers. Thus, it is more likely that a business will have an accounts receivable subsidiary ledger than an accounts payable subsidiary ledger.

Since the use of credit cards has become a major method of payment at the retail level, special systems must be designed so that businesses can have control over this procedure. To gain this control, businesses will establish a credit department that is responsible for credit approval, and an accounts receivable department that is responsible for recording all claims on and payments by customers. Of course, if the business accepts only credit cards issued by banks, such as VISA or MasterCard, these tasks will be passed on to the bank.

Credit department: responsible for approving the granting of credit to customers.

Credit Department

When a customer wishes to obtain a store credit card, he or she is sent to the credit department. The procedure followed by this department was studied in Chapter 6. The credit department will contact the local credit bureau or a national credit rating institution such as Dun & Bradstreet in order to run a credit check on the applicant. Based on the information obtained from the credit bureau, and using its own guidelines for granting credit, the business decides whether to grant credit. A limit may be placed on the amount that can be charged. As the customer shows his or her reliability in making payments, the limit may be raised. The same procedure is followed by VISA, MasterCard, and other major credit card issuers.

Accounts Receivable Ledger

When a firm has thousands of customers buying on account, the presentation of all of their names on a trial balance, worksheet, or balance sheet would be very difficult. As was the case with accounts payable, a system that makes use of an accounts receivable subsidiary ledger makes the accounting system more efficient. A business that previously maintained individual accounts in the general ledger for each of its charge customers will remove them from the general ledger and place them in an accounts receivable subsidiary ledger. A business that grouped all charge customers together under Accounts Receivable will establish separate accounts for them in the accounts receivable subsidiary ledger. In order to keep the general ledger in balance, the individual accounts are replaced with one control account, in this case, the Accounts Receivable control account.

The sales cycle consists of all steps involved in making the sale, until payment has been received. All source documents issued by the business that are related to sales on account are sent to the **accounts receivable clerk** first. The tasks performed by the accounts receivable clerk are as follows:

Accounts receivable clerk: records all changes in the accounts receivable subsidiary ledger.

1. checking source documents and entering the data in the subsidiary ledger
2. preparing a schedule of accounts receivable
3. issuing statements of account to customers

Each of these tasks is outlined below. As with the accounts payable subsidiary ledger system, the accounting supervisor alone is responsible for the general journal and general ledger entries.

1. Checking Source Documents and Entering the Data in the Subsidiary Ledger

When a sale is made on account, a prenumbered sales invoice is completed by the sales clerk. A copy is given to the customer, and the original is given to the accounts receivable clerk. Each day the previous day's invoices will be available for posting.

The accounts receivable clerk checks to ensure that all the invoices are included, by checking the numerical sequence. A check is made of the accuracy of the invoice, and then the data is entered in the accounts receivable subsidiary ledger as a debit to the customer's account. Direct posting has occurred again: going directly from a source document to a subsidiary ledger account.

ACCOUNTS RECEIVABLE SUBSIDIARY LEDGER

ACCOUNT Murphy Enterprises					NO	
DATE 1992	PARTICULARS	PR	DEBIT	CREDIT	DR/CR	BALANCE
June 22	Sales Invoice #55-6449		782 –		DR	782 –

The document is initialled, dated, and forwarded to the accounting supervisor (unless a copy was forwarded). The supervisor then makes an entry in the general journal, posts it to the general ledger, and files the source document numerically.

GENERAL JOURNAL

PAGE 601

DATE 1992	PARTICULARS	PR	DEBIT	CREDIT
June 22	Accounts Receivable	120	782 –	
	Sales	420		680 –
	GST Payable	230		47 60
	PST Payable	240		54 40
	Sales Invoice #55-6449, Murphy Enterprises			

It is this entry that keeps the control account in balance with the accounts receivable ledger, for the posting of the $782 debit to the control account matches the amount that was posted to Murphy Enterprises in the accounts receivable subsidiary ledger.

GENERAL LEDGER

Accounts Receivable	120		Sales	420
dr.	cr.		dr.	cr.
June 22 782.00				June 22 680.00

GST Payable	230		PST Payable	240
dr.	cr.		dr.	cr.
	June 22 47.60			June 22 54.40

Note that again the work of the clerk and the accounting supervisor will agree. The accounts receivable clerk has made a debit entry to the account of Murphy Enterprises, and the accounting supervisor has made a debit entry to the Accounts Receivable control account.

FIGURE 10-13 ACCOUNTING PROCEDURES FOR PROCESSING A SALES INVOICE

Accounts Receivable Clerk

Check Source Document
(sales invoice)
↓
Post to Accounts Payable Ledger
↓
Forward Document to Supervisor ⟶

Accounting Supervisor

Journalize in General Journal
↓
Post to General Ledger

Figure 10-13 summarizes the accounting procedures carried out in processing the sales invoice.

When cash receipts arrive from customers paying on account, a list of these is prepared, indicating the name of the customer and the amount. These receipts can either arrive by mail, or by the customer coming into the business to make payment. A copy of the list is given to the accounts receivable clerk so that changes can be made in the accounts receivable subsidiary ledger. A copy is also sent, with the cheques, to the treasurer for deposit.

The accounts receivable clerk makes an entry in the accounts receivable subsidiary ledger showing a decrease in the claim the business has on the customer.

ACCOUNTS RECEIVABLE SUBSIDIARY LEDGER

ACCOUNT Murphy Enterprises   NO

DATE 1992		PARTICULARS	PR	DEBIT	CREDIT	DR CR	BALANCE
June	22	Sales Invoice #55-6449		782 —		DR	782 —
	29	Cash Receipt Slip #33-6689			782 —	—	∅

The list is then forwarded to the accounting supervisor to be entered in the general journal, and posted to the general ledger.

GENERAL JOURNAL

PAGE 603

DATE 1992		PARTICULARS	PR	DEBIT	CREDIT
June	29	Cash	100	782 —	
		Accounts Receivable	120		782 —
		Cash Receipt Slip #33-6689, Murphy Enterprises			

GENERAL LEDGER

Cash	100		Accounts Receivable	120
dr.	cr.		dr.	cr.
June 29 782			June 22 782	June 29 782

Figure 10-14 summarizes the accounting procedures carried out by the accounts receivable clerk and the accounting supervisor in processing a cash receipt slip.

FIGURE 10-14 ACCOUNTING PROCEDURES FOR PROCESSING A CASH RECEIPT SLIP

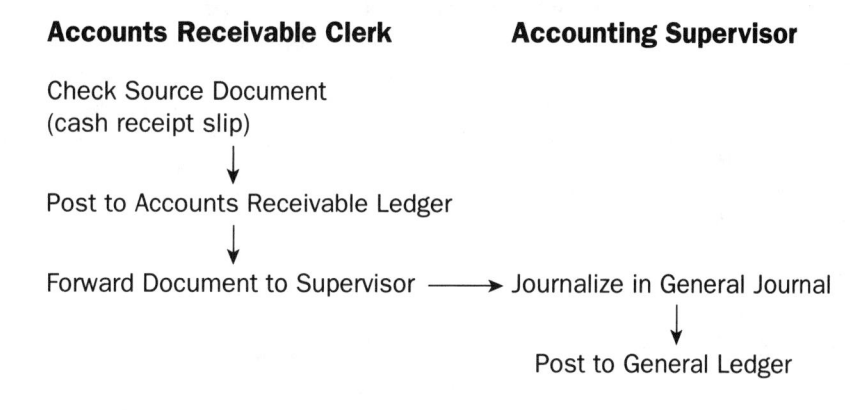

Accounts Receivable Clerk

Check Source Document
(cash receipt slip)
↓
Post to Accounts Receivable Ledger
↓
Forward Document to Supervisor ⟶

Accounting Supervisor

Journalize in General Journal
↓
Post to General Ledger

Schedule of accounts receivable: a list of all debtors, and the amount of the claim that the business has on them.

2. Preparing a Schedule of Accounts Receivable

At the end of the month, the accounts receivable clerk prepares a **schedule of accounts receivable** which lists all accounts receivable and their balances.

FIGURE 10-15 A SCHEDULE OF ACCOUNTS RECEIVABLE PREPARED AT MONTH END

Algor Computer Services
Schedule of Accounts Receivable
June 30, 1992

	Debit
Commerce High School	$12 458
Dakon Printers Ltd.	4 920
Fielding Motors Ltd.	1 243
Murphy Enterprises	4 220
New Visions Travel	(18)
Westview Visual Arts	11 659
	$34 482

Since these claims on customers are assets, they should all have debit balances. It is possible, however, for an Accounts Receivable account to have a credit balance. This credit balance can result from an overpayment, a return or allowance, or a correction of an error. Theoretically, accounts with credit balances should be listed as current liabilities. However, in practice, if they are not significant in amount, they are combined with the accounts receivable that have debit balances.

This schedule is forwarded to the accounting supervisor who compares it to the balance of the Accounts Receivable control account. The two must agree; if not, the discrepancy must be found.

3. Issuing Statements of Account

Once the schedule of accounts receivable is found to be correct, statements of account are sent to customers. A **statement of account** shows all the changes that have taken place in the customer's account during the month, and the amount owing as of the statement date. By law, a statement of account must also outline any interest charges that apply if the outstanding balance is not paid by the date shown.

Statement of account: *a document sent to a debtor to indicate changes in his or her account during the month, and the balance owing at the statement date.*

FIGURE 10-16 A STATEMENT OF ACCOUNT SENT TO WESTVIEW VISUAL ARTS BY ALGOR

TO Westview Visual Arts
    44 King George Drive
    Ottawa, ON
    K2V 3N9

ALGOR
COMPUTER
SERVICES

55 Eastern Parkway
Kanata, ON
K2L 2B1
(613) 500-1212

Date	Particulars	Debits/Credits
12 JUN 92	Services — Inv. 55-6433	543.60
16 JUN 92	Computer Equipment — Inv. 55-6482	2 920.80
21 JUN 92	Payment Received — Thank you	2 360.00
24 JUN 92	Computer Equipment — Inv. 55-6494	8 755.40

Account Number	Previous Balance	Total Credits	Total Debits	New Balance
422 820	2 360.00 −	2 360.00 +	12 219.80 =	12 219.80
Statement Date	30 June/92	Due Date	21 July/92	

Payments must reach Algor Computer Services by due date.

Interest Rate 2% per month

See reverse for further explanation concerning payments.

> **Cycle billing:**
> the sending of statements of account to different customers on different days of the month.

Due to the enormous number of statements of account that must be sent out by some businesses, cycle billing is used. Under this system, statements are sent out at different times of the month to different customers. Thus, statements for customers whose last name starts with the letters A to C might be sent out the first day of the month, D to F the second day, and so on. There are several advantages to this system:
- the task of preparing statements is spread over the month;
- the receipt of payments on account will usually be spread over the month, providing a better cash flow.

Summary of the Accounts Receivable Procedure

All source documents related to accounts receivable must be given to the accounts receivable clerk. These documents include the following:
- Sales invoices
- Cash receipt slips
- Credit memos issued
- Debit memos issued
- Memos for unusual transactions

The key to understanding the accounts receivable subsidiary ledger is to note that the accounts receivable clerk only deals with source documents that relate to accounts receivable. Every time the accounts receivable clerk makes an entry to a customer's account in the accounts receivable subsidiary ledger, the accounting supervisor must make a change to the Accounts Receivable control account. After all the posting has been completed at month end, the following must be true:

$$\text{Total of all customer accounts in accounts receivable ledger} = \text{Balance of Accounts Receivable control account}$$

Collecting Accounts Receivable

One of the more important tasks of the accounts receivable department is the collection of overdue accounts. A number of procedures can be used to encourage customers to pay their accounts on time. First, as outlined in Chapter 6, discounts can be offered. Thus, terms of 2/10, n/30 on a sale provide for a 2 percent discount if the invoice is paid within 10 days of the date of the invoice. If the customer does not have enough cash to pay the amount owing, it might be advantageous for the customer to obtain a loan from the bank in order to take advantage of the discount. In the majority of cases, the interest charges of the lending institution are less than the amount lost by not taking advantage of the discount.

A second way of encouraging customers to pay their accounts on time is to add interest to overdue accounts. The laws of each province require that the business state the credit charges on the monthly statement, both in percentage terms and as examples in dollar terms. Figure 10-17 shows the rules for interest charges for VISA:

FIGURE 10-17 VISA INTEREST CHARGES

INTEREST CHARGES / CALCULATION

PURCHASES — You will not be charged interest on purchases appearing on a statement for the first time provided the full balance of that statement is paid within 21 days of the "Statement Date" i.e. by the "Due Date". If payment in full is not received by the "Due Date", interest is charged from the day each purchase was posted to your account until the day payment in full is credited to the account.

CASH ADVANCES AND VISA CHEQUES — You pay interest on cash advances from the day the advances were obtained, and on cheques from the day the cheques are charged to the account, until repaid in full. Please note that payments are applied against cash advances and cheques in the manner outlined below in the Payments section.

CALCULATION
When your balance is made up of charges for which you have previously been billed and / or current cash advances or cheques, this becomes your "interest-bearing balance". Interest on this balance is calculated at the annual rate of interest shown on the front of the statement: the daily rate is calculated by dividing the annual rate of interest by the number of days in the year. This interest-bearing balance is reduced by the amount of payments received. As such, you minimize your interest charge by paying as early as possible: the earlier your payment, the lower your interest-bearing balance will be.

Since interest accrues up to receipt of payment, the final charge can only be calculated and shown on the statement which reflects your payment. No interest is charged on billed interest or service fees.

The advantage to the business of adding interest to overdue accounts is that the interest provides an additional source of revenue. That revenue helps to cover the cost of operating a credit system, which is significant when one considers all the related costs, such as wages, computer costs, mailings, and losses due to bad debts.

When an interest charge is added to an account, a journal entry is required, as well as an entry in the accounts receivable ledger. Algor Computer Services made a sale to J. Chaplin. The entry to record that sale was as follows:

Sept. 11   Sales Invoice #55-6498: To J. Chaplin, $400 plus taxes.

GENERAL JOURNAL

PAGE   619

DATE 1992		PARTICULARS	PR	DEBIT	CREDIT
Sept.	11	Accounts Receivable	120	460 —	
		Sales	420		400 —
		GST Payable	230		28 —
		PST Payable	240		32 —
		Sales Invoice #55-6498, J. Chaplin			

Algor Computer Services should have received payment from Chaplin by October 11. From this date on, interest charges will be added to his account. When his statement is sent out on November 1, 20 days of interest will be added. A memo is prepared to indicate the interest charge, and the amount is added to J. Chaplin's account. The memo is forwarded to the accounts receivable clerk, who increases the claim that the business has on Chaplin by making a debit entry for interest in his account. The accounting supervisor also makes an entry, as follows:

Nov. 1   Memo #76: $6.16 added to the account of J. Chaplin for interest on overdue account.

GENERAL JOURNAL

PAGE 633

DATE 1992		PARTICULARS	PR	DEBIT	CREDIT
Nov.	1	Accounts Receivable	120	6 16	
		Accounts Receivable: Interest	450		6 16
		Memo #76, interest on J. Chaplin's account			

When payment is received from Chaplin, a cash receipt slip is completed and given to the accounts receivable clerk. The clerk makes an entry to reduce the business's claim on Chaplin. The receipt is then forwarded to the accounting supervisor, who makes the following entry:

Nov. 10   Cash Receipt Slip #33-6968: Receipt on account from J. Chaplin, $466.16.

GENERAL JOURNAL

PAGE 637

DATE 1992		PARTICULARS	PR	DEBIT	CREDIT
Nov.	10	Cash	100	466 16	
		Accounts Receivable	120		466 16
		Cash Receipt Slip #33-6968, J. Chaplin			

A third way of encouraging customers to pay on time is to require a deposit before a service will be given. This procedure is frequently followed by utility companies, especially when providing a service to renters. If the customer does not pay, any overdue amount is taken from the deposit. The amount of the deposit is recorded as a liability to the customer, and will be paid back should the customer no longer require the service.

Collection agency: a service business that tries to collect accounts receivable on behalf of businesses.

Collection Agencies

When a business has difficulty collecting from a customer, it may enlist the services of a **collection agency**. For a fee, the agency will try to locate the customer and obtain payment. Of course, the cost of the service reduces the profit that the business makes on the sale. All of these costs are added on to the price of goods and services by a business.

Lesson Review

27. What is the key function of the credit department?

28. Where can a business obtain information about a credit applicant?

29. What is the daily task of the accounts receivable clerk?

30. For a sale on account, what entry does
    (a) the accounts receivable clerk make?
    (b) the accounting supervisor make?

31. For a payment received on account, what entry does
    (a) the accounts receivable clerk make?
    (b) the accounting supervisor make?

32. What two tasks does the accounts receivable clerk have at month end? Why is each performed?

33. Describe the process of cycle billing.

34. What are the five source documents handled by the accounts receivable clerk?

35. What are the three ways of encouraging customers to pay their accounts on time?

36. What function is carried out by a collection agency?

Lesson Applications

37. Sandy Theriault is appointed accounts receivable clerk for Fuoco's Tool Rentals Ltd. As part of her training, she is told that only certain source documents are to be entered in the accounts receivable subsidiary ledger.
    (a) State the four main source documents that Sandy will be handling.
    (b) State whether the source documents increase or decrease the customer accounts.
    (c) What other source document might Sandy handle? Give an example of the transaction.

38. Paul Vista is the accounts receivable clerk for the new Vista Travel Service. The following sales invoices are on his desk after the first four days of business. Open customer accounts as needed, and enter the sales invoices in the accounts receivable subsidiary ledger.

Date	Inv.	Customer	Amount	GST	PST	Total
Nov. 1	1	Kim Wozniak	$ 74.35	$ 5.20	$ 5.95	$ 85.50
	2	Shannon Fagan	192.42	13.47	15.39	221.28
2	3	Katie Pettifer	439.10	30.74	35.13	504.97
	4	Chris Moll	87.24	6.11	6.98	100.33
3	5	Carol Belsher	118.24	8.28	9.46	135.98
	6	Kim Wozniak	313.04	21.91	25.04	359.99
4	7	Carol Belsher	84.50	5.92	6.76	97.18
	8	Shannon Fagan	429.17	30.04	34.33	493.54
	9	Katie Pettifer	111.50	7.81	8.92	128.23
	10	Kim Wozniak	93.25	6.53	7.46	107.24

39. (a) Using the accounts receivable subsidiary ledger from Question 38, enter the following source documents that arrived on Paul Vista's desk the fifth and sixth day of business.

Date	Document	#	Customer	Total	Explanation
Nov. 5	Cash Receipt Slip	1	Kim Wozniak	$ 85.50	On account
	Sales Invoice	11	Shannon Fagan	142.60	Sale $124.00, GST $8.68, PST $9.92
	Debit Memo	1	Carol Belsher	18.98	Error on Sales Invoice #5, $16.50, GST $1.16, PST $1.32
6	Sales Invoice	12	Katie Pettifer	332.93	Sale $289.50, GST $20.27, PST $23.16
	Cash Receipt Slip	2	Kim Wozniak	359.99	On account
	Credit Memo	1	Chris Moll	100.33	Refund, sale $87.24, GST $6.11, PST $6.98

(b) Prepare a schedule of accounts receivable as at November 6. The accounting supervisor shows a balance of $2 182.93 in the Accounts Receivable control account. Compare the balances.

40. Jane Winterwerb is the accounts receivable clerk for Beechburg Distributors Ltd. The accounts receivable ledger that she maintains has the following customer names and balances as of May 13:

J. Baillergeon	36 Westend Lane	$139.92
D. Curley	144 Norton Drive	435.90
G. Johnston	1101 Deer Drive	84.29
S. Kinsey	29 Westminster Avenue	717.34
M. Stevens	543 Roosevelt Street	128.00

(a) Open an accounts receivable ledger with the above information.
(b) From the source documents given, select those that apply to

Jane's job, and enter them in the ledger. Open new accounts as necessary.

May 14 Sales Invoices:
#422 to G. Johnston, sale $244.50, GST $17.12, PST $19.56, total $281.18.
#423 to S. Kinsey, sale $300.00, GST $21.00, PST $24.00, total $345.00.
#424 to D. Curley, sale $900.00, GST $63.00, PST $72.00, total $1 035.00.
Cash Receipt Slip #153, from J. Baillergeon, $139.92 on account.
Purchase Invoice #284A from Computer Bits, $864.00 plus $56.00 GST, for a new disk drive.
Debit Memo #11 issued to S. Kinsey, $24.50 plus GST $1.72 and PST $1.96, total $28.18, for error on Sales Invoice #398.
Bank Debit Memo for $24.00 for service charges.

May 15 Credit Note #59 received from St. Laurent garage, $50.00 plus $3.50 GST and $4.00 PST, for error on Purchase Invoice #591 for car repairs.
Purchase Invoice #491, from Bridlewood Importers, $1 290.00 plus GST of $90.30, for merchandise.
Sales Invoices:
#425 to M. Stevens, sale $490.00, GST $34.30, PST $39.20, total $563.50.
#426 to D. Curley, sale $1 200.00, GST $84.00, PST $96.00, total $1 380.00.
#427 to S. Kinsey, sale $920.00, GST $64.40, PST $73.60, total $1 058.00.
#428 to R. Villeneuve, sale $70.00, GST $4.90, PST $5.60, total $80.50.
Cash Receipt Slips:
#154 from D. Curley, $435.90 on account.
#155 from M. Stevens, $128.00 on account.
Cheque Copies:
#448 to Beaumont Realty, $900.00 plus $63.00 GST, for monthly rent.
#449 to Peter Wolf, $800.00 for wages.
Credit Note #12 issued to G. Johnston, sale $40.00, GST $2.80, PST $3.20, total $46.00, for error on Sales Invoice #422.

41. The schedule of accounts receivable and the Accounts Receivable control account totals differ by the following amounts at different times. In each instance, indicate the probable type of error that either the accounts receivable clerk or the accounting supervisor has made. Assume that only one error was made.

(a) $3 000.00   (c) $434.00
(b) $1 919.25   (d) $22.25

42. Westboro Auto Repairs utilizes the three-ledger system, along with a general journal. The documents are first given to the respective subsidiary ledger clerks, who check them and make entries in the subsidiary ledgers. The documents are then given to the accounting supervisor who makes the necessary journal entry and posts to the general ledger.
    (a) Set up the accounts payable ledger with the following suppliers and their balances as of November 26.

Chow Tires Ltd.	62 Westport Road	$ 984.25
Leigh Auto Body Parts	443 Bentley Road	1 842.50
Mandarin Auto Body Parts	147 Broadview Avenue	722.36
Trask Auto Glass Ltd.	99 Yonge Street	449.32

(b) Set up the accounts receivable ledger with the following customers and their balances as of November 26.

Erin Bennett	44 Chimo Road	$123.98
Laura Donovan	89 Beaufort Drive	982.16
John McEachern	924 Nanook Crescent	452.87
Lee O'Connor	1212 Katimavik Road	339.04
Simon Robertson-Palmer	214 Peary Way	722.00

(c) Enter all transactions that apply to the accounts payable clerk in the accounts payable ledger. Open new accounts as required.
(d) Enter all transactions that apply to the accounts receivable clerk in the accounts receivable ledger. Open new accounts as required.
(e) Complete the schedules of accounts receivable and accounts payable. The accounting supervisor shows a balance of $5 735.47 in the Accounts Receivable control account, and a balance of $3 199.33 in the Accounts Payable control account. Compare the balances of the control accounts with the totals of the schedules.

November 27
Purchase Invoices:
#398 from Chow Tires Ltd., $420.00 plus GST of $29.40, for merchandise; terms n/30.
#413 from Mandarin Auto Body Parts, $220.00 plus GST of $15.40, for merchandise; terms 2/10, n/30.
Sales Invoices:
#244 to Lee O'Connor, sale $350.00, GST $24.50, PST $21.00, total $395.50.
#245 to John McEachern, sale $220.00, GST $15.40, PST $13.20, total $248.60.

#246 to Erin Bennett, sale $412.00, GST $28.84, PST $24.72, total $465.56.
#247 to Agam Dashi, sale $375.00, GST $26.25, PST $22.50, total $423.75.
Credit Invoice received from Trask Auto Glass Ltd., $98.00 plus GST of $6.86, for merchandise returned.
Bank Credit Memo: Bank loan for $3 000.00 made in order to take advantage of discounts offered by suppliers.
Cheque Copies:
#491 to Leigh Auto Body Parts $924.88, for Purchase Invoice #663 in the amount of $942.50 less discount of $17.62.
#492 to Chow Tires Ltd. $965.85, for Purchase Invoice #316 in the amount of $984.25 less discount of $18.40.
#493 to BC Tel, $205.07 plus GST of $13.54, for monthly phone bill.
Cash Receipt Slip #96 from Erin Bennett, $136.22 for Sales Invoice #192 in the amount of $138.67, less discount of $2.45.

November 28
Purchase Invoices:
#452 from Mandarin Auto Body Parts, $1 490.00 plus GST of $104.30, for merchandise.
#819 from Travis Auto Glass Ltd., $982.00 plus GST of $68.74, for merchandise.
Debit Memos:
#42 from Travis Auto Glass Ltd., $81.00 plus GST of $5.67, for undercharge on Purchase Invoice #819.
#61 to John McEachern, sale $40.00, plus GST of $2.80 and PST of $2.40, total $45.20; for undercharge on Sales Invoice #221.
Sales Invoices:
#248 to Dessi Frenette, sale $248.00, GST $17.36, PST $14.88, total $280.24.
#249 to Laura Donovan, sale $272.00, GST $19.04, PST $16.32, total $307.36.
#250 to John McEachern, sale $122.00, GST $8.54, PST $7.32, total $137.86.
#251 to Simon Robertson-Palmer, sale $732.00, GST $51.24, PST $43.92, total $827.16.
#252 to Erin Bennett, sale $101.00, GST $7.07, PST $6.06, total $114.13.
Cheque Copies:
#494 to R. Zuro, $250.00 for wages.
#495 to Western Gas Co., $822.00 plus GST of $57.54, for natural gas for heating.
#496 to Mandarin Auto Body Parts, $1 264.40 for Purchase Invoice

#396 in the amount of $1 048.60 less discount of $19.60, and for Purchase Invoice #413 in the amount of $235.40 with no discount.

#497 to Leigh Auto Body Parts, $883.18 for Purchase Invoice #19923 in the amount of $900.00, less discount of $16.82.

Memo #29: To add the following amounts to the accounts shown, as interest on overdue accounts:

Erin Bennett	$1.24
Laura Donovan	6.22
Lee O'Connor	1.27

10.4 Other Design Aspects of Subsidiary Ledger Systems

You may have wondered why an entry was made in the general journal for every transaction even though individual entries were made to supplier and customer accounts. For example, if there were 100 sales invoices issued on one day for computer services, 100 entries would be made by the accounts receivable clerk in the accounts receivable ledger, one to each of the customers' accounts. One hundred entries would be made by the accounting supervisor in the general journal, one for each source document. The general journal entry would debit and credit the same accounts for each of the 100 source documents, as shown below for one of them.

GENERAL JOURNAL

PAGE 640

DATE 1992		PARTICULARS	PR	DEBIT	CREDIT
Nov.	17	Accounts Receivable		202 40	
		Computer Services			1 76 —
		GST Payable			12 32
		PST Payable			14 08
		Sales Invoice #55-6366, Willlard Business			

By making each general journal entry to record a sale individually, 400 postings to the general ledger are required! Instead of making 100 separate journal entries and the resulting 400 postings to the general ledger, batch journalizing can be used. **Batch journalizing** is the grouping of the same source documents for any one day into a single entry. The amounts of the 100 sales invoices for November 17 are added together, and one entry for the total is made.

Batch journalizing: the grouping of the same source documents for any one day into a single entry.

Nov. 17   Sales Invoices #55-6366 – #55-6465: Sales on account for the day for computer services $12 320.00, GST $862.40, PST $985.60.

GENERAL JOURNAL

PAGE 640

DATE 1992		PARTICULARS	PR	DEBIT	CREDIT
Nov.	17	Accounts Receivable		14 168 —	
		Computer Services			12 320 —
		GST Payable			862 40
		PST Payable			985 60
		Sales Invoices #55-6366 – #55-6465			

Batch journalizing can occur because the individual customers' accounts have been changed in the accounts receivable subsidiary ledger by the accounts receivable clerk. The source documents are bundled, with an adding machine tape put on the top of the bundle showing the date of the source documents, the total for each account, and the initials of the person making the journal entry.

There are several advantages to using batch journalizing:
• journalizing is reduced, saving time and space
• posting is reduced, saving time and space
• the chance of error is reduced due to less journalizing and posting.

Other source documents that are the same can also be batched. Cash receipts on account can be batch journalized as follows:

Nov. 17 Cash Receipt Slips #33-7497–#33-7521: Cash receipts on account for the day, $15 269.14.

GENERAL JOURNAL

PAGE 640

DATE 1992		PARTICULARS	PR	DEBIT	CREDIT
Nov.	17	Cash		15 269 14	
		Accounts Receivable			15 269 14
		Cash Receipt Slips #33-7497–#33-7521			

Purchase invoices can also be batched, but different items may have been purchased, so the debits will be to different accounts. The credit will be to accounts payable.

Purchase Invoices #322: for equipment, $900.00 plus $63.00 GST and $72.00 PST;

#982: for supplies, $129.00 plus $9.03 GST and $10.32 PST;

#1187: for supplies, $100.00 plus $7.00 GST and $8.00 PST;

#22A: for delivery of merchandise, $187 plus $13.09 GST.

GENERAL JOURNAL

PAGE 640

DATE 1992		PARTICULARS	PR	DEBIT	CREDIT
Nov.	17	Equipment		972 —	
		Supplies		247 32	
		Delivery Expense		187 —	
		GST Recoverable		92 12	
		Accounts Payable			1 498 44
		Purchase Invoices #322, #982, #1187, #22A			

Cash payments can also be batch journalized but, again, different debits may exist.

Cheque Copies #983 on account, $942
　　　　　　　#984 on account, $820
　　　　　　　#985 on account, $122
　　　　　　　#986 for heating gas, $780 plus $54.60 GST

GENERAL JOURNAL

PAGE 640

DATE 1992		PARTICULARS	PR	DEBIT	CREDIT
Nov.	17	Accounts Payable		1 884 —	
		Utilities Expense		780 —	
		GST Recoverable		54 60	
		Cash			2 718 60
		Cheque Copies #983 – #986			

Direct and Indirect Posting

In some businesses, a different procedure from direct posting, which was previously described, may be followed for posting to the accounts payable or accounts receivable subsidiary ledgers. These businesses use **indirect posting**: they enter all source documents in the general journal first, and then post to all ledgers from the journal.

Indirect posting: the entering of data from a source document to a general journal, and then posting to a ledger.

Using the indirect system, transactions that change Accounts Payable, for instance, must be double posted. The posting to the Accounts Payable control account is indicated by placing the number of the Accounts Payable account in the PR column of the journal. The posting to the supplier's account in the accounts payable subsidiary ledger is indicated by placing a ✓ in the PR column of the journal. The transaction shown in Figure 10-18 for the purchase of merchandise on account illustrates the journalizing and indirect posting procedure.

FIGURE 10-18

GENERAL JOURNAL

PAGE 640

DATE 1992		PARTICULARS	PR	DEBIT	CREDIT
Nov.	17	Purchases	500	21 000 —	
		GST Recoverable	135	1 470 —	
		Accounts Payable (California Computers)	200✓		22 470 —
		Purchase Invoice #489, California Computers			

GENERAL LEDGER

ACCOUNT Purchases   NO 500

DATE 1992		PARTICULARS	PR	DEBIT	CREDIT	DR CR	BALANCE
Nov.	17		J640	21 000 —		DR	21 000 —

ACCOUNT GST Recoverable   NO 135

DATE 1992		PARTICULARS	PR	DEBIT	CREDIT	DR CR	BALANCE
Nov.	17		J640	1 470 —		DR	1 470 —

ACCOUNT Accounts Payable   NO 200

DATE 1992		PARTICULARS	PR	DEBIT	CREDIT	DR CR	BALANCE
Nov.	17		J640	22 470 —		CR	22 470 —

ACCOUNTS PAYABLE SUBSIDIARY LEDGER

ACCOUNT California Computers   NO

DATE 1992		PARTICULARS	PR	DEBIT	CREDIT	DR CR	BALANCE
Nov.	17		J640		22 470 —	CR	22 470 —

Changes in accounts receivable are treated in the same manner using the indirect system.

Comparison of Direct and Indirect Posting

The direct posting system is called that because entries are posted to the accounts payable ledger or the accounts receivable ledger *directly* from the source document. The indirect posting system is called that because amounts are entered first in the general journal, and then posted to the accounts payable ledger or the accounts receivable ledger. An indirect path has been taken.

FIGURE 10-19 DIRECT POSTING COMPARED TO INDIRECT POSTING

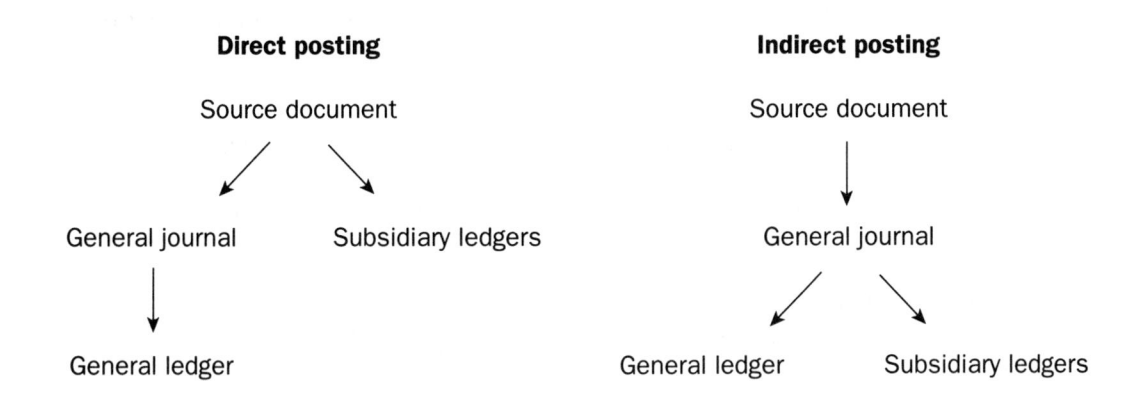

```
      Direct posting                          Indirect posting

      Source document                         Source document
        ↙        ↘                                   ↓
General journal   Subsidiary ledgers         General journal
     ↓                                          ↙        ↘
General ledger                          General ledger    Subsidiary ledgers
```

The indirect system is not used frequently, for it requires that the accounting supervisor and the subsidiary ledger clerk both use the general journal. When one is using it, the other cannot do his or her work. The indirect system also does not permit the use of batch journalizing.

Subsidiary Ledger System Overview

Figure 10-20 summarizes the responsibilities of the accounts payable clerk, the accounts receivable clerk, and the accounting supervisor when a subsidiary ledger system is used by a business.

It might be necessary for a firm to use other subsidiary ledgers if the quantity of work is too much for the accounting supervisor. For example, a business with a very large truck fleet may have a subsidiary ledger for trucks. Similarly, one could be established for equipment or for payroll. The main criterion for establishing such ledgers is to divide the accounting tasks among personnel.

Advantages of Subsidiary Ledger Systems

The use of subsidiary ledgers is dependent upon the size of a business. As a business grows, the management will have to decide when it becomes advantageous to change from having all of the accounts payable and accounts receivable listed in a general ledger to having subsidiary ledgers for them. In most cases, the volume of transactions will demand that the change be made, for one person alone will not be able to manage the accounting. A decision to adopt a new system is made when the accountants and auditors of the business review the accounting procedures at year end.

FIGURE 10-20 SUMMARY OF RESPONSIBILITIES OF THE ACCOUNTS PAYABLE CLERK, THE ACCOUNTS RECEIVABLE CLERK, AND THE ACCOUNTING SUPERVISOR

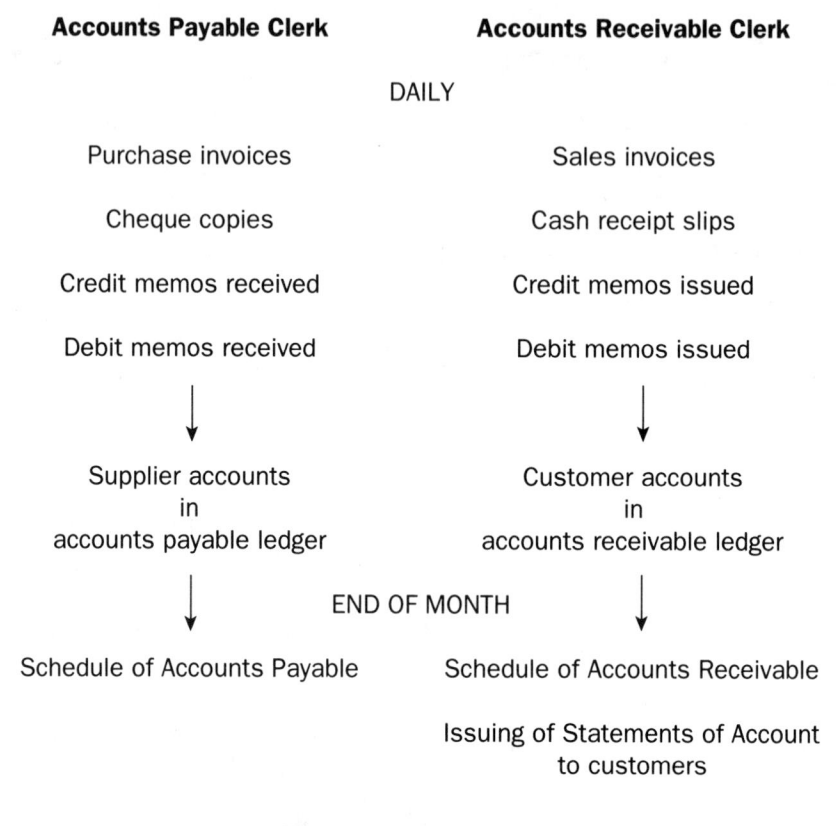

Accounts Payable Clerk	**Accounts Receivable Clerk**
DAILY	
Purchase invoices	Sales invoices
Cheque copies	Cash receipt slips
Credit memos received	Credit memos issued
Debit memos received	Debit memos issued
↓	↓
Supplier accounts in accounts payable ledger	Customer accounts in accounts receivable ledger
↓	↓
END OF MONTH	
Schedule of Accounts Payable	Schedule of Accounts Receivable
	Issuing of Statements of Account to customers

Accounting Supervisor

DAILY

All Source Documents
↓
General journal
↓
General ledger

MONTHLY

↓
Trial balance
↓
Worksheet
↓
Financial statements

YEARLY

↓
Journalize and post adjusting entries
↓
Journalize and post closing entries
↓
Post-closing trial balance

The advantages of using a subsidiary ledger system are:
- Division of labour and specialization: more than one person is able to perform accounting functions when direct posting to subsidiary ledgers is followed. As well, accounts payable and accounts receivable clerks get to know the names of the various suppliers and customers that the business deals with. Such familiarity reduces the chance of error.
- Internal control: the schedules of the subsidiary ledgers prepared by the accounts payable and accounts receivable clerks must balance with the control accounts maintained by the accounting supervisor. Since the work of the various parties must agree, there is less chance that any of them will be able to defraud the business.
- Batch journalizing: the process of batch journalizing allows the accounting supervisor to journalize many transactions of the same type at one time. The time saved by such a procedure allows the supervisor to devote time to other accounting tasks.

LESSON REVIEW

43. (a) Describe batch journalizing.
    (b) What are three advantages of batch journalizing?

44. Prepare a diagram to distinguish between direct and indirect posting.

45. Why is indirect posting not frequently used?

46. Briefly describe the job specifications of the accounts payable clerk, the accounts receivable clerk, and the accounting supervisor under a three-ledger system.

47. What are the three advantages of using a subsidiary ledger system?

LESSON APPLICATIONS

48. The following source documents were either received or issued by Downsview Fireplace Designs. The firm uses batch journalizing, and has a subsidiary ledger for both accounts payable and accounts receivable. Prepare the general journal entries, using appropriate account names, that would be completed by the accounting supervisor. The firm uses direct posting to the subsidiary ledgers. All source documents are dated March 2. PST of 8 percent is calculated on the base price, and GST is 7 percent.

    Purchase Invoices:
    #443, from Vesta Fireplaces, $2 580 for merchandise, plus GST.

#92, from Brantford Office Suppliers, $129 for office supplies, plus taxes.
#911, from Bill's Service Station, $423 plus taxes, for truck repairs.

Cheque Copies:
#24, to Willard Real Estate, $2 450 plus GST for rent.
#25, to V. Lemay, owner, $550 for personal use.
#26, to Bell Canada, $286 for telephone expenses, plus taxes.
#27, to Vesta Fireplaces, $5 600 on account.

Sales Invoices:
#256, to Art Mason, $350 plus taxes.
#257, to Sue Draper, $822 plus taxes.
#258, to Bill Tupper, $1 420 plus taxes.

Cash Receipt Slips:
#192, from M. Hardy, $942 on account.
#193, from D. Piche, $1 300 on account.
#194, from V. Emond, $1 122 on account.

Cash Sales Slips:
#456 to #464, $9 350 plus taxes.

Memos:
#524, to record interest charges for overdue accounts to the following customers: $9.92 to J. Mabbutt, $14.35 to D. MacQuaig, $3.29 to C. Warchow.
#525, to record withdrawal from the business of $122 worth of merchandise by the owner. (Don't forget to calculate the taxes.)

49. Highland Park Sports' accounting system consists of a general journal and three ledgers. The firm uses indirect posting, and batch journalizes where possible.
    (a) Using appropriate account names, journalize the source documents. The documents are all dated August 27. PST of 8 percent is calculated on the base price only, and GST is 7 percent.
    (b) Using appropriate account numbers, show how the PR column of the journal would appear after the posting to the ledgers has been completed. Remember that the firm uses indirect posting.

Purchase Invoices:
#356, from Bauer Ltd., $440 for merchandise, plus GST.
#591, from Watertown Sports, $592 for merchandise, plus GST.
#401D, from Speedy Delivery Services, $622 for delivery expense, plus GST.

Cheque Copies:
#201, to Renaldo Delivery, $24.50 plus GST, for transportation-in.

#202, to Nike Canada Ltd., $5 600 on account.
#203, to Peter Kahn, owner, $540 for personal use.

Sales Invoices:
#1239, to D. Kittell, $520 plus taxes.
#1240, to P. Raicevic, $142 plus taxes.
#1241, to Sir Robert Borden High School, $2 350 plus taxes.

Cash Receipt Slips:
#902, $940 from Sir Wilfrid Laurier High School, on account.
#903, $129 from T. Mokohonuk, on account.

Cash Sales Slips:
#441 to #496, $3 401 plus taxes.

Memos:
#42, to record interest on overdue accounts: $3.59 to P. Bura, $14.25 to V. Fretwell, and $17.89 to C. Steeves.

CHAPTER REVIEW AND SKILL DEVELOPMENT

Accounting Principles and Concepts

- A **subsidiary ledger system** is created if a business has a large number of accounts of one type, such as Accounts Receivable and Accounts Payable.

- A **control account** is placed in the general ledger to take the place of accounts that are removed from the general ledger to make a subsidiary ledger.

- For every entry made in the subsidiary ledger, there must be a corresponding entry made in the **control account**.

- A **matching of documents** should occur before invoices are paid.

- **Batch journalizing** allows for the journalizing of many source documents of one type on the same day in a single journal entry.

- **Direct** or **indirect posting** may be done from source documents to a subsidiary ledger.

Knowing the Terms

For each of the following terms, indicate the term being defined.

(a) The process of comparing the purchase order, packing slip, and purchase invoice.
(b) A request by someone in a business that goods or services be purchased by the business.
(c) The network of related procedures initiated to perform some major business activity.
(d) An account found in the general ledger, the balance of which represents the total of all accounts in a subsidiary ledger.
(e) A document sent with a shipment to indicate the contents of the shipment.
(f) A journal entry that groups the same source documents for any one day into a single journal entry.
(g) The person responsible for updating the accounts payable subsidiary ledger, which shows amounts owing to suppliers.
(h) The transferring of information directly from a source document to a subsidiary ledger.

(i) An extra ledger containing accounts of one type.
(j) A document that lists suppliers and amounts owing to them.

Food for Thought

1. An accounts receivable clerk indicated that he was not overly concerned about a customer's account being incorrect, since the customer would be sent a statement at month end. The clerk said that it was the customer's responsibility to correct any errors that exist. Why should the clerk ensure that the errors are corrected before the statements are sent?

2. Subsidiary ledgers are frequently looked after by persons who have not obtained a specialized accounting certificate. Why?

3. A new employee, who was to work in accounts receivable, was being trained by another accounts receivable clerk. The new employee was familiar with the concept of double-entry accounting. However, she could not understand why the accounts receivable clerk was making a debit to an account when handling a sales invoice, and not making any corresponding credit. Explain why.

4. Some accounts receivable ledgers are in alphabetical order according to the customer name, while others are in a numerical order. Give the reason.

5. Access to the accounts payable tickler file should be restricted to specific accounting personnel. Explain why that is true.

6. It is customary to ensure that the accounts receivable and accounts payable ledgers are up to date on a daily basis, while it is not as important to do so for the general ledger. Explain why.

7. The accounts receivable clerk notices, while reading the business section of the newspaper, that a debtor of the company has declared bankruptcy. What should be done with the account?

8. The accounts receivable clerk notices, while reading the newspaper, that a debtor of the company has died. What should be done with the account?

9. In a small business, the accounts receivable clerk is also responsible for receiving cash on account from customers and completing the cash receipt slips. Criticize this policy.

10. In a small business, the accounts payable clerk is also responsible for approving invoices for payment, and issuing the cheques. Criticize this policy.

11. What aspect of the purchasing procedure discourages employees in the receiving department from stealing merchandise when it arrives?

12. A clerk in the accounts payable department matches a purchase invoice with the packing slip. She indicates that it is not necessary to compare it with the missing purchase order. Explain why it is also necessary to match the documents with the purchase order before payment approval is given.

13. Answer the following questions, which relate to Figure 10-5 on page 445.
    (a) Why would Algor Computer Services want the three items included in the Note to be a part of the Purchase Order?
    (b) What items would be included in the tax information?

14. Answer the following questions, which relate to Figure 10-6 on page 446.
    (a) Why would the supplier want to know

who filled the order, checked it, and packed it?
(b) What does B/O stand for?
(c) Why is there an amount column on the form, even though amounts are not entered?

Organizing

Figure 10-21 shows a division of tasks between the accounts payable clerk, the accounts receivable clerk, and the accounting supervisor. Prepare and complete a similar chart in your notebook. In the Other Account column, provide the appropriate account name and the type of entry.

Applications

Team Sportswear is owned and operated by Sue Tyrell. The firm uses a three-ledger system. Direct posting is done to the subsidiary ledgers, and batch journalizing is used where possible. PST of 8% is calculated on the base price, and GST is 7%.

In this exercise, you will perform the duties of the accounts payable clerk, the accounts receivable clerk, and the accounting supervisor.

(a) Open the three ledgers, and enter the information given in Figures 10-22, 10-23, and 10-24. Provide appropriate account numbers.
(b) Perform the tasks of the accounts payable clerk by posting directly into the

FIGURE 10-21

Source Document	Subsidiary Ledger Changes			General Ledger Changes				
	Which ledger is affected?	Will the account be increased or decreased?	Will the account be debited or credited?	Accounts Receivable Dr.	Cr.	Accounts Payable Dr.	Cr.	Other Account Dr./Cr.
Purchase Invoice								
Cheque Copy								
Credit Memo received								
Debit Memo received								
Sales Invoice								
Cash Receipt Slip								
Credit Memo issued								
Debit Memo issued								

FIGURE 10-22

Team Sportswear Schedule of Accounts Payable April 30, 19–9	
Barrister Sports Clothing Ltd.	$12 902.45
Moore Athletic Wear	1 450.82
Sealand Equipment Limited	2 345.10
Team Uniforms Limited	8 560.00
	$25 258.37

FIGURE 10-23

Team Sportswear Schedule of Accounts Receivable April 30, 19–9	
Leaside High School	$ 4 235.60
Merivale High School	2 309.20
Stanton Baseball Association	4 029.50
West Side Football Club	1 906.50
	$12 480.80

FIGURE 10-24

Team Sportswear General Ledger Trial Balance April 30, 19–9		
Cash	$ 4 325.09	
Accounts Receivable	12 480.80	
Merchandise Inventory	22 301.50	
GST Recoverable	1 435.00	
Furniture & Equipment	14 509.00	
Accounts Payable		$15 258.37
GST Payable		1 982.00
PST Payable		2 309.18
S. Tyrell, Capital		13 551.84
S. Tyrell, Drawings	4 000.00	
Sales		31 400.00
Rent Expense	1 300.00	
Utilities Expense	980.00	
Wages Expense	2 450.00	
Miscellaneous Expense	720.00	
	$64 501.39	$64 501.39

supplier accounts in the accounts payable subsidiary ledger. Prepare a schedule of accounts payable for May 31.

(c) Perform the tasks of the accounts receivable clerk by posting directly into the customer accounts in the accounts receivable subsidiary ledger. Prepare a schedule of accounts receivable for May 31.

(d) Perform the tasks of the accounting supervisor by journalizing all the source documents. Prepare a general ledger trial balance as of May 31, 19–9.

May 1 Purchase Invoices:
#402, from Team Uniforms Limited, for merchandise, $2 350 plus GST.
#91, from Moore Athletic Wear, for merchandise, $3 456 plus GST.
Memo #11: A $400 debit to Purchases had been incorrectly made on Purchase Invoice #331 from Sealand Equipment Ltd. The debit should have been to Furniture & Equipment.

2 Sales Invoices:
#513, Leaside High School, $745 plus GST (PST does not apply).
#514, Stanton Baseball Association, $920 plus taxes.

4 Cash Receipt Slips:
#46, from Leaside High School, $2 620.

#47, from Merivale High School, $2 309.20.

Memo #12: The owner invested an additional $15 000 in the business.

7 Cheque Copies:
#98, to Moore Athletic Wear, $1 450.82.
#99, to Rosemount Real Estate, $1 300 plus GST, for rent expense.
#100, $547.00 to the Receiver General of Canada, for GST. The GST Recoverable had been deducted from the $1 982.00 owing.

9 Cash Sales Slips:
#422 to #431, $1 928.00 plus taxes.

10 Purchase Invoices:
#0992, from Barrister Sports Clothing Ltd., $1 430.00 plus GST.
#322, from Sealand Equipment Limited, $980.00 plus taxes, for office furniture.

11 Sales Invoice #515: To West Side Football Club, $1 400.00 plus taxes.

12 Cheque Copies:
#101, to Barrister Sports Clothing Ltd., $4 920.00.
#102, for wages, $1 225.00.
#103, for delivery expense, $34.00, plus GST.
#104, for the balance owing to Team Uniforms Limited.

14 Cash Receipt Slips:
#48, West Side Football Club, $1 906.50.
#49, Stanton Baseball Association, $2 029.50.

16 Purchase Invoice #442: From Sealand Equipment Limited, $450.00 plus taxes, for a new printer.

Cash Sales Slips #432 to #448: $2 304.00 plus taxes.

17 Cash Receipt Slip #50: From West Side Football Club, $1 610.00.

18 Cheque Copies:
#105, $500.00 to the owner for personal use.
#106, $4 512.55 to Barrister Sports Clothing Ltd.
#107, $2 309.18 to the Provincial Treasurer for sales tax.

21 Sales Invoices:
#516, Merivale High School, $840.00 plus GST (PST does not apply).
#517, West Side Football Club, $320.00 plus taxes.

23 Cheque Copies:
#108, $230.00 plus taxes to Bell Canada for telephone usage.
#109, $141.00 plus GST for heating fuel.
Cash Receipt Slips:
#51, from Leaside High School, $1 412.75.
#52, from Stanton Baseball Association, $2 000.00.

24 Cash Sales Slips #449 to #501; $2 092 plus taxes.

25 Cheque Copy #110:
$1 225.00 for wages.

28 Purchase Invoices:
#922, from Moore Athletic Wear, $980.00 plus GST.
#811, from Team Uniforms Limited, $1 230.00 plus GST.

29 Cheque Copies:
#111, $200.00 donation to United Appeal.
#112, $350.00 to the West Side Football Club as a donation.

30 Cash Receipt Slip #53: From Merivale High School, $898.80.

31 Cash Sales Slips #502 to #541: $3 290.00 plus taxes.

Applications — Comprehensive

Using the information in Figure 10-25 for C.B. Paints, prepare the following for the month, and provide the appropriate account numbers:
(a) a worksheet, with adjustments, using the following data as of August 31.
   Estimate of bad debts, $820, using the balance sheet method;
   Merchandise inventory, $31 450;
   Supplies inventory, $140;
   Furniture & Equipment and Truck depreciation are at capital cost allowance rates.
(b) the financial statements;
(c) the adjusting entries and closing entries in general journal form;
(d) the working capital and current ratio;

Focussing

1. Accounting Procedures

Geraldine Armor is an accounting supervisor. She has received from the accounts receivable clerk the 522 sales invoices from the previous day.
(a) What should Geraldine do first with these invoices, before journalizing them?
(b) What does Geraldine know that the accounts receivable clerk has already done with the invoices? (Give at least three items.) How does Geraldine know that the clerk has done each task with each invoice?
(c) How will Geraldine know if one of the invoices is missing? What should she do in this case?
(d) What should Geraldine do if she cannot read the total on one of the sales invoices? Why should she do this?
(e) What journalizing technique should Geraldine use in order to record these items? How many journal entries and postings will it save her?
(f) What jobs does Geraldine do at month end that the other accounting personnel are not responsible for?

FIGURE 10-25

C. B. Paints
Trial Balance
August 31, 19–7

Account	Debit	Credit
Cash	$ 12 400	
Accounts Receivable	17 800	
Allowance for Doubtful Accounts		$ 120
Merchandise Inventory	34 560	
GST Recoverable	1 230	
Supplies	720	
Furniture & Equipment	14 200	
Acc. Dep.: F & E		6 340
Truck	16 700	
Accounts Payable		10 408
Bank Loan (2 years)		8 250
GST Payable		1 928
PST Payable		2 340
B. DeMontigny, Capital		43 435
B. DeMontigny, Drawings	4 000	
Sales		54 800
Sales Returns & Allowances	160	
Sales Discounts	112	
A/R: Interest		422
Purchases	18 900	
Freight-in	171	
Purchases Returns & Allowances		540
Purchases Discounts		60
Wages Expense	4 240	
Rent Expense	2 100	
Interest Expense	80	
Truck Expense	300	
Advertising Expense	400	
Utilities Expense	350	
Miscellaneous Expense	220	
	$128 643	$128 643

2. Correcting a Subsidiary Ledger and Control Account

At the end of September, the accounting supervisor for Dinardo Ceramics noticed that the accounts receivable subsidiary ledger and the control account were not in agreement. In trying to locate the error with the accounts receivable clerk, the following errors were discovered:

1. A cash receipt on account for $320 from D. Norton was not posted to the subsidiary ledger.

2. A sales invoice for $550 was posted in the subsidiary ledger as $505.

3. A sales invoice for $600 was posted in the subsidiary ledger as $60.

4. A sales invoice for $895 was not posted in the general ledger.

5. A sales invoice for $420 was posted as a credit in the subsidiary ledger.

6. A sales invoice for $350 was not posted in the subsidiary ledger or the general ledger.

7. A cash receipt for $720 on account from J. Bradley was not posted in the subsidiary ledger.

8. A cash receipt for $228 on account from C. Elliott was posted as a debit to the Accounts Receivable control account.

(a) Calculate the correct total for the subsidiary ledger and the control account. The accounts receivable subsidiary ledger total was $12 506 before the above errors.
(b) Calculate the Accounts Receivable account balance before the above errors were found.
(c) Indicate the type of errors illustrated by items 2 and 3.

Evaluate and Assess — Internal Control

Martin Gastineau and Marvin Gastineau are in charge of the accounting for a business. Martin carries out the tasks of the accounting supervisor as well as those of the treasurer in that he issues cheques and makes deposits. Marvin is in charge of the accounts receivable ledger.

The two have set up a scheme to defraud the owner. They take sales invoices, cut out the amounts, put smaller amounts under the invoice on a separate page, and photocopy them. The new invoice has a smaller amount as well as the signature of the person responsible for issuing it. When the cheque is received from the customer, the lower amount is credited to his or her account, and the difference is paid out as a "refund" of overpaid amounts. The cheque, however, is made out to a fictitious company that the two have set up.

(a) What basic accounting principle have the Gastineaus managed to circumvent?
(b) How might the fraud be discovered? Give at least three ways.

Synthesize and Conclude

1. Accounts Payable Procedures

In the small ceramic shop of Crystal & Daughter, the accounting is done by the owner Crystal Knowlton. Crystal is very careful about collecting accounts receivable, and she collects them within one month. She does this when the students come to ceramics class.

For accounts payable, Crystal puts purchase invoices in a file folder and pays them when she receives a statement from the supplier. The accounting entry made at the time is a debit to what was purchased, and a credit to cash. Her balance sheet therefore never shows any accounts payable, even though there may be a file folder full of them when the statements are made. Crystal

finds this to be an advantage when she goes to borrow money from the bank.
(a) What accounting principle is Crystal not following?
(b) Has Crystal done anything wrong by not disclosing the accounts payable to the bank?
(c) What might Crystal not be taking advantage of due to the system that she uses for filing purchase invoices?

2. Matching of Source Documents
Read the following newspaper article:
(a) What accounting principle has not been followed by the companies that paid the invoices but did not order the service?
(b) Where could the firms have obtained information about the supplier?

Users of facsimiles target of a bill fraud

The Globe and Mail

Let the faxer beware.

A variation on an old scam has come back to haunt the users of facsimile machines, particularly in large organizations. Boiler room operations in Europe and Britain are sending Canadian companies what appear to be invoices demanding payment for listings in international fax directories.

The documents look just like a typical invoice, complete with reference numbers and in some cases discounts for paying within 21 days. But buried at the bottom, in tiny type, most of them say "if you agree please remit the amount shown."

Many people, especially in large organizations where it can be a difficult task to track down an order, simply pay.

"The industry now is filled with all kinds of opportunists who see there is a boom and want to take advantage of it," said Lori Jeffrey, vice-president of Fax Directory Inc. of Toronto, which publishes the Official Fax Directory.

Ms Jeffrey said she has had about 50 complaints from customers in the past year who receive bills for directory listings and believe they are being charged by her company.

"It seems to be the big companies who get hit the hardest," she said.

One large accounting firm received what appeared to be a bill from List of Telefax Subscribers of Canada for $725. They sent a cheque for that amount to Fax Directory Inc., believing that is where the bill originated. In fact Fax Directory does not charge for listings in its directory. The $725 invoice appears to have originated in West Germany.

She had other documents that appeared to be invoices from companies such as the Telefax Directory of Canadian Subscribers, in Zurich, and the World Telefax Edition, in London.

Ms Jeffrey said she returns the cheques with an explanation and a warning. Don't pay for anything you haven't ordered.

Likewise, James Crammond, general manager of Faxlist Publishers Inc. of Toronto, which publishes a business directory called the Ultimate Source, said he gets about 50 complaints a year from clients who have received bogus invoices.

"This has been going on for a long time," Mr. Crammond said. "They target large organizations where the likelihood of something getting through the payables process without scrutiny is greater." He said Faxlist customers don't have to pay for any order that they haven't signed. But he said the boiler room operations are still hurting business.

"Anybody who has fallen prey to one of these things tends to be a little more leery about getting involved in another directory."

ACCOUNTING AT WORK

Leslie Nishina
Accounts Receivable Clerk

Leslie Nishina works as an Accounts Receivable clerk with Ginger Pet Supply Enterprises. Ginger is a dog food distribution centre located in Metropolitan Toronto that caters to the pet care needs of various retail pet supply stores in the Metro Toronto Area. In addition to dog food, their products include pet care related merchandise, such as grooming items, training equipment, and pet toys.

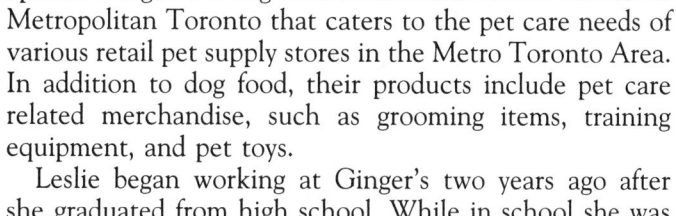

Leslie began working at Ginger's two years ago after she graduated from high school. While in school she was enrolled in various business courses including accounting and computer classes. It was in high school that she was first exposed to computer accounting software. With her computer skills she found a part-time/summer job with Ginger's as an assistant to the Accounts Supervisor. As a part-time summer student her duties were primarily clerical, but as she showed an interest and an ability with accounting she was given more responsibility working with individual accounts. Upon graduating from high school, she was able to obtain a full-time position with the company.

As an Accounts Receivable clerk, Leslie is responsible for monitoring incoming sales, posting the transactions to an Accounts Receivable Ledger, and then forwarding any new entries to the Accounts Supervisor. Leslie makes sure that no discrepancies exist between the Accounts Receivable Ledger and the source documents (sales slips, invoices). She also prepares a list of all accounts receivable and their balances. She then issues a Statement of Accounts and keeps track of payments received and those still outstanding.

Leslie finds that knowledge of computer software has enhanced her job a great deal. Monitoring debits and the varying interest charges on overdue accounts often requires daily updating. As a result, computerized accounting not only reduces time spent in recording information, but also increases the efficiency in operating a credit/debit system. Leslie knows this significantly increases her value as an employee. She hopes that she will be recognized for her contribution to the company and gain advancement in the Accounting Department.

Leslie wants to develop her skills and education. She is taking computer upgrading courses and plans to enrol in more Accounting classes. She also has plans to go to college and obtain a business degree. Although Leslie is happy with her current position, she would eventually like to see herself in a supervisory position in the Accounting Department.

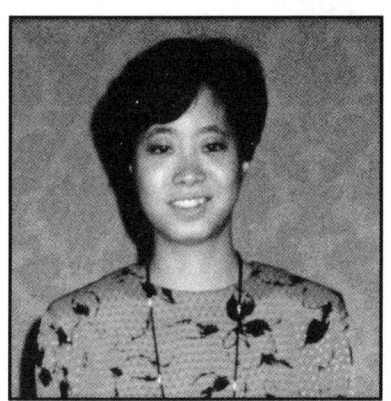

ACCOUNTS RECEIVABLE CLERK

One of Canada's leading automotive component manufacturers requires an Accounts Receivable Clerk. This person will be responsible for maintaining the accounts receivable system and will report directly to the Accounts Supervisor.

The ideal candidate will have a minimum of three years' experience, will be self-motivated, with good work habits. Education preferred — community college.

We offer salary: $23-$25K with excellent company benefits. Rush résumé (no phone calls please)

**Plant Superintendent
2625 Main St
Ingersoll   N4P 2Z1**

ACCOUNTS PAYABLE CLERK

Major food wholesaler seeks an accounts payable clerk with a minimum of three years' experience. A working knowledge of payroll, WordPerfect 5.1, ACCPAC, and Quick Check is required. Salary/benefits governed by Collective Agreement.

JANICE STEIN, 555-6767

---

1. What advantage was there to Leslie of obtaining a summer job?
2. What are five tasks for which Leslie is responsible in her position as an Accounts Receivable clerk?
3. What skills are required to be an accounts receivable clerk?

Business Career Skills

1. Report Writing — Systems Analysis and Design

The Widmark Furniture Company grew from a small family firm to a large multinational corporation. The firm still has only a few suppliers, but, by using its own credit system, its credit customers have grown to over 4 000. It is expected that the number will more than triple in the next two years. The company started its accounting system with only a general ledger. Based on the huge growth of accounts receivable, prepare a report for Widmark concerning the following matters:

(a) Recommend the various departments that they should operate in their business, and the basis for your conclusions.
(b) Recommend the best accounting system to use, outlining specifically what ledger(s) should be used. Give the basis for your conclusions.
(c) Recommend the jobs that should be performed by the personnel in each of the departments.

2. Decision Making — Credit Approval

The task of the credit approval office of a business is to decide to which customers the company should extend the privilege of buying on credit.

(a) In groups, brainstorm to develop a list of information that you would want to obtain about a person before extending credit.
(b) On your own, rank the information that you obtain, from most important to least important.
(c) In groups, compare your rankings.
(d) What are three procedures that can be followed in order to collect accounts receivable on time?
(e) A business was able to claim, "We have no bad debts — all our approved credit customers pay on time." Does this

indicate that the credit approval office is doing a great job? Comment.

3. Communication — Credit Granting

The income statements and balance sheets in Figures 10-26 and 10-27 are for two firms that approach you, as assistant credit manager, for credit privileges with your firm. Analyze the data, and

(a) prepare a report to the credit manager indicating your recommendation, with supporting reasons that refer to the data.
(b) prepare a business letter to each of the firms indicating your decision, along with any conditions that you might wish to include.

FIGURE 10-26

Income Statements
for the year ended April 30

	Company A		Company B	
Revenue		$176 900		$156 800
Cost		80 600		68 600
Gross Profit		96 300		88 200
Expenses				
Bad Debts	$ 1 400		$ 700	
Interest	2 457		2 652	
Other	54 300	58 157	52 900	56 252
		$ 38 143		$ 31 948

FIGURE 10-27

Balance Sheets
as at April 30

	Company A	Company B
Assets		
Cash	$ 12 000	$ 9 000
Accounts Receivable (net)	33 400	14 800
Merchandise Inventory	26 700	44 500
Other Assets	152 000	146 800
Total Assets	$224 100	$215 100
Liabilities and Owner's Equity		
Accounts Payable	$ 41 200	$ 22 300
Bank Loan	18 900	20 400
Owner's Equity	164 000	172 400
Total Liabilities and Owner's Equity	$224 100	$215 100

COMPUTER ACCOUNTING
SUBSIDIARY LEDGERS AND COMPUTER ACCOUNTING SOFTWARE

Of all the computer accounting programs available, the general ledger package is the most important, since its primary task is to provide the data needed to prepare the income statement and balance sheet, as well as other financial reports. It is an important cost and operating consideration whether a firm buys a general ledger system as a separate system and adds modules later to tie in with payables, receivables, payroll, inventory, project or job costing, bank reconciliation, and order entry — all necessary procedures that eventually have an effect on the financial matters and statements of the business. Many of the accounting software packages on the market today offer at least two companion modules, usually accounts receivable and accounts payable, that work with the general ledger. If a company requires additional subsidiary modules not offered by the accounting package under consideration, further research and assessment are necessary.

Exercise

Sara Mendel, a graduate of a two-year financial management program from a local junior college, has been hired to assist you in a special project that your employer, Sutcliffe Company, has decided to implement as of July 1. Jim Sutcliffe, the President of the company, has, on the advice of a data processing consultant, purchased a microcomputer system for the business. Plans call for the computer system to be integrated into all phases of the company's operations. The first priority is to use the system for word processing and to convert most of the existing manual accounting system to a computerized system utilizing a commercial software package suitable to the specific needs of the firm. Currently, payroll is prepared using the one-write system, however, there are plans to convert to the accounting software's payroll module when staff are sufficiently trained in its operation.

The trial balance for Sutcliffe Company, as of June 30 of this year, is given in Figure 10–28 and a list of accounts receivable and accounts payable follows. All postings have been done for June. As has been stated, the company must now begin to convert its manual accounting system (which consists of sales, purchases, cash receipts, and cash disbursements journals and a general journal, a general ledger, and two subsidiary ledgers — accounts receivable and accounts payable) to a microcomputer-based system. A decision has been made to initially utilize only the general ledger, and the accounts payable and accounts receivable modules. Also, on the advice of the consultant, the staff intend to run both systems parallel to one another for July and August in order to minimize conversion problems and to ensure the integrity of the transaction data. Sara's job is to monitor the manual system and also to work closely with you to convert the existing accounting system to the newly acquired computer system. The accounting year begins on March 1.

Procedure

1. Use your accounting software package to prepare the necessary modules including the entry of the appropriate historical data as of July 1.

FIGURE 10-28

	Sutcliffe Company Trial Balance June 30, 19--	
100 Cash	$ 45 000	
110 Marketable Securities	17 000	
120 Accounts Receivable	4 955	
130 Notes Receivable	7 000	
140 Merchandise Inventory	12 302	
150 GST Recoverable	1 240	
160 Equipment	35 800	
170 Accumulated Depreciation: Equipment		$ 2 950
200 Accounts Payable		3 600
210 Notes Payable		5 000
220 GST Payable		2 320
230 PST Payable		2 650
300 J. Sutcliffe, Capital		82 956
310 J. Sutcliffe, Drawings	12 000	
400 Sales		119 030
410 Sales Discounts	1 877	
420 Interest Earned		128
500 Purchases	62 450	
510 Purchase Returns and Allowances		8 720
520 Purchase Discounts		593
600 Rent Expense	8 000	
610 Salaries Expense	16 000	
620 Office Expense	3 540	
630 Interest Expense	783	
	$227 947	$227 947

2. When your modules are ready, enter the transaction data for July. Remember that you must add any new customer or vendor details from the list provided in Figure 10-29 before entering transactions affecting these new accounts.

Accounts Receivable:

Sales Invoice #450, June 3rd $1 612
S. Holoway
840 Cahill Drive West
Ottawa, Ontario
K4T 8W3

Sales Invoice #455, June 28th $3 343
M. Lawton
17 BankView Place
Ottawa, Ontario
K1R 2Y8

Accounts Payable:

Purchase Invoice #556, Terms 2/10, n/30 $3 650
Payless Supply Company
1800 Woodward Drive
Ottawa, Ontario
K6G 4U9

Transactions

Apply GST where appropriate and calculate PST at 6% on the base price.

July 2 Purchase Invoice 449876 from Kepler Wholesale Co., $8 943 plus GST, for merchandise; terms n/15.
- 2 Cash Receipt Slip #824 from Stan Holoway, $1 612, to pay Sales Invoice #450 in full.
- 2 Cheque Copy #549 to Eastern Office Management Co., $2 000 plus GST, for monthly rent.
- 5 Cash Receipt Slip #825 from Fred Chapman, $5 075, in full payment of his promissory note including interest owing of $75.
- 7 Sales Invoice #459 to C. Tonnenberg, $1 600 plus taxes.
- 8 Cheque Copy #550 to Trident Equipment Co., $5 120 to repay a note payable for $5 000. (Cheque includes the interest cost.)
- 9 Cheque Copy #551 to Payless Supply Company $3 650, to pay Purchase Invoice #556 in full.
- 11 Sales Invoice #460 to M. Lawton, $2 272 plus taxes.
- 12 Purchase Invoice 22336 from Abblass Trading Co., $15 176 plus GST, for merchandise; terms n/10.
- 14 Cheque Copy #552 to Kepler Wholesale Co., $9 569.01, in full payment of Purchase Invoice 449876.
- 15 Purchase Invoice 450176 from Kepler Wholesale Co., $592 plus GST, for merchandise; terms n/15.
- 17 Purchase Invoice 44589 from Massey Equipment Co., $2 000 plus taxes, for additional equipment; terms 1/10, n/30.
- 17 Sales Invoice #461 to L. Noonen, $750 plus taxes.
- 17 Cash Receipt Slip #826 from C. Tonnenberg, $1 776.00 for Sales Invoice #459 in the amount of $1 808.00, less a discount of $32.00.
- 19 Cash Receipt Slip #827 from Payne & Co., $2 500, less $75 brokerage fee for investments sold by the brokerage firm.
- 20 Cheque Copy #553 to Abblass Trading Co., $16 238.32, in full payment of Purchase Invoice 22336.
- 22 Sales Invoice #462 to M. Lawton, $2 000 plus taxes.
- 22 Purchase Invoice #590 from Payless Supply Company, $245 plus taxes, for office supplies; terms 1/10, n/30.
- 26 Sales Invoice #463 to L. Noonen, $1 550 plus taxes.
- 27 Cash Receipt Slip #828 from M. Lawton, $3 343, for Sales Invoice #455.
- 27 Cash Receipt Slip #829 from L. Noonen, $832.50 for Sales Invoice #461 in the amount of $847.50, less a discount of $15.00.
- 29 Cheque Copy #554 to J. Sutcliffe, $3 000 for the owner's personal use.
- 30 Sales Invoice #464 to S. Holoway, $1 792 plus taxes.
- 30 Bank Debit Memo, $4 000, for the transfer of funds from the firm's current account to the payroll bank account, for the monthly payroll.

At the end of the month

1. Print a trial balance and summaries of the accounts receivable and accounts payable.

2. Your teacher should have the trial balance and schedules of accounts receivable and accounts payable that Sara Mendel was responsible for producing from the manual accounting system. Use these to verify your data.

FIGURE 10-29

Addresses for new customers:	**Addresses for new vendors:**
C. Tonnenberg 244 Lennox Drive Hull, Quebec K4Y 8I3 L. Noonen 309 Baseline Road Ottawa, Ontario K3F 4B5	Kepler Wholesale Co. 844 Gatineau Avenue Ottawa, Ontario K1T 1R7 Abblass Trading Co. 450 Pender Street Nepean, Ontario K6P 2H7 Massey Equipment Co. 4566 Moodie Street Ottawa, Ontario K8U 4R9

CHAPTER ELEVEN

Columnar Journals

LEARNING OBJECTIVES

At the end of this chapter you should be able to
- enter transactions in a columnar journal;
- discuss the advantages and disadvantages of a columnar journal;
- post from a columnar journal;
- enter transactions in a five-journal system;
- discuss the advantages and disadvantages of a five-journal system;
- discuss the types of business in which a five-journal system would be appropriate;
- use a spreadsheet program to format a columnar journal.

LANGUAGE OF ACCOUNTING

You will see the following terms in this chapter:
columnar journal
cross balancing
five-journal system
journalless system
mainframe computers
synoptic journal
VisiCalc

11.1 Designing an Accounting System: The Columnar Journal

One of an accountant's important tasks is to determine the best accounting system for a particular business. A good accounting system is one that is efficient, follows generally accepted accounting principles, and provides needed information in the form of reports. The cost of the

FIGURE 11-1 TYPICAL COLUMN HEADINGS THAT COULD BE USED BY A SMALL BUSINESS, USING A COLUMNAR JOURNAL

DATE	CUSTOMER/SUPPLIER	REF. NO.	CASH DR	CASH CR	ACCOUNTS RECEIVABLE DR	ACCOUNTS RECEIVABLE CR	✓
1							

FIGURE 11-2 TYPICAL COLUMN HEADINGS THAT COULD BE USED BY A STUDENTS' COUNCIL, USING A COLUMNAR JOURNAL

DATE	CUSTOMER/SUPPLIER	REF. NO.	CASH DR	CASH CR	DANCES DR	DANCES CR
1						

system is also a factor, which is why many small businesses still do their accounting manually. There are a number of books of record that can be used, and a number of ways of actually recording the information and deriving reports from it. As we saw in the last chapter, a subsidiary ledger is one of the first considerations of a growing business. In this chapter we will examine different journal systems.

The first journal system that we studied used only a general journal. In fact, the general journal is rarely used alone in business; often it is combined with other journals. It is introduced by itself in basic accounting texts in order to illustrate the fundamentals of accounting. However, even in a small organization such as a school club, there are more efficient systems that can be used. Two of the more common systems employed, the columnar journal and the five-journal system, are examined here. The former is used where a small accounting system is required, the latter where a large accounting system is required.

The Columnar Journal

The columnar journal, sometimes referred to as a synoptic journal or multipurpose journal, is used by many small businesses. It is called a columnar journal because there are more than the two columns used in the general journal. The term synoptic journal is appropriate, for "synopsis" means "summary," as in a weather synopsis. As you will see, the synoptic journal lends itself to a business that does not have a great many transactions other than those dealing with accounts receivable and payable, and therefore has a small number of accounts in the general ledger. Thus, all the business's transactions can be entered in it. It may be the only journal used in a business, or it may be used in combination with a general journal. It is especially suited to small businesses with one or only a few accounting personnel.

> "A columnar journal can be used alone, or in conjunction with a general journal."

A partial columnar journal for a small service business is illustrated in Figure 11-1. Note the column headings.

A columnar journal for a students' council is illustrated in Figure 11-2. Note that some of the columns are the same as for the preceding

COLUMNAR JOURNAL

PAGE NO. _____

CUSTOMIZING FEES CR		GST PAYABLE CR	GST RECOVERABLE DR	OTHER ACCOUNTS		
				ACCOUNT	PR	DR	CR

COLUMNAR JOURNAL

PAGE NO. _____

GRANTS/CLUBS DR	COKE MACHINE CR	POPCORN MACHINE CR	STUDENT FEES CR	OTHER ACCOUNTS		
				ACCOUNT	PR	DR	CR

business, but others are not. There are no Accounts Receivable or Accounts Payable columns because the council does its accounting on a cash basis: entries are made only when cash is received and cheques are issued.

Columns can be added to the journal in order to accommodate the particular needs of the business. Revenue columns can be divided in order to keep a record of different sources. For example, a golf course may have columns for green fees, driving range fees, lessons, clubhouse storage fees, and merchandise sales. Separate columns are maintained only for accounts that are used frequently. Accounts that are not used frequently are entered in the Other Accounts columns. The following examples for Marco Iannucci, a freelance software programmer and customizer, show how transactions are recorded in a columnar journal. Remember that when you make entries in a columnar journal the basic theory of double-entry accounting still applies! Total debits must equal total credits. The transaction is first entered in the general journal below so that you can see the debits and credits. Obviously, the transaction would really only be entered in one journal.

"Separate columns are maintained for frequently occurring transactions."

Transaction 1

April 22   Cash Sales Slip #862: Customizing Microsoft Works, $198, plus GST of $13.86, total $211.86.

In a general journal, the transaction would appear as follows:

GENERAL JOURNAL

PAGE 141

DATE 1992		PARTICULARS	PR	DEBIT	CREDIT
Apr.	22	Cash		211 86	
		Customizing Fees			198 –
		GST Payable			13 86
		Cash Sales Slip #862			

In a columnar journal, the transaction would appear as in Figure 11-3.

FIGURE 11-3

	DATE 1992		CUSTOMER/SUPPLIER	REF. NO.	CASH DR	CASH CR	ACCOUNTS RECEIVABLE DR	ACCOUNTS RECEIVABLE CR	✓
1	Apr.	22	Cash sale	862	211 86				

FIGURE 11-4

	DATE 1992		CUSTOMER/SUPPLIER	REF. NO.	CASH DR	CASH CR	ACCOUNTS RECEIVABLE DR	ACCOUNTS RECEIVABLE CR	✓
1	Apr.	22	Cash sale	862	211 86				
2		22	Universal Computer Products Ltd.	286					
3									

Notice the following:

(1) the explanation is entered in the Customer/Supplier column;

(2) the number of the source document is entered in the Ref. No. column. The type of source document will be evident when examining the transaction, as in this example. A debit to Cash and a credit to Customizing Fees indicates a cash sales slip.

(3) the debit and credit amounts are entered on the same line in their appropriate columns. (Sometimes it will be necessary to use more than one line to complete an entry.)

(4) total debits equal total credits.

Transaction 2
April 22   Purchase Invoice #286: From Universal Computer Products Ltd., for equipment, $1 443, plus GST of $101.01 and PST of $115.44.

In a general journal, the transaction would appear as follows:

GENERAL JOURNAL

PAGE 141

DATE 1992		PARTICULARS	PR	DEBIT	CREDIT
Apr.	22	Equipment		1558 44	
		GST Recoverable		101 01	
		Accounts Payable			1659 45
		Purchase Invoice #286, Universal Computer			
		Products Ltd.			

In a columnar journal, the transaction would appear as in Figure 11-4.

COLUMNAR JOURNAL

PAGE NO. 36

CUSTOMIZING FEES CR	GST PAYABLE CR	GST RECOVERABLE DR	OTHER ACCOUNTS			
			ACCOUNT	PR	DR	CR
198 –		13 86					1

COLUMNAR JOURNAL

PAGE NO. 36

CUSTOMIZING FEES CR	GST PAYABLE CR	GST RECOVERABLE DR	OTHER ACCOUNTS				
			ACCOUNT	PR	DR	CR	
198 –		13 86					1
		101 01	Equipment		1558 44		2
			Accounts Payable			1659 45	3

Note the following:

(1) the month is not repeated in the date;

(2) there is no blank line between entries;

(3) the transaction required more than one line in the journal.

Remember that GST paid on any purchase is going to be recovered. Since there will likely be many purchases by the business, a special column has been established for GST Recoverable.

Transaction 3
April 23   Sales Invoice #892: Customized dBase IV for Neighbourhood Watch, $850, plus GST of $59.50 for a total of $909.50.

In a general journal, the transaction would appear as follows:

GENERAL JOURNAL
PAGE 141

DATE 1992		PARTICULARS	PR	DEBIT	CREDIT
Apr.	23	Accounts Receivable		909 50	
		Customizing Fees			850 —
		GST Payable			59 50
		Sales Invoice #892, Neighbourhood Watch			

In a columnar journal, the transaction would appear as in Figure 11-5.

FIGURE 11-5

	DATE 1992	CUSTOMER/SUPPLIER	REF. NO.	CASH DR	CASH CR	ACCOUNTS RECEIVABLE DR	ACCOUNTS RECEIVABLE CR	✓
4	23	Neighbourhood Watch	892			909 50		

FIGURE 11-6

	DATE 1992	CUSTOMER/SUPPLIER	REF. NO.	CASH DR	CASH CR	ACCOUNTS RECEIVABLE DR	ACCOUNTS RECEIVABLE CR	✓
5	23	Royal Bank			9 —			

Transaction 4

April 23   Bank Debit Memo: The bank withdrew $9 for service charges.

In a general journal, the transaction would appear as follows:

GENERAL JOURNAL

PAGE 141

DATE 1992		PARTICULARS	PR	DEBIT	CREDIT
Apr.	23	Bank Expense		9 –	
		Cash			9 –
		Royal Bank Debit Memo, service charges			

In a columnar journal, the transaction would appear as in Figure 11-6.

Since service charges on the business's bank account occur only once a month, it is not necessary to have a special column for bank charges. The account name is therefore put in the Other Accounts column, and the amount is put in the appropriate money column, in this case the debit column.

Transaction 5

April 23   Memo #98: Received $1 500 cash from the owner, Marco Iannucci, as an additional investment.

COLUMNAR JOURNAL

PAGE NO. 36

CUSTOMIZING FEES CR		GST PAYABLE CR	GST RECOVERABLE DR	OTHER ACCOUNTS				
				ACCOUNT	PR	DR	CR	
850 –		59 50						4

COLUMNAR JOURNAL

PAGE NO. 36

CUSTOMIZING FEES CR		GST PAYABLE CR	GST RECOVERABLE DR	OTHER ACCOUNTS				
				ACCOUNT	PR	DR	CR	
				Bank Expense		9 –		5

In a general journal, the transaction would appear as follows:

GENERAL JOURNAL

PAGE 141

DATE 1992		PARTICULARS	PR	DEBIT	CREDIT
Apr.	23	Cash		1500 –	
		M. Iannucci, Capital			1500 –
		Memo #98, to record additional owner investment			

In a columnar journal, the transaction would appear as in Figure 11-7.

The credit to M. Iannucci, Capital is recorded in the Other Accounts credit column. A special column is not required for M. Iannucci, Capital because the account is not frequently used.

Transaction 6
April 24 Purchase Invoice #858: From Willson Supplies Ltd., $555.45, for office supplies, $133.92, and a new office desk, $387.72. GST is $33.81.

FIGURE 11-7

	DATE 1992		CUSTOMER/SUPPLIER	REF. NO.	CASH DR	CASH CR	ACCOUNTS RECEIVABLE DR	ACCOUNTS RECEIVABLE CR	✓
6		23	Marco Iannucci	98	1500 –				

FIGURE 11-8

	DATE 1992		CUSTOMER/SUPPLIER	REF. NO.	CASH DR	CASH CR	ACCOUNTS RECEIVABLE DR	ACCOUNTS RECEIVABLE CR	✓
7		24	Willson Supplies Ltd.	858					
8									
9									

Chapter 11: Columnar Journals

In a general journal, the transaction would appear as follows:

GENERAL JOURNAL

PAGE 141

DATE 1992		PARTICULARS	PR	DEBIT	CREDIT
Apr.	24	Office Supplies		133 92	
		Office Equipment		387 72	
		GST Recoverable		33 81	
		Accounts Payable			555 45
		Purchase Invoice #858, Willson Supplies Ltd.			

In a columnar journal, the transaction would appear as in Figure 11-8.

Note that the entry requires three lines, because three accounts must be entered in the Other Accounts column. It is acceptable to use as many lines as necessary to enter a transaction in the columnar journal.

Transaction 7
April 24 Cash Refund Slip #22: Cash refund on customizing work, given to Lloyd Jarvis, $27 plus GST of $1.89, for a total of $28.89.

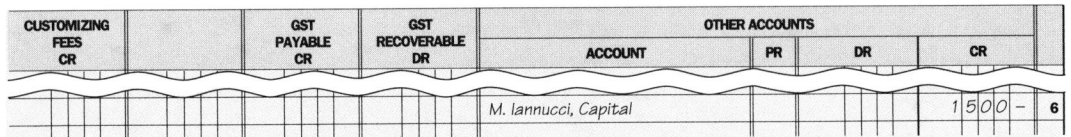

COLUMNAR JOURNAL

PAGE NO. 36

CUSTOMIZING FEES CR	GST PAYABLE CR	GST RECOVERABLE DR	OTHER ACCOUNTS			
			ACCOUNT	PR	DR	CR
			M. Iannucci, Capital			1500 —	6

COLUMNAR JOURNAL

PAGE NO. 36

CUSTOMIZING FEES CR	GST PAYABLE CR	GST RECOVERABLE DR	OTHER ACCOUNTS				
			ACCOUNT	PR	DR	CR	
		33 81	Office Supplies		133 92		7
			Office Equipment		387 72		8
			Accounts Payable			555 45	9

In a general journal, the transaction would appear as follows:

GENERAL JOURNAL

PAGE 141

DATE 1992		PARTICULARS	PR	DEBIT	CREDIT
Apr.	24	Customizing Fees		27 —	
		GST Payable		1 89	
		Cash			28 89
		Cash Refund Slip #22, to Lloyd Jarvis			

In a columnar journal, the transaction would appear as in Figure 11-9.

"*Debit entries may be placed in a credit column, and vice versa, if they are entered in red or circled.*"

Note that debit entries may be made in credit columns, and credit entries in debit columns. To indicate that the amount has an effect opposite to the column debit or credit heading, the amount is either circled or entered in red. When the column is totalled in order to forward it to the next journal page or to post it at month end, amounts circled or entered in red must be subtracted rather than added.

Alternate entries to the one shown in Figure 11-9 would be

(1) to enter the debits for GST Payable and for Refunds in the Other Accounts column; or

(2) to make a separate column in the journal for Refunds or for Sales Returns and Allowances.

FIGURE 11-9

	DATE 1992		CUSTOMER/SUPPLIER	REF. NO.	CASH DR	CASH CR	ACCOUNTS RECEIVABLE DR	ACCOUNTS RECEIVABLE CR	✓
10		24	Lloyd Jarvis	22		28 89			

FIGURE 11-10 ALL TRANSACTIONS HAVE BEEN ENTERED IN THE COLUMNAR JOURNAL

	DATE 1992		CUSTOMER/SUPPLIER	REF. NO.	CASH DR	CASH CR	ACCOUNTS RECEIVABLE DR	ACCOUNTS RECEIVABLE CR	✓
1	Apr.	22	Cash sale	862	211 86				
2		22	Universal Computer Products Ltd.	286					
3									
4		23	Neighbourhood Watch	892			909 50		
5		23	Royal Bank			9 —			
6		23	Marco Iannucci	98	15 00 —				
7		24	Willson Supplies Ltd.	858					
8									
9									
10		24	Lloyd Jarvis	22		28 89			

Figure 11-10 shows a columnar journal with all of the entries included.

Forwarding a Columnar Journal

Unlike what happens with the general journal, during the month columnar journals must be totalled at the bottom of the page and the column balances forwarded to the top of the next page. This procedure is followed until the end of the month. At that time, posting of column totals takes place.

In order to forward, the following procedure is carried out. (See Figures 11-11 and 11-12.)

(1) Reserve the last two lines on the page for forwarding. Draw a single ruled line in ink immediately beneath the last entry in the journal.

(2) Foot each money column, showing the amount as a pencil footing.

(3) **Cross balance** the page; that is, prove that the total debits equal the total credits. This can be done on a separate piece of paper, or with a printing calculator. Staple the calculation to the page when complete.

> "Forwarding of each page of a columnar journal is done until the end of the month."

> **To cross balance:** to prove that debits equal credits for the column totals.

COLUMNAR JOURNAL
PAGE NO. 36

CUSTOMIZING FEES CR		GST PAYABLE CR	GST RECOVERABLE DR	ACCOUNT	PR	DR	CR	
27 —		1 89						10

COLUMNAR JOURNAL
PAGE NO. 36

CUSTOMIZING FEES CR		GST PAYABLE CR	GST RECOVERABLE DR	ACCOUNT	PR	DR	CR	
1 98 —		13 86						1
			10 1 01	Equipment		1 558 44		2
				Accounts Payable			1 659 45	3
8 50 —		59 50						4
				Bank Expense		9 —		5
				M. Iannucci, Capital			15 00 —	6
			3 3 81	Office Supplies		1 33 92		7
				Office Equipment		3 87 72		8
				Accounts Payable			555 45	9
27 —		1 89						10

FIGURE 11-11 COLUMNAR JOURNAL SHOWING FORWARDING AT THE END OF A PAGE

DATE 1992		CUSTOMER/SUPPLIER	REF. NO.	CASH DR	CASH CR	ACCOUNTS RECEIVABLE DR	ACCOUNTS RECEIVABLE CR	✓
28				8 3 6 9 76	1 8 4 5 92	3 8 1 0 —	2 6 7 0 —	
29		28 Forwarded		8 3 6 9 76	1 8 4 5 92	3 8 1 0 —	2 6 7 0 —	

FIGURE 11-12 COLUMNAR JOURNAL SHOWING FORWARDING TO THE TOP OF THE NEXT PAGE

DATE 1992		CUSTOMER/SUPPLIER	REF. NO.	CASH DR	CASH CR	ACCOUNTS RECEIVABLE DR	ACCOUNTS RECEIVABLE CR	✓
1	Apr.	28 Forwarded		8 3 6 9 76	1 8 4 5 92	3 8 1 0 —	2 6 7 0 —	

(4) If the debits equal the credits, enter the final totals in ink beneath the pencil totals, and double rule all money columns immediately beneath the totals. Write "forwarded" in the Customer/Supplier column. If the debits do not equal the credits, then the error must be found before the totals are entered in ink. A common error made when entering transactions in a columnar journal is to put the amount in a debit column when it should be in a credit column, or vice versa. Therefore, when you have found the total debits and total credits for the page, and they are not equal, the correction procedures described in earlier chapters should be followed. The most important test will be to divide the difference between the total debits and total credits by two, and look for the amount of the answer in the journal. The divide-by-two test finds those numbers that are entered on the wrong side, if there is only one error on the page.

(5) On the first line at the top of the next page, enter the exact information that was written on the last line of the previous page, omitting the single and double rules.

FIGURE 11-13

DATE 1992	CUSTOMER/SUPPLIER	REF. NO.	CASH DR	CASH CR	ACCOUNTS RECEIVABLE DR	ACCOUNTS RECEIVABLE CR	✓
10			12 0 7 0 88	3 9 2 0 01	4 6 9 5 —	4 2 1 0 —	
11			12 0 7 0 88	3 9 2 0 01	4 6 9 5 —	4 2 1 0 —	

Totalling, Balancing, and Ruling the Columnar Journal

At the end of the month, the columnar journal should be totalled, balanced, and double ruled. Before the totals are entered in ink and double ruled, one should be certain that the total debits equal the total credits. If one does not have a calculator, the Customer/Supplier column can be used to list the column headings, and the first two money columns can be used to list column totals, either debit or credit. The two columns can then be added to prove whether debits equal credits.

Cross balancing Figure 11-13, we get the following:

	Debit	Credit
Cash	$12 070.88	$ 3 920.01
Accounts Receivable	4 695.00	4 210.00
Customizing Fees		7 215.00
GST Payable		505.05
GST Recoverable	362.73	
Other Accounts	12 461.16	13 739.71
	$29 589.77	$29 589.77

Lesson Review

1. What is a columnar journal?

2. What alternative names are used for a columnar journal? Why are they used?

3. When designing the columnar journal, what rationale is used to decide the column headings?

4. What are each of the following columns used for in the columnar journal: (a) Customer/Supplier? (b) Ref. No.?

5. Why are Other Accounts columns necessary in a columnar journal?

6. How many lines can be used when a transaction is entered in a columnar journal?

7. State two ways that columnar journal entries differ from general journal entries.

8. State four ways that the debit for a sales return transaction can be entered in a columnar journal.

9. Why is forwarding necessary in a columnar journal? Summarize the procedure for forwarding.

Lesson Applications

10. (a) Journalize each of the following transactions on page 76 of a columnar journal. Use the following extra column headings: Sales Cr., GST Payable Cr., and PST Payable Cr. Create other accounts as required. GST is 7 percent and PST is 8 percent, calculated on the base price.
    (b) Total, balance, and rule the journal.

    June 1   Voucher #12: Received $2 000 from the owner, K. Linesman, as an additional investment in the business.

          1   Cheque Copy #45: Paid the monthly rent, $980 plus GST.

          4   Sales Invoice #93: Sale on account to R. Cunneyworth, $240 plus taxes.

          4   Purchase Invoice #819: Purchased a new computer from Computex, $4 320 plus taxes.

          6   Cash Sales Invoice #32: Cash sale of $2 800, plus taxes.

          7   Purchase Invoice #52: Purchased merchandise on account from Sundstrom Bedding Limited, $320 plus GST; terms 2/10, n/30.

          9   Bank Debit Memo: The bank returned an NSF cheque that the business had deposited. The cheque for $128

had been issued by R. Pivonka. Service charge was $15, to be recovered from client.

9 Cash Receipt Slip #87: Received $420 on account from R. Gould.

10 Cheque Copy #46: Deposited to Payroll account for wages to three employees, $865 each.

10 Cheque Copy #47: Paid Computex $2 320 on account.

10 Sales Invoice #94: Sale to R. Tambellini, $900 plus taxes.

11. (a) Journalize each of the following transactions on page 116 of a columnar journal. Use the following extra column headings: Sales Cr., GST Payable Cr., and GST Recoverable Dr. Create other accounts as required. Assume that there is no PST, but the GST is 7 percent. The names of source documents have been omitted.

(b) Total, balance, and rule the journal.

Sept. 3 Sold merchandise on account to D. Arca, $360 plus GST.

4 Issued a cheque, $250, to the owner, D. Ryan, for personal use.

4 Purchased office equipment, valued at $900 plus GST, on account from Nagel Office Furnishings Ltd.

5 Issued a cheque to *Brandon Sun* for advertising, $139 plus GST.

5 The owner, Dave Ryan, took $23 worth of supplies home for personal use. (Remember to calculate GST.)

6 Issued a cheque, $97 plus GST, to Manitoba Tel, for monthly telephone usage.

6 Issued a cheque, $3 280, for biweekly wages.

6 Sale on account to R. Martin, $880 plus GST.

8 Issued a cheque, $963, to Nagel Office Furnishings Ltd., on account.

9 Cash sales, $620 plus GST.

10 Purchased merchandise on account from Westway Office Products Ltd., $700 plus GST.

10 Sold merchandise on account to V. Williamson, $320 plus GST.

11 Issued a cheque, $749, to Westway Office Products Ltd., on account.

11 Cash sales, $411 plus GST.

12 Purchased a telephone answering machine, $145 plus GST, on account from OE Inc.

12. (a) Journalize each of the following transactions for Sunnyside Auto Centre on page 45 of a columnar journal. Insert extra column headings for Sales (credit), GST Payable

(credit), and PST Payable (credit). GST is 7 percent and PST is 6 percent, calculated on the base price.

(b) Total, balance, and rule the journal.

May 1 Voucher #17: Received $5 000 from the owner, Chris Yzerman, as an investment.
    1 Cheque Copy #661: Paid monthly rent, $1 200 plus GST.
    5 Cash Receipt Slip #438: Received $900 on account from Martin Building Service.
    6 Cash Sales Slips #694 to #719: Cash sales for the week, $19 540 plus taxes.
    6 Sales Invoice #1428: To Z. Bradkowski, sale of $428 plus taxes. Terms 2/10, n/30.
    6 Sales Invoice #1429: To M. Peacock, sale of $1 400 plus taxes. Terms 2/10, n/30.
    6 Cheque Copy #662: Purchased office supplies, $319 plus taxes.
    7 Purchase Invoice #725A: Purchased merchandise on account from Norton Tire Suppliers, $4 320 plus GST.
   11 Purchase Invoice #762: Purchased merchandise on account from Delco Batteries, $1 246 plus GST. Terms 2/10, n/30.
   13 Cash Sales Slips #720 to #798: Cash sales for the week, $21 870 plus taxes.
   13 Voucher #18: The owner withdrew $72 worth of merchandise for personal use. (Remember to adjust for taxes here.)

13. (a) Continue the columnar journal for Sunnyside Auto Centre in Question 12 by forwarding the totals from page 45 to page 46.

(b) Journalize the following transactions using page 46 of the columnar journal.

May 16 Cheque Copy #663: To BC Tel for telephone, $97 plus taxes.
   16 Cheque Copy #664: To Norton Tire Suppliers, $2 000 on account.
   16 Cheque Copy #665: To Delco Batteries, $1 308.30 for Purchase Invoice #762, in payment of $1 333.22 owing on account. Discount of $24.92 taken.
   16 Cash Receipt Slip #439: Received $475.08 on account for Sales Invoice #1428, $483.64. Sales discount of $8.56 was taken.
   17 Sales Invoice #1430: To J. Pandeya, sale of $2 760 plus taxes. Terms 2/10, n/30.
   17 Sales Invoice #1431: To T. Murphy, sale of $1 489 plus taxes. Terms 2/10, n/30.
   18 Bank Debit Memo: Bank charges of $38.

18 Debit Memo #41: Error on Sales Invoice #1430; undercharged J. Pandeya $200 plus taxes.
19 Bank Debit Memo: The bank returned an NSF cheque that the business had deposited. The cheque for $122.50 had been issued by R. Callander, and a sales discount of $2.21 had been granted when it was received. The business intends to collect the $18 service charge from the client.

11.2 Posting Procedures Using a Columnar Journal

The most important advantage of using a columnar journal is the time that is saved in posting. If there were 300 debits to Cash in a month, using a general journal, 300 postings would have to be made. Using a columnar journal, the same 300 debits require only one posting. That is because column totals are posted instead of all the individual entries.

During the month either direct posting from source documents to the subsidiary ledgers, or indirect posting from the columnar journal is carried out. It is important to post on a daily basis because customer and supplier balances are needed during the month. A customer who comes to the business to pay his or her account before leaving on a holiday will not want to wait while the accountant searches for the source documents relating to that person and then posts them. In many cases a subsidiary ledger will not be required by a business that chooses to use a columnar journal, for by its very nature it can only be used by small businesses.

FIGURE 11-14 COMPARISON OF PROCEDURES USING DIRECT AND INDIRECT POSTING WHEN A COLUMNAR JOURNAL IS USED WITH A SUBSIDIARY LEDGER SYSTEM

POSTING TO SUBSIDIARY LEDGERS

If Direct Posting is Used	If Indirect Posting is Used
Source Document	Source Document
↓	↓
Subsidiary Ledger	Columnar Journal
	↓
	Subsidiary Ledger

If indirect posting is used, the completion of the posting from the columnar journal to the subsidiary ledger is indicated by placing a check mark in the √ column, as shown in Figure 11-15.

FIGURE 11-15 COLUMNAR JOURNAL WITH A CHECK MARK IN THE ✓ COLUMN, WHICH SHOWS THAT A POSTING HAS BEEN MADE TO A SUBSIDIARY LEDGER

	DATE 1992		CUSTOMER/SUPPLIER	REF. NO.	CASH DR	CASH CR	ACCOUNTS RECEIVABLE DR	ACCOUNTS RECEIVABLE CR	✓
5		28	Edna Bartholomew	900			240 75		✓

The subsidiary ledger account PR column indicates that the amount entered in it was posted from the columnar journal.

ACCOUNTS RECEIVABLE SUBSIDIARY LEDGER

ACCOUNT Edna Bartholomew   NO

DATE 1992		PARTICULARS	PR	DEBIT	CREDIT	DR CR	BALANCE
Apr.	28	Sales Invoice #900	C37	240 75		DR	240 75

At the end of the month, the columnar journal is posted to the general ledger. The following procedure is completed and illustrated in Figures 11-16, 11-17, and 11-18.

(1) Cross balance the journal.

"Column totals are posted from the columnar journal to the general ledger."

(2) Post column totals. The total of the Cash debit column is posted to the debit column of the Cash account. The Cash account number is put beneath the total of the Cash debit column in the columnar journal in brackets to show that the posting is complete. The total of the Cash credit column is then posted to the credit column of the Cash account, and the Cash account number is entered under the column total in the columnar journal in brackets. Note that the *difference* between the debit

FIGURE 11-16

	DATE 1992		CUSTOMER/SUPPLIER	REF. NO.	CASH DR	CASH CR	ACCOUNTS RECEIVABLE DR	ACCOUNTS RECEIVABLE CR	✓
1	Apr.	28	Forwarded		8369 76	1845 92	3810 —	2670 —	
2		28	Doug Davies	898			644 25		✓
3		28	Madhu Ranadive	C921	1540 —			1540 —	✓
4		28	Linda Scott	899	1663 74				
5		28	Edna Bartholomew	900			240 75		✓
6		29	Cash refund — Future Shop	F343	497 38				
7		30	Dell Computers	1284		2074 09			
8		30	Hay Stationery	722					
9									
10					12070 88	3920 01	4695 —	4210 —	
11					12070 88	3920 01	4695 —	4210 —	
12					(101)	(101)	(111)	(111)	

Chapter 11: Columnar Journals

COLUMNAR JOURNAL

PAGE NO. 37

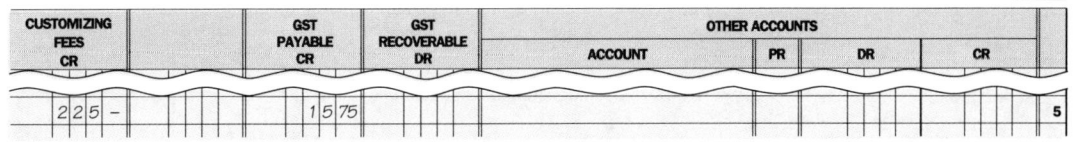

CUSTOMIZING FEES CR		GST PAYABLE CR	GST RECOVERABLE DR	OTHER ACCOUNTS			
				ACCOUNT	PR	DR	CR
2 25 –		1 5 75					5

and credit is *not* posted: the debit and credit are posted separately. As well, note that the symbol entered in the general ledger PR column to indicate that the information was obtained from the columnar journal is a C.

FIGURE 11-17 GENERAL LEDGER CASH ACCOUNT SHOWING DOUBLE POSTING FROM THE COLUMNAR JOURNAL ON APRIL 30

GENERAL LEDGER

ACCOUNT Cash   NO 101

DATE 1992		PARTICULARS	PR	DEBIT	CREDIT	DR CR	BALANCE
Apr.	30	Forwarded	✓			DR	14 23 6 92
	30		C37	12 0 7 0 88		DR	26 3 0 7 80
	30		C37		3 9 2 0 01	DR	22 3 8 7 79

The totals for the Accounts Receivable columns are then posted, followed by the Customizing Fees, and so on, except for the totals of the Other Accounts columns.

The entry in the ledger should show:
- the last day of the month;
- the columnar journal page number where the information came from, indicated by C for columnar journal.

COLUMNAR JOURNAL

PAGE NO. 37

CUSTOMIZING FEES CR		GST PAYABLE CR	GST RECOVERABLE DR	OTHER ACCOUNTS				
				ACCOUNT	PR	DR	CR	
4 8 3 3 –		3 3 8 31	1 6 6 81			8 9 7 1 23	11 6 3 0 57	1
6 0 2 10		4 2 15						2
								3
1 5 5 4 90		1 0 8 84						4
2 25 –		1 5 75						5
			(3 0 28)	Computer Software	126		4 6 7 10	6
			1 2 6 25	Computer Equipment	131	1 9 4 7 84		7
			9 9 95	Office Furniture	136	1 5 4 2 09		8
				Accounts Payable	211		1 6 4 2 04	9
7 2 1 5 –		5 0 5 05	3 6 2 73			12 4 6 1 16	13 7 3 9 71	10
7 2 1 5 –		5 0 5 05	3 6 2 73			12 4 6 1 16	13 7 3 9 71	11
(4 0 1)		(2 2 1)	(1 2 1)					12

FIGURE 11-18 THE COLUMNAR JOURNAL SHOWS THE POSTING OF THE ENTRY IN THE OTHER ACCOUNTS COLUMN, EQUIPMENT, TO THE GENERAL LEDGER ACCOUNT

	DATE 1992		CUSTOMER/SUPPLIER	REF. NO.	CASH DR	CASH CR	ACCOUNTS RECEIVABLE DR	ACCOUNTS RECEIVABLE CR	✓
2		22	Universal Computer Products Ltd.	286					
3									

> "The accounts in the Other Accounts column in the columnar journal are posted individually to the general ledger."

(3) The Other Accounts columns should then be posted. The totals of these columns cannot be posted, for the entries are to a variety of general ledger accounts. Therefore, each amount in these columns is posted individually. To show in the columnar journal that an entry has been posted, the account number is entered in the PR column. Figure 11-18 shows the posting of the entry in the Other Accounts column to the Equipment account.

The general ledger account, Equipment, will show the posting from the columnar journal as follows:

GENERAL LEDGER

ACCOUNT Equipment						NO 145	
DATE 1992		PARTICULARS	PR	DEBIT	CREDIT	DR CR	BALANCE
Apr.	21		C35	100 –		DR	26 502 25
	22		C36	1558 44		DR	28 060 69

Adjusting Entries and Closing Entries

Adjusting entries and closing entries are prepared in a journal. These entries may be made in the columnar journal, using the Other Accounts columns. However, it is easier to use a general journal for adjusting and closing entries. Uncommon entries such as refunds can also be entered

FIGURE 11-19 COMPARISON OF A COLUMNAR JOURNAL SYSTEM WITH A TWO-JOURNAL SYSTEM

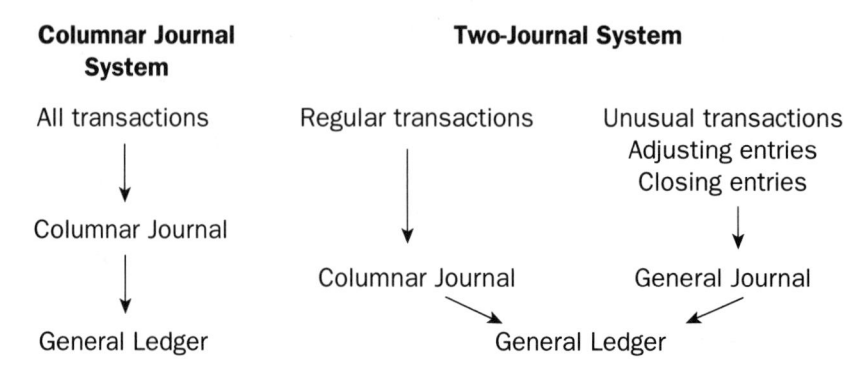

```
        Columnar Journal              Two-Journal System
            System

        All transactions        Regular transactions    Unusual transactions
                                                        Adjusting entries
                                                        Closing entries
                ↓                       ↓                       ↓
        Columnar Journal                                General Journal
                                Columnar Journal
                ↓                       ↘               ↙
        General Ledger                  General Ledger
```

COLUMNAR JOURNAL

PAGE NO. 36

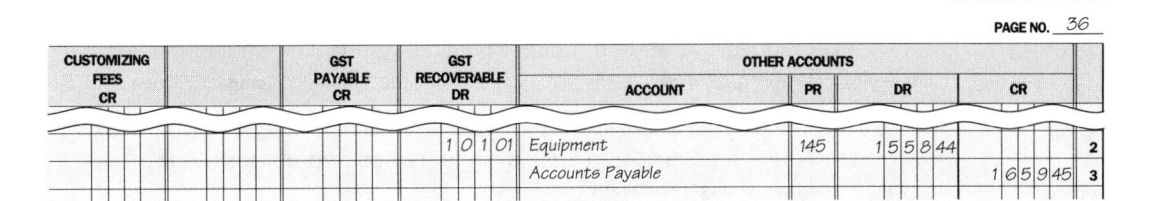

CUSTOMIZING FEES CR		GST PAYABLE CR	GST RECOVERABLE DR	OTHER ACCOUNTS			
				ACCOUNT	PR	DR	CR
			1 01 01	Equipment	145	1558 44	2
				Accounts Payable			1659 45 3

in the general journal. For this reason, businesses will design their system to make use of both of these journals rather than just the columnar journal.

Advantages and Disadvantages of the Columnar Journal

When deciding whether to use a columnar journal as part of the accounting system, there are a number of factors that should be considered. The advantages of the system are mainly related to the saving of time, which of course translates into a reduction in labour expenses for a business.

Advantages of the Columnar Journal

1. Less time is required for journalizing, because account names for most transactions do not have to be written.

2. Time is saved when posting, because column totals are posted instead of each individual entry, with the exception of the entries in the Other Accounts columns.

3. There are fewer errors when posting. Posting from a general journal is one of the most time-consuming tasks in accounting, and because of the repetition involved it leads to errors. Since column totals are posted when using a columnar journal, rather than individual entries in the column, the chance of error is reduced.

4. Since all journal entries are on one page, and in chronological order, it is easy to refer to any one transaction.

Disadvantages of the Columnar Journal

1. The columnar journal system is only useful to a small business, in which one person does the accounting.

2. There is an increased risk of error when journalizing, as compared to the journalizing done in a general journal. This is due to the number of columns in the columnar journal, and to the procedure of circling or entering amounts in red. The large number of columns also makes it cumbersome to use.

LESSON REVIEW

14. Distinguish between a direct posting system and an indirect posting system as they apply to a columnar journal combined with a subsidiary ledger.
15. When is posting to a subsidiary ledger carried out for a columnar journal system? Why?
16. When is posting to a general ledger carried out for a columnar journal system? Why?
17. Describe the posting procedure that is followed at month end for a columnar journal system.
18. What column totals in a columnar journal are not posted?
19. Why is a general journal sometimes part of a columnar journal system?
20. Summarize the advantages and disadvantages of a columnar journal system.

LESSON APPLICATIONS

21. (a) The trial balance for Sudbury Business Consultants as of January 31 is shown in Figure 11-20. Open a general ledger, providing appropriate account numbers, and enter the account balances.
    (b) Journalize the following transactions in a columnar journal. Create new accounts, as required. GST is 7 percent and PST is 8 percent, calculated on the base price. All terms are n/20.
    (c) Total, balance, and rule the journal.
    (d) Post the transactions from the columnar journal to the general ledger, and prepare the February 28 trial balance.

    Feb. 1 Sales Invoices:
    #445, to True North Resources, $6 500 plus GST.
    #446, to Delti Furniture Ltd., $880 plus GST.
    #447, to Barnum Delicatessen, $800 plus GST.
    #448, to Pat's Moving and Storage, $1 000 plus GST.

    4 Cash Receipt Slips:
    #123, from Quinlan Floral Shops, $932 on account.
    #124, from Delti Furniture Ltd., $1 284 on account.
    #125, from Pat's Moving and Storage, $950 on account.

    5 Cheque Copies:
    #327, to Sault Business Equipment, $1 349 on account.
    #328, to Northern Business Suppliers Ltd., $1 734 on account.

FIGURE 11-20

Sudbury Business Consultants
Trial Balance
January 31, 19–4

Cash	$ 44 600	
Accounts Receivable	3 166	
Allowance for Bad Debts		$ 380
GST Recoverable	1 890	
Business Supplies	1 980	
Automobiles	38 850	
Accumulated Depreciation: Auto		6 810
Furniture & Equipment	46 504	
Accumulated Depreciation: F & E		22 394
Accounts Payable		3 083
Auto Loan Payable		14 630
GST Payable		3 404
H. Kinnear, Capital		62 496
H. Kinnear, Drawings	35 000	
Consultation Fees		373 748
Rent Expense	48 000	
Wages Expense	198 000	
Advertising Expense	14 800	
Automobile Expense	27 300	
Utilities Expense	21 314	
Interest Expense	1 341	
General Expense	4 200	
	$486 945	$486 945

6 Cheque Copies:
#329, to the Receiver General of Canada, $1 514 for GST.
#330, to Innovative Real Estate, $4 500 plus GST, for rent.
#331, to Esso Canada, $926 plus GST, for gas and oil for automobiles.

8 Sales Invoices:
#449, to Barnum Delicatessen, $520 plus GST.
#450, to Quinlan Floral Shops, $500 plus GST.

8 Cash Receipt Slip:
#126, from True North Resources, $6 955 on account.

9 Purchase Invoices:
#958B, from Computer Specialists Ltd., $2 400 plus taxes, for fax machine.
#1993, from Tillway Equipment, $5 200 plus taxes, for new office furniture.

11 Cheque Copies:
   #332, $900 plus GST to the *Sudbury Star*, for advertising.
   #333, $1 200 plus GST to CHNO, for advertising.
12 Credit Invoice Issued:
   #24, to Delti Furniture Ltd., $240 plus GST, for billing error.
12 Purchase Invoices:
   #439, from Northern Business Suppliers Ltd., $300 plus taxes, for business supplies.
   #494, from Sault Business Equipment, $2 400 plus taxes, for furniture.
15 Cheque Copies:
   #334, $9 000 for semi-monthly wages.
   #335, $1 000 for loan payment on the automobile. (Includes $490 interest.)
   #336, $2 400 to the owner, for personal use.
15 Sales Invoices:
   #451, to True North Resources, $6 500 plus GST.
   #452, to Delti Furniture Ltd., $600 plus GST.
   #453, to Pat's Moving and Storage, $350 plus GST.
18 Cash Receipt Slips:
   #127, from Barnum Delicatessen, $856 on account.
   #128, from Delti Furniture Ltd., $684.80 on account.
   #129, from Pat's Moving and Storage, $1 070 on account.
18 Credit Invoice Received:
   #933D, from Computer Specialists Ltd., $250 plus taxes, for damages to the fax machine.
19 Purchase Invoices:
   #912C, from Computer Specialists Ltd., $210 plus taxes, for an answering machine.
   #2047, from Tillway Equipment, $2 600 plus taxes, for office furniture.
   #511, from Sault Business Equipment, $1 400 plus taxes, for furniture.
19 Cheque Copies:
   #337, to Canada Post, $50 plus GST, for postage stamps.
   #338, to Ontario Hydro, $294 plus GST, for electricity.
   #339, to Gerrard's Garage, $192.50 plus taxes, for automobile tune-up.
   #340, to Computer Specialists Ltd., $2 760 on account.
   #341, to Tillway Equipment, $5 980 on account.
22 Sales Invoices:
   #454, to Quinlan Floral Shops, $720 plus GST.
   #455, to Barnum Delicatessen, $540 plus GST.

22 Cash Receipt Slips:
  #130, from Quinlan Floral Shops, $535 on account.
  #131, from True North Resources, $6 955 on account.
22 Purchase Invoices:
  #922, from Computer Specialists Ltd., $3 200 plus taxes, for a laser printer.
  #592, from Northern Business Suppliers Ltd., $230 plus taxes, for business supplies for the computer.
22 Cheque Copies:
  #342, to Sault Business Equipment, $2 760 on account.
  #343, to Northern Business Suppliers Ltd., $345 on account.
25 Cheque Copies:
  #344, $82.50 to Culligan for water.
  #345, $280 plus GST to I.C.G. Utilities for gas for heating.
  #346, $450 plus GST to CHNO for advertising.
26 Sales Invoice:
  #456, to Ontario Northland, $4 600 plus GST.
26 Credit Memo Received:
  #499, from Northern Business Suppliers Ltd., $110 plus taxes, for returned business supplies.
28 Bank Debit Memo:
  For bank service charges, $52.
28 Cash Receipt Slip:
  #132, from Barnum Delicatessen, $556.40 on account.
28 Cheque Copies:
  #347, $123 plus GST for courier services.
  #348, $9 000 for semi-monthly wages.

22. Continue the accounting procedures for Sudbury Business Consultants begun in Question 21.
   (a) Set up an accounts receivable ledger and an accounts payable ledger with the following balances as of January 31.
   Accounts Receivable:
   Barnum Delicatessen   nil
   Delti Furniture Ltd. $1 284
   Pat's Moving and Storage   950
   Quinlan Floral Shops   932
   Accounts Payable:
   Computer Specialists Ltd.   nil
   Northern Business Suppliers Ltd. $1 734
   Sault Business Equipment   1 349
   Tillway Equipment   nil

(b) Using indirect posting, post from the columnar journal to the accounts receivable and accounts payable ledgers, and add accounts as required.
(c) Prepare schedules of accounts receivable and accounts payable. Compare your answers to the control accounts.
(d) When would the posting to the subsidiary ledgers normally be done?

11.3 Designing an Accounting System: Special Journals

As businesses expand, they not only require subsidiary ledgers to keep a record of customers and suppliers, but also a better system of journalizing. As already mentioned, the columnar journal is adequate for a small business, but not for one that handles thousands of transactions a day. Imagine one person working at a columnar journal trying to enter the transactions for the largest business in your area. The task would be formidable! To handle that situation, many businesses rely on special-purpose columnar journals, which usually comprise a five-journal system. Such a system is especially adaptable to computer usage, and therefore is the basis for many software programs. As well, such a system puts into application the advantages of the columnar journal: the saving of time in journalizing and posting.

The five-journal system consists of five special journals, one for each of the most common types of transactions of a business. The order in which they are listed below matches the flow of goods through a business. The journals are:

- Purchases Journal
- Cash Payments Journal
- Sales Journal
- Cash Receipts Journal
- General Journal

Our assumption is that the five-journal system used by large businesses with many transactions each day allows for one person to specialize in the use of each journal. If the business is not large enough for such specialization, one person could handle all items related to purchasing (Purchases Journal and Cash Payments Journal) and another person could deal with all items related to sales (Sales Journal and Cash Receipts Journal).

Because of this type of specialization, the source documents that either arrive at a business or are completed by the business each day can be directed to the one person who will make the entry in a journal. The five journals, and the source documents that are entered in each, are summarized in Figure 11-21.

FIGURE 11-21 SUMMARY SHOWING INTO WHICH JOURNAL IN A FIVE-JOURNAL SYSTEM THE VARIOUS SOURCE DOCUMENTS ARE ENTERED

Source Document	Journal
Purchase Invoices Credit Memos Received Debit Memos Received	Purchases Journal
Cheque Copies Bank Debit Memos	Cash Payments Journal
Sales Invoices Credit Memos Issued Debit Memos Issued	Sales Journal
Cash Sales Slips or Cash Register Summaries Cash Receipt Slips Bank Credit Memos	Cash Receipts Journal
Memos/Vouchers Other transactions (adjusting, closing)	General Journal

From Figure 11-21 one can see that the person handling the Purchases Journal need only handle purchase invoices, and credit memos and debit memos received from suppliers. The person handling the cash payments journal need only receive cheque copies and bank debit memos. Such specialization allows a person to complete the following tasks more quickly: journalizing, finding errors, and locating a particular entry. A five-journal system makes use of our previous accounting knowledge, and the principle of double-entry accounting still applies to each transaction: debits must equal credits. Each of the journals is a columnar journal: special columns are made in the appropriate journal for routine transactions, and non-routine transactions can either be entered in the Other Accounts columns, or the general journal, or as circled items in a special journal. Each of the four special journals in the five-journal system is discussed below.

Purchases Journal

The purchases journal is used to record all transactions involving the buying of goods or services on account. Goods or services paid for in cash, or immediately on receipt of the invoice, are entered in the cash payments journal. The source document for purchases on account is a purchase invoice. Therefore, Accounts Payable will always appear as a credit column in the purchases journal. Figure 11-22 shows the flow of the source documents, assuming that direct posting is made to subsidiary ledgers.

FIGURE 11-22

Source Document	Accounts Payable Clerk	Accounting Supervisor
Purchase Invoices Credit Memos Received Debit Memos Received	→ Accounts Payable Ledger →	Purchases Journal and General Ledger

What debit column headings should the journal have? When designing a special journal, a separate column should be used for frequently occurring transactions. Algor Computer Services will frequently purchase merchandise, so one column should be Purchases (debit). Since the firm frequently buys office and computer supplies, special columns are added for these items. As well, the firm is entitled to a GST input tax credit for merchandise that it purchases, so a special column is added for GST Recoverable. In order to handle non-routine transactions, Other Accounts columns are included.

Credit invoices received can also be entered in the purchases journal. Also, if returns and allowances on purchases are going to occur frequently, separate columns for Accounts Payable (debit) and Purchases Returns and Allowances (credit) can be made. If returns and allowances are not going to occur frequently, the entries can be circled or entered in red in the existing columns, or entered in the Other Accounts columns. In some businesses, credit invoices received are entered in the general journal if they are non-routine.

The following source documents have been entered in the purchases journal for Algor Computer Services in Figure 11-23:

Mar. 1   Purchase Invoice #622: From Norwood Suppliers Ltd., $820 plus GST, for merchandise.
     2   Purchase Invoices:
           #142, from Willson Office Supplies Ltd., $20.87 plus taxes for office supplies.
           #98, from Computequick, $714.78 plus taxes for computer supplies.
     3   Purchase Invoices:
           #81A, from Brunswick Office Equipment, $285.22 plus taxes for an office desk.
           #333, from Shell Canada Ltd., $210.43 plus taxes for auto expenses.

FIGURE 11-23 A COMPLETED PURCHASES JOURNAL

	DATE 1992		PARTICULARS	SD NO.	OTHER ACCOUNTS DR			PURCHASES DR
					ACCOUNT	PR	AMOUNT	
1	Mar.	1	Norwood Suppliers Ltd.	622				820 —
2		2	Willson Office Supplies Ltd.	142				
3		2	Computequick	98				
4		3	Brunswick	81A	Equipment		308 04	
5		3	Shell Canada Ltd.	333	Automobile Expense		227 26	
6		4	Delta Computer Services	938D				
7							535 30	820 —

4 Credit Memo #938D Received: From Delta Computer Services and Repairs, $322 plus GST, for merchandise returned.

The month-end procedure for a purchases journal is the same as that for all columnar journals. It must be totalled, balanced, and ruled at the end of the month.

Cross balancing Figure 11-23, we get the following:

	Debit	Credit
Other Accounts	$ 535.30	
Purchases	820.00	
Office Supplies	22.54	
Computer Supplies	771.96	
GST Recoverable	121.05	
Purchases Ret. & All.		$ 322.00
Accounts Payable	344.54	2 293.39
	$2 615.39	$2 615.39

Posting to the general ledger follows the same two steps:

(1) column totals are posted, except for the Other Accounts totals, and the account number is placed under the total in brackets;

(2) the Other Accounts column is posted individually, and the account numbers are placed in the PR column of the journal.

Posting to the accounts payable subsidiary ledger may be done either directly or indirectly. If done indirectly, from the journal to the subsidiary ledger, a check mark must be placed in the check mark column of the purchases journal.

Cash Payments Journal

The cash payments journal (sometimes called the cash disbursements journal) is used to record all transactions that directly reduce the balance of the Cash account. The credit will therefore always be to Cash. Source documents that reduce the Cash account are cheque copies, and bank debit memos for such items as service charges. Figure 11-24 shows the flow of the source documents, assuming that direct posting is made to subsidiary ledgers.

PURCHASES JOURNAL
PAGE NO. 41

OFFICE SUPPLIES DR	COMPUTER SUPPLIES DR	GST RECOVERABLE DR	PURCHASES RET + ALL CR	ACCOUNTS PAYABLE DR	✓	ACCOUNTS PAYABLE CR	
		57 40				877 40	1
22 54		1 46				24 −	2
	771 96	50 03				821 99	3
		19 97				328 01	4
		14 73				241 99	5
		(22 54)	322 −	344 54			6
22 54	771 96	121 05	322 −	344 54		2293 39	7

FIGURE 11-24

Source Document	Accounts Payable Clerk	Accounting Supervisor
Cheque Copies	Accounts Payable Ledger	Cash Payments Journal and
Bank Debit Memos	(if on account)	General Ledger

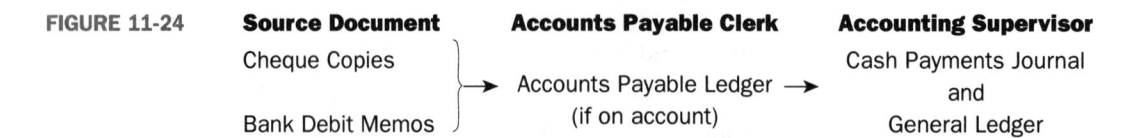

When a purchase is partly on account and partly paid for immediately, the cash payments journal is used, rather than the purchases journal. The purchases journal is strictly reserved for entire purchases on account.

The following cheque copies and bank debit memo have been entered in Algor Computer Services' cash payments journal shown in Figure 11-25.

Mar. 2 Cheque Copies:
#724, to Bell Canada, for monthly telephone bill, $74.43 plus taxes.
#725, to M. Bergin, for weekly wages, $880.
#726, to Computequick, $159.18 on account, after taking a cash discount of $2.82.
3 Bank Debit Memo: From Royal Bank, $22 for service charges.
3 Cheque Copies:
#727, to V. Marshall, owner, $300 for personal use.
#728, to Elston's Restaurant, for lunch purchased by owner, $11.50.

Cross balancing Figure 11-25, we get the following:

	Debit	Credit
Other Accounts	$ 338.71	
Wages Expense	880.00	
Utility Expense	80.38	
Discounts Earned		$ 2.82
Accounts Payable	162.00	
Cash		1 458.27
	$1 461.09	$1 461.09

FIGURE 11-25 A COMPLETED CASH PAYMENTS JOURNAL

	DATE 1992		PARTICULARS	SD NO.	OTHER ACCOUNTS DR			WAGES EXPENSE DR
					ACCOUNT	PR	AMOUNT	
1	Mar.	2	Bell Canada	724	GST Recoverable		5 21	
2		2	M. Bergin	725				880 –
3		2	Computequick	726				
4		3	Royal Bank	DM	Bank Expense		22 –	
5		3	V. Marshall	727	Drawings		300 –	
6		3	V. Marshall	728	Drawings		11 50	
7							338 71	880 –

Sales Journal

The sales journal is used to record all sales on account. Sales of items such as furniture used in the business are usually non-routine transactions and are therefore recorded in the general journal. Sales on account always have a debit to Accounts Receivable, and credits to the proper Sales account, PST Payable, and GST Payable, so six columns are required, although more may be added.

The sales journal may be used to record sales returns and allowances from credit invoices issued. The entry should then be circled, or entered in red. Should the firm wish to keep a record of sales returns and allowances separate from sales, a separate column headed Sales Returns and Allowances (debit) will be required. The flow of the source documents is as follows, assuming that direct posting is made to subsidiary ledgers:

Source Document	Accounts Receivable Clerk	Accounting Supervisor
Sales Invoices Credit Memos Issued Debit Memos Issued	→ Accounts Receivable Ledger →	Sales Journal and General Ledger

The sales journal for Algor Computer Services is shown in Figure 11-26. The following sales invoices and credit memos issued have been entered into it, and the month-end procedure completed.

Mar. 2   Sales Invoices:
#55-5243, to J. Bull, computer services, $164.20, GST $11.49, PST $13.14, total $188.83.
#55-5244, to R. Wainwright, software lessons, $114.00, GST $7.98, total $121.98.
#55-5245, to R. Milligan, computer services, $236.00, GST $16.52, PST $18.88, total $271.40.

2   Credit Memo Issued:
#77-0521, to O. Florescu for reduction on computer services, $45.00, GST $3.15, PST $3.60, total $51.75.

CASH PAYMENTS JOURNAL

PAGE NO. 78

AUTO EXPENSE DR	UTILITY EXPENSE DR	DISCOUNTS EARNED CR		ACCOUNTS PAYABLE DR	✓	CASH CR	
	80 38					85 59	1
						880 —	2
		2 82		162 —		159 18	3
						22 —	4
						300 —	5
						11 50	6
Ø	80 38	2 82		162 —		1458 27	7

FIGURE 11-26 A COMPLETED SALES JOURNAL

	DATE 1992		PARTICULARS	SD NO.	OTHER ACCOUNTS DR			COMPUTER SERVICES CR
					ACCOUNT	PR	AMOUNT	
1	Mar.	2	J. Bull	5243				164 20
2		2	R. Wainright	5244				
3		2	R. Milligan	5245				236 —
4		2	O. Florescu		521 Refunds		45 —	
5		3	J. Cacciotti	5246				97 —
6		3	V. Wormleighton	5247				
7							45 —	497 20

3   Sales Invoices:
    #55-5246, to J. Cacciotti, warranty $97.00, GST $6.79, PST $7.76, total $111.55.
    #55-5247, to V. Wormleighton, software lessons, $121.00, GST $8.47, total $129.47.

Cross balancing Figure 11-26, we get the following:

	Debit	Credit
Other Accounts	$ 45.00	
Computer Services		$497.20
Software Lessons		235.00
GST Payable		48.10
PST Payable		36.18
Accounts Receivable	823.23	51.75
	$868.23	$868.23

Cash Receipts Journal

The cash receipts journal is used to record all transactions that directly result in an increase in the bank balance. Source documents entered in this journal include cash sales slips, cash register summaries, cash receipt slips, and bank credit memos. The debit for all these source documents is Cash.

FIGURE 11-27 A COMPLETED CASH RECEIPTS JOURNAL

	DATE 1992		PARTICULARS	SD NO.	OTHER ACCOUNTS CR			COMPUTER SERVICES CR
					ACCOUNT	PR	AMOUNT	
1	Mar.	2	O. Florescu	5674				
2		2	B. Warner	5675				
3		2	V. Marshall	5676	Capital		1000 —	
4		2	Cash sales					494 —
5		2	Bank Credit Memo	CM	Bank Expense		45 —	
6		3	R. Singh	5677				
7		3	Cash sales					400 —
8							1045 —	894 —

SALES JOURNAL

PAGE NO. 92

SOFTWARE LESSONS CR	SALES CR	GST PAYABLE CR	PST PAYABLE CR	ACCOUNTS RECEIVABLE DR	✓	ACCOUNTS RECEIVABLE CR	
		11 49	13 14	188 83			1
	114 –	7 98		121 98			2
		16 52	18 88	271 40			3
		3 15	3 60			51 75	4
		6 79	7 76	111 55			5
	121 –	8 47		129 47			6
	235 –	Ø	48 10	36 18	823 23		51 75	7

When there is a sale that is partly on account and partly for cash, the cash receipts journal is used, not the sales journal. The sales journal is strictly reserved for sales on account. The flow of the source documents is as follows, assuming that direct posting is made to subsidiary ledgers:

Source Document	Accounts Receivable Clerk	Accounting Supervisor
Cash Receipt Slips Cash Sales Slips Bank Credit Memos Cash Register Summaries	→ Accounts Receivable Ledger →	Cash Receipts Journal and General Ledger

The cash receipts journal for Algor Computer Services is shown in Figure 11-27. The following transactions have been entered into it, and the month-end procedure completed.

Mar. 2 Cash Receipt Slips:
#33-5674, from O. Florescu, $220 on account.
#33-5675, from B. Warner, $16 on account.
#33-5676, from V. Marshall, owner, $1 000 investment.

2 Cash Sales Slips:
#99-7973 to #99-7979, cash sales $494.00, GST $34.58, PST $39.52, total $568.10.

2 Bank Credit Memo:
Reversal of a previous service charge due to an error, $45.

CASH RECEIPTS JOURNAL

PAGE NO. 91

SOFTWARE LESSONS CR	GST PAYABLE CR	PST PAYABLE CR	SALES DISCOUNTS DR	ACCOUNTS RECEIVABLE CR	✓	CASH DR	
				220 –		220 –	1
				16 –		16 –	2
						1 000 –	3
	34 58	39 52				568 10	4
						45 –	5
			11 59	620 –		608 41	6
174 –	40 18	32 –				646 18	7
174 –	74 76	71 52	11 59	856 –		3 103 69	8

3 Cash Receipt Slips:
#33-5677, from R. Singh, $608.41, $620.00 on account less a discount of $11.59.
3 Cash Sales Slips:
#99-7980 to #99-7986, cash sales $574.00 (Computer Services $400.00, Software Lessons $174.00), GST $40.18, PST $32.00, total $646.18.

Cross balancing Figure 11-27, we get the following:

	Debit	Credit
Other Accounts		$1 045.00
Computer Services		894.00
Software Lessons		174.00
GST Payable		74.76
PST Payable		71.52
Sales Discounts	$ 11.59	
Accounts Receivable		856.00
Cash	3 103.69	
	$3 115.28	$3 115.28

General Journal

What transactions are left for the general journal in a five-journal system? Non-routine transactions are entered in the general journal. As previously noted, such transactions might include both purchases returns and allowances and sales returns and allowances. When designing the system, the firm must decide on this matter. The adjusting entries and the closing entries will be entered in the general journal.

Forwarding Special Journals

The forwarding procedure used in any of the special journals of the five-journal system is exactly the same as that used in a columnar journal. At the bottom of a page, a line is left to foot the columns; if the page cross balances the totals should be written in ink, double ruled, and carried forward to the first line on the next page. Remember: the reason that forwarding must be done is to take advantage of the posting of column totals at month end.

Summary of Posting Procedures for a Special Journal

The posting procedure used for any journal of the five-journal system is the same as that used for a columnar journal:
(a) Posting during the month: from special journals and the general journal to subsidiary ledgers if indirect posting is used. (If direct posting is used, the information from source documents is posted directly from the source document to the subsidiary ledgers, without using any of the five journals.)

(b) Posting at month end: amounts in the Other Accounts columns are posted individually, and all other column totals are posted.

The abbreviations used in the Posting Reference column of the general ledger, and of the subsidiary ledger if indirect posting is used, are as follows:

Purchases Journal	P
Cash Payments Journal	CP
Sales Journal	S
Cash Receipts Journal	CR

It does not matter in which order the journals are posted, but one must be careful of opposite balances in the general ledger accounts. For example, if the Cash (credit) column in the cash payments journal is posted before the Cash (debit) column in the cash receipts journal, the balance in the Cash account will temporarily be a credit. This balance will (hopefully!) revert to a debit balance when the cash receipts journal is posted. A trial balance should not be prepared at month end until all the journals have been totalled, ruled, balanced, and posted.

Batch Journalizing and the Five-Journal System

Batch journalizing can also be used with the five-journal system. As previously noted, if batch journalizing does occur, direct posting to subsidiary ledgers must occur. The subsidiary ledger accounts will then be brought up to date by the clerks. Using such a system, there will only be one entry in the special journals per day for many types of transactions. For example, all the sales on account for a day would be entered in the sales journal as one transaction.

A Journalless Accounting System

Journalless system: postings are made directly from a batch of source documents to the general ledger, eliminating one or more of the journals in a five-journal system.

If batch journalizing is used, there may be only one journal entry per business day in some journals, such as the sales journal. Rather than establish a sales journal, some businesses prefer to use a "journalless" system. Obviously a general journal is necessary in order to record non-routine transactions, as well as adjusting and closing entries. The other journals may be eliminated, depending upon the complexity of the journal entries that would normally be entered in them.

If a business used a journalless system with no sales journal, all the sales invoices would be given to the accounts receivable clerk for entry in the accounts receivable subsidiary ledger. The clerk would forward the sales invoices to the accounting supervisor. The supervisor would total the amount of the sales, GST Payable, and PST Payable on the invoices, bundle them, and put the tape showing the totals on the top of the bundle. An entry would then be made directly into the general ledger, using the tape as the source document. The entry would require a debit to Accounts Receivable, and credits to Sales, GST Payable, and PST Payable. The supervisor would date and sign the tape, and indicate beside each of the totals the account number to which the total has been posted. Under this system, transactions related to sales, such as sales returns and allowances and adjustments in sales amounts, would be entered in the general journal. The major advantage of the journalless system is the saving of establishing a journal. However, the use of the system could lead to errors in posting to the general ledger, for a debit or a credit may easily be omitted. The reduction of this type of error is the main reason that journals were established.

Advantages of a Five-Journal System

A business would adopt a five-journal system because it has the following advantages:

(1) Depending upon the size of the business, a person can specialize in handling all transactions dealing with one journal only.

(2) Because a special journal only has transactions dealing with a few source documents, it is easy to find any particular transaction.

(3) Because special journals are columnar, they have the advantages that relate to that type of journal: time is saved in both journalizing and posting. The use of batch journalizing accentuates this time saving.

LESSON REVIEW

23. Under what circumstances would a business adopt a five-journal system?

24. For each of the five journals in the system, state the source documents that would be entered in them.

25. Describe four ways in which purchases returns and allowances can be entered in a purchases journal.

26. Why is there a necessity for a general journal in a five-journal system?

27. Why is forwarding necessary in a special journal?

28. What posting is done from a special journal
    (a) during the month?
    (b) at the end of the month?

29. Describe how postings are made to a general ledger under a journalless system.

30. Describe the advantages and disadvantages of a five-journal system.

LESSON APPLICATIONS

31. For each of the following transactions, indicate the source document that would provide the information, and in which journal of the five-journal system it would be entered.
    (a) Purchased $5 000 worth of equipment on account.
    (b) Received $600 on account from I. Robertson.
    (c) Bank deposited interest, $55, in our account.
    (d) Paid rent for the month, $1 200.
    (e) Merchandise returned to a supplier, $2 300.
    (f) Paid the owner $5 000 for personal use.
    (g) Purchased $6 000 worth of merchandise.
    (h) Refunded $50 cash for merchandise returned.
    (i) Bank charged $25 for an NSF cheque.
    (j) Sale of merchandise on account, $550.
    (k) Received notice that a $400 error had been made on a purchase invoice for equipment.
    (l) Issued a notice that a $24 error had been made on a sales invoice.

32. (a) Journalize each of the following transactions on page 42 of a purchases journal. Prepare column headings as follows: Purchases Returns and Allowances Cr., and GST Recoverable Dr. GST is 7 percent and PST is 8 percent, calculated on the base price.
    (b) Total, balance, and rule the journal.

    Feb. 4 Purchase Invoice #422: Purchased merchandise from Ledyard Clothing Ltd., $5 900 plus GST; terms 2/10, n/30.
    5 Purchase Invoice #761: Purchased computer supplies from Computemart Ltd., $219 plus taxes; terms n/30.
    5 Purchase Invoice #24A: Purchased merchandise from Modern Fashions Ltd., $2 190 plus GST; terms 2/10, n/30.
    6 Purchase Invoice #39: Purchased an office desk from Capital Office Furniture, $1 200 plus taxes. Terms n/30.
    11 Credit Memo #12: Received from Computemart Ltd., $18 plus taxes, due to overcharge on Feb. 5 purchase of computer supplies.
    12 Debit Memo #95: Received from Modern Fashions Ltd., $43 plus GST, due to error on invoice of Feb. 5.
    12 Credit Memo #312: Received from Ledyard Clothing Ltd., $224 plus GST, due to damaged merchandise received under Purchase Invoice #422.
    12 Purchase Invoice #493: Purchased merchandise from Ledyard Clothing Ltd., $1 200 plus GST; terms 2/10, n/30.

12 Purchase Invoice #33: Purchased advertising on account from Modern Visuals, $500 plus GST.

33. (a) Journalize each of the following transactions on page 67 of a cash payments journal. Use the following column headings: Wages Expense Dr., Drawings Dr., and Purchases Discounts Cr. Choose appropriate account names. The question uses information from Question 32.
(b) Total, balance, and rule the journal.
Feb. 4 Cheque Copy #845: $900 plus GST for the monthly rent.
     4 Cheque Copy #846: $224 plus GST for the monthly electricity bill which was received today.
     7 Cheque Copy #847: $872 for the weekly wages.
     9 Cheque Copy #848: $2 700 on account to Martino's Fashions Ltd.
    10 Bank Debit Memo: $900 for the monthly payment on the bank loan. (Includes $630 interest.)
    11 Bank Debit Memo: $63; $58 for an NSF cheque that had been deposited by the business, plus a $5 service charge. The cheque had been issued by P. Buskas, a customer. The service charge is passed on to the customer.
    14 Cheque Copy #849: $5 959.80 issued to Ledyard Clothing Ltd. for Purchase Invoice #422 less Credit Memo #312. A discount of $113.52 was taken.
    14 Cheque Copy #850: Paid the weekly wages, $852.
    15 Cheque Copy #851: $2 344.65 for Purchase Invoice #24A plus Debit Memo #95 from Modern Fashions Ltd. A discount of $44.66 was taken.
    15 Cheque Copy #852: $480 to the owner B. McKinnon, for personal use.

34. (a) Journalize the following transactions, using page 12 of the purchases journal and page 31 of the cash payments journal. The names of source documents have been omitted. The firm uses the purchases journal for purchases returns and allowances. Use the following column headings:
Purchases Journal: GST Recoverable Dr., and Purchases Returns and Allowances Cr.
Cash Payments Journal: Wages Expense Dr., Drawings Dr., and Purchases Discounts Cr.
GST is 7 percent and PST is 8 percent, calculated on the base price.
(b) Total, balance, and rule the journals.
June 4 Purchased a telephone answering machine on account from Bell Canada, $190 plus taxes.

6 Issued a cheque, $117 plus GST, to *Nepean Clarion* for advertising.
9 Issued a cheque, $249, to Motion Video Ltd. on account.
11 Purchased merchandise from Motion Video Ltd. on account, $390 plus GST; terms 2/10, n/30.
12 Bank debit memo, $12 for monthly service charge.
12 Bank debit memo, total $137; NSF cheque for $127 issued by D. Barber was returned, plus $10 service charge. (Service charge is passed on to customer.)
16 Credit memo received from Vista Video for merchandise returned, $820 plus GST.
18 Issued a cheque, $400, to the owner R. Murrill for her personal use.
20 Debit memo received, $11 plus GST, from Bell Canada for overcharge on answering machine.
21 Issued a cheque, $409.50, on account to Motion Video Ltd.; $7.80 discount taken.
23 Purchased an office file cabinet, $220 plus taxes, from Willson Office Equipment Ltd. on account.
25 Purchased office supplies, $38 plus taxes, from Willson Office Equipment Ltd. on account.
27 Issued a cheque, $1 100, for employees' wages.
29 Issued a cheque, $335, to Barton Catering Services on behalf of the owner, R. Murrill, for personal use.
30 Issued a cheque, $600, to Seaway Services, on account.

35. (a) Journalize the following sales on account on page 86 of a sales journal. Use the following column headings: Sales Cr., GST Payable Cr., and PST Payable Cr. Terms are 2/10, n/30. GST is 7 percent and PST is 6 percent of the base price.
(b) Total, balance, and rule the journal.

Jan. 16 Sales Invoice #922: To D. Cousineau, $300 plus taxes.
Sales Invoice #923: To D. McAskin, $311 plus taxes.
17 Sales Invoice #924: To T. Lukacs, $122 plus taxes.
18 Sales Invoice #925: To L. Bronkhorst, $217 plus taxes.
Sales Invoice #926: To J. Seth, $93 plus taxes.
Sales Invoice #927: To H. Wood, $117 plus taxes.
Credit Memo #22: Issued to D. McAskin, $45 plus taxes.
19 Debit Memo #11: Issued to J. Seth, due to undercharging on Sales Invoice #926, $40 plus taxes.
Sales Invoice #928: To A. Millar, $211 plus taxes.
Sales Invoice #929: To T. Hallett, $141 plus taxes.

36. (a) Journalize the following transactions in a cash receipts journal, page 117. Add the column heading Sales Cr. to the journal. Choose appropriate account names. The question uses information from Question 35.

(b) Total, balance, and rule the journal.

Jan. 20 Cash Sales Slips #121–#146: Total sales for the day, $1 140 plus taxes.

20 Voucher #22: Received $1 100 as an additional investment by the owner, G. Wallace.

20 Cash Receipt Slip #57: $333 from D. Cousineau for Sales Invoice #922, less a discount of $6.

20 Cash Receipt Slip #58: $345.21 from D. McAskin for Sales Invoice #923, less a discount of $6.22. She had inadvertently ignored Credit Memo #22.

20 Bank Credit Memo: $110 for account receivable of K. Barker collected on the business's behalf. The bank had deducted a $5 service charge from the collection.

25 Cash Receipt Slip #59: $240.87 from L. Bronkhorst for Sales Invoice #925, less a discount of $4.34.

25 Cash Receipt Slip #60: $422 from G. Lecky for Sales Invoice #911; no discount was taken.

26 Cash Sales Slips #147–#162: Total sales for the day, $1 295 plus taxes.

26 Bank Credit Memo: $22 for bank error on service charge of previous month.

27 Cash Receipt Slip #61: $129.87 from H. Wood for Sales Invoice #927, less a discount of $2.34.

27 Cash Receipt Slip #62: $119.88 from J. Marshman for Sales Invoice #901; no discount was taken.

30 Cash Receipt Slip #63: $135.42 from T. Lukacs for Sales Invoice #924, less a discount of $2.44. (The customer was not entitled to this discount.)

37. (a) Journalize the following transactions on page 62 of a sales journal and page 97 of a cash receipts journal. Use the same *column headings* as in Questions 35 and 36. Choose appropriate account names. All sales are 2/10, n/30. GST is 7 percent and PST is 8 percent, calculated on the base price.
(b) Total, balance, and rule the journals.

June 5 Sales Invoices
#412: To R. Lafontaine, sale $92, plus taxes.
#413: To B. A. Friend, sale $64, plus taxes.

8 Cash Receipt Slip #72A: From R. Lomax, $191.89 on account.

8 Cash Sales Slips #198–#214: Total sales, $1 947 plus taxes.

10 Sales Invoice #414: To A. Sanscartier, sale $73.50, plus taxes.
12 Cash Receipt Slip #73A: From A. Sanscartier, for Sales Invoice #411, $117.20, less a 2% discount.
14 Bank Credit Memo: $17 for overcharge on previous month's bank charges.
14 Cash Receipt Slip #74A: From B. A. Friend, for Sales Invoice #413, $73.60, less a 2% discount.
14 Cash Sales Slips #215–#272: Total sales, $2 043 plus taxes.
17 Sales Invoice #415: To R. Lafontaine, sale $111.40, plus taxes.
19 Credit Memo #31: Issued to A. Sanscartier, sales return $73.50, plus taxes.
21 Sales Invoice #416: To T. Lomax, sale $431, plus taxes.
21 Sales Invoice #417: To D. Barber, sale $141, plus taxes.
22 Cash Sales Slips #273–#302: Total sales, $2 916.08 plus taxes.
25 Credit Memo #32: Issued to B. A. Friend, $100 plus taxes.
27 Cash Receipt Slip #75A: From R. Lafontaine, for Sales Invoice #410, $261.05, less a 2% discount. (The customer was not entitled to this discount.)
30 Cash Sales Slips #303–#329: Total sales, $1 732.60 plus taxes.
30 Debit Memo #5: Issued to B. A. Friend, $12 plus taxes, for undercharge on Sales Invoice #404.

38. (a) Open a general ledger with the following accounts and account balances as of June 3. The firm is in its first year of operation, so there is no merchandise inventory or depreciation of assets recorded as yet.

100	Cash	$12 400	400 Sales	$22 400
110	Accounts Receivable	9 870	410 Sales Discounts	122
130	GST Recoverable	420	420 Sales Ret. & Allow.	56
140	Office Supplies	560	500 Purchases	14 800
150	Furn. & Equip.	4 562	510 Purchases Discounts	140
200	Accounts Payable	14 560	520 Purchases Ret. & Allow.	45
210	GST Payable	392	600 Wages Expense	14 680
220	PST Payable	648	610 Advertising Expense	800
230	Bank Loan	6 803	620 Miscellaneous Expense	679
300	R. Murrill, Capital	15 561		
310	R. Murrill, Drawings	1 600		

(b) Open an accounts payable subsidiary ledger and an accounts receivable subsidiary ledger with the following accounts and balances as of June 3.

Accounts Payable Subsidiary Ledger

Motion Video Ltd.	$ 3 560
Seaway Services	600
Vista Video	6 024
Willson Office Equipment Ltd.	4 376
	$14 560

Accounts Receivable Subsidiary Ledger

D. Barber	$1 202
B. A. Friend	3 240
R. Lafontaine	980
R. Lomax	3 032
A. Sanscartier	1 416
	$9 870

(c) Post the purchases journal and cash payments journal used in Question 34 to the general ledger, and to the accounts payable subsidiary ledger using indirect posting.
(d) Post the sales journal and cash receipts journal used in Question 37 to the general ledger, and to the accounts receivable subsidiary ledger using indirect posting.
(e) Prepare schedules and compare with control accounts.

CHAPTER REVIEW AND SKILL DEVELOPMENT

Accounting Principles and Concepts

- A business designs its **accounting system** according to its needs.

- A **columnar journal** accommodates a small business that has repetitive transactions of the same type.

- A **five-journal system** accommodates a business that has many repetitive transactions of the same type, which cannot be handled by one person.

Knowing the Terms

For each of the following statements, indicate the term being defined.
(a) The procedure of proving that column debit totals equal column credit totals in a columnar journal.

(b) The process of transferring column totals from the bottom of one columnar journal page to the top of another.
(c) Journal in which credit memos issued are entered.
(d) Posting from a special journal to a subsidiary ledger.
(e) A synonym for a columnar journal.
(f) When posting to subsidiary ledgers should be done.
(g) Posting from a source document to a subsidiary ledger.
(h) An accounting system that has one journal for common entries, and one journal for unusual entries including adjusting and closing.
(i) An accounting system that has one journal for transactions of a similar type.
(j) Journal in which credit memos received are entered.

Food for Thought

1. A business has 1 000 transactions during a month. Five hundred of the transactions relate to sales, either on account or for cash. Each of these transactions requires four lines in a general journal. Two hundred and fifty of the transactions relate to purchases, either on account or for cash. Each of these transactions requires three lines. One hundred and fifty of the transactions relate to receipts of cash on account and payments of cash on account. Each of these transactions requires two lines. The other 100 transactions are varied. Half require two lines and the other half require three lines in a general journal.
   (a) If the transactions were entered in a general journal, how many postings would be required?
   (b) If the transactions were entered in a columnar journal, how many postings would be required? Assume that all items related to the sales and purchase entries have special columns, and that either the debit or the credit of the varied transactions are entered in the Other Accounts columns.

2. A business uses a five-journal system, with direct posting to subsidiary ledgers. Assuming that batch journalizing is used, how many entries will there be for sales invoices on any particular day? Explain your answer.

3. A business that uses a five-journal system and subsidiary ledgers must decide, when designing its system, whether to use direct posting or indirect posting to subsidiary ledgers. Prepare a list of the advantages and disadvantages of each method.

4. An accounts receivable clerk indicates that it would not be beneficial for a firm that uses an accounts receivable subsidiary ledger, and direct posting, to use a journalless system for sales invoices. He bases his opinion on the fact that if such a system is used, the firm will not be able to trace errors made in posting to the general ledger from each day's batch of sales invoices. Comment on the clerk's viewpoint.

5. You are asked to design a columnar journal for a small business that sells crafts. How would you decide on what column headings to use? On what basis would you change the column headings later in the life of the business?

6. A business has a substantial increase in the number of daily transactions. In order to accommodate the increase, the business changes from a columnar journal to a five-journal system. In order to do so, the firm must also hire one more employee. Prepare a list of the

costs to the firm of changing its accounting system.

7. During the month, a firm uses a total of 12 columnar journal pages. The accounting clerk does not forward each page. Instead, she posts the totals at the bottom of each page to their respective ledger accounts. What is the disadvantage of this system? Assuming that there are 16 columns in the journal, calculate the number of postings under each system. (Ignore the posting of the Other Accounts column, for it will be the same under either system.)

8. What other journals could be added to a five-journal system?

9. An accountant totalled, balanced, and ruled the sales journal at the end of the month. After doing so, she noticed that she had forgotten to enter one of the sales invoices. Where could she make the entry? What problems might occur due to the procedure that you select?

10. If a business uses a five-journal system with subsidiary ledgers, would it be preferable to use direct posting or indirect posting to the subsidiary ledgers? Support your decision.

11. You open up a columnar journal. By looking at it you should be able to tell whether the business uses direct or indirect posting. How should you know this?

Organizing

1. Prepare a diagram to illustrate the following:
   (a) the five journals in a five-journal system
   (b) the source documents that would be entered in each of the five journals.

2. Prepare examples of different types of transactions that go with each of the journals in a five-journal system. The first one has been done for you.

Journal	Description of Transaction
Sales	Sold merchandise to F. Neely on account, $500 plus taxes.

Applications

1. The White Swan Gift Shop is started by Tracy Bushnik. It operates in a shopping centre, where Tracy rents store space. The following is the chart of accounts for the shop. There are no accounts receivable, because all sales on account are made through VISA or MasterCard. GST is 7 percent. PST of 7 percent is calculated on the base price only.

Assets
100 Cash
102 Merchandise Inventory
103 GST Recoverable
104 Supplies
105 Displays and Equipment

Liabilities
201 Accounts Payable
202 Trust Co. Loan
203 GST Payable
204 PST Payable

Equity
301 T. Bushnik, Capital
302 T. Bushnik, Drawings

Revenue
401 Sales

Cost
501 Purchases
502 Purchases Returns
503 Purchases Discounts
504 Transportation-in

Expenses
505 Credit Card Discount Expense
506 Wages Expense
507 Rent Expense
508 Utilities Expense
509 Advertising Expense
510 Miscellaneous Expense

(a) Open a general ledger using the above accounts.
(b) Journalize the following transactions on page 1 of a columnar journal. Use the following column headings:

GST Recoverable Dr., Sales Cr., GST Payable Cr., and PST Payable Cr.

Oct. 3 Received a $20 000 investment from the owner.
3 Borrowed $14 000 from Guaranteed Trust Co.
3 Purchased a business licence from the municipality, $30 plus GST.
3 Purchased merchandise from Glassworks Ltd. on account, $4 800 plus GST; terms 2/10, n/30.
3 Cheque issued to Accounting Services Ltd., $320 plus taxes, for accounting supplies.
3 Purchased a cash register, $1 900 plus taxes, on account from Business World; terms n/30.
3 Purchased display cabinets on account from Melton's Display Equipment Ltd., $4 500 plus taxes.
4 Cheque issued to Western Transport Ltd., $138 plus GST, for transportation of display cabinets.
4 Cheque issued to *Brandon Times Colonist*, $120 plus GST, for advertising.
4 Cheque issued to Meridian Properties Ltd., $1 800 plus GST for monthly rent.
4 Cash sales, $760 plus taxes.
6 Cheque issued to Manitoba Tel, $274 plus taxes, for installation of phone.
6 Cash sales, $1 240 plus taxes.
7 Purchased merchandise on account from Millington's Importers and Gifts, $5 600 plus GST; terms 2/10, n/30.
8 Cash sales, $1 400 plus taxes.
8 Cheque issued for weekly payment of wages, $1 520.
8 Cheque issued to owner, $200, for personal use.
8 Deposit of VISA drafts for the week: sales were $2 120 plus taxes, less discount of $80.34.
8 Deposit of MasterCard drafts for the week: sales were $1 270 plus taxes, less discount of $43.43.
11 Received credit memo from Millington's Importers and Gifts, $120 plus GST, for return of merchandise. Discount date extended to October 21.
12 Cheque issued to Glassworks Ltd., $5 040, for purchase invoice of October 3 less discount of $96.
12 Cash sales, $1 700 plus taxes.
12 Cash refund of $47 plus taxes.
12 Debit memo received from Melton's Display Equipment Ltd., $100 plus taxes, for undercharge on cabinets.
15 Cheque issued for weekly payment of wages, $1 520.
15 Cheque issued to owner, $250, for personal use.
15 Deposit of VISA drafts for the week: sales were $3 300 plus taxes, less discount of $142.56.
15 Deposit of MasterCard drafts for the week: sales were $3 604 plus taxes, less discount of $123.26.
15 Bank debit memo: $240 for the first payment on the trust company loan.
15 Cheque issued to Millington's Importers and Gifts, $5 754, for purchase invoice of October 7 less credit memo of October 11 and discount of $109.60.

(c) Total, balance, and rule the journal.
(d) Post the transactions from the columnar journal to the general ledger.
(e) Take off a trial balance on October 15.

2. Martin Hamelin has been elected treasurer of his students' council. Martin approaches his accounting teacher, who recommends that Martin establish a synoptic journal in order to keep track of the council's books. All accounting is done on the cash basis. Since the students' council is part of an educational institution, no taxes are collected or paid. The following column headings are decided upon:

Cash, debit and credit
Grants to Clubs, debit
Student Fees, credit
Dance Revenue, credit
Dance Expense, debit
Coke Machine, credit
Other Accounts, debit and credit

(a) Set up page 1 of a columnar journal using the headings given.
(b) Set up a general ledger with the following account names. Provide appropriate account numbers.

Assets
Cash

Equity
Surplus

Revenue
Dance Revenue
Student Fees Revenue
Coke Machine Revenue

Expenses
Dance Expense
Donations Expense
Decorating Expense
Grants to Clubs Expense
Band Expense
Coke Machine Expense
Miscellaneous Expense

(c) Martin noted that the bank book showed a balance of $2 321 from the previous year. Enter in the ledger a debit to Cash and a credit to Surplus for that amount on September 5.
(d) Journalize the following transactions in the columnar journal.

Sept. 6 Received student fees of $1 800.
7 Cheque issued for $720 for expenses for Grade 9 welcoming barbecue.
9 Received student fees of $300.
12 Received final amount of student fees, $240.
12 Purchased decorating supplies for September 30 dance, $240.
12 Cheque issued for $400 as down payment for band.
12 Cheque issued for $200 as grant to Photography Club.
16 Cheque issued for $120, grant to Outers Club.
16 Cheque issued for $150, for student leadership camp.
16 Cheque issued for $10 for miscellaneous supplies.
16 Cheque issued for $12 for cash box.
19 Cheque received from School Chocolate Promotions Ltd. for share of chocolate bar drive the previous year, $800.
23 Donation of $100 made to United Appeal.
23 Cheque issued for dance refreshments, $428.
26 Advance sale of dance tickets, $300.
28 Advance sale of dance tickets, $1 100.
29 Advance sale of dance tickets, $200.
30 Cheque issued as final payment to band, $800.
30 Revenue from dance tickets at door, $1 200.
30 Revenue from dance refreshments, $511.

(e) Total, balance, and rule the journal.
(f) Post the transactions from the columnar journal to the general ledger.
(g) Take off a trial balance.
(h) Prepare an income statement for the students' council for the dance only.
(i) Prepare an income statement for the students' council for the month of September.

Applications — Comprehensive: Five-Journal System to Trial Balance

(a) Echo Bay Trading Company uses a five-journal system. Set up each of the journals using the following information.

(i) Using page 24 of the purchases journal, prepare the following column headings: Freight-in Dr., GST Recoverable Dr., and Purchases Returns and Allowances Cr.
(ii) Using page 45 of the cash payments journal, prepare the following column headings: Wages Expense Dr., Drawings Dr., Purchases Discounts Cr., and GST Recoverable Dr.
(iii) Using page 32 of the sales journal, prepare the following column headings: Sales Cr., and Sales Returns and Allowances Dr.
(iv) Using page 38 of the cash receipts journal, prepare the column heading Sales Cr.
(v) Use page 15 of the general journal to journalize any other transactions.

(b) Set up a general ledger from the combined chart of accounts and general ledger trial balance shown in Figure 11-28. Provide appropriate account numbers.

FIGURE 11-28

Echo Bay Trading Company
General Ledger Trial Balance
September 30, 19–9

Cash	$ 21 460	
Accounts Receivable	14 502	
GST Recoverable	980	
Merchandise Inventory	26 910	
Supplies	452	
Equipment	8 705	
Accumulated Depreciation: Equipment		$ 2 684
Accounts Payable		22 504
GST Payable		1 315
PST Payable		1 503
C. Sulek, Capital		47 353
C. Sulek, Drawings	3 480	
Sales		77 608
Sales Returns and Allowances	442	
Sales Discounts	158	
Purchases	46 802	
Purchases Returns and Allowances		554
Purchases Discounts		704
Freight-in	699	
Bank Charges	110	
Delivery Expense	90	
Utilities Expense	1 980	
Rent Expense	10 870	
Wages Expense	15 680	
Miscellaneous Expense	905	
	$154 225	$154 225

(c) Set up the accounts payable subsidiary ledger as of September 30, using the following information.

T. Morrison Ltd.	$ 7 890
R.S.L. Transport	680
Wellington & Sons	12 390
Western Suppliers	1 544

(d) Set up the accounts receivable subsidiary ledger as of September 30, using the following information.

V. Leung	$4 640
D. Lum	2 690
T. Pantridge	3 250
P. Vogt	3 922

(e) Journalize each of the following transactions. You have been provided with the base price for each of the transactions listed below. GST is 7 percent and PST is 8 percent, calculated on the base price only. Apply these taxes as necessary. Post directly from the source documents to the subsidiary ledgers on a daily basis. Create accounts as required.

(f) Total, balance, and rule the journals.

(g) Post to the general ledger.

(h) Prepare a trial balance, schedule of accounts payable, and schedule of accounts receivable.

Date		Source Document	No.	Customer/Supplier	Particulars	Base Price
Oct.	1	Cheque Copy	231	Porter Realty	Rent for Oct.	$ 1 500
	2	Purchase Invoice	333	T. Morrison Ltd.	Merchandise	7 800
	2	Bank Debit Memo		Royal Bank	Service Charge	85
	5	Sales Invoice	492	T. Pantridge	On account	900
	5	Credit Memo received	56D	Wellington & Sons	Merchandise returned	440
	6	Cash Sales Slip	88	V. Renaldo	Merchandise	128
	6	Purchase Invoice	883	Western Suppliers	Equipment	1 200
	6	Memo	28	Error: debit Freight-in	Cancel debit to Delivery Exp.	120
	7	Cheque Copy	232	T. Morrison Ltd.	On account	7 890
	7	Cheque Copy	233	Bell Telephone	Monthly	225
	7	Sales Invoice	493	D. Lum	On account	3 200
	8	Cash Receipt Slip	912	V. Leung	On account	4 640
	8	Bank Debit Memo		Royal Bank/J. Verity	NSF cheque	620
					Service charge to be passed on to customer	10
	8	Cheque Copy	234	Computel	Equipment	6 805
	8	Cheque Copy	235	Receiver General	GST — Sept. (Credit of $980 deducted)	335
	9	Cheque Copy	236	Payroll	Wages	2 220
	9	Bank Credit Memo		Royal Bank	Bank Loan	15 000
	9	Cheque Copy	237	Southway Travel	Owner's holiday	2 400
	12	Sales Invoice	494	P. Vogt	On account	3 008

Date	Source Document	No.	Customer/Supplier	Particulars	Base Price
14	Cash Receipt Slip	913	D. Lum	On account	2 690
15	Cheque Copy	238	Provincial Treasurer	Sales tax — Sept.	1 503
15	Purchase Invoice	33C	R.S.L. Transport	Freight-in	390
16	Credit Note issued	57	P. Vogt	Return	120
16	Cheque Copy	239	Ontario Hydro	Electricity	223
16	Cheque Copy	240	Payroll	Wages	2 220
19	Cash Sales Slip	89	D. Hucul	Merchandise	1 245
20	Sales Invoice	495	T. Pantridge	On account	3 402
21	Cheque Copy	241	Delta Delivery	Delivery	320
21	Cash Receipt Slip	914	T. Pantridge	On account	3 250
22	Cash Sales Slip	90	V. Dossa	Merchandise	840
22	Memo	29	C. Sulek, Drawings	Supplies	125
23	Sales Invoice	496	D. Lum	On account	1 825
26	Cash Receipt Slip	915	P. Vogt	On account	3 922
26	Memo	30	Owner withdrawal	Merchandise	400
26	Credit Note issued	58	D. Lum	Allowance	450
27	Cheque Copy	242	Cash	Postage	100
28	Purchase Invoice	928	Wellington & Sons	Merchandise	8 850
28	Credit Memo received	49	Western Suppliers	Equipment returned	200
29	Purchase Invoice	87C	R.S.L. Transport	Freight-in	235
30	Cheque Copy	243	Payroll	Wages	2 220
30	Cheque Copy	244	C. Sulek, Drawings	Personal use	1 500
31	Cheque Copy	245	Wellington & Sons	On account	11 950

Focussing

Each of the following errors were either made in one of the special journals or in posting to either the general ledger or a subsidiary ledger. They were noticed after the journals had been totalled, balanced, ruled, and posted. In each case
(a) indicate how the error will likely be found;
(b) prepare a journal entry to correct the error, if necessary.

1. A $5 500 debit total in the Purchases column of the purchases journal was posted as a credit to the Purchases account.

2. A $400 entry in the purchases journal was entered in the Wages debit column, but should have been entered in the Office Equipment debit column.

3. A $750 cheque copy on account to Williams & Sons was entered in the cash receipts journal as a receipt on account from T. Williams.

4. The accounts receivable account of V. Dance was added incorrectly, showing an overcharge of $300.

5. A $1 200 investment by the owner, N. Kumagai, recorded in the Other Accounts column of the cash receipts journal as a credit to N. Kumagai, Capital, was posted as a debit to the owner's Drawings account.

Evaluate and Assess

John Knickerson is the accountant for Nouveau Laundry Services. He uses a columnar journal, with a general ledger that includes all the accounts receivable in individual accounts. There are approximately 100 individual accounts receivable. On average, each day there are 20 sales on account, usually to hotels, motels, and dining establishments. John is finding that he is using a large number of columnar journal pages each month. As well, because of the limited number of columns in his columnar journal, he is doing a large number of postings from the Other Accounts column each day.

(a) Criticize the accounting system used by John.
(b) Indicate changes that John could make to his system in order to improve it.

Synthesize and Conclude

You are hired by a new medium-sized business to design an accounting system. The owner indicates to you that there will be approximately two or three purchases on account and 80 sales on account each day. He also estimates that there will be five cheques issued and five cash receipts each day. Cash sales should number 100 per day.

(a) Give the advantages and disadvantages of each of the following alternatives to the owner:
  - a columnar journal, with a general ledger and subsidiary ledgers;
  - a five-journal system, with a general ledger and subsidiary ledgers;
  - a journalless system with a general journal, and a cash receipts journal with a general ledger and subsidiary ledgers. Purchase invoices, sales invoices, and cheque copies are posted directly to the general ledger in batch form on a daily basis.

(b) Indicate which system you would recommend, and the reasons for selecting it.

Accounting At Work

Wendy Craig
Systems Analyst

Wendy Craig is a partner for Entrepreneurial Services with Ernst & Young Management Consultants. She manages the microcomputer services for clients in the Toronto area. The company's aim is to help small- to medium-sized businesses master computer technology.

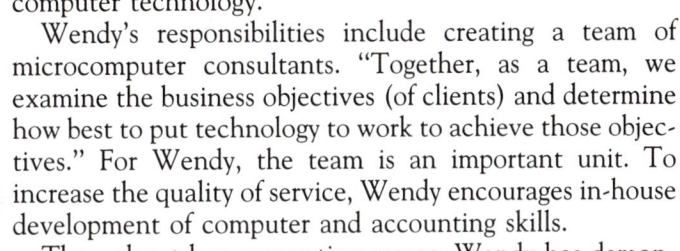

Wendy's responsibilities include creating a team of microcomputer consultants. "Together, as a team, we examine the business objectives (of clients) and determine how best to put technology to work to achieve those objectives." For Wendy, the team is an important unit. To increase the quality of service, Wendy encourages in-house development of computer and accounting skills.

Throughout her accounting career, Wendy has demonstrated interest in being well informed about new developments in computer accounting. Wendy graduated from the University of Manitoba with a Bachelor of Commerce (Hons.) degree. She then took the CICA's (Canadian Institute of Chartered Accountants) CA program and wrote the UFE (Uniform Final Exam) in 1979 scoring as a Gold Medallist. She did her computer audit training with Dunwoody & Company in Winnipeg, where she gained practical experience performing EDP (Electronic Data Processing) reviews on major clients. In her next position, she worked as a computer consultant with Hardie & Associates in Mississauga, Ontario. While there, she developed and taught microcomputer courses designed especially for chartered accountants. These courses were subsequently offered by the CICA. She went on to create and manage a microcomputer consulting practice for Collins Barrow, a national firm of chartered accountants. Wendy is currently developing a specialized microcomputer training program for CAs, which she will also be teaching for the CICA.

Her introduction to computer accounting began just as the field was emerging. With no precedents to follow, she had to define her own policies and procedures. This ability to build new techniques from previous experiences has helped her adapt. "As this area of consulting is still relatively new and undefined (versus an area like tax consulting), my past experience and education has laid the foundation for my position today." To ensure that her clients are satisfied, she must continue to keep abreast of new developments and new technology. She anticipates moving into a national role with her firm, so she will continue to build on her past experience. Wendy Craig's future looks promising based on her strong reputation, which she has worked hard to achieve in the microcomputer industry.

> One of Canada's leading producers of financial documents and forms is currently looking for individuals to join our young and aggressive information Systems team.
>
> ## SYSTEMS ANALYST
>
> The successful candidate has a university education with a minimum of five years' programming, analysis, and design experience in a relational database environment. Excellent communication, analytical, and problem-solving skills are essential for this potential supervisory position. Experience with Oracle is required.
>
> ## PROGRAMMER ANALYST
>
> The successful candidate has a university education with a minimum of two years' programming experience, preferably in a relational database environment. Good communication skills are essential. Experience with Oracle is a definite asset.
>
> We offer competitive salaries and a comprehensive benefits program including profit-sharing. Apply to:
>
> File #2272
> 2625 Stampede Court
> Calgary T6C 4V2

1. Briefly describe the job of a Systems Analyst.
2. Briefly describe Wendy Craig's career path.
3. State other skills, as indicated by the advertisement or Wendy Craig's career profile, that are beneficial or necessary to a systems analyst.

Business Career Skills

1. Decision Making
The following problems were on the agenda for a management meeting. In groups, brainstorm to obtain a list of advantages and disadvantages for each of the items.
(a) Should employees be permitted to accept gifts from suppliers?
(b) Should music be played softly in work areas?
(c) Should reserved parking spots be allotted to employees, with management having those closest to the offices?
(d) Should a profit sharing plan be offered to employees, with a corresponding reduction of two percent in the wage increase being offered for the coming year?

2. Report Writing
For any two of the agenda items given in Question 1, prepare a report to management with your recommendations, and supporting arguments.

3. Decision Making
The owner of a large merchandising firm continually makes withdrawals of merchandise from the business without recording them as drawings. She does this to avoid paying the retail price for the items, as

well as the sales taxes. She indicates to the accountant that the inventory will just show a smaller amount. Furthermore, she orders things through the business which the business does not need, and she withdraws these items as well. On a number of occasions, she has also ordered things for her penthouse apartment, and charged them to the firm. She indicates to the accountant that because the business is hers, she can do as she wishes.

(a) The owner's conduct has an effect on a number of groups. Indicate what these groups might be, and the effect that it has on them.
(b) Using the decision-making model shown in the "To the Teacher" at the front of the text, indicate what action you would take if you were the accountant.

COMPUTER ACCOUNTING
COMPUTERIZING THE COLUMNAR JOURNAL

Many of the application programs used on microcomputers are natural extensions of similar programs that have already been used on **mainframe computers**. One example of this phenomenon is accounting software. Accounting programs were first designed for use on mainframe computers, and when reliable and inexpensive disk storage systems and printers became available for microcomputers, these same programs were scaled down for use on these new machines.

Electronic spreadsheets, however, were not developed in this way. While financial modelling programs had been used on mainframes for some time, the **VisiCalc** program, designed by Daniel Bricklin and Robert Frankston for the Apple microcomputer, was the first electronic spreadsheet. *VisiCalc*, which stands for "visible calculating," was a new idea whose time had come because of the microcomputer.

This was the first program to really move computing power away from large data processing departments and onto the desks of the people who use spreadsheets as decision-making tools. As a result, *VisiCalc* now has many imitators by such names as *Microsoft Works*, *SuperCalc*, *Multiplan*, and *Lotus 1-2-3*. The latest versions of spreadsheet programs have many new features that make them easier to use and more powerful. These features, along with the increased memory and processing speed of new computers, make the electronic spreadsheet a very powerful and useful tool indeed.

Exercise

Recently the Mid Valley Minor Hockey Association held its Annual General Meeting. One of the new directors of the board was Shawn Carmichael who accepted the position of Treasurer. Shawn has access to a microcomputer and would like to computerize the association's financial records for the coming season. Since he has had considerable experience working with spreadsheets, he has decided to design an electronic worksheet similar to the columnar journal that is presently being used to manually record the organization's financial transactions. A copy of the columnar journal currently being used by the association is reproduced in Figure 11-29.

FIGURE 11-29

	DATE	CUSTOMER/SUPPLIER	REF. NO.	CASH		ACCOUNTS PAYABLE		✓
				DR	CR	DR	CR	
1								
2								
3								
4								
5								
6								
7								
8								
9								
10								
11								
12								
13								
14								
15								
16								
17								
18								
19								
20								
21								
22								
23								
24								
25								
26								
27								
28								

Assume that you too have been elected to a similar position in your local association. Load your spreadsheet program and prepare a computerized columnar journal comparable to the one used by the Mid Valley Minor Hockey Association.

After you have completed the design of the electronic columnar journal, enter the following transactions for the month of September. Create accounts as required.

Sept. 1 Balance forward: Cash in bank current account, $6 400.
 1 The Registrar, Sandra Kerembenios, submitted a reconciliation slip of the registration fees ($11 181.50 including GST of $731.50) collected at the registration session held the previous weekend. Attached to the reconciliation were the cheques to be deposited by you.
 2 The Equipment Manager, Wayne Nishi, submitted an invoice from ProSports Equipment Ltd. for $2 599, including GST of $161; terms n/30. The invoice listed the purchase of pucks, pylons, and goalie sticks for use in the coming season.
 3 Jim Sangha, the Director-at-Large,

who is responsible for securing sponsors for the association's 31 teams, submitted cheques totalling $4 800.
4. A bill for $508.50, including GST of $31.50, was received from Village Shoe Repair for repairs made to association goalie pads, catching gloves, and blockers over the summer period. Terms are n/30.
6. A bill for $321, including GST of $21, from *The Optimist*, a local newspaper, for running three advertisements announcing registration dates and times in August was received. The bill allows the Association 30 days to pay for the advertising.
7. A cheque for $600 was made out in the name of Doug Langlais, the referee allocator, to pay for referees and linesmen for the upcoming exhibition series of games for rep and house league teams.
7. Sandra Kerembenios submitted a reconciliation slip ($25 461.72 including GST of $1 665.72) with cheques, totalling this figure, attached for player registrations completed this past week.

9 Gail Choy, the Secretary of the Association, submitted a bill from Ideal Office Supplies for $368.38 including GST of $22.82 for letterhead stationery and envelopes and other general office supplies.

11 A bill for $1 240.13, including GST of $81.13, was received from Promo Plus Advertising for association pins, buttons, and pennants. Terms n/30. These are subsequently sold throughout the year by the Mother's Auxilliary.

15 Pat Bentley, the head coach of the association, submitted a bill from Garth Dion for $374.50, including GST of $24.50, for power skating sessions held from Sept. 1 to Sept. 14.

16 Bill Heimlicher submitted the Summer Hockey School financial statements and a cheque for $1 239, which represented the surplus of revenue over expenses.

18 A cheque for $267.50, including GST of $17.50, was sent to the District Coaching Co-ordinator as the fee for a coaching level clinic held on Sept. 6.

28 Jack McKeon, whose job is to allocate the ice time made available to the association, submitted the monthly ice bill from the municipality's Leisure Service Department. The bill totals $2 568 which includes GST of $168, and is payable by the tenth of the following month.

28 A cheque in the amount of $3 702.20, including GST of $242.20, was sent to the Provincial Hockey Association governing body to cover player registration fees and liability insurance costs. This amount is based on the previous year's enrolment figures with a reconciliation to be made in the new year when actual figures have been confirmed for this playing year.

29 September registrations totalled 135 players. This resulted in an additional deposit of $25 209.20 in cheques, which included GST of $1 649.20. A reconciliation was given to you by the Registrar with the cheques attached.

29 Rep team fees totalling $17 815.50, including GST of $1 165.50, were submitted jointly by the First and Second Vice-Presidents Dan Leeman and Mike Takeuchi, who administer and are responsible for rep teams from the Atom Division to the Midget Division.

29 Bank statement indicates that $214 in bank interest has been credited to the account, and a bank service charge of $12.40 has been debited to the account.

30 After consultation with the President, Norm Stonehouse, $25 000 was transferred into a 90-day, 7.5 percent term deposit at the bank, and $25 000 was invested in a Guaranteed Investment Certificate at 10.75 percent.

Total and balance the columns. Print a hard copy of the columnar journal at month end. The president of the association has requested interim financial statements for the upcoming executive meeting. Use your spreadsheet program and the printed columnar journal to prepare financial statements for this meeting.

Project 3 — THE ACCOUNTING CYCLE

The Thames River Electrical Mart specializes in providing electrical products for electricians and do-it-yourself home-owners. It uses a five-journal accounting system. Its fiscal year end is May 31.

(a) Open the four special journals using the following column headings. Enter the amount shown after each account on the first line, and indicate that it has been forwarded. Select your own page numbers.

Purchases: Purchases Dr. $26 400; Accounts Payable Cr. $28 802.80; Supplies Dr. $940; Purchases Returns and Allowances Cr. $360; GST Recoverable Dr. $1 822.80.

Cash Payments: Accounts Payable Dr. $29 872; Purchases Discounts Cr. $736; Cash Cr. $38 777; Other Accounts Dr. $9 641.

Sales: Accounts Receivable Dr. $19 669.60; Sales Cr. $17 230; PST Payable Cr. $1 368.32; GST Payable Cr. $1 197.28; Sales Returns and Allowances Dr. $126.

Cash Receipts: Cash Dr. $20 074; Sales Discounts Dr. $48.20; Accounts Receivable Cr. $7 320; Sales Cr. $7 960; PST Payable Cr. $636.80; GST Payable Cr. $557.20; Other Accounts Cr. $3 648.20.

(b) Open a general ledger using the trial balance shown in Figure A as of May 1, 19–7. Provide appropriate account numbers.

(c) Open an accounts receivable ledger using the following accounts and account balances as of May 24, 19–7. (The total will not equal the accounts receivable control account because direct posting has been used for the entries previous to May 24.)

M. Kilgour	$ 7 580.27
J. Mayne	6 820.50
T. Rahman	4 392.19
T. Walsworth	11 399.93
	$30 192.89

FIGURE A

Thames River Electrical Mart
Trial Balance
May 1, 19–7

	Debit	Credit
Cash	$ 25 896.90	
Accounts Receivable	17 843.29	
Allowance for Doubtful Accounts		$ 510.00
Merchandise Inventory	288 403.80	
GST Recoverable	1 456.00	
Supplies	3 260.00	
Equipment	47 800.00	
Accumulated Depreciation: Equipment		16 843.00
Vans	51 340.00	
Accumulated Depreciation: Vans		28 970.00
Accounts Payable		92 540.10
Trust Co. Loan		21 350.08
PST Payable		4 890.55
GST Payable		4 279.23
G. Seguin, Capital		426 031.02
G. Seguin, Drawings	54 600.00	
Sales		672 450.00
Sales Returns and Allowances	8 750.00	
Sales Discounts	9 870.40	
Purchases	398 400.80	
Transportation-In	14 327.80	
Purchases Returns and Allowances		11 430.00
Purchases Discounts		6 420.00
Advertising Expense	24 510.65	
Van Expense	32 340.87	
Rent Expense	44 000.00	
Wages Expense	192 300.00	
Utilities Expense	58 500.40	
Bank Charges	848.00	
Interest Expense	4 152.00	
Miscellaneous Expense	7 113.00	
	$1 285 713.90	$1 285 713.90

(d) Open an accounts payable ledger using the following accounts and account balances as of May 24, 19–7. (The total will not equal the accounts payable control account because direct posting has been used for the entries previous to May 24.)

Intrepid Paints Ltd.	$33 211.30
Renfrew Tape Ltd.	6 780.50
Stanley Tools Ltd.	23 760.00
Sudbury Metals Ltd.	21 098.30
Wellington Business Fixtures Ltd.	8 759.20
	$93 609.30

(e) Record the following transactions in the appropriate journals. The GST is 7 percent, and the PST is 8 percent, calculated on the base price. It is the accounting policy of the firm to record all credit memos received and issued (except bank credit memos) in the general journal. Use direct posting to subsidiary ledgers.

May 27 Cash Sales Slips #588-#597: Sales, $2 346.40 plus taxes.

27 Purchase Invoices:
#459, from Stanley Tools Ltd., $1 400 plus GST, for merchandise.
#92-446, from Sudbury Metals Ltd., $3 690.50 plus GST, for merchandise.

27 Bank Credit Memo: A cheque from Bart Norton for $184.50 was returned NSF. The bank charged a $15 fee, which will be passed on to the customer.

27 Credit Memo #98: Issued to T. Walsworth, $890 plus taxes, for return of a table saw.

27 Memo #39: The owner took home $190 worth of merchandise for her personal use.

27 Cheque Copy #243: To the Receiver General, $3 434.55 for GST. The balance of the GST Recoverable account was $1 456.

28 Sales Invoices:
#970, to J. Mayne, $720 plus taxes.
#971, to T. Rahman, $1 240.50 plus taxes.

28 Cheque Copies:
#244, to G. Seguin, owner, for personal use, $3 000.
#245, to Gryphon Real Estate, for rent, $4 000 plus GST.
#246, to Bell Telephone, $192.50 plus taxes for telephone.
#247, to Intrepid Paints, $8 000 on account.

28 Purchase Invoice #93003: From Intrepid Paints, $2 450 plus GST, for merchandise.

28 Cash Receipt Slip #447: $1 238 from T. Rahman on account.
29 Cash Sales Slips #598-#624: Sales, $4 880.50 plus taxes.
29 Cash Receipt Slips:
    #448, from J. Mayne, $2 718, on account.
    #449, from M. Kilgour, $780.27, on account.
    #450, from T. Walsworth, $3 200.50, on account.
29 Credit Memo #49: Received from Renfrew Tape Ltd., $240 plus GST, for merchandise returned.
29 Cheque Copies:
    #248, to Intrepid Paints, $11 900, on account.
    #249, to Stanley Tools Ltd., $5 000, on account.
    #250, to Westboro News, $300 plus GST, for advertising.
30 Cash Sales Slips #625-#688: Sales, $3 784.94 plus taxes.
30 Purchase Invoices:
    #93084 from Intrepid Paints, $2 360 plus GST, for merchandise.
    #1422, from Office Specialty Ltd., $3 200 plus taxes for a fax machine.
30 Credit Memo #99: Issued to J. Mayne, $800 plus taxes.
30 Memo #40: An invoice in the amount of $124 for a personal dinner of the owner was charged to Supplies in error, and is to be corrected.
30 Sales Invoices:
    #972, to T. Walsworth, $2 890 plus taxes.
    #973, to J. Mayne, $400 plus taxes.
30 Credit Memo #884: Received from Wellington Business Fixtures Ltd., $1 200 plus taxes for store equipment returned.
30 Cheque Copies:
    #251, to weekly wages, $4 200.
    #252, to CFPL for television advertising, $2 400 plus GST.
    #253, to G. Seguin, owner, $34 for personal use.
    #254, to London Fastball League, $250 for sponsorship of a team.
    #255, $8 000 to Stanley Tools Ltd., on account.
31 Cash Sales Slips #689-#724: Sales, $4 509 plus taxes.
31 Sales Invoices:
    #974, to M. Kilgour, $450 plus taxes.
    #975, to T. Walsworth, $720 plus taxes.
    #976, to T. Rahman, $3 200 plus taxes.

31 Cash Receipt Slips:
#451, from J. Mayne, $3 826.53.
#452, from T. Walsworth, $2 030.33.
31 Bank Debit Memo: $85 for bank service charges.
31 Cheque Copies:
#256, to London PUC, $345.80 for water.
#257, Forest City Motors Ltd., $10 400 for a new van, which cost $21 400 plus taxes. A van purchased for $19 500 with an accumulated depreciation of $10 400 was traded in.
#258, to Renfrew Tape Ltd., $3 220.50, on account.
#259, to City of London, $144 plus GST, for vendor's licence.
#260, to CFPL radio station, $2 340 plus GST, for advertising.
#261, to Shell Canada Ltd., $2 143 plus taxes, for van expenses.
31 Credit Memo #183: Received from Office Specialty Ltd., $3 200 plus taxes, for a returned fax machine.
31 Purchase Invoice #446: From Wellington Business Fixtures Ltd., $2 300 plus taxes, for equipment.
31 Credit Memo #100: Issued to T. Rahman, $327 plus taxes.

(f) Take off a trial balance, schedule of accounts receivable, and schedule of accounts payable at May 31.
(g) Prepare an eight-column worksheet, using the following data:
Allowance for Doubtful Accounts, $13 400, using the balance sheet method;
Merchandise Inventory, $259 400;
Supplies on hand, $420;
Depreciation rates using the
declining-balance method: store, 5 percent
van, 30 percent
(h) Prepare an income statement and balance sheet.
(i) Journalize and post the adjusting and closing entries.
(j) Take off a post-closing trial balance.

CHAPTER TWELVE

Internal Control Over Cash

LEARNING OBJECTIVES

At the end of this chapter you should be able to
- discuss the importance of internal control over cash;
- describe system designs that lead to a division of duties;
- describe the operation of a petty cash fund;
- outline procedures for handling cash receipts;
- prepare a bank reconciliation and the corresponding journal entries;
- use a spreadsheet program as a tool in the internal control process;
- use a spreadsheet program to prepare a bank reconciliation template.

LANGUAGE OF ACCOUNTING

You will see the following terms in this chapter:
- audit trail
- auditor
- bank reconciliation
- cash short and over
- cash float
- certified cheque
- computer fraud
- issuer/drawer
- payee
- petty cash
- stale dated

12.1 Internal Control

When Algor Computer Services was establishing its procedures for internal control over its assets, it realized that one of its most important assets was cash. Yet cash is also one of the most difficult assets to have internal control over. This problem exists because the bills and coins used by the employees and by the business are the same, and are small in size. Once mixed with those of the employee, they are impossible to identify as belonging to the business. Procedures must be instituted to minimize the opportunity for fraud in the handling of cash.

Besides the protection of cash from fraud, procedures must also be maintained so that too much cash, or too little cash, is not on hand at any time. The inability to maintain a proper cash flow has resulted in the bankruptcy for many businesses because they were insolvent. Insolvency means that a business cannot pay its debts as they become due. Factors that influence solvency are debt-collecting techniques, which were examined in Chapter 6, and proper planning for the payment of liabilities. The efficient use of cash is also important, for cash that lies idle in a chequing account does not earn revenue. It can better be used making short- or long-term investments, obtaining more merchandise, or investing in expansion.

The various policies that Algor Computer Services established for internal control over cash are examined in the remainder of this chapter.

Division of Duties

> "*The division of duties results in one person's work serving as a check on another person's work.*"

The first principle that should be established for the handling of cash is that one person should not have responsibility for all of the tasks that result from the receipt of cash: receiving cash, issuing a receipt, making the entry in the accounting records for the receipt, and making the deposit. Similarly, on the payment side, one person should not have responsibility for all of the tasks involved in payments: authorizing payment, issuing the cheque, keeping the accounting records, and doing the bank reconciliation. Policies should be established to minimize the chance of fraud.

At Algor Computer Services, for example, a cashier who received cash on account also issued a receipt to the customer. A list of cash receipts was forwarded to the accounts receivable clerk who made the entries in the accounts receivable subsidiary ledger. This list was forwarded to the accounting supervisor, who made an entry in the general journal. Another copy of the list of cash receipts was sent by the cashier to the treasurer, who was responsible for the deposit of all funds. At month end, the schedule of accounts receivable was matched with the control account. As well, the banking records were matched with the cash receipts journal to ensure that all deposits were made.

It is difficult for many small businesses to achieve this division of duties, and in such circumstances audit procedures should ensure that fraud is not occurring.

LESSON REVIEW

1. Why is internal control over cash difficult to achieve?
2. What is the first principle for internal control over cash?
3. Why is cash flow so important in a business?
4. What does insolvency mean?
5. What can be done with excess cash?
6. Why is division of duties so important in a business?

12.2 Petty Cash Fund

When Algor Computer Services established its accounting system, the systems analyst recommended that a petty cash fund be established. The reason for the recommendation was twofold:

- Small payments, such as for transportation-in, are frequently due immediately. When payment is due on receipt of an item or service, it is said to arrive C.O.D. (cash on delivery). Other times, suppliers of goods or services do not accept payment by cheque because the amount may not be very large and it may not be worth the company's while to set up an invoicing and accounts receivable system for any NSF cheques they receive. As well, employees may be required to purchase items that are needed quickly on behalf of the firm. The person responsible for issuing a cheque may not be present at the time, or the exact amount required by the employee for the purchase might not be known, so the employee uses his or her own cash.
- The cost of issuing a cheque and making the resulting accounting entries is high, and may even be more than the amount owing.

Algor Computer Services, in consultation with its systems analyst, decided to establish a petty cash fund. In such a fund the amount of cash on hand plus the total of the vouchers and/or receipts should always equal the total of the petty cash fund.

> *"Payments of small amounts are frequently made in cash."*

> *"In a petty cash fund, the total of the petty cash fund is equal to the cash on hand plus the vouchers and/or receipts."*

Total of petty cash fund = Cash on hand + Vouchers + Receipts

Procedures were to be established so that the firm's policy manual would answer the following questions:

(1) Who should be in possession of the money?

(2) How much should be in the fund?

(3) At what minimum amount should the fund be replenished?

(4) What payments should be permitted, and for how much?

(5) Who will have final authority to decide what payments should be made?

(6) Where should the money be kept?

(7) What proof should a person requesting money from the fund have that a payment was made on behalf of the firm?

(8) What proof should there be that payments from the fund have been made?

(9) What record keeping system should be used for the fund?

(10) Can personal cheques be cashed with funds from the system?

The following policies were established:

FIGURE 12-1 PETTY CASH FUND PROCEDURES FOR ALGOR COMPUTER SERVICES

ALGOR COMPUTER SERVICES: ACCOUNTING PROCEDURES AND POLICIES
Petty Cash Fund Procedures

Amount of Fund
The fund shall be established with $150. The controller (chief accountant) shall use discretion in increasing or decreasing the fund as need be.

Fund Custodian
The office manager shall be the custodian of the fund. The cash and related documents shall be kept in a locked cash box. The box is to be placed in the office vault each night.

Payments from the Fund
Individual payments from the fund shall not exceed $25. The petty cashier shall only issue payments for business-related matters. When making payments,
(a) a bill of sale for the expenditure shall be received from the person who made a payment on behalf of the business or from the person requesting payment from the business for an item or service.
(b) a voucher shall be completed; the voucher form is shown in appendix xi [see Figure 12.2 on page 559]. The voucher shall be signed by both the petty cashier and the person requesting funds. The petty cashier shall stamp the bill of sale "paid."

If the petty cashier believes that a payment should not be made from the fund for whatever reason, the person refused may present the receipt to the controller who has the final authority to authorize payment.

There shall not be any loans made from the petty cash fund, nor will personal cheques be cashed.

Replenishing the Fund
The fund shall be replenished when there is a cash balance of $25 or less. The petty cashier shall give to the controller the receipts, the vouchers, and a petty cash summary when requesting that the fund be replenished. The vouchers shall be stamped "paid."

Establishing the Petty Cash Fund

To establish the petty cash fund, a cheque was issued to the petty cashier, Dale Webster, for $150. (Some businesses issue the cheque to Cash, however, any person may cash a cheque made out to "cash," so it is safer to make it payable to the petty cashier.) Dale cashed the cheque and put the money in the petty cash box. The required journal entry by the accountant is as follows (note that journal entries are given in general journal form for illustration purposes — in actual procedure, they would be entered in a cash payments journal):

July 4 Cheque Copy #463: $150 to Dale Webster, petty cashier, for establishment of the petty cash fund.

GENERAL JOURNAL

PAGE 605

DATE 1992		PARTICULARS	PR	DEBIT	CREDIT
July	4	Petty Cash		150 —	
		Cash			150 —
		Cheque Copy #463, to establish the petty cash fund			

"Petty Cash is a current asset."

The explanation for the entry is as follows:
- Petty Cash, a current asset, is debited to increase the asset.
- Cash is credited to reduce the asset.

Increasing and Decreasing the Fund

Should the controller find that the fund is being replenished frequently, the firm may decide to increase the fund. The journal entry is as follows:

GENERAL JOURNAL

PAGE 612

DATE 1992		PARTICULARS	PR	DEBIT	CREDIT
Aug.	14	Petty Cash		100 —	
		Cash			100 —
		Cheque Copy #490, to increase the petty cash fund to $250			

If, instead, the business had found that the fund was not used very much, it might decide to decrease the amount of the petty cash fund because in this case the cash would be lying idle. The entry to reduce the fund would be:

Chapter 12: Internal Control Over Cash

GENERAL JOURNAL

PAGE 612

DATE 1992		PARTICULARS	PR	DEBIT	CREDIT
Aug.	14	Cash		50 —	
		Petty Cash			50 —
		Memo #49, to reduce the petty cash fund to $100			

Payments from the Petty Cash Fund

"A petty cash voucher is completed each time a payment is made from the petty cash fund."

Each time a payment is made from the petty cash fund, a petty cash voucher must be completed. The purpose of the petty cash voucher is to summarize the reason for the payment, and to obtain the signature of the petty cashier and the person receiving the cash as proof of payment.

FIGURE 12-2 A PETTY CASH VOUCHER

```
PETTY CASH VOUCHER
                     NO.: 22-0017
Date:   August 14, 1992
Amount: $7.49
Paid to: Arrowspeed Delivery
Signature: Wanda Elichuk
Explanation: Transportation of supplies

Authorized by: D. Webster
Charge to Account: Transportation-in $7.00;
GST Recoverable $0.49
```

Replenishing the Petty Cash Fund

"A petty cash summary is prepared when the fund is to be replenished."

Each time a payment is made from petty cash, the total value of the vouchers increases and the amount of available cash decreases. When Dale Webster notices that the petty cash fund has been reduced to below $25, he prepares a petty cash summary as shown below.

FIGURE 12-3 PETTY CASH SUMMARY FOR AUGUST 29, 1992

Petty Cash Summary
August 29, 1992

Office Supplies	$ 24.35
Freight-in	21.03
Miscellaneous Expense	67.99
V. Marshall, Drawings	20.53
GST Recoverable	8.79
	$142.69

> "The petty cash summary, used vouchers, and voided receipts are taken to the treasurer when the fund is replenished."

Dale then takes the summary, the petty cash vouchers, and the receipts to the treasurer and receives a cheque in the amount of $142.69 from the treasurer. When the cheque is cashed and the funds are put in the petty cash box, the total cash in the box will be $150. The vouchers, receipts, and cheque copy are passed on to the accounting department.

FIGURE 12-4 THE FLOW OF DOCUMENTS FOR REPLENISHING THE PETTY CASH FUND

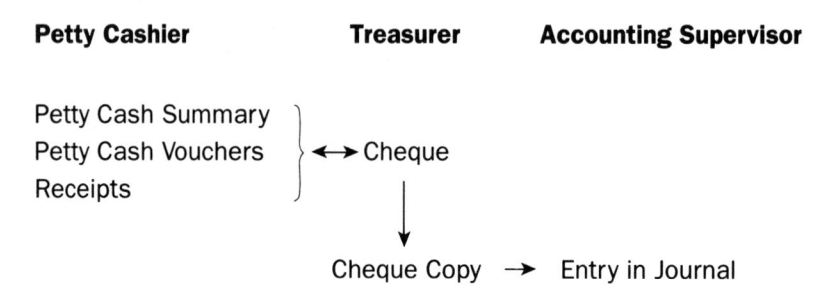

Petty Cashier	Treasurer	Accounting Supervisor
Petty Cash Summary Petty Cash Vouchers Receipts } ↔	Cheque	
	↓	
	Cheque Copy →	Entry in Journal

The following entry is made in the cash payments journal by the accounting department:

Aug. 29   Cheque Copy #548: $142.69, to Dale Webster, petty cashier, for Petty Cash Summary of August 29.

GENERAL JOURNAL

PAGE 614

DATE 1992		PARTICULARS	PR	DEBIT	CREDIT
Aug.	29	Office Supplies	150	24 35	
		Freight-in	510	21 03	
		Miscellaneous Expense	760	67 99	
		V. Marshall, Drawings	310	20 53	
		GST Recoverable	135	8 79	
		Cash	100		142 69
		Cheque Copy #548, to replenish petty cash			

GENERAL LEDGER

Office Supplies 150		Freight-in 510		Miscellaneous Expense 760	
dr.	cr.	dr.	cr.	dr.	cr.
Aug. 29 24.35		Aug. 29 21.03		Aug. 29 67.99	

V. Marshall, Drawings 310		GST Recoverable 135		Cash 100	
dr.	cr.	dr.	cr.	dr.	cr.
Aug. 29 20.53		Aug. 29 8.79			Aug. 29 142.69

The explanation for the entry is as follows:
- A debit is made to charge each account with its share of the reimbursement, hence the debits to the assets Office Supplies and GST Recoverable, the cost account Freight-in, the expense account Miscellaneous Expense, and the contra-equity account Drawings. Note that a debit is not made to Petty Cash, for the total amount in the fund has not increased.
- A credit is made to Cash to reduce the asset.

> "Cash Short and Over is debited when there is a cash shortage."

When replenishing the fund, the cashier may find that there is a shortage or excess due to an error. Should there be frequent shortages of significant amounts, an internal audit should take place. In shortage situations, a debit is made to Cash Short and Over. The replenishing entry for a cash shortage is as follows:

Sept. 14 Cheque Copy #592: $147.00, to Dale Webster, petty cashier, for Petty Cash Summary of September 14.

GENERAL JOURNAL

PAGE 620

DATE 1992		PARTICULARS	PR	DEBIT	CREDIT
Sept.	14	Miscellaneous Expense		34 28	
		Office Expense		27 54	
		V. Marshall, Drawings		76 06	
		GST Recoverable		8 94	
		Cash Short and Over		18	
		Cash			147 —
		Cheque Copy #592, to replenish petty cash			

> "Cash Short and Over is credited when there is an excess in cash."

For excesses, a credit is made to Cash Short and Over. The replenishing entry when there is cash over is as follows:

Oct. 22 Cheque Copy #663: $143.50, to Dale Webster, petty cashier, for Petty Cash Summary of October 22.

GENERAL JOURNAL

PAGE 629

DATE 1992		PARTICULARS	PR	DEBIT	CREDIT
Oct.	22	Miscellaneous Expense		50 52	
		Office Expense		67 81	
		V. Marshall, Drawings		17 83	
		GST Recoverable		8 83	
		Cash Short and Over			1 49
		Cash			143 50
		Cheque Copy #663, to replenish petty cash			

> "Cash Short and Over may appear as either an expense account, or a revenue account."

The Cash Short and Over account is listed on the income statement as an expense if it has a debit balance at the end of the fiscal period, or a revenue account if it has a credit balance.

Cash Short and Over	
dr.	cr.
Cash is short (expense)	Cash is over (revenue)

> "The petty cash fund should be replenished at the end of the fiscal period."

The petty cash fund should be replenished at the fiscal year-end so that the respective accounts that are to be charged for payments from the fund will have the correct balances for the preparation of the financial statements. Correspondingly, the petty cash fund should have the maximum amount of cash in it at fiscal year-end, because it will be shown on the balance sheet as a current asset for that amount.

Balance Sheet Presentation of Petty Cash

As indicated in Chapter 1, cash includes all items that would be accepted as a deposit by the bank. Thus, the petty cash fund is recognized as being cash. For this reason, the account usually does not have a separate listing in the current asset section of a condensed balance sheet, but rather is combined with cash. This combining also follows the principle of materiality. It does, of course, have a separate ledger account and will be shown as a current asset on balance sheets that are not in condensed form.

LESSON REVIEW

7. What is the purpose of a petty cash fund?

8. What relationship must always exist in a petty cash fund?

9. For each of the ten questions listed on page 556, indicate how the policies established by the firm solved the problem.

10. (a) What type of account is Petty Cash?
    (b) In what section of what statement is the Petty Cash account found?

11. What is the difference between establishing a petty cash fund and replenishing the fund?

12. An accountant made a debit to Petty Cash and a credit to Cash when replenishing the petty cash fund. Criticize the entry.

Chapter 12: Internal Control Over Cash

13. What internal control is obtained by requiring that an employee sign the voucher and the receipt when receiving a payment from the petty cashier?

14. What internal control is obtained by requiring that all receipts be stamped "paid" when payments are made from petty cash?

15. What account is used to record shortages and excesses in a petty cash fund? The account can be one of two types, depending on its balance. Explain how this is possible.

16. State the two occasions when a petty cash fund should be replenished. Give the reason for each.

17. In what way does the petty cash system violate the principle that all payments be made by cheque? In what way does it follow the principle?

18. Petty Cash is a ledger account, the balance of which is allowed to be incorrect during the fiscal year. Give examples of other accounts whose balances are allowed to be incorrect during the fiscal year. Compare how this account balance is corrected at the end of the fiscal period with the method used for the other examples that you gave.

LESSON APPLICATIONS

19. Complete a petty cash voucher for each of the following items that are submitted to the petty cashier for payment. You are the petty cashier.
    (a) #67: May 26, $25.00 to Mary Cornish. Charge Office Supplies, $23.48 and GST Recoverable, $1.52.
    (b) #68: May 27, $15.00 to S. Psovsky, driver for Psovsky Bros. Delivery. Charge Freight-in, $14.02 and GST Recoverable, $0.98.
    (c) #69: May 27, $13.50 cash to the owner, C. Turcotte, for personal use.
    (d) #70: May 29, $28.94 to T. Elliott, building supervisor, for an electric power bar. Charge Miscellaneous Expense, $27.18 and GST Recoverable, $1.76.
    (e) #71: May 30, $26.00 to D. Nygaard, for computer paper. Charge Office Supplies, $24.42 and GST Recoverable, $1.58.
    (f) #72: May 30, $26.49 to D. Nygaard, for Fax ribbon. Charge Office Supplies, $24.88 and GST Recoverable, $1.61.

20. Journalize each of the following transctions on page 21 of the general journal:

Sept. 4 Cheque Copy #25: $150.00 to D. Kaminski, petty cashier, to establish a petty cash fund.

15 Cheque Copy #68: $137.51 to D. Kaminski, petty cashier, for replenishing the petty cash fund. The petty cash summary is as follows: Office Supplies, $36.16; Freight-in, $39.25; W. Kurush, Drawings, $50.00; Miscellaneous Expense, $6.58; GST Recoverable, $5.52.

18 Cheque Copy #93: $100.00 to D. Kaminski, petty cashier, to increase the amount of the petty cash fund.

Oct. 5 Cheque Copy #173: $231.60 to D. Kaminski, petty cashier, to replenish the petty cash fund. The petty cash summary is as follows: Office Supplies, $36.16; Freight-in, $112.15; W. Kurush, Drawings, $35.00; Miscellaneous Expense, $35.78; GST Recoverable, $12.51.

21. Journalize each of the following transctions on page 584 of the general journal. Cheques were made out to George Kovacs, petty cashier.

May 14 Cheque Copy #476: $200.00, to establish a petty cash fund.

29 Cheque Copy #632: $187.91, to replenish the petty cash fund. The accounts to be charged are: Miscellaneous Expense, $71.83; Office Supplies, $40.58; Freight-in, $63.75; GST Recoverable, $11.75.

June 5 Cheque Copy #701: $100.00, to increase the amount of the petty cash fund.

24 Cheque Copy #893: $278.41, to replenish the petty cash fund. The accounts to be charged are: Miscellaneous Expense, $96.53; Office Supplies, $119.59; Freight-in, $43.25; GST Recoverable, $17.04; Cash Short and Over, $2.00.

July 23 Cheque Copy #1007: $188.27, to replenish the petty cash fund. The accounts to be charged are: T. Kellett, Drawings, $80.00; Miscellaneous Expense, $30.52; Office Supplies, $82.32; Freight-in, $36.56; GST Recoverable, $9.87. The fund had cash over of $1.00. Management had decided to reduce the fund by $50.00.

22. Complete a petty cash summary for the petty cash fund from which payments were made in Question 19. Assume that the fund maximum was $150.00 and that there was a $1.00 shortage.

12.3 Internal Control Over Cash Receipts

An internal control system for cash receipts must ensure that:
- the receipts are protected from improper usage, or theft, and
- proper records are maintained.

The control system for cash receipts should have many of the internal control elements already described: prenumbered source documents, the issuing of receipts for all cash received, the daily deposit of cash, and a division of duties including separation of the accounting task from the custodianship of the cash. Figures 12-5 and 12-7 show the division of duties among the employees at Algor Computer Services for cash receipts.

Remember that a business basically receives cash for two reasons: cash sales and cash receipts on account.

FIGURE 12-5 CONTROL PROCEDURE FOR CASH SALES

ALGOR COMPUTER SERVICES: ACCOUNTING PROCEDURES AND POLICIES

Sales Clerk	Supervisor	Treasurer	Accounting Department
Completes cash sales slip	──→		Checks numerical sequence of slips
Completes cash summary →	Verifies cash summary →	Compares to cash received	
Removes cash float and forwards cash ──────────→		Prepares cash deposit slip →	Prepares journal entry in cash receipts journal

"A cash float is given to cashiers each day so that they may make change for sales."

For cash sales, the sales clerk is given a cash float of the same amount each day. The float is a change fund, so that proper change can be made if required for the cash sales of the day. The procedure for handling cash sales at the point of sale varies from business to business. Procedures must be in place so that many sales people do not have access to the same register. If they do, responsibility for errors may be difficult to trace, and remedial action will be difficult to effect. In some businesses, clerks have their own portable cash drawer that they put into the cash register when they arrive and remove when they leave. No other sales person has access to that cash register, or that particular cash drawer.

The cash summary prepared by the clerk at the end of the day appears as in Figure 12-6.

FIGURE 12-6 A CASH REGISTER PROOF

CASH REGISTER PROOF						
ACTUAL CASH IN DRAWER				GENERAL JOURNAL		
8 X $ 1.00 =	$ 8.00				DEBIT	CREDIT
6 X 2.00 =	12.00			CASH	917 50	
2 X 5.00 =	10.00					
6 X 10.00 =	60.00			ACCTS. REC. (CH)		
28 X 20.00 =	560.00			CASH SHORT	2 50	
1 X 50.00 =	50.00					
2 X 100.00 =	200.00			ACCTS. REC. (RA)		
CHANGE =	17.50			SALES (SA)		800 —
TOTAL	$ 917.50					
CASH SUMMARY				GST PBL		56 —
CASH SALES (CA) RECD ON ACC'T. (RA)		920 —		PST PBL		64 —
CASH COUNT SHOULD BE ACTUAL CASH IN DRAWER		920 — 917 50		CASH OVER		
CASH (SHORTAGE) OVER		(2 50)		TOTALS	920 —	920 —

The journal entry required to record the above cash summary is as follows:

GENERAL JOURNAL
PAGE 580

DATE 1992		PARTICULARS	PR	DEBIT	CREDIT
May	14	Cash		917 50	
		Cash Short and Over		2 50	
		Sales			800 —
		GST Payable			56 —
		PST Payable			64 —
		To record Cash Sales Slips #99-8872 – #99-8898			

Since the Cash Short and Over account can be either an expense account or a revenue account, depending upon its balance at the end of the fiscal year, the business must establish policies concerning cash short or over. Who will receive cash over, and who is to bear the cost of cash short? What action will the firm take if cash is consistently short?

In Figure 12-5 it is important to note that the work of one person is checked by another person. The procedure for checking that deposits were properly made will be examined in the next section on reconciliation statements. The audit will, of course, check on the accounting procedures.

Figure 12-7 is the procedure chart for cash receipts on account, received in the mail and paid in person.

FIGURE 12-7 PROCEDURES FOR INTERNAL CONTROL OVER CASH RECEIVED ON ACCOUNT, EITHER BY MAIL OR IN PERSON

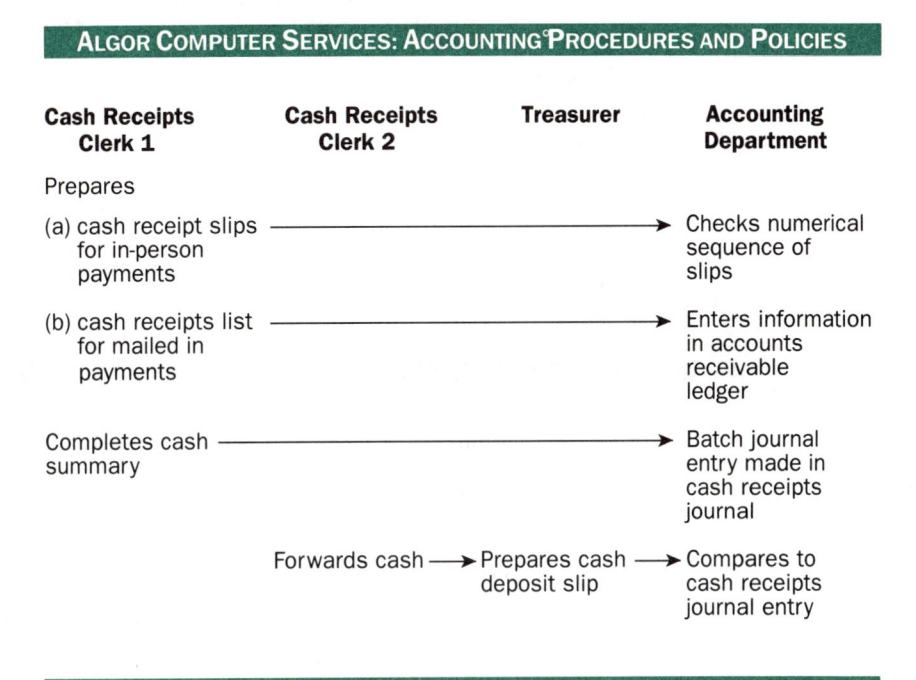

ALGOR COMPUTER SERVICES: ACCOUNTING PROCEDURES AND POLICIES

Cash Receipts Clerk 1	Cash Receipts Clerk 2	Treasurer	Accounting Department
Prepares			
(a) cash receipt slips for in-person payments	⟶		⟶ Checks numerical sequence of slips
(b) cash receipts list for mailed in payments	⟶		⟶ Enters information in accounts receivable ledger
Completes cash summary	⟶		⟶ Batch journal entry made in cash receipts journal
	Forwards cash ⟶	Prepares cash deposit slip ⟶	Compares to cash receipts journal entry

Note that the work of one person checks the work of another. The list of cash receipts received by mail appears in Figure 12-8. It is not necessary to prepare a cash receipt slip for each mail receipt, since the accounts receivable clerk will make the necessary changes in the account. The customer will be advised of the change on the next statement sent by mail.

Some customers may also have sent post-dated cheques. The issuer of a post-dated cheque has made the date on the cheque later than the day on which it was written. Customers do this so that the cheque will not be cashed until a later date when they have sufficient money in their account to cover the cheque. A separate tickler file should be maintained for these cheques, so that they can be deposited and credited to the customer's account on the appropriate date. A person can be charged with a criminal offence if they issue a cheque knowing that there are not sufficient funds in the account to cover the amount of the cheque on the day on which the cheque is dated.

FIGURE 12-8 DAILY LISTING OF CASH RECEIPTS

```
           Algor Computer Services
        Daily Cash Receipts for July 4, 1992

   R. Anderson                               $   430.50
   L. Jarvis                                     220.00
   H. Kaufmann                                    75.00
   M. Murtagh                                  1 420.30
   G. Rowan                                       51.75
   Total                                      $2 197.55

   Clerk's Signature:    Sue Martin
```

LESSON REVIEW

23. Internal control over cash receipts must ensure what two items?

24. Referring to Figure 12-5, what are four situations in which one person's work checks another's?

25. What is the purpose of a float?

26. What type(s) of account can Cash Short or Over be? Why?

27. Referring to Figure 12-7, what are four situations in which one person's work checks another's?

12.4 Bank Reconciliation

Businesses avail themselves of the services of financial institutions in order to protect their cash assets. A business will make use of the institution to, among other things, deposit cash, clear cheques, and obtain loans. Algor Computer Services uses a bank for its financial transactions. All transactions that affect the Cash account of the business also affect the bank's records, but in the opposite way. A deposit by the business is recorded in the business's books as an asset; the same transaction is recorded by the bank as a liability, for it owes the money left in its care to the business.

FIGURE 12-9 THE BUSINESS'S AND THE BANK'S BOOKS SHOW OPPOSITE ENTRIES FOR EACH TRANSACTION

Business's Cash Account		Bank's Account Payable	
dr.	cr.	dr.	cr.
Cash receipts	Cash payments	Cash payment on behalf of the customer	Cash receipts deposited by the customer

At any given time, however, transactions recorded by the business will not be recorded by the bank. For example, a cheque written by the business and recorded in its books on April 17 may not be received by the bank for many months because the payee does not cash it.

April 17 Cheque issued and recorded in the books of Algor Computer Services.

April 18 Cheque mailed to the payee.

May 31   Cheque cashed by the payee.

June 3   Cancelled cheque received by the Algor Computer Services' bank.

Similarly, certain transactions recorded by the bank that change the business's bank account will not be recorded immediately by the business. For example, the bank does not notify the business the same day when service charges are deducted from an account. To notify the business of all changes occurring in its account during the month, a statement, as shown in Figure 12-12 on page 572, is mailed by the bank. The bank statement indicates that the business has forty-five days in which to bring any errors to the attention of the bank, therefore, the business must compare the bank statement to its own records in a search for discrepancies.

> *A reconciliation statement compares the business's records with the bank's records.*

In order to make this comparison, the business prepares a reconciliation statement. To reconcile means to make agree. Theoretically, when all the business and bank activities that affect the bank account are recorded by each party, the bank's records and the business's records should be exactly the same.

Reconciling Items in the Business's Books

The bank statement sent at month end informs the business that certain cheques that it issued have been charged against the account, and that deposits were made for specific amounts on specified dates. In addition, the bank statement informs the business of other changes that were made to the account balance during the month by the bank, which the bank is entitled to do according to the agreement entered into at the time of opening the account. Such changes could include the following:

- bank charges: The bank charges for services that it renders on behalf of the business. Such services include returning NSF cheques, cashing cheques, issuing statements, and sending cancelled cheques back to the business. On the bank statement this amount is referred to as a Service Charge. The business must reduce its Cash account by the amount of the service charge.
- errors made by the bank: The bank may have made an error in recording an item.

- amounts collected by the bank on behalf of the business: Banks will provide the service of collecting accounts on behalf of the business. A charge is made for this service. These amounts will result in an increase in the Cash account.

"*An NSF cheque results when there is not enough funds in the issuer's account to cover the amount of the cheque.*"

- NSF cheques: Any cheques deposited by the business and subsequently not honoured by the issuer's bank are deducted from the business's account by the bank. On the bank statement they are referred to as a Returned Item. The business must reduce its Cash account by the amount of the NSF cheque and set up or adjust its Accounts Receivable ledger account to reflect this situation. Depending on the company's policy, the NSF charges may be passed on to the client too.

Cheques deposited by the business are sent to a clearing house and then forwarded to the issuer's bank. (See Figure 12-10.)

FIGURE 12-10 PATH THAT A CHEQUE FOLLOWS FROM THE TIME THAT IT IS ISSUED UNTIL IT IS RETURNED TO THE ISSUER

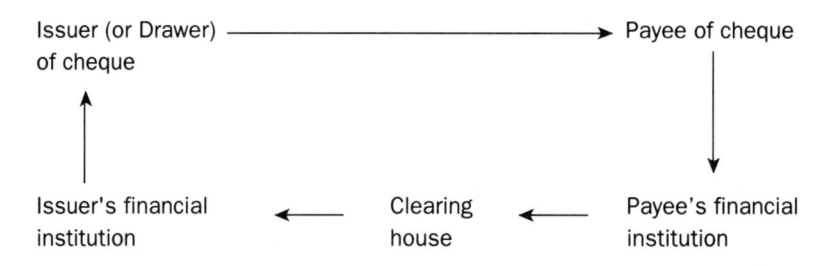

"*A clearing house calculates the settlement of balances between financial institutions.*"

```
Issuer (or Drawer)  ──────────────────▶  Payee of cheque
of cheque                                      │
   ▲                                           │
   │                                           ▼
Issuer's financial  ◀──────  Clearing  ◀──────  Payee's financial
institution                  house              institution
```

"*A stale-dated cheque is one for which the issue date is now more than six months ago.*"

The issuer's financial institution may refuse to honour the cheque for a variety of reasons: the issuer's account does not have sufficient funds to cover the cheque; the cheque was issued more than six months prior to being cashed and is therefore stale dated; or the cheque is improperly issued.

For any of these reasons, the issuer's bank will return the cheque to the payee's bank, and the payee must then try to collect the funds from the issuer.

Reconciling Items in the Bank's Books

The business compares the bank statement to its own books to find those items that have caused the discrepancy between the bank's balance and the business's Cash account balance. These items may include:
- cheques issued by the business that have not yet cleared the bank (called outstanding cheques);
- deposits made by the business on the last day of the month, but not recorded by the bank until the first day of the following month (these are called outstanding deposits);
- errors made by the business.

THE FACTS SPEAK...

Clearing systems totals for 1989: 2 038 million items
$16 709 billion

Preparing the Bank Reconciliation Statement

When preparing the reconciliation statement, the accountant must decide whether it is the business's or the bank's records that are not up to date, or have an error. A number of documents are required in order to compare the records:
- the previous month's reconciliation statement;
- the balance of the Cash account from the general ledger;
- the cash receipts journal;
- the cash payments journal;
- the current month's bank statement.

The bank statement is shown in Figure 12-12; other items will be shown as they are required for the reconciliation.

The following steps are carried out when making the reconciliation statement, as shown here at the end of August:

(1) The balances of the Cash account and the bank statement as at August 31 are entered. (The ending bank balance from the July bank statement should be compared to the beginning balance on the August statement to ensure that they are the same. Assume this has been done.)

GENERAL LEDGER

ACCOUNT Cash						NO 100	
DATE 1992	PARTICULARS	PR	DEBIT	CREDIT	DR/CR	BALANCE	
Aug. 31		CP 11		11 292 92	DR	19 099 16	

FIGURE 12-11 BANK RECONCILIATION STATEMENT WITH BALANCES FOR THE BUSINESS'S CASH ACCOUNT AND THE BANK STATEMENT ENTERED

Algor Computer Services
Bank Reconciliation
August 31, 1992

Balance in Cash ledger account	$19 099.16
Balance on August 31 bank statement	16 981.57

FIGURE 12-12 ALGOR'S BANK STATEMENT

THE ROYAL BANK OF CANADA

ACCOUNT STATEMENT

PLEASE NOTIFY US OF ANY CHANGE IN YOUR ADDRESS

Algor Computer Services
55 Eastern Parkway
Kanata, ON
K2L 2B1

ACCOUNT NO. 625-040-8
STATEMENT DATE August 31, 1992
ENCLOSURES 16 | PAGE 8

BALANCE FORWARD ▶ 13 094.21

DESCRIPTION - DEBITS / CHEQUES		DEPOSITS / CREDITS	DATE M D	NEW BALANCE
Deposit		2 970.00	08 03	16 064.21
Returned Item	116.22		08 03	15 947.99
Cheque #382	216.55		08 04	15 731.44
Deposit		144.93	08 05	15 876.37
Cheque #377	147.56		08 07	15 728.81
Credit Memo		220.00	08 07	15 948.81
Cheque #384	29.43		08 07	15 919.38
Cheque #385	1 209.33		08 10	14 710.05
Deposit		2 655.49	08 12	17 365.54
Cheque #383	422.22		08 12	16 943.32
Cheque #386	36.77		08 13	16 906.55
Cheque #388	711.12		08 17	16 195.43
Deposit		1 644.00	08 19	17 839.43
Cheque #387	122.78		08 20	17 716.65
Cheque #390	2 440.00		08 21	15 276.65
Cheque #391	322.08		08 24	14 954.57
Cheque #389	14.34		08 24	14 940.23
Deposit		3 560.87	08 25	18 501.10
Cheque #392	172.93		08 25	18 328.17
Cheque #393	916.40		08 28	17 411.77
Cheque #397	73.60		08 31	17 338.17
Cheque #395	321.60		08 31	17 016.57
Service Charge	35.00		08 31	16 981.57

NO. DEBITS	TOTAL AMOUNT - DEBIT	NO. CREDITS	TOTAL AMOUNT - CREDIT	
17	7 307.93	6	11 195.29	

PLEASE CHECK THIS STATEMENT WITHOUT DELAY
THE BANK MUST BE NOTIFIED IN WRITING OF ANY ERROR WITHIN 45 DAYS AFTER THE ABOVE STATEMENT DATE

(2) Deposits are recorded in the cash receipts journal of the business, and then taken to the bank for deposit. The Deposits/Credits column of the bank statement (credit column, since the bank owes this money to the business and it is therefore recorded as a liability) is therefore matched with the Cash Dr. column of the cash receipts journal and the outstanding deposits listed on July's reconciliation statement. Each item is checked off if it matches an item on the opposite records.

FIGURE 12-13 A COMPARISON OF THE INCREASES IN THE BANK BALANCE RECORDED BY THE BUSINESS WITH THE BANK'S RECORDS

Business's Records		Bank's Records	
Bank reconciliation statement		From the bank statement:	
July 31, 1992 shows:		Date	Deposits/Credits
o/s deposit	$2 970.00	Aug. 3	$2 970.00
		5	144.93
From the cash receipts		8	220.00
journal Cash Debit column:		12	2 655.49
Aug. 3	$ 144.93	19	1 644.00
10	2 655.49	25	3 560.87
17	1 644.00		
24	3 560.87		
31	2 991.76		

(a) The only item from the Cash Dr. column in the cash receipts journal not appearing in the Deposits/Credits column of the bank statement is the $2 991.76 deposit of August 31. It is recorded in the business's books, but not the bank's; it must therefore be added to the bank side of the statement because it will increase the bank balance when recorded by the bank.

FIGURE 12-14 A PARTIALLY COMPLETED BANK RECONCILIATION STATEMENT, SHOWING CHANGES DUE TO INCREASES IN THE BANK BALANCE

Algor Computer Services
Bank Reconciliation
August 31, 1992

Balance in Cash ledger account	$19 099.16
Add: Credit memo, B. Snelgrove	220.00
	$19 319.16
Balance on August 31 bank statement	$16 981.57
Add: o/s deposit, August 31	2 991.76
	$19 973.33

(b) The only item from the Deposits/Credits column of the bank statement not appearing in the Cash Dr. column of the cash receipts journal is the $220 entry. The Credit Memo returned with the bank statement indicates that the bank collected an accounts receivable from B. Snelgrove on behalf of the business. The amount is to be added to the Cash account balance.

(3) Cheques are recorded in the cash payments journal of the business, and on the bank statement in the debit column when they have been paid by the bank. If not yet paid by the bank, they will not appear on the bank statement. As noted previously, many of the cheques issued by Algor Computer Services will not have been received by Algor's bank by month end, for the payees will not have cashed them, or the cheques will not have been cleared through the clearing house. The Debits/Cheques column of the bank statement is therefore matched with the Cash Cr. column of the cash payments journal and to the outstanding cheques listed on July's reconciliation state-

FIGURE 12-15 A COMPARISON OF THE DECREASES IN THE BANK BALANCE RECORDED BY THE BUSINESS WITH THE BANK'S RECORDS

Business's Records			Bank's Records	
Bank reconciliation statement July 31, 1992 shows:			From the bank statement:	
			Date	Debits/Cheques
o/s cheques	#377	$147.56	Aug. 3	$ 116.22
	#382	216.55	4	216.55
			7	147.56
From the cash payments journal Cash Credit column:			7	29.43
			10	1 209.33
Aug. 3		$ 422.22	12	422.22
3		29.43	13	36.77
5		1 209.33	17	711.12
7		36.77	20	122.78
10		122.78	21	2 440.00
12		711.12	24	322.08
17		14.34	24	14.34
18		2 440.00	25	172.93
18		322.08	28	916.40
21		127.93	31	73.60
26		916.40	31	321.60
27		439.01	31	35.00
28		321.60		
28		200.00		
29		73.60		
31		211.38		

ment. Each item is checked off if it matches an item on the opposite records.

(a) Any items from the Cash Cr. column in the cash payments journal or the previous month's reconciliation not appearing in the Debits/Cheques column of the bank statement represent outstanding cheques that the bank has not paid. Since these cheques have been recorded by the business in its books, they should be deducted from the balance on the bank statement.

(b) Any items from the Debits/Cheques column of the bank statement not appearing in the Cash Dr. column of the cash payments journal represent items not recorded in the business's records. Two items have Service Charge and Returned Item (a non-sufficient funds cheque) beside them. The $35 service charge is the monthly bank charge for operation of the account. The NSF cheque of $116.22 was received from T. Farriera. Both of these items reduce the business's Cash account balance.

(c) In checking off items, the accountant may notice that an error has been made by the business or by the bank. For example, cheque #392 was recorded on the bank statement as $172.93 but was incorrectly recorded in the business's books as $127.93. The cheque had been issued to Martin Rapid Transport for transportation-in. The error is $45.

Figure 12-16 shows the completed reconciliation statement.

FIGURE 12-16 A COMPLETED BANK RECONCILIATION STATEMENT FOR ALGOR

Algor Computer Services
Bank Reconciliation
August 31, 1992

Balance in Cash ledger account		$19 099.16
Add: Credit memo, B. Snelgrove		220.00
		19 319.16
Less: Error on cheque #392	$ 45.00	
Service charge	35.00	
NSF cheque of T. Farriera	116.22	196.22
		$19 122.94
Balance on August 31 bank statement		$16 981.57
Add: o/s deposit, August 31		2 991.76
		19 973.33
Less: o/s cheques		
#394	$439.01	
#396	200.00	
#398	211.38	850.39
True balance for bank statement		$19 122.94

Updating the Business Records

All those items listed as changes to the business records require a journal entry to update the books. Those four items are:

(1) the account receivable collected by the bank;

(2) the NSF cheque;

(3) the bank service charge;

(4) the error on cheque #392, which had been issued for transportation-in.

The journal entries are shown in Figure 12-17.

FIGURE 12-17

GENERAL JOURNAL

PAGE 615

DATE 1992		PARTICULARS	PR	DEBIT	CREDIT
Aug.	31	Cash		220 —	
		Accounts Receivable			220 —
		To record payment to bank by B. Snelgrove			
	31	Accounts Receivable		116 22	
		Cash			116 22
		NSF cheque of T. Farriera			
	31	Bank Charges		35 —	
		Cash			35 —
		To record bank service charge			
	31	Transportation-in		45 —	
		Cash			45 —
		To correct recording error on cheque #392			

The updated balance shown in the Cash ledger account will be the same figure as that shown on the reconciliation statement. It is important that the cheque stub in the bank book also be updated with this new balance (see Figure 12-18); otherwise the treasurer will issue cheques while being unaware of the correct balance.

The business must notify the bank of any bank errors made on the bank statement within the forty-five-day time limit shown on the bank statement. The outstanding cheques and deposits on the bank side of the statement will be recorded on future bank statements.

Other Reconciling Items

Certified cheque: When a cheque is certified, the bank on which it is issued guarantees payment. The payee of a cheque sometimes requests that the debtor make payment with a certified cheque. When Algor Computer Services was a young business, a supplier, West Coast Electronics, requested a certified cheque for a large purchase. Algor Com-

> "A certified cheque is guaranteed by the bank on which it is drawn; the amount is removed from the issuer's account and is held by the bank for the payee."

FIGURE 12-18 AN UPDATED CHEQUE STUB, SHOWING THE EFFECTS OF THE BANK RECONCILIATION STATEMENT

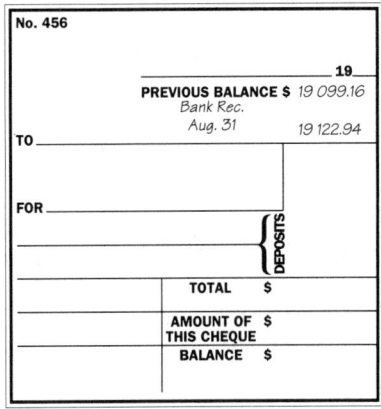

```
No. 456
                                              19___
                    PREVIOUS BALANCE  $ 19 099.16
                         Bank Rec.
                         Aug. 31        19 122.94
TO _____

FOR _____
                                        } DEPOSITS

                         TOTAL       $
                         AMOUNT OF  $
                         THIS CHEQUE
                         BALANCE     $
```

puter Services took the cheque to the bank, which withdrew the funds from Algor Computer Services' account, and kept them in trust for the payee. The bank stamped on the cheque that it had been certified. Algor Computer Services then mailed the cheque to West Coast Electronics. West Coast Electronics knew that the cheque was good, for the certification stamp placed on the cheque by the bank meant that the money had been removed from Algor Computer Services' account.

When preparing a bank reconciliation statement, a certified cheque should not be listed as outstanding if it is not returned with the bank statement, for the money was removed from the account at the time of certification. The withdrawal at the time of certification will be indicated on the bank statement by Certified Cheque.

Stale-dated cheque: A cheque that bears a date of at least six months prior to the date when it is presented for payment does not have to be accepted by a financial institution. Thus, a cheque dated June 30 is valid until December 31. After that time, if refused by the bank, the payee would have to obtain a new cheque from the issuer. Patti Ronald requested Algor Computer Services to replace a cheque that she had inadvertently not cashed. In doing so, Algor Computer Services indicated on the previous month's reconciliation statement that the old cheque had been cancelled, and a new one issued. A journal entry was made in the general journal to cancel the old cheque, and in the cash payments journal to issue the new one.

A Summary of Internal Control Procedures

The following internal control procedures were discussed in this chapter:
- Division of duties
- Petty cash fund

- Fixed amount of float
- Daily cash summary
- Daily cash deposit
- Payment by cheque
- Reconciliation statement

Lesson Review

28. What relationship exists between a business and its financial institution?
29. Give an example of a situation in which the business has recorded changes in its Cash account, but the bank will not have recorded changes in the bank account. When will the bank become aware of them?
30. How does the bank notify the business that it has made changes in the business's bank account?
31. What is a bank reconciliation statement? When is one prepared?
32. What are four items of change that the bank statement can inform the business of?
33. What purpose does a clearing house fulfill?
34. Why might the issuer's bank refuse to accept a cheque drawn on a particular account?
35. What is an outstanding deposit? An outstanding cheque?
36. Summarize the steps required to prepare a reconciliation statement.
37. How does one know that a cheque has been certified? What is the purpose of having the issuer of a cheque certify it?
38. When does a cheque become stale dated?

Lesson Applications

39. Indicate whether the business's books or the bank's books will be incorrect due to the following items, and explain why. Also indicate whether they will cause an increase, a decrease, or have no effect on the cash balance.
    (a) an NSF cheque

(b) an outstanding deposit
(c) a bank service charge
(d) an outstanding cheque
(e) a certified cheque
(f) interest credited to a bank account

40. Using the following information, prepare a reconciliation statement for Beaverbrook Craft Studio for the month of June.
    (a) Balance in Beaverbrook ledger account for Cash, $2 590.50.
    (b) Balance on bank statement dated June 30, 19-9, $1 480.14.
    (c) Information from bank statement:
        Bank charges, $14.50.
        Debit Memos: NSF cheque of C. Villeneuve, $143.59.
                     NSF cheque of P. Cathcart, $48.91.
    (d) Information from cash payments journal:
        Outstanding cheques: #391 $153.30
                               #393   40.93
                               #396   22.10
                               #397   101.43
    (e) Information from cash receipts journal:
        Outstanding deposit: June 30, $1 212.12
        Deposit of June 16 for sales on that date had been recorded in the journal as $98.72 instead of $89.72.

41. Using the following information, prepare a reconciliation statement for Western Home Hardware for the month of August.
    (a) Balance in Western's ledger account for cash, $53 920.00.
    (b) Balance on bank statement dated August 31, 19-4, $54 590.64.
    (c) Information from bank statement:
        Bank charges, $22.50.
        Debit Memos: NSF cheque of V. Chiu, $316.20.
                     NSF cheque of C. Janz, $21.49.
                     NSF cheque of P. Bonderud, $31.24.
    (d) Information from cash payments journal:
        Outstanding cheques: #90-329 $143.87
                               #90-334   52.39
                               #90-335   901.28
                               #90-336   57.49
                               #90-338   843.27
    (e) Information from cash receipts journal:
        Outstanding deposit: August 31, $945.23.
        Deposit of August 23 for sales on that date had been recorded in the journal as $167.50 instead of $176.50.

42. Prepare the necessary journal entries for the bank reconciliations completed in (a) Question 40, and (b) Question 41.

43. Figure 12-19 is the bank reconciliation for Salhany's Restaurant, for July 31, 19–5.

FIGURE 12-19

Salhany's Restaurant
Reconciliation Statement
July 31, 19–5

Cash per books		$5 205.01	Cash per bank statement		$5 834.58
Less:			Add: Deposit in transit		2 038.64
Service charge	$ 6.30				7 873.22
NSF cheque	121.43	127.73	Less: Outstanding cheques		
Adjusted cash balance		$5 077.28	#442	$1 809.50	
			443	833.93	
			444 (certified)	150.00	
			446	20.50	
			447	132.01	2 795.94
			Adjusted cash balance		$5 077.28

(a) Indicate where the balances "cash per books" and "cash per bank statement" would have been obtained.
(b) Indicate what items would have been compared to find the following items:
  (i) the service charge
  (ii) the NSF cheque
  (iii) the outstanding cheques
  (iv) the outstanding deposit
(c) Why is cheque #444 not included in the total of the cheques?
(d) What journal entries are required at the end of the month?

44. (a) Using the following information, prepare a reconciliation statement for Victoria Flyers Hockey Team for the month of December.
   (b) Prepare journal entries for the reconciliation.
      (i) Balance in Flyer's ledger account for Cash, $12 389.06.
      (ii) Balance on bank statement dated December 31, $13 982.71.
      (iii) Information from bank statement:
         Bank charges, $15
         Debit Memos: NSF cheque of C. Savard, $135.40
                      NSF cheque of D. Hull, $40.50
         Loan payment of $340.00 plus $3.80 interest
      (iv) Information from cash payments journal:
         Outstanding cheques: #566 $ 483.92
                                #575   185.18
                                #583   123.93
                                #584   1 022.88
                                #585   332.01
                                #587   73.02

(v) Information from cash receipts journal:
Outstanding deposit: December 31, $92.59

45. (a) Using the following information, prepare a reconciliation statement for Britannia Weekly Chronicle for the month of June.
(b) Prepare journal entries for the bank reconciliation of June 30.
  (i) Balance in Britannia's ledger account for Cash, $19 235.82.
  (ii) Information from bank statement:
    Balance, $16 982.71
    Bank charges, $30
    Debit Memos: NSF cheque of K. Jabbar, $902.20
                 NSF cheque of B. Cousy, $114.50
    Loan payment of $1 540 plus interest, $15.70
  (iii) Information from cash payments journal:
    Outstanding cheques: #348 $ 246.91
                           #349   368.15
                           #351   1 835.93
                           #354   472.51
                           #355   2 500.00 (certified)
                           #357   743.82
    Cheque #346, issued for the purchase of supplies, was recorded as $53.69 instead of $53.96.
  (iv) Information from cash receipts journal:
    Outstanding deposit: June 30, $3 317.76

CHAPTER REVIEW AND SKILL DEVELOPMENT

Accounting Principles and Concepts

- **Internal control over cash** requires systems analysis and design.

- **Division of duties** decreases the possibility of fraud.

- A **petty cash system** is established in order to make small payments in cash.

- A **reconciliation** is prepared at month end to compare the records of the business with the records of the bank.

Knowing the Terms

For each of the following statements, indicate the term being defined.
(a) A cheque for which the bank guarantees payment.
(b) A cheque on which the date is more than six months old.
(c) The person who makes out a cheque.
(d) A cheque for which the issuer does not have the amount in his or her account when it is presented for payment.
(e) An institution that calculates the amount that banks owe to each other for cheques cashed.

(f) The person who receives a cheque.
(g) The statement made at month end to find the reason for discrepancies between the financial institution's books and the business's books.
(h) The document received by a business from its financial institution at month end.
(i) A cheque that has been issued but not cashed.
(j) A cheque that has been cashed.

Food for Thought

1. Juan Marichal began his own business, with one office person. He assigned all accounting activities to this one person. How can he ensure that fraud is not being committed?

2. Cheryl's cash position shows $122 000 on hand; the accountant informs Cheryl that her business only requires $60 000 in the short term to meet its liabilities. What should Cheryl consider before making a long-term investment?

3. At Harvard's School Supplies, daily cash counts showed between $25 and $30 missing on cash receipts averaging $12 000. Four clerks shared one cash register. Do you consider the cash short a significant amount based on the size of receipts? Justify your view.

4. The auditors for Chinwisky's Restaurant indicated that up to $25 of cash was missing each day based on the cash count. Miss Chinwisky, the owner, indicates that she does not consider any action to be necessary because she does not want to affect employee morale. Why should she take action?

5. Brenda Jackson is a golf pro at the Pineridge Golf Club and operates the pro shop. Each day she puts the cash from the cash register in her pocket, and tells the pro shop clerk, who also does the accounting, to prepare the records from the cash register tape and the sales invoices. What weaknesses are there in Brenda's procedure?

6. State why the journal entry in Figure 12-20 is incorrect (assume that the explanation is correct).

7. Give reasons why each of the following should not be allowed.
   (a) borrowing by employees from a petty cash fund
   (b) cashing cheques for employees from a petty cash fund

8. In what way does the Petty Cash system violate the principle that all payments be made by cheque? In what way does it follow the principle?

9. Some businesses use a Petty Cash Record similar to a multicolumn journal for recording payments from a petty cash fund. The petty cashier makes an entry each time a payment is made from the fund. What advantage is there to following this method?

FIGURE 12-20

GENERAL JOURNAL

PAGE 665

DATE 19–		PARTICULARS	PR	DEBIT	CREDIT
May	1	Petty Cash		87 23	
		Cash			87 23
		To replenish petty cash			

10. How does the Petty Cash system support the objectivity principle?

11. What internal control is obtained by requiring that an employee sign the voucher when receiving a payment from the petty cashier?

12. What internal control is obtained by requiring that all receipts be stamped "paid" when payments are made from petty cash?

13. Why should the replenishing cheque for petty cash be made out to the petty cashier and not to "Cash" or "Petty Cash"?

14. You are appointed to make an audit of the petty cash fund. What procedure would you follow?

15. While completing a prenumbered petty cash voucher Giuseppe Gucci made an error, and had to prepare a new one. What should be done with the spoiled voucher?

16. Good internal control procedures provide for the separation of the accounting function from the custodianship of cash. Indicate how this is shown in Figures 12-5 and 12-7.

17. A customer remits cash in the mail to pay the amount owing on his account. Why is this a poor procedure from (a) the business's point of view? (b) the customer's point of view? What should the business do to inform customers that it is a poor procedure?

18. A corner store takes in an average of $5 600 a day in cash sales. What procedures should be followed to ensure that the cash is safely deposited each day?

19. Victoria Furniture Centre accepts many post-dated cheques on account. What problems may occur if a business does accept post-dated cheques? What procedure should the firm follow in order to ensure that the cheques are deposited on the date of the cheque?

20. Barton's Outdoor Pools decides that, in order to save time, it will only do its reconciliation statement on a bimonthly basis. What are the disadvantages of this policy?

21. Paul Martin, bookkeeper for Norton's Hardware, is going on holidays for two weeks. He made the bank reconciliation statement three weeks late and found a bank error. He decides to put off calling the bank to have the error corrected until he returns. What difficulty might be caused?

22. As treasurer, Marlene writes cheques and also has been given the responsibility of doing the bank reconciliation. She wrote herself a $100 cheque, and didn't record it in the cash payments journal. When the cheque was returned from the bank, she removed it. To make the balance of the bank agree with that of the business on her reconciliation, she recorded a bank error of $100. What procedures can be established to ensure that this does not happen?

23. Banks impose a charge for NSF cheques. Why? Why would a business pass the charge on to the issuer (drawer)?

24. Tricia is examining the accountant's books for her business, which uses a five-journal system. She does not understand why there are three postings to the Cash account at the end of the month after the postings from the Cash Payments Journal and the Cash Receipts Journal. Explain what they probably are.

25. Gaston is asked by his supervisor to prepare a balance sheet. He looks at

the bank statement and sees that there is $4 500 in the account. He assumes that since that is the amount in the bank, that that is the amount the business must have in cash, so he enters it on the balance sheet. Why is Gaston's assumption incorrect?

26. It has been said that there is no such thing as computer fraud. To refer to fraud in computerized systems as computer fraud is thought to be the equivalent to referring to fraud in manual systems as pencil fraud. Provide a critical comment on this assertion.

Organizing

Reconciliation Statement
Prepare a list of the steps that should be followed in preparing a reconciliation statement. For each of the steps, indicate the documents that will be needed.

Applications

1. Journalize each of the following transactions on page 123 of the general journal:
   Apr. 22 Established a petty cash fund, $200.00.
   30 Replenished the petty cash fund, $192.99. The vouchers indicated payments had been made as follows: Miscellaneous Expense, $82.40; Postage Expense, $23.36; Transportation-in, $30.61; D. Pollard, Drawings, $47.50; GST Recoverable, $9.12.
   May 5 Management decided to increase the amount of the petty cash fund to $300.00. A cheque was issued to increase the fund.

2. Journalize each of the following transactions on page 222 of the general journal:
   June 4 Established a petty cash fund, $150.00.
   6 Cash sales $192.00, GST $13.44, PST $13.44. The cash count showed $219.41.
   8 Paid bank loan, $600.00 plus interest of $6.12.
   9 Cash sales $120.00, GST $8.40, PST $8.40. The cash count showed $137.68.
   10 Cash sales $208.20, GST $14.57, PST $14.57. The cash count showed $236.77.

3. Journalize each of the following transactions on page 369 of the general journal:
   May 4 Received a bank debit memo for the bank loan, $3 279.80: principal of $3 250, and interest of $29.80.
   4 Cash sales $942.93, GST $66.01, PST $75.43. The cash count showed $1 085.96.
   5 Cash sales $1 083.93, GST $75.88, PST $86.71. The cash count showed $1 253.85.
   5 Cash received on account, $593.
   6 Received a post-dated cheque on account for May 31, $423.
   6 Received $3 000.00 from the owner, J. Ahmed, as an additional investment.

4. (a) Prepare a reconciliation statement for the Wilkinson Hardware Co. as at June 30.
   (b) Prepare journal entries for the reconciliation statement prepared in (a).
   (c) Indicate what procedure should be followed concerning the bank error.
      (i) Balance as per bank statement, $23 740.00.

(ii) Cash balance as per general ledger, $21 895.00.

(iii) Outstanding cheques: #166 — $155.93; #480 — $235.22; #484 — $245.60; #485 — $1 290.33; #487 — $122.30; #488 — $100.25; #489 — a certified cheque, $1 500.00. Cheque #166 for $155.93 issued on November 16 of the previous year to Walter Cheng has been returned by Mr. Cheng because it is stale-dated.

(iv) Service charge for the month is $43.25.

(v) NSF cheque from Martha Pimm, $103.28.

(vi) The accountant made an error in recording cheque #481 which had been issued for the purchase of computer supplies. The cheque was for $762.39 but had been recorded as $726.39.

(vii) The bank had charged a cheque in the amount of $122.10 to our account, but it was issued by Wilkinson Trading Company.

5. (a) Prepare a bank reconciliation statement as of May 31 for Computer Bits, using the following information and Figure 12-22.
   (i) Ledger account for Cash (See Figure 12-21.)

(ii) The bank reconciliation for the month of April showed the following to be outstanding:

Deposit of April 30	$1 437.50
Cheques: #526	94.67
#529	435.07
#530	14.50
#531	1 202.33

(iii) The columnar journals for May showed the following:

Cash Payments Journal		Cash Receipts Journal	
Cheques issued		Deposits made	
#532	$ 432.56	05 08	$ 901.20
#533	122.35	05 10	2 390.10
#534	57.35	05 13	1 024.61
#535	209.80	05 19	772.01
#536	223.56	05 20	2 910.29
#537	550.01	05 26	1 501.28
#538	1 222.56	05 30	550.43
#539	122.51	05 31	1 409.00
#540	812.43		
#541	990.00		
#542	101.90		
#543	341.10		
#544	998.01		
#545	111.03		
#546	76.92		

(b) Prepare journal entries for the reconciliation.

FIGURE 12-21

GENERAL LEDGER

ACCOUNT Cash   **NO** 100

DATE 19–	PARTICULARS	PR	DEBIT	CREDIT	DR CR	BALANCE
May 1					DR	17 611 66
31		CR21	11 458 92		DR	29 070 58
31		CP24		6 372 09	DR	22 698 49

FIGURE 12-22

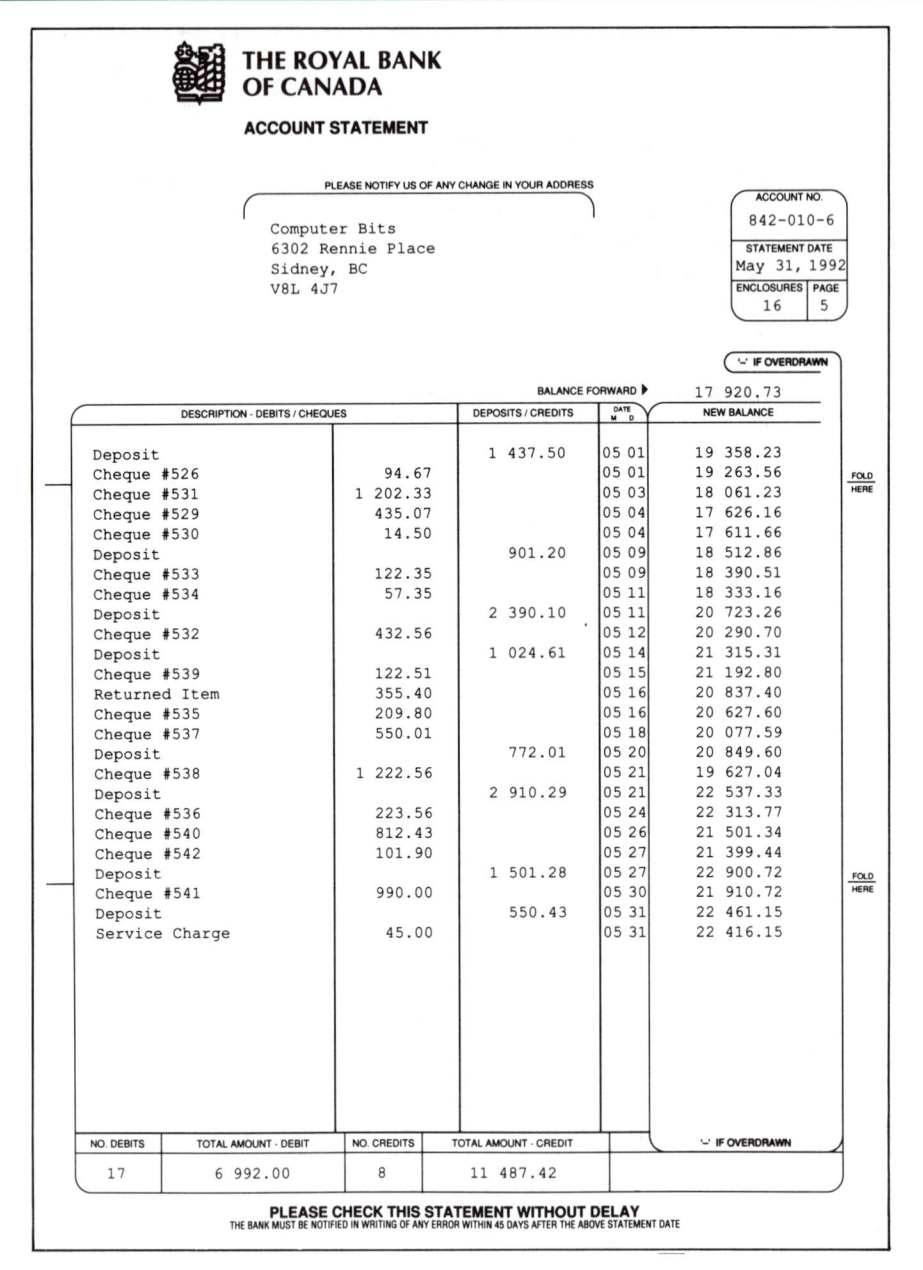

THE ROYAL BANK OF CANADA
ACCOUNT STATEMENT

PLEASE NOTIFY US OF ANY CHANGE IN YOUR ADDRESS

Computer Bits
6302 Rennie Place
Sidney, BC
V8L 4J7

ACCOUNT NO. 842-010-6
STATEMENT DATE May 31, 1992
ENCLOSURES 16 PAGE 5

BALANCE FORWARD 17 920.73

DESCRIPTION - DEBITS / CHEQUES		DEPOSITS / CREDITS	DATE M D	NEW BALANCE
Deposit		1 437.50	05 01	19 358.23
Cheque #526	94.67		05 01	19 263.56
Cheque #531	1 202.33		05 03	18 061.23
Cheque #529	435.07		05 04	17 626.16
Cheque #530	14.50		05 04	17 611.66
Deposit		901.20	05 09	18 512.86
Cheque #533	122.35		05 09	18 390.51
Cheque #534	57.35		05 11	18 333.16
Deposit		2 390.10	05 11	20 723.26
Cheque #532	432.56		05 12	20 290.70
Deposit		1 024.61	05 14	21 315.31
Cheque #539	122.51		05 15	21 192.80
Returned Item	355.40		05 16	20 837.40
Cheque #535	209.80		05 16	20 627.60
Cheque #537	550.01		05 18	20 077.59
Deposit		772.01	05 20	20 849.60
Cheque #538	1 222.56		05 21	19 627.04
Deposit		2 910.29	05 21	22 537.33
Cheque #536	223.56		05 24	22 313.77
Cheque #540	812.43		05 26	21 501.34
Cheque #542	101.90		05 27	21 399.44
Deposit		1 501.28	05 27	22 900.72
Cheque #541	990.00		05 30	21 910.72
Deposit		550.43	05 31	22 461.15
Service Charge	45.00		05 31	22 416.15

NO. DEBITS	TOTAL AMOUNT - DEBIT	NO. CREDITS	TOTAL AMOUNT - CREDIT
17	6 992.00	8	11 487.42

PLEASE CHECK THIS STATEMENT WITHOUT DELAY
THE BANK MUST BE NOTIFIED IN WRITING OF ANY ERROR WITHIN 45 DAYS AFTER THE ABOVE STATEMENT DATE

Applications — Comprehensive

(a) Prepare a bank reconciliation statement for Algonquin Mapping Ltd. for October, using the following information and Figure 12-24.

  (i) Ledger account for Cash (See Figure 12-23.)

(ii) The bank reconciliation for the month of September showed the following to be outstanding:

Deposit of Sept. 30, $2 590.91
Cheques: #394 $ 97.00
          #439   88.00
          #440   722.00

FIGURE 12-23

GENERAL LEDGER

ACCOUNT Cash **NO** 100

DATE 1992		PARTICULARS	PR	DEBIT	CREDIT	DR CR	BALANCE
Sept.	30		J78	742 –		DR	18 106 62
Oct.	31		CR21	12 510 18		DR	30 616 80
	31		CP24		8 901 10	DR	21 715 70

FIGURE 12-24

THE ROYAL BANK OF CANADA

ACCOUNT STATEMENT

PLEASE NOTIFY US OF ANY CHANGE IN YOUR ADDRESS

Algonquin Mapping Ltd.
2742 Beaver Creek Blvd.
Kearney, ON
P0A 1M0

ACCOUNT NO. 408-625-9
STATEMENT DATE October 31, 1992
ENCLOSURES 20 PAGE 10

BALANCE FORWARD ▶ 16 422.71

DESCRIPTION - DEBITS / CHEQUES		DEPOSITS / CREDITS	DATE M D	NEW BALANCE
Deposit		2 590.91	10 01	19 013.62
Cheque #442	1 239.00		10 02	17 774.62
Returned Item	445.00		10 02	17 329.62
Cheque #444	142.00		10 03	17 187.62
Cheque #394	97.00		10 04	17 090.62
Deposit		1 409.32	10 04	18 499.94
Cheque #441	1 902.00		10 05	16 597.94
Deposit		2 092.90	10 08	18 690.84
Cheque #440	722.00		10 09	17 968.84
Cheque #439	88.00		10 11	17 880.84
Deposit		1 222.00	10 12	19 102.84
Cheque #443	101.00		10 12	19 001.84
Cheque #445	91.03		10 16	18 910.81
Cheque #448	440.29		10 16	18 470.52
Cheque #449	111.91		10 17	18 358.61
Deposit		2 309.78	10 17	20 668.39
Cheque #446	21.20		10 18	20 647.19
Cheque #450	1 092.09		10 18	19 555.10
Deposit		1 293.99	10 19	20 849.09
Deposit		122.50	10 22	20 971.59
Cheque #447	223.45		10 23	20 748.14
Cheque #453	119.95		10 23	20 628.19
Returned Item	22.50		10 24	20 605.69
Cheque #454	20.02		10 25	20 585.67
Deposit		1 872.23	10 25	22 457.90
Cheque #451	309.87		10 26	22 148.03
Credit Memo (interest)		25.00	10 26	22 173.03
Cheque #452	733.24		10 29	21 439.79
Cheque #456	88.00		10 30	21 351.79
Deposit		1 222.98	10 31	22 574.77
Service Charge	45.00		10 31	22 529.77

NO. DEBITS	TOTAL AMOUNT - DEBIT	NO. CREDITS	TOTAL AMOUNT - CREDIT
21	8 054.55	10	14 161.61

PLEASE CHECK THIS STATEMENT WITHOUT DELAY
THE BANK MUST BE NOTIFIED IN WRITING OF ANY ERROR WITHIN 45 DAYS AFTER THE ABOVE STATEMENT DATE

(iii)

Cash Receipts Journal for Oct. Deposits		Cash Payments Journal for Oct. Bank Cr.	
Oct. 3	$1 409.32	#441	$1 902.00
7	2 092.90	442	1 239.00
11	1 222.00	443	101.00
16	2 309.78	444	142.00
18	1 293.99	445	91.03
21	122.50	446	21.20
24	1 872.23	447	223.45
30	1 222.98	448	440.29
31	964.48	449	111.91
		450	1 092.09
		451	309.87
		452	733.24
		453	119.95
		454	20.02
		455	223.86
		456	88.00
		457 (void)	77.02
		458	120.19
		459	1 922.00

(b) Prepare journal entries for the reconciliation.

Focussing

1. Journal Entries Omitted

Fatuma Awada diligently prepares a bank reconciliation statement for the month of November. However, she forgets to prepare the necessary journal entries resulting from the reconciliation. Entries were required to show:
 (i) bank charges of $86
 (ii) an NSF cheque for $278 from Doug Yee
 (iii) a loan payment of $350
State the effect that the missing journal entries will have on
 (a) the income statement
 (b) the balance sheet

2. Designing a System

Draw a procedure diagram to show the flow of information through the business for a system that has the following characteristics:
 (a) one cash register, operated by one person;
 (b) cash on account is accepted at the cash register, where cash receipts are given;
 (c) refunds, both cash and on account, are made by the one cashier;
 (d) a treasurer receives cash for deposit;
 (e) an accountant keeps the books.

Evaluate and Assess

The owner of Wilma's Gym sells memberships and also accepts cash customers. Wilma issues receipts to those who buy memberships, because she knows that in an audit the receipts would be checked against the membership cards which she has to issue. However, for cash customers, Wilma regularly does not issue a receipt for the day and she pockets the cash. Wilma says that it is her business and that she can do as she likes.
 (a) What law(s) has Wilma violated?
 (b) Wilma states that half of the money would just go to the "income tax department." State ten benefits that she, and others, receive from her payment of income tax.
 (c) As Wilma's accountant, and being aware of her methods, what options do you have? Indicate which one you would follow and why.

Synthesize and Conclude

Sangeeta and Diane work at a movie theatre. Sangeeta sells the tickets, and Diane is the ticket taker. They decide that, because they think their employer does not pay them enough, they will take some of the cash. They decide that Diane will not give some of the ticket stubs to the movie goers, but instead return them to Sangeeta. She will sell them again, and pocket the money. Each night she and Diane split the money on their way home.

(a) Brainstorm to develop procedures that could be implemented to prevent this fraud.

(b) Prepare a procedure diagram that would illustrate your flow of cash and documents.

(c) Prepare policies which will accompany the procedure diagram. Organize your policies under two headings: Ticket Seller and Ticket Taker.

ACCOUNTING AT WORK

Murray Sutherland
Bank Manager

Murray Sutherland is a Branch and Area Manager with the Bank of Montreal in Edmonton. For Murray, much of the satisfaction he derives from his job comes from helping his depositors realize their goals. From buying a car to assisting with a mortgage or helping to expand a business, Murray enjoys the challenge of working within the banking system to help his clients.

Murray is responsible for managing all aspects of his branch. He is also responsible for five other branches in his community, which employ over 70 people. Meeting clients' individual demands is an important objective for Murray. He believes a well-trained staff is more easily motivated, better able to meet those demands, and able to provide a higher level of customer service.

After graduating from high school, Murray obtained a B.Comm and eventually received his Chartered Accountant (CA) designation and became a Fellow of the Institute of Canadian Bankers. Murray feels that his strong background in accounting and finance gives him an advantage over his contemporaries. In order to be fully aware of how various deposits and loans operate, Murray believes that a strong financial background is essential. "By understanding financial statements, you are better equipped to discuss a customer's loan request while also protecting the bank's (interests) on an existing loan." The banking environment has also been a source of education for Murray. He began his banking career in Commercial Accounts, where he handled small business and small commercial depositors. From there he moved into Real Estate Lending, then into Commercial Account Management, and eventually into his present position as Branch and Area Manager. In each position, the bank always provided training that enhanced his formal education. As a result, Murray gained knowledge in other areas of business, such as marketing, law, and international trade.

The greatest challenge Murray faces is being able to recognize whether a deal will be mutually beneficial to both a commercial customer and the bank. The banking industry must compete with other large Canadian banks, trust companies, credit unions, and a variety of other financial institutions. Murray must often convince his customers to rethink their goals while maintaining their loyalty. Murray explains that, "Sometimes, for reasons of risk, . . . you are unable to help your . . . customer. Having to decline your customers and leave them feeling positive about the bank is a difficult task."

Management Trainees

International Banking

A leading financial institution seeks exceptional candidates to assume entry-level training positions within its International Banking Division.

The positions are initially Montreal based but following training, successful candidates may be required to serve in less developed countries and to relocate regularly in order to acquire the range of experience that makes them suitable for career advancement.

The successful candidate will be a confident, self-motivated, bright, energetic individual with superior oral and written communication skills and a highly developed sense of responsibility. You will hold a university degree in business and you will be numerate and fluent in *at least* one other language. On your résumé indicate what skills, experience, or events in your life suggest that you are an out of the ordinary candidate.

A competitive entry-level remuneration and benefits package is offered. Please forward your application by February 22 to:

**Box 212
Station C Montreal**

---

1. Outline Murray Sutherland's career path until he became an area manager with the Bank of Montreal.

2. What education did Murray have in order to obtain his position?

3. What is the greatest challenge that Murray faces?

4. What is an "entry-level training position" as described by the advertisement?

5. What skills are necessary to be a successful candidate as a management trainee?

Business Career Skills

1. Policy Development
Prepare policies that will overcome the following problem situations, by
(a) brainstorming in groups to develop a list of possible policies
(b) selecting one policy for each problem. List the advantages and disadvantages of the policy.
  (i) The petty cashier is currently numbering the petty cash vouchers. It is suspected that he has at times destroyed the original voucher and completed a new voucher with an inflated amount, taking the difference for himself.
  (ii) The petty cashier has stolen receipts that he has already presented to the treasurer for reimbursement. He has then reused the receipts, keeping the money for himself. He has merely been changing the year on them.
  (iii) The petty cashier accepts phony receipts from a friend. They split the money between them.

2. Value Judgement
Bill, the petty cashier, and Sandi, the treasurer, work for a small firm that installs furnaces. Bill returns with a receipt from a small personal purchase that he has made, and submits it, along with the other receipts and petty cash vouchers, to Sandi for reimbursement. He tells Sandi that the purchase was for personal use, and she says that she will reimburse him anyway. Bill then realizes how easy it would be to continue to make these small purchases, as long as Sandi will agree to pay him for them. He suggests to her that he will give her half of the profit if she reimburses him for these personal purchases.
(a) Who is more dishonest, Sandi or Bill? Why?
(b) How will the fraud be found, if at all?

3. Problem Solving
Using a problem-solving method, prepare a company policy for cash short or over. The policy is to specify
(a) who will be responsible for cash short;
(b) who will receive the benefit of cash over. Assume that the business has twenty cash stations, with a pair of clerks working at each station, but using the same cash register. Each sales station takes in an average of $1 100 in cash sales and $2 000 in sales on account daily.

COMPUTER ACCOUNTING
INTERNAL CONTROL — A CONCERN OF ALL COMPANIES

The integrity and efficiency of a company's information system rely upon effective internal control. Controls can be classified either as administrative in nature, relating to management's authorization of transactions for the purpose of achieving a company's objectives, or as accounting in nature, primarily concerned with safeguarding assets and reasonably assuring the reliability of financial records.

The general control features that should be incorporated into any accounting system include the following: limiting access to assets; separating duties; utilizing accountability procedures such as duty authorization, prenumbering source documents, and verifying records; hiring qualified personnel; and subjecting controls to an independent review. In all cases, a business must evaluate the benefits of an internal control relative to the cost of implementing the particular control as the basis for designing and installing its internal control system.

The **audit trail** is an important element of control, particularly in providing the independent **auditor** with a means of verifying the legitimacy of recorded transactions and the absence of unrecorded transactions. The audit trail takes many forms depending on the type of processing system utilized by a company. Such systems range from a cardboard box holding original documents to a computerized real-time database that instantaneously updates inventory and permits the offering of such services as advance seating reservations on an airline.

The computerization of accounting systems is becoming more common as the costs of computers decline and, thus, the availability of microcomputers increases, and the quantity of transactions being processed grows. The advantages deriving from the use of computers include the reduction of data processing costs, the availability of better information for management control, and access to quick responses to system queries. However, such advantages come at the cost of increased exposure to **computer fraud**. Such exposure is particularly acute in the absence of adequate controls over computer programming and computer access, and in the presence of only limited computer expertise within a business, particularly in its internal audit department.

Exercises

1. Use your spreadsheet program and the model in Figure 12-25 to prepare a bank reconciliation template. Remember to enter the appropriate formulas.

   Starlook Company received a bank statement on June 30 that reported a bank balance of $46 000. With the statement were included: cheques numbered 201 to 305 and 308, deposits made weekly through June 24, a debit memo reporting an NSF cheque from Mr. Noonen (deposited on June 8), a credit memo for $1 700 collection of a promissory note and interest (the interest portion was $300), and a debit memo for bank service charges of $40.

According to the company's records, cheques numbered 201 through 310 have been written, deposits were made weekly, including one on June 30 for $7 600, and the cheque received from Mr. Noonen was in the amount of $430. Detailed information follows:

Cheques	Amount
#201 through #305	$185 000
#306	3 000
#307	1 000
#308	860
#309	2 400
#310	300

The cash account in the general ledger and the current chequebook stub both show a balance of $45 670.

Prepare a bank reconciliation for Starlook Company based on this information.

FIGURE 12-25

```
                        BANK RECONCILIATION
Date:
Bank Balance as per statement                              $
Add deposits in transit                   $
                                          $
                                          $
Total deposits in transit                                  $
                                                           $

Subtract outstanding cheques
      #         $              #         $
      #         $              #         $
      #         $              #         $
      #         $              #         $
      #         $              #         $
Total outstanding cheques                                  $
Adjusted Bank Statement Balance                            $

Cash balance as per accounting records                     $
Add credit memos
                  $
                  $
                  $
                                                           $
                                                           $

Subtract debit memos and NSF cheques
                  $
                  $
                  $
                  $
                                                           $
Adjusted Cash Account Balance                              $
```

2. You have been hired as an accounting clerk for the Triple-O Company to start work on November 1. On your first day on the job you have discovered that the owner, Sam Weeks, has kept records of a sort and is concerned about the number of overdue accounts and the subsequent cash flow problem that this has created. You have suggested that an Aged List of Receivables be prepared as of October 31 so that he can make decisions regarding the collection of overdue accounts and the determination of the bad debt accounts. Terms of all the credit sales were net 30 days. Use the following list and your spreadsheet program to design a schedule that will age the accounts receivable.

Name	Date	$ Sales	Paid	Date	Paid	Date	Paid In Full
Able & Co.	May 15	1 000	500	June 3	500	July 7	
Smith Bros.	May 16	750	700	Aug. 12			
ABC Co Ltd.	May 30	800	300	July 30	300	Sept. 30	
Black & White	June 4	200					
Jones Bros.	June 15	600	300	Aug. 26			
Triple A Co.	June 28	1 000	600	Sept. 2	400	Oct. 28	
Alpha Products	July 8	400					
Jones Bros.	July 17	400	400	July 26			
Ess-Jay	July 24	950					
Alpha Products	Aug. 6	1 400	800	Sept. 6			
Jones Bros.	Aug. 16	200					
Scott & Son	Aug. 27	300	200	Sept. 27			
Ess-Jay Ltd.	Sept. 2	1 250	700	Sept. 3			
Alpha Products	Sept. 12	400					
White & Co.	Sept. 21	100					
Scott & Son	Oct. 2	300					
White & Co.	Oct. 14	450					
XYZ Co. Ltd.	Oct. 29	550					
ABC Co. Ltd.	Oct. 30	250					

CHAPTER THIRTEEN

Payroll Accounting

LEARNING OBJECTIVES

At the end of this chapter you should be able to
- calculate payroll deductions, using formulas and tables;
- complete a payroll register;
- complete journal entries required to record a payroll register;
- complete journal entries required to record payment of payroll liabilities;
- set up and access accounting data files for a merchandising firm;
- enter transactions into the computer using the general ledger, accounts receivable, accounts payable, and payroll modules of an accounting software package;
- display and print accounting transactions and reports.

LANGUAGE OF ACCOUNTING

You will see the following terms in this chapter:
at source
benefits
collective agreement
employer's cost of payroll
indexed
net claim code
payroll system
payroll taxes
portable
taxable benefit
workers' compensation

13.1 Calculating Gross Pay

The design of the payroll accounting system for Algor Computer Services took a number of factors into consideration. First, it was recognized that the procedure would be repetitive: the employees would be paid each week. As well, much of the data required from one pay period to the next would be the same, for most of the employees would be working the full week, with only a few entitled to work overtime. Second, it was recognized that the provincial and federal governments had passed legislation that influenced the payroll calculation. The payroll clerk therefore had to be very familiar with the legislation and keep up-to-date on it, because it changed on a yearly basis. Finally, a number of documents had to be prepared during the year and at year end. The system would have to be designed so that the data to be inserted in them was readily available. After some time had passed, the firm had to negotiate a contract with its employees who had joined a union. The payroll clerk had to become familiar with the terms of the contract because they too affect the payroll calculation.

The largest expense for many businesses is labour expense, because of the number of employees needed to operate these businesses. Small businesses, such as Algor Computer Services, have only a few employees. Other businesses are labour intensive, which means that labour expenses are a significant part of their total expenses. The school board that employs your teachers runs a labour-intensive operation, for its largest expense is probably wages and salaries. Most service businesses are labour intensive. Merchandising and manufacturing businesses are not as labour intensive, especially in the modern era of computerization and robots. However, labour costs for these businesses are usually a significant percentage of total expenses.

> "The payroll is a listing of the employees and a calculation of the pay due to them for a pay period."

> "The pay period indicates how often the employees are paid."

The payroll is a listing of the employees and a calculation of the pay due to them for a pay period. The pay period indicates how often the employees are paid: usually it is weekly, biweekly (every two weeks), semi-monthly (twice monthly), or monthly. The process of completing the payroll includes a variety of tasks that form the payroll cycle described in Figure 13-1. Some steps in the cycle are performed each pay period, and others are done on a yearly basis.

FIGURE 13-1

PAYROLL CYCLE

TASK	RESPONSIBILITY
Each Pay Period	
1. Complete Payroll Register: — wages calculated from time cards — salaries entered from salary sheets — deductions entered from tables and policies	Payroll Department
2. Total and prove Payroll Register — prepare cheque requisitions	Payroll Department
3. Issue Paycheques/Direct Transfers	Treasurer
4. Either (a) post from Payroll Register directly to General Ledger *or* (b) prepare General Journal entries from Payroll Register and post to General Ledger	Accounting Department
5. Journalize employer's payroll liabilities	Accounting Department
6. Journalize payment of employees from cheque stubs	Accounting Department
As Required by Law	
7. Pay payroll liabilities Data from cheque requisitions prepared by Payroll	Treasurer
8. Journalize payment of employer's share of payroll liabilities	Accounting Department
By February 28 of following year	
9. Issue T4 slips (Statement of Remuneration Paid) to show earnings and deductions for the year	Payroll Department

As the cycle indicates, the calculation of an employee's pay is an extensive process. The system used to record payroll depends upon the number of employees, the frequency of the pay period, and the cost of the system. Small businesses can do the payroll by hand, while larger businesses will use computer systems, or have a financial institution or another business specializing in payroll do it for them. In some businesses, the task is so large that a separate department, the payroll division, is formed. For obvious reasons, it will have close ties to the accounting department, or even be a branch of it.

Businesses are required by both the provincial and federal governments to maintain records of all hiring, paying, retiring, and firing of employees. These records must be kept for a minimum of six years, after which permission must be obtained to destroy them. The data is necessary for the governments to know the amounts that are owed to them for income tax, and for them to regulate the various insurances and pensions under their control. Some federal acts apply to all employees, and they are:

    Income Tax Act
    Canada Pension Plan Act
    Unemployment Insurance Act

Provincial legislation that applies to all employees includes:

    Workers' Compensation laws
    Hospital Insurance Plan laws

> *The* Constitution Act *(1867) indicates which level of government has jurisdiction over an occupation.*

Other laws that govern an employer and employee may be found in federal or provincial Acts, depending upon the type of job involved. The *Constitution Act* (1867) indicates which level of government is responsible for which type of job. A business in an occupation that falls under federal control would look to the Canada Labour Code for information on matters such as hiring, hours of work, holidays, and firing. A business in an occupation that falls under provincial control would look to the province's Act governing employment standards.

> *A collective agreement is an agreement between a union, representing its members, and an employer.*

The payroll division must not only be aware of government legislation that affects the employee payroll, but also the terms of the contract that the employer has entered into with the employees. The contracts may be individual contracts for each employee, or collective agreements (contracts) for groups of or all of the employees. These latter contracts would have been negotiated between the union, representing its members, and the employer. The terms of the contract may provide pay and benefits for the employees in excess of those specified in the various acts.

Hiring An Employee

When an employee is hired, the personnel department informs the payroll division of the job to be performed by the new employee and the gross pay level. The gross pay is the amount of pay an employee is entitled to before various deductions.

Gross pay = Regular pay + Overtime pay

In order to determine the amount of gross pay, the payroll division must know the basis on which the pay is to be determined. There are basically four methods of calculating gross pay: salary, wages, commissions, and piece work.

> **Salary:** *a fixed sum of money paid to a person for working a specified length of time or for completing a specific job.*

Salary   A **salary** is a fixed sum of money to be paid to a person for working a specified length of time, such as a year, or for completing a specified job. The hours that a person works each day may be specified, but it is more common that the person has to work hours sufficient to complete the job. Your teacher earns a salary, which means that the pay period is for the school year. Although the number of hours that the teacher must be in school are specified by law, much longer hours are usually required to complete the job. It is assumed that these extra hours are included in the salary. Some businesses pay salaried employees a bonus if the extra hours become excessive.

A salaried person usually is allowed to stay home for a specified number of sick days without losing any pay. A clerk in each department is usually assigned the task of recording days absent for the salaried employees and forwarding this information to payroll before the end of each pay period. In recent years, considerable attention has been directed at ways of reducing the amount of employee absenteeism, for it is an added cost to the business. The employee is still paid when on sick leave, and either a replacement has to be paid or there is a loss in productivity. As well, if a salaried employee is released without cause before the term of the job contract is up, such as a coach of a sports team, the complete salary is usually still payable.

In order to calculate the gross pay for each pay period, the salary is divided by the number of pay periods in the term of the contract. Thus, for a person with a $60 000 salary who is paid weekly, the calculation is as follows:

$$\text{Gross pay per pay period} = \frac{\text{Salary}}{\text{Number of pay periods}}$$
$$= \frac{\$60\ 000.00}{52}$$
$$= \$1\ 153.85 \text{ per week}$$

> *"Wage employees are paid based on the number of hours, days, or weeks worked."*

Wages   Employees who are wage earners are paid a gross pay based on the number of hours, days, or weeks worked. To maintain a record of the hours, a time card is frequently used. A time card may be completed manually by a supervisor, or by the employee using a time clock. The time card in Figure 13-2 is for Mike Bergin, who earns $16.50 an hour and is paid weekly. Each day Mike must "punch in" and "punch out,"

FIGURE 13-2 TIME CARD FOR MIKE BERGIN

TIME CARD

NAME: _Mike Bergin_

WEEK ENDED: _May 11_   EMPLOYEE NO.: _410_

DAY	MORNING		AFTERNOON		EXTRA		TOTAL HOURS
	IN	OUT	IN	OUT	IN	OUT	
M	8:30	12:04	1:00	5:33	7:00	9:03	
T	8:24	12:03	12:54	5:38	7:00	9:31	
W	8:39	12:01	12:56	5:30			
T	8:26	12:04	12:59	5:32			
F	8:27	12:02	12:55	5:30			

TOTAL

	HOURS	RATE	EARNINGS
REGULAR TIME		$16 50	
OVERTIME		$24 75	
		GROSS PAY	

which means that he puts his time card into the time clock when he arrives and when he leaves. The clock punches the time on his card.

At the end of the week, Mike totals the number of hours worked and gives it to a payroll clerk who checks Mike's calculations. To calculate the gross pay, the total number of hours worked is calculated from the time card using the following procedure. (This procedure is to be used for calculations throughout this text.)

- The regular hours and overtime hours must be calculated separately, because the pay rates are different. Times are rounded off to the nearest *following* quarter-hour for "in" times. Thus, if an employee enters any time from 8:16 to 8:29, the time entered would be considered as 8:30 for pay purposes. Times are rounded off to the nearest *previous* quarter-hour for "out" times. Thus, if an employee leaves at any time from 4:31 to 4:44, the time entered would be considered as 4:30 for pay purposes.
- A regular work week consists of a five-day week, eight hours per day, for a total of 40 hours per week. Overtime consists of any work over 40 hours.
- Lateness is calculated as follows:
  — one quarter of an hour is deducted for lateness of one to 15 minutes (starting time is 8:30)

— thirty minutes is deducted for lateness of 16 to 30 minutes, etc.

- Overtime is applied at one and a half times the regular rate. Mike's gross pay is calculated as follows on his time card shown in Figure 13-3:

$$\text{Gross pay} = (\text{Regular hours} \times \text{Regular rate}) + (\text{Overtime hours} \times \text{Overtime rate})$$

Gross pay = Regular pay + Overtime pay

FIGURE 13-3 MIKE BERGIN'S COMPLETED TIME CARD

TIME CARD

NAME: Mike Bergin

WEEK ENDED: May 11   EMPLOYEE NO.: 410

DAY	MORNING IN	MORNING OUT	AFTERNOON IN	AFTERNOON OUT	EXTRA IN	EXTRA OUT	TOTAL HOURS
M	8:30	12:04	1:00	5:33	7:00	9:03	10
T	8:24	12:03	12:54	5:38	7:00	9:31	10.5
W	8:39	12:01	12:56	5:30			7.75
T	8:26	12:04	12:59	5:32			8
F	8:27	12:02	12:55	5:30			8
						TOTAL	44.25

	HOURS	RATE	EARNINGS
REGULAR TIME	40	$16.50	$660.—
OVERTIME	4.25	$24.75	$105.19
		GROSS PAY	$765.19

Commissions A person earns a commission based on sales made. In many cases, pay is a combination of a salary or wages and a commission because of the possibility that there may be slow sales periods. A salesperson who earns a biweekly salary of $700 plus 5 percent of sales made would have the following gross pay for sales of $24 000 during the period:

"*Commissions are based on sales made.*"

$$\begin{aligned}\text{Gross pay} &= \text{Salary} + 5\% \text{ of sales} \\ &= \$700 + (0.05 \times \$24\,000) \\ &= \$700 + \$1\,200 \\ &= \$1\,900\end{aligned}$$

"*Piece work means that the employee's pay is based on the number of items produced.*"

Piece Work Piece work means that the employee's pay is based on the number of items produced. The piece work method is frequently used to determine pay levels for persons who make crafts at home, or for those who work in the garment industry. At the end of the pay period, the gross pay is calculated by multiplying the number of items produced by the rate per item. For a person knitting 30 sweaters, with a pay rate of $40 per sweater, the calculation would be as follows:

$$\begin{aligned}\text{Gross pay} &= \text{Number produced} \times \text{Rate per item} \\ &= 30 \times \$40 \\ &= \$1\,200\end{aligned}$$

Social Insurance Number (SIN)

"A Social Insurance Number (SIN) is required by all employees."

It is necessary that the payroll division obtain two pieces of information from the employee when he or she is hired: a social insurance number and a Personal Tax Credit Return (commonly known as a TD1), which is a form showing deductions to which the employee is entitled when determining the amount of income tax payable.

The social insurance number system is maintained by the federal government. It is necessary for a person to have a social insurance number for the following reasons:

(1) to complete a TD1 when hired, because the employer should not pay an employee who does not have a SIN;

(2) to complete a personal income tax return each year;

(3) to receive unemployment insurance benefits;

(4) to make contributions to and receive benefits from the Canada Pension Plan.

A social insurance number can be obtained by applying at a Canada Employment Centre. The number will be the same for a person's entire lifetime, because it identifies that person to the government. In fact, it is illegal to have more than one social insurance number.

Personal Tax Credit Return (TD1)

"A TD1 form is completed by an employee in order that the income tax deduction can be calculated."

All income earners above a certain dollar amount are required to pay income tax to the provincial and federal governments. There is an amount deducted from each pay, so that the amount owing is spread over the year. In order for the employer to know how much income tax to deduct from an employee's pay, the person's income for the year and various other pieces of data must be known. The employee provides this data to the employer by completing a Personal Tax Credit Return (TD1) form.

A TD1 form for 1990 is shown in Figure 13-4. The top part of the form identifies the employee, giving name, address, employee number, SIN, and date of birth — in this case for Mike Bergin, an employee at Algor Computer Services. It also indicates which workers must complete the form. The balance of the form is used to calculate a Net Claim

FIGURE 13-4
A TD1 FORM

1990 PERSONAL TAX CREDIT RETURN

Revenue Canada Taxation / Revenu Canada Impôt

page 1.
TD1 (E) Rev. 1990

FAMILY NAME (Please Print): BERGIN
ADDRESS: 276 Glenhome Drive, Ottawa
Postal Code: K2G 4R6
USUAL FIRST NAME AND INITIALS: MIKE R.
For NON-RESIDENTS ONLY — Country of Permanent Residence:
EMPLOYEE NUMBER: 410
SOCIAL INSURANCE NUMBER: 999 999 999
DATE OF BIRTH: Day 27 / Month 08 / Year 43

Instructions

- Please fill out this form so your employer or payer will know how much tax to deduct regularly from your pay. Regular deductions will help you avoid having to pay when you file your income tax return.
- **You must complete this form if you receive**
  - salary, wages, commissions or any other remuneration;
  - superannuation or pension benefits including an annuity payment made under a superannuation or pension fund or plan;
  - Unemployment Insurance benefits including training allowances.
- You may also complete this form if you receive annuity payments under registered retirement income funds and registered retirement savings plans.
- Give the completed form to your employer or payer. Otherwise, you will be allowed **only** the basic personal amount of $6,169.
- All amounts on this form should be rounded to the nearest dollar.
- **Need Help?** If you need help to complete this form, you may ask your employer or payer, or call the Source Deductions Section of your local Revenue Canada district taxation office. Before you do this, please refer to the additional information on page 2 under "Notes to Employees and Payees."

1. **Are you a non-resident of Canada?** (see note 1 on page 2). If so, and **less than** 90 per cent of your 1990 total world income will be included when calculating taxable income earned in Canada, enter 0 in the box on line 17 and sign the form. If you are a resident of Canada, go to item 2.

2. **Basic personal amount.** (everyone may claim $6,169) .... $6,169 .... 2.

3. (a) **Are you married and supporting your spouse?** (see notes 4 and 5 on page 2)
   or
   (b) **Are you single, divorced, separated or widowed and supporting a relative who lives with you** who is either your parent or grandparent, OR who is under 19 at the end of 1990, OR 19 or older and infirm? (see notes 2, 3 and 4 on page 2)
   Note: A spouse or dependant claimed here cannot be claimed again on lines 4 or 5.
   If you answered yes to either (a) or (b) and your spouse's or dependant's 1990 net income will be
   - under $514, CLAIM $5,141
   - between $514 and $5,655, CLAIM (e)
   - over $5,655, CLAIM $0

   Minus: spouse or dependant's net income $5,655 (c)
   ___ (d)
   Claim (c minus d) ___ (e) ..... 3.

4. **Do you have any dependants who will be under 19 at the end of 1990?** (see notes 2 and 4 on page 2). If so, and your 1990 net income will be **higher** than your spouse's, calculate the amount to claim for **each** dependant. If you are not married, please refer to notes 2, 3 and 4 on page 2.
   Note: If you have three or more dependants who will be under 19 years old at the end of the year, you do not have to claim them in the order they were born. You may claim them in the **most beneficial** order. For example, a dependant who is 16 years old with a net income of $3,500 could be claimed as the first dependant (claim 0) while the other two, with no income, could be claimed as second and third dependants.

   First and second dependant:
   If your dependant's 1990 net income will be
   - under $2,570, CLAIM $399
   - between $2,570 and $2,969, CLAIM (e)
   - over $2,969, CLAIM $0

   Minus: $2,969 (c)
   dependant's net income 2,700 (d)
   Claim (c minus d) 269 (e)

   dependants
   1st 269
   2nd 399

   Third and each additional dependant:
   If your dependant's 1990 net income will be
   - under $2,570, CLAIM $798
   - between $2,570 and $3,368, CLAIM (e)
   - over $3,368, CLAIM $0

   Minus: $3,368 (c)
   dependant's net income ___ (d)
   Claim (c minus d) ___ (e)

   3rd ___
   4th ___
   5th ___

   Total 668 ▶ 668 .... 4.

5. **Do you have any infirm dependants who will be 19 or older at the end of 1990?** (see notes 2 and 4 on page 2). If so, and your dependant's net income will be
   - under $2,570, CLAIM $1,512
   - between $2,570 and $4,082, CLAIM (e)
   - over $4,082, CLAIM $0

   Minus: $4,082 (c)
   dependant's net income ___ (d)
   Claim (c minus d) ___ (e)

   dependants
   1st ___
   2nd ___
   3rd ___
   Total ___ ▶ ___ .... 5.

6. **Do you receive eligible pension income?** (see note 6 on page 2). If so, claim your pension income amount or $1,000, whichever is less. .... ▶ ___ .... 6.

7. **Will you be 65 or older at the end of 1990?** If so, claim $3,327. .... ▶ ___ .... 7.

8. **Are you disabled?** (see note 7 on page 2). If so, claim $3,327. .... ▶ ___ .... 8.

9. **Are you a student?** If so, claim
   - tuition fees paid for courses you take in 1990 to attend either a university, college or a certified educational institution. If you receive any scholarships, fellowships or bursaries in 1990, subtract the amount over $500 from your tuition fees before you claim them.
   - $60 for each month in 1990 that you will be in **full-time attendance** in a qualifying program, at either a university, college or a school offering job re-training courses.

   Total ___ ▶ ___ .... 9.

10. Total (add lines 2 to 9 — please enter this amount on line 11 on page 2) .... 6837 .... 10.
    (See reverse)

11.	Total (from line 10 on page 1)	6837
12.	Are you claiming any transfers of unused pension income, age, disability, tuition fees and education amounts from your spouse and/or dependants? (see note 10 below) • If your **spouse receives eligible pension income**, you may claim any unused balance to a maximum of $1,000 (see note 6 below). • If your **spouse will be 65 or older** in 1990, you may claim any unused balance to a maximum of $3,327. • If your **spouse and/or dependants are disabled**, you may claim any unused balance to a maximum of $3,327 for each (see note 7 below). • If you are supporting a **spouse and/or dependants who are attending either a university, college or a certified educational institution**, you may be entitled to claim the unused balance to a maximum of $3,529 for each (see item 9 on page 1). Total	
13.	**Total Claim Amount** - Add lines 11 and 12.	6837
14.	Will you or your spouse receive family allowance (baby bonus) payments in 1990? If so, and your 1990 net income will be **higher** than your spouse's, enter the amount of family allowance payments you will receive in 1990. If you are not married, see note 3 below.	799.92
15.	**NET CLAIM AMOUNT** - Line 13 minus line 14.	6037.08
16.	Is your estimated total income for 1990 (excluding family allowance payments) less than your net claim amount on line 15? If so, enter E in the box on line 17 and tax will **not** be deducted from your pay. Otherwise, go to line 17.	
17.	**NET CLAIM CODE** - Match your net claim amount from line 15 with the net claim code table below to determine your net claim code, and enter this code in the box. If you already have a code in the box, go to line 18.	1
18.	Do you want to increase the amount of tax to be deducted from your salary or from other amounts paid to you such as pensions, commissions etc.? (see note 8 below). If so, state the amount of additional tax you wish to have deducted from each payment. The amount must be a multiple of $5, for example, 5, 10, 15, 20 etc.	
19.	Will you live in the Yukon, Northwest Territories or another prescribed area for more than six months in a row beginning or ending in 1990? If so, claim $225 for each 30-day period that you live in a prescribed area, **or** if you maintain a "self-contained domestic establishment" in a prescribed area and you are the only person within that establishment claiming this deduction, claim $450 for each 30-day period. You **cannot** claim more than 20 per cent of your net income for 1990 (see note 9 below).	

I HEREBY CERTIFY that the information given in this return is correct and complete.

Signature *Mike Bergin*   Date *Jan 2, 1990*

Complete a new return within seven days of any change in your claim. It is an offence to make a false return.

An exemption:
a deduction from income for living costs, and the amounts spent supporting dependent relatives.

Code. This code is used by the employer to determine the amount that should be deducted each pay period for income tax purposes. In order to determine the code number, the Net Claim Amount must be calculated. The higher the net claim amount, the less income tax that has to be paid. The net claim amount is the total of Mike's exemptions minus the family allowance payments received. An **exemption** is a deduction from income to help cover personal costs as well as costs incurred in supporting dependent relatives. Note the following points that Mike considered in filling out his TD1 form:

(1) Resident vs non-resident in Canada. For tax purposes, the broad definition of a non-resident is someone who does not reside in Canada for at least 183 days a year and does not have an occupational exemption such as being an ambassador at a foreign embassy or being a member of the armed forces. Other tests are applied by Revenue Canada to establish residency vs non-residency.

(2) Personal exemption — for the employee; Mike Bergin claims $6 169.

(3) Married exemption — for the spouse of the employee; the amount of the deduction is based on the amount that the spouse earns; Mike claims nothing, as his wife is employed and earns over $5 655.

Equivalent to married exemption — a person who is single, divorced, separated, or a widow(er) is entitled to claim one dependant as being equivalent to a spouse; Mike claims nothing because he is married.

(4) Wholly dependant children — Mike claims $668; he claims $269 for his 18-year-old son Gerald and $399 for his 14-year-old daughter Cynthia. The amount for Gerald is based on his earning $2 700. The following calculation is therefore made:

Basic exemption	$2 969
Minus:	
Child's net income	2 700
Claim	$ 269

There is a higher claim available if the claimant has more than two dependant children.

(5) Infirm dependant — a child or other relative, 19 years of age or older, who is infirm and financially dependent on the taxpayer. Mike makes no claim.

(6) Pension income — a person who receives any amount from a pension fund is entitled to a deduction up to $1 000. Mike does not receive a pension so he cannot claim this amount.

(7) Age exemption — if over 65 a claim of $3 327 is made. Mike is under 65 so he cannot claim this amount.

(8) Disability exemption — a person who is severely mentally or physically impaired and has a Disability Credit Certificate from his/her doctor claims $3 327. Mike cannot claim this amount.

(9) Student exemption — for students at a university or college or an institution offering job retraining courses. The student may claim the tuition fees less any scholarship, fellowship or bursary in excess of $500. Also $60 may be claimed for each month that the student is in full-time attendance. Mike claims nothing.

The exemptions are totalled, and from this figure the taxable family allowance payments are deducted to give the net claim amount, as on page 2 of Figure 13-4. The family allowance for the family must be included on Mike's form, because he is going to claim the children as exemptions when he files his income tax. He does this because his income is higher than his wife's income.

$$\begin{aligned}\text{Net claim amount} &= \text{Total claim amount} \\ &\quad - \text{Family allowance payments} \\ &= \$6\,837 - 799.92 \\ &= \$6\,037 \text{ (rounded to the nearest dollar)}\end{aligned}$$

The $6 037 figure is compared to the Net Claim Codes shown in Figure 13-5, which indicates that Mike has a claim code of 1. Mike enters a 1 on line 17 of the form as his net claim code. If Mike's claim was over $19 773, a manual formula provided by Revenue Canada Taxation would be used and an X would be indicated. If the annual income is less than the net claim amount, an E would be entered.

FIGURE 13-5 NET CLAIM CODES

1990 NET CLAIM CODES	
net claim amount over–not over	claim code
NO claim amount	0
$ 0– 6,169	1
6,169– 7,680	2
7,680– 9,192	3
9,192–10,704	4
10,704–12,215	5
12,215–13,726	6
13,726–15,238	7
15,238–16,749	8
16,749–18,260	9
18,260–19,773	10
19,773 and over	X
NO tax withholding required	E

This code will be used by the employer to find the amount of taxes to deduct from Mike's pay. The procedure for finding this amount is outlined later in this chapter. It should be noted that the amounts for the net claim codes, and for the family allowance, change each year due to inflation or at the will of the federal government. It is not necessary, however, to fill in a new TD1 form each year since your net claim code will not change unless your family circumstances change. In that case it is advisable to review your Personal Tax Credit Return.

LESSON REVIEW

1. What factors must be considered when designing a payroll system?
2. What is a payroll? What is a pay period?
3. (a) State the federal Acts that apply to payroll.
   (b) State the provincial Acts that apply to payroll.
4. Why does the payroll division have to be aware of an employee's contract or the collective agreement?
5. What is the formula for calculating gross pay?
6. Prepare and complete the following chart:

Pay Calculation Method	Advantages	Disadvantages
Salary		
Wages		
Commission		
Piece Work		

7. What two pieces of information must an employer obtain after hiring an employee? Why is each needed?
8. What is a tax exemption?
9. For what types of dependants may a person claim an exemption?
10. What other exemptions are available to a taxpayer?
11. Why would a person claim all the exemptions to which he or she is entitled?

LESSON APPLICATIONS

12. Calculate the net claim amount and then the net claim code for each of the following employees using the TD1 form shown in Figure 13-4. Assume that each married person has an income higher than their spouse, and will therefore claim the children as an exemption. Assume that family allowance payments total $400 per year per child.

Winnie Garcia	Married, spouse's annual income will be nil.
Sophia Doja	Married, spouse's annual income will be $42 000; children 12 and 14 with annual income under $2 570.

Nick Chahal   Divorced, 53 years of age, receiving a pension income of $18 000 per year, and supporting his 20-year-old infirm son whose income will be $2 500. Nick is also taking a university course, with tuition fees of $320.

Winston Dunn   Retired, 67 years of age, receiving a pension income of $15 000 per year, supporting his spouse of the same age whose income will be $1 800.

Fera Newton   Married, spouse has an income of $29 000, child 15 with income of $2 500, child 17 with income of $2 600, and child 18 whose income will be $2 700.

Des Topshee   Single, attends university full-time for 9 months a year, tuition fees of $1 800.

13. Calculate the weekly gross pay for each of the following employees. Regular and overtime rules are as shown on pages 599–600.
    (a) Debbie Martin: salary of $37 000.
    (b) Jim Watters: salary of $48 000.
    (c) Vera Derocher: salary of $22 000, plus commission of 3 percent. Her sales this week were $21 000.
    (d) Denise Cousineau: salary of $16 000, plus commission of 5 percent. Her sales this week were $17 000.
    (e) Barry Bickerton: he is paid $14.20 per hour. His time card is as follows:

TIME CARD

NAME: Barry Bickerton

WEEK ENDED: March 28   EMPLOYEE NO.: 604

DAY	MORNING		AFTERNOON		EXTRA		TOTAL HOURS
	IN	OUT	IN	OUT	IN	OUT	
M	8:00	12:04	1:00	5:30	7:00	9:33	
T	8:34	12:03	12:59	5:38	7:00	9:31	
W	8:49	12:00	12:56	5:50			
T	8:26	12:04	12:39	5:32	7:00	9:30	
F	8:27	12:02	12:55	5:30			

		TOTAL	
	HOURS	RATE	EARNINGS
REGULAR TIME		$14 20	
OVERTIME		$21 30	
		GROSS PAY	

(f) Sue Snuggs: she is paid $18 per hour. Her time card is as follows:

TIME CARD

NAME: Sue Snuggs

WEEK ENDED: March 28   EMPLOYEE NO.: 612

DAY	MORNING		AFTERNOON		EXTRA		TOTAL
	IN	OUT	IN	OUT	IN	OUT	HOURS
M	8:00	12:03	1:00	5:05			
T	8:00	12:08	12:45	5:15			
W	7:58	12:03	12:58	5:30			
T	7:49	12:05	12:57	5:03			
F	8:00	12:15	12:55	5:15			
						TOTAL	

	HOURS	RATE	EARNINGS
REGULAR TIME		$18 00	
OVERTIME		$27 00	
		GROSS PAY	

14. Ron Negrych has been employed by a clothing store. Ron has a choice of
    (i) a weekly salary of $420;
    (ii) a weekly salary of $180 and a 3 percent commission on all sales;
    (iii) a commission of 5 percent on all sales.
    It is estimated that Ron should be able to make sales of $9 000 per week.
    (a) Calculate the weekly pay for each option, assuming that Ron does make sales of $9 000 per week.
    (b) Which pay option would you select if you were Ron?
    (c) What are the advantages to Ron of selecting each option?
    (d) What are the disadvantages to Ron of selecting each option?

15. For each of the following employees, indicate the gross pay that would be received under each of the payroll periods given. Barb earns $49 800 and Tom earns $38 000 per year.

	Weekly	Biweekly	Semi-monthly	Monthly
Barb Fulton				
Tom Tol				

16. Complete the chart using the rules given on pages 599–600.

Employee	Total Hours	Regular Hours	Overtime Hours	Regular Rate	Overtime Rate	Gross Pay
V. Bell	44			$10.00		
P. Cote	46			10.50		
C. Kemp	45			12.30		
T. Walt	44			13.40		

17. Using the time cards for Peter Fu and Art Johnson,
    (a) calculate the total regular and overtime hours (use the rules given on pages 599–600 to determine hours worked);
    (b) calculate the regular and overtime earnings;
    (c) calculate the gross pay.

TIME CARD

NAME: Peter Fu
WEEK ENDED: July 5   EMPLOYEE NO.: 345

DAY	MORNING IN	MORNING OUT	AFTERNOON IN	AFTERNOON OUT	EXTRA IN	EXTRA OUT	TOTAL HOURS
M	8:00	12:02	12:59	5:02			
T	7:55	12:01	1:00	5:05			
W	7:58	12:00	12:58	5:01	7:00	8:30	
T	8:00	12:05	12:59	5:02			
F	7:50	12:00	12:57	5:01			

	HOURS	RATE	EARNINGS
REGULAR TIME		$15.00	
OVERTIME		$22.50	
		GROSS PAY	

TIME CARD

NAME: Art Johnson
WEEK ENDED: July 5   EMPLOYEE NO.: 294

DAY	MORNING IN	MORNING OUT	AFTERNOON IN	AFTERNOON OUT	EXTRA IN	EXTRA OUT	TOTAL HOURS
M	7:59	12:01	1:00	5:02			
T	8:00	12:04	1:02	5:02			
W	7:56	12:00	1:00	5:00	7:00	9:30	
T	7:59	12:00	1:00	5:04	6:58	9:03	
F	8:03	12:01	12:57	5:00			

	HOURS	RATE	EARNINGS
REGULAR TIME		$16.50	
OVERTIME		$24.75	
		GROSS PAY	

18. Gino Giannandrea is employed to produce components for automobile stereo systems. He is paid by the piece, earning $2.20 for each component produced. Calculate Gino's gross pay for the week, given the following production totals.

	Mon.	Tues.	Wed.	Thurs.	Fri.
Components produced	64	71	78	72	68

13.2 Calculating Net Pay

Net pay, the amount that is actually given to the employee, is calculated using the following formula:

Net pay (or take-home pay) = Gross pay − Deductions

The deductions from an employee's pay are also known as **payroll deductions** or **payroll taxes**. For some employees the deductions are few, for others many. They include payments for unemployment insurance, Canada Pension Plan, income tax, and union dues. The purpose of some deductions is to provide the employee with insurance against risks, such as unemployment, hospitalization, or dental claims. The purpose of other deductions is to provide for retirement. In cases where the employer pays a share or all of the cost of a deduction, it is referred to as a **taxable benefit** or **allowance**.

Other deductions are made at the source so that each employee does not have to send in his or her own payment to an organization. Such deductions include donations and union dues. To deduct **at the source** means to deduct an amount from the gross pay before the employee receives it. The employer can then remit to the appropriate agency the amount deducted from all the employees. Instead of an insurance company receiving 3 000 individual cheques for premiums from the employees of a large business, it receives one cheque from the employer, who has deducted the required amount from the employees' cheques. The employee must pay income tax on the amount the employer remits as if it were income.

Deductions can be divided into three categories:

(1) compulsory deductions required by law, such as Canada Pension Plan, unemployment insurance, income tax, and possibly hospital insurance (depending on the province);

(2) compulsory deductions required by the employee's contract, such as dental, life, and medical insurance;

(3) voluntary deductions, such as United Way or Canada Savings Bonds.

The employer is required by law to contribute to the Canada Pension Plan and unemployment insurance on behalf of the employees. For other forms of insurance, the employer may agree to pay part of the cost.

Compulsory Deductions Required by Law

Federal legislation requires that three deductions be made from an employee's pay: Canada Pension Plan, Unemployment Insurance, and income tax. As well, some provinces require that deductions be made for the provincial hospital program.

Net pay (or take-home pay) = Gross pay − Deductions

Payroll deductions or **payroll taxes:** amounts deducted from gross pay.

Taxable benefits or **allowances:** items in addition to one's pay for which the employer pays all or a share of the cost.

At the source: the employee's share of the premium for the benefit is deducted from his or her pay.

Canada Pension Plan

The Canada Pension Plan (CPP) is a federal government initiative to provide pensions for those who have contributed to the plan during their working years. According to the *Canada Pension Plan Act*, a deduction must be made from the employee's pay for the CPP, and the employer must contribute an equal amount. Quebec operates its own pension plan for residents of that province, so they do not pay into CPP. The plans are "portable," which means that a person moving from one province to another province has the pension benefits transferred as well. The pension is also "indexed," which means that it increases each year in accordance with the cost of living.

Contributions generally must be made to CPP by all employees over 18 and under 70. There are a large number of exceptions, which are detailed in the *Act*. Contribution to the plan provides a full pension at age 65, or a reduced pension at age 60. A person may receive the pension and also be working at the age of 60.

Calculating the Canada Pension Plan Deduction

The amount to be deducted each pay period for CPP can be obtained by calculation or from tables provided by the federal government. As well, Revenue Canada provides computer users with a formula and tables which can be used on their systems.

(a) CPP calculation by formula

Canada Pension Plan is calculated as 2.2 percent of a person's gross earnings above a specified basic exemption until the maximum payable is reached. This maximum in 1990 was $574.20. The basic exemptions for some common pay periods are shown in Figure 13-6. Corresponding exemptions are available for other pay periods.

FIGURE 13-6 BASIC EXEMPTIONS FOR CPP IN 1990

Weekly	$ 53.84
Biweekly	107.69
Semi-monthly	116.66
Monthly	233.33

A person who earns less than the exempt amount pays no CPP, while a person who earns over the exempt amount pays 2.2 percent of the earnings until the maximum payable for the year is reached. The following chart illustrates the income amounts for which CPP would be payable for a person who is paid weekly:

Gross Earnings	CPP Paid
0 to $53.84	nil
Over $53.84	2.2 percent until $574.20 has been paid for the year

"*CPP = (Gross earnings − Basic exemption) × 2.2%*"

As noted in Figure 13-3, Mike Bergin earned $765.19 for the week ended May 11th while working at Algor Computer Services. He would therefore pay the following amount:

$$\begin{aligned} \text{CPP} &= (\text{Gross earnings} - \text{Basic exemption}) \times 2.2\% \\ &= (\$765.19 - \$53.84) \times 2.2\% \\ &= \$711.35 \times 0.022 \\ &= \$15.65 \end{aligned}$$

If Mike's number of hours worked remained constant, he would have $15.65 deducted each weekly pay period until the maximum payable for a year, $574.20, was reached. Subsequent pay periods in that year would have no deduction for Canada Pension Plan. New tables are provided to employers yearly, or whenever the rate changes.

"*Employer CPP costs = Employee CPP costs*"

The employer must contribute an amount equal to that deducted from the employees' pays. The employer must therefore remit to the government the amount deducted from the employees' pays plus the employer's contribution. The employer has acted as a tax collector for the government and as a funder of the employees' pension plan.

(b) CPP calculation by using the tables

CPP tables are provided in a booklet which also includes the unemployment insurance tables, and is called *Canada Pension Plan Contributions and Unemployment Insurance Premiums*. The booklet is available from your nearest district tax office.

The Canada Pension Plan tables are divided into sections according to the length of the pay period: weekly, biweekly, semi-monthly, and monthly. A small part of the tables for a person paid on a weekly basis is shown in Figure 13-7. Additional tables for use in doing application

FIGURE 13-7 CANADA PENSION PLAN CONTRIBUTIONS BY THE EMPLOYEE FOR REMUNERATION OF $746.34 TO $886.33

Remuneration / Rémunération		C.P.P. / R.P.C.
From-*de*	To-*à*	
746.34 −	756.33	15.34
756.34 −	766.33	15.56
766.34 −	776.33	15.78
776.34 −	786.33	16.00
786.34 −	796.33	16.22
796.34 −	806.33	16.44
806.34 −	816.33	16.66
816.34 −	826.33	16.88
826.34 −	836.33	17.10
836.34 −	846.33	17.32
846.34 −	856.33	17.54
856.34 −	866.33	17.76
866.34 −	876.33	17.98
876.34 −	886.33	18.20

questions are shown in Appendix A at the end of this chapter. The amount to be deducted from Mike Bergin's pay when he earns $765.19 is shown in the tables to be $15.56. (The difference of 9 cents is not significant, for whether the tables are used or the formula is used, the person will pay a maximum of $574.20 per year.)

Unemployment Insurance

According to the *Unemployment Insurance Act*, an employer must deduct unemployment insurance premiums from an employee's pay, and also contribute an amount equal to 1.4 times the employee's contribution.

In general, all employees are required to contribute to the unemployment insurance fund. If no contribution is made, no benefits can be received when the person is unemployed. Those who do not have to pay premiums include workers who have worked less than 15 hours in any week and have earned less than 20 percent of the maximum weekly insurable earnings, and casual employees. As well, there is a minimum earnings figure below which a person does not have to pay, and a range between the minimum and maximum earnings figures for which the employee only has to pay 2.25 percent. No premiums are paid on earnings beyond the maximum amount for the pay period.

The maximum and minimum earnings figures are shown in the table below. Included are also the maximum premium deductions for each frequency of pay period. It is calculated as 2.25% of the maximum earnings.

	Minimum Earnings	Maximum Earnings	Maximum Premium
Weekly	$128.00	$ 640.00	$14.40
Biweekly	256.00	1 280.00	28.80
Semi-monthly	277.33	1 386.65	31.20
Monthly	554.66	2 773.30	62.40

The deduction from the employee's pay can be calculated either by formula or by using the tables. Revenue Canada also provides a program with a formula and tables for computer systems.

"*Unemployment Insurance deduction = Gross pay × 2.25%*"

(a) Calculating the Unemployment Insurance deduction by formula
The formula for obtaining the Unemployment Insurance deduction is:

Unemployment Insurance deduction = Gross pay × 2.25%

THE FACTS SPEAK...

Unemployment insurance benefits paid to Canadians in 1989 were $11.53 billion.

THE FACTS SPEAK...

The average weekly unemployment insurance payment in 1989 was $215.88.

Remember though that there is a maximum premium deduction for each type of pay period. Use the lesser of the calculated deduction or the maximum deduction in each case.

For Mike Bergin, the calculation would therefore be

$$\begin{aligned}\text{Unemployment Insurance deduction} &= \text{Gross pay} \times 2.25\% \\ &= \$765.19 \times 0.0225 \\ &= \$17.22\end{aligned}$$

But the maximum deduction for a weekly pay frequency is $14.40. Therefore, Mike would have $14.40 deducted from each weekly pay provided his gross pay figure remained the same.

(b) Unemployment Insurance deduction calculation from the tables

The amount of the gross pay is found on the tables and the appropriate deduction is made. Figure 13-8 shows the cutoff point for gross pay and deductions for weekly pay frequencies. For Mike Bergin, the deduction will be $14.40 since his gross pay exceeds the maximum weekly insurable income level of $640.22. Additional tables in Appendix A, at the end of this chapter, can be used for the application questions.

FIGURE 13-8 UNEMPLOYMENT INSURANCE TABLE MARKED TO SHOW THE CUTOFF POINT FOR INSURABLE GROSS PAY AND DEDUCTIONS FOR WEEKLY PAY PERIODS

Unemployment Insurance Premiums

Gross Pay Range	Premium
634.45 - 634.88	14.28
634.89 - 635.33	14.29
635.34 - 635.77	14.30
635.78 - 636.22	14.31
636.23 - 636.66	14.32
636.67 - 637.11	14.33
637.12 - 637.55	14.34
637.56 - 637.99	14.35
638.00 - 638.44	14.36
638.45 - 638.88	14.37
638.89 - 639.33	14.38
639.34 - 639.77	14.39
639.78 - 640.22	14.40
640.23 - 640.66	14.41
640.67 - 641.11	14.42

Employer's Contribution to Unemployment Insurance

Employer's UI premium = 1.4 × Employee premium

The employer must contribute to the unemployment insurance fund an amount equal to 1.4 times that paid by the employee. In Mike Bergin's case, his premium of $14.40 must be matched by a $20.16 payment by the employer.

If an employee is released from a job, the employer must provide a Record of Employment within five days after earnings are interrupted.

The record will show the first and last day of work for the employee, the earnings per pay period, and the number of weeks of insurable employment. As well, the reason for the issuing of the record must be given. This document, when presented to Employment Canada, will determine if the person is eligible for unemployment insurance, the amount of benefits allowed, and the length of time for which benefits will be paid.

Income Tax

The largest payroll deduction for most employees is income tax. The *Income Tax Act* was introduced in 1917 as a temporary measure to finance Canada's efforts in World War I. The tax has been in effect ever since. The tax is, generally, on all income earned. The employer must deduct income tax each pay period from each employee's employment income, referred to as income tax deduction at source. The employee must calculate the exact amount of income tax due each year and file an income tax return (T1) by April 30th of the following year. This filing is necessary so that the citizen pays tax on all sources of income, not just employment income. Other sources of income could include interest, rental income, and alimony. As well, additional deductions for the citizen could have occurred during the year, such as getting married, having a child, starting to pay alimony, or taking a university course.

The provincial governments have all initiated a personal income tax as well, and the employer must also deduct amounts for this. When the federal rate and the provincial rate are considered together, the following are the top tax rates, which apply to any income exceeding $83 000, as of 1990.

FIGURE 13-9 TOP TAX RATES FOR INCOME EXCEEDING $83 000

Alberta	46.4%	Nova Scotia	50.3%
British Columbia	46.3%	Ontario	48.2%
Manitoba	50.4%	Prince Edward Island	49.5%
Newfoundland	49.3%	Quebec	50.5%
New Brunswick	48.7%	Saskatchewan	49.8%
North West Territories	44.1%	Yukon Territory	44.4%

Thus a person in Nova Scotia must pay 50.3 percent of taxable earnings exceeding $83 000 in income tax. The lowest rates on taxable incomes of approximately $6 500 to $28 000 fall in the 25–27 percent range in all provinces.

Except in Quebec, the employer remits both types of income tax deducted to the federal government, which then forwards the appropriate amounts to the provinces. (In Quebec, a separate remittance must be made to the provincial government.) In order that the employer

THE FACTS SPEAK...

Eighty-three percent of all personal income tax paid is deducted from taxpayers' wages or salaries by employers and sent to Revenue Canada Taxation.

knows how much to deduct, Revenue Canada Taxation provides a set of tables for employers in each of the provinces. There must be separate provincial tax tables, for the provincial income tax rates vary. A formula is again provided for computer systems. The figures in the tables provided by Revenue Canada include both the provincial and the federal tax to be deducted, so the payroll clerk only needs to look up one amount.

In order to look up the amount of tax to be deducted using the tables, the taxable income must first be calculated. Taxable income is equal to earnings less amounts considered to be tax deductions.

> "Taxable income = Gross earnings − Amounts considered to be tax deductions."

Taxable earnings = Gross earnings −
(Registered Pension Plan contributions + Union dues + Deduction for living in a prescribed area + Other amounts authorized by Revenue Canada (alimony payments, child care etc.))

Previous to 1989, CPP and unemployment insurance would also be on this list, but since that time these deductions have been built into the tables. RPP stands for registered pension plan, which is a pension fund contributed to through one's employment and participation is usually mandatory according to the contract with the employer. In most cases, the employer also makes a contribution to the cost of the fund. If an employee makes such a contribution, the amount is deducted from taxable income when the contribution is made. Income tax will be paid on the money when it is taken out of the pension.

A deduction from gross earnings is allowed to persons who live in prescribed areas, which include the Yukon Territory and Northwest Territories, for a period of not less than six consecutive months. The amounts are equal to

(i) 20 percent of the net income for the year, or
(ii) $225 for each 30-day period in the year the person resided in the prescribed area.

> "Taxable income may be reduced by special items with the permission of Revenue Canada."

A person may also apply to Revenue Canada Taxation to have taxable income reduced by special items. These items include contributions to RRSPs, alimony, maintenance, child care, donations, and medical expenses. Thus, a person who pays alimony can have the amount of the payment deducted from gross earnings in order to determine taxable income. Revenue Canada informs the employer of its permission to allow these deductions. In addition, a person can request that income tax greater than the required amount be deducted each pay period. This might be done because the person is going to receive income during the year which will not have any tax deducted from it, but for which tax will have to be paid when a T1 is filed. Interest income is an example of this.

For Mike Bergin, the calculation of taxable earnings would be:

$$\begin{aligned}\text{Taxable earnings} &= \$765.19 - (\text{RPP} + \text{Union dues}) \\ &= \$765.19 - (\$45.91 + \$15) \\ &= \$704.28\end{aligned}$$

The taxable earnings figure is then used with the tables to find the amount of tax due. However, the net claim code, which was calculated on a TD1 when the employee was hired, must also be used. Remember that the higher the net claim code, the more exemptions a person has. And the more exemptions one has, the less tax paid. Using the tax table for employees paid weekly, which is shown in Figure 13-10, find the line that shows Mike Bergin's taxable earnings of $704.28. You should notice that an employee with weekly taxable earnings of $704.28 and a net claim code of 0 pays $204.65 and a person with the same weekly taxable earnings but a net claim code of 10 pays only $106.40. Mike Bergin has a net claim code of 1 and has a taxable income of $704.28. The amount of income tax that should be deducted from Mike's pay is $172.75.

The employer does not, of course, pay any income tax on behalf of the employee.

FIGURE 13-10 INCOME TAX TABLE, SHOWING DEDUCTIONS REQUIRED FOR WEEKLY PAY PERIODS, FOR TAXABLE INCOME AMOUNTS OF $691 TO $771

ONTARIO — WEEKLY TAX DEDUCTIONS — Basis — 52 Pay Periods per Year

TABLE 1

ONTARIO — RETENUES D'IMPÔT PAR SEMAINE — Base — 52 périodes de paie par année

WEEKLY PAY Use appropriate bracket PAIE PAR SEMAINE Utilisez le palier approprié		IF THE EMPLOYEE'S "NET CLAIM CODE" ON FORM TD1 IS SI LE CODE DE DEMANDE NETTE DE L'EMPLOYÉ SELON LA FORMULE TD1 EST DE										
From - De	Less than Moins que	0	1	2	3	4	5	6	7	8	9	10
		DEDUCT FROM EACH PAY — RETENEZ SUR CHAQUE PAIE										
691.-	699.	201.35	169.50	165.60	157.75	149.95	142.15	134.45	126.55	118.75	110.95	103.10
699.-	707.	204.65	172.75	168.85	161.05	153.25	145.45	137.75	129.80	122.00	114.20	106.40
707.-	715.	207.90	176.05	172.15	164.35	156.55	148.70	141.00	133.10	125.30	117.50	109.70
715.-	723.	211.20	179.35	175.45	167.65	159.80	152.00	144.30	136.40	128.60	120.80	112.95
723.-	731.	214.50	182.60	178.70	170.90	163.10	155.30	147.60	139.70	131.90	124.05	116.25
731.-	739.	217.80	185.90	182.00	174.20	166.40	158.60	150.90	142.95	135.15	127.35	119.55
739.-	747.	221.05	189.20	185.30	177.50	169.70	161.85	154.15	146.25	138.45	130.65	122.85
747.-	755.	224.35	192.50	188.60	180.75	172.95	165.15	157.45	149.55	141.75	133.95	126.10
755.-	763.	227.65	195.75	191.85	184.05	176.25	168.45	160.75	152.85	145.00	137.20	129.40
763.-	771.	230.90	199.05	195.15	187.35	179.55	171.75	164.05	156.10	148.30	140.50	132.70

Health Insurance

Each province in Canada operates a health insurance program for its residents. The program provides for

(1) basic hospital expenses

(2) doctors' fees for required treatment

The health program is financed in Manitoba, Ontario, and Quebec by imposing a health tax on employers and from general tax revenues. In Ontario, for example, the health tax provides about 16 percent of the annual health spending; the other 84 percent is from general tax revenues. In Manitoba, the employer tax is called the Health and Post-Secondary Education Tax. The following table shows the tax rates applied to employers in respect of this tax for all three provinces that use this type of financing for their provincial health program.

HEALTH TAX RATE STRUCTURE

Ontario

Gross Payroll	Rate
up to $200 000	0.980%
$200 001–$230 000	1.101%
$230 001–$260 000	1.223%
$260 001–$290 000	1.344%
$290 001–$320 000	1.465%
$320 001–$350 000	1.586%
$350 001–$380 000	1.708%
$380 001–$400 000	1.829%
$400 001 and up	1.950%

Quebec

Gross Payroll	Rate
on all amounts	3.45%

Manitoba

Gross Payroll	Rate
less than $600 000	0%
$600 000–$1 200 000*	4.5%
over $1 200 000**	2.25%

* on the amount over $600 000

** on the full amount

In the other provinces, the financing is done through each citizen paying a premium and from general tax revenues. Persons with low income and those over 65 may have their fees subsidized. The fee is either a family rate or a single rate. The family rate is for a person with any number of dependants. In many cases, unions and employees have negotiated for their employer to pay all or part of the premium as a benefit. Where the cost is borne by the employees, the premium is quoted as an annual rate and each pay period a proportional amount is deducted. The rates used in this text for examples where the citizen and/or employer pay the premium are:

Family rate = $520 per year
Single rate = $260 per year

The amount to be deducted for each weekly pay period would be as follows:

$$\text{Family rate} = \$520/52 = \$10$$
$$\text{Single rate} = \$260/52 = \$5$$

Compulsory Deductions According to a Contract

When hired, an employee may enter into an individual contract with the employer, or become part of a collective agreement that a union has negotiated with the employer. The collective agreement would have been negotiated with the employer by members of the union on behalf of all the employees, thus the term collective. In either case, the employer may provide certain benefits on a voluntary or a compulsory basis.

> "Payroll deductions may be offered on a voluntary or a compulsory basis."

Compulsory deductions are those benefits for which the employee must pay. Such deductions might include basic life insurance, dental insurance, and long-term disability insurance. The insurances might be compulsory because the employer has been able to find an insurer who will provide the coverage at a very low premium cost if all employees in the business belong to the plan, or, the insurer might require that to offer dental insurance, for example, the life insurance and long-term disability must be compulsory. In any case, the cost to employees is usually much less than if they tried to buy their own individual coverage.

> "Benefits paid by the employer are taxable."

In many cases, the employer will pay part or all of the premium for each employee. When the employer pays the premium on behalf of the employee, it is sometimes treated as a taxable benefit and the amount is added to the income in order to calculate the income tax to be deducted.

In recent years, the number of deductions from an employee's pay has greatly increased as unions have sought from their employers new benefits to cover certain risks. Some of the more common deductions are outlined below.

> "Supplementary health insurance provides coverage for many items not included in provincial health insurance plans."

<u>Group life insurance:</u> an amount of money will be paid to beneficiaries of the employee should he or she die. The rates for life insurance depend upon the age of the employee and the amount of coverage. As well, different rates may apply to smokers and to non-smokers. A table of rates to be used for the exercises is provided in Appendix A on page 666.

<u>Supplementary health insurance:</u> the employee is covered for many medical items not covered by provincial health insurance plans. For example, the plan may provide for home health care, semi-private or private hospital accommodation, physiotherapy, prescription drugs, and braces. Rates to be used for the exercises are also included in Appendix A on page 666.

> "Long-term disability insurance (LTD) provides an employee with a percentage of his or her wages/salary if unable to work for health reasons."

<u>Long-term disability insurance:</u> the employee will receive a portion of his or her wages/salary if unable to work for health reasons. (If the employer pays the premiums, the income is taxable in the hands of the

The Facts Speak...

An all-inclusive employee benefit plan costs the average Canadian firm more than $11 700 per employee per year.

employee. If the employee pays the premiums, the income is not taxable. Obviously, it is an advantage to the employee to pay these premiums alone.)

Registered Pension Plans (RPP): many businesses provide the opportunity for the employee to contribute to a "company" pension where part of the pay is invested for retirement. This pension would be in addition to the CPP and any private retirement savings plan the employee may purchase.

Union dues: dues are paid to the union so that it can carry out its activities on behalf of the employees. The employer does not, of course, contribute any share of the employees' union dues.

Dental care, vision care, and legal assistance: these three items are the most recent additions to deductions.

Voluntary Payroll Deductions

In addition to the above deductions, an employee may wish to have other amounts deducted from his or her pay and forwarded to the appropriate party. Such deductions might include:

Charity: many businesses will deduct amounts from employees' pays and forward them to the appropriate charity, such as United Way.

Canada Savings Bonds: each year the federal government sells bonds to the general public in order to help finance its activities. Employees can frequently pay for the bond by payroll deduction. Thus, a $1 000 bond could be purchased over a number of pay periods instead of in one lump sum.

Credit unions: a credit union is similar to a bank, except that it is owned by the depositors, who are usually a group of people in the same profession. Members can authorize payroll deductions in order to deposit money in savings accounts and earn interest, or to pay off loans.

Lesson Review

19. What is the formula for calculating net pay?

20. Distinguish between each of the following terms:
    (a) payroll tax   (b) benefit   (c) deduction

21. Into what three categories do deductions fall?

22. What benefits must the employer contribute to on behalf of the employees? Does the employer contribute to other benefits? Explain.

Chapter 13: Payroll Accounting

23. Who must contribute to Canada Pension Plan?
24. Explain the terms "portable" and "indexed" as they relate to pensions.
25. Who must contribute to Unemployment Insurance?
26. What two methods are used to calculate CPP and UI?
27. What must be calculated first in order to use the income tax tables? What is the formula?
28. What is the advantage to an employee of buying insurance as a member of a group?
29. Outline the benefit received for each of the following payroll deductions:
    (a) Supplementary health insurance
    (b) Long-term disability insurance
    (c) Registered pension plan
30. List five voluntary payroll deductions.

LESSON APPLICATIONS

Where tables are required, use those found in Appendix A on pages 660 to 666.

31. Calculate the weekly CPP and UI deductions for each of the following, using a formula. Show your calculations.
    (a) Martin Wesley   Gross earnings $29 430
    (b) Sue Smart   Gross earnings $42 900
    (c) Alain Cosier   Gross earnings $15 200

32. Obtain the CPP and UI deductions for each of the following employees, using the tables. Also show the amount of the employer's contribution.

Employee	Weekly Earnings	CPP Employee	CPP Employer	UI Employee	UI Employer
Jay Allan	$772.80				
Wendy Grassie	898.40				
Bart McGuire	974.50				
Ernie Ruzylo	863.90				

33. (a) Complete the chart to obtain the taxable earnings for the week. The RPP deduction is equal to 5 percent of gross earnings, and union dues are $10 per week.

(b) Total and prove the columns by showing that
Gross earnings − (RPP + Union dues) = Taxable earnings.

Employee	Gross Earnings	RPP Deduction	Union Dues	Taxable Earnings
P. Coutts	$920			
C. Gillissie	880			
F. Minai	830			
P. Twynham	960			
Totals				

34. (a) Complete the following chart to show the net earnings after income tax for the week. RPP is 6 percent of gross earnings, and union dues are $8 per week.
(b) Total and prove the chart.

Employee	Net Claim Code	Gross Earnings	RPP Deduction	Union Dues	Taxable Earnings	Income Tax	Net Earnings after Tax
V. Donkor	3	$892					
R. Ingram	5	894					
C. Ruhs	6	845					
H. Urbach	4	880					
Totals							

35. (a) Complete the following chart to show the net earnings after income tax for the week. RPP is 5.5 percent of gross earnings, and union dues are $8.50 per week.
(b) Total and prove the chart.

Employee	Net Claim Code	Gross Earnings	RPP Deduction	Union Dues	Taxable Earnings	Income Tax	Net Earnings after Tax
V. Carmasino	3	$ 870					
K. Gruber	7	980					
P. Lagrois	1	1 050					
G. Sandhu	4	820					
C. Sardoz	5	870					
F. Taylor	1	880					
Totals							

36. Calculate the monthly payroll deduction for life insurance based on the following data. The employees pay the complete cost.

	Employee	Age	Amount of Coverage	Smoking Habit	Payroll Deduction
(a)	C. Ballantyne	40	$40 000	Non	
(b)	N. Darshi	37	30 000	S	
(c)	Y. Majerus	26	35 000	Non	
(d)	M. Warwick	54	25 000	Non	

37. Calculate the monthly payroll deduction for life insurance based on the following data. The employees pay 25 percent and the employer pays 75 percent of the cost.

	Employee	Age	Amount of Coverage	Smoking Habit	Payroll Deduction
(a)	T. Foley	31	$50 000	S	
(b)	C. Misra	43	35 000	Non	
(c)	G. Pilsworth	29	40 000	Non	
(d)	S. Tiwari	53	45 000	S	

38. Calculate the payroll deductions and the net weekly earnings for each of the employees using the data given below.
    (a) RPP is 5 percent of gross earnings.
    (b) Union dues are $10 per week.
    (c) Each employee has purchased $30 000 of life insurance; all are married non-smokers.
    (d) The employer pays 75 percent of the health and life insurance.

Employee	Age	Net Claim Code	Gross Earnings	RPP Deduction	Union Dues	Taxable Earnings	Income Tax	Health Insurance	Life Insurance	Net Weekly Earnings
T. Au	34	4	$920							
G. Mai	27	1	890							
A. Pal	43	6	940							
F. Luzzi	39	3	925							

13.3 Recording Payroll in the Payroll Register

The methods for calculating gross pay and net pay have been described in the previous sections. A business must establish a payroll accounting system that will meet the following criteria:
(1) it must be efficient and accurate, given that pay periods are frequent, and that a great deal of data is required for each employee for each pay period;
(2) it must reflect that the same basic calculations are made for each employee and for each pay period;
(3) it must reflect that the same information is recorded on a number of documents:
   • the books of the business
   • the employee's pay voucher
   • reports filed with the government, insurance companies, and other businesses that receive payments due to payroll deductions
   • year-end reports related to each of the above

To satisfy the above requirements, payroll is first recorded in a payroll register, which is similar to the multi-column journals studied

FIGURE 13-11 THE COLUMN HEADINGS FOR A PAYROLL REGISTER

PAYROLL REGISTER FOR THE ______ ENDED ______ 19____

EMPLOYEE	NET CLAIM CODE	EARNINGS			DEDUCTIONS									TOTAL DED'NS	NET PAY
		REGULAR	OVERTIME	GROSS	UNION DUES	RPP	TAXABLE INCOME	TAX DED'N	CPP	UI	HEALTH INS.	GROUP LIFE			

previously. The register shown in Figure 13-11 for Algor Computer Services, has columns organized so that each step in the calculation of the payroll follows consecutively. Because much of the data will be transferred to other documents, it helps if the columns are designed so that the information can be entered in the same order on all of the documents.

The Payroll Register

Gross Pay

The gross pay is first entered in the payroll register, using the information found on the time cards of wage employees or on a report completed for salary employees. The register shows the regular earnings, overtime earnings, and gross earnings.

FIGURE 13-12 CALCULATION OF GROSS EARNINGS IN A PAYROLL REGISTER

PAYROLL REGISTER FOR THE *week* ENDED *May 11* 19*90*

EMPLOYEE	NET CLAIM CODE	EARNINGS			DEDUCTIONS									TOTAL DED'NS	NET PAY
		REGULAR	OVERTIME	GROSS	UNION DUES	RPP	TAXABLE INCOME	TAX DED'N	CPP	UI	HEALTH INS.	GROUP LIFE			
Mike Bergin	1	660 –	105 19	765 19											

Calculating Taxable Earnings

The next two columns list the deductions taken to arrive at the taxable earnings; the union dues and RPP. The calculation is:

$$\text{Taxable income} = \text{Gross pay} - (\text{Union dues} + \text{RPP})$$

This amount is then used to find the required income tax deduction according to the tax tables. For Mike Bergin taxable income is $704.28.

FIGURE 13-13 PAYROLL REGISTER SHOWING CALCULATION OF TAXABLE INCOME AND INCOME TAX DEDUCTION FOR MIKE BERGIN

PAYROLL REGISTER FOR THE *week* ENDED *May 11* 19*90*

EMPLOYEE	NET CLAIM CODE	EARNINGS			DEDUCTIONS									TOTAL DED'NS	NET PAY
		REGULAR	OVERTIME	GROSS	UNION DUES	RPP	TAXABLE INCOME	TAX DED'N	CPP	UI	HEALTH INS.	GROUP LIFE			
Mike Bergin	1	660 –	105 19	765 19	15 –	45 91	704 28	172 75							

Other Deductions and Net Pay

The other deductions for each employee are then entered in the payroll register. For Mike Bergin, these consist of CPP and UI (both premiums taken from the tables), health insurance, and group life insurance. Employees participate in a supplementary health insurance plan and have purchased $200 000 of group life insurance. Deductions are totalled and net pay, or take-home pay, is then calculated as follows:

$$\text{Net pay} = \text{Gross pay} - \text{Deductions}$$

FIGURE 13-14 PAYROLL REGISTER SHOWING CALCULATION OF NET PAY FOR MIKE BERGIN

PAYROLL REGISTER — FOR THE _week_ ENDED _May 11_ 19 _90_

EMPLOYEE	NET CLAIM CODE	EARNINGS			DEDUCTIONS									TOTAL DED'NS	NET PAY
		REGULAR	OVERTIME	GROSS	UNION DUES	RPP	TAXABLE INCOME	TAX DED'N	CPP	UI	HEALTH INS.	GROUP LIFE			
Mike Bergin	1	660 —	105 19	765 19	15 —	45 91	704 28	172 75	15 56	14 40	3 50	2 79		269 91	495 28

Completing the Payroll Register

Once the payroll information for each employee has been entered in the register, the columns are totalled and the following proofs are made to ensure that the register is correct:
- Regular earnings + Overtime earnings = Gross earnings
- Total of all deduction columns = Total deductions
- Gross earnings − Total deductions = Net earnings

The payroll register is ruled once the proofs have been completed.

FIGURE 13-15 A COMPLETED PAYROLL REGISTER FOR THE ONE-WEEK PAY PERIOD ENDING MAY 11

PAYROLL REGISTER — FOR THE _week_ ENDED _May 11_ 19 _90_

EMPLOYEE	NET CLAIM CODE	EARNINGS			DEDUCTIONS									TOTAL DED'NS	NET PAY
		REGULAR	OVERTIME	GROSS	UNION DUES	RPP	TAXABLE INCOME	TAX DED'N	CPP	UI	HEALTH INS.	GROUP LIFE			
Mike Bergin	1	660 —	105 19	765 19	15 —	45 91	704 28	172 75	15 56	14 40	3 50	2 79		269 91	495 28
Dean Dorsey	4	800 —	140 —	940 —	15 —	56 40	868 60	222 25	19 52	14 40	3 50	2 79		333 86	606 14
Sue Martin	8	780 —	140 —	920 —	15 —	55 20	849 80	181 15	19 08	14 40	3 50	4 04		292 37	627 63
Peter Turner	3	700 —	210 —	910 —	15 —	54 60	840 40	216 90	18 86	14 40	1 75	1 25		322 76	587 24
Dale Webster	5	740 —	170 —	910 —	15 —	54 60	840 40	201 30	18 86	14 40	3 50	2 60		310 26	599 74
		3680 —	765 19	4445 19	75 —	266 71	4103 48	994 35	91 88	72 —	15 75	13 47		1529 16	2916 03

Paying the Employees
The Statement of Earnings

> "A statement of earnings must be given to each employee."

By law, each employee is required to receive a statement of earnings that shows the calculation of his or her own pay. By designing the statement of earnings with columns in the same order as those in the payroll register, a rapid manual transfer of the data can be made. For computer systems such as the one used by Algor, the data can be printed in any desired format on the statement.

FIGURE 13-16 A PAYCHEQUE WITH A STATEMENT OF EARNINGS

Payroll Account	ALGOR COMPUTER SERVICES 55 EASTERN PARKWAY KANATA ON K2L 2B1		982
			May 18, 19 90
PAY TO THE ORDER OF	Mike Bergin		$ 495.28
SUM OF	Four Hundred Ninety-Five		28/100 DOLLARS
THE ROYAL BANK OF CANADA	25 EASTERN PARKWAY KANATA, ON K2L 2B1	PER	V. Marshall
		PER	M. Ranadive
17⋅85721⋅ ⋅:18122⋅⋅⋅5651⋅: 672755 ⋅⋅⋅ 249⋅			

DATE: May 18, 1990			STATEMENT OF EARNINGS				982	
EARNINGS			DEDUCTIONS			DEDUCTIONS		
Regular	660	—	Union Dues	15	—	CPP	15	56
Extra	105	19	RPP	45	91	UI	14	40
Gross	765	19	Income Tax	172	75	Health Insurance	3	50
Total Deductions	269	91				Group Life	2	79
Net Pay	495	28						

Transfer of Pay to the Employees

The actual payment to the employees can be done in a number of ways. The employer and employee will agree as to the method.

> "A currency requisition shows the quantities of coins and bills needed to pay employees in cash."

Cash Payment in cash is not frequently used for it requires that the employer obtain change from a financial institution in order to pay each employee the exact amount of pay due. If payment is made by cash, a currency requisition is completed showing the number of each coin and bill required, and is given to the treasurer. (See Figure 13-17.) A cheque is issued for the total amount of the payroll. The currency requisition and cheque are taken to the bank where the required total numbers of each coin and bill are received.

FIGURE 13-17 A CURRENCY REQUISITION

PAYROLL CURRENCY REQUISITION   FOR THE Pay Period ENDED May 11 19 92

EMPLOYEE	NET PAY		$50	$20	$10	$5	$2	$1	25¢	10¢	5¢	1¢
Mike Bergin	495	28	9	2		1				2	1	3
Dean Dorsey	606	14	12			1		1		1		4
Sue Martin	627	63	12	1		1	1		2	1		3
Peter Turner	587	24	11	1	1	1	1			2		4
Dale Webster	599	74	11	2		1	2		2	2		4
	$2 916	03	55	6	1	5	4	1	4	8	1	18

Once the change required has been received from the bank, the payroll clerk must prepare an envelope for each employee with the exact amount of pay. Each employee must sign a form as proof that the cash was received.

Payment by cash is not favored by employers because it is more time consuming than payment by cheque or bank deposit, and more risky due to the transportation of the cash.

Cheque   The most common method of payment is by cheque. A separate bank account is usually opened, and the total of the payroll is transferred to it from the regular bank account. Cheques with the words "Payroll Account" on them are then issued to the employees. When each employee has cashed his or her cheque, the balance of the payroll account will be zero. The entry to record payment to the payroll bank account from the regular bank account will be:

> "A separate payroll account is frequently opened at a financial institution."

GENERAL JOURNAL

PAGE 372

DATE 1990		PARTICULARS	PR	DEBIT	CREDIT
May	18	Payroll Account		2 9 1 6 03	
		Cash			2 9 1 6 03
		Cheque Copy #401, to meet payroll of May 7 to May 11			

The use of a payroll bank account reduces the number of outstanding cheques on the normal bank account when employees are paid at the end of the month. The bank reconciliation, studied in Chapter 12, is therefore easier to complete for both the business's regular bank account and its payroll bank account. The cancelled cheques are returned to the business and serve as proof that the employee was paid.

Direct deposit   Many businesses are now paying employees by direct deposit to the employee's bank, trust company, or credit union account. The business obtains from each employee the name of the institution and the account number to which they wish the deposit to be made. The transfer of funds is then carried out electronically by the business's bank from a listing of employees and their net pay provided by the business.

> "Direct deposit of pay results in the employee's bank account being credited for the amount of the pay for the payroll period."

Some businesses purchase a payroll service from a financial institution or business specializing in payroll accounting. The business provides all the payroll information for each pay period, usually through a computer terminal. The payroll service prepares the payroll, issues cheques and statements of earnings, and prepares reports for the firm.

LESSON REVIEW

39. What key factors must be considered when designing a payroll system?

40. In what ways is the payroll register similar to the multi-column journal? In what ways is it different?

41. What proofs are done for the payroll register?

42. What is a statement of earnings? What legal requirement exists concerning it?

43. Describe three methods of paying the employees. For each method, complete a chart with the following headings:

Method of Payment	Advantages		Disadvantages	
	To Employer	To Employee	To Employer	To Employee

44. What is a currency requisition?

45. What is the advantage to a business of establishing a separate payroll account at a financial institution?

LESSON APPLICATIONS

Where tables are required, use those found in Appendix A on pages 660 to 666.

46. (a) Set up a payroll register with the required deduction columns.
    (b) Use the following information and the tables in Appendix A to calculate the weekly payroll for Wellington Industries.
       (i) The pay period is for the week ending November 18.
       (ii) Union dues are $7 for each employee.
    (c) Balance the payroll register.

Employee		Net Claim Code	Time Card Summary		Donations
No.	Name		Regular	Overtime	
4	Joy Davey	5	$990	$ 30	$3
2	Diane Proulx	3	820	80	2
1	Terry Begin	8	880		3
3	Mike Whyte	1	910	140	2

47. (a) Set up a payroll register with the required deduction columns.
    (b) Use the following information and the tables in Appendix A to calculate the weekly payroll for British Columbia Auto Parts Distributors.

(i) The pay period is for the week ending May 13.
(ii) Registered pension plan is 5 percent of gross earnings.
(iii) Union dues are $13.50 for each employee.
(iv) The employer pays 75 percent of the health insurance premium.
(v) Donations are as shown below for each employee.
(c) Balance the payroll register.

Employee		Marital Status	Net Claim Code	Time Card Summary		
No.	Name			Regular	Overtime	Donations
4	Tsang Hui	M	4	$870		$10
2	Raj Renton	M	4	940	$50	5
5	Neera Malhotra	S	1	820		10
1	Bea Martin	S	1	840	30	5
3	Vera Wingare	M	5	820	60	5

48. Complete a payroll register for Two Sisters Sports Wear using the data given below and the tables in Appendix A. Establish appropriate headings for the various columns.
    (i) The pay period is for the week ending August 27.
    (ii) Registered pension plan is 5 percent of gross earnings.
    (iii) Union dues are $10 for each employee.
    (iv) Each employee has purchased $30 000 of life insurance; all are non-smokers.
    (v) The employer pays three quarters of the health and life insurance premiums.

Employee	Marital Status	Age	Net Claim Code	Gross Earnings
D. Gould	M	32	6	$854
R. Grodzki	S	27	1	802
B. Lemay	M	44	3	841
W. Wood	M	38	5	895

49. Complete a payroll register for Fortune's Financial Services using the data given below, the tables in Appendix A, and Figure 13-18. Establish appropriate headings for the various columns.
    (i) The pay period is for the week ending May 13.
    (ii) Registered pension plan is 5 percent of gross earnings.
    (iii) Union dues are $2.50 for each employee.
    (iv) The employer pays 75 percent of the health and life insurance premiums.
    (v) Donations are as shown for each employee.

FIGURE 13-18

Employee		Marital Status	Age	Net Claim Code	Time Card		Life Insurance	Donations
No.	Name				Reg.	Over		
3	V. Gledhill	M	45	2	$850	$30	$30 000(non)	$5
2	B. Ironmonger	S	41	7	980		30 000	4
6	M. Islam	M	32	4	970		20 000(non)	5
1	G. Podolsky	M	51	7	950	20	20 000(non)	5
4	M. Racicot	M	29	1	900	50	10 000(non)	0
5	A. Twynham	S	33	4	880		20 000(non)	5

13.4 Updating the Books for Payroll

Employee's Individual Earnings Record

"A T4 slip shows the gross earnings of the employee, along with any items deducted from pay that will influence the income tax payable for the year."

The *Income Tax Act* requires that an employer provide all employees with a T4 slip (Statement of Remuneration) by the end of February of the following year. The form must show the gross earnings of the employee, along with any items deducted from pay that will influence the income tax payable for the year. The employee will then use the data to prepare his or her annual tax return. A T4 slip is shown in Figure 13-19.

FIGURE 13-19 A T4 SLIP, SHOWING EARNINGS AND DEDUCTIONS WHICH AFFECT INCOME TAX, FOR THE YEAR

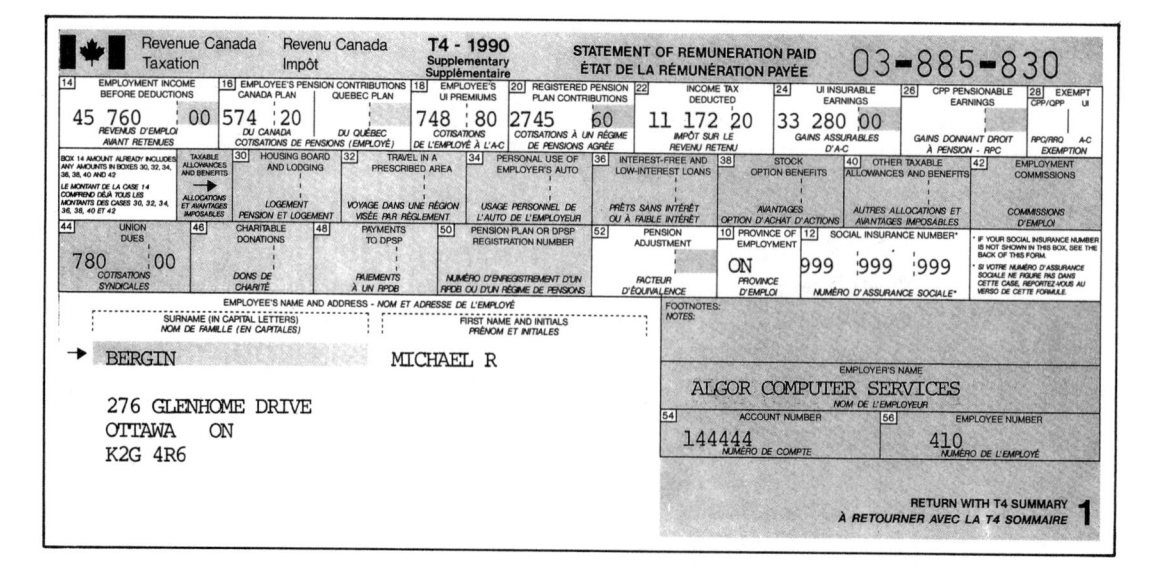

Chapter 13: Payroll Accounting

"*The employee's individual earnings record, showing pay and deductions for each employee, is updated after each pay period.*"

The data necessary for preparing the T4 for each employee can be found in the payroll register. However, to use the register as the source of information would mean that the person preparing the T4 would have to turn to each pay period and total the pay and deductions for each employee. Rather than wait to year end, an employee's individual earnings record is updated after each pay period. This accumulated record of pay to individual employees also shows the amount paid to CPP during the year, which can be referred to in order to ensure that the employee (and the employer) does not overpay this item.

The columnar design of the payroll register and the employee earnings record is the same in order to facilitate the transfer of information. Note that there are additional columns in the employee earnings record that provide the cheque number and the CPP totals for the year. The employee earnings record for Mike Bergin showing data for the weekly pay periods ending May 11 to June 8 is shown in Figure 13-20.

FIGURE 13-20 EMPLOYEE EARNINGS RECORD FOR MIKE BERGIN FOR THE WEEKLY PAY PERIODS ENDING MAY 11 TO JUNE 8

EMPLOYEE EARNINGS RECORD

NAME: Mike Bergin
ADDRESS: 276 Glenhome Dr., Ottawa, ON K2G 4R6
SIN: 999 999 999
MARITAL STATUS: Married
PHONE: 555-6666
NET CLAIM CODE: 1
BIRTHDATE: 27/08/43
EMPLOYMENT DATE: Jan. 2, 1990
DEPARTMENT: Sales

PAY PERIOD	EARNINGS			DEDUCTIONS								TOTAL DED'NS	NET PAY	CHEQUE NUMBER	CPP TO DATE
	REGULAR	EXTRA	GROSS	UNION DUES	RPP	TAXABLE INCOME	TAX DED'N	CPP	UI	HEALTH INS.	GROUP LIFE				
Forwarded	11880 –	3960 –	15840 –	270 –	950 40	14619 60	4410 90	327 60	259 20	63 –	50 22	6331 32	9508 86		327 60
May 7 – 11	660 –	105 19	765 19	15 –	45 91	704 28	172 75	15 56	14 40	3 50	2 79	269 91	495 28	982	343 16
May 14 – 18	660 –	148 50	808 50	15 –	48 51	744 99	189 20	16 66	14 40	3 50	2 79	290 06	518 44	987	359 82
May 21 – 25	660 –	185 63	845 63	15 –	50 74	779 89	205 65	17 32	14 40	3 50	2 79	309 40	536 23	992	377 14
May 28 – June 1	660 –	198 –	858 –	15 –	51 48	791 52	208 90	17 76	14 40	3 50	2 79	313 83	544 17	997	394 90
June 4 – 8	660 –	204 19	864 19	15 –	51 85	797 34	212 20	17 76	14 40	3 50	2 79	317 50	546 69	1002	412 66

When the calendar year ends, the columns are totalled and a check is made to ensure that the record balances. A T4 can then be prepared from the information. A copy of the T4 slip is kept by the employer, two copies are sent to the employee, and one copy is sent to Revenue Canada. When the employee files his or her tax return, a copy of the T4 is also sent, and it is matched with the copy sent by the employer.

Updating the General Ledger

The general ledger must be updated to reflect the various changes in the accounts related to payroll. Journal entries are made, and posted, in order to:

(1) record the data that was entered in the payroll register

(2) record the employer's share of payroll taxes

(3) record payment of the employees

(4) record payment of the various payroll liabilities.

The various journal entries are illustrated below.

Recording Data from the Payroll Register

> "Either of two systems can be used for transferring data from the payroll register to the general ledger."

In some businesses the payroll register is considered to be a journal, and column totals are posted directly from the register to the ledger as with other multi-column journals. However, all columns do not have to be posted because some are used only for calculation purposes, such as regular and overtime earnings. As well, the column headings do not have Debit or Credit on them, which may cause difficulties when posting. For this reason, many businesses prepare a general journal entry to summarize the payroll register, and then post to the general ledger. Figure 13-21 summarizes these two possible procedures.

FIGURE 13-21 TWO POSSIBLE PROCEDURES FOR TRANSFERRING PAYROLL DATA TO A GENERAL LEDGER; THE FIRST IS PREFERRED

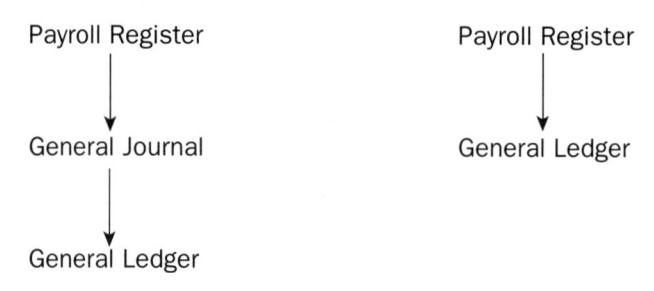

```
     Payroll Register              Payroll Register
            |                             |
            v                             v
     General Journal               General Ledger
            |
            v
     General Ledger
```

The general journal entry to record the payroll for the pay period ending May 11, 1990, is shown in Figure 13-22. The data comes from the payroll register, as shown in Figure 13-15.

The explanation for the journal entry is as follows:
- A debit is made to Wages Expense for the amount from the Gross Earnings column. This reflects the total pay for each employee.
- A credit is made for each deduction, to show that the amount has been deducted from the pay and is owing to a third party, such as Revenue Canada or an insurance company.

FIGURE 13-22

GENERAL JOURNAL

PAGE 372

DATE 1990		PARTICULARS	PR	DEBIT	CREDIT
May	18	Wages Expense	600	4445 19	
		Union Dues Payable	265		75 -
		RPP Payable	262		266 71
		Income Tax Payable	260		994 35
		CPP Payable	250		91 88
		UI Payable	255		72 -
		Health Insurance Payable	270		15 75
		Group Life Insurance Payable	280		13 47
		Wages Payable	205		2916 03
		To record payroll register for pay period ending May 11			

- A credit is made to Wages Payable to show the net amount owing to the employees for the pay period. Individual cheques will be issued to employees from the payroll bank account to satisfy this liability.

The following summarizes the journal entry made from the payroll register:

```
Earnings
   Regular               $3 680.00
   Overtime                 765.19
   Total Gross Pay                    $4 445.19  } Debit to
                                                   Wages Expense
Deductions
   Union Dues                75.00
   RPP                      266.71
   Income Tax               994.35
   CPP                       91.88                } Credit to
   UI                        72.00                  Current Liabilities
   Health Insurance          15.75
   Group Life Insurance      13.47
   Total Deductions                    1 529.16
Net Pay                                $2 916.03 } Credit to
                                                   Wages Payable
```

Recording the Employer's Contributions to Benefits

In our discussion of payroll deductions, we noted that by law the employer must make a contribution for some benefits, and may agree with the employees to do so for other items. A journal entry is required to record these liabilities, sometimes referred to collectively as "payroll taxes."

Employer's Contribution to Canada Pension Plan

"The employer must contribute an amount to CPP that is equal to that of the employees."

Under the *Canada Pension Plan Act*, the employer must match the employees' contribution. The payroll register shows that the employees' premium was $91.88, therefore the employer must also contribute $91.88. The required journal entry is:

GENERAL JOURNAL

PAGE 372

DATE 1990		PARTICULARS	PR	DEBIT	CREDIT
May	18	CPP Expense	610	91 88	
		CPP Payable	250		91 88
		Employer's CPP premiums for pay period ending May 11			

The explanation for the journal entry is as follows:
- A debit is made to CPP Expense to show the employer's contribution to the plan. This is a normal operating cost.
- A credit is made to CPP Payable to record the liability to the federal government.

Employer's Contribution to Unemployment Insurance

"The employer is required to contribute to UI an amount equal to 1.4 times that of the employees' contribution."

Under the *Unemployment Insurance Act*, the employer must contribute 1.4 times the employees' contribution. The payroll register shows that the employees' premium was $72.00, and therefore the employer must contribute $100.80. The required journal entry is:

GENERAL JOURNAL

PAGE 372

DATE 1990		PARTICULARS	PR	DEBIT	CREDIT
May	18	UI Expense	620	100 80	
		UI Payable	255		100 80
		Employer's UI premium for pay period ending May 11			

The explanation for the journal entry is as follows:
- A debit is made to UI Expense to show the employer's contribution to the fund. This is a normal operating cost.
- A credit is made to UI Payable to record the liability to the federal government. The liability will be paid at the same time as the CPP liability.

Employer's Health Tax

Since Algor is located in Ontario, it must also pay the province's Employer Health Tax, which has replaced premium payments to the Ontario Hospital Insurance Plan. The rate applied to Algor's gross payroll is 1.101%. The required journal entry to record Algor's liability for this tax is shown in Figure 13-23.

FIGURE 13-23

GENERAL JOURNAL

PAGE 372

DATE 1990		PARTICULARS	PR	DEBIT	CREDIT
May	18	Health Tax Expense	622	48 94	
		Health Tax Payable	258		48 94
		Health tax owing for pay period ending May 11			

The explanation for the journal entry is as follows:
- A debit is made to Health Tax Expense to show the employer's tax liability for the pay period. This is a normal operating cost in Ontario.
- A credit is made to Health Tax Payable to record this liability to the provincial government. This liability will be paid on the 15th of the month after the second quarter of the calendar year has been completed, i.e., July 15.

Employer's Contribution to Other Benefits

A journal entry is required to record the contributions the employer has agreed to make to other benefits on behalf of the employees. For Algor Computer Services this consists of a matching amount (50 percent of the total cost) to the registered pension plan and health insurance, and three times the employee premium (75 percent of the total cost) for the group life insurance. Separate journal entries can be made for each item, or one entry for all of them. Using the data from Figure 13-15, the employer's contributions are calculated as follows:

	Employees' Contribution	Employer's Contribution
Registered Pension Plan	$266.71 = 50%	$266.71 = 50%
Health Insurance	$15.75 = 50%	$15.75 = 50%
Group Life Insurance	$13.47 = 25%	$40.41 = 75%

The required journal entry is:

GENERAL JOURNAL

PAGE 372

DATE 1990		PARTICULARS	PR	DEBIT	CREDIT
May	18	RPP Expense	625	266 71	
		Health Insurance Expense	630	15 75	
		Group Life Insurance Expense	640	40 41	
		RPP Payable	262		266 71
		Health Insurance Payable	270		15 75
		Group Life Insurance Payable	280		40 41
		Employer's contributions for pay period ending May 11			

The explanation for the journal entry is as follows:
- A debit is made to each of the expenses to show the employer's contribution. These are normal operating costs of the business and are therefore recorded as expenses.
- A credit is made to each of the payables to record the liability to each of the insurance carriers. The liabilities will be paid as agreed with the carriers.

The general ledger accounts affected by payroll will appear as follows:

GENERAL LEDGER

Wages Payable		205
dr.	cr.	
	May 18 2 916.03	

CPP Payable		250
dr.	cr.	
	May 18 91.88	
	18 91.88	

UI Payable		255
dr.	cr.	
	May 18 72.00	
	18 100.80	

Health Tax Payable		258
dr.	cr.	
	May 18 48.94	

Income Tax Payable		260
dr.	cr.	
	May 18 994.35	

RPP Payable		262
dr.	cr.	
	May 18 266.71	
	18 266.71	

Union Dues Payable		265
dr.	cr.	
	May 18 75.00	

Health Insurance Payable		270
dr.	cr.	
	May 18 15.75	
	18 15.75	

Group Life Insurance Payable		280
dr.	cr.	
	May 18 13.47	
	18 40.41	

Wages Expense		600
dr.	cr.	
May 18 4 445.19		

CPP Expense		610
dr.	cr.	
May 18 91.88		

UI Expense		620
dr.	cr.	
May 18 100.80		

Health Tax Expense		622
dr.	cr.	
May 18 48.94		

RPP Expense		625
dr.	cr.	
May 18 266.71		

Health Insurance Expense		630
dr.	cr.	
May 18 15.75		

Group Life Insurance Expense		640
dr.	cr.	
May 18 40.41		

Alternate Method of Recording the Payroll Costs

In some businesses, rather than make entries to the individual expenses, only one account is used, called Payroll Expenses. The entry to record the various expenses for Algor Computer Services as shown above would then be as follows:

GENERAL JOURNAL

PAGE 372

DATE 1990		PARTICULARS	PR	DEBIT	CREDIT
May	18	Payroll Expenses		564 49	
		CPP Payable			91 88
		Health Tax Payable			48 94
		UI Payable			100 80
		RPP Payable			266 71
		Health Insurance Payable			15 75
		Group Life Insurance Payable			40 41
		To record the employer's share of payroll expenses for			
		pay period ending May 11			

Recording Payment of the Employees

To record payment of the employees, the *net pay* figure is used because it represents the take-home pay. The required entry to cancel the liability established previously is as follows:

GENERAL JOURNAL

PAGE 372

DATE 1990		PARTICULARS	PR	DEBIT	CREDIT
May	18	Wages Payable	205	2 916 03	
		Payroll Account	108		2 916 03
		To record payment of employees for pay period ending May 11			

When the individual paycheques are issued, the balance of each account returns to zero until the next time payroll is prepared.

GENERAL LEDGER

Payroll Account			108
dr.		cr.	
May 18	2 916.03	May 18	495.28
	0	18	606.14
		18	627.63
		18	587.24
		18	599.74

Wages Payable			205
dr.		cr.	
May 18	2 916.03	May 18	2 916.03
			0

Recording Payment of the Payroll Liabilities

It is the responsibility of the employer to remit the amounts deducted from the employees' pays, as well as the employer's contributions, to the proper governments, insurance carriers, and other agencies. Amounts are due to the Receiver General for CPP, UI, and income tax according to the schedule in Figure 13-4, which depends upon the amount withheld from the payroll.

FIGURE 13-24

Monthly Withholding Amount	Due
up to $14 999	by 15th of the following month
$15 000 to $49 999	by 25th of the month for pay dates in the first 15 days of the month; by 10th of the following month for pay dates after the 15th of the month.
$50 000 and over	by 10th if pay is on 1st to 7th of the month; by 17th if pay is on 8th to 14th of the month; by 24th if pay is on 15th to 21st of the month; by 3rd day of the following month if pay is on 22nd to end of the month.

FIGURE 13-25

GENERAL JOURNAL

PAGE 380

DATE 1990		PARTICULARS	PR	DEBIT	CREDIT
June	15	Health Insurance Payable		126 —	
		Cash			126 —
		Cheque Copy #412, payment of health insurance premiums			
		for month of May to True North Insurance			
	15	Group Life Insurance Payable		215 52	
		Cash			215 52
		Cheque Copy #413, life insurance premiums for month of			
		May paid to Seaboard Life			
	15	Union Dues Payable		300 —	
		Cash			300 —
		Cheque Copy #414, union dues for month of May			
		forwarded to URW			
	15	CPP Payable		735 04	
		UI Payable		691 20	
		Income Tax Payable		3977 40	
		Cash			5403 64
		Cheque Copy #415, payment to Receiver General for May			
		payroll deductions			
	15	RPP Payable		2133 68	
		Cash			2133 68
		Cheque Copy #416, payment to NN Financial for pension			
		funds collected in May			

Revenue Canada provides a form, PD7AR, for the employer to use when remitting the source deductions. The amount must be *received* by Revenue Canada or a financial institution on the due date. There is a penalty for late or deficient payments, and interest is also charged.

For other agencies, the amount is forwarded as per the agreement between the employer and the agency. The entries for payment of various payroll liabilities are shown in Figure 13-25. At this time Algor is accumulating the Health Tax for payment to the Provincial Treasurer at a later date. Since Algor is a small business, remittance does not have to be made until the fifteenth of the following month. For the purpose of illustration, it is assumed that the remittances are for the four pay periods in May, and that amounts for each pay period were the same.

The general ledger accounts with the accumulation and payment of the May payroll liabilities are shown in Figure 13-26.

FIGURE 13-26 GENERAL LEDGER PAYROLL LIABILITY ACCOUNTS SHOWING THE EFFECTS OF FOUR PAYROLL PERIODS IN MAY, AND PAYMENT OF THOSE LIABILITIES IN JUNE

GENERAL LEDGER

CPP Payable			250
dr.		cr.	
June 15 735.04	May 4	91.88	
	4	91.88	
	11	91.88	
	11	91.88	
	18	91.88	
	18	91.88	
	25	91.88	
	25	91.88	

UI Payable			255
dr.		cr.	
June 15 691.20	May 4	72.00	
	4	100.80	
	11	72.00	
	11	100.80	
	18	72.00	
	18	100.80	
	25	72.00	
	25	100.80	

Income Tax Payable			260
dr.		cr.	
June 15 3 977.40	May 4	994.35	
	11	994.35	
	18	994.35	
	25	994.35	

RPP Payable			262
dr.		cr.	
June 15 2 133.68	May 4	266.71	
	4	266.71	
	11	266.71	
	11	266.71	
	18	266.71	
	18	266.71	
	25	266.71	
	25	266.71	

Union Dues Payable			265
dr.		cr.	
June 15 300.00	May 4	75.00	
	11	75.00	
	18	75.00	
	25	75.00	

Health Insurance Payable			270
dr.		cr.	
June 15 126.00	May 4	15.75	
	4	15.75	
	11	15.75	
	11	15.75	
	18	15.75	
	18	15.75	
	25	15.75	
	25	15.75	

Group Life Insurance Payable			280
dr.		cr.	
June 15 215.52	May 4	13.47	
	4	40.41	
	11	13.47	
	11	40.41	
	18	13.47	
	18	40.41	
	25	13.47	
	25	40.41	

Workers' Compensation

> "Workers' Compensation provides for those who are injured on the job, or who suffer from occupational diseases."

In all of the provinces a work-related disability plan, Workers' Compensation, is in effect to assist those employees who are injured on the job, or who suffer occupational disease. Before the plan came into effect, an injured worker had to sue his employer for negligence causing the accident. More often than not, the injured employee was not able to pursue the matter effectively, while the employer had plentiful resources to defend the firm against an action in court. To reduce the amount of employer-employee litigation and to assist the injured employee quickly, Workers' Compensation was enacted. For this gain, the worker gives up the right to sue the employer.

Each employer contributes an amount to the plan in relation to the type of business, the size of the business, and its accident record. The entry to record payment to the fund by the employer is as follows:

GENERAL JOURNAL

PAGE 379

DATE 1990		PARTICULARS	PR	DEBIT	CREDIT
May	30	Workers' Compensation Expense		2500 —	
		Cash			2500 —
		Cheque Copy #407, to record payment of Workers'			
		Compensation			

The fund, administered by the Workers' Compensation Board, makes payments to workers injured by accident for a reason "arising out of and in the course of employment." If the employee dies due to an accident, payment is made to the dependants. Application must be made to the Board for compensation.

Vacation Pay

Vacation pay must be given to wage employees. The amount of the vacation pay is equal to four percent of the gross pay. Although the timing of the vacation is usually negotiated, the employer has the right to indicate when the vacation will be taken. As well, the employer may give more than two weeks holiday, and more than four percent vacation pay.

A number of accounting procedures can be followed to record the liability with respect to the vacation pay. Many businesses that have a weekly payroll recognize one fiftieth of the liability each pay period. The liability is then cancelled when the pay is distributed to the employee at vacation time. An employee is still entitled to receive vacation pay if

THE FACTS SPEAK...

There were 617 997 work-related injuries or illnesses reported in Canada in 1988.

a vacation is not taken. In such cases it must be paid within ten months after the employee has earned the vacation. The journal entry to record the vacation pay each pay period for Algor Computer Services is as follows:

GENERAL JOURNAL

PAGE 372

DATE 1990		PARTICULARS	PR	DEBIT	CREDIT
May	18	Wages Expense		177 81	
		Vacation Pay Payable			177 81
		To record the vacation pay for all employees; Wages Expense × 4%			

When Mike Bergin takes his vacation, he receives his accumulated vacation pay. The entry to record payment of the vacation pay is as follows:

GENERAL JOURNAL

PAGE 385

DATE 1990		PARTICULARS	PR	DEBIT	CREDIT
Aug.	15	Vacation Pay Payable		1126 40	
		Cash			1126 40
		Cheque Copy #492, to record payment of vacation pay due to M. Bergin			

If an employee resigns or is fired, he or she is entitled to receive his or her outstanding vacation pay within seven days of termination.

LESSON REVIEW

50. What is an employee's individual earnings record? What purpose does it serve?
51. What is a T4 slip? Where is the information to prepare it found?
52. What use is made of a T4 slip by an employee?
53. Why is there a "CPP to Date" column in an employee earnings record?
54. What four sets of journal entries are required to complete the payroll?
55. Why is the information found in a payroll register usually summarized in a general journal entry?
56. What single account can be used to record the employer's share of benefits?

57. What is the purpose of Workers' Compensation? What right does it take away from the employee?

58. On what basis is the amount paid by the employer into the Workers' Compensation fund determined?

59. When is vacation pay due to an employee? How is the amount of vacation pay due to an employee determined?

LESSON APPLICATIONS

60. The following payroll register is for Delta Fresh Fruit Suppliers for the week ending December 31.

PAYROLL REGISTER — FOR THE _week_ ENDED _Dec. 31_ 19 _90_

EMPLOYEE	NET CLAIM CODE	EARNINGS			DEDUCTIONS									TOTAL DED'NS	NET PAY
		REGULAR	OVERTIME	GROSS	UNION DUES	RPP	TAXABLE INCOME	TAX DED'N	CPP	UI	HEALTH INS.	GROUP LIFE	DENTAL		
M. Glustien	7	1020 —		1020 —	12 —	61 20	946 80	229 25	21 28	14 40	6 —	3 —	11 —	358 13	661 87
K. Kuehn	4	940 —		940 —	12 —	56 40	871 60	222 25	19 52	14 40	6 —	3 —	11 —	344 57	595 43
B. Moneypenny	5	870 —	90 —	960 —	12 —	57 60	890 40	221 —	19 96	14 40	6 —	3 —	11 —	344 96	615 04
J. Poulsen	3	1000 —	200 —	1200 —	12 —	72 —	1116 —	330 70	25 24	14 40	6 —	3 —	11 —	474 34	725 66
M. Takahashi	6	910 —	120 —	1030 —	12 —	61 80	956 20	242 10	21 50	14 40	6 —	3 —	11 —	371 80	658 20
		4740 —	410 —	5150 —	60 —	309 —	4781 —	1245 30	107 50	72 —	30 —	15 —	55 —	1893 80	3256 20

(a) Transfer the payroll data from the payroll register to the employee earnings record for each of the employees, on the line after the subtotals in the Working Papers.
(b) Update the "CPP to Date" column.
(c) Calculate year-end totals in the employee earnings records.
(d) Prepare a T4 slip for each employee. Provide the missing data.

61. The selected T-accounts in Figure 13-27 are for Halifax Shoe Centre, after the posting of the payroll for the week ending October 16. This represents the third payday in October.
   (a) Why are there three amounts on the credit side of the Union Dues Payable account?
   (b) Why are there six amounts on the credit side of the CPP Payable account?
   (c) Why are the two credit amounts for each date for CPP Payable the same?
   (d) What do the two debit entries to CPP Payable indicate?
   (e) Why are there three amounts on the debit side of the CPP Expense account?
   (f) Why are there six amounts on the credit side of the UI Payable account?

FIGURE 13-27

Union Dues Payable

dr.	cr.
	Oct. 2 563.74
	9 563.74
	16 563.74

CPP Payable

dr.	cr.
Oct. 6 6 480	Oct. 2 3 240
12 6 480	2 3 240
	9 3 240
	9 3 240
	16 3 240
	16 3 240

UI Payable

dr.	cr.
Oct. 6 7 956	Oct. 2 3 315
12 7 956	2 4 641
	9 3 315
	9 4 641
	16 3 315
	16 4 641

Group Life Insurance Payable

dr.	cr.
	Oct. 2 121.90
	9 121.90
	16 121.90

CPP Expense

dr.	cr.
Oct. 2 3 240	
9 3 240	
16 3 240	

UI Expense

dr.	cr.
Oct. 2 4 641	
9 4 641	
16 4 641	

(g) Why are there three amounts on the debit side of the UI Expense account?

(h) Why are the two credit amounts for each date for UI Payable not the same?

(i) There is no T-account for Group Life Insurance Expense in the business, but there is one for Group Life Insurance Payable. What does this indicate?

(j) There is no debit entry in the CPP Payable and UI Payable accounts on October 16. Why?

62. The following payroll register is for Moncton Auto Body Repairs for the week ending June 22.

PAYROLL REGISTER FOR THE __week__ ENDED __June 22__ 19 _-3_

EMPLOYEE	NET CLAIM CODE	EARNINGS			DEDUCTIONS									TOTAL DED'NS	NET PAY
		REGULAR	OVERTIME	GROSS	UNION DUES	RPP	TAXABLE INCOME	TAX DED'N	CPP	UI	HEALTH INS.	GROUP LIFE	UNITED WAY		
J. Blaszczak	5	850 –		850 –	7 –	51 –	792 –	181 60	17 54	14 40	4 –	2 –	2 50	280 04	569 96
A. Coleman	7	780 –	130 –	910 –	7 –	54 60	848 40	189 –	18 86	14 40	4 –	2 –	2 50	292 36	617 64
M. Ihnat	7	880 –		880 –	7 –	52 80	820 20	179 10	18 20	14 40	8 –	2 –	2 50	284 –	596 –
J. McCalla	3	940 –		940 –	7 –	56 40	876 60	233 35	19 52	14 40	4 –	2 –	2 50	339 17	600 83
A. Radia	4	900 –		900 –	7 –	54 –	839 –	209 10	18 64	14 40	8 –	2 –	2 50	315 64	584 36
		4350 –	130 –	4480 –	35 –	268 80	4176 20	992 15	92 76	72 –	28 –	10 –	12 50	1511 21	2968 79

Prepare general journal entries on page 129 to record:

(a) the payroll register

(b) the employer's share of payroll costs (assume that the employer contributes only to those items required by law)

(c) the paying of the employees (use a Payroll account)

(d) the remittance of all deductions on the fifteenth of the following month. Assume that there were five pay dates in June, and that the pay data was the same for each date.

63. The following payroll register is for the Victoria Home Renovation Centre for the week ending May 20.

PAYROLL REGISTER — FOR THE week ENDED May 20 19-4

EMPLOYEE	NET CLAIM CODE	REGULAR	OVERTIME	GROSS	UNION DUES	RPP	TAXABLE INCOME	TAX DED'N	CPP	UI	HEALTH INS.	GROUP LIFE	DENTAL INS.	TOTAL DED'NS	NET PAY
H. Andreassen	9	1020 –		1020 –	11 –	61 20	947 80	213 65	21 28	14 40	10 –	2 30	8 –	341 83	678 17
C. Barraco	5	880 –	140 –	1020 –	11 –	61 20	947 80	244 85	21 28	14 40	10 –	1 90	8 –	372 63	647 37
J. Kiang	6	1000 –		1000 –	11 –	60 –	929 –	232 20	20 84	14 40	10 –	2 30	8 –	358 74	641 26
R. Orthaber	4	900 –		900 –	11 –	54 –	835 –	209 10	18 64	14 40	5 –	2 85	3 50	318 49	581 51
J. Wan	8	860 –		860 –	11 –	51 60	797 40	161 45	17 76	14 40	10 –	3 20	8 –	277 41	582 59
		4660 –	140 –	4800 –	55 –	288 –	4457 –	1061 25	99 80	72 –	45 –	12 55	35 50	1669 10	3130 90

Prepare general journal entries on page 408 to record:
(a) the payroll register
(b) the employer's share of payroll costs (assume that the employer matches the amount paid by the employees to the registered pension plan)
(c) the paying of the employees (assume the use of a Payroll account)
(d) the remittance of all deductions on the fifteenth of the following month. Assume that there were four pay dates in the month of May and that the pay data was the same for each date.

64. The following data is from the payroll register of the Newfoundland Tannery Ltd. for the week ending September 21, 19-8.

Gross earnings: $24 389

Mandatory deductions:
CPP $ 609.73
UI   707.28
Income Tax 5 609.47

Other deductions:
Group life $ 432.00
Supplementary health   145.00
Donations   62.00
Union dues   86.00
RPP   1 463.34

Prepare general journal entries on page 201 to record:
(a) the payroll register
(b) the employer's share of payroll costs (assume that the employer matches the amount paid by the employees to the registered pension plan, and pays all of the health insurance, $180)
(c) the paying of the employees (assume the use of a Payroll account)
(d) the remittance of all deductions on the fifteenth of the following month. The donations are to be sent to the Canadian Cancer Society. Assume that there were four pay dates in the month of September and that the pay data was the same for each date.

CHAPTER REVIEW AND SKILL DEVELOPMENT

Accounting Principles and Concepts

An employer is required by law to:
- pay only those employees who have a SIN;
- keep a record of pay and deductions for each employee;
- make deductions for Canada Pension Plan, Unemployment Insurance, and Income Tax;
- remit to the appropriate organization amounts deducted from an employee's pay within the time specified;
- provide employees with a T4 slip by February 28th of the year following the earning of the income;
- contribute to Workers' Compensation.

Knowing the Terms

For each of the following statements, indicate the term being defined.
(a) Paid by the employer, to provide an insurance fund for workers injured on the job.
(b) Completed by the employee to show income taxes owing, and sent to the government by April 30th of the year following the earning of the income.
(c) Benefits to which the employer must contribute.
(d) An agreement between a union and the employer.
(e) Used to determine the amount of income tax to deduct from an employee's pay.
(f) Pension which increases in relation to the cost of living.
(g) A benefit paid for by the employer, for which the employee must pay income tax.
(h) To deduct from a pay, rather than have the employee pay for the benefit on his or her own.
(i) Form that the employer must provide to the employee, which shows gross pay and deductions related to income tax.
(j) Record that summarizes the pay and deductions for each employee.

Food for Thought

1. An employee could not understand why there were no deductions for CPP on his December paycheques. Explain why there might be none.

2. One of the costs to an employer is the "cost of compliance" with various laws that apply to the collecting and remitting of taxes to the government. What taxes does the employer have to collect and remit to the government? What are the costs to the employer of this process?

3. Many firms are contracting out their payroll preparation. Firms that specialize in offering accounting services, including banks, offer this service to employers. What are the advantages to a business of contracting out its payroll function?

4. A provincial government decides that it will pass a law requiring that employers pay the complete cost of the provincial health premium for their employees. State the two financial benefits that the employee will receive as a result of this law.

5. An employee wishes to have no income tax deducted from his pay, and indicates that he will pay all of it the following April 30th when he is responsible for filing his T1. Why will the government not permit the employer to accept this request?

6. A payroll clerk believed that it was a waste of time to separate the regular from the

overtime pay. Why would a firm want to know the cost of overtime pay?

7. An employer deducts, as required by law, amounts from the pay of her employees. Instead of making payments to Revenue Canada Taxation, she uses the money to pay the liabilities of the business. Can she legally do this?

8. An employee enters into an agreement with her employer to have no unemployment insurance deducted from her pay. In return, the employee states that she will never attempt to collect unemployment insurance. Why does the law prohibit this type of agreement?

Organizing

1. Prepare a chart with the headings "Deductions Required by Law," "Deductions Which May Be Required by Contract," and "Voluntary Deductions." Under each heading, list the deductions that apply.

2. Prepare a summary to show the four basic general journal entries that are required for payroll.

Applications

Where tables are required, use those in Appendix A on pages 660 to 666.

1. (a) Set up a payroll register with the required deduction columns.
   (b) Use the following information and Figure 13-28 to calculate the weekly payroll for Nanaimo Outdoor Garden Ltd.
      (i) The pay period is for the week ending June 7.
      (ii) Registered pension plan is 5 percent of gross earnings.
      (iii) Union dues are $3 per week for each employee.
      (iv) Use the formula to calculate UI.
      (v) Use the tables in Appendix A to calculate CPP and Income Tax.
      (vi) The employer pays 75 percent of the health insurance premium and group life insurance. Again, use the tables and rates in Appendix A.
      (vii) Long-term disability insurance costs a total of $10 per week per employee, with 75 percent paid by the employer.
   (c) Prepare the general journal entry on page 69 to record the payroll register.
   (d) Prepare the general journal entries to record the employer's share of payroll costs.
   (e) Prepare the general journal entry to record the paying of the employees.
   (f) Prepare an employee earnings record for D. Empringham and B. Watanabe, assuming that this is their first pay. Supply any missing information.
   (g) Transfer the payroll data from the payroll register to the employee's individual earnings record for Empringham and Watanabe.

FIGURE 13-28

Employee		Marital Status	Age	Net Claim Code	Time Card		Life Insurance
No.	Name				Regular	Overtime	
5	R. Ahmed	M	42	5	$680		$20 000(N)
2	D. Empringham	S	21	1	540	$120	10 000(S)
3	M. Nanjappa	M	44	1	680		30 000(S)
4	P. Shanahan	M	33	7	550	100	10 000(N)
1	B. Watanabe	S	26	3	660		20 000(N)

2. The following data is provided concerning the October payroll for Northside Beauty Salons:

Gross earnings	$24 500.00
Income tax deducted	4 390.00
CPP deducted from employees' pay	585.23
UI deducted from employees' pay	723.19
Long-term disability insurance	325.00
Health Insurance deducted from employees' pay (The employer pays 75 percent of the cost.)	220.00
Group Life insurance deducted from employees' pay (The employer pays 75 percent of the cost.)	140.00

(a) Set up T-accounts showing balances as at November 1 to reflect the above information. Supply the appropriate account numbers. Assume that the employees have been paid all amounts owing to them using a Payroll account.

(b) The following totals are in the payroll register for the Northside Beauty Salon for the month of November.

Gross earnings	$23 409.00
CPP contributions	585.23
UI contributions	723.19
Income tax	4 328.50
Health insurance	220.00
Long-term disability insurance	325.00
Group life insurance	140.00

Show the T-accounts as they would appear after all the information related to the payroll for November has been posted.

(c) Balance the T-accounts.

3. The following are the totals shown for a payroll register for the month ending June 28.

Gross earnings	$87 980.00
Union dues	610.00
Registered pension plan	4 399.00
Taxable earnings	82 971.00
CPP contributions	1 647.00
UI contributions	2 064.24
Income tax	19 764.00
Health insurance	1 098.00
Life insurance	228.50
Net earnings	58 169.26

(a) Prepare entries in the general journal on page 625 to record:
  (i) the payroll register
  (ii) the employer's share of payroll costs (assume that the employer contributes to those items required by law, and pays one-half of the registered pension plan, and 75 percent of the health and life insurance premiums)

(b) Prepare entries on page 94 of the cash payments journal to record:
  (i) the paying of the employees
  (ii) the remittance of all deductions on the fifteenth of the following month.

Applications — Comprehensive

Worksheet to Closing Entries with Payroll

The trial balance in Figure 13-29 is for Speedex Ski Equipment and Maintenance.

(a) Complete the worksheet providing appropriate account numbers. Use the additional information for the adjustments for the year ended August 31, 19-9.

(b) Prepare an income statement and a classified balance sheet.

(c) Prepare the closing entries from the worksheet on page 82 of the general journal.

FIGURE 13-29

Speedex Ski Equipment and Maintenance
Trial Balance
August 31, 19–9

	Debit	Credit
Cash	$ 24 500	
Accounts Receivable	39 240	
Allowance for Doubtful Accounts		$ 900
Merchandise Inventory	98 420	
GST Recoverable	2 150	
Prepaid Insurance	4 500	
Maintenance Supplies	4 200	
Equipment	14 400	
Accumulated Depreciation: Equipment		2 000
Accounts Payable		23 620
CPP Payable		216
UI Payable		238
Income Tax Payable		2 400
GST Payable		4 200
Union Dues Payable		80
Group Life Insurance Payable		370
Trust Co. Loan Payable		8 900
D. Prakash, Capital		82 123
D. Prakash, Drawings	44 500	
Sales		573 800
Sales Returns and Allowances	2 350	
Maintenance Fees		36 200
Purchases	284 500	
Purchases Discounts		1 740
Rent Expense	36 800	
Wages Expense	129 600	
CPP Expense	2 851	
UI Expense	4 536	
Group Life Insurance Expense	19 240	
Utilities Expense	24 600	
General Expense	400	
	$736 787	$736 787

Additional Information

1. Merchandise inventory, August 31, 19–9, is $96 750.

2. Allowance for doubtful accounts, by ageing method, $1 250.

3. Insurance policy is a one-year policy, purchased February 1, 19–9.

4. Supplies inventory, $320.

5. Depreciation is at capital cost rates.

Evaluate and Assess

Wade Skube has recently been hired as a word processor. Wade's salary is to be $28 000 a year. In conversation with his friend Peter Sidwell, Wade states that it is only costing the firm $28 000 a year to have him as an employee. Peter disagrees, and says that it is costing the firm much more than the $28 000 to have Wade as an employee. Outline reasons that would support Peter's viewpoint.

Synthesize and Conclude

1. The following is a digest of news coverage. "Over $15 billion is stolen each year by employees. This is the estimated cost to employers of those who steal time. Time theft includes arriving late, leaving early, taking extended lunches or breaks, socializing with other employees, making personal phone calls, and taking care of personal chores. The loss of time, of course, leads to a reduction in productivity, which in turn leads to a lower income for the business. The loss due to time theft is greater than the combined costs of employee pilferage, embezzlement, insurance fraud, vandalism, kickbacks, arson, and other business crimes. Statistics showed that weekly time theft averaged three hours and forty-two minutes per employee."
   (a) What action can management take to penalize employees who are late?
   (b) How many lates should an employee be allowed before being penalized?
   (c) What action can management take to reward employees who are not late? Should there be rewards for not being late?
   (d) What should management do with employees who abuse sick leave by taking it when they are really not sick?

2. Cindy Sigouin is in charge of the payroll department for a department store. In order to increase her earnings, Cindy decides to add a fictitious person to the payroll. To do so, she obtains permission to hire another person for her department. Instead of actually doing so, she indicates to the personnel department the name of the person that she has supposedly interviewed and hired. She adds a phony time sheet to those processed each week, and takes the cheque when she signs all the paycheques on behalf of the company. She was able to open an account at a local trust company in the fictitious name, so she has no problems cashing the cheque.

   What internal control procedures should be in place in order for Cindy's scheme to be detected?

ACCOUNTING AT WORK

Anne Marie Tossan
Payroll Supervisor

Anne Marie Tossan did not set out to pursue a career in accounting, but the enjoyment she gets from working with others and her natural affinity for accounting made a career in payroll management ideal.

Anne Marie is employed as a payroll supervisor with Giffels Associates Ltd., an engineering consulting company located in Toronto. She supervises the overall payroll operation for over 400 employees. As supervisor, Anne Marie has two primary goals: to be a highly efficient paymaster and to satisfy the requirements of various government agencies, such as Revenue Canada, Employment and Immigration Canada, and the Workers' Compensation Board. The challenge is to maintain a proper balance between the needs of individual employees and the task of working within the structured guidelines necessary for maintaining a responsible payroll system. Her duties include liaising with external organizations, such as RRSP carriers, medical and dental insurance companies, and other financial institutions that affect the wages of the employees.

Anne Marie graduated from the University of Hawaii with a BA in Business Administration. Throughout her career, Anne Marie has been able to upgrade her professional skills. She supplemented her business background with courses in accounting, and then further specialized in payroll management with the Canadian Payroll Association (CPA), through which she gained basic professional knowledge and competence in payroll administration. Her academic qualifications and practical experience combine well in her chosen career path.

Anne Marie points out, "As the business of paying wages has graduated from a simple bookkeeping task to a complex, computerized system, it is imperative that the payroll personnel calculate with accuracy both the amount to be paid as well as the amount to be deducted."

Anne Marie attributes her success in accomplishing that task to the training and education she received. She now hopes to build on that success by moving up to the position of payroll manager. Her enthusiasm for a future in payroll demonstrates the satisfaction Anne Marie gets from her work. Although accounting was not her initial aim, it has turned out to be an ideal career for Anne Marie.

PAYROLL & BENEFITS

A large distribution company requires an experienced payroll and benefits person.

Applicants should be mature, responsible, extremely well organized, and able to work independently. TD Bank payroll experience preferred. Union and staff payrolls are prepared on a biweekly basis. An accounting background is an asset for payroll reconciliations and monthly journal entries. Lotus 1-2-3 is a definite asset.

Salary is commensurate with experience. We offer a congenial atmosphere and 100% company-paid benefits.

Applications should be submitted to:

Box 174
Station A
Vancouver, British Columbia
V6P 3P7

1. What are the two goals that Anne Marie Tossan has in her job as payroll supervisor?

2. Briefly outline the education path of Anne Marie.

3. What skills would Anne Marie use in her liaising with outside organizations?

4. Why is computer experience so important in obtaining a job in payroll?

Business Career Skills

1. Problem Solving — Sexual Harassment
L. Hansen, the accountant for R. Wilson Paint Supplies, is in charge of a department of six junior accountants. John, one of the male junior accountants, is continually talking with Ramona, a female employee. She has finally complained to Mr. Hansen that she finds John's conversations harassing. John keeps asking her out, and making suggestive references to her dress and figure.
(a) Using a problem-solving technique, decide what Mr. Hansen should do about the complaint?
(b) Are there laws that govern John's conduct? Explain.

2. Decision Making — The Job Interview
As supervisor of the accounting department, you are required to interview people for various positions in your department. In groups, brainstorm to develop a list of
(a) questions that you would ask prospective candidates for a job as accounts receivable clerk;
(b) questions that you should not ask candidates according to human rights legislation;
(c) attributes that the successful candidate should demonstrate that you would look for in the interview.

3. Communication — Letter Writing
Write a letter to a person who was not selected for the position that you were interviewing for in Question 2 above. Indicate to the person that they were not successful in being hired for the job. The reason that the person did not receive the job is that the successful candidate had more experience for the tasks required in the position.

4. Decision-Making — Drug Testing
The owner of the firm comes to you, the accounting supervisor, and asks that you sit on a committee to determine whether the firm should introduce compulsory testing of employees for drug use.
(a) In groups, brainstorm to develop a list of reasons for, and against, the compulsory testing of employees for drug use.
(b) Write a brief report to the owner, giving your opinion of the proposal for the introduction of compulsory testing of employees for drug use.

5. Analysis of Accounting Data
The owner of Bradkowski's Computer Equipment asks the accountant to prepare a report on the percentage increase in wages that the firm should offer its employees.
(a) Brainstorm to develop a list of items that should be considered when preparing the report.

(b) Use the financial statements in Figures 13-30 and 13-31 to assist you in preparing your report.
(c) Include in your report a list of advantages and disadvantages in offering to pay 50 percent of the cost of employee health and insurance premiums. (Total cost for the employees is $5 000.) Assume that the firm currently contributes nothing to the cost of benefits.

FIGURE 13-30

Bradkowski's Computer Equipment
Income Statement
for the year ended June 30, 19–4

Revenue		
Revenue (net)	$560 000	
Cost of Goods Sold	290 000	
Gross Profit		$270 000
Expenses		
Wages	160 000	
Other	90 000	
Total Expenses		250 000
Net Income		$ 20 000

FIGURE 13-31

Bradkowski's Computer Equipment
Balance Sheet
as at June 30, 19–4

Assets

Current Assets		
Cash	$ 40 000	
Accounts Receivable	10 000	
Merchandise Inventory	90 000	
Other Assets	140 000	
Total Current Assets		$280 000
Fixed Assets (net)		420 000
Total Assets		$700 000

Liabilities and Owner's Equity

Current Liabilities		
Accounts Payable	$ 60 000	
Bank Loan	30 000	
Total Current Liabilities		$ 90 000
Long-Term Liabilities		490 000
Total Liabilities		580 000
Owner's Equity		
Capital, July 1, 19–3	100 000	
Net Income	20 000	
Capital, June 30, 19–4		120 000
Total Liabilities and Owner's Equity		$700 000

COMPUTER ACCOUNTING
PAYROLL ACCOUNTING

As a computerized function, payroll has probably been around the longest of any business computer application. Even though it is the oldest program, it is the one that seems to give most people problems. The reason for this is the many payroll variations that exist from one organization to another, one city to another, and one province to another. A few years ago, most small business owners would have been well advised to make out paycheques and the required reports by hand or, at best, to let their accountant or a specialized company do it for a low cost per cheque per payroll period. With the arrival of full accounting programs for small computers, business owners and managers are well advised to seek out a payroll system that will fit in with the general ledger system they are currently using. In this manner, the effects that wage and salary disbursements have on the financial statements can be handled automatically.

Payroll, due to its liquidity and magnitude, requires strong internal controls to guard against loss from embezzlement. Employee payroll data is typically maintained collectively and with individual earnings records to facilitate the preparation of information and tax returns for both employees and government departments. As we are all aware, the gap between gross earnings and take-home pay is due to the combination of deductions required by federal and provincial laws, and other items such as pensions, insurance, savings bonds, and charitable donations.

An **employer's cost of payroll** includes matching the CPP contribution of each employee, an unemployment insurance payment of 1.4 times each employee's contribution, and payments for numerous fringe benefits. In addition, substantial costs are associated with record keeping as well as with acting as a collector for the government and other organizations.

To service these requirements there are many payroll systems on the market, and a business should ensure that the one selected will work easily in the company's overall accounting system. A good **payroll system** should accept data for employee master records and also for calculating the salaries and wages to be paid; produce the payroll cheques and a payroll journal; print a copy of the employee master file, employee earnings records, monthly federal tax reports, and annual T4 statements when required; and post all accounting entries to the general ledger data files.

Exercise

FarWest Lumber Products

Instructional Objectives

You have completed the study of individual topics in the accounting cycle for service and merchandising businesses, including the preparation of the company payroll and adjusting entries. Those systems may have included special journals and the general journal or a columnar journal, the general ledger and two subsidiary ledgers — accounts payable and accounts receivable, and a manual payroll system. You are now ready to learn how such manual accounting systems can be converted to a computerized accounting system.

Upon completion of this exercise you will be able to:

1. Load your accounting software program.

2. Set and access accounting data files for a sole proprietorship merchandising business.

3. Convert an existing manual accounting system to one using an integrated accounting software package.

4. Enter transactions into the computer using the General Ledger Module, Accounts Receivable Module, Accounts Payable Module, and the Payroll Module.

5. Display and print accounting transactions and reports.

6. Save your data entries and exit the accounting software program.

Information about the Business Enterprise

You have taken a position as accounting clerk for the FarWest Lumber Products Company located at 1700 River Road, Delta, BC V3M 2L6. You are to commence your duties on December 15, 1991, the arrangement being that you are to work with the present accounting clerk who is leaving at the end of the month. It is expected that during this time you will become sufficiently acquainted with the firm's accounting records and company procedures to enable you to assume full responsibility for the conversion of the existing accounting system to one utilizing microcomputer equipment.

During the first two weeks, you learn the following facts and information:

1. The business was formed two years ago by Bob Waterman.

2. The company's fiscal year coincides with the calendar year.

3. Provincial Sales Tax is currently at 6 percent and is levied on all sales.

4. All employees are paid on a semi-monthly basis.

5. As a condition of employment, each employee must contribute to the company registered pension plan. Contributions are made at the rate of 6 percent of the gross pay on each pay period. The employer matches the employees' contributions. Contributions made by the employees and the employer are accumulated by the company and remitted to AK Wong & Associates by the 10th of the following month.

6. The provincial medical services plan contributions for each employee are: Howard Ashley $18; Lisa Ellis $22; Douglas Scott $36; You $18.

7. As per Revenue Canada regulations, employees' income taxes and employees' and employers' contributions to the Unemployment Insurance Plan and the Canada Pension Plan are remitted to the Receiver General in one cheque by the fifteenth of the following month and detailed on form PD7AR.

8. The business uses the periodic system for accounting for merchandise inventory.

9. PST is remitted to the Provincial Treasurer by the fifteenth of each month for the deductions of the previous month. GST is remitted to the Receiver General by the fifteenth of each month for the deductions of the previous month.

10. The amount owing to the bank was borrowed on a demand note basis with interest at 11 percent per annum. Interest payments must be made monthly and remitted to the bank by the tenth of each month.

11. All credit sales are on a net 30 days basis.

On December 31, 1991, you assemble the following information necessary for a successful conversion to the computer system. (See Figures 13-32 to 13-36.)

FIGURE 13-32

CHART OF ACCOUNTS

101 Cash	260 PST Payable
102 Petty Cash	301 B. Waterman, Capital
104 Payroll Account	302 B. Waterman, Drawings
105 Accounts Receivable	401 Sales
110 Merchandise Inventory	501 Cost of Goods Sold
111 GST Recoverable	502 Purchases
112 Office Supplies	503 Freight-in
113 Prepaid Insurance	511 Maintenance Expense
120 Land	512 Dep. Expense: Building
121 Building	513 Dep. Expense: Off Equip.
122 Accumulated Dep.: Building	514 Dep. Expense: Trucks
125 Office Equipment	515 Insurance Expense
126 Accumulated Dep.: Office Equip.	516 Interest Expense
130 Trucks	517 Office Expense
131 Accumulated Dep.: Trucks	518 Office Supplies Expense
201 Bank Loan	519 Wages Expense
220 Accounts Payable	520 UI Expense
231 UI Payable	521 CPP Expense
232 CPP Payable	522 Utilities Expense
233 Income Tax Payable	523 Telephone Expense
240 Registered Pension Plan Payable	524 Registered Pension Plan Expense
241 MSP Contributions Payable	525 Truck Expense
250 GST Payable	526 Miscellaneous Expense

FIGURE 13-33

ACCOUNTS PAYABLE LEDGER

BC Forest Products　　　　　　　　Invoice 4567　$5 689
9515 Hopcott Street　　　　　　　　Terms n/30
Delta, BC　　　　　　　　　　　　　December 16
V5M 2L9

Absolutely Hardwoods　　　　　　　Invoice L654　$2 340
5689 Edmonds Street　　　　　　　　Terms n/30
Sudbury, Ontario　　　　　　　　　　December 5
M3R 2T6

Sunbury Cedar Products　　　　　　Invoice 3322　$1 456
10008 River Road West　　　　　　　Terms n/30
Delta, BC　　　　　　　　　　　　　December 22
V2T 5U8

Taiga Forest Products　　　　　　　Invoice 1298　$2 387
3209 Ewen Street　　　　　　　　　 Terms n/30
New Westminster, BC　　　　　　　　December 10
V6P 9E7

FIGURE 13-34

ACCOUNTS RECEIVABLE LEDGER	
Bayview Builders 2441 Vaxhall Road Richmond, BC V3E 4Y7	Invoice S1008 $1 000.27 December 14
Gentile's Cabinets Plus Ltd. 6038 Portland Street Burnaby, BC V4R 8J6	Invoice S1003 $1 589.00 November 30
Homemaster Building Ltd. 7987 McPherson Avenue North Vancouver, BC V3D 2T9	Invoice S1011 $1 896.43 December 27
Kedco Construction Co. 110 Front Street New Westminster, BC V5R 3S2	Invoice S0801 $567.00 April 23
MJD Construction Co. 210-4567 Granville Street Vancouver, BC V9L 5C9	Invoice S1012 $1 400.00 December 28
Pioneer Designs 110-56th Street Delta, BC V6W 1L8	Invoice S0907 $680.90 September 24
Reliable Construction 7531 Lombard Avenue West Vancouver, BC V2S 1F7	Invoice S1004 $446.80 December 12
Westlake Contracting Ltd. 78889 167th Street Surrey, BC V8U 3A8	Invoice S1010 $1 456.90 December 18

In addition, the company controller has given you the following information necessary to make the January end-of-month adjusting entries so that accurate and relevant financial statements can be prepared.

1. A physical inventory is taken at the end of the business day on the last day in the month. Merchandise Inventory is then updated by a series of adjusting entries transferring the beginning balance of Merchandise Inventory and the month-end balances of Purchases, Freight-in, and Purchases Returns and Allowances as well as the ending merchandise inventory to the Cost of Goods Sold account.

2. The annual insurance premium is $7 200 payable in advance on September 1 of each year.

3. The fixed assets — Building, Office Equipment, and Trucks — are depreciated in accordance with the rules and regulations as set down by Revenue Canada.

FIGURE 13-35

PAYROLL DATA

Employee 1 — Howard Ashley
636 8th Avenue
New Westminster, BC
V9N 9E1
Phone (604) 766-5438
SIN 706-828-512
Birthdate October 25, 1953
Net Claim $11 310/year
Regular $14/hour
OT $21/hour

Employee 2 — Lisa Ellis
117-480 Bute Street
Vancouver, BC
V2G 3X7
Phone (604) 872-8630
SIN 718-808-627
Birthdate January 14, 1956
Net Claim $10 779/year
Salary $750/period

Employee 3 — Douglas Scott
6006 Dogwood Drive
Delta, BC
V4M 1B9
Phone (604) 943-4407
SIN 706-919-611
Net Claim $6 800/year
Birthdate November 17, 1960
Salary $1 500/period

Employee 4 — You
Record your own personal data
Net Claim — Use Figure 13-4
Salary $1 300/period

Asset	Rate of Depreciation (Declining Balance Method)
Building	5%
Office Equipment	20%
Trucks	30%

Solution

You will use your data files disk to create a file directory for this company if this is part of your accounting software requirements. After recording the company name and other data you will need to use the information you have gathered to prepare the modules you will require and also set up the Chart of Accounts to meet the requirements of your software.

After converting the account balances from the year-end information, you will journalize the transactions for the month of January. You will print or display your general journal and a trial balance to determine if your data entries are correct.

Journalizing the Transactions

Enter the accounting data for the transactions using the appropriate module. You are told directly about *most* of the transactions but some you must remember to originate yourself, from the information you have gathered. Apply GST of 7% and PST of 6% to the base price given for each sale. Otherwise, apply taxes as indicated.

Jan. 2 Sales Invoice S1014 to Homemaster Building Ltd., $6 456.
2 Cash Receipt Slip R1122 from Gentile's Cabinets Plus Ltd., $1 589, in full payment of Sales Invoice S1003.
3 Sales Invoice S1015 to Westlake Contracting Ltd., $4 247.
5 Cheque Copy 125 to Absolutely Hardwoods, $2 340, in full payment of Purchase Invoice L654.
7 Purchase Invoice 3456 from Sunbury Cedar Products, $1 500 plus GST, for merchandise; terms n/30.
8 Cheque Copy 126 to Esso Canada Petroleum, $650 plus GST, for gas and oil used in the trucks (received billing statement today).
8 Sales Invoice S1016 to Gentile's Cabinets Plus Ltd., $3 400.
9 Cheque Copy 129 to Taiga Forest Products, $2 387, in full payment of Purchase Invoice 1298.
9 Cheque Copy 130 to Moore Business Forms, $690 plus taxes,

FIGURE 13-36

FarWest Lumber Products
Post-Closing Trial Balance
December 31, 1991

	Debit	Credit
Cash	$ 28 500.00	
Petty Cash	100.00	
Accounts Receivable	9 037.30	
Merchandise Inventory	36 812.00	
GST Recoverable	1 750.00	
Office Supplies	700.00	
Prepaid Insurance	4 800.00	
Land	60 000.00	
Building	140 000.00	
Accumulated Depreciation: Building		$ 26 600.00
Office Equipment	6 200.00	
Accumulated Depreciation: Office Equip.		2 232.00
Trucks	45 000.00	
Accumulated Depreciation: Trucks		24 200.00
Bank Loan		15 000.00
Accounts Payable		11 872.00
UI Payable		201.60
CPP Payable		168.12
Income Tax Payable		1 486.80
Registered Pension Plan Payable		934.00
MSP Contributions Payable		188.00
GST Payable		3 045.00
PST Payable		2 610.00
B. Waterman, Capital		244 361.78
	$332 899.30	$332 899.30

for office stationery and computer forms.

10 Purchase Invoice L876 from Absolutely Hardwoods, $6 234 plus GST, for merchandise; terms n/30, FOB Sudbury.

10 Cheque Copy 131 to CP Rail, $456 plus GST, for Freight Bill 459.

11 Sales Invoice S1017 to MJD Construction Co., $4 809.

11 Cash Receipt Slip R1123 from Homemaster Building Ltd., $1 896.43, in full payment of Sales Invoice S1011.

12 Cash Receipt Slip R1124 from MJD Construction Co., $1 400, in full payment of Sales Invoice S1012.

13 Cash Receipt Slip R1125 from Westlake Contracting Ltd., $1 456.90, in full payment of Sales Invoice S1010.

14 Purchase Invoice 4765 from BC Forest Products, $1 410 plus GST, for merchandise; terms n/30.

15 Cheque Copy 135 to BC Forest Products, $5 689, in full payment of Purchase Invoice 4567.

15 Cheque Copy 136 to B. Waterman, $2 500, for the owner's personal use.

16 Cheque Copy 137 to Payroll Account for the semi-monthly payroll. Howard Ashley the only hourly-rated employee worked a total of 80 regular hours and 6 hours of overtime.

16	Sales Invoice S1018 to Pioneer Designs, $4 869.		Construction Co., $5 434.17, in full payment of Sales Invoice S1017.
17	Cash Receipt Slip R1126 from Homemaster Building Ltd., $7 295.28, in full payment of Sales Invoice S1014.	27	Cash Receipt Slip R1131 from Reliable Construction, $446.80, in full payment of Sales Invoice S1004.
18	Cash Receipt Slip R1127 from Westlake Contracting Ltd., $4 799.11, in full payment of Sales Invoice S1015.	28	Cheque Copy 140 to BC Hydro & Power Authority, $850 plus GST, for electricity and natural gas consumption.
19	Sales Invoice S1019 to Homemaster Building Ltd., $5 238.	29	Cheque Copy 141 to BC Telephone Company, $233 plus taxes.
20	Purchase Invoice 1467 from Taiga Forest Products, $1 870 plus GST, for merchandise; terms n/30.	30	Cheque Copy 142 to B. Waterman, $2 500, for owner's personal use.
21	Cheque Copy 138 to Sunbury Cedar Products, $1 456, in full payment of Purchase Invoice 3322.	31	Cheque Copy 143 to Payroll Account for the semi-monthly payroll. Howard Ashley worked 80 regular hours.
21	Cheque Copy 139 to Lisa Ellis, petty cashier, for $76.50, to replenish the petty cash fund. Petty Cash Requisition Form 23 lists the following disbursements: Miscellaneous Expense, $22.13; Office Supplies, $17.73; Office Expense, $31.90; GST Recoverable, $4.74.	31	Lisa Ellis submitted an inventory of $250 for the office supplies on hand.
		31	At the end of the business day the closing inventory of lumber products as determined by a physical count was $36 789.

Chapter 13: Payroll Accounting

(Continuing)

16 Sales Invoice S1018 to Pioneer Designs, $4 869.
17 Cash Receipt Slip R1126 from Homemaster Building Ltd., $7 295.28, in full payment of Sales Invoice S1014.
18 Cash Receipt Slip R1127 from Westlake Contracting Ltd., $4 799.11, in full payment of Sales Invoice S1015.
19 Sales Invoice S1019 to Homemaster Building Ltd., $5 238.
20 Purchase Invoice 1467 from Taiga Forest Products, $1 870 plus GST, for merchandise; terms n/30.
21 Cheque Copy 138 to Sunbury Cedar Products, $1 456, in full payment of Purchase Invoice 3322.
21 Cheque Copy 139 to Lisa Ellis, petty cashier, for $76.50, to replenish the petty cash fund. Petty Cash Requisition Form 23 lists the following disbursements: Miscellaneous Expense, $22.13; Office Supplies, $17.73; Office Expense, $31.90; GST Recoverable, $4.74.
22 Sales Invoice S1020 to Reliable Construction, $5 786.
23 Purchase Invoice 3568 from Sunbury Cedar Products, $1 150 plus GST, for merchandise; terms n/30.
23 Cash Receipt Slip R1128 from Pioneer Designs, $680.90, in full payment of Sales Invoice S0907.
23 Cash Receipt Slip R1129 from Gentile's Cabinets Plus Ltd., $3 842, in full payment of Sales Invoice S1016.
25 Purchase Invoice 4856 from BC Forest Products, $1 068 plus GST, for merchandise; terms n/30.
26 Sales Invoice S1021 to Westlake Contracting Ltd., $6 098.
26 Cash Receipt Slip R1130 from MJD Construction Co., $5 434.17, in full payment of Sales Invoice S1017.
27 Cash Receipt Slip R1131 from Reliable Construction, $446.80, in full payment of Sales Invoice S1004.
28 Cheque Copy 140 to BC Hydro & Power Authority, $850 plus GST, for electricity and natural gas consumption.
29 Cheque Copy 141 to BC Telephone Company, $233 plus taxes.
30 Cheque Copy 142 to B. Waterman, $2 500, for owner's personal use.
31 Cheque Copy 143 to Payroll Account for the semi-monthly payroll. Howard Ashley worked 80 regular hours.
31 Lisa Ellis submitted an inventory of $250 for the office supplies on hand.
31 At the end of the business day the closing inventory of lumber products as determined by a physical count was $36 789.

Month-end Activities

Before printing any of the requested reports, have your teacher check the trial balance.

Print a hard copy of the following:

1. General Journal
2. General Ledger
3. Income Statement
4. Balance Sheet
5. Accounts Payable Reports
6. Accounts Receivable Reports
7. Payroll Reports

Evaluation

You will now use your printouts or access information from your data disk to complete:

1. An audit test of the accuracy of the accounting records of the business.
2. Analysis exercises.

APPENDIX A

TABLE 1

ONTARIO
WEEKLY TAX DEDUCTIONS
Basis — 52 Pay Periods per Year

ONTARIO
RETENUES D'IMPÔT PAR SEMAINE
Base — 52 périodes de paie par année

IF THE EMPLOYEE'S "NET CLAIM CODE" ON FORM TD1 IS
SI LE CODE DE DEMANDE NETTE DE L'EMPLOYÉ SELON LA FORMULE TD1 EST DE

WEEKLY PAY / PAIE PAR SEMAINE		0	1	2	3	4	5	6	7	8	9	10
From - De	Less than / Moins que	\multicolumn{11}{l}{DEDUCT FROM EACH PAY — *RETENEZ SUR CHAQUE PAIE*}										
451.-	459.	117.10	85.25	81.30	73.50	65.70	57.90	50.20	42.30	34.50	26.70	18.85
459.-	467.	119.15	87.30	83.40	75.55	67.75	59.95	52.25	44.35	36.55	28.75	20.90
467.-	475.	121.20	89.35	85.45	77.60	69.80	62.00	54.30	46.40	38.60	30.80	22.95
475.-	483.	123.25	91.40	87.50	79.70	71.85	64.05	56.35	48.45	40.65	32.85	25.00
483.-	491.	125.30	93.45	89.55	81.75	73.90	66.10	58.40	50.50	42.70	34.90	27.10
491.-	499.	127.35	95.50	91.60	83.80	75.95	68.15	60.45	52.55	44.75	36.95	29.15
499.-	507.	129.40	97.55	93.65	85.85	78.05	70.20	62.50	54.60	46.80	39.00	31.20
507.-	515.	131.45	99.60	95.70	87.90	80.10	72.25	64.55	56.65	48.85	41.05	33.25
515.-	523.	133.50	101.65	97.75	89.95	82.15	74.35	66.60	58.70	50.90	43.10	35.30
523.-	531.	135.55	103.70	99.80	92.00	84.20	76.40	68.70	60.75	52.95	45.15	37.35
531.-	539.	137.60	105.75	101.85	94.05	86.25	78.45	70.75	62.80	55.00	47.20	39.40
539.-	547.	139.70	107.80	103.90	96.10	88.30	80.50	72.80	64.85	57.05	49.25	41.45
547.-	555.	142.75	110.90	107.00	99.20	91.35	83.55	75.85	67.95	60.15	52.35	44.55
555.-	563.	145.95	114.10	110.20	102.40	94.60	86.75	79.05	71.15	63.35	55.55	47.75
563.-	571.	149.20	117.35	113.45	105.65	97.80	90.00	82.30	74.40	66.60	58.80	50.95
571.-	579.	152.45	120.55	116.65	108.85	101.05	93.25	85.55	77.65	69.85	62.00	54.20
579.-	587.	155.70	123.80	119.90	112.10	104.30	96.50	88.80	80.85	73.05	65.25	57.45
587.-	595.	158.90	127.05	123.15	115.35	107.55	99.70	92.00	84.10	76.30	68.50	60.70
595.-	603.	162.15	130.30	126.40	118.60	110.75	102.95	95.25	87.35	79.55	71.75	63.95
603.-	611.	165.40	133.55	129.60	121.80	114.00	106.20	98.50	90.60	82.80	74.95	67.15
611.-	619.	168.65	136.75	132.85	125.05	117.25	109.45	101.75	93.85	86.00	78.20	70.40
619.-	627.	171.85	140.00	136.10	128.30	120.50	112.70	104.95	97.05	89.25	81.45	73.65
627.-	635.	175.10	143.25	139.35	131.55	123.70	115.90	108.20	100.30	92.50	84.70	76.90
635.-	643.	178.35	146.50	142.60	134.75	126.95	119.15	111.45	103.55	95.75	87.95	80.10
643.-	651.	181.60	149.75	145.85	138.05	130.25	122.45	114.75	106.80	99.00	91.20	83.40
651.-	659.	184.90	153.05	149.15	141.35	133.55	125.70	118.00	110.10	102.30	94.50	86.70
659.-	667.	188.20	156.35	152.45	144.60	136.80	129.00	121.30	113.40	105.60	97.80	89.95
667.-	675.	191.50	159.60	155.70	147.90	140.10	132.30	124.60	116.70	108.85	101.05	93.25
675.-	683.	194.75	162.90	159.00	151.20	143.40	135.60	127.90	119.95	112.15	104.35	96.55
683.-	691.	198.05	166.20	162.30	154.50	146.65	138.85	131.15	123.25	115.45	107.65	99.85
691.-	699.	201.35	169.50	165.60	157.75	149.95	142.15	134.45	126.55	118.75	110.95	103.10
699.-	707.	204.65	172.75	168.85	161.05	153.25	145.45	137.75	129.80	122.00	114.20	106.40
707.-	715.	207.90	176.05	172.15	164.35	156.55	148.70	141.00	133.10	125.30	117.50	109.70
715.-	723.	211.20	179.35	175.45	167.65	159.80	152.00	144.30	136.40	128.60	120.80	112.95
723.-	731.	214.50	182.60	178.70	170.90	163.10	155.30	147.60	139.70	131.90	124.05	116.25
731.-	739.	217.80	185.90	182.00	174.20	166.40	158.60	150.90	142.95	135.15	127.35	119.55
739.-	747.	221.05	189.20	185.30	177.50	169.70	161.85	154.15	146.25	138.45	130.65	122.85
747.-	755.	224.35	192.50	188.60	180.75	172.95	165.15	157.45	149.55	141.75	133.95	126.10
755.-	763.	227.65	195.75	191.85	184.05	176.25	168.45	160.75	152.85	145.00	137.20	129.40
763.-	771.	230.90	199.05	195.15	187.35	179.55	171.75	164.05	156.10	148.30	140.50	132.70
771.-	779.	234.20	202.35	198.45	190.65	182.80	175.00	167.30	159.40	151.60	143.80	136.00
779.-	787.	237.50	205.65	201.75	193.90	186.10	178.30	170.60	162.70	154.90	147.10	139.25
787.-	795.	240.80	208.90	205.00	197.20	189.40	181.60	173.90	166.00	158.15	150.35	142.55
795.-	803.	244.05	212.20	208.30	200.50	192.70	184.85	177.15	169.25	161.45	153.65	145.85
803.-	811.	247.35	215.50	211.60	203.80	195.95	188.15	180.45	172.55	164.75	156.95	149.15
811.-	819.	250.65	218.75	214.85	207.05	199.25	191.45	183.75	175.85	168.05	160.20	152.40
819.-	827.	253.95	222.05	218.15	210.35	202.55	194.75	187.05	179.10	171.30	163.50	155.70
827.-	835.	257.20	225.35	221.45	213.65	205.85	198.00	190.30	182.40	174.60	166.80	159.00
835.-	843.	260.50	228.65	224.75	216.90	209.10	201.30	193.60	185.70	177.90	170.10	162.25
843.-	851.	263.80	231.90	228.00	220.20	212.40	204.60	196.90	189.00	181.15	173.35	165.55
851.-	859.	267.05	235.20	231.30	223.50	215.70	207.90	200.20	192.25	184.45	176.65	168.85
859.-	867.	270.35	238.50	234.60	226.80	218.95	211.15	203.45	195.55	187.75	179.95	172.15
867.-	875.	273.65	241.80	237.90	230.05	222.25	214.45	206.75	198.85	191.05	183.25	175.40
875.-	883.	276.95	245.05	241.15	233.35	225.55	217.75	210.05	202.15	194.30	186.50	178.70
883.-	891.	280.20	248.35	244.45	236.65	228.85	221.00	213.30	205.40	197.60	189.80	182.00

APPENDIX A (continued)

TABLE 1

ONTARIO
WEEKLY TAX DEDUCTIONS
Basis — 52 Pay Periods per Year

ONTARIO
RETENUES D'IMPÔT PAR SEMAINE
Base — 52 périodes de paie par année

WEEKLY PAY Use appropriate bracket — PAIE PAR SEMAINE Utilisez le palier approprié		IF THE EMPLOYEE'S "NET CLAIM CODE" ON FORM TD1 IS SI LE CODE DE DEMANDE NETTE DE L'EMPLOYÉ SELON LA FORMULE TD1 EST DE									
		0	1	2	3	4	5	6	7	8	9	10
From - De	Less than Moins que	DEDUCT FROM EACH PAY — RETENEZ SUR CHAQUE PAIE										
891.-	903.	284.30	252.45	248.55	240.75	232.95	225.15	217.45	209.50	201.70	193.90	186.10
903.-	915.	289.25	257.40	253.50	245.70	237.85	230.05	222.35	214.45	206.65	198.85	191.05
915.-	927.	294.20	262.30	258.40	250.60	242.80	235.00	227.30	219.40	211.55	203.75	195.95
927.-	939.	299.10	267.25	263.35	255.55	247.75	239.90	232.20	224.30	216.50	208.70	200.90
939.-	951.	304.05	272.20	268.30	260.45	252.65	244.85	237.15	229.25	221.45	213.65	205.80
951.-	963.	308.95	277.10	273.20	265.40	257.60	249.80	242.10	234.15	226.35	218.55	210.75
963.-	975.	313.90	282.05	278.15	270.35	262.50	254.70	247.00	239.10	231.30	223.50	215.65
975.-	987.	318.85	286.95	283.05	275.25	267.45	259.65	251.95	244.05	236.20	228.40	220.60
987.-	999.	323.75	291.90	288.00	280.20	272.40	264.55	256.85	248.95	241.15	233.35	225.55
999.-	1011.	328.70	296.85	292.90	285.10	277.30	269.50	261.80	253.90	246.10	238.25	230.45
1011.-	1023.	333.60	301.75	297.85	290.05	282.25	274.45	266.75	258.80	251.00	243.20	235.40
1023.-	1035.	338.55	306.70	302.80	295.00	287.15	279.35	271.65	263.75	255.95	248.15	240.30
1035.-	1047.	343.50	311.60	307.70	299.90	292.10	284.30	276.60	268.70	260.85	253.05	245.25
1047.-	1059.	348.40	316.55	312.65	304.85	297.00	289.20	281.50	273.60	265.80	258.00	250.20
1059.-	1071.	353.35	321.45	317.55	309.75	301.95	294.15	286.45	278.55	270.75	262.90	255.10
1071.-	1083.	358.25	326.40	322.50	314.70	306.90	299.10	291.35	283.45	275.65	267.85	260.05
1083.-	1095.	363.30	331.40	327.50	319.70	311.90	304.10	296.40	288.50	280.65	272.85	265.05
1095.-	1107.	368.80	336.90	333.00	325.20	317.40	309.60	301.90	294.00	286.15	278.35	270.55
1107.-	1119.	374.30	342.40	338.50	330.70	322.90	315.10	307.40	299.50	291.65	283.85	276.05
1119.-	1131.	379.80	347.90	344.00	336.20	328.40	320.60	312.90	304.95	297.15	289.35	281.55
1131.-	1143.	385.30	353.40	349.50	341.70	333.90	326.10	318.40	310.45	302.65	294.85	287.05
1143.-	1155.	390.80	358.90	355.00	347.20	339.40	331.60	323.90	315.95	308.15	300.35	292.55
1155.-	1167.	396.30	364.40	360.50	352.70	344.90	337.10	329.40	321.45	313.65	305.85	298.05
1167.-	1179.	401.75	369.90	366.00	358.20	350.40	342.60	334.90	326.95	319.15	311.35	303.55
1179.-	1191.	407.25	375.40	371.50	363.70	355.90	348.10	340.40	332.45	324.65	316.85	309.05
1191.-	1203.	412.75	380.90	377.00	369.20	361.40	353.60	345.90	337.95	330.15	322.35	314.55
1203.-	1215.	418.25	386.40	382.50	374.70	366.90	359.10	351.35	343.45	335.65	327.85	320.05
1215.-	1227.	423.75	391.90	388.00	380.20	372.40	364.55	356.85	348.95	341.15	333.35	325.55
1227.-	1239.	429.25	397.40	393.50	385.70	377.90	370.05	362.35	354.45	346.65	338.85	331.05
1239.-	1251.	434.75	402.90	399.00	391.20	383.40	375.55	367.85	359.95	352.15	344.35	336.55
1251.-	1263.	440.25	408.40	404.50	396.70	388.90	381.05	373.35	365.45	357.65	349.85	342.05
1263.-	1275.	445.75	413.90	410.00	402.20	394.40	386.55	378.85	370.95	363.15	355.35	347.55
1275.-	1287.	451.25	419.40	415.50	407.70	399.85	392.05	384.35	376.45	368.65	360.85	353.05
1287.-	1299.	456.80	424.90	421.00	413.20	405.35	397.55	389.85	381.95	374.15	366.35	358.55
1299.-	1311.	462.40	430.40	426.50	418.70	410.85	403.05	395.35	387.45	379.65	371.85	364.05
1311.-	1323.	468.00	435.90	432.00	424.20	416.35	408.55	400.85	392.95	385.15	377.35	369.55
1323.-	1335.	473.60	441.40	437.50	429.70	421.85	414.05	406.35	398.45	390.65	382.85	375.05
1335.-	1347.	479.20	446.90	443.00	435.20	427.35	419.55	411.85	403.95	396.15	388.35	380.50
1347.-	1359.	484.80	452.40	448.50	440.65	432.85	425.05	417.35	409.45	401.65	393.85	386.00
1359.-	1371.	490.40	457.90	454.00	446.15	438.35	430.55	422.85	414.95	407.15	399.35	391.50
1371.-	1383.	496.00	463.55	459.55	451.65	443.85	436.05	428.35	420.45	412.65	404.85	397.00
1383.-	1395.	501.60	469.15	465.15	457.20	449.35	441.55	433.85	425.95	418.15	410.35	402.50
1395.-	1407.	507.20	474.75	470.75	462.80	454.85	447.05	439.35	431.45	423.65	415.85	408.00
1407.-	1419.	512.80	480.35	476.35	468.40	460.45	452.55	444.85	436.95	429.15	421.30	413.50
1419.-	1431.	518.40	485.95	481.95	474.00	466.05	458.10	450.35	442.45	434.65	426.80	419.00
1431.-	1443.	524.00	491.55	487.55	479.60	471.65	463.70	455.85	447.95	440.15	432.30	424.50
1443.-	1455.	529.60	497.15	493.15	485.20	477.25	469.30	461.45	453.45	445.60	437.80	430.00
1455.-	1467.	535.20	502.75	498.75	490.80	482.85	474.90	467.05	459.00	451.10	443.30	435.50
1467.-	1479.	540.80	508.35	504.35	496.40	488.45	480.50	472.65	464.60	456.65	448.80	441.00
1479.-	1491.	546.40	513.95	509.95	502.00	494.05	486.10	478.25	470.20	462.25	454.30	446.50
1491.-	1503.	552.00	519.55	515.60	507.60	499.65	491.70	483.85	475.80	467.85	459.90	452.00
1503.-	1515.	557.65	525.15	521.20	513.20	505.25	497.30	489.45	481.40	473.45	465.50	457.55
1515.-	1527.	563.25	530.75	526.80	518.85	510.85	502.90	495.05	487.00	479.05	471.10	463.15
1527.-	1539.	568.85	536.35	532.40	524.45	516.45	508.50	500.65	492.60	484.65	476.70	468.75
1539.-	1551.	574.45	541.95	538.00	530.05	522.05	514.10	506.25	498.20	490.25	482.30	474.35

CANADA PENSION PLAN CONTRIBUTIONS — COTISATIONS AU RÉGIME DE PENSIONS DU CANADA

WEEKLY PAY PERIOD — *PÉRIODE HEBDOMADAIRE DE PAIE*

446.34 — 1016.33

Remuneration / Rémunération From-de — To-à	C.P.P. R.P.C.	Remuneration / Rémunération From-de — To-à	C.P.P. R.P.C.	Remuneration / Rémunération From-de — To-à	C.P.P. R.P.C.	Remuneration / Rémunération From-de — To-à	C.P.P. R.P.C.
446.34 - 446.79	8.64	479.07 - 479.52	9.36	511.80 - 512.24	10.08	544.53 - 544.97	10.80
446.80 - 447.24	8.65	479.53 - 479.97	9.37	512.25 - 512.70	10.09	544.98 - 545.43	10.81
447.25 - 447.70	8.66	479.98 - 480.43	9.38	512.71 - 513.15	10.10	545.44 - 545.88	10.82
447.71 - 448.15	8.67	480.44 - 480.88	9.39	513.16 - 513.61	10.11	545.89 - 546.33	10.83
448.16 - 448.61	8.68	480.89 - 481.33	9.40	513.62 - 514.06	10.12	546.34 - 546.79	10.84
448.62 - 449.06	8.69	481.34 - 481.79	9.41	514.07 - 514.52	10.13	546.80 - 547.24	10.85
449.07 - 449.52	8.70	481.80 - 482.24	9.42	514.53 - 514.97	10.14	547.25 - 547.70	10.86
449.53 - 449.97	8.71	482.25 - 482.70	9.43	514.98 - 515.43	10.15	547.71 - 548.15	10.87
449.98 - 450.43	8.72	482.71 - 483.15	9.44	515.44 - 515.88	10.16	548.16 - 548.61	10.88
450.44 - 450.88	8.73	483.16 - 483.61	9.45	515.89 - 516.33	10.17	548.62 - 549.06	10.89
450.89 - 451.33	8.74	483.62 - 484.06	9.46	516.34 - 516.79	10.18	549.07 - 549.52	10.90
451.34 - 451.79	8.75	484.07 - 484.52	9.47	516.80 - 517.24	10.19	549.53 - 549.97	10.91
451.80 - 452.24	8.76	484.53 - 484.97	9.48	517.25 - 517.70	10.20	549.98 - 550.43	10.92
452.25 - 452.70	8.77	484.98 - 485.43	9.49	517.71 - 518.15	10.21	550.44 - 550.88	10.93
452.71 - 453.15	8.78	485.44 - 485.88	9.50	518.16 - 518.61	10.22	550.89 - 551.33	10.94
453.16 - 453.61	8.79	485.89 - 486.33	9.51	518.62 - 519.06	10.23	551.34 - 551.79	10.95
453.62 - 454.06	8.80	486.34 - 486.79	9.52	519.07 - 519.52	10.24	551.80 - 552.24	10.96
454.07 - 454.52	8.81	486.80 - 487.24	9.53	519.53 - 519.97	10.25	552.25 - 552.70	10.97
454.53 - 454.97	8.82	487.25 - 487.70	9.54	519.98 - 520.43	10.26	552.71 - 553.15	10.98
454.98 - 455.43	8.83	487.71 - 488.15	9.55	520.44 - 520.88	10.27	553.16 - 553.61	10.99
455.44 - 455.88	8.84	488.16 - 488.61	9.56	520.89 - 521.33	10.28	553.62 - 554.06	11.00
455.89 - 456.33	8.85	488.62 - 489.06	9.57	521.34 - 521.79	10.29	554.07 - 554.52	11.01
456.34 - 456.79	8.86	489.07 - 489.52	9.58	521.80 - 522.24	10.30	554.53 - 554.97	11.02
456.80 - 457.24	8.87	489.53 - 489.97	9.59	522.25 - 522.70	10.31	554.98 - 555.43	11.03
457.25 - 457.70	8.88	489.98 - 490.43	9.60	522.71 - 523.15	10.32	555.44 - 555.88	11.04
457.71 - 458.15	8.89	490.44 - 490.88	9.61	523.16 - 523.61	10.33	555.89 - 556.33	11.05
458.16 - 458.61	8.90	490.89 - 491.33	9.62	523.62 - 524.06	10.34	556.34 - 566.33	11.16
458.62 - 459.06	8.91	491.34 - 491.79	9.63	524.07 - 524.52	10.35	566.34 - 576.33	11.38
459.07 - 459.52	8.92	491.80 - 492.24	9.64	524.53 - 524.97	10.36	576.34 - 586.33	11.60
459.53 - 459.97	8.93	492.25 - 492.70	9.65	524.98 - 525.43	10.37	586.34 - 596.33	11.82
459.98 - 460.43	8.94	492.71 - 493.15	9.66	525.44 - 525.88	10.38	596.34 - 606.33	12.04
460.44 - 460.88	8.95	493.16 - 493.61	9.67	525.89 - 526.33	10.39	606.34 - 616.33	12.26
460.89 - 461.33	8.96	493.62 - 494.06	9.68	526.34 - 526.79	10.40	616.34 - 626.33	12.48
461.34 - 461.79	8.97	494.07 - 494.52	9.69	526.80 - 527.24	10.41	626.34 - 636.33	12.70
461.80 - 462.24	8.98	494.53 - 494.97	9.70	527.25 - 527.70	10.42	636.34 - 646.33	12.92
462.25 - 462.70	8.99	494.98 - 495.43	9.71	527.71 - 528.15	10.43	646.34 - 656.33	13.14
462.71 - 463.15	9.00	495.44 - 495.88	9.72	528.16 - 528.61	10.44	656.34 - 666.33	13.36
463.16 - 463.61	9.01	495.89 - 496.33	9.73	528.62 - 529.06	10.45	666.34 - 676.33	13.58
463.62 - 464.06	9.02	496.34 - 496.79	9.74	529.07 - 529.52	10.46	676.34 - 686.33	13.80
464.07 - 464.52	9.03	496.80 - 497.24	9.75	529.53 - 529.97	10.47	686.34 - 696.33	14.02
464.53 - 464.97	9.04	497.25 - 497.70	9.76	529.98 - 530.43	10.48	696.34 - 706.33	14.24
464.98 - 465.43	9.05	497.71 - 498.15	9.77	530.44 - 530.88	10.49	706.34 - 716.33	14.46
465.44 - 465.88	9.06	498.16 - 498.61	9.78	530.89 - 531.33	10.50	716.34 - 726.33	14.68
465.89 - 466.33	9.07	498.62 - 499.06	9.79	531.34 - 531.79	10.51	726.34 - 736.33	14.90
466.34 - 466.79	9.08	499.07 - 499.52	9.80	531.80 - 532.24	10.52	736.34 - 746.33	15.12
466.80 - 467.24	9.09	499.53 - 499.97	9.81	532.25 - 532.70	10.53	746.34 - 756.33	15.34
467.25 - 467.70	9.10	499.98 - 500.43	9.82	532.71 - 533.15	10.54	756.34 - 766.33	15.56
467.71 - 468.15	9.11	500.44 - 500.88	9.83	533.16 - 533.61	10.55	766.34 - 776.33	15.78
468.16 - 468.61	9.12	500.89 - 501.33	9.84	533.62 - 534.06	10.56	776.34 - 786.33	16.00
468.62 - 469.06	9.13	501.34 - 501.79	9.85	534.07 - 534.52	10.57	786.34 - 796.33	16.22
469.07 - 469.52	9.14	501.80 - 502.24	9.86	534.53 - 534.97	10.58	796.34 - 806.33	16.44
469.53 - 469.97	9.15	502.25 - 502.70	9.87	534.98 - 535.43	10.59	806.34 - 816.33	16.66
469.98 - 470.43	9.16	502.71 - 503.15	9.88	535.44 - 535.88	10.60	816.34 - 826.33	16.88
470.44 - 470.88	9.17	503.16 - 503.61	9.89	535.89 - 536.33	10.61	826.34 - 836.33	17.10
470.89 - 471.33	9.18	503.62 - 504.06	9.90	536.34 - 536.79	10.62	836.34 - 846.33	17.32
471.34 - 471.79	9.19	504.07 - 504.52	9.91	536.80 - 537.24	10.63	846.34 - 856.33	17.54
471.80 - 472.24	9.20	504.53 - 504.97	9.92	537.25 - 537.70	10.64	856.34 - 866.33	17.76
472.25 - 472.70	9.21	504.98 - 505.43	9.93	537.71 - 538.15	10.65	866.34 - 876.33	17.98
472.71 - 473.15	9.22	505.44 - 505.88	9.94	538.16 - 538.61	10.66	876.34 - 886.33	18.20
473.16 - 473.61	9.23	505.89 - 506.33	9.95	538.62 - 539.06	10.67	886.34 - 896.33	18.42
473.62 - 474.06	9.24	506.34 - 506.79	9.96	539.07 - 539.52	10.68	896.34 - 906.33	18.64
474.07 - 474.52	9.25	506.80 - 507.24	9.97	539.53 - 539.97	10.69	906.34 - 916.33	18.86
474.53 - 474.97	9.26	507.25 - 507.70	9.98	539.98 - 540.43	10.70	916.34 - 926.33	19.08
474.98 - 475.43	9.27	507.71 - 508.15	9.99	540.44 - 540.88	10.71	926.34 - 936.33	19.30
475.44 - 475.88	9.28	508.16 - 508.61	10.00	540.89 - 541.33	10.72	936.34 - 946.33	19.52
475.89 - 476.33	9.29	508.62 - 509.06	10.01	541.34 - 541.79	10.73	946.34 - 956.33	19.74
476.34 - 476.79	9.30	509.07 - 509.52	10.02	541.80 - 542.24	10.74	956.34 - 966.33	19.96
476.80 - 477.24	9.31	509.53 - 509.97	10.03	542.25 - 542.70	10.75	966.34 - 976.33	20.18
477.25 - 477.70	9.32	509.98 - 510.43	10.04	542.71 - 543.15	10.76	976.34 - 986.33	20.40
477.71 - 478.15	9.33	510.44 - 510.88	10.05	543.16 - 543.61	10.77	986.34 - 996.33	20.62
478.16 - 478.61	9.34	510.89 - 511.33	10.06	543.62 - 544.06	10.78	996.34 - 1006.33	20.84
478.62 - 479.06	9.35	511.34 - 511.79	10.07	544.07 - 544.52	10.79	1006.34 - 1016.33	21.06

APPENDIX A *(continued)*

CANADA PENSION PLAN CONTRIBUTIONS — COTISATIONS AU RÉGIME DE PENSIONS DU CANADA

WEEKLY PAY PERIOD — *PÉRIODE HEBDOMADAIRE DE PAIE*

1016.34 — 3806.33

Remuneration / Rémunération From-de — To-à	C.P.P. R.P.C.	Remuneration / Rémunération From-de — To-à	C.P.P. R.P.C.	Remuneration / Rémunération From-de — To-à	C.P.P. R.P.C.	Remuneration / Rémunération From-de — To-à	C.P.P. R.P.C.
1016.34 - 1026.33	21.28	1736.34 - 1746.33	37.12	2456.34 - 2466.33	52.96	3176.34 - 3186.33	68.80
1026.34 - 1036.33	21.50	1746.34 - 1756.33	37.34	2466.34 - 2476.33	53.18	3186.34 - 3196.33	69.02
1036.34 - 1046.33	21.72	1756.34 - 1766.33	37.56	2476.34 - 2486.33	53.40	3196.34 - 3206.33	69.24
1046.34 - 1056.33	21.94	1766.34 - 1776.33	37.78	2486.34 - 2496.33	53.62	3206.34 - 3216.33	69.46
1056.34 - 1066.33	22.16	1776.34 - 1786.33	38.00	2496.34 - 2506.33	53.84	3216.34 - 3226.33	69.68
1066.34 - 1076.33	22.38	1786.34 - 1796.33	38.22	2506.34 - 2516.33	54.06	3226.34 - 3236.33	69.90
1076.34 - 1086.33	22.60	1796.34 - 1806.33	38.44	2516.34 - 2526.33	54.28	3236.34 - 3246.33	70.12
1086.34 - 1096.33	22.82	1806.34 - 1816.33	38.66	2526.34 - 2536.33	54.50	3246.34 - 3256.33	70.34
1096.34 - 1106.33	23.04	1816.34 - 1826.33	38.88	2536.34 - 2546.33	54.72	3256.34 - 3266.33	70.56
1106.34 - 1116.33	23.26	1826.34 - 1836.33	39.10	2546.34 - 2556.33	54.94	3266.34 - 3276.33	70.78
1116.34 - 1126.33	23.48	1836.34 - 1846.33	39.32	2556.34 - 2566.33	55.16	3276.34 - 3286.33	71.00
1126.34 - 1136.33	23.70	1846.34 - 1856.33	39.54	2566.34 - 2576.33	55.38	3286.34 - 3296.33	71.22
1136.34 - 1146.33	23.92	1856.34 - 1866.33	39.76	2576.34 - 2586.33	55.60	3296.34 - 3306.33	71.44
1146.34 - 1156.33	24.14	1866.34 - 1876.33	39.98	2586.34 - 2596.33	55.82	3306.34 - 3316.33	71.66
1156.34 - 1166.33	24.36	1876.34 - 1886.33	40.20	2596.34 - 2606.33	56.04	3316.34 - 3326.33	71.88
1166.34 - 1176.33	24.58	1886.34 - 1896.33	40.42	2606.34 - 2616.33	56.26	3326.34 - 3336.33	72.10
1176.34 - 1186.33	24.80	1896.34 - 1906.33	40.64	2616.34 - 2626.33	56.48	3336.34 - 3346.33	72.32
1186.34 - 1196.33	25.02	1906.34 - 1916.33	40.86	2626.34 - 2636.33	56.70	3346.34 - 3356.33	72.54
1196.34 - 1206.33	25.24	1916.34 - 1926.33	41.08	2636.34 - 2646.33	56.92	3356.34 - 3366.33	72.76
1206.34 - 1216.33	25.46	1926.34 - 1936.33	41.30	2646.34 - 2656.33	57.14	3366.34 - 3376.33	72.98
1216.34 - 1226.33	25.68	1936.34 - 1946.33	41.52	2656.34 - 2666.33	57.36	3376.34 - 3386.33	73.20
1226.34 - 1236.33	25.90	1946.34 - 1956.33	41.74	2666.34 - 2676.33	57.58	3386.34 - 3396.33	73.42
1236.34 - 1246.33	26.12	1956.34 - 1966.33	41.96	2676.34 - 2686.33	57.80	3396.34 - 3406.33	73.64
1246.34 - 1256.33	26.34	1966.34 - 1976.33	42.18	2686.34 - 2695.33	58.02	3406.34 - 3416.33	73.86
1256.34 - 1266.33	26.56	1976.34 - 1986.33	42.40	2696.34 - 2706.33	58.24	3416.34 - 3425.33	74.08
1266.34 - 1276.33	26.78	1986.34 - 1996.33	42.62	2706.34 - 2716.33	58.46	3426.34 - 3436.33	74.30
1276.34 - 1286.33	27.00	1996.34 - 2006.33	42.84	2716.34 - 2726.33	58.68	3436.34 - 3446.33	74.52
1286.34 - 1296.33	27.22	2006.34 - 2016.33	43.06	2726.34 - 2736.33	58.90	3446.34 - 3456.33	74.74
1296.34 - 1306.33	27.44	2016.34 - 2026.33	43.28	2736.34 - 2746.33	59.12	3456.34 - 3466.33	74.96
1306.34 - 1316.33	27.66	2026.34 - 2036.33	43.50	2746.34 - 2756.33	59.34	3466.34 - 3476.33	75.18
1316.34 - 1326.33	27.88	2036.34 - 2046.33	43.72	2756.34 - 2766.33	59.56	3476.34 - 3486.33	75.40
1326.34 - 1336.33	28.10	2046.34 - 2056.33	43.94	2766.34 - 2776.33	59.78	3486.34 - 3496.33	75.62
1336.34 - 1346.33	28.32	2056.34 - 2066.33	44.16	2776.34 - 2786.33	60.00	3496.34 - 3506.33	75.84
1346.34 - 1356.33	28.54	2066.34 - 2076.33	44.38	2786.34 - 2796.33	60.22	3506.34 - 3516.33	76.06
1356.34 - 1366.33	28.76	2076.34 - 2086.33	44.60	2796.34 - 2806.33	60.44	3516.34 - 3526.33	76.28
1366.34 - 1376.33	28.98	2086.34 - 2096.33	44.82	2806.34 - 2816.33	60.66	3526.34 - 3536.33	76.50
1376.34 - 1386.33	29.20	2096.34 - 2106.33	45.04	2816.34 - 2826.33	60.88	3536.34 - 3546.33	76.72
1386.34 - 1396.33	29.42	2106.34 - 2116.33	45.26	2826.34 - 2836.33	61.10	3546.34 - 3556.33	76.94
1396.34 - 1406.33	29.64	2116.34 - 2126.33	45.48	2836.34 - 2846.33	61.32	3556.34 - 3566.33	77.16
1406.34 - 1416.33	29.86	2126.34 - 2136.33	45.70	2846.34 - 2856.33	61.54	3566.34 - 3576.33	77.38
1416.34 - 1426.33	30.08	2136.34 - 2146.33	45.92	2856.34 - 2866.33	61.76	3576.34 - 3586.33	77.60
1426.34 - 1436.33	30.30	2146.34 - 2156.33	46.14	2866.34 - 2875.33	61.98	3586.34 - 3596.33	77.82
1436.34 - 1446.33	30.52	2156.34 - 2166.33	46.36	2876.34 - 2886.33	62.20	3596.34 - 3606.33	78.04
1446.34 - 1456.33	30.74	2166.34 - 2176.33	46.58	2886.34 - 2896.33	62.42	3606.34 - 3616.33	78.26
1456.34 - 1466.33	30.96	2176.34 - 2186.33	46.80	2896.34 - 2906.33	62.64	3616.34 - 3626.33	78.48
1466.34 - 1476.33	31.18	2186.34 - 2196.33	47.02	2906.34 - 2916.33	62.86	3626.34 - 3636.33	78.70
1476.34 - 1486.33	31.40	2196.34 - 2206.33	47.24	2916.34 - 2926.33	63.08	3636.34 - 3646.33	78.92
1486.34 - 1496.33	31.62	2206.34 - 2216.33	47.46	2926.34 - 2936.33	63.30	3646.34 - 3656.33	79.14
1496.34 - 1506.33	31.84	2216.34 - 2226.33	47.68	2936.34 - 2946.33	63.52	3656.34 - 3666.33	79.36
1506.34 - 1516.33	32.06	2226.34 - 2236.33	47.90	2946.34 - 2956.33	63.74	3666.34 - 3676.33	79.58
1516.34 - 1526.33	32.28	2236.34 - 2246.33	48.12	2956.34 - 2966.33	63.96	3676.34 - 3686.33	79.80
1526.34 - 1536.33	32.50	2246.34 - 2256.33	48.34	2966.34 - 2976.33	64.18	3686.34 - 3696.33	80.02
1536.34 - 1546.33	32.72	2256.34 - 2266.33	48.56	2976.34 - 2986.33	64.40	3696.34 - 3706.33	80.24
1546.34 - 1556.33	32.94	2266.34 - 2276.33	48.78	2986.34 - 2996.33	64.62	3706.34 - 3716.33	80.46
1556.34 - 1566.33	33.16	2276.34 - 2286.33	49.00	2996.34 - 3006.33	64.84	3716.34 - 3726.33	80.68
1566.34 - 1576.33	33.38	2286.34 - 2296.33	49.22	3006.34 - 3016.33	65.06	3726.34 - 3736.33	80.90
1576.34 - 1586.33	33.60	2296.34 - 2306.33	49.44	3016.34 - 3026.33	65.28	3736.34 - 3746.33	81.12
1586.34 - 1596.33	33.82	2306.34 - 2316.33	49.66	3026.34 - 3035.33	65.50	3746.34 - 3756.33	81.34
1596.34 - 1606.33	34.04	2316.34 - 2326.33	49.88	3036.34 - 3046.33	65.72	3756.34 - 3766.33	81.56
1606.34 - 1616.33	34.26	2326.34 - 2336.33	50.10	3046.34 - 3056.33	65.94	3766.34 - 3776.33	81.78
1616.34 - 1626.33	34.48	2336.34 - 2346.33	50.32	3056.34 - 3066.33	66.16	3776.34 - 3786.33	82.00
1626.34 - 1636.33	34.70	2346.34 - 2356.33	50.54	3066.34 - 3076.33	66.38	3786.34 - 3796.33	82.22
1636.34 - 1646.33	34.92	2356.34 - 2366.33	50.76	3076.34 - 3086.33	66.60	3796.34 - 3806.33	82.44
1646.34 - 1656.33	35.14	2366.34 - 2376.33	50.98	3086.34 - 3096.33	66.82		
1656.34 - 1666.33	35.36	2376.34 - 2386.33	51.20	3096.34 - 3106.33	67.04		
1666.34 - 1676.33	35.58	2386.34 - 2396.33	51.42	3106.34 - 3116.33	67.26		
1676.34 - 1686.33	35.80	2396.34 - 2406.33	51.64	3116.34 - 3126.33	67.48		
1686.34 - 1696.33	36.02	2406.34 - 2416.33	51.86	3126.34 - 3136.33	67.70		
1696.34 - 1706.33	36.24	2416.34 - 2426.33	52.08	3136.34 - 3146.33	67.92		
1706.34 - 1716.33	36.46	2426.34 - 2436.33	52.30	3146.34 - 3156.33	68.14		
1716.34 - 1726.33	36.68	2436.34 - 2446.33	52.52	3156.34 - 3166.33	68.36		
1726.34 - 1736.33	36.90	2446.34 - 2456.33	52.74	3166.34 - 3176.33	68.58		

"For remuneration in excess of the above amount refer to "Employee's Contribution — Calculation Method"."

"*Si la rémunération dépasse le montant ci-dessus se reporter à la rubrique «Cotisation de l'employé — Méthode par le calcul.»*"

APPENDIX A (continued)

UNEMPLOYMENT INSURANCE PREMIUMS / COTISATIONS À L'ASSURANCE-CHÔMAGE

For minimum and maximum insurable earnings amounts for various pay periods see Schedule II. For the maximum premium deduction for various pay periods see bottom of this page.

Les montants minimum et maximum des gains assurables pour diverses périodes de paie figurent en annexe II. La déduction maximale de primes pour diverses périodes de paie figure au bas de la présente page.

Remuneration / Rémunération From-de	To-à	U.I. Premium Cotisation d'a.-c.	Remuneration / Rémunération From-de	To-à	U.I. Premium Cotisation d'a.-c.	Remuneration / Rémunération From-de	To-à	U.I. Premium Cotisation d'a.-c.	Remuneration / Rémunération From-de	To-à	U.I. Premium Cotisation d'a.-c.
768.23 -	768.66	17.29	800.23 -	800.66	18.01	832.23 -	832.66	18.73	864.23 -	864.66	19.45
768.67 -	769.11	17.30	800.67 -	801.11	18.02	832.67 -	833.11	18.74	864.67 -	865.11	19.46
769.12 -	769.55	17.31	801.12 -	801.55	18.03	833.12 -	833.55	18.75	865.12 -	865.55	19.47
769.56 -	769.99	17.32	801.56 -	801.99	18.04	833.56 -	833.99	18.76	865.56 -	865.99	19.48
770.00 -	770.44	17.33	802.00 -	802.44	18.05	834.00 -	834.44	18.77	866.00 -	866.44	19.49
770.45 -	770.88	17.34	802.45 -	802.88	18.06	834.45 -	834.88	18.78	866.45 -	866.88	19.50
770.89 -	771.33	17.35	802.89 -	803.33	18.07	834.89 -	835.33	18.79	866.89 -	867.33	19.51
771.34 -	771.77	17.36	803.34 -	803.77	18.08	835.34 -	835.77	18.80	867.34 -	867.77	19.52
771.78 -	772.22	17.37	803.78 -	804.22	18.09	835.78 -	836.22	18.81	867.78 -	868.22	19.53
772.23 -	772.66	17.38	804.23 -	804.66	18.10	836.23 -	836.66	18.82	868.23 -	868.66	19.54
772.67 -	773.11	17.39	804.67 -	805.11	18.11	836.67 -	837.11	18.83	868.67 -	869.11	19.55
773.12 -	773.55	17.40	805.12 -	805.55	18.12	837.12 -	837.55	18.84	869.12 -	869.55	19.56
773.56 -	773.99	17.41	805.56 -	805.99	18.13	837.56 -	837.99	18.85	869.56 -	869.99	19.57
774.00 -	774.44	17.42	806.00 -	806.44	18.14	838.00 -	838.44	18.86	870.00 -	870.44	19.58
774.45 -	774.88	17.43	806.45 -	806.88	18.15	838.45 -	838.88	18.87	870.45 -	870.88	19.59
774.89 -	775.33	17.44	806.89 -	807.33	18.16	838.89 -	839.33	18.88	870.89 -	871.33	19.60
775.34 -	775.77	17.45	807.34 -	807.77	18.17	839.34 -	839.77	18.89	871.34 -	871.77	19.61
775.78 -	776.22	17.46	807.78 -	808.22	18.18	839.78 -	840.22	18.90	871.78 -	872.22	19.62
776.23 -	776.66	17.47	808.23 -	808.66	18.19	840.23 -	840.66	18.91	872.23 -	872.66	19.63
776.67 -	777.11	17.48	808.67 -	809.11	18.20	840.67 -	841.11	18.92	872.67 -	873.11	19.64
777.12 -	777.55	17.49	809.12 -	809.55	18.21	841.12 -	841.55	18.93	873.12 -	873.55	19.65
777.56 -	777.99	17.50	809.56 -	809.99	18.22	841.56 -	841.99	18.94	873.56 -	873.99	19.66
778.00 -	778.44	17.51	810.00 -	810.44	18.23	842.00 -	842.44	18.95	874.00 -	874.44	19.67
778.45 -	778.88	17.52	810.45 -	810.88	18.24	842.45 -	842.88	18.96	874.45 -	874.88	19.68
778.89 -	779.33	17.53	810.89 -	811.33	18.25	842.89 -	843.33	18.97	874.89 -	875.33	19.69
779.34 -	779.77	17.54	811.34 -	811.77	18.26	843.34 -	843.77	18.98	875.34 -	875.77	19.70
779.78 -	780.22	17.55	811.78 -	812.22	18.27	843.78 -	844.22	18.99	875.78 -	876.22	19.71
780.23 -	780.66	17.56	812.23 -	812.66	18.28	844.23 -	844.66	19.00	876.23 -	876.66	19.72
780.67 -	781.11	17.57	812.67 -	813.11	18.29	844.67 -	845.11	19.01	876.67 -	877.11	19.73
781.12 -	781.55	17.58	813.12 -	813.55	18.30	845.12 -	845.55	19.02	877.12 -	877.55	19.74
781.56 -	781.99	17.59	813.56 -	813.99	18.31	845.56 -	845.99	19.03	877.56 -	877.99	19.75
782.00 -	782.44	17.60	814.00 -	814.44	18.32	846.00 -	846.44	19.04	878.00 -	878.44	19.76
782.45 -	782.88	17.61	814.45 -	814.88	18.33	846.45 -	846.88	19.05	878.45 -	878.88	19.77
782.89 -	783.33	17.62	814.89 -	815.33	18.34	846.89 -	847.33	19.06	878.89 -	879.33	19.78
783.34 -	783.77	17.63	815.34 -	815.77	18.35	847.34 -	847.77	19.07	879.34 -	879.77	19.79
783.78 -	784.22	17.64	815.78 -	816.22	18.36	847.78 -	848.22	19.08	879.78 -	880.22	19.80
784.23 -	784.66	17.65	816.23 -	816.66	18.37	848.23 -	848.66	19.09	880.23 -	880.66	19.81
784.67 -	785.11	17.66	816.67 -	817.11	18.38	848.67 -	849.11	19.10	880.67 -	881.11	19.82
785.12 -	785.55	17.67	817.12 -	817.55	18.39	849.12 -	849.55	19.11	881.12 -	881.55	19.83
785.56 -	785.99	17.68	817.56 -	817.99	18.40	849.56 -	849.99	19.12	881.56 -	881.99	19.84
786.00 -	786.44	17.69	818.00 -	818.44	18.41	850.00 -	850.44	19.13	882.00 -	882.44	19.85
786.45 -	786.88	17.70	818.45 -	818.88	18.42	850.45 -	850.88	19.14	882.45 -	882.88	19.86
786.89 -	787.33	17.71	818.89 -	819.33	18.43	850.89 -	851.33	19.15	882.89 -	883.33	19.87
787.34 -	787.77	17.72	819.34 -	819.77	18.44	851.34 -	851.77	19.16	883.34 -	883.77	19.88
787.78 -	788.22	17.73	819.78 -	820.22	18.45	851.78 -	852.22	19.17	883.78 -	884.22	19.89
788.23 -	788.66	17.74	820.23 -	820.66	18.46	852.23 -	852.66	19.18	884.23 -	884.66	19.90
788.67 -	789.11	17.75	820.67 -	821.11	18.47	852.67 -	853.11	19.19	884.67 -	885.11	19.91
789.12 -	789.55	17.76	821.12 -	821.55	18.48	853.12 -	853.55	19.20	885.12 -	885.55	19.92
789.56 -	789.99	17.77	821.56 -	821.99	18.49	853.56 -	853.99	19.21	885.56 -	885.99	19.93
790.00 -	790.44	17.78	822.00 -	822.44	18.50	854.00 -	854.44	19.22	886.00 -	886.44	19.94
790.45 -	790.88	17.79	822.45 -	822.88	18.51	854.45 -	854.88	19.23	886.45 -	886.88	19.95
790.89 -	791.33	17.80	822.89 -	823.33	18.52	854.89 -	855.33	19.24	886.89 -	887.33	19.96
791.34 -	791.77	17.81	823.34 -	823.77	18.53	855.34 -	855.77	19.25	887.34 -	887.77	19.97
791.78 -	792.22	17.82	823.78 -	824.22	18.54	855.78 -	856.22	19.26	887.78 -	888.22	19.98
792.23 -	792.66	17.83	824.23 -	824.66	18.55	856.23 -	856.66	19.27	888.23 -	888.66	19.99
792.67 -	793.11	17.84	824.67 -	825.11	18.56	856.67 -	857.11	19.28	888.67 -	889.11	20.00
793.12 -	793.55	17.85	825.12 -	825.55	18.57	857.12 -	857.55	19.29	889.12 -	889.55	20.01
793.56 -	793.99	17.86	825.56 -	825.99	18.58	857.56 -	857.99	19.30	889.56 -	889.99	20.02
794.00 -	794.44	17.87	826.00 -	826.44	18.59	858.00 -	858.44	19.31	890.00 -	890.44	20.03
794.45 -	794.88	17.88	826.45 -	826.88	18.60	858.45 -	858.88	19.32	890.45 -	890.88	20.04
794.89 -	795.33	17.89	826.89 -	827.33	18.61	858.89 -	859.33	19.33	890.89 -	891.33	20.05
795.34 -	795.77	17.90	827.34 -	827.77	18.62	859.34 -	859.77	19.34	891.34 -	891.77	20.06
795.78 -	796.22	17.91	827.78 -	828.22	18.63	859.78 -	860.22	19.35	891.78 -	892.22	20.07
796.23 -	796.66	17.92	828.23 -	828.66	18.64	860.23 -	860.66	19.36	892.23 -	892.66	20.08
796.67 -	797.11	17.93	828.67 -	829.11	18.65	860.67 -	861.11	19.37	892.67 -	893.11	20.09
797.12 -	797.55	17.94	829.12 -	829.55	18.66	861.12 -	861.55	19.38	893.12 -	893.55	20.10
797.56 -	797.99	17.95	829.56 -	829.99	18.67	861.56 -	861.99	19.39	893.56 -	893.99	20.11
798.00 -	798.44	17.96	830.00 -	830.44	18.68	862.00 -	862.44	19.40	894.00 -	894.44	20.12
798.45 -	798.88	17.97	830.45 -	830.88	18.69	862.45 -	862.88	19.41	894.45 -	894.88	20.13
798.89 -	799.33	17.98	830.89 -	831.33	18.70	862.89 -	863.33	19.42	894.89 -	895.33	20.14
799.34 -	799.77	17.99	831.34 -	831.77	18.71	863.34 -	863.77	19.43	895.34 -	895.77	20.15
799.78 -	800.22	18.00	831.78 -	832.22	18.72	863.78 -	864.22	19.44	895.78 -	896.22	20.16

Maximum Premium Deduction for a Pay Period of the stated frequency.
Déduction maximale de prime pour une période de paie d'une durée donnée.

Weekly - Hebdomadaire	14.40	
Bi-Weekly - Deux semaines	28.80	
Semi-Monthly - Bi-mensuel	31.20	
Monthly - Mensuellement	62.40	
10 pp per year - 10 pp par année	74.88	
13 pp per year - 13 pp par année	57.60	
22 pp per year - 22 pp par année	34.04	

APPENDIX A (continued)

UNEMPLOYMENT INSURANCE PREMIUMS / COTISATIONS À L'ASSURANCE-CHÔMAGE

For minimum and maximum insurable earnings amounts for various pay periods see Schedule II. For the maximum premium deduction for various pay periods see bottom of this page.

Les montants minimum et maximum des gains assurables pour diverses périodes de paie figurent en annexe II. La déduction maximale de primes pour diverses périodes de paie figure au bas de la présente page.

Remuneration / Rémunération		U.I. Premium / Cotisation d'a.-c.	Remuneration / Rémunération		U.I. Premium / Cotisation d'a.-c.	Remuneration / Rémunération		U.I. Premium / Cotisation d'a.-c.	Remuneration / Rémunération		U.I. Premium / Cotisation d'a.-c.
From-de	To-à		From-de	To-à		From-de	To-à		From-de	To-à	
896.23 -	896.66	20.17	928.23 -	928.66	20.89	960.23 -	960.66	21.61	992.23 -	992.66	22.33
896.67 -	897.11	20.18	928.67 -	929.11	20.90	960.67 -	961.11	21.62	992.67 -	993.11	22.34
897.12 -	897.55	20.19	929.12 -	929.55	20.91	961.12 -	961.55	21.63	993.12 -	993.55	22.35
897.56 -	897.99	20.20	929.56 -	929.99	20.92	961.56 -	961.99	21.64	993.56 -	993.99	22.36
898.00 -	898.44	20.21	930.00 -	930.44	20.93	962.00 -	962.44	21.65	994.00 -	994.44	22.37
898.45 -	898.88	20.22	930.45 -	930.88	20.94	962.45 -	962.88	21.66	994.45 -	994.88	22.38
898.89 -	899.33	20.23	930.89 -	931.33	20.95	962.89 -	963.33	21.67	994.89 -	995.33	22.39
899.34 -	899.77	20.24	931.34 -	931.77	20.96	963.34 -	963.77	21.68	995.34 -	995.77	22.40
899.78 -	900.22	20.25	931.78 -	932.22	20.97	963.78 -	964.22	21.69	995.78 -	996.22	22.41
900.23 -	900.66	20.26	932.23 -	932.66	20.98	964.23 -	964.66	21.70	996.23 -	996.66	22.42
900.67 -	901.11	20.27	932.67 -	933.11	20.99	964.67 -	965.11	21.71	996.67 -	997.11	22.43
901.12 -	901.55	20.28	933.12 -	933.55	21.00	965.12 -	965.55	21.72	997.12 -	997.55	22.44
901.56 -	901.99	20.29	933.56 -	933.99	21.01	965.56 -	965.99	21.73	997.56 -	997.99	22.45
902.00 -	902.44	20.30	934.00 -	934.44	21.02	966.00 -	966.44	21.74	998.00 -	998.44	22.46
902.45 -	902.88	20.31	934.45 -	934.88	21.03	966.45 -	966.88	21.75	998.45 -	998.88	22.47
902.89 -	903.33	20.32	934.89 -	935.33	21.04	966.89 -	967.33	21.76	998.89 -	999.33	22.48
903.34 -	903.77	20.33	935.34 -	935.77	21.05	967.34 -	967.77	21.77	999.34 -	999.77	22.49
903.78 -	904.22	20.34	935.78 -	936.22	21.06	967.78 -	968.22	21.78	999.78 -	1000.22	22.50
904.23 -	904.66	20.35	936.23 -	936.66	21.07	968.23 -	968.66	21.79	1000.23 -	1000.66	22.51
904.67 -	905.11	20.36	936.67 -	937.11	21.08	968.67 -	969.11	21.80	1000.67 -	1001.11	22.52
905.12 -	905.55	20.37	937.12 -	937.55	21.09	969.12 -	969.55	21.81	1001.12 -	1001.55	22.53
905.56 -	905.99	20.38	937.56 -	937.99	21.10	969.56 -	969.99	21.82	1001.56 -	1001.99	22.54
906.00 -	906.44	20.39	938.00 -	938.44	21.11	970.00 -	970.44	21.83	1002.00 -	1002.44	22.55
906.45 -	906.88	20.40	938.45 -	938.88	21.12	970.45 -	970.88	21.84	1002.45 -	1002.88	22.56
906.89 -	907.33	20.41	938.89 -	939.33	21.13	970.89 -	971.33	21.85	1002.89 -	1003.33	22.57
907.34 -	907.77	20.42	939.34 -	939.77	21.14	971.34 -	971.77	21.86	1003.34 -	1003.77	22.58
907.78 -	908.22	20.43	939.78 -	940.22	21.15	971.78 -	972.22	21.87	1003.78 -	1004.22	22.59
908.23 -	908.66	20.44	940.23 -	940.66	21.16	972.23 -	972.66	21.88	1004.23 -	1004.66	22.60
908.67 -	909.11	20.45	940.67 -	941.11	21.17	972.67 -	973.11	21.89	1004.67 -	1005.11	22.61
909.12 -	909.55	20.46	941.12 -	941.55	21.18	973.12 -	973.55	21.90	1005.12 -	1005.55	22.62
909.56 -	909.99	20.47	941.56 -	941.99	21.19	973.56 -	973.99	21.91	1005.56 -	1005.99	22.63
910.00 -	910.44	20.48	942.00 -	942.44	21.20	974.00 -	974.44	21.92	1006.00 -	1006.44	22.64
910.45 -	910.88	20.49	942.45 -	942.88	21.21	974.45 -	974.88	21.93	1006.45 -	1006.88	22.65
910.89 -	911.33	20.50	942.89 -	943.33	21.22	974.89 -	975.33	21.94	1006.89 -	1007.33	22.66
911.34 -	911.77	20.51	943.34 -	943.77	21.23	975.34 -	975.77	21.95	1007.34 -	1007.77	22.67
911.78 -	912.22	20.52	943.78 -	944.22	21.24	975.78 -	976.22	21.96	1007.78 -	1008.22	22.68
912.23 -	912.66	20.53	944.23 -	944.66	21.25	976.23 -	976.66	21.97	1008.23 -	1008.66	22.69
912.67 -	913.11	20.54	944.67 -	945.11	21.26	976.67 -	977.11	21.98	1008.67 -	1009.11	22.70
913.12 -	913.55	20.55	945.12 -	945.55	21.27	977.12 -	977.55	21.99	1009.12 -	1009.55	22.71
913.56 -	913.99	20.56	945.56 -	945.99	21.28	977.56 -	977.99	22.00	1009.56 -	1009.99	22.72
914.00 -	914.44	20.57	946.00 -	946.44	21.29	978.00 -	978.44	22.01	1010.00 -	1010.44	22.73
914.45 -	914.88	20.58	946.45 -	946.88	21.30	978.45 -	978.88	22.02	1010.45 -	1010.88	22.74
914.89 -	915.33	20.59	946.89 -	947.33	21.31	978.89 -	979.33	22.03	1010.89 -	1011.33	22.75
915.34 -	915.77	20.60	947.34 -	947.77	21.32	979.34 -	979.77	22.04	1011.34 -	1011.77	22.76
915.78 -	916.22	20.61	947.78 -	948.22	21.33	979.78 -	980.22	22.05	1011.78 -	1012.22	22.77
916.23 -	916.66	20.62	948.23 -	948.66	21.34	980.23 -	980.66	22.06	1012.23 -	1012.66	22.78
916.67 -	917.11	20.63	948.67 -	949.11	21.35	980.67 -	981.11	22.07	1012.67 -	1013.11	22.79
917.12 -	917.55	20.64	949.12 -	949.55	21.36	981.12 -	981.55	22.08	1013.12 -	1013.55	22.80
917.56 -	917.99	20.65	949.56 -	949.99	21.37	981.56 -	981.99	22.09	1013.56 -	1013.99	22.81
918.00 -	918.44	20.66	950.00 -	950.44	21.38	982.00 -	982.44	22.10	1014.00 -	1014.44	22.82
918.45 -	918.88	20.67	950.45 -	950.88	21.39	982.45 -	982.88	22.11	1014.45 -	1014.88	22.83
918.89 -	919.33	20.68	950.89 -	951.33	21.40	982.89 -	983.33	22.12	1014.89 -	1015.33	22.84
919.34 -	919.77	20.69	951.34 -	951.77	21.41	983.34 -	983.77	22.13	1015.34 -	1015.77	22.85
919.78 -	920.22	20.70	951.78 -	952.22	21.42	983.78 -	984.22	22.14	1015.78 -	1016.22	22.86
920.23 -	920.66	20.71	952.23 -	952.66	21.43	984.23 -	984.66	22.15	1016.23 -	1016.66	22.87
920.67 -	921.11	20.72	952.67 -	953.11	21.44	984.67 -	985.11	22.16	1016.67 -	1017.11	22.88
921.12 -	921.55	20.73	953.12 -	953.55	21.45	985.12 -	985.55	22.17	1017.12 -	1017.55	22.89
921.56 -	921.99	20.74	953.56 -	953.99	21.46	985.56 -	985.99	22.18	1017.56 -	1017.99	22.90
922.00 -	922.44	20.75	954.00 -	954.44	21.47	986.00 -	986.44	22.19	1018.00 -	1018.44	22.91
922.45 -	922.88	20.76	954.45 -	954.88	21.48	986.45 -	986.88	22.20	1018.45 -	1018.88	22.92
922.89 -	923.33	20.77	954.89 -	955.33	21.49	986.89 -	987.33	22.21	1018.89 -	1019.33	22.93
923.34 -	923.77	20.78	955.34 -	955.77	21.50	987.34 -	987.77	22.22	1019.34 -	1019.77	22.94
923.78 -	924.22	20.79	955.78 -	956.22	21.51	987.78 -	988.22	22.23	1019.78 -	1020.22	22.95
924.23 -	924.66	20.80	956.23 -	956.66	21.52	988.23 -	988.66	22.24	1020.23 -	1020.66	22.96
924.67 -	925.11	20.81	956.67 -	957.11	21.53	988.67 -	989.11	22.25	1020.67 -	1021.11	22.97
925.12 -	925.55	20.82	957.12 -	957.55	21.54	989.12 -	989.55	22.26	1021.12 -	1021.55	22.98
925.56 -	925.99	20.83	957.56 -	957.99	21.55	989.56 -	989.99	22.27	1021.56 -	1021.99	22.99
926.00 -	926.44	20.84	958.00 -	958.44	21.56	990.00 -	990.44	22.28	1022.00 -	1022.44	23.00
926.45 -	926.88	20.85	958.45 -	958.88	21.57	990.45 -	990.88	22.29	1022.45 -	1022.88	23.01
926.89 -	927.33	20.86	958.89 -	959.33	21.58	990.89 -	991.33	22.30	1022.89 -	1023.33	23.02
927.34 -	927.77	20.87	959.34 -	959.77	21.59	991.34 -	991.77	22.31	1023.34 -	1023.77	23.03
927.78 -	928.22	20.88	959.78 -	960.22	21.60	991.78 -	992.22	22.32	1023.78 -	1024.22	23.04

Maximum Premium Deduction for a Pay Period of the stated frequency.
Déduction maximale de prime pour une période de paie d'une durée donnée.

Weekly - Hebdomadaire	14.40
Bi-Weekly - Deux semaines	28.80
Semi-Monthly - Bi-mensuel	31.20
Monthly - Mensuellement	62.40
10 pp per year - 10 pp par année	74.88
13 pp per year - 13 pp par année	57.60
22 pp per year - 22 pp par année	34.04

GROUP LIFE INSURANCE ANNUAL PREMIUMS PER THOUSAND OF INSURANCE		
Age	Smoker	Non-smoker
20–35	$ 2.40	$ 1.30
36–40	2.70	1.50
41–45	3.70	2.00
46–50	5.30	2.90
51–55	7.70	4.20
56–60	10.80	6.00
61–65	16.60	10.00

SUPPLEMENTARY HEALTH INSURANCE PREMIUMS	
Coverage	Weekly Cost
Single	$3.50
Family	7.00

CHAPTER FOURTEEN

Analyzing Financial Statements

LEARNING OBJECTIVES

At the end of this chapter you should be able to
- calculate various financial ratios;
- comment on the financial activities of the business in relation to the ratios;
- prepare financial statements showing horizontal analysis;
- prepare financial statements showing vertical analysis;
- comment on the financial activities of the business in relation to the trends;
- use a spreadsheet program to analyze the decisions a business must continually make.

LANGUAGE OF ACCOUNTING

You will see the following terms in this chapter:
accounts receivable turnover
acid-test ratio
activity ratios
common size statements
coverage ratios
forecasting instrument
inventory turnover
liquidity ratios
profit margin on sales
profitability ratios
quick ratio
rate of return on investment
trends

14.1 Ratios

As we have seen in previous parts of the text, an important use of accounting reports is in analyzing the past history of the business and planning its future path. We have already begun to look at analysis through the calculation of working capital and the current ratio, and carried out a horizontal analysis of financial statements. The analysis of financial information provides management with data it uses in order to examine the firm's present financial position. The results of this analysis are then included in the decision-making process.

The various users of financial statements have different needs: management wishes to improve the firm's net income position; creditors focus on the business's short-term debt-paying ability; union workers focus on the net income, and so on. Therefore, when analyzing financial statements, it is necessary to have a clear understanding of the type of information that is required before selecting the instrument for analysis.

A figure taken from a financial statement is, in itself, not very significant. For example, to state that a business had a net income of

$800 000 only indicates an absolute dollar amount. Yet it can be used to determine a number of things, among them, whether the business was more successful in absolute dollar terms than in previous years and whether it earned more than other firms of the same size in the industry. However, the absolute net income amount itself is not overly significant in that it does not indicate whether the business is solvent, whether or not the net income has increased over the previous year's net income when inflation is considered, or many other things which will be examined below. The fact that a firm has earned a net income does not in itself mean success. It is the job of the firm's accountant to not only prepare the accounting reports, but also assist management in its interpretation of them so that decisions can be made that will meet the goals of the firm. These decisions are not only related to the accounting function. A newspaper article on a draft report on the focus that audits should take stated the following:

"The draft emphasizes the importance of the control environment, which includes factors such as
- general management philosophy and operating style
- the function of the board of directors and its committees, particularly the audit committee
- organizational structure
- methods of assigning responsibility
- management control methods
- systems development methodology
- personnel policies and practices
- management reaction to external influences
- internal audit"

There are many factors other than the financial data that are important to the success or failure of a firm, so complete reliance should not be placed upon this data by users.
- A government might impose strict environmental regulations, which would be an additional cost to the firm, or award a large contract to it, which would increase its probability of making a profit.
- Competitors can adversely influence the profitability of a firm, by introducing an improved product, or by running a better advertising campaign.
- The state of the economy has a tremendous effect on profitability. In 1990, during a recession, many businesses went bankrupt, laid off employees, or witnessed a decrease in net income. Also, hiring a new person for the management team has at times been the best change that a business could make to improve its bottom line.

Instruments of analysis can basically be broken into two categories: ratios, and comparisons or trends. A **ratio** compares two items. We

Ratio: *a comparison of two items.*

have already examined two ratios: the working capital ratio and the current ratio. Trends have also been examined, specifically the horizontal examination of the balance sheet and income statement. In this chapter we shall introduce other ratios and trend analysis so that a more detailed examination of financial statements can be made, and their interpretation can lead to better business decisions.

The ratios that we will employ fall into four categories:
(1) liquidity ratios, which measure the ability of the business to meet its short-term commitments;
(2) activity ratios, which indicate how effectively certain assets are being used;
(3) profitability ratios, which measure the success of the business in relation to net income for a given period of time;
(4) coverage ratios, which measure the degree of protection for long-term creditors and investors.

Liquidity Ratios

Liquidity ratios: ratios that measure the ability of the business to meet its short-term commitments.

As indicated previously, it is important that a business remain solvent, which means able to pay its current liabilities as they become due. The use of **liquidity ratios** will give some indication of the solvency of the business. The basic liquidity ratios, the current ratio and the acid-test ratio, are shown below.

Current Ratio

Current ratio: a ratio that compares current assets to current liabilities.

The **current ratio** compares current assets to current liabilities. The data in the financial statements for Algor Computer Services, shown in Figures 14-1 and 14-2, will be used for calculating all of the following ratios.

The current ratio would be calculated as follows:

$$\text{Current ratio} = \frac{\text{Current assets}}{\text{Current liabilities}}$$

$$= \frac{180\ 177}{46\ 161}$$

$$= 3.90$$

For Algor, this ratio indicates that there is $3.90 in current assets available to pay each $1 in current liabilities. What is a good ratio? To answer this question, one must look at the ratios of successful firms in similar businesses. Their ratios may be found from an examination of their financial statements if they are public companies, or from financial information firms such as Dun and Bradstreet. In general, it can be said that a ratio of 2 : 1 is looked upon as being favourable. That means that

FIGURE 14-1 AN INCOME STATEMENT FOR ALGOR COMPUTER SERVICES

Algor Computer Services
Income Statement
for the year ended May 31, 1991

Revenue
Computer Services			$312 400.00
Software Lessons			26 700.00
Sales			176 337.00
Gross Revenue			515 437.00
Less: Refunds		$ 2 140.00	
Sales Returns and Allowances		1 364.00	
Sales Discounts		2 267.00	5 771.00
Net Revenue			509 666.00

Cost of Goods Sold
Inventory, June 1, 1990		89 600.00	
Purchases	$86 200.00		
Freight-in	1 439.00		
Gross Purchases	87 639.00		
Less: Purchases Discounts	468.00		
Net Purchases		87 171.00	
Cost of Goods Available for Sale		176 771.00	
Less: Ending Inventory		87 200.00	
Cost of Goods Sold			89 571.00
Gross Profit			420 095.00

Expenses
Wages	244 309.00	
Bank	368.00	
Interest	30 133.00	
Visa Discount	7 460.00	
Advertising	10 400.00	
Utilities	29 400.00	
Automobile	5 227.00	
Miscellaneous	1 436.00	
Bad Debts	1 200.00	
Depreciation Expense: Building	10 288.50	
Depreciation Expense: Office Equipment	275.50	
Depreciation Expense: Computer Equipment	6 703.20	
Depreciation Expense: Automobile	1 837.50	
Insurance	1 600.00	
Office Supplies	640.00	
Computer Supplies	2 160.00	
Total Expenses		353 437.70
Net Income		$ 66 657.30

FIGURE 14-2 A BALANCE SHEET FOR ALGOR COMPUTER SERVICES

Algor Computer Services
Balance Sheet
as at May 31, 1991

Assets

Current Assets
Cash			$ 44 600.00
Accounts Receivable		$ 42 700.00	
Less: Allowance for Doubtful Accounts		1 400.00	41 300.00
Merchandise Inventory			87 200.00
GST Recoverable			1 605.00
Prepaid Insurance			3 200.00
Office Supplies			1 125.00
Computer Supplies			1 147.00
Total Current Assets				$180 177.00

Fixed Assets
Land			124 600.00	
Building		228 000.00		
Less: Accumulated Depreciation		32 518.50	195 481.50	
Office Equipment		14 500.00		
Less: Accumulated Depreciation		12 020.50	2 479.50	
Computer Equipment		65 600.00		
Less: Accumulated Depreciation		29 959.20	35 640.80	
Automobile		12 500.00		
Less: Accumulated Depreciation		8 212.50	4 287.50	
Total Fixed Assets				362 489.30
Total Assets				$542 666.30

Liabilities and Owner's Equity

Current Liabilities
Accounts Payable			$ 27 205.00	
Short-Term Loans			14 612.00	
GST Payable			1 976.00	
PST Payable			2 368.00	
Total Current Liabilities				$ 46 161.00

Long-Term Liabilities
Mortgage Payable   236 500.00

Owner's Equity
Capital, June 1, 1990			234 148.00	
Net Income		$ 66 657.30		
Less: Drawings		40 800.00		
Increase in Capital			25 857.30	
Capital, May 31, 1991				260 005.30
Total Liabilities and Owner's Equity				$542 666.30

there is $2 in current assets to pay every $1 in current liabilities. However, there are difficulties in accepting the current ratio as the sole indicator of debt-paying ability in the short term. Other factors must be considered. For example, the current asset figure includes accounts receivable and merchandise inventory. Are these liquid — are debtors paying their accounts on time, and does merchandise inventory consist of an up-to-date stock, and is it selling?

Poor ratios are looked upon as being well above 2:1 or below 2:1. For example, a ratio of 8:1 indicates that there may be too much money tied up in current assets, which could better be put to use as a long-term investment. As a simple comparison, money invested with a financial institution for a long term will bring a higher rate of return than for a short term. At the other extreme, a ratio of 1:1 indicates that there is only $1 in current assets for each $1 owed in current liabilities. This ratio does not provide for emergencies. As well, current assets include accounts receivable and merchandise inventory, yet these items are not necessarily converted to cash at the same time that the current liabilities are due. The 1:1 ratio also includes current assets such as supplies, which, rather than being converted to cash, will be used in the business operations. These prepaid assets do not improve the cash position of the business.

Acid-Test Ratio

Acid-test ratio or quick ratio: *a ratio that compares the quick assets to the current liabilities.*

In order to overcome some of the weaknesses of the current ratio, the **acid-test ratio**, or the **quick ratio** as it is sometimes called, is used. This ratio eliminates from the comparison to current liabilities those assets which may not contribute to the short-term debt-paying ability of the business: merchandise inventory and prepaid expenses. The current assets that remain are referred to as the quick assets: cash, marketable securities, and accounts receivable — cash plus those assets that can quickly be converted into cash. The acid-test ratio for Algor Computer Services is calculated as follows:

$$\text{Acid-test ratio} = \frac{\text{Cash + Marketable securities + Net receivables}}{\text{Current liabilities}}$$

$$= \frac{44\,600 + 41\,300}{46\,161}$$

$$= \frac{85\,900}{46\,161}$$

$$= 1.86$$

A 1:1 ratio is generally looked upon as being an acceptable quick ratio, for it indicates that there is $1 in quick assets for each dollar in current liabilities. The 1.86:1 ratio for Algor Computer Services is therefore very acceptable. Acceptable acid-test ratios are obviously lower than acceptable current ratios because some of the less liquid current assets have been excluded. The two ratios together will indicate the general ability of the business to remain solvent.

Activity Ratios

Activity ratios: ratios that indicate how effectively certain assets are being used.

Activity ratios indicate how effectively the assets are being used, as well as how liquid accounts receivable and merchandise inventory are. The more effective the use of assets the better the cash position of the business. If merchandise inventory, for example, can be quickly converted to cash, then replenished, then converted to cash, and so on, the cash flow for the business will be good. However, should the firm not be able to sell its merchandise quickly, the cash flow will be poor. Two activity ratios that indicate how well assets are being utilized are accounts receivable turnover and inventory turnover.

Accounts Receivable Turnover

Accounts receivable turnover: the number of times that accounts receivable have been converted into cash during the year.

The **accounts receivable turnover** shows the number of times that accounts receivable have been converted into cash during the year. The higher the ratio, the less the investment in accounts receivable. For example, should one business have a turnover of ten times, and another six times, the firm with a turnover of ten times is in a better position, for it requires less investment in its accounts receivable. It is receiving the cash from them faster. Obviously, a firm prefers to have the cash rather than the accounts receivable, for then it can invest in other things. Again, what is acceptable will depend upon the type of business, but the time should be close to the credit terms offered by the business. The formula for the receivable turnover ratio is calculated by dividing net sales on account by average accounts receivable. If net sales on account are not available, total sales may be used, but the same formula should be used on a year-to-year basis, according to the consistency concept. Also, to calculate average accounts receivable, the beginning and ending account balances can be used, dividing their sum by two to get an average. (This calculation could not be used if the business was seasonal.) The ratio for Algor Computer Services is shown below, assuming an average accounts receivable figure of $44 000.00:

$$\text{Accounts receivable turnover} = \frac{\text{Net sales}}{\text{Average accounts receivable}}$$

$$= \frac{509\ 666}{44\ 000}$$

$$= 11.58$$

This figure indicates that the accounts receivable turn over 11.58 times per year, or every 31.5 days. The higher the turnover figure, the lower the number of days required for collection of the receivable. The general rule is that the number of days for accounts receivable turnover should not exceed the terms allowed for payment of the net amount by more than 10 to 15 days. Thus, if a firm offers terms of net 30 days, the accounts receivable should be turning over at least every 45 days. The figure for Algor Computer Services is therefore within the range of acceptability.

Inventory Turnover

> **Inventory turnover:** a ratio that indicates how quickly inventory is sold.

The **inventory turnover** indicates how quickly inventory is sold. In order to calculate the turnover, the Cost of Goods Sold is divided by the average inventory. As with the accounts receivable turnover, the inventory turnover can be divided into 365 days in order to calculate the average number of days that it takes to sell the inventory. Also, the average inventory can be calculated by taking the sum of the beginning and the ending inventory and dividing it by two. (As with the accounts receivable inventory, this method of calculating the average cannot be used if the business is seasonal.)

A high inventory turnover ratio may indicate that the business's sales are good, the presence of old inventory is low, and there is a good cash flow. However, it may also indicate that, because the amount of inventory on hand is low, only a small inventory is being turned over rapidly. That is certainly not a good situation. The inventory turnover for Algor Computer Services is calculated as follows:

$$\text{Inventory turnover} = \frac{\text{Cost of goods sold}}{\text{Average inventory}}$$

$$= \frac{89\,571}{87\,200}$$

$$= 1.03$$

In order for this figure to be relevant, it should be compared to other years. The higher the figure, however, the better, for that means that inventory is turning over frequently. In the case of Algor Computer Services, the figure is very poor, for the inventory is only turning over once per year. Algor is a young business focussing on the service side however, and therefore this figure, though disturbing to management, is not indicative of the overall performance of the business.

Profitability Ratios

> **Profitability ratios:** ratios that measure the success of the business in relation to net income for a given period of time.

Two **profitability ratios**, profit margin on sales and rate of return on investment, measure the success of the business in relation to net income for a given period of time.

Profit Margin on Sales

> **Profit margin on sales:** a ratio that compares net sales to net income.

To calculate the **profit margin on sales**, the net sales are compared to the net income. Surveys of the public usually show that people think businesses have a profit margin of 40 to 50 percent. In reality, the figure is usually under ten percent. The profit margin on sales for Algor Computer Services is calculated as follows:

$$\text{Profit margin on sales} = \frac{\text{Net income} \times 100}{\text{Net sales}}$$

$$= \frac{66\,657.30 \times 100}{509\,666.00}$$

$$= 13.1\%$$

To evaluate the profit margin on sales, there must be a comparison to previous years, and to other businesses in the same industry. Consideration must also be given to whether there was increased investment in the business, and to external economic factors. Though Algor Computer Services was not very profitable on the merchandise side of the operation, it was profitable on the service side. For a proprietorship, the return on its sales was significant.

Rate of Return on Investment

An owner of a business would like to know what the return on his or her investment is so that a comparison can be made to alternative investments. An entrepreneur with $200 000 to invest has many alternatives, and would like to invest where the return will be maximized. This individual would compare the rate of return on the investment in the business to alternatives such as bonds, stocks, savings certificates, or investing in alternate businesses. The **rate of return on investment** is calculated by dividing net income by average capital. The calculation for Algor Computer Services is as follows, using the average capital of $247 076.65:

Rate of return on investment: a ratio that compares net income to average capital.

$$\text{Rate of return on investment} = \frac{\text{Net income} \times 100}{\text{Average capital}}$$

$$= \frac{66\,657.30 \times 100}{247\,076.65}$$

$$= 27.0\%$$

The 27.0 percent rate of return on investment should be compared to the return generated in previous years, to the rate of return for other businesses of the same size in the same field, and to the rate that could be earned if Vijay Marshall, the owner, were to close the business and invest his money elsewhere. Obviously, the rate of return is very high in this case.

Coverage Ratios

Coverage ratios measure the degree of protection for long-term creditors and investors. The objective of each of these two groups in examining the financial statements is very different. The creditor wants to ensure that the firm is solvent, whereas the investors will want a large return on their investment, and potential for growth.

> **Coverage ratios:** ratios that measure the degree of protection for long-term creditors and investors.

Debt to Total Assets

The **debt to total assets ratio** provides important information about the ability of the firm to service its debt load and to absorb losses without affecting the creditors' status. The debt to total assets ratio for Algor is calculated as follows:

> **Debt to total assets ratio:** a ratio that measures the ability of the firm to service its debt load or absorb losses.

$$\text{Debt to total assets} = \frac{\text{Debt} \times 100}{\text{Total assets}}$$

$$= \frac{282\,661 \times 100}{542\,666.30}$$

$$= 52.1\%$$

The lower the ratio the better for creditors, for it is easier for the company to pay the interest on its debt and there will be fewer creditors having a claim against the assets in the case of a bankruptcy. A low ratio makes it easier to obtain financing from other creditors, for these potential creditors know that they have a good chance of receiving payment for their loan. If the ratio is high, the creditor might still loan the money but impose a higher interest rate. In Algor's case, the creditors have a rather large claim against the assets of the business, approximately 52.1 percent. This is due mainly to the large mortgage that Algor Computer Services is responsible for, which is not unusual for a young business. Since the bulk of this debt is long term, Algor should not have problems meeting its payments.

Equity to Total Assets

The parallel calculation to debt to total assets is equity to total assets, since liabilities plus owner's equity is equal to assets. The two calculations should add to 100 percent. **Equity to total assets** measures the owner's investment as a portion of total assets. The equity to total assets ratio is calculated as follows:

> **Equity to total assets:** a ratio that measures the owner's investment as a portion of total assets.

$$\text{Equity to total assets} = \frac{\text{Owner's equity} \times 100}{\text{Total assets}}$$

$$= \frac{260\,005.30 \times 100}{542\,666.30}$$

$$= 47.9\%$$

It is to the advantage of the owners to have this percentage very low, and to the creditors to have it as high as possible. If you were the owner of a business with earnings at a satisfactory level and low interest rates, you would prefer to have the creditors contribute a large percentage of the assets, for then you would not have to have your funds tied up in the business and could have them invested in other areas. It is preferable to earn an income using somebody else's money, rather than your own.

LESSON REVIEW

1. What is the purpose of calculating various ratios and trends?

2. Why is an absolute dollar amount for net income not by itself a very important figure?

3. What are the two main instruments of analysis? Describe each.

4. What does a liquidity ratio show? What are the two main liquidity ratios?

5. What do the accounts receivable and inventory activity ratios indicate? Why does a firm want a high figure in both cases?

6. What are the two main profitability ratios? Why is each calculated?

7. Distinguish between the two coverage ratios.

8. What percentage must the debt to assets and equity to assets ratios always add to?

9. If you were a creditor, which would you rather see as the larger percentage: debt to assets, or equity to assets? Why?

LESSON APPLICATIONS

10. (a) Given the following data, calculate the working capital, current ratio, and quick ratio (or acid-test ratio).

Cash	$ 5 000	Accounts Payable	$ 3 000
Accounts Receivable	6 000	Bank Loan (current)	2 000
Merchandise Inventory	10 000	Mortgage	12 000
Prepaid Expenses	200		

    (b) Comment on the firm's ability to remain solvent.

11. (a) Given the following data, calculate the accounts receivable turnover and inventory turnover, and the number of days required for each to turn over.

Average accounts receivable (net)	$ 65 000
Average merchandise inventory	120 000
Net credit sales	385 000
Cost of Goods Sold	940 000

(b) Comment on each of the turnover ratios.

12. (a) Given the following data, calculate the accounts receivable turnover and inventory turnover, and the number of days required for each to turn over.

Average accounts receivable (net)	$ 80 000
Average merchandise inventory	70 000
Net credit sales	940 000
Cost of Goods Sold	820 000

(b) Comment on each of the turnover ratios.

13. (a) Given the following data, calculate the profit margin on sales and the rate of return on investment.

Net income	$ 760 000
Net sales	8 400 000
Average Capital	12 400 000

(b) Comment on each of the profitability ratios.

14. (a) Given the following data, calculate the profit margin on sales and the rate of return on investment.

Net income	$ 420 000
Net sales	7 800 000
Average Capital	12 400 000

(b) Comment on each of the profitability ratios.

15. (a) Given the following data, calculate the ratios of debt to total assets and equity to total assets.

Total assets	$490 000
Total debt	330 000
Owner's equity	160 000

(b) Comment on each of the ratios, assuming that you are a creditor of the firm.

16. (a) Given the following data, calculate the ratios of debt to total assets and equity to total assets.

Total assets	$680 000
Total debt	260 000
Owner's equity	420 000

(b) Comment on each of the ratios, assuming that you are the owner of the firm.

17. Figure 14-3 shows the summarized financial statement data for a small merchandising firm.

FIGURE 14-3

Balance Sheet

Assets		Liabilities and Owner's Equity	
Cash	$ 500	Current Liabilities	$ 900
Accounts Receivable (net)	500	Mortgage Payable	4 000
Merchandise Inventory	1 000	N. Deen, Capital	2 110
Prepaid Expenses	10		
Fixed Assets	5 000		
	$7 010		$7 010

Income Statement

Sales	$2 500
Cost of Goods Sold	1 200
Gross Profit	1 300
Operating Expenses	300
Net Income	$1 000

(a) Calculate the following ratios:
   (i) Current ratio
   (ii) Working capital
   (iii) Quick ratio
   (iv) Accounts receivable turnover (assume that the average accounts receivable is equal to the year-end figure, and all sales are on credit)
   (v) Inventory turnover (assume that the average merchandise inventory is equal to the year-end figure)
   (vi) Profit margin on sales
   (vii) Rate of return on investment
   (viii) Debt to total assets
   (ix) Equity to total assets
(b) Comment on the financial stability of the business by reference to each of the ratios.

18. Figures 14-4 and 14-5 show the summarized financial statement data for a variety store.

FIGURE 14-4

Balance Sheet

Assets		Liabilities and Owner's Equity	
Cash	$ 300	Current Liabilities	$1 900
Accounts Receivable (net)	400	Mortgage Payable	5 000
Merchandise Inventory	900	C. Fraser, Capital	720
Prepaid Expenses	20		
Fixed Assets	6 000		
	$7 620		$7 620

FIGURE 14-5

Income Statement

Sales	$4 000
Cost of Goods Sold	3 000
Gross Profit	1 000
Operating Expenses	800
Net Income	$ 200

(a) Calculate the following ratios:
   (i) Current ratio
   (ii) Working capital
   (iii) Quick ratio
   (iv) Accounts receivable turnover (assume that the average accounts receivable is equal to the year-end figure, and all sales are on credit)
   (v) Inventory turnover (assume that the average merchandise inventory is equal to the year-end figure)
   (vi) Profit margin on sales
   (vii) Rate of return on investment
   (viii) Debt to total assets
   (ix) Equity to total assets
(b) Comment on the financial stability of the business by reference to each of the ratios.

14.2 Trends

The analysis of trends is very important for a business, for it provides an overview of the business's growth rather than a description of what has occurred in the current year, which ratios provide. **Trend analysis** involves the analysis of financial statement data for a number of years. The CICA Handbook recommends that the previous periods' financial data be given when it is meaningful. Most publicly held firms provide a minimum of five years of data with their financial statements for comparison purposes. Again, trends alone cannot be relied on when evaluating the current health and future prospects for the business. However, the extent of the growth in various significant areas can be determined from trends. As well, the data can be used as a point of comparison to other businesses in the industry, industry averages, and other industries.

> **Trend analysis:** the analysis of financial statement data for a number of years.

Trend analysis is done using percentages. The analysis can either be a horizontal analysis, or a vertical analysis, the results of which are sometimes referred to as common size statements. Horizontal analysis was examined in Chapter 3 in relation to income statements. It included the dollar and percentage change over two years for the income statement. In Chapter 5 horizontal analysis of balance sheets was carried out. Figures 14-6 and 14-7 show the horizontal analysis of a condensed balance sheet and income statement for Algor, for the years 1990 and 1991.

> "**Horizontal analysis of financial statements** compares the percentage change in items for two or more years."

FIGURE 14-6 A CONDENSED, COMPARATIVE BALANCE SHEET

Algor Computer Services
Comparative Balance Sheet
as at May 31

	1991	1990	Net Incr. or (Decr.)	% Change
Assets				
Current Assets				
Cash	$ 44 600.00	$ 42 400.00	$ 2 200.00	5.2
Accounts Receivable (net)	41 300.00	36 700.00	4 600.00	12.5
Merchandise Inventory	87 200.00	74 800.00	12 400.00	16.6
GST Recoverable	1 605.00	n.a.	1 605.00	—
Prepaid Expenses	5 472.00	5 580.00	(108.00)	(1.9)
Total Current Assets	180 177.00	159 480.00	20 697.00	13.0
Fixed Assets				
Land	124 600.00	124 600.00	0	0
Building & Equipment	320 600.00	318 060.00	2 540.00	0.8
Total Fixed Assets	445 200.00	442 660.00	2 540.00	0.6
Less: Accumulated depreciation	82 710.70	70 170.50	12 540.20	17.9
Net Fixed Assets	362 489.30	372 489.50	(10 000.20)	(2.7)
Total Assets	$542 666.30	$531 969.50	$10 696.80	2.0
Liabilities and Owner's Equity				
Current Liabilities				
Accounts Payable	$ 27 205.00	$ 22 557.50	$ 4 647.50	20.6
Short-Term Loans	14 612.00	26 784.00	(12 172.00)	(45.4)
Sales Taxes Payable	4 344.00	1 980.00	2 364.00	119.4
Total Current Liabilities	46 161.00	51 321.50	(5 160.50)	(10.1)
Long-Term Liabilities				
Mortgage Payable	236 500.00	246 500.00	(10 000.00)	(4.1)
Owner's Equity				
Opening Capital, June 1	234 148.00	209 258.00	24 890.00	11.9
Net Income	66 657.30	40 790.00	25 867.30	63.4
Less: Drawings	40 800.00	15 900.00	24 900.00	156.6
Net increase in Capital	25 857.30	24 890.00	967.30	3.9
Closing Capital, May 31	260 005.30	234 148.00	25 857.30	11.0
Total Liabilities and Owner's Equity	$542 666.30	$531 969.50	$10 696.80	2.0

FIGURE 14-7 A CONDENSED COMPARATIVE INCOME STATEMENT

Algor Computer Services
Comparative Income Statement
for the year ended May 31

	1991	1990	Net Incr. or (Decr.)	% Change
Net Revenue	$509 666.00	$460 800.00	$48 866.00	10.6
Cost of Goods Sold	89 571.00	73 090.00	16 481.00	22.5
Gross Profit	420 095.00	387 710.00	32 385.00	8.4
Expenses	353 437.70	346 920.00	6 517.70	1.9
Net Income	$ 66 657.30	$ 40 790.00	$25 867.30	63.4

Vertical Analysis

"Vertical analysis requires the converting of financial statements to percentages for comparison purposes."

In order to carry out a vertical analysis, or common size statement analysis (Figure 14-8), the dollar amounts are converted to percentages of a base. The base for the income statement is net sales, for the balance sheet the total assets, or liabilities plus owner's equity. Vertical analysis can also be done for more than one year for purposes of trend analysis. The vertical analysis for Algor Computer Services is shown in Figure 14-8 (income statement) and Figure 14-9 (balance sheet).

FIGURE 14-8 A COMMON SIZE INCOME STATEMENT

Algor Computer Services
Common Size Income Statement
for the year ended May 31, 1991

Revenue		
Net Revenue	$509 666.00	100.0%
Cost of Goods Sold	89 571.00	17.6
Gross Profit	420 095.00	82.4
Expenses	353 437.70	69.3
Net Income	$ 66 657.30	13.1%

For the above percentages to be significant, comparisons must again be made. They should be made to other years, to other businesses in the same sector, and to other industries. Obviously, the firm's objective is to improve its net income from year to year, both in absolute terms and as a percentage of net revenue. In establishing its goals, the firm must consider strategies that can be implemented in order to increase the revenue, decrease the cost of goods sold or decrease expenses, which are the three ways of changing "the bottom line."

In the case of Algor Computer Services, the Cost of Goods Sold only appeared on income statements once it began to sell merchandise, for initially it was a service business. In the beginning, because its merchandise turnover ratio was not very good, the firm needed to focus on better management of this side of the business. Regular management strategy sessions were held to implement plans to increase revenue, and decrease expenses. The data for Algor Computer Services, as a young merchandising firm, should be compared to that for the established firm Sears Canada Inc., as shown in the accompanying The Facts Speak. It should be noted that the data for Sears Canada Inc. does not include the calculation of gross profit. Many firms prefer not to disclose this information to their competitors, so they combine it with expense information.

The Facts Speak...

Common size income statement for Sears Canada Inc. for the year ended December 31, 1989. (Dollars are in millions.)

Revenue	$4 562	100.0%
Deductions:		
Cost of merchandise sold, operating, administrative and selling expenses	4 129	90.5
Depreciation	45	1.0
Interest on long-term obligations	102	2.2
Other interest	69	1.5
Municipality realty and business taxes	47	1.0
Total Deductions	4 392	96.2
Earnings from operations before taxes	170	3.8
Income taxes	75	1.6
Earnings from operations	$ 95	2.2%

FIGURE 14-9 A COMMON SIZE BALANCE SHEET

Algor Computer Services
Common Size Balance Sheet
as at May 31, 1991

Assets		
Current Assets	$180 177.00	33.2%
Fixed Assets		
Land	124 600.00	23.0
Building & Equipment (net)	237 889.30	43.8
Total Assets	$542 666.30	100.0%
Liabilities and Owner's Equity		
Current Liabilities		
Accounts Payable	$ 27 205.00	5.0%
Short-Term Loans	14 612.00	2.7
Sales Taxes Payable	4 344.00	0.8
Total Current Liabilities	46 161.00	8.5
Long-Term Liabilities		
Mortgage Payable	236 500.00	43.6
Owner's Equity		
Capital, May 31, 1991	260 005.30	47.9
Total Liabilities and Owner's Equity	$542 666.30	100.0%

The common size balance sheet for Algor Computer Services (Figure 14-9) shows that approximately 33 percent of the total assets is represented by current assets, the balance by fixed assets. The firm's main concern is that it have sufficient current assets on hand to remain solvent. Again, for these figures to have significance, they should be compared to those of previous years. One should compare these ratios for Algor Computer Services, a young company, to those for the established firm, Sears Canada Inc., as shown in the accompanying The Facts Speak.

When making an analysis of financial statements, it is necessary to not only calculate ratios, but also to examine trends. As noted in Chapter 1 on page 3, concerning the Three Buoys Houseboats, the failure of the owners to examine the facts as prepared by the accountants was a significant reason for the failure of the firm. A business that examines its financial statements, calculates ratios, examines trends, and considers the many other factors that can influence its success will have a good chance to be successful.

THE FACTS SPEAK...

Common size balance sheet for Sears Canada Inc., 1989. (Dollar figures are in millions.)

Sears Canada Inc.
Common Size Balance Sheet
as at December 31, 1989

Assets

Current Assets	$2 667.7	84.2%
Investments and other assets	26.7	0.8
Fixed Assets	365.2	11.5
Deferred Charges	108.9	3.4
Total Assets	$3 168.5	

Liabilities and Owner's Equity

Current Liabilities	$1 251.9	39.5%
Long-Term Obligations	871.1	27.5
Deferred Income Taxes	75.4	2.4
Owners' Equity	970.1	30.6
Total Liabilities and Owners' Equity	$3 168.5	

LESSON REVIEW

19. What is a trend?

20. Does trend analysis have significance on its own? Explain.

21. Distinguish between horizontal and vertical analysis.

22. Describe how one prepares a common size income statement and a common size balance sheet.

23. What should the trends in a business be compared to?

24. Why do some firms include the Cost of Goods Sold with expenses?

LESSON APPLICATIONS

25. Using the following data for Ford Motor Company for the year ended December 31, 1989, prepare a common size income statement. Dollar figures are in millions.

Sales	$15 312
Operating Costs	
Costs, excluding items listed below	14 151
Marketing and administration	369
Depreciation/amortization	309
Employee pension plans	21
Operating Income	462
Other Income	62
Income before income taxes	524
Income Taxes	210
Net Income	$ 314

26. Using the following data for British Columbia Telephone Company for the years ended December 31, 1989, and 1988, prepare common size income statements. Dollar figures are in millions.

	1989	1988
Revenue	$1 690	$1 634
Operating Expenses		
Operations	953	864
Depreciation	286	322
Property taxes	31	30
Operating Earnings	420	418
Interest, etc. on debt	126	115
Earnings before income taxes	294	303
Income Taxes	125	147
Earnings from Operations	$ 169	$ 156

27. (a) Using the following data for Time Air Corporation for the years ended December 31, 1989, and 1988, prepare common size balance sheets. Dollar figures are in millions.

	1989	1988
Assets		
Current Assets	$ 36 720	$ 30 125
Fixed Assets	161 594	111 188
Less Depreciation	(24 357)	(17 699)
Liabilities		
Current Liabilities	21 639	19 020
Long-Term Debt	84 411	50 029
Deferred Income Taxes	18 287	12 195
Owners' Equity	49 620	42 370

(b) Compare the data for the two years, and prepare a brief report as to any significant changes.

28. (a) Using the following data for Shell Canada Limited for the years ended December 31, 1989, and 1988, prepare common size income statements. Dollar figures are in millions.

	1989	1988
Revenues	$4 917	$5 060
Expenses		
Purchases	2 287	2 146
Operating	934	933
Selling and General	850	806
Exploration and predevelopment	126	97
Depreciation, etc.	283	288
Interest on long-term debt	76	89
Total Expenses	4 556	4 359
Earnings before taxes	361	701
Income taxes	149	274
Earnings for the year	$ 212	$ 427

(b) Using the following data for Shell Canada Limited for the years ended December 31, 1989, and 1988, prepare common size balance sheets. Dollar figures are in millions.

	1989	1988
Assets		
Current Assets	$1 622	$1 855
Investments	120	115
Fixed Assets	3 926	3 645
Liabilities		
Current Liabilities	598	890
Long-Term Liabilities	904	649
Other Liabilities	1 090	1 113
Owners' Equity	3 076	2 963

(c) Prepare a brief report concerning the most significant changes in the data shown.

29. (a) Using the following data for Canadian Tire Corporation, Limited for the years ended December 31, 1989, and 1988, prepare common size income statements. Dollar figures are in millions.

	1989	1988
Revenue	$2 957	$2 641
Expenses		
Cost of merchandise sold and all expenses except as below	2 636	2 341
Interest	39	37
Depreciation	30	27
Employee profit sharing plans	18	14
Operating Earnings	234	222
Interest and Investment Income	21	17
Earnings before income taxes	255	239
Income taxes	105	109
Earnings from operations	$ 150	$ 130

(b) Using the following data for Canadian Tire Corporation, Limited for the years ended December 31, 1989, and 1988, prepare common size balance sheets. Dollar figures are in millions.

	1989	1988
Assets		
Current Assets	$1 107	$1 011
Long-term receivables/investments	15	20
Property and Equipment	606	499
Other Assets	2	1
Liabilities		
Current Liabilities	495	516
Long-term Liabilities	308	181
Deferred Income Taxes	6	10
Owners' Equity	921	824

(c) Compare the data for the two years, and prepare a brief report as to any significant changes.

CHAPTER REVIEW AND SKILL DEVELOPMENT

Accounting Principles and Concepts
- **Ratios** are calculated in order to evaluate a business's activities for the current year.
- **Trends** are calculated in order to evaluate a business's activities for two or more years.
- **Ratios and trends** in themselves do not indicate the success of a business.

Knowing the Terms
For each of the following statements, indicate the term being defined.
(a) Ratios that measure the ability of the business to meet its short-term commitments.
(b) The analysis of financial statement data that covers a number of years.
(c) Ratios that measure the degree of protection for long-term creditors and investors.
(d) Ratios that indicate how effectively assets are being used.
(e) Ratio that compares the net income to net sales.
(f) Analysis in which the items on the statements indicate the change over two or more years.
(g) Ratios that measure the success of the business in relation to net income for a given period of time.
(h) Ratio that compares net income to average capital.
(i) Analysis in which the items on the statements are restated as a percentage.
(j) Ratio that compares net sales to average accounts receivable.

Food for Thought
1. The government of Canada imposed a 7 percent GST, effective January 1, 1991. The tax replaced a 13 percent manufacturer's sales tax imposed only on goods manufactured in Canada. What effect would this tax have on
   (a) a retail business;
   (b) a service business, which previously was not being taxed?

2. Wage settlements in the paper industry in 1990 in the United States were in the 3 percent range, whereas settlements in Canada were in the 7 percent range. What effect does this difference have for Canadian producers?

3. In 1990, during a recession, the resale value of houses in some parts of Canada plunged by over 30 percent in a few months. What types of businesses would be affected by this decrease?

4. On average, Canadians drink approximately 115 litres of soft drinks per person per year, as compared to 210 litres for the average U.S. consumer. What strategies could Canadian soft drink manufacturers employ in order to increase sales?

5. The Canadian government was proposing, in 1990, an open skies policy. This policy would mean that Canadian airlines would have to compete openly with the larger U.S. airlines. What effect would this policy have on revenue for the major Canadian airlines?

6. "Financial statement data in itself is not very significant." Explain why this statement is true.

7. An accounting student indicated that the current ratio can never be too high. Criticize this statement.

8. When calculating the inventory turnover for a business, an accounting student indicated that it is not necessary to work out the average merchandise figure for the year. He indicated that the year-end figure would suffice. Why should the average be calculated? When can the end-of-year figure be used?

9. An owner of a firm indicated to her accountant that she would prefer to increase the ratio of debt to total assets instead of equity to total assets. Why would the owner prefer to have that situation? Why might it be difficult for an owner to meet this objective?

10. McDuff Boating Supplies is very seasonal in nature. Would its current ratio normally be better during its busy season or its slow season? Based on your answer, during which season should it choose its year end? Why?

Locate and Record

1. Using the annual report that you obtained in Chapter 4, calculate the following ratios, where possible:
   (a) working capital
   (b) current ratio
   (c) quick ratio
   (d) accounts receivable turnover (assume that the year-end amount is the average)
   (e) inventory turnover (assume that the year-end amount is the average)
   (f) profit margin on sales
   (g) rate of return on investment
   (h) debt to total assets
   (i) equity to total assets

2. Using the annual report obtained in Chapter 4,
   (a) prepare a common size balance sheet
   (b) prepare a common size income statement
   (c) prepare a horizontal analysis for the latest two-year period.

Organizing

Prepare a chart showing
(a) the names of the ratios discussed in the text
(b) the formulas for the ratios
(c) a brief description of what the ratio illustrates.

Applications

1. Figure 14-10 summarizes the results for Air Canada for the years ended December 31, 1988 and 1989. Dollar figures are in millions.
   (a) Prepare a horizontal analysis for the two years.
   (b) Indicate items of significance that you think should have footnotes in the annual report.
   (c) Calculate the following ratios: profit margin on sales, and rate of return on investment (equity was $1 062 million).
   (d) Calculate the effect on net income if there is a 10 percent increase in the cost of aircraft fuel.

2. Figure 14-11 summarizes the results for Mitel Corporation for the years ended March 31, 1988 and 1989. Figures are in millions of Canadian dollars.
   (a) Prepare a horizontal analysis for the balance sheet.
   (b) Calculate the following ratios: current ratio, working capital, quick ratio, and debt to total assets and equity to total assets.
   (c) Comment on the financial position of the business by referring to the calculations done in (a) and (b).

FIGURE 14-10

Air Canada
Consolidated Statement of Income
for the years ended December 31

	1989	1988
Operating Revenues		
Passenger	$2 909	$2 596
Cargo	398	503
Other	369	327
Operating Expenses		
Salaries, wages and benefits	1 142	1 101
Aircraft fuel	526	481
Depreciation, etc.	150	148
Other	1 735	1 582
Operating income before undernoted	123	114
Provision for staff reduction and retirement costs	(16)	(6)
Operating Income	107	108
Non-operating income (expense)	124	10
Income before income taxes and minority interest	231	118
Provision for deferred income taxes	(82)	(30)
Minority Interest	—	1
Net Income	$ 149	$ 89

FIGURE 14-11

Mitel Corporation
Consolidated Balance Sheet
as at March 31

	1989	1988
Assets		
Current Assets		
Cash and short-term investments	$128.7	$119.4
Accounts receivable	99.8	97.2
Inventories	68.3	84.9
Prepaid expenses	2.9	3.3
Fixed Assets	129.7	139.0
Other Assets	6.0	2.1
	$435.4	$445.9
Liabilities and Owners' Equity		
Current Liabilities		
Accounts payable and accrued liabilities	$106.4	$110.1
Income tax and other taxes payable	10.2	10.4
Current portion of long-term debt	5.7	7.2
Long-term and other debt	10.0	18.6
Owners' Equity	303.1	299.6
	$435.4	$445.9

3. Figures 14-12 and 14-13 show the statement of income and balance sheet for McDonald's Corporation for the years ended December 31, 1989 and 1988. Figures are in millions of dollars.
   (a) Prepare a horizontal analysis of the income statement and balance sheet.
   (b) Prepare a common size income statement and balance sheet for both years.
   (c) Calculate the following for each of the two years: working capital, current ratio, acid-test ratio, accounts receivable turnover, profit margin on sales, rate of return on investment, debt to total assets, and equity to total assets. (For accounts receivable turnover, assume that the year-end figure is the average.)
   (d) Prepare a brief report, referring to the changes between the 1989 and 1988 figures, as to whether McDonald's financial situation is improving.

FIGURE 14-12

McDonald's Corporation
Consolidated Statement of Income
for the years ended December 31

	1989	1988
Revenues		
Sales by Company-operated restaurants	$4 601	$4 196
Revenues from franchised restaurants	1 464	1 325
Other revenues — net	77	45
Total Revenues	6 142	5 566
Costs and Expenses		
Company-operated restaurants		
Food and paper	1 560	1 442
Payroll	1 021	936
Depreciation, etc.	221	192
Rent	86	69
Other operating expenses	891	815
	3 779	3 454
Franchised restaurants		
Depreciation, etc.	143	132
Rent	98	86
	241	218
General, administrative and selling expenses	663	611
Interest expense (net)	302	237
Total costs and expenses	4 985	4 520
Income before provision for taxes	1 157	1 046
Provision for income taxes	430	400
Net Income	$ 727	$ 646

FIGURE 14-13

McDonald's Corporation
Consolidated Balance Sheet
as at December 31

	1989	1988
Assets		
Current Assets		
Cash and equivalents	$ 137	$ 184
Accounts receivable	207	179
Notes receivable	27	25
Inventories, at cost	46	49
Prepaid expenses and other current assets	78	80
Total Current Assets	495	517
Other Assets	596	527
Property and equipment		
Property and equipment, at cost	9 874	8 647
Accumulated depreciation, etc.	(2 116)	(1 847)
Net property and equipment	7 758	6 800
Intangible assets	326	315
Total Assets	$9 175	$8 159
Liabilities and Owners' Equity		
Current liabilities		
Notes payable	$ 76	$ 115
Accounts payable	413	453
Income taxes	71	34
Other taxes	67	60
Accrued interest	128	125
Other accrued liabilities	203	174
Current maturities of long-term debt	59	43
Total current liabilities	1 017	1 004
Long-term debt	3 901	3 111
Security deposits by franchisees	94	88
Deferred income taxes	613	543
Owners' Equity	3 550	3 413
Total Liabilities and Owners' Equity	$9 175	$8 159

Applications — Comprehensive

Using the trial balance in Figure 14-14 for Ranadive's Games & Books for the year ended June 30, 1990,

(a) prepare a worksheet with adjustments, providing appropriate account numbers;

Adjusting data:
Prepaid expenses	$12 200 used
Inventory, June 30	$340 900
Building, depreciation	5% per annum (declining-balance method)
Furniture & Fixtures, depreciation	10% per annum (declining-balance method)
Interest earned on investments	$9 140
Interest due on long-term debt	$3 400

(b) prepare the financial statements;
(c) prepare a common size income statement and balance sheet;
(d) calculate the following ratios: working capital, current ratio, acid-test ratio,

FIGURE 14-14

Ranadive's Games & Books
Trial Balance
June 30, 1990

Cash	$ 24 900	
Accounts Receivable	116 400	
Inventories	312 600	
Prepaid expenses and other assets	16 300	
Investments	92 800	
Land	230 000	
Building	210 000	
Accumulated Depreciation: Building		$ 140 400
Furniture & Fixtures	78 900	
Accumulated Depreciation: Furn. & Fix.		37 500
Accounts Payable		124 600
Long-term debt due within one year		22 500
Long-Term Debt		245 600
M. Ranadive, Capital		428 400
M. Ranadive, Drawings	45 000	
Sales		984 600
Cost of Goods Sold	522 300	
Wages Expense	200 400	
Utilities	24 000	
Advertising	89 000	
Other Expenses	21 000	
	$1 983 600	$1 983 600

accounts receivable turnover, inventory turnover, profit margin on sales, rate of return on investment, debt to total assets, and equity to total assets. (Assume that the accounts receivable figure is the average; average the beginning and ending inventory to obtain the average.)

Focussing

The following ratios were obtained for a firm which was engaged in the merchandising of sportswear:
Current ratio: 1.3
Acid-test: 0.8
Accounts receivable turnover: 6.14 (the firm's terms were n/30)
Inventory turnover: 5.98
Rate of return on investment: 3%
Debt to total assets: 67%
Equity to total assets: 33%
For each of the above ratios, indicate whether it reflects a poor ratio or not, and why. The ratios were obtained for a year in which the economy went through a recession, which means that sales were poor for most firms in this sector of the economy.

Evaluate and Assess

Two firms in the same business sector, shoe sales, have the following financial data at the end of 19–8. Figures are in thousands of dollars.

	Co. A	Co. B
Cash	$ 110	$ 120
Accounts Receivable (net)	150	120
Inventory	190	310
Current Liabilities	220	580
Net Credit Sales	800	650
Net Sales (cash and credit)	1 400	1 300
Cost of Goods Sold	1 045	1 130

1. Compare the firms by calculating five ratios that can be done with the data given. (Use year-end figures of receivables and inventory as if they were averages.)

2. Compare the firms as if you were the owner. Which would you prefer to own? Why?

3. Compare the firms as if you were a creditor. Which would you prefer to sell $30 000 worth of merchandise inventory to on credit? Why?

Synthesize and Conclude

Wimarck is a firm engaged in the merchandising of furniture. The firm's condensed financial statements are in Figures 14-15 and 14-16. Figures are in thousands of dollars.

FIGURE 14-15

Wimarck Furniture
Income Statement
for the year ended December 31, 19–9

Revenue	$525 900
Cost and Expenses	
Cost of sales, selling and administrative expenses	398 000
Depreciation of fixed assets	31 900
	429 900
Operating income	96 000
Interest on debt	18 000
Earnings before income tax	78 000
Income taxes	24 500
Net earnings for the period	$ 53 500

FIGURE 14-16

Wimarck Furniture
Balance Sheet
as at December 31, 19–9

Current Assets	
Cash	$ 3 000
Accounts Receivable	5 984
Inventories	24 905
Prepaid expenses and other assets	2 450
	36 339
Investments	18 000
Fixed assets	126 808
Other assets	5 320
	$186 467
Liabilities	
Current liabilities	
Accounts payable	$ 16 400
Accrued liabilities	6 800
Long-Term Liabilities	92 400
C. Wimarck, Capital	70 867
	$186 467

1. Calculate the liquidity, activity, profitability, and coverage ratios outlined in this chapter. (Use the accounts receivable and merchandise inventory amounts on the statement as the average.)
2. The firm wanted to meet each of the following goals for the next year:
   (a) increase net income, by focussing on decreasing costs and expenses
   (b) increase receivables turnover
   (c) increase merchandise inventory turnover

   Give at least three control procedures that can be put in place that will contribute to each of the above goals being achieved.

Accounting At Work

Swati Joshi
Financial Analyst

Swati Joshi is a financial analyst with a government security commission agency. Her clients include individual investors as well as the general public. The field of accounting has provided her with many opportunities to work with people of varying backgrounds and, as a result, she has learned to work in many different environments.

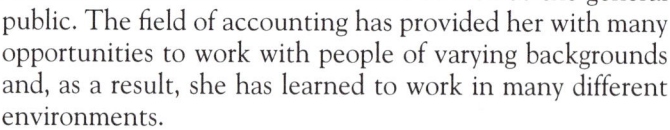

Swati helps her clients make informed investment decisions. She examines and analyzes disclosure documents related to the issuance of securities and reviews financial statements and related financial information to ensure they meet the requirements of the *Securities Act* and comply with *Securities Regulations*. She also works with her clients and a Filing Solicitor to resolve problems that arise from inconsistency between financial disclosure documents and the *Securities Act/Regulations*.

In addition, Swati deals with the public by responding to inquiries related to securities and franchise issues. Her contact with the public is invaluable, because she also assists in developing policies and amendments to address issues in the capital markets. Her input into policy-making, consequently, takes into account the concerns and needs of the public.

Her education and career have taken Swati from Western Canada to many parts of the world. After graduation from the University of British Columbia with a Bachelor of Commerce degree, she articled at an accounting firm to achieve her Chartered Accountant (CA) designation. In her subsequent position, she was an internal auditor for a hotel chain for which she performed audits throughout North and South America, Asia, and Africa.

The extensive experience she gained working among other cultures and new environments has taught Swati to maintain flexibility in her work schedule. As her work is dependent on changeable capital markets and the economy, Swati feels that strong communication skills are the key to maintaining stability in her job. Many of the professionals she works with have their own area of expertise. Often a great deal of effort and negotiation is required to reach a consensus on specific issues.

Swati has a number of opportunities open in the future. She sees potential in industry where she would have the chance to manage a company's investment portfolio. Alternatively, she might go into investment counselling, or become a private consultant. The experience she has gained from working with many different people in a variety of environments has given Swati promising opportunities for advancing her career in financial analysis.

ANALYST

Bouvier International Funds Management is responsible for worldwide investments, and requires an Analyst to do financial analysis of these holdings.

Minimum education — Bachelor's degree in business, engineering, or mathematics together with advanced computer skills.

Reporting to the Vice-President, the successful candiate will be responsible for maintaining the investment database and for producing detailed analysis on new and current investment portfolios.

Excellent benefits package. Salary commensurate with experience. Send résumé outlining work experience to:

**Box 346
Station Q
Halifax NS**

---

1. What is a financial analyst?

2. What education is required to be a financial analyst?

3. What is an investment portfolio, as stated in the advertisement?

4. Why would it be necessary to have a good accounting background to be a financial analyst?

Business Career Skills

1. Team Building

The owner of a large business dealing in the merchandising of clothing noticed that morale among his staff of 20 salespeople was poor, and cliques were developing. The staff were frequently complaining about one another, concerning lateness, and the effort put into serving customers and various other jobs, such as rearranging stock on the shelves. As well, they argued with one another over when they would be on duty, when holidays were going to be taken, and even when coffee breaks would be taken. The owner realized that this poor morale was having an effect on sales, and thus on his profit. The staff consisted mainly of young people who were just out of high school or college, or part-time high school students. The manager was an elderly lady who was concerned mainly with sales and not team building.

(a) In groups, brainstorm to obtain a list of strategies that the owner could use in order to increase morale among his staff.

(b) Write a brief report outlining the strategies that you would use to deal with the situation, and why you would use the ones that you chose.

2. Decision Making

The following problems were brought to the accounting supervisor for her decision. For each of the problems, prepare a brief answer outlining your decision, and the reason for your decision.

(a) Employees of the business were required to make frequent air trips to other cities. Their expenses were completely paid. The travel points which airlines offered to frequent flyers could be accumulated in order to take free trips at a later time. The business could either keep the points and use them towards future business trips, or allow the employees to keep the points and use them for pleasure trips. Which system should the business adopt?

(b) Management had put in position a number of years ago an evaluation system for employees, which required that each person report on the people for whom they are responsible. Management was considering the adoption of a system that would require each employee to report on the supervisor to whom they were responsible. Should such a system be adopted?

(c) Concern had developed that the personnel department was allowing its employees to favour their own relatives when hiring for full-time positions, and part-time positions, such as summer jobs. Other members of the business were making the complaint, for their relatives were not being considered. What can be done concerning the complaints?

(d) The telephone costs of a firm had risen substantially, mainly due to long distance calls by employees, for which they were not billed. The main reason for not billing was that it was difficult to pin point which employees had actually made the calls. What can be done to stop the abuse?

3. Report Writing

Using the annual report that you obtained in Chapter 4, write a report of not less than 800 words, outlining the following concerning the business:

(1) the type of business, and its location(s);

(2) the goals of the business;

(3) a review of the current operations;

(4) anything special or different about the firm;

(5) the future prospects for the firm;

(6) the financial position of the firm.

Submit your copy of the annual report with your report.

COMPUTER ACCOUNTING
Getting Down to Business

Computer spreadsheets were invented by two Harvard Business School graduate students in the late 1970s — Daniel Bricklin and Robert Frankston. The inventors were looking for an easier way of "keeping the books" and solving financial problems that involved numerous calculations. They initially envisioned a spreadsheet as a way for a computer to maintain the ledger accounts that accountants deal with.

The current primary use of a spreadsheet, is as a **forecasting instrument**. Today, spreadsheets are used to predict elections, estimate populations of returning salmon, and make other calculations where mathematical formulas are involved. Many business executives rely on spreadsheets to analyze the decisions a business must continually make.

Exercises

1. The determination of the price of an airline ticket necessarily includes a detailed analysis of several factors such as supply and demand, the competition, and the day of the week. However, decisions on fares are ultimately based on mathematics. Airline executives continually "play with figures" to maximize their profits.

In this exercise you will play the role of an airline executive who is analyzing flights from Toronto to three cities. As in a real business, you will have a number of questions to answer. Your computer spreadsheet will serve as a problem-solving tool in helping you to find the "figures" you are after.

As president of All Canada Airways, you have decided to analyze the revenue from three of your regular flights. Here are the current prices:

TORONTO TO:	CALGARY	$283
	WINNIPEG	$210
	VANCOUVER	$315

You have decided to find out how much revenue your company would generate if 100 people purchased tickets on each of these flights. Your template (model) should be set up so that you can alter both the number of passengers and the ticket prices. Complete the formulas in column D in Figure 14-17 to find the revenue by multiplying the number of passengers by the ticket price.

Load your spreadsheet program and key in the template from Figure 14-17 to solve the following problems. Do not consider the aspect of airplane capacity at this time.

FIGURE 14-17

```
       File    Edit   Print   Select   Format   Options   Chart   Window

       A                    B                C                  D
   1   CITY                 FARE             PASSENGERS         REVENUE
   2   CALGARY              283              100                B2*C2
   3   WINNIPEG             210              100                -----
   4   VANCOUVER            315              100                -----
```

(a) Which of the following will generate the greatest amount of revenue for the company?
  (i) 46 passengers to Vancouver
  (ii) 50 passengers to Calgary
  (iii) 68 passengers to Winnipeg
(b) Which of the following will generate the least amount of revenue?
  (i) 95 passengers to Vancouver
  (ii) 111 passengers to Calgary
  (iii) 145 passengers to Winnipeg
(c) (i) How much revenue will you receive if 200 people buy tickets to Vancouver?
  (ii) How many tickets to Winnipeg do you need to sell to receive the same amount of revenue?
(d) For each destination, what number of tickets must be sold to generate $100 000 of revenue?
(e) You are considering increasing the price of the Winnipeg fare by $20. You predict that the price increase will reduce the number of passengers who choose your company by 5 percent (to 95%). Will you increase your gross revenue by raising the price?

2. You are still president of All Canada Airways. Your airline has four types of aircraft, each with a different seating capacity. You are to use your spreadsheet program to assist you in making business decisions that will make your company run most efficiently.

As has already been stated, businesses use spreadsheets as a tool to help them make important decisions. Spreadsheets allow businesses to quickly examine different possibilities. The type of questions asked when using the spreadsheet often begin with the words "What If?"

These are the aircraft that you have available in your company fleet.

AIRCRAFT TYPE	PASSENGER CAPACITY
737	90
727	131
767	195
DC-10	370

Use the data in the template in Figure 14-18. Notice that the formulas in column D multiply the aircraft's capacity by the number of flights each day to get a total daily capacity. As president, you want to be able to change the number of flights in column C to analyze your daily capacity possibilities in column D.

Load your spreadsheet program and key in the template in Figure 14-18 to help you answer the following scheduling questions.

(a) (i) Over 1 100 people fly with your airline between Vancouver and Honolulu, Hawaii each day. How many 727s would be needed to carry this many people?
  (ii) If you used DC-10s for this route, how many aircraft would you then need?
(b) (i) Presently you have six flights daily from Calgary to Regina. All are

FIGURE 14-18

```
       File    Edit    Print   Select   Format   Options   Chart   Window

        A                B                 C                D
1    PLANE           CAPACITY           FLIGHTS          DAILY CAP.
2    737                90                 2              B2*C2
3    727               131                 2             ----------
4    767               195                 2             ----------
5    DC-10             370                 2             ----------
```

737s. How many passengers can you carry?
(ii) If you used 767s, how many flights would be needed?

(c) (i) Four DC-10s make the Montreal to Vancouver run daily. What is the daily capacity?

(ii) If you tried 767s on this run, what would the daily capacity be?

(d) If you have ten flights each day on each of the four types of aircraft you own, how many passengers can your airline handle on a daily basis?

Credits

p.2 Universal Press Syndicate; p.27 Steven Stober Photography; p.28 Giltspur Exhibits of Canada Inc.;p.86 David Rattray; p.87 Bombardier Inc.;p.94 Margaret Stewart; p.129 Bob McLeod; p.130 Toronto-Dominion Bank; p.139 Universal Press Syndicate; p.169 Chris Earle; p.210 Shirley Reilly; p.211 McIntyre Rowan Executive Recruitment Syndicate; p.222 The Royal Bank of Canada; p.224 The Royal Bank of Canada; p.233 The Royal Bank of Canada p.234 The Royal Bank of Canada; p.253 The Royal bank of Canada; p.255 The Royal Bank of Canada; p. 264 Lee White/First Light p.309 Delores Lawrence; p. 422 Michael Iannou; p.464 The Royal Bank of Canada; p.486 p.245 Stephen Homer/First Light; p.542 Wendy Craig; p.572 The Royal Bank of Canada; p.589 Murray Sutherland; p. 649 Ann Marie Tossan; p.696 Jim Russell/First Light.

Index

Note: Page numbers that appear in **boldface** type indicate where terms are defined in the margin.

A

Account, defined, **57**
Accountant
  role of, 2-5
  skills of, 6
Accounting
  accrual basis of, 290
  computer, see Computer accounting
  defined, **2**
  double-entry, 63-64
  as language of business, 3
  standards, see Generally Accepted Accounting Principles
Accounting cycle, 202
  complete, 313
  defined, 159
  merchandise business, 391-96
Accounting department
  organization of, 4-6
  personnel, tasks of, 441
Accounting equation,
  fundamental, **9**
  revenue transactions, 105
Accounting function, 2-3
Accounting information, users of, 3

Accounting period, **96**
Accounting software, 172, 173
Accounting supervisor, **448**, 476
  accounts receivable, 460-461
  making entries in general journal, 448-51
  posting to the general ledger, 448-51
Accounting systems
  columnar journal, 494-505
  five-journal system, 518
  journalless, 527-28
  special journals, 518-28
Account names, in general journal, 138
Accounting period, **96**
Accounting year, **97**
Accounts
  balancing, 70-74
  chart of, 57-58
Accounts payable
  defined, **5**, **14**
  procedure, summary of, 452
  and purchasing procedure, 423-53
  schedule of, 451-52
Accounts payable clerk,
  443, 448, 476
  approving payment, 446-48
  making entries in accounts payable ledger, 448
  matching documents, 446-48
  preparing schedule of accounts payable, **451**-52

Accounts payable department,
  payment of liabilities, 449-51
Accounts payable ledger, **439**,
  440, 441, 448
  errors in, 452
Accounts receivable
  aging of, 374-75
  collecting, 463-65
  cycle billing, **463**
  defined, **5**
  deposit on, 465
  discounts on, 463
  interest on overdue accounts, 464-65
  net, 373
  schedule of, 461-62
Accounts receivable clerk,
  458, 476
  checking source documents, 458-61
  entering data in subsidiary ledger, 458-61
  issuing statements of account, 462-63
  preparing schedule of accounts receivable, **461**-62
  tasks, 458
Accounts receivable ledger,
  458-59
Accounts receivable turnover,
  673-74
Accrued liabilities, **314**
Acid-test ratio, 672-73
Activity ratio, **673**

Adjusting entries
  accrual basis of accounting, 290
  computer applications, 311-12
  defined, 270
  depreciation of fixed assets, 280-90
  8-column worksheet, 293-97
  interest payable, 314-17
  interim statements, 273
  journalizing and posting, 300
  for period expenses, 271-78
  types of, 271
  unearned revenue, 321-22
  unrecorded expenses, 314-19
  unrecorded revenue, 323-24
  wages, 317-19
Aging of accounts receivable, 374-75
Allowance for Doubtful Accounts, 372-73
Assets
  current, **194**
  debit balance of, 61
  defined, **7**, 8
Assets, fixed, 13, **194**
  classification under Income Tax Act, 288-89
  depreciation of, 280-90
  net book value, 282
At the source, 612
Audit, defined, **5**, 74, **175**
Audit trail, **146**

B
Bad debts, 372-79
  estimating, 373-77
  balance-sheet method, 374-75
  income-statement method, 373-74
  writing off an uncollectable, 378-79
Balance sheet
  accounts, debit and credit rules for, 64-66
  for a business, 10-15
  classified, 194
  comparative, 200-202
  defined, **7**
  from 8-column worksheet, 299

errors, correcting, 12-13
estimating bad debts, 374-75
items included on, 13-14
merchandise business, 389, 390
owner's equity section, 116, 117-18
personal, 7-9
report form, **116**, 117
steps in preparing, 10-13
Balancing accounts, 70-74
Bank reconciliation, 568-77
  in bank's books, 570
  in business's books, 569-70
  statement, 569, 571-75
  updating business records, 575
Bank reconciliation statements, 569, 571-75
Batch journalizing, 471-73
  and five-journal system, 527
Bookkeeping, defined, **2**
Book of original entry, **136**
Books of account, **138**
Business, basic transactions of, 35-36
Business records, updating, 576

C
CICA Handbook, 18
Canada Pension Plan
  deduction, calculating, 611-13
  by formula, 611-12
  using tables, 612-13
  employer's contribution to, 634
Canadian Business Corporations Act, 18
Canadian Certified General Accountants Association, 18
Canadian Institute of Chartered Accountants, 18
Capital account, 103
Capital cost allowance, **288**-89
Cash, on business balance sheet, **13**
Cash float, 565
Cash payments journal, 521-22
Cash receipts
  internal control over, 565-68
  slip, **39**, 40

Cash receipts journal, 524-26
Cash sale slip, **38**
Cash Short and Over, 561-62
Certified General Accountant, 210-11
Certified Management Accountant, 169
Chartered accountants, 128-29
Cheques
  certified, 576-77
  copy, **37**-38
  NSF, **222**, 570
  payroll, for, 627
  post-dated, 567
  stale-dated, 570-577
  stub, **37**-38
Clearing house, 570
Closing entries, 329-36
  net income situation, 330-35
  net loss situtation, 335-36
  posting, 336
  types, 329
  worksheets, merchandise business, 394-96
Collateral, defined, **14**
Collection agencies, **465**
Collective agreement, 597
Columnar journal, 494-505
  adjusting entries, 512-13
  advantages, 513
  charaacteristics of, 495-96
  closing entries, 512-13
  computerizing, 545
  debit entries, 502
  disadvantages, 513
  forwarding, 503-504
  posting procedures, 509-12
  totalling, balancing, and ruling, 505
Columnar paper, **12**
Commissions, 600
Compound entry, **138**
Computer accounting, 30-33
  accounting package, 172
  adjustments and, 311-12
  analyzing accounting data with spreadsheet, 133
  columnar journal, 545
  computerized restaurant, 266-67
  creating file directory, 174

data diskette preparation, 174
displaying general journal, 183-83
exiting *Bedford*, 175
forecasting instrument, 701
general ledger module, 172
internal control, 591-94
inventory control, 424-25
journalizing transactions, 178-82
loading *Bedford*, 174-75
loading operating system, 173-74
making general ledger module ready, 177-78
payroll, 653
preparing general ledger module, 175-77
preparing for general ledger operation, 177
printing financial reports, 183
printing hard copy of general journal, 183
printing hard copy of general ledger, 183
printing trial balance, 183
reasons to computerize, 213
saving work, 175
software, 347-48
subsidiary ledgers, 490
what if questions, 133
Computer accounting modules, 311-12
Computer analyst/programmer, 422-23
Computer funds transfers, 252
Condensed statements, **100**
Conservatism, **290**
Constitution Act, 1867, 597
Contra-asset account, **282**
    Accumulated Depreciation: Automobile, **282**
    Allowance for Doubtful Accounts, 372-73
Contra-cost account, 356
    Purchases Discounts account, 358-60
    Purchases Returns and Allowances, 356-58

Contra-equity account, 111
Contra-revenue account
    defined, 231
    refund entries to, 231-32
    Sales Discounts, 369-71
    Sales Returns and Allowances, 368-69
Control account, **440**, 449
    accounts receivable, 458
Controller, defined, **4**
Cost account, 352-53
Coverage ratios, **678**
Credit applications, 250
Credit bureau, 250-51
Credit cards, 248
    advantages, 249
    disadvantages, 249
    financial institution, 252-53
    accounting procedures for, 254-56
    merchant sales recap, 254
Credit department
    defined, **457**
    accounts receivable procedure, 457-65
    duties of, 457-58
Credit memo
    business, 225-26
    issued, 229-32
    received, 226-29
    financial institution, 223-24
Creditor, defined, 3, **14**
Cross balance, **503**
Currency requisition, 626
Current ratio, 198-99, 669, 672
Cycle billing, **463**

D

Debtor, defined, **8**
Depreciation entry, 281
Delivery Expense, **367**
Demand loans, **314**
Direct posting, **448**
Discounts
    on accounts receivable, 463
    on purchases, 358-60
    sales transactions, 369-72
Division of duties, 555
Double-entry accounting, 63-64

in general journal, 138
revenue transactions, 105
Double rule, for totals, 188
Drawings Accounts, **110**-11, 367

E

Employee
    hiring, 597-601
    individual earning record (T4), 630-31
    paying, 625-27
    recording payment of, 637
    statement of earnings, 625-26
    transfer of pay to, 626-27
    cash, 626-27
    cheque, 627
    direct deposit, 627
Employer's contribution to other benefits, 633-36
Employer's health tax, 634-35
Entity, defined, **10**
Entrepreneur, 309-310
    defined, **7**
Equities, defined, **14**
Equity account, 93
Equity to total assets ratio, **676**-77
Errors
    in accounts payable ledger, 452
    correcting, 12-13
    in general journal, 157-58
    in general ledger, 156-57
    in trial balance, 152-56
    in general journals, 139
    when posting accounts, 145
    shortcut techniques to find, 152-54
    slide, 153
    transposition, 152-53
    in trial balances, 72, 74
    on worksheet, locating, 189-90
Exceptional balance, **71**
Exemption, on TD1, **603**-607
Expenses
    defined, **95**
    unrecorded, adjusting entries for, 314-19
Extending, 186-87

F

F.O.B. (free on board), 354-55
   F.O.B. destination, **355**
   F.O.B. shipping point, **355**
Financial analyst, 696-97
Financial reports, defined, 3
Financial statements
   analyzing, 667
   comparative, 100, 199-202
   condensed, 100
   frequency of, 185-86
   horizontal analysis, 680-82
   income statement, 93
   preparing, from work-
     sheet, 193-96
   principle of materiality, 290
   trend analysis, 680-84
   vertical analysis, 682-85
Financial worksheet, 31
Fiscal period, 96
Fiscal year, **97**
Five-journal system
   advantages of, 528
   cash payments journal, 521-22
   cash receipts journal, 524-26
   general journal, 526
   purchases journal, 519-21
   sales journal, 523-24
Foot, 70
Forwarding notation, 147
Freight-in, **354**-55
Full disclosure principle, **9**, 289-90

G

GST Payable account, 241
GST Recoverable account, **240**
General journal, 526
   advantages of, 139
   compound entry, 138
   correcting errors in, 157-58
   defined, **136**
   opening entry, 138
   rules for journalizing in, 138-39
   two-column, 136, 137
General ledger, **57**, 66
   Chart of accounts, **57**
   correcting errors in, 156-57
   credit side, **57**
   Debit side, **57**
   entering transactions into, 61-63
   forwarding notation, 147
   making an entry, 59
   numbering system for, 58-59
   opening, 59
   opening balance, 60
   payroll accounts, 632
   recording employer's contribu-
     tion to benefits, 633-36
Generally Accepted Accounting
   Principles (GAAPs), 17-20
   business entity concept, **19**
   full disclosure principle,
     20, 289-90
   global, **18**
   going concern assumption, **19**-20
   historical cost principle, **19**
   matching principle, 272-73
   monetary unit concept, **19**
   principle of materiality, 290
   recognition of cost principle,
     354
Goods and Sevices Tax (GST),
   238-42
   tax-exempt items, **239**
   tax-free (zero-rated) items, **239**
   tax input credit, **238**
Gross pay, calculating, 595-605
   commissions, 600
   lateness, 599
   overtime, 600
   personal tax credit return
     (TD1), 602
   piece work, 600-601
   salary, 598
   wages, 598-**600**

H

Health insurance, deductions for,
   618-19
Horizontal analysis of financial
   statements, 680-82

I

Income statement
   comparative, **100**, 199-200
   defined, **93**
   from 8-column worksheet,
     298-99
   estimating bad debts, 373-74
   expenses, 95
   merchandise business, 385-89
   perpetual inventory system, 409
   month-end procedures, 116
   multi-step, 388
   net uncome/net loss, 96
   owner's drawing account, 110-11
   preparing, from work-
     sheet, 193-96
   quarterly, 93
   revenue, 93-95
   single-step, 389
   steps in preparing, 97-99
   time-period principle, 96-97
   transaction analysis, 103-110
   uses of, 99-100
Income Summary Account, **329**-30
Income tax, 615-17
Insurance
   adjusting for, 275-77
   liability, **275**
   premium, 275
Integrated accounting system,
   311-12
Interest
   defined, **315**
   on overdue accounts, 464
   payable, adjusting
     entries for, 314-17
   simple, formula for
     calculating, **315**
Interim statements, adjustments
   to, 273
Internal control, 555-77
   bank reconciliations, 568-77
   cash receipts, 565-68
   computer applications, 591
   petty cash, 556-62
   summary of procedures, 577
Inventory
   counting, 384
   ending, 393
   opening, 393
   physical, 383, 407
   pricing, 384-85
   taking, **274**
Inventory control, computer
   accounting, 424-25

Inventory turnover, **674**
Investment, defined, **8**
Invoice, 37
    defined, **36**
    purchase, 36
    sales, **39**

J
Journal, defined, **136**
Journal entry, **136**
Journalizing, **136**
Journalless accounting system, 527-28

L
Land, valuation of, 284
Liabilities
    accrued, **314**
    business, **14**
    credit balances of, 61
    current, **194**-95
    defined, **7**, **8**, **9**
    long-term, **195**
    maturity rule, **15**
    payment of, 449-51
Liability insurance, 275
Liquidity, order of, 15
Liquidity ratios, **669**
Loans, 14

M
Manufacturers' sales tax, 238
Marketable security, defined, **8**
Matching principle, **110**, 272-73
Memo, **40**
Merchandise business
    accounting cycle, 391-96
    accounting system with perpetual inventory system, 401-409
    balance sheet for, 389, 390
    defined, **7**, **350**
    income statement, 385-89
        cost of goods sold, 386-87
        expenses, 387-89
        revenue, 385-86
    purchase transactions, 352-60
    worksheet, 391-93

Merchandise Inventory account, closing entries, 395
Merchant sales recap, 254
Microcomputer systems, 213
Month-end procedures, 115-18
Mortgage payable, 14
Multipurpose journal, see Columnar journal

N
Neatness, importance of, 12
Net accounts receivable, **373**
Net book value, **282**
Net income, **93**, 96
    calculating, 187
    uses for, 99
Net loss, **93**, 96
Net pay, calculating, 600-20
    deductions, 610
    compulsory, contract, 610-20
    statutory, 610-19
    voluntary, 620
Net worth, defined, **9**
Numbers, standard way of reading, 13

O
Objectivity principle, **41**
Office supplies, 13
On account, **35**
Opening balance, **60**
Opening entry, general journal, **138**
Opening a ledger, **59**
Order of liquidity, **15**
Organization chart, **4**
Owner's drawings account, 110-12
Owner's equity, 14
    credit balance of, 61
Owner's security, 9

P
Pacioli, Luca, 2
Packing slip, **446**
    particulars column, general ledger accounts, 145, 146-47
Payroll accounting, 595-641
    alternate method of recording costs, 636-37

computer applications, 653
gross pay, calculating, 595-605
net pay, calculating, 610-20
recording payroll in payroll register, 623-27
updating books, 630-41
vacation pay, 640-41
workers' compensation, 640
Payroll cycle, 596-97
Payroll deductions, 610
Payroll liabilities, recording payment of, 637-39
Payroll register
    completing, 625
    gross pay, 624
    net pay, 625
    other deductions, 625
    recording data from, 632-33
    taxable earnings, calculating, 624
Payroll supervisor, 649-50
Payroll taxes, recording, 633-36
Pencil footings, **70**
Periodic inventory system,
    advantages, 351
    defined, 350
    disadvantages, 351
    merchandise business:
    completing accounting cycle for, 383-96
    sales transactions, 364-7
    purchase transactions, 352-60
Perpetual inventory system
    defined, **351**
    physical inventory, 407
    merchandise business:
    accounting system for, 401-409
    completing cycle, 408-409
    journal entries, 402-408
    purchase/payment cycle entries, 402-403
    purchase discounts, 404-405
Purchases Returns and Allowances, 356, 403-404
    sales/collection cycle entries, 405-408
Personal Tax Credit return (TD1), 601-605
    exemptions, 603-605

net claim codes, 605
Petty cash fund, 556-62
  balance sheet presentation of, 562
  establishing, 558
  increasing/decreasing, 558
  payments from, 559
  procedures for, 556-57
  replenishing, 559-62
Petty cash summary, 559
Petty cash voucher, 559
Physical inventory, **383**, 407
Piece work, 600-601
Pin totals, **70**
Post-closing trial balance, 336-37
Posting
  in a columnar journal, 509-12
  defined, **143**
  error correction, 157
  from journal to ledger, 144-45
  to running-balance ledger accounts, 143-47
  to special journals, 526-27
Posting, direct
  to columnar journal, 509
  compared to indirect, 474-75
Posting, indirect, 473-74
  to columnar journal, 509
  compared to direct, 474-75
Posting reference (PR) column, 145, 146
Premium, insurance, **275**
Prepaid cards, 249, 257
Prepaid expenses
  adjustments for, **271**-78
  insurance, 275-77
  rent, 277-78
  supplies, 273-75
Principal, loan, **314**
Principle of materiality, **290**
Profit, as goal of business, 3
Profitability ratios, **674**
Profit margin on sales, **674**-75
Proprietorship, defined, **7**
  provincial sales tax (PST), see Retail Sales Tax, provincial
Provincial Sales Tax Payable Account, 245
Purchase invoice, 36

batch journalizing, 472
Purchase orders, 443, **444**-45
Purchase requisition, **443**-44
Purchases account, **352**, 357
Purchases Discounts account, **358**-60
Purchases journal, 519-21
Purchases Returns and Allowances, 356-58
  combined with Purchases account, 357-58
Purchasing department, 443-53
  checking purchase requisitions, 443-44
  issuing purchase orders, 443, 444-45
Purchasing procedure, **443**

Q
Quarterly statements, 185
  accounting cycle for, 159

R
Rate of return on investment, **675**
Ratios, 667-77
  accounts receivable turnover, 673-74
  acid-test, 672-73
  activity, 673
  coverage, 676
  current, **198**, **669**
  debt to total assets, **676**
  equity to total assets, **676**-77
  defined, **668**
  inventory turnover, 674
  liquidity, **669**
  profitability, **674**
  profit margin on sales, **674**-75
  rate of return on investment, 675
Receiving report, **446**
Recognition of cost principle, 354
Refunds, making, 231-32
Rent, prepaid, 277-78
  adjusting entries for, 277-78
Residual claim, defined, **14**
Restaurant, computerized, 266-67
Retailer, defined, 350
Retail sales tax, provincial (PST), 242-46, 365

calculating, 243
collecting, 244-45
exempt categories, 243
goods for resale, 242
remitting, 245
tax commission, 245-46
vendor's licence, 243
Revenue
  defined, **93**
  transaction analysis, 104-107
Revenue recognition principle, **109**
Ruled accounts, **336**
Running-balance account, defined, 145
Running-balance ledger accounts, posting to, 143-47

S
Salary, **598**
Sales, 364-67
  defined, **365**
Sales Discount account, **369**-71
  combined with sales return or allowance, 372
  taking discounts after discount date, 371
Sales journal, 523-24
Sales Returns and Allowances account, **368**-69
Sales tax, 238-46. *See also Retail sales tax, provincial.*
Sales tax commission, 245-46
Sales transactions
  bad debts allowance, 372-79
  delivery expense, 367-68
  sales, 364-67
  sales discounts, 369-71
  sales returns and allowances, 368-69
Services business, defined, **7**
Shipping terms, 354-55
Skip, defined, **372**
Social insurance numbers, 601
Society of Management Accountants of Canada, 18
Software, 213
Source deductions, remitting, 637-39

Source documents, **36**-41
   cash receipt slip, 39, 40
   cash sales slip, 38, 104
   cheque copy, 37-38
   form, 88
   in general journal, 138
   memo/voucher, 40
   missing, 41
   objectivity principle, 41
   purchase invoice, 36-37
   sales invoice, 39, 104
   void, 41
Special journals, 518-28. *See also Five-journal system.*
   forwarding, 526
   summary of posting procedures for, 526-27
Spreadsheet
   electronic, 89
   as forecasting instrument, 699
Spreadsheet program, source document form, 88
Statement of account, **462**-63
Statement of earnings, 625-26
Straight line method, **286**
Subsidiary ledger system, 438-41
   accounts receivable procedure, 457-63
   advantages of, 475, 477
   batch journalizing, **471**-73
   computer accounting software, 490
   control account, 440
   defined, **439**
   direct posting, 448
   direct/indirect posting, **473**-75
   payments of liabilities, 449-51
   systems analysis and design, **439**
Supplies, adjusting for, 273-75
Synoptic journal, *see Columnar journal*
Systems analysis and design, 439

T

T-account, 57
   vs. running-balance ledger account, 143-44
TD1, *see Personal Tax Credit Return*

T4 slip, 630-31
Taxable benefits, 610
Tax input credit (GST), **238**
Temporary accounts, **329**
Term of loan, **314**
Three Buoys, 1
Tickler file, **449**
Time-period principle, 96-**97**
Transaction analysis
   expense transactions, 107-108
   income statement accounts, 103-110
   matching principle, **110**
   revenue recognition principle, 109
   revenue transactions, 104-107
Transaction analysis sheet, 46-52
Transactions, 34-41
   on account, 35
   analyzing, 35, 46-52
   buying, 35
   defined, **34**
   recording, 36
   selling, 35
   source documents, 36-41
   types of, 35
Treasurer, defined, **4**
Trend analysis, **680**-84
Trial balance, 72-74
   correcting errors in, 152-56
   formal, **72**
   informal, 72
   month-end procedures, 115-18
   post-closing, 336-37
   tape, 72
   on work sheet, 186

U

UPC, 401
Unearned items, 322
Unearned revenue, **321**
   adjustments for, 321-22
Unemployment insurance deduction, calculating, 613-15
   by formula, 613-14
   using tables, 61
   employer's contribution to, **614**-15, 634
Unrecorded expenses, defined, **314**

Unrecorded revenue, **323**
   adjustments for, 323-24

V

Vacation pay, 640-41
Vertical analysis of financial statements, 682-85
Voucher, **40**

W

Wage employees, 598
Wages, adjusting entries for, 317-19
Wholesaler, defined, 350
Workers' compensation, 640
Working capital, defined, 198
Worksheet
   completing, where net loss, 188
   defined, 185
   locating errors in, 189-90
   for merchandise business, 391-93
   closing entries, 394-96
   perpetual inventory system, 408
   self-balancing nature of, 189
   steps in preparing, 186-88
Worksheet, eight-column, 293-97
   automobile, 297
   building, 295-96
   equipment, 296
   footnotes, 293
   office supplies, 295
   prepaid insurance, 294-95
   preparing, 293
   using, 298-99
Worksheet, ten-column, 298
Writing off an uncollectable, **378**-79

Y

Year-end adjustments
   fixed assets, 281-82
   insurance, 276-77
   rent, 277-78
   supplies used, 274-75